2750

DATE DUE

A RINGING GLASS
The Life of Rainer Maria Rilke

Rainer Maria Rilke (passport photograph *c.* 1922)

A RINGING GLASS

The Life of
Rainer Maria Rilke

DONALD PRATER

CLARENDON PRESS · OXFORD
1986

Oxford University Press, Walton Street, Oxford OX2 6DP
Oxford New York Toronto
Delhi Bombay Calcutta Madras Karachi
Kuala Lumpur Singapore Hong Kong Tokyo
Nairobi Dar es Salaam Cape Town
Melbourne Auckland
and associated companies in
Beirut Berlin Ibadan Nicosia

Oxford is a trade mark of Oxford University Press

Published in the United States
by Oxford University Press, New York

First published 1986 by Oxford University Press

British Library Cataloguing in Publication Data
Prater, Donald
A ringing glass: the life of Rainer Maria Rilke.
1. Rilke, Rainer Maria—Biography   2. Poets,
German—19th century—Biography
I. Title
831'.912   PT2635.165Z/
ISBN 0–19–815755–X

Library of Congress Cataloging in Publication Data
Prater, Donald A., 1918–
A ringing glass.
Bibliography: p. 450
Includes indexes.
1. Rilke, Rainer Maria, 1875–1926—Biography.
2. Authors, German—20th century—Biography.   I. Title.
PT2635.I65Z836 1985   831'.912 [B]   85–7830
ISBN 0–19–815755–X

Typeset by Latimer Trend & Company Ltd, Plymouth
Printed and bound in Great Britain
at the University Press, Oxford
by David Stanford
Printer to the University

A RINGING GLASS:
The Life of Rainer Maria Rilke

Be ahead of all departure, as if it were
behind you like the winter that's just passed.
. . . .
Be here among the vanishing in the realm of entropy,
be a ringing glass that shatters as it rings.
Be—and at the same time know the implication
of non-being, the endless ground of your inner vibration,
so you can fulfil it fully just this once . . .

(*Sonnets to Orpheus*, ii. 13)

For Patricia

Preface

'From indescribable transforming flashes
such figuration—: Feel and trust!
We know too well how flames can turn to ashes:
in art, though, flame is kindled out of dust.'

(Rilke, 'Magic')

Do we need to know a poet's personal and private life? Is it not true, as Orwell said, that a writer's private character has little or nothing to do with his literary personality? It is certainly possible to read and admire the work of Rainer Maria Rilke, perhaps the greatest lyric genius of our century—his *Elegies*, the *Sonnets to Orpheus*, *Malte Laurids Brigge*, and especially the *New Poems*—as free-standing works of art unconnected with a real existence; and it may be felt superfluous to wish to discover more of their author than that he was born in Prague in 1875, wrote in German and sometimes in French, wandered through Europe, and died in Switzerland in 1926.

Rilke himself, however, fully realized the significant interconnection between how he lived and what he produced. That is quite clear from the care with which he preserved his papers, and especially from his specific authorization, in his will, of the publication of the letters to which he had confided so much of himself. It could not be otherwise: for he was a rare instance of a poet who contrived an existence exclusively dedicated to his art, who made indeed a work of his life; and if we are fully to appreciate the written words we cannot leave out of account the circumstances in which they came into being—the peripeteias, the *misères et grandeurs*, the existential crises, and above all the human relationships, that left their imprint. There is so much of magic in what Rilke wrote that we must know what manner of man it was who could become the magician.

Such was not the view of Rilke's literary executors. In the decade up to the Second World War their selection of letters for publication had the avowed aim of revealing only what 'related to the poetical work and to the experiences directly concerned with its creation', and of excluding, as far as possible, everything about the poet's private life. This selectivity, coupled with the undoubted difficulty of obtaining letters in other hands, could not but contribute further to the image of the poet as high priest and philosopher which the work *in vacuo* tended to foster: a being whose earthly life is largely irrelevant, and about whom everything, as Eudo Mason ruefully observed, is 'conducive to hyperbole and to the evolution of legends'.

Though a number of studies on particular periods of Rilke's life appeared before and after the war—notably J. R. von Salis's admirable account of the last years in Switzerland, drawing on personal reminiscences and then unpublished letters—attempts at a full biography, even as late as the 1950s, lacked anything approaching an adequate basis. Only in comparatively recent years, after the gradual publication of memoirs and important correspondence, the accession to the major library collections of more letters as yet unpublished, and the appearance of Ingeborg Schnack's detailed *Rilke-Chronik* and Ernst Zinn's scholarly edition of the *Complete Works*, has it become possible to tell a fuller story.

To do so is the aim of the present work. In contrast to the 'Life and Work' form adopted in other studies, whose emphasis is on the interpretation of Rilke's work, often making the life itself seem incidental, this is strictly a 'Life', to give a portrait of the man and to show the background against which he wrote and the conditions in which his ideas were developed. The reader will have to look elsewhere for an interpretation and critical appreciation, for example, of the *Elegies*: but I hope that he may be better equipped to follow such exegeses after this account of how they grew and the part they played in Rilke's life. My quotation from the works, therefore, is limited, and designed only to show this process and what each signified for Rilke at a particular stage in his life. The translations are those which I felt best suited to achieve this, even if they may not be the most accomplished aesthetically, and regardless of the controversy over Rilke's 'translatability'. Quotations from the verse in French, however, are left in the original.

His letters, by contrast, are quoted extensively—not because they are necessarily the 'truth', but because they illustrate, better perhaps than for any other poet, the feelings behind the work, the hopes and fears and the continuing struggle for achievement. For this reason, and also for reasons of space, many of his correspondents familiar to those already versed in Rilke's life—Gräfin Sizzo, Gudi Nölke, Elisabeth von Schmidt-Pauli, and a host of others—are not named in the text: in such cases it was more important to show what Rilke was saying than to specify to whom he was saying it. As far as possible I have selected hitherto unpublished letters, which often add something new or give a fresh turn to what was already known. All quotations, except where otherwise stated, are in my own translation.

In this respect, and with the benefit of other testimonies both oral and written, this account, as far as space would allow, is fuller than its predecessors. It is by no means yet, alas, definitive. The Rilke Archive in Gernsbach contains much material still to be opened up: although Christoph and Hella Sieber-Rilke gave me much help, which I most gratefully acknowledge, practical difficulties made it impossible to see more than a fraction of this material, and in particular Rilke's notebooks, diaries, and letters to his mother, one day to be published, had to be left out of account. I was however greatly privileged to read Carl Sieber's sequel to his *René Rilke*, a biography of the later years, in a manuscript completed just before his death in 1945: the inclusion of excerpts from unpublished letters in the Rilke Archive made it invaluable, and the extent of my indebtedness will be clear from the Notes.

These document all quotations, in as brief a form as possible, to avoid an overburden of apparatus. For Rilke's works, references are to the *Sämtliche Werke*, edited by Ernst Zinn (Frankfurt a.M., 1955–66). For permission to reprint translations, by the authors named (see p. 452), grateful acknowledgement is made to: St. John's College, Oxford, and the Hogarth Press (J. B. Leishman); Houghton Mifflin Company, Boston (A. Poulin Jr.); Random House Inc., New York (Stephen Mitchell); Anvil Press Poetry Ltd, and Michael Hamburger; David H. Kitton (Eudo C. Mason); the Trustees of the Estate of B. J. Morse.

My debt of gratitude is great, not only to Christoph and Hella Sieber-Rilke for their kindness and support, and to the publishers for great forbearance, but also to many other friends and colleagues whose scholarship and generosity with documentation, advice, and suggestions were of inestimable value to the work: Dr Joachim W. Storck (Marbach); Dr Ernst Pfeiffer (Göttingen); Dr Ingeborg Schnack (Marburg); Professor Klaus W. Jonas (Pittsburgh); Professor J. R. von Salis (Brunegg); Dr Rätus Luck (Berne); Dr Karl Klutz (Bad Ems). For personal memories and other substantial assistance I owe thanks to Prince Raimondo della Torre e Tasso (Duino), Gräfin von Clary (Salzburg), Madame Roland de Margerie (Paris), Elisabeth Bergner (London), Director and Mrs L. Rehnquist (Stocksund), and to the late Frau Frieda Baumgartner and Madame Jeanne de Sépibus; to Frau Greta Lauterburg, Madame A. Vincens-de Bonstetten, Frau Magda Kerényi, Madame Monique Desarzens, and Madame Ernest Abravanel.

My thanks must also go, for their ready co-operation, to the many institutions housing Rilke documentation: Deutsches Literaturarchiv, Marbach; Schweizerische Landesbibliothek, Berne; Nationalbibliothek and Stadt- und Landesbibliothek, Vienna; Stadtbibliothek and Bayerische Staatsbibliothek, Munich; Rilke Collection, Hôtel de Ville, Sierre; Kungliga Biblioteket, Stockholm; Universitetsbiblioteket, Lund; Landsarkivet and Universitetsbiblioteket, Gothenburg; Houghton Library, Harvard University; Goethe- und Schiller-Archiv, Weimar; British Library, London; Kongelige Biblioteket, Copenhagen; Jewish National and University Library, Jerusalem; Bibliothek der Universität Bremen; Staatsbibliothek (Preussischer Kulturbesitz), Berlin; National Museum Archives, Prague; University College, Cardiff.

Thanks, finally, to my friends of the Rilke-Gesellschaft, and to all those others, too numerous to mention individually, whose interest in the work and whose help in a multitude of ways was an unfailing encouragement on a long road. I trust that they and the others to whom I owe so much will feel the result rewards their goodwill. 'If it blazes, it has worth.'*

Gingins, Switzerland

*SW ii. 442.

Contents

List of Plates

—◦❧❦◦—

I

A Boyhood in Bohemia
1875–1896

—◦❧☙◦—

'This Prague is an old city of magic ... a place where many
essences flow together and also many wondrous, inconceivable
things come to pass—things, words, characters and incidents
never seen elsewhere. It is fertile soil for magic powers and
spells.'

(Johannes Urzidil, *The Nine Devils*)

I

'An anxious, heavy childhood'
(Rilke to Ellen Key, 14. 2. 1904)

Shortly after midnight on Saturday, 4 December 1875, at seven months 'in a
hurry to get into the world',[1] René Karl Wilhelm Johann Josef Maria Rilke
was born, in an apartment rented by his parents at 19 Heinrichsgasse
(Jindřisská ulice), Prague. The day before his unexpected arrival they had
been early astir, though the snow lay thick, to pay a visit to his maternal
grandmother Caroline Entz, and on the way home had bought a little gold
cross as the first present for this longed-for child, whose sister had died, only a
few days old, the previous year. On 19 December they ventured out with him
for his baptism in the Catholic faith at the Church of St. Heinrich near by, and
he was endowed with the series of pretentious forenames.

The province of Bohemia, of which Prague was the capital city, formed at
that time a part of the great supra-national Austro-Hungarian Empire of the
Habsburgs, the second-largest state system in Europe, extending from Croatia
and Slovenia in the south to the Erzgebirge in the north, and from the
Vorarlberg in the west to Galicia and Bukovina in the east. This remarkable
amalgam of widely differing races, languages, and customs was held together
in an imperial and royal framework that to many of its citizens—or at any rate
to those of German tongue—seemed destined to endure for ever, an appar-
rently ideal combination of benevolence with regulation and tolerance with
firm rule. The stirrings of national sentiment in the provinces, though
increasingly marked and sometimes militant, had not yet shown signs of
turning to revolution, and, where national independence was dreamed of, it

was mostly seen as no more than self-determination within a commonwealth which, under the steady if unimaginative hand of King-Emperor Franz Josef, could claim to be eminently workable.

Outside Austria itself there were nevertheless distinctions, sometimes sharp, between the German-speakers and those of different mother tongues, tending to correspond to those of social class. The population of Bohemia was German-speaking to about one-third of its numbers, and these were the upper classes—the merchants, officials, military, and nobility—who shunned contact with the Czechs. This was the case even among the less prosperous, like Rilke's parents. In Prague itself, where the Czechs preponderated, with barely 7 per cent of the population German-speaking, the result, as has been aptly remarked, was a 'double ghetto' for the Germans, behind the walls of both language and class. Under this apartheid the upper middle class of Germans and of Jews (recently liberated from their actual ghetto) congregated mainly in the area between the Stadtpark (Sady Vrchlickcho) and the Graben (Na Příkopě)—the 'better quarter' of the city. This remained the background to Rilke's early years; and the stifling atmosphere it generated was a potent factor in his departure before his twenty-first birthday from a city he was always reluctant to revisit, feeling as though swallowed up by 'this great silent fish' and repelled by 'those dark streets amid whose terrors my lonely childhood longed for the sun, like a pale, shivering blossom.'[2]

His family's view of their superior status had long been bolstered by a tradition that they were the descendants of a noble line, the 'German-ness' of which was reinforced by claiming its origins in Carinthia, where indeed certain knights of Rülko had flourished between the thirteenth and sixteenth centuries. Rilke himself held throughout his life to the pleasant notion of this ancestry, but neither his own researches nor those of his uncle could yield any firm evidence for it. His earliest attested forebears, it is now undisputed, were prosperous and well-respected farmers in the early seventeenth century, in the village of Türmitz bei Aussig (Termiče) in Bohemia, not far from Teplitz and near the border with Saxony. The evidence of these more modest beginnings does not entirely rule out the possibility that the family tradition and Rilke's own instinct may well have been right. There were Rülkos, or Rylkes, in Saxony in the fourteenth and fifteenth centuries, one Johann being documented in 1348 as a town official in Freiberg, in a mining district south-west of Dresden, and the family as owning estates at Langenau and Linda around 1450. The knightly title is absent, it is true, but the greyhound device on that Johann's crest is similar to that on the coat of arms of the Carinthian Rülkos. A century later, a Franz Rülike was bailiff at the castle of Brüx in Bohemia, not far from Türmitz. Diligent genealogical researches have so far failed to establish any link, apart from geography, between him and the Rilkes of Türmitz, or between either of the Saxony/Bohemia lines and that of Carinthia. But two facts may lend colour to the oral tradition. One is that Johann

Franziskus of Türmitz, Rilke's great-great-grandfather, owned a silver seal with the Carinthian coat of arms: 'party per pale, sable and argent, two greyhounds salient confrontés', with the motto 'Veritate firmitas, firmitate veritas'. The other is the discovery in 1960, in the Hilprant Castle library at Mlada Vožice in Bohemia, of a 1554 Basel edition of Pliny the Younger, inscribed in 1585 as owned by one Christophorus Rülcko of Gamelitz, Carinthia.

With the Türmitz family we are on firmer ground. Its fortunes suffered during the Thirty Years War, and Michael Rilke (1653–1710) turned butcher as well as farmer, while his son Johannes (1679–1750) was a tailor; but his grandson Johann Franziskus (born 1719) was mayor of Türmitz in 1774. In 1806 Rilke's great-grandfather Johann Joseph (born 1755) had so far restored the position as to be able to purchase a considerable estate at Kamenitz an der Linde, an imposing manor some hundred kilometres south-east of Prague: but he could maintain himself there only for a few years before being forced to sell and take a post as land agent on the Nostitz estates at Tschochau. His son, Johann Baptist Joseph (1788–1853), Rilke's grandfather, occupied a similar position for the property of Count Hartig at Schwabitz, where Josef, Rilke's father, was born in 1838.

Josef was the third of four sons. His mother, Wilhelmine née Reiter, was the daughter of a town councillor at Budin in Bohemia. After the death of her husband she lived, until she died in 1879, in Kremsier in central Moravia, where René visited her. The eldest of the family, Jaroslav, entered the law, while the other three brothers all embarked on military careers: Emil dying in his early twenties as a Lieutenant of the 12th Uhlan Regiment in the Ruhr, and Hugo at fifty-one as an artillery Captain, by his own hand at disappointment over promotion. The only sister, Gabriele, youngest of the children, married a Prague lawyer, Wenzel von Kutschera. Josef's military career found a less dramatic end than that of his brothers. After ten years of correct and not undistinguished service in the artillery as a cadet, notably in the Austrian campaign in Italy in 1859, where for a short time he found himself in independent command, a persistent throat ailment ruled him out for the coveted commission. Embittered, he sought his discharge at the age of twenty-seven, and, thanks to Jaroslav's good offices, found a post as an official with the newly-constructed Turnau-Kralup-Prague railway. Though he progressed in due time to inspector and head of personnel with the North Bohemia railway, he remained a fish out of water in a bewildering world outside the confines of army regulations. Still on the reserve of his regiment, upright of bearing, elegant, and conventional, he maintained for himself the illusion of the ex-soldier whose son should follow in his footsteps and one day reach the officer rank he had himself failed to attain.

On 24 May 1873 he married Sophie, the twenty-two-year-old daughter of a Prague merchant and Imperial Councillor, Carl Joseph Entz, and his wife

Caroline née Kinzelberger. The origins of this established Prague family are
less well documented, but an earlier generation of Entzes was believed to have
emigrated from Alsace—another tradition which appealed to Rilke, as explaining the strong affinity he always felt for France and the French. As a director of
the Bohemia Savings Bank and with a father-in-law the owner of a prosperous
colour and chemical business, Carl Entz's circumstances were comparatively
wealthy. They lived in the Kinzelbergers' romantic baroque *palais* in the
Herrengasse (Panská ulice), and here Phia, as she always wanted to be known,
was born. It was a family whose worldly success contrasted with the relatively
modest achievements of the Rilkes, and whose outstanding trait was the strong
will which Rilke inherited from both mother and grandmother.

As a young girl, Phia had indeed been self-willed, with dreams of
emancipation and a life in high society. With marriage to Josef Rilke she soon
discovered behind the elegant charm of the suitor the dullness of a plain,
sometimes rough soldierly husband, with whom it was impossible to satisfy
either her longing for love or the social aspirations she had brought with her.
They were a temperamentally ill-assorted couple, and in her disappointment
she sought refuge, like him, in a life of outward show. Much effort went into
creating an impression of social standing in the furnishings of the Heinrichsgasse apartment, and she was not above garnishing with quality labels the
bottles of *vin ordinaire* she served when they entertained. Josef's family
connections were not unimpressive—there was an uncle Josef von Weissen-
burg, with an estate in Moravia—and the Rilke tradition of noble descent held
great attraction for Phia. Her expectations from the marriage were all the more
frustrated when she found that for the new hereditary title of Ritter von
Rüliken, to which Jaroslav had just been elevated, no documentary antece-
dents could be established in his researches, ruling out any claim to
distinguished ancestry for her husband.

She dressed always in black and affected the demeanour of a *grande dame*
and the vapours of a fashionable hypochondria. Religious observance and the
ritual of the Catholic Church occupied her to the point of bigotry, and in later
life almost of mania, as she sought not only solace for an unkindly fate but also
the protection of the Virgin Mary against the dangers of a spirit world in which
she firmly believed. Intellectually she felt, and indeed was, superior to her
more stolid and humourless husband, keeping a diary, writing poems, noting
in aphoristic brevity her observations of the human condition. These,
published in a slim volume entitled *Ephemeriden* at the turn of the century,
show a certain shrewdness and form a commentary, sometimes bitter, on her
unsuccessful marriage, as well as reflecting determination to free herself from
it: 'Many a betrothal is only a prayer before the battle' . . . 'Sometimes even the
entire mineral kingdom cannot provide enough stones to cast at a happy
woman' . . . 'A woman who has not loved has not lived' . . . 'Misfortune does
but strengthen our will.' It would have been surprising to find so strong a

personality submitting for long to the narrow confines of her married lot, or, seeking liberation, showing the timidity of an Emma Bovary.

Precocious as he was, the child was not slow to sense the worsening relationship between his parents, and to recognize the falseness of their life in the Heinrichsgasse. 'A very dark childhood,' he called it at twenty-two: and a few years later: 'My parents' marriage was already in decline when I was born ... My mother was highly nervous, slim, black, a woman who wanted something from life, something undefined. And so she has remained. ... I had to wear fine clothes, and until I went to school was dressed as a girl; for my mother I was a plaything, I think, like a big doll. She was always pleased when people called her "Miss". She wanted to appear young, suffering, unhappy. And she was unhappy, too, I dare say. I think we all were.'[3] It was natural that she should spoil the young René, treating him at first as the girl she had lost, and, fearful that his premature birth would make him delicate, surrounding him with suffocating care: equally natural that the result in him was a fundamental antagonism towards her which he never lost. He never ceased to write to her, especially at Christmas, but the dutiful letters held only what he knew she wanted to hear and rarely expressed his true feelings.

Every time he saw her, he wrote at twenty-nine, he relived his struggle as a child to get away from her, and felt that, after years of running, he had still not got far enough—that somewhere within him there were still reflections of her gestures, fragments of memories which she carried around broken with her— ' and then I shudder at her distracted godliness, her stubborn belief, especially the distorted and deformed faith which she had hung on to ... And to think that I am yet her child: that my way into the world was some hardly distinguishable concealed door in this irrelevant, faded wall.'[4] Her religiosity and superstitious turn were overwhelming for a child at such an impressionable age. On every visit to church he was made to kiss Christ's wounds on the crucifix, and he was constantly regaled with stories of spirit manifestations.

> Poor saints of wood
> to whom my mother brought her gifts
>
> . . . .
> For her searing troubles
> they certainly knew no gratitude
>
> . . . .
> But my mother came and brought them flowers,
> flowers my mother plucked,
> all of them, out of my life.[5]

Such early exposure was enough to turn him away in adolescence from the outward forms of received religion, and, despite a profound belief in a realm beyond our perceptions, to leave him unconvinced by its alleged revelation through mediums.

His father's stiff conventionality gave little room for love. Looking back, long after Josef's death in 1906, he said that 'right to the end he had a kind of inexpressible fear of the heart towards me, a feeling against which I was very nearly defenceless, but which must have cost him more than the most intense love.'[6] These were indeed 'anxious, heavy' days,[7] with parents whose only concern seemed to be that he should be dressed well and not catch anything. 'If there had been someone to show me animals or flowers, or taught me how to be happily alone with a book, what love, what blessing I would have had in my heart for him. Instead of which, I walked myself to a standstill ... and *passed* the time ... which I would later find never long enough. Theseus came into the world in an underground chamber, no matter, he came up like a shoot from a plant: but I grew up in absolute nothingness, up towards nothing ...'.[8]

2

'What I suffered ... in these five years, is a life apart: a long, hard life.'

(To Ellen Key, 5. 4. 1903)

Many people tend to idealize their childhood days. Rilke, as we have seen, was not of their number, but even he could occasionally admit that there had been some happy times for him in these early years. The excitement of Christmas preparations in his boyhood returned each year in later life as a vivid memory, and there were summer holidays with Phia in the country which he clearly enjoyed, 'eating like a horse, sleeping like a log',[1] climbing trees, imagining himself a cavalry officer. At home, on the rare occasions when other children were invited, the favourite game was playing house and pretending to cook: but he had tin soldiers too—commanded of course by Wallenstein—and a rocking-horse, helmet, and sword as presents from his uncles; loved to draw knights errant and heroes falling in battle; and enjoyed his father's tales of military exploits.

School began for him in 1882, at the establishment of the Piaristen Order. This was regarded as the socially more acceptable of the two *Volksschulen* available for German-speaking children, and thus in Phia's eyes to be preferred, notwithstanding the poor reputation of the brothers both as men and teachers ('Piaristians—rotten Christians!' was a popular catcall to which the pupils were subjected in the streets). It was only a stone's throw from home, but she saw to it that René was escorted to and fro each day. He was not entirely kept in cotton wool and denied the excitement of a normal boy's life, however. Though kept out of the routine fights with boys from the neighbour-ing Czech school, and unable to join his schoolmates in their journeys of discovery in the labyrinths of Prague, he could sometimes escape to cross Charles Bridge over to the 'Kleinseite' (Malá Strana), 'all the corners I loved as a boy; whenever I could I ran over and followed the most remarkable trails.'[2]

Such ventures away from Phia's enveloping concern, however, were doubtless rare, and he remained a rather lonely mother's boy, lost in his own thoughts and an outsider in the carefree games of the others. Photographs show him as sturdy enough; but he was certainly prey to disturbing fevers as well as all the normal childish ailments, and was kept away from school for long periods, in his third year missing two whole terms. After a slow start, his third-year reports, in spite of the long absences, were 'very good' in all subjects except drawing and singing, which were merely 'good'. The curriculum included Czech, in which he made a good grounding. French he was learning from Phia herself, who made a point of teaching him a few words every day; and she had him early getting poetry by heart or listening to her reciting Schiller as she went about the household chores or sat by his sick-bed. From copying out poems he liked he soon graduated to trying his own hand at rhyming, in which she was alert to encourage him, somewhat to his father's dismay; and the first recorded effort is a verse to his parents on their eleventh wedding anniversary in May 1884. Ironically, this was when Phia was beginning to assert her independence, with frequent absences from home, and later that same year Josef agreed to their separation for good, Phia setting up for the time being in her own quarters in Prague.

It was time for decision on the next stage of the boy's education, for which she was to remain responsible but which had to be arranged in agreement with her husband. The break-up of the home, making some form of boarding-school essential, was obviously an important factor as they weighed the possibilities: at the same time, money was short for either this or a normal progress of secondary schooling through the Gymnasium. His father, though equally concerned for his health, had never abandoned the idea that he should follow him into the army, so that the military college system, where there was a good chance of a free place for the son of an ex-serviceman, was for him the ideal solution; and René himself seems to have welcomed it. Thus it was decided. But it is hard to see anything but selfishness in Phia's consent to surrender an over-protected child to such conditions. Perhaps conscious of this, she took him with her in the summer of 1885 to Canale, in Gorizia north of Trieste — his first experience of Italy and, as he later remarked, 'a kind of primer for my nomadic existence'[3] — from where he wrote to his father that he was practising his poetry with diligence, to be worthy, if he could keep it up, of the 'laurel crown' when he returned. After his final year with the Piaristen, the doctor pronounced him fit and his bodily development 'appropriate for his age'.[4] On 1 September 1886 Phia escorted him, in the prescribed uniform and his hair in regulation crop, to the Militär-Unterrealschule at St. Pölten, in Lower Austria.

On his four years here, and the year which followed at the senior college in

Weisskirchen (Hraniče) in Moravia, much has been written, not least by Rilke himself. In his memory it remained a traumatic experience, on which he looked back with horror and loathing: the culmination of what he called, in a characteristic use of words, his 'ungeleistete Kindheit'—a childhood unachieved, incomplete, we may translate. It was like being totally submerged for five whole years, he once said: 'no one has stayed under water longer'.[5] The sensitive poet of later years gained much sympathy for this from his admirers, and many biographers made much of the tempting pathos it offered, so that the 'military period' as an intolerably cruel blow of fate long constituted an essential part of the Rilke legend. Others tended to the opposite extreme, minimizing the drama of his military school days and dismissing the picture he drew of a fearful ordeal as merely another instance of his tendency to 'self-stylization', if not (in one case) as 'emasculate self-pity'. The truth must lie somewhere between.

The official record at St. Pölten certainly shows little evidence of a boy in an agony of unhappiness. His conduct improved from 'very good' at the start to 'excellent' in his third and fourth years; his character, judged at first as 'hesitant', was marked 'quiet and good-tempered' throughout, and gained in the final years the additional comment of 'industrious'; his 'adjustment' in the first year 'needed watching', but thereafter he was found 'neat and orderly'. In the purely academic subjects, notably languages (including Czech) and divinity, his performance showed steady improvement. On the military side of the curriculum he appears to have just passed muster in drill, target-shooting, and knowledge of army regulations, but not in fencing and gymnastics, in which he had to take extra tests before being passed out for acceptance in the senior college. His low first-year class order, 35th out of 51, improved remarkably to 7th out of 53 in the second and 8th out of 48 in the third, but dropped then to 18th out of 51 at the end of the fourth, clearly because of his less satisfactory physical performance and not for any lack of application. The scanty medical records show him as weakly developed and anaemic, but from his letters to his mother he does not appear to have been unduly sick until his last year.[6]

There is not much independent testimony, however, to fill out these bare facts. The padre, Horaček, remembered René as a quiet, serious, highly talented lad, tending to stand alone, and patient under the pressures of a school in barracks. To one of his contemporaries, writing many years later, he seemed as though from another world: modest, good-willed, never breaking the rules, neat and correct in appearance, 'like a girl in uniform'. What was striking, recalled this class-mate, was his consciousness of his poetic gift. Often, before the start of the German lesson, he would rise silently from his place at the back and bring some poems up to the teacher, who always allowed him to read them to the class. 'We knew little about poetry, and were silent, for us a sign of great respect, and no one poked fun. He was a personality.'[7]

Physically he was below par, and could not, according to this account, have been more awkward at gymnastics, fencing, and games: but he never complained. The officer who taught German—also, it must be noted, writing many years later, when this young 'personality' had become the famous poet and he himself was a Major-General on the reserve—recalled in a letter to Rilke the red ink he had lavished in criticism of his 'imaginative and verbose essays', but also the understanding he had shown for the 'book-worm' and his sympathy for the duffer at gym exposed to the contempt of his fellows.[8]

Rilke himself, when he spoke or wrote of these days, stressed as the mainspring of his misery his increasing isolation, a 'painful training in loneliness among the crowd'.[9] And it cannot be doubted that, coming at the age of ten from a sheltered life into the rough-and-tumble of boarding-school and military discipline, he found it an ordeal. 'When the lonely, helpless heart is treated with unreasoning brutality after unhealthy pampering', as he put it himself, 'then comes the moment of truth: a child becomes either indifferent or unhappy. For me it was the latter.' He sought consolation in an exaggerated piety, to which his mother's fervid religiosity had already made him prone: sometimes, after specially brutal bullying, praying for an illness, or even death, positively enjoying a 'false sense of martyrdom'.[10] 'I suffered, and endured.'[11] Above all, and especially in his third year, he sought refuge in his poetry, which now became more for him than just an occupation for idle moments— poems sometimes expressing adolescent longing for love or idealizing the comradeship he could not find, but more often devoted to themes of battle and heroic deeds. He also began to write a history of the Thirty Years War, for which his interest had already been evoked at school in Prague, trying to picture the great men of the time, Wallenstein, Gustav Adolph, Tilly, against a backdrop of devastation and decay, and interlarding his prose text with verse celebrating their power of leadership in the warring faiths. The school notebooks of 1888 and 1889 which contain these poems and the beginning of this manuscript bear witness to a sudden bursting forth of poetic talent, his 'first modest sacrifice' at the altar of the Muse 'when I awoke out of the night of my spirit'.[12] The wish-fulfilment apparent is of a piece with the 'false sense of martyrdom' and evidence of the will to prove himself against all odds. It was accompanied in his fourth year at St. Pölten by a progressive deterioration in his health. His medical condition on leaving was characterized by 'nervous- ness', and a bout of pneumonia proved sufficiently disturbing for him to be sent during the summer of 1890 to Salzburg for a salt-water cure before going up to Mährisch-Weisskirchen.

For the start of the school year there in September he arrived late, and was almost immediately complaining in a letter to his mother, of fever and headaches 'worse than ever'.[13] In November he was in the sick-bay for a fortnight, and was clearly still so unfit when discharged that he was sent home on 6 December, well before the end of term, for which there is thus no

performance record. How long he actually remained after returning in the
New Year is not clear. He spoke of riding lessons, but also spoke of long
periods in the sick-room, 'more spiritually troubled than ill in body', when he
seemed to find greater clarity and self-assurance in his essays at poetry and 'the
oft-repressed urge for solace now freely blossomed forth'.[14] What is certain is
that he had now become desperate to get out as soon as ever possible, and that
he somehow convinced his father that he should be withdrawn on grounds of
health. Josef, as is shown by one of the rare communications of his to Phia
which have been preserved, put this crisis down to the disturbing influence of
her letters to René, exciting instead of calming him. Be that as it may, he gave
in, and his official application obtained the boy's release on 4 June 1891.

3

'The strings of my lyre are not rusting'
(To Sedlakowitz, 30. 12. 1892)

One of the legends which long surrounded Rilke's school-days was that his
sufferings had rendered his formal education unavailing, and that the powers
he revealed later were all the more remarkable for being those of a largely self-
taught adult. It is now evident that this was wide of the mark. For, after having
forced his parents to spare him any further 'tortures' at the hands of the
military system, he was able without any special coaching to join the
Commercial Academy at Linz, where they decided to enter him that autumn,
at the level appropriate to his age, omitting the preparatory first stage and
moving straight into the second-year class. The military college curriculum
was broadly modelled on that of the civil educational system in Austria, and
Rilke's academic performance at St. Pölten, as we have seen, had been
excellent: so that his transfer in September 1891 to the Linz Academy,
corresponding in level to the senior college at Weisskirchen, presented no
difficulty on that score.

His illnesses had been largely psychosomatic, induced by the feeling of
isolation and abandonment rather than by any resistance to the idea of a
military career, and he was quickly restored. Most of the summer he spent at a
villa rented by his uncle Jaroslav at Smichov, then still a suburb of Prague,
where he went for long walks—still in uniform, for, as he wrote to Phia, it
gained him more respect. The new-found freedom had not, indeed, yet
tempted him to give up a military future. For the moment, he told her, he was
'entirely a literary man', and among other things was busy on the second part
of the 'Thirty Years War'; but later, from Linz, he avowed that the army was
the only career for which he was suited. 'I have taken off the Emperor's
uniform only to don it again before long—for always: and rest assured I shall
wear it honourably.'[1] He will no doubt have written in similar strain to his

father, for in a poem for Josef's birthday, on 25 September, he promised hard work 'to keep his word'.[2] At Linz, a garrison town where army officers were held in high regard, friends of his own age heard the same story.

It was not the relative freedom of civilian student life which most marked the change for him. The lonely outsider now found acceptance and respect among his fellows, his unusual background and friendly approach to all lending him a standing he had never so far enjoyed. Awkwardness at games and physical shortcomings no longer weighed in the balance against academic performance, and he quickly came to be regarded as an asset to the establishment. Lodgings with a responsible guardian had to be found for a student still under sixteen: but with the family of Hans Drouot, the respected chief clerk and later owner of the Court printing works at Linz, the way was open for a light-hearted social life he had not known before, with balls, the theatre, carnival occasions, even a shooting party with Drouot. Uniform had given way to an elegant dark suit with white tie, velvet-collared overcoat, silver-headed cane, and grey bowler. A studio portrait of him in this rig, with level, assertive gaze, shows how quickly this 'personality' had developed in the new conditions into a self-assured young man, confident in his ability to find his way.

His aura of literary achievement added an undoubted cachet. Already from Smichov he had succeeded in getting a poem into print, his entry for a competition in a Vienna magazine (not a prize-winner, but judged among the best),[3] and his gift for rhyming could now be given full rein before a more receptive audience than the army trainers and trainees. His reputation as a poet grew: he now had friends who were delighted to have his verse inscribed in their albums; he was called on by the class to write the poem celebrating their teacher's name-day; and his effort for the Academy Director's jubilee was highly praised in the local press. Another Viennese journal, *Bohemia's German Poetry and Art*, encouraged him to send in his contributions, and published one at Easter 1892—significantly, a robust and fervently patriotic reply to Bertha von Suttner's pacifist call against armaments.[4]

As he wrote to Phia, it was a delight to be there. The Academy's curriculum was designed to combine 'a scientifically based general education with a comprehensive preparation for the various commercial professions'. In his first semester there was less emphasis on the second aim, though his performance was 'satisfactory' in commercial mathematics and business theory; in arts and science subjects, on the other hand, notably French, history, chemistry, natural history, and physics, he excelled, and in spite of a rather high number of absences he had no difficulty in achieving an overall 'pass' and being placed second in a class of over fifty.[5] Out of school, his evenings were not all social occasions. He read Tolstoy and Schlosser's *World History* in the Drouots' 'highly elegant drawing-room',[6] and wrote many poems which were later to appear in his first published volume of verse. There was a welcome for him in the home of a school-mate, Arnold Wimhölzel, with whom he had struck up a close friendship. Here he met two charming sisters, cousins of Arnold's, and, as befitted his new image, responded to their admiration in letters strewn with verse, protesting his love and blessing the good fortune which had brought him to Linz.

Here I was to know what love means ... it cannot be just chance? How lonely and drearily I passed my days till now ... Spring! Spring is here, inside me, in my soul and in nature ... Now I am *truly* happy—Oh! do not destroy this beautiful illusion, let me go on believing that—you both—like me a little, that there is a modest place in your hearts for your—René.[7]

Distance now lent enchantment even to the misery of St. Pölten. In a letter to the German teacher there he said he looked back on his time not without pleasure, for even though some days had been hard, there were still many 'radiant in the sunshine of overflowing youthful spirits: and in times to come these will remain islands of promise amid the surging seas of earthly sorrows'.[8]

For the moment, such sorrows seemed a long way off. Early in the New Year he was noticed to be 'walking out' with Olga Blumauer, an attractive blonde employed as a children's nurse, meeting her in the mornings before going to school. Frau Drouot was informed of this by the guardian of another pupil, whom he feared was being led astray by René's bad influence and not working as he should; and she was therefore suspicious when her charge announced his intention of going to the theatre for the end of season performance on 30 March. With reason, as it turned out: for enquiry with Olga's employer revealed that she too had been given the evening off for the theatre, but neither was to be found there when Frau Drouot—evidently an energetic Mrs Grundy—actually checked the audience. She gave René the edge of her tongue when he came in at a quarter to eleven, and telegraphed his father to come the following day, who extracted a promise that he would give up this 'liaison'. But he soon lapsed again, with the result that father was once more summoned, at the end of April, and again received his solemn vow to forget Olga.

It did not escape the notice of the vigilant Frau Drouot when he failed once again to keep his promise, but she was not prepared for the dénouement. On Sunday 21 May he went out early, and was presumed to be viewing the town's decorations for the Choir Festival due that day. Only when he failed to return, and after Olga too was found to have given notice, ostensibly to join her mother in Vienna, was the alarm raised. Telegrams were sent to Josef and Phia, to see if René was with them; the school was notified; and after two days the police informed. It was not until 24 May that the couple were found to have registered in an obscure Vienna hotel, and René was fetched back via Linz to Prague. No one seems to have paid much attention to the fate of the girl. He had given no inkling of his plans to Arnold Wimhölzel, who of course as his friend was closely questioned. In the record of the drama which Arnold subsequently wrote up for posterity, and which has only recently come to light, he draws a fascinating picture of the scandalized Frau Drouot bemoaning this ungrateful behaviour from a boy she had liked so much and treated as one of her own.[9]

Later, in September, René wrote to his mother to say he felt happy now that he could recognize his error and could regret it—couching his letter in the high-flown terms calculated to secure her indulgence: the divine spark 'kindled by heaven in every breast' could become a holy Vestal flame, but it could also start 'a disastrous consuming fire, fanned by the violent storms of passion, to destroy everything it has previously created'—and for him this fire had been kindled by a 'stupid flirtation'. 'Thank God I feel freed from the bonds of this liaison.'[10] But his true motives for this sudden break seem fairly clear. The military dream had faded; in its place, if he completed his course at the Commercial Academy, there loomed the nightmare of a 'desolate counting-house future'.[11] He was sure he deserved better than that, and felt there must be a way to escape it. It had been flattering to bask in the admiration of friends, but the reception of his verse in the wider world of the Vienna literary scene encouraged hope for greater things, away from the provincial social life of Linz. To run off with Olga to Vienna offered him the chance he wanted. For, whatever consuming fire had been kindled by this 'stupid flirtation', it is certain that he kept a cool head while in the capital, taking the opportunity to call twice on Eduard Kastner, the editor who had already published him and with whom he had been in correspondence. With Kastner he left a manuscript notebook of the poems he had written at Linz, in the hope of further publication.[12] We need not discount the erotic appeal of the adventure to realize that it was also a startling demonstration of refusal to follow the path laid down for him, and that the month of May 1892 marked his decision for himself that, come what might, he would be a poet.

Phia, who now planned to move to Vienna, was soon to be asked to help him place his poems in journals; but Josef, though indulgent, was not one to conceive of poetry as anything but a spare-time diversion. His concern was how to finish the boy's education in a way that would fit him for some sort of 'normal' career—and how to pay for it. Jaroslav, who felt himself responsible for his younger brothers as the head of the family since their father's death, was at first furious over René's escapade. Having lost both his own sons from illness at an early age, he saw in his nephew the last hope for the Rilkes' future. René had obviously suffered from his mother's influence, he wrote to Josef on 4 June—an unhealthy inheritance which, coupled with his unsystematic reading, had over-excited him, and excessive praise at too early an age had gone to his head.[13] Nevertheless he said he was prepared to put up a monthly allowance of 200 gulden ('except during the holidays') for private tuition for the school certificate, followed by law studies at university, after which René would be in line to join his own practice and one day, he hoped, succeed him.[14] With the exception of this ultimate aim, René asked for nothing better. He would work hard, but he would be free also to pursue his own goal.

For the rest of the summer he was sent up to Schönfeld, in northern Bohemia, staying with a tutor who had been engaged to begin his study programme. On his return to Prague in September a room was found for him with his aunt Gabriele von Kutschera, now also separated from her husband, in the Wassergasse (Vodičkova Ulice). Here he settled down with a will to a severe schedule of work, to catch up in three years on the normal Gymnasium eight-year curriculum for Latin, Greek, and the other subjects he had so far missed. Every morning from 6.30 till noon the tutors succeeded each other; every six months he was examined at the German secondary school at Prague-Neustadt (Nové Mesto), acquitting himself with distinction each time. It was work he enjoyed, as can be seen from his letters to Phia: but what made him most happy was the freedom to do his own writing. The strings of his lyre, far from rusting, sounded purer notes than ever, he wrote in another letter to the St. Pölten teacher.[15]

The manuscript notebook, returned by Kastner in Vienna, had now become the manuscript of a volume of verses which he planned to entitle *Life and Songs* (*Leben und Lieder*), and towards the end of 1892 he sent some of the poems to Franz Keim, a poet-schoolmaster in St. Pölten he had been too diffident to approach before, for his opinion. Keim was evidently encouraging, though rightly urging him to more stringent self-criticism. He received favourable comments too from Dr Alfred Klaar, Prague teacher in the history of German Literature and president of the 'Concordia' literary society. Thus fortified, he offered the volume in the New Year to the Stuttgart publishing house of Cotta. Though it was refused, he was not cast down, more especially as he had just found new inspiration in another love-affair, this time on a plane more appealing to his artistic pretensions.

Valerie von David-Rhonfeld, or Vally as she was called, came from a family who were frequent visitors at the Entz home in the Herrengasse. A year or so older than René, she was a friend of one of his cousins, and the niece of the Czech poet Julius Zeyer. She liked to paint porcelain and write novellas, and cultivated her artistic leanings in a delicately eccentric bohemianism, affecting a red Empire-style dress and a shepherdess's crook—altogether an understandably attractive figure to a young man eager himself to break loose from the bonds of bourgeois philistinism, and he was declaring his love in verse the very day after their first meeting. She lived in another district of Prague, the Weinberge (Vinohrady), and he often took refuge there with his work in the afternoons. It was a welcome relief from the lonely room in the Wassergasse, which looked out on a noisy courtyard, and from the 'gloomy, sober atmosphere round the relations who are so far removed from me'.[16] The appearance in his life of this agreeably unconventional creature gave him new heart for his school work at a time when his future had become uncertain with the unexpected death of his benefactor Uncle Jaroslav in December.

She claimed later that only thanks to her was he able to finish his cramming and not succumb to despair—that, despised by his family and friendless, he even talked sometimes of suicide. No doubt the welcome in her aesthetically pretentious room, and her appreciation of his still näive verses, gave him the spur he stood in need of. Indeed, it was she who, when he finally found a publisher for *Life and Songs*, contrived to get together the money required to finance it, after having rescued the manuscript from a pond in to which he had thrown it in another fit of despair—or so she said. G. E. Kattentidt, who issued from Strasbourg and Leipzig a literary fortnightly and a similar annual almanac, was among those who had accepted some of René's poems from these student days, and one of the few who were prepared to enter into a personal correspondence with him, becoming friend as well as publisher. To editors in Vienna, Dresden, Hamburg, and Prague, René Maria Rilke was now an increasingly familiar name: but it was Kattentidt who, once assured of having the printing costs covered, brought out *Life and Songs* in November 1894, with its dedication to Vally.

Standard themes in an imitative style characterize these verses, with only a rare glimpse of an original turn and in most an unredeemed sentimentality. It was not long, indeed, before he came himself to concede the shortcomings of *Life and Songs*. 'My talent was so small then,' he wrote to Ellen Key in 1904, 'my feelings immature and timorous, and into the bargain I chose for all my first publications the worst and most impersonal of all my efforts, for I could not bring myself to reveal what was really close to my heart.'[17] He fervently hoped the book would be forgotten; and in fact only a handful of copies have survived.

In these and his other efforts we can discern little promise of the later Rilke. Unlike the young Hofmannsthal a few years earlier, he did not emerge fully-fledged to astonish the literary world with instant mastery. Trying his hand at everything—lyric poetry, prose stories and sketches, drama—in dogged determination to succeed, he showed astonishing industry, and the urge to write, not as the amanuensis of some divine inspiration, but as the conscious apprentice to a craft. He sought advice and help from 'authoritative' personalities—always addressed as 'Master'—and corresponded indefatigably with, as it were, the trade journals. He had not yet reached that serene independence he would recommend a few years later in his turn to a young poet seeking his advice; but he had asked himself the question: 'Can I live without writing? *must* I write?' and answered with an unhesitating, a 'strong and simple "*I must*"'.[18] All else, the externals of ordinary life, the passing of examinations, the demands of family and friends, the call of love, were already subordinate to this imperative.

It led to a preoccupation with himself, a drive of which he was half-aware to make his life fit his 'work': and we find now the first manifestations of that lifelong tendency to 'self-stylization' which has by turns fascinated and irritated friends and critics. Where others would confide in a diary, or transmute the autobiographical into literature, Rilke's need was almost always to communicate directly, in letters which are simultaneously both personal and impersonal, and which, as he himself acknowledged at the end of his life, form an essential part of his work. Thus now, on his nineteenth birthday, in a long missive to Vally in which he looked forward to their life together—going forward into the twentieth century as two artists in harmony, 'in their love and creative activity forgetting the world and pitying or despising their fellow men'—he re-created his life so far in bleak contrast to this bright vision.

You know the dark story of my missed childhood and you know whose fault it was that I have little or nothing joyful to record from those early days. . . . I had love and care only from my father, but generally was left to myself, and there was no one to whom I could confide my little pleasures and sorrows. . . . What I suffered then can be compared with the worst torment known in this world, although I was but a child—or rather just because I was one, because I had as yet no power of resistance or the experience to see that this was only boyish exuberance and nothing more.
. . . To my childish mind, my forbearance seemed to bring me close in merit to Jesus Christ: and one day, when I received a hard blow in the face, so that my knees trembled, I said quietly—I can hear it now—to my unjust attacker: 'I suffer this in peace and without complaint, for that is how Christ suffered, and when you hit me, I prayed to my good Lord that He may forgive you.' . . . I sought refuge always in the farthest window corner, bit back my tears till they could flow hot and uncontrolled at night time when the noise of the boys' regular breathing filled the dormitory. And it was one night, on one of my birthdays, that I kneeled up in bed and prayed with folded hands for death. Even an illness would have been a sign that my prayer had been heard, but it did not come. Instead at that time the urge to write grew stronger in me, which had already in my childish efforts given me comfort. . . . So in these dreary days the often-repressed urge for solace now freely blossomed forth . . . For I had never encountered even a friendly approach, let alone love, and yet this was what I longed for and demanded. . . . My heart was empty before I met you, Vally. . . . Then came the time you know about, of which the bitter disappointments and vagaries are now buried in your forgiveness. . . . I was already on the point of giving up my academic future, the continual unsuccessful work unconnected with what I wanted from life, when you, my beloved dearest Vally, found me, strengthened, healed and comforted me and gave me life, existence, hope and future . . .[19]

There is much of self-pity here: but we should not allow this to obscure the evidence it gives of determination to overcome what he saw as a fearful handicap. For this version of his childhood, which became for him the 'truth', was to strengthen him in his conviction that the artist must necessarily stand alone against the incomprehension of his fellow men, and in his will to succeed even against these odds.

Letters were for him a form of self-analysis, and Vally was the first in a long

Joseph and Phia Rilke on their engagement

Rilke aged three

Rilke as a schoolboy, 1883

The cadet at the Military College,
Mährisch-Weisskirchen

Rilke in Linz

Valerie von David-Rhonfeld

line of 'healers and comforters' to receive them. Yet, although he afterwards often referred to the hell of his military school-days, he seems to have been anxious to suppress its memory. In a short story, 'Pierre Dumont', written earlier in 1894, he had described vividly the parting of a mother, an officer's widow, from her young son at the start of the autumn term at a military college: but this was never published. A brief cameo, 'The Gym Class' ('Die Turnstunde'), first written as a diary entry in November 1899, was actually published three years later. It reflects more directly his antipathy to the military atmosphere, in describing the death of a weakly boy in a desperate attempt to prove himself. Apart from these, however, the 'military novel' he long had in mind could never be brought to paper.

Meanwhile the independence he enjoyed was sweet, and his continued allowance was ample enough to cover summer holidays away from Prague. After passing with distinction his final examinations in June 1894 he spent some time in Dittersbach, in north Bohemia, and on the Baltic coast at Misdroy—his first sight of the sea, 'like violet-blue, heavy satin'.[20] Greater freedom still now lay before him, when he would enrol at the university; and the ties to Vally, which only eight months before he had celebrated with such fervour, began to loosen. His feeling of new power, as master of his fate, found expression in his signature 'René Maria *Caesar* Rilke' under a poem for the daughter of a Prague doctor whom he chanced to meet in Misdroy. Back in Prague in the autumn, he broke off the still unofficial engagement to Vally, writing afterwards, to thank her 'for the gift of freedom', in a letter of suffocating banality:

You showed greatness and nobility even in this moment of trial, more than I. My blessing rests on your head. You were a bright shooting star in a dark life! Farewell. And if you ever need a friend—then call on me.—No one can be more of a friend to you than your René.[21]

It is doubtful whether her affection for him had ever been more than a part of the role she was playing, with the added attraction of earning her parents' diapproval when she preferred the prospect-less student to the more suitable matches they proposed. But when it came to parting, she took it hard, and in fact never married, her memories of the episode turning to bitterness as she watched his progress. In its way, the relationship was a prototype of that with all the women in his life: the initial attraction, often to someone older than himself and an artist, the temptation of a 'normal' life together, the conflict then between the life and his work, with sooner or later—and mostly sooner—the inevitable stern decision that his work must come first, and that he could realize what was in him only in solitude. In an apparently gentle nature, such ruthlessness was surprising. More surprising still, and it says much for his charm, was that, of all the women to whom this happened (and none failed eventually to record their feelings and memories), Vally was the only one to bear him any lasting ill will.

4

'There is no one like me, there never has been'

(*Ewald Tragy*)

The project of grooming René Rilke to succeed to his uncle's practice had not been affected by Jaroslav's death so soon after setting it in motion. The surviving daughters, Paula and Irene, had agreed to continue the monthly allowance, so there was no obstacle to the next stage. But with René's enrolment at the Carl-Ferdinand University for the winter term of 1895 came his first open demurral, though not yet open rebellion, against the plan which had been set for him. Instead of reading law, as Jaroslav would certainly have insisted had he lived, he chose history of art, history of literature, and philosophy as his field. At nearly twenty, he was older than his fellows, if not more mature; and in the liberation of university life he found the opportunity not only to emerge in person on the literary scene where he had hitherto made his mark from relative obscurity, but also to discover the life of the city itself outside the German culture in which he had been brought up.

The themes of the next volume of verse he was planning reflected both these worlds. *Offerings to the Lares* (*Larenopfer*), which was published in December and for which he again had Vally's help, this time in designing the cover, has 'strong roots in Bohemia', as he wrote himself in a puff for the book[1]—a Bohemia with both a German and a Czech past and present, and which to the patriots of the '48' had been a single fatherland, not the preserve of one or the other party. The work is a curious mixture: a Baedeker-like tour of Prague's memorials to its long history, new-romantic evocations of its atmosphere, sentimental naturalistic pictures of 'the people', in their poverty and dreary lives, and tributes to admired contemporaries among the Czech poets, such as Jaroslav Vrchlický and Julius Zeyer (Vally's uncle, the 'master' to whom he sent in October a copy of *Life and Songs* with a fulsome dedication). Rilke is seen here still as a beginner, open to all the literary influences of the time, following and imitating: but also as a sharp observer of real life. As some reviewers noted, he had begun to shed the immaturity and unreality of *Life and Songs*. Replying in January to some appreciative lines from a Czech writer, he characterized his purpose as the 'sounding of a gentle chord of peace amid the clash of battle', the expression of 'the sympathy I feel for your people and their artistic endeavours' and 'a witness to my recognition of a supreme empire above the caste divisions of the nations; the empire on which the sun of art never sets'.[2]

There was no sign yet of the antipathy towards Prague which often coloured his later memories. On the contrary, in this first university year he seems to have eagerly sought out and hugely enjoyed the new literary and artistic contacts which now offered themselves. He became an active member of the leading associations, appeared in the café circles, and pushed himself forward assiduously, seeking out the 'moderns', fertile in ideas and full of projects of his own. Already in his first term he published at his own expense the first number of a free pamphlet-journal of poems, and had proposed to Kattentidt that he should take over the editing of a new venture, *Young Germany and Young Austria*, a fortnightly to appear alongside the publisher's *Young Germany and Young Alsatia* to which he was still contributing. These enterprises were short-lived, but his enthusiasm was unabated. Increasingly self-confident, he wrote ceaselessly, and saw much of his work published, in such varying forms and styles that it is sometimes hard to credit them to the same pen. Now the aesthete, the poet of romantic melancholy, who was indeed occasionally to be seen in this persona, making his way through the crowds on the Graben, dressed in black and carrying a single long-stemmed iris; now the author of dramatic monologues ('psycho-dramas') and crassly naturalistic stories and dramatic episodes, outdoing Hauptmann in their dreary themes of the downtrodden poor and their outspoken criticism of society; now the self-appointed 'house poet' to Láska van Oestéren of Schloss Veleslavin, the daughter of a family of the minor nobility and a writer herself. But always the self-advertiser, avid for attention and recognition as a writer. In January 1896 his draft entry for a lexicon of nineteenth-century German poets and prose-writers ran: 'René Maria Caesar Rilke ... currently editor of "Young Germany and Young Austria". My motto: patior ut potiar. For the present I nourish a striving towards light; for the future, one hope and one fear. The hope: inner peace and joy of creation. The fear (burdened as I am with an hereditary nervous condition): madness! I am active in the fields of drama (*Free and Equal, Hoar-Frost*), the novella and sketch (many scattered in over 20 journals, soon to be collected), lyric poetry, psychodrama, criticism, etc.'[3] As has rightly been said, this year in Prague was perhaps the only one in his life in which he could see a successful career in the conventional sense opening before him.[4]

The idea of publishing his own journal of 'Songs as a Gift to the People' seems to have been inspired by Karl Henckell's *Sunflowers* (*Sonnenblumen*), which was appearing in Zurich with contributions from a number of prominent poets and which René reviewed in a Prague newspaper in December 1895. Henckell, a refugee socialist from Bismarck's Germany, saw his journal as an instrument of workers' education. René resolved to go one better. His, entitled *Wild Chicory* (*Wegwarten*), the wayside weed, would be distributed gratis to the workers and the poor wherever he could find them. That same month, immediately after *Larenopfer*, the first number appeared, with a score of his poems selected from the ample stores of the previous three years and a foreword in which he proclaimed the need for art to be free for the poor. 'Cheap editions are not enough: even two kreuzer is too much if the choice is book or bread. If you want to give to all—then give! According to Paracelsus, the wild chicory becomes a living being once every century: and the legend may well be fulfilled in these songs—perhaps they will awake to a higher life in the soul of the people. I am myself poor: but this hope makes me rich.—"Wild Chicory" will appear once or twice a year. Pluck them, and may they be a joy to you!'[5] He had doubts himself whether his offering would in fact reach the people, as he sent it off to various craft guilds and workers' associations, hospitals and booksellers, or left copies lying about in public places. He was hardly in a position to afford sufficient numbers to saturate the market, and 'a few hundred copies just sink without trace'. But he could hope that here and there chance would still carry one 'into a lonely room where these simple songs may awaken a little joy and light'.[6]

Behind the genuine idealism lay probably a more practical, if subconscious, purpose. Sending copies to his already extensive address list of 'masters' and to others who might not yet have heard of him—Theodor Fontane, or Arthur Schnitzler—was a more striking and original way of bringing himself to their notice. It was significant that the journal was exclusively devoted to René Rilke, unlike Henckell's anthologies of contemporaries; and the second number in April 1896 abandoned the idea altogether of 'songs for the people' in favour of his abysmally naturalistic drama *Now and in the Hour of our Departing . . . (Jetzt und in der Stunde unseres Absterbens . . .)*, a grim tale of grinding landlords, incest, and death in poverty—hardly a source of light and joy for the lonely worker's room. With equal enthusiasm he had simultaneously pressed himself on Kattentidt as editor, from the New Year, of *Young Germany and Young Austria*, which with its promising list of potential subscribers he was confident he could 'raise to the level of its well-proven sister journal'[7]—and which incidentally could also serve the reputation of its energetic editor. But within a few weeks he was already complaining of his powerlessness to change this 'asylum for dilettantes'[8] which he reproached Kattentidt for creating. The flood of subscribers he had expected turned out a trickle: there proved in fact to be no readership for a separate edition. By March he had laid down the burden as quickly as he had taken it up, recording a loss of over 19 gulden—for his circumstances quite substantial.

In his correspondence with Kattentidt, with whom he remained on the best of terms in spite of the irritation he must have caused the editor, he could be condescending about the self-advertising of other aspiring young poets, confident in the position he had established for himself on loftier heights. Certainly, with so much of his own published, he was becoming a name in Prague. He rarely missed the meetings of the sedate literary society 'Concordia', presided over by his patron Klaar, where he could demonstrate his remarkable gift for improvisation in verse before distinguished visitors such as Karl-Emil Franzos, or the regular Thursday evenings in the 'peaceable, moderated Anti-Concordia'[9] of the Fine Arts Association, where there was livelier and more congenial company in the persons of the dramatist Rudolf Christoph Jenny and the artist Emil Orlik. Here he could listen to talks by the artists on their work and technique, or to Jenny reading his plays; his own novellas found a receptive audience, and he could rhyme for this anti-Establishment younger generation a call for a 'bold *Sezession*'. But all this was still not enough: he must needs form a society himself—a 'league of true moderns', complementary rather than in competition with the two established associations, with a journal of its own (for which *Wegwarten* stood ready made) and an 'intimate theatre' for connoisseurs of drama where plays excluded from the regular stage could be produced. He dreamed of an entirely new structure, 'the fantastic house of a free guild of artists, reaching up high into the blue, a palace from whose golden turret flutters the oriflamme of enthusiasm'.[10]

The idea had in fact originated with his friend Harry Louis von Dickinson, of Dresden, who was writing verse and prose like his under the pseudonym Bodo Wildberg (and also publishing at his own expense). The two rapidly agreed that the society of 'like-minded spirits' should be highly select (that is, selected by them), and not be limited to Prague but extend by correspondence over Austria and Germany—Vienna, Berlin, Göttingen. By May, in the summer semester at the University when René finally transferred to the law faculty in deference to the family's wishes, they had drummed up sufficient support to plan *Wegwarten* as the official organ, to which all the members would contribute their work, the artists providing a new title-page for each issue. Also, and much more important, the members would subscribe to cover the printing costs of a hundred copies each. With every member reaching his own circle of friends, René was optimistic for an 'enormous circulation' for a journal still to be distributed gratis but destined now for the élite, no longer for the lonely worker:[11] a new vehicle for 'modern creation' under the spell of 'intimate imaginative atmosphere'.[12] And it would be all the more effective as the product of a small group, united in its aims and free of the quarrels inevitable in anything larger.

He had already pushed for the creation of a 'free theatre' in Prague, and this too he could hope for from the new league. He had a fully-equipped stage in mind, Jenny would make a magnificent producer, and actors, both 'professionals and sensible amateurs', would soon be found. Oddly, however, for such an enthusiast for naturalism, his aim with it was to produce—Maeterlinck: 'the drama whose most eloquent speech is silence and where the catastrophe is "repose that cries out". Hermann Bahr wrote to me that [Maeterlinck's] *Les aveugles* would be suitable for such a presentation.'[13] Anything further removed from his own recent efforts—*Hoar-frost, Now and in the Hour* . . .—is hard to imagine. His 'free theatre' never materialized, and the grandiose concept of the league of moderns itself petered out after the third and last number of *Wegwarten*: but the conflicting pulls of naturalism and symbolism remained a long time unresolved, explaining perhaps his eventual renunciation of the drama as a form of expression. The whole episode—and it was very brief—was simply part, as he recognized later, of his 'impatient desire to prove to a hostile environment my right to such activity . . . the only time in my life that I was not struggling inside the work itself but striving for recognition by presenting its inadequate beginnings.'[14] In his idea of a meeting of 'like-minded spirits', however, we can see a trait which remained an essential element in his make-up. Linked with them, he felt he would no longer be writing a confession to the lifeless walls of his room, but whispering a confidence to a 'deeply sensitive people, whose limpid soul reflects the image of my own being'.[15] This need to communicate and elaborate his work to friends, or to unknown correspondents in whom he sensed an affinity, soon became much more powerful than the desire to see it published.

For the moment publication, and the search for recognition, remained paramount. He was feverishly active in every possible direction: placing his own productions and pressing to get them noticed, helping with anthologies of translations from the Czech, reviewing, planning collections of his prose stories and sketches, arranging for a performance of *Now and in the Hour* . . . at the German Volkstheater in Prague and conducting a vast correspondence. In practice, the league of moderns was little more than a mutual admiration society, the few members reviewing each other's work. Hans Benzmann received René's glowing praise for his volume of verse (the reader being urged to *buy* it) and in his turn noticed *Larenopfer* favourably; Jenny's play *Necessity Knows No Law*—a 'drama of the people'—with its 'clearly developed action' and the 'Hogarthian realism' of its characters,[16] gained useful advance publicity from René for its sole Prague performance in May. His university lectures he presumably did not entirely cut, but there is never a mention of this less absorbing work in his letters, which bubble over with the latest literary and theatre gossip.

At Whitsun he accompanied Jenny to Vienna, and then journeyed on to Budapest to see the millennial Festival and Exhibition. Distant relations there had invited him, and he was due to stay until the middle of June. Although he found them 'miles better' than those at home, the prospect of so long in the company of people with petty interests, whose horizon was bounded by the parish church, was not appealing, however, and he was able to beat a polite retreat a few days earlier than planned.[17]

Prague itself was becoming too narrow for him. Where his early letters and contributions to editors, apart from Kattentidt, had once ranged no further than the confines of Austria, they now reached out to Berlin, Bremen, and Munich. Planning a new volume of verse, he looked for a publisher, not in Prague, but in Wiesbaden, or even Zurich—'never in Austria!';[18] and during the summer another of his revered 'masters', Richard Zoozmann, impressed with the quality of this new manuscript, helped him to place it with

Friesenhahn in Leipzig, generously meeting half the publishing costs himself. He grew increasingly restive under the restraints of provincial life: not only the indifference, even hostility, of his father and relations to his endeavours, but also the limitations of the literary establishment itself, notwithstanding the benevolence of Klaar and of August Sauer, who had been his professor in the history of literature. He had managed to see beyond the walls of the German 'ghetto' in Bohemia, and learned to respect the aspirations of the Czechs. But his brief year of independence had shown him ever more clearly that, if he was to make his name as a poet in the German language, he must abandon this distant outpost.

Many before and after him, who grew up on the periphery of the German culture and language, felt this strong gravitational pull from the centre, and its influence was especially powerful on his contemporaries, at a time when the non-German peoples of Austria-Hungary were beginning to press more urgently their claims to self-determination. Franz Werfel went to Hamburg and Leipzig, Kafka to Berlin; Emil Orlik from Prague and Arthur Holitscher from Budapest to Munich. And Munich was René Rilke's choice. He had already corresponded with Holitscher, on the editorial staff of the new journal *Simplizissimus*, over contributions of poems; the city was the home of many of his admired masters, including the playwright Max Halbe and the dramatist-poet Ludwig Ganghofer; here he would surely find a true 'league of moderns'. After the atmosphere of Prague, he would find fresh air indeed in a 'city of art' where he could 'purify and clarify my taste and judgement'.[19] In July, the summer semester scarcely over, he was already thinking of a move there, and the plan soon became firm. His university studies could continue in Munich, and with that assurance he contrived to persuade his father, not only to agree, but also to provide a modest allowance over and above that which his cousins, much against their will, consented to continue.

The production of his play on 6 August he registered as a 'great success', writing to Zoozmann and to Ludwig Jacobowski in Berlin, splendidly staged and less stark and brutal in its effect than the reading version.[20] The notices were in fact reasonably good. One Prague paper, describing its 'heaped-up misery' as a 'ballad in everyday clothing, but no drama', nevertheless praised the dramatic talent shown in the 'anticipation and compression of the short succession of scenes, some powerful dashes of colour and the bold use of contrasts'.[21] The Vienna theatrical publisher Eirich took it into his list, and René had hopes that *Hoar-Frost* too would be produced. His plans for a collection of novellas and sketches, several times announced when individual stories were published, had not so far materialized, and he was continually revising his selection. The verse volume, however, 'modern, better poems than those of *Larenopfer*', which he hoped would reach the Christmas market,[22] made good progress. On Zoozmann's advice, he curtailed their number and limited the themes, and changed the title from *New Poems* to *Crowned with Dreams* (*Traumgekrönt*), with a respectful dedication to his patron. He was busy too on the preparation of the third number of *Wegwarten*.

Social occasions were not lacking amid all this industry. After many months of correspondence with Láska van Oestéren, his 'admired colleague', pouring out to her at great length all his hopes and plans and a great deal of occasional verse, he had finally succeeded in getting himself invited in July to Schloss Veleslavin, near Prague, where the family spent the summers. In the first days of August came another invitation, to a great ball at the Castle, given by the Baroness van Oestéren for Láska and her other daughters; and in the carriage she sent for him René found another guest, a young man in the dress uniform of a lieutenant of dragoons, one Siegfried Trebitsch, temporarily in Prague on his second term of military service. This fellow poet and writer, as he proved to be (remembered now chiefly as the translator into German of George Bernard Shaw), was a congenial companion: for like René he too was seeking to justify his vocation against his stepfather's wish for him to succeed him in his business in Vienna. They talked long in the garden of the castle, away from the crowd, and René confided in him his own decision: 'I shall either become a poet that people will listen to, or leave this earth, disappearing into the darkness.' In the carriage home Trebitsch recited some of his own verses, and was greatly heartened by the other's words: 'You are under an obligation to sweep aside every distraction and dedicate yourself with all your might to the work that destiny sets you. We have no choice, men like you and I.'[23] Shortly afterwards came a copy of *Larenopfer*, inscribed with a poem of dedication 'to the secret, sensitive poet, in remembrance of the homeward drive from Veleslavin'.[24] Thanks to Rilke's example of determination, he too succeeded in shaking the parental grip, and was grateful all his life for that evening.

As though sensing that his departure for Munich would be an irrevocable break with his homeland, René left soon after the performance of his play to spend ten days in Obergrund, on the upper Elbe, in the mountains of northern Bohemia. Here, not far from his father's birthplace, he revisited 'the old familiar places, whose temple magic banishes trouble and discontent from the spirit', listening to the brooks in the gorges and drinking in the sun on the peaks.[25] It was a much-needed rest, for although his health had been generally good, he had suffered considerable nervous tension and occasional migraines. He spent a day or two in nearby Dresden while there, a city whose art galleries he would often return to in later years. After two days back in Prague, he left again later in August, this time for the Salzkammergut to visit a cousin, but chiefly, it seems, to follow an actress from the Prague German Volkstheater, Jenny Carsen, who was making a guest appearance in Gmunden. His 'dear, evening-red-blonde friend' found little time for him, however, which was perhaps just as well: restful days in Goisern near Bad Ischl, 'not having to think of anything', were a 'fountain of youth for the nerves'.[26]

In Prague again in early September, he began to prepare for his leap into the unknown at the end of the month. The confidence he had expressed to Trebitsch may well have ebbed at the prospect. So much is clear from one of his few truly autobiographical works, the novella *Ewald Tragy*, written a year or so later: the longing to be gone, to be away from the constrictions and incomprehension of the family, to prove himself; but at the same time the love for his father and the gnawing self-doubt. Ewald is shown as two years younger than René, but otherwise every detail seems exact—so exact, indeed, in the delineation of the father, the absent mother, and the aunts and cousins, that there is no wonder he did not publish the story.

On Ewald's last Sunday before he goes off to Munich, 'I still don't know what you really want,' says his father, the 'elegant and respected' Inspector, on their way to the weekly lunch with his aunts:

'One doesn't just go off like that, into the blue. Just tell me, what are you going to do in Munich?' Ewald has his answer pat: 'Work.' 'So—as if you couldn't work here! . . . You have your room, your food, everybody wishes you well. And after all, we are known here, and if you treat people right, the best houses are open to you—' 'Oh, people! Always people . . . you seem to recognize only two things, people and money. Fall on your knees before people, and crawl on your belly to money, that's the goal, isn't it?' . . . 'Without money, one becomes a worthless scoundrel and brings shame on one's good and honourable name. After all we are not upstarts.' 'That's just it! you're the past, anno domini, outdated, dusty, dried-up—'

And the Inspector crosses to the other side of the street, which seems as they go on to grow wider and wider between them. The generation gap seems unbridgeable.

The luncheon, with three aunts, four cousins, little Egon, and his French governess, is described with delicate satire: the ineffable dullness, the trivial conversation before they move to table, the silences 'like long, long threads of faded wool', the parrot to whom they make animal noises and who bows towards them with the 'demeanour of a Jewish music-teacher', the over-eating, the predictable remarks with every course—and Ewald's frustrated hope that *someone*, as they raise their liqueur glasses in toasts, will surely remember that it is his *last* Sunday. As they doze off in the drawing-room, he confides quietly in the governess, who alone is interested in why he should be leaving when he does not have to. 'Are you a poet?' she asks.

'That's just it, I don't know. And one should really know, one way or the other. *Here* I can't get it clear: one can't get outside oneself, I need quiet, and room, and perspective . . .' 'But your father must be pleased, and your—' 'Mother, you mean. Well, yes, a lot of people have said that. You know, my mother is sick. You will have heard, probably—although they avoid mentioning her name here. She has left my father. She travels. She only takes with her what she needs for the journey, even love—I haven't heard about her for a long time, for we haven't written for a year now. But I'm sure, in the railway carriage, between two stations, she tells everyone: "My son is a poet"—

. . .yes, and then my father. He is a fine person. I love him. He is so distinguished, and he has a heart of gold. But people ask him: "What is your son?" And he is ashamed, and becomes embarrassed. What can he say? *Only* a poet? That's simply ridiculous. Even if it were possible—it's not any kind of position. It has no standing, no rank, no pension rights, in short—no connection with life. . . . You must understand that I never show my father anything, or anyone here: for they don't judge my efforts, they hate them from the start, and hate me in them. And I have so many doubts myself. Really—I lie awake sometimes the whole night, with folded hands, and torment myself with the question: "Am I worthy?" '[27]

II

Munich, Russia, and
Worpswede
1896–1902

'Ever longing for a reality, a home, people ... everyday life—
what a mistake that was'

(To Lou Andreas-Salomé, 8.8.1903)

I

'I feel the times ripening in my soul,
The new age we don't yet understand'
(Dedication to *Crowned with Dreams*)

Prague, for all his respect for its tradition and history, remained always a
memory of dark, narrow streets, and the contrast of this 'new, light city' of
Munich[1] strengthened his resolve to make good in his fresh start. He found
accommodation in the Briennerstrasse, on the ground floor but looking out to
the back, a 'quiet dreamer's room'.[2] Enrolling at the University, he abandoned
law in favour of philosophy, but spread his interests wide—renaissance art,
aesthetics, Darwinism. From the contacts he already had, a wider circle
developed and a social life as active as he cared to enjoy among artists and
writers, the 'moderns' he had admired from afar. Michael Georg Conrad,
whose Munich journal *Die Gesellschaft* had been the vehicle for the early phase
of naturalism, he respected as the eloquent advocate of a 'modern creative
spirit' in society, literature, art, and science, 'bursting the bonds of the old
forms, throwing off all constraints on the free mind, declaring war on
deception'.[3] This revolutionary trend he found among others of the older
generation: Ludwig Ganghofer, Max Halbe, the witty journalist and novelist
Ernst von Wolzogen, the artist Heinrich von Reder, the painter-authoress
Hermione von Preuschen. In the Café Luitpold he consorted with those of his
own age: Jakob Wassermann, struggling in poverty with his first novel, Wilhelm
von Scholz, the ex-officer poet; his Prague friend Emil Orlik and the young
composer Oskar Fried, also from Bohemia; Láska van Oestéren's brother
Werner. Solitude, however, was often his 'dearest friend: I feel so well when
her cool evening hands caress my brow feverish with longings.'[4]

In these new surroundings the *Wegwarten* project seemed to take on a new life, and he had a letterhead with the title made for his correspondence. By the end of October the third number was ready, subtitled 'Modern German verse (appearing irregularly)', with himself and Bodo Wildberg as editors and the cover-page drawn by a Dresden artist.[5] They had assembled a wider range of contributors, including some well-established poets such as Gustav Falke, of Lübeck, as well as beginners such as René's actress friend Jenny Carsen and the young Christian Morgenstern. There was no more mention of 'poetry for the poor': as he wrote to Richard Dehmel seeking a contribution for the next issue, these were to be anthologies of 'sensitive, genuine lyric poetry for more intimate circles; perhaps they will gradually generate wider ripples in the pool of incomprehension and indifference'.[6]

Though the fourth number never saw the light, the record of those he approached for it is in itself a fair indication of the continuing uncertainty of his own direction. The 'modernity' of the older generation took many forms: Julius Hart in Berlin, poet and playwright, who with his brother had been the forerunner of naturalism in the 1870s; Dehmel, whose revolutionary lyric poetry had been strongly influenced, not only by the Harts, but also by Nietzsche; Prince Emil von Schönaich-Carolath, author of verse without a trace of 'relevance' or engagement; Gustav Falke, poet in the simple folk-song and Romantic tradition; and Detlev von Liliencron, the former officer who took to writing when his debts forced resignation of his commission, and whose forceful language and disregard for convention in his ballads and lyrics—perhaps also his military background—held great appeal for René Rilke. All these were north Germans. Those closer at hand were his contemporaries and friends, such as Wilhelm von Scholz, Emanuel von Bodman, and Dickinson-Wildberg, or Richard von Schaukal in Vienna, and were lyric poets in a neo-Romantic style.

His greatest enthusiasm seemed reserved for Dehmel and Liliencron. Dehmel's verse volume *Woman and World* and 'Master' Detlev's *Poggfred*, an epic poem in the *Childe Harold* tradition, would mark out for posterity, he felt, 'the glorious year 96 in which they were born'.[7] He still hoped (in vain) for productions of *Hoar-Frost* and *Now and in the Hour* in Munich, Vienna, and Berlin; but in his efforts at drama he began now to move away from the simplistic naturalism of those earlier pieces, and the desire to see them produced was not from the idea that they had any great merit. 'I have to prove to my relations that I have not given up hope of outward success—which of course is not the main object for me,' he wrote to Rudolf Jenny in November, asking him to put in a word with the Raimund Theatre in Vienna.[8] Setting *Now and in the Hour* alongside one of his later works, as he wrote to his mother on 8 December, he felt he had left behind the unhealthy, destructive side of his *Sturm und Drang*. In *Vigils* (*Vigilien*), based on an outline of Werner van

Oesterén's and written just before he left Prague, there is at least a change of milieu, though more than a touch of the macabre: a student, bringing his friends and their girls back to his house for revelry at midnight, eventually lights the lamps to discover the body of his mother already cold in the armchair. But the short scene *Little Mother* (*Mütterchen*) he wrote that winter, to be part apparently of a cycle of three one-act plays, of which the others have not survived, is a more sensitive study of bourgeois family life, without the earlier crudities of plot.

The evocations of atmosphere in *Crowned with Dreams*, his own contribution to the 'glorious year of 96', had a much quieter lyrical quality than Dehmel's or Liliencron's. It appeared in the early days of December, and copies went, as usual with his careful dedications, to friends, colleagues, and the 'masters'. Those for his parents were perhaps the most important; after all, he could confidently expect a new publication on his twenty-first birthday to weigh in the scales of justification of the path he was following. For his father, hoping it would bring joy and 'a new proof of the honesty of my artistic endeavours',[9] he inscribed on the flyleaf a long poem, describing his life as a joyous ride through spring valleys towards the distant mountains, spurring forward, every day an adventure of youth, reconciled with the world amid his dreams and songs—'You are my best friend, and full of care about me, but you will see that I am succeeding in what I wanted: I shall borrow silver from the stars, and the sun himself comes to give me gold—not to the *professor* or the *judge*, but to your grateful, loyal son, the poet!' In the copy for his 'dear, good Mama' he was somewhat more enigmatic, with a brief verse recalling times of struggle and searching, with 'black-winged folly fluttering round the white blossom of my longings like a moth round the lilac'; 'but I conquered it, and see deep within me peace and fulfilment, and round me there is a ringing of bells as though I walk a Sunday through . . .'.[10]

To Master Detlev he sent a battle-cry against the philistines: 'Attaque! Forward against hatred and mockery, we rally to *your* standard, Liliencron!'[11] He had heard of the poet's straitened circumstances, and, discussing with von Scholz what his young admirers could do to help, had had the idea of giving a talk, with readings from Liliencron's works, when he returned to Prague for the Christmas holidays. He would win a new public for him there, and the proceeds could go some way towards alleviating his distress. He was also not averse to a prominent public appearance like this on his home ground, which would show the prodigal as a man of achievement, worthy of respect. As if to underline his independence, he did not seek to stay with his aunt in the Wassergasse; and it was significant too that he included Czech literati among those he sought to interest in the event.[12] The performance took place in the German Dilettante Society, on the Graben, on 13 January 1897, and he was delighted beyond measure, in spite of the next day's rather reserved notices, at his success: 'I am sending our beloved Detlev today 300 marks and the assurance of new enthusiastic devotees!' he wrote to von Scholz. 'Heil Liliencron!'[13]

He did not exaggerate, for Liliencron was invited to Prague the following May, his first visit to the Bohemian capital since his days as a cavalry lieutenant with the invading Prussian army in 1866, and was received with almost overwhelming enthusiasm. Long afterwards Rilke looked back on this distant master as the man who had shown him, 'a city-child whose road to distinction was still strewn with tears', the way to the 'open heath' of real life.[14] He would never forget, he wrote towards the end of his life, 'that it was Detlev von Liliencron who was one of the first to encourage me ... when I read his letters addressed "My splendid René Maria", it seemed to me (and I strove to transmit the conviction to my family) that the words stood as a reliable signpost to the boldest of futures.'[15]

By February he had moved his rooms to Blütenstrasse, a little further north and nearer Schwabing, Munich's 'left bank'. Less hesitant now in society, he was an assiduous attender of the 'at home' afternoons which succeeded each other almost daily, given by the writers, artists, music directors, and theatrical personalities of the city. His letters give no sign that solitude and quiet creation was his dream: on the contrary, his retailing of the latest literary gossip, vivid descriptions of the mad whirl of the Carnival—a new experience indeed for the young man from Bohemia—and critiques of the current theatre productions show that he missed little of the social and cultural scene. To this somewhat exhausting round, and at least some university lectures, he added the 'heavy toil' of the editorial work for the next *Wegwarten*[16] and the preparation of the manuscript for another volume of verse.

But he was finding the time to seek his own way. Unlike his other self, Ewald Tragy, he did not wake up one morning in Munich to discover he had a philosophy: but these were months in which he thought deeply about 'last things', and in which his ideas on religion were setting into the form they would take for the rest of his life. Though he discounted his mother's simple credulity for the supernatural, the mysteries of extra-sensory perception held an attraction understandable in one whose gift was to be the expression of inwardness and the visionary. He eagerly delved into the recent works of Baron Du Prel on spiritualism, in the expectation, as he wrote to their author, that 'with word and pen it may be granted to me to make one of the comrades of the new faith which reaches high above the church-tower's cross'. He had the feeling, he said, that with his *Visions of Christ* he would be coming close to that company.[17]

This cycle of long poems, which he at first thought of publishing but then decided against, is crucial to an understanding of his religious ideas. Ewald Tragy, before leaving Prague, had 'lost God': René Rilke had lost, not God, but Christ. Already in 'Confession of Faith', a poem written in 1893 and also not published, he had declared his revulsion against 'the trap of Christianity', the gospel of reward in another world for renunciation of this one. 'I am satisfied with this *one* world . . . the doctrine I follow is that of love, love is my religion.' And in 'Christ on the Cross', about the same time: 'he was a man, like me—but trusted too much in his own strength. He was great, with noble aims. But *one* thing made him small—in excess of presumption he denied he was a simple human being. . . . Rather bore he shame, contempt, mockery, rather would he suffer and die on the cross—as a god. Now I know why I cannot love him . . . or pray to him: a man, he could have remained divinely great, only as God does he seem humanly small!'[18] Now, in stark and sometimes fearful *Visions*, he drew Christ faced with modern life, a figure sad in eternal remorse for his false teachings, for the presumptuous interposing of himself between man and God. Driven like a dry leaf through the world, he is an Ahasverus 'who daily dies, each day to live again', an 'eternal delusion', 'the hereditary curse of the world', warning the people, and especially children, against himself. Lying with a whore, he whispers: 'They brought me once to judgement . . . "Are you the son of God?" . . . I cried to them: "Yes, I am. My throne is at the right hand of my Father!"—Why do you laugh? Yes, spit in my face, it is my desert. And my remorse. No, I am not he, I am no God!'[19]

The *Visions*, to which he added in the coming few years, remained unpublished until over twenty years after his death. Only then, and with the gradual publication of his letters, did his deeply-held view of Christ as a superfluous intermediary between man and God emerge—to the dismay of those who had thought to see in his known work the revelation of a poet-priest of fundamentally Christian belief. In Spain in 1912 he described in a letter his 'almost rabid anti-Christianity', applauding Mahomet's direct contact with God, 'without the telephone "Christ" where the constant call: Hallo, who's there? goes unanswered'.[20] But apart from the confession of faith the *Visions* represent, their most striking feature is the strength of poetic utterance. It was ironic that, though eager to justify himself, he did not feel able to publish poems which were the first true manifestation of his genius.

Wassermann—'the dark little man with broad shoulders and shabby coat'[21]—was an almost daily guest at the lunch-table of his pension. René had reason to be grateful for the novelist's common-sense approach to literature as work rather than the product of high-flown aesthetic theory, and for correcting his tendency to the vague and indeterminate in his writing. To Wassermann also he owed his introduction now to the works of Turgenev, and especially of the Dane Jens Peter Jacobsen, the 'lonely poet'. Jacobsen remained for many years 'a companion in spirit and a presence in the mind: it sometimes seemed to me an unbearable want that he should no longer be alive'.[22] In his 'gentleness and secret lyrical tenderness', wrote Stefan Zweig, Jacobsen was the 'poet of poets' for a whole generation in Germany around the turn of the century, and the melancholy love-story *Niels Lyhne* their *Werther*.[23] His novels reflect many of the themes of Rilke's later life and work: the unheard music of the soul, the allure of old furniture, the concept of all gods as the creation of men, Lyhne's thirst for knowledge, the notion that each man should die his own death (*Maria Grubbe*). 'I could not say what I recognized in these books: but I was determined to live with them,' he wrote in 1907; 'it was primarily to them that I owe my readiness for unselective observation and my determination to admire, and they strengthen in me ... the inner certainty that even for the most imperceptible, the most unintelligible strains within us there are physical equivalents in nature which must let themselves be found.'[24]

Among the many new friends in Munich were Mathilde Nora Goudstikker and her sister Sophie, who ran the photography studio 'Elvira'. René's first visit there, where he duly had himself photographed, had been with a young American fellow student, Nathan Sulzberger. The independent young sisters were indeed true 'moderns', and he was greatly attracted to Nora. For the spring vacation his mother invited him to join her at Arco in the South Tyrol (then still within the borders of the Austrian Empire, at the head of Lake Garda). He was short of money, and her offer to meet his expenses was welcome; and the prospect of seeing Nora Goudstikker there, if only for a short time, was an added incentive. Arriving in Arco on 16 March, he found Sulzberger had also come south, and was staying at nearby Riva. Though greatly tempted by his friend's generous offer to take him on a three-week tour of Italy, René felt his pride could not permit him to accept more than a few days in Venice: but the promise of this experience, his first visit, greatly excited him, and he read all he could lay his hands on about the city, including Goethe's 'very un-modern' account of Venice in the *Italian Journey*.[25]

The four days there he likened to a crowning 'golden dome' on the 'palace of heavenly treasures' of his three weeks' holiday. 'I gaze, and gaze, and am like a child.'[26] Its 'stone fairy-tale' surpassed all the imaginings of his childhood,[27] and with Sulzberger he eagerly explored the labyrinth of the city that, after Paris, he was to know and love best of all Europe: back and forth over the bridges, suddenly confronted by an impasse and then surrounded by a horde of laughing children demanding a ransom to let him go free; sharing Goethe's admiration for Palladio's masterpieces, especially the cloisters of Maria della Carità; penetrating to the old Jewish quarter, its houses piled high 'as though stretching their thin arms in helpless despair to the gloomy heavens', 'glassless windows and frightened little doors leading to cold, dim, dirty corridors', its singular seclusion reminding him of the Prague ghetto. The midnight bells seemed like 'an echo from the infinite, hovering with heavy beat of wings over the lagoon', making him sit up among the pillows with the vague feeling that he was to encounter something new, which would make him 'much better, or much more wretched—but certainly different'. In these days of 'the many poems', which he set down among his impressions in long letters to Nora Goudstikker and some of which he selected for his next verse volume *Advent* at the end of the year, he was able to capture some of the atmosphere of 'this most singular of all historical settlements'. But the 'great profusion of newness' it represented for him would find its expression only later.[28]

Back in Austria on 1 April, he sent his heartfelt thanks to Sulzberger the next day, from Bolzano, for having made the experience possible. Joining his mother in Merano, he found the contrast of Austria striking: from feeling like 'a little Doge', one became just a statistic for the authorities, reminded at every bridge, 'by a categorical imperative', of the tolls due—'9 kreuzer there, 9 kreuzer back. I would have held it an inconceivable injustice if Venice had stayed in Austria. The imperial-royal administration spins its grey orderliness round the most charming of poetry.' All the same, he found a softer, more human environment than among the 'marble houses' of Venice: castles like little old people dreaming in the sun, thankful for every new day; simple, good, and true folk, with a vision of Christ very different from his own, carving Him in their own image 'dressed like a peasant from the Eisacktal with knee-stockings, a pointed hat in His hand', a tired wanderer from afar. In the warm sunlight and bright valleys of the South Tyrol he had the same feeling as in Venice, of something new in store, a 'great preparation' for he knew not what.[29]

When he returned to Munich a week later, his mind, it seems, was made up. Somehow, he would find his way to independence from the family, quit his studies, and begin in earnest a career as a poet and writer. To leave the university was easy: to find a source of income independent of the family was another matter. Von Scholz, whose marriage he had attended early in March, had invited him to visit his parents in Konstanz over Easter; and before leaving he drew up with some care a long letter to Ludwig Ganghofer, setting out his problem and reminding him of his earlier promise to give him any help he could. Apart from Max Halbe, less responsive to René's admiration, Ganghofer was the only one of the older generation of established writers with whom he had been able to enter into a personal relationship, and after writing to him enthusiastically over his poetic drama *Phosphorescence* (*Meerleuchten*) he had been encouraged by the other's approbation for his efforts. Ganghofer's standing and influence would, he felt sure, create for him the opening he sought to earn a modest living with a publisher or a journal.

The letter was the first of many such he was to write over the years, and is a classic among them in its illustration of his single-minded devotion to his purpose. More factually than in that to Vally, two years earlier, it rehearsed for his 'honoured Master' the story of his 'dark childhood', the military college, the Linz episode, and the private study thanks to his uncle's generosity. 'He no doubt left this world with the feeling that nothing much was to be made of me. The only provision in his will was that his daughters, my cousins, should grant me the means to complete my school certificate and possibly to study at the university.'

And in my two years of university I have gained the rather strong impression that for the two ladies I represent a burdensome duty. More troublesome still for me is the feeling of helpless, slave-like dependence at an age when others are already able to support their parents. And then: it is a road on which I have *absolutely no goal*. For all I do is cost more and more money, and even with a doctorate, if I am not to starve as an assistant teacher, more money still will be required to gain me a professorship—a prospect which anyway has no appeal for me.

With every day that passes I see more clearly how right I was to resist from the start, with all my strength, the catch-phrase beloved of my relations: that art is just something for leisure hours after coming home from the office or whatever.—I find that a frightful statement. For me, it is an article of faith that he who does not devote himself to art with all his desires and everything in him can never reach the highest goal. He is simply not an artist. And it cannot be overweening pride if I confess that I feel myself an artist, maybe weak and hesitant in power and boldness, but still conscious of a luminous aim, of the seriousness, splendour, and truth of all artistic creation. I don't see art as a martyrdom, but as a battle which the chosen one must fight, with himself and with those around him, to strive pure in heart towards the great objective, the one great day of festival, and to pass on with full hands, to those who come after, the serene reconciliation achieved. But that needs the whole man! not just a few free hours of weariness. . . .

You may well greet this turbulent anger of youth with a wise smile, but I hope you may still pardon it.—Now I am free from the university.—The time has come. You once offered me help if ever I should need it. Well: here I am. What I would like is, through an agreement with some publisher or a firm commitment to a paper, to be able to earn enough to live on by my own efforts. I should like to spare my cousins the need for benevolence, and to make it possible for my father, who is not in the best of health, to look after himself more, by thankfully renouncing my monthly allowance. I cannot work in peace until that has been done. For myself I need little.

He went on to list the works he had ready: the *Visions of Christ*, five of which Michael Conrad was considering for publication in *Die Gesellschaft*, but which otherwise, like the drama *Hoar-Frost*, three one-act plays, and a substantial verse volume, had as yet no publisher; and a volume of stories, under consideration by the Berlin house of Schuster & Loeffler. 'And if I only had the security and quiet to create more! . . . With the deepest confidence I place this whole confession in your hands, and ask you, in all openness: advise me, help me.' When he returned after Easter perhaps there might be an opportunity to discuss in person. 'Be assured that I will never abuse any recommendation from you.' There is no mistaking the sincerity, and one can only admire him for adding a plea on behalf of someone else: a 'dear colleague', Franziska Countess Reventlow, 'who has contributed to the Fischer review, among others, and has achieved something of a name, but who is in rather difficult circumstances.' He trusted the master would not be vexed at someone himself badly in need of help trying to help another.[30]

Franziska, daughter of a north German nobleman and some four years older than René, was indeed in difficult circumstances. After an unhappy childhood and adolescence in Husum and Lübeck, headstrong and at odds with her strictly conventional parents, she had qualified as a teacher, and during the student years had joined the stream of youthful revolt for which the patron saints were Ibsen and Nietzsche and the watchword free love. Her dream was always to paint, however, and, marrying a young lawyer in Hamburg in 1894, she persuaded him after a year to let her study art in Munich. There, love-affairs in hectic succession brought a near breakdown and in January 1897 the news that she was with child. Her husband, from whom she had concealed nothing, divorced her. Depression and loneliness alternated with the joy of coming motherhood, to which with great courage she showed single-minded devotion. And through it all—Rilke. 'Every morning a poem in my letterbox, I like that.'[31] Money was desperately short, but she contrived to keep her head just above water with translations, stories, contributions to journals. René was among the friends who tried to help, and she went with him on his Easter weekend to Konstanz (perhaps the reason for the 'empty pockets' to which he referred—without complaint—in a letter to his mother later).[32] The memory of that journey, he wrote to Franziska a few years afterwards, remained dear to him: 'I felt that I did you good, and that you needed me, although I could really do nothing for you . . . a guardian angel of wood, but at least a guardian angel . . .'.[33] Her situation was undoubtedly the inspiration for another one-act play he wrote on his return, *Mountain Air* (*Höhenluft*), in which the heroine, an unmarried mother, shows the same defiance of convention and determination to find her own way to happiness in independence.

But he dedicated the piece to Nora Goudstikker, to whom he had written from Konstanz, and whom he saw often after his return. He seemed relaxed now that his future lay in capable hands: and his confidence was at least partially justified when he saw Ganghofer towards the end of April 1897. It was a very cordial interview, he reported to Nora: 'he encouraged me to withdraw the novellas from Schuster & Loeffler and send them to him, as he would like to put them to his own publisher—if he feels they merit his recommendation after he has read them.' This he did at once, sending a selection of twelve to Ganghofer. 'His publisher has the reputation of paying well . . . This hope . . . and a return to wonderful solitude and gentle thoughts of you, has made me more contented and happier.[34]

Nothing had actually changed for him, he was still the dependent student, not even a prodigal son. Yet the 'security and quiet to create' seemed to be at hand, plans for new work developed, and he no longer felt anxious 'looking beyond the next few days into the wider world of what is to come'. In his 'holy solitude', as 'rich, pure, and broad as an awakening garden',[35] he would work through till the late afternoon, walking down then to the Wiener Café to read the papers (only the *feuilleton*, 'politics I avoid like the plague'), or into the English Garden. This 'life of an anchorite' was interrupted now and then by a

visit to the theatre, or an evening with Nora, reading her his verse or just
sitting silent in brotherly companionship.[36]

> Within me a thousand unruly questions rise.
> Called aloud, they bring me only echo,
> No answer. Yet, through all my days,
> They stand like watch-towers on the ramparts,
> I see the longing of their pinnacles soar
> And thrust towards the stars above,
> And sometimes bells awaken in them
> Ringing the dawn of a rejoicing day.
>
> But her I seek, who tolling them
> May strongly grasp the hidden ropes:
> Far from the crowds I search,
> Hesitant on unfamiliar ways,
> And if I find her, there will blaze a festive day,
> I'll snatch it down from heaven
> To earth below, where my delight
> Will wake a hundred echoes.[37]

His premonition in Venice of an encounter with something new, to make him
'much better, or much more wretched—but certainly different', was soon to be
fulfilled, when she whom he sought, in this vague longing, entered his life.

2

'It may be that God is as yet only foreshadowed in life'
(H. G. Wells, *The Undying Fire*)

On the evening of 12 May 1897, René was introduced at Jakob Wassermann's
to 'two splendid women', as he wrote to his mother afterwards: 'the famous
authoress Lou Andreas-Salomé and the African explorer Frieda von Bülow'.[1]
They had just arrived in Munich, for a stay of a few months, and had taken
rooms in a pension in the nearby Schellingstrasse. René was no doubt anxious
to impress his mother: 'notorious' would perhaps better have described Lou
Andreas-Salomé at this time, after the well-known scandal of Nietzsche's
fruitless pursuit of her fifteen years earlier and the brief months of what the
world saw as a *ménage à trois* with him and Paul Rée, which had made more of
a stir than the success of her books on Nietzsche and Ibsen and three novels.
Born Louise von Salomé in St. Petersburg in 1861, the daughter of a Russian
general of Huguenot descent and a German mother, she had early shown great
intelligence and an intense thirst for knowledge. After her father's death she
had travelled with her mother in Europe, becoming one of the earliest women
university students when she read theology and philosophy in Zurich, and
making a considerable mark in intellectual circles, notably in Rome with

Malwida von Meysenbug. She was strikingly beautiful; but, although thoroughly 'liberated' in ideas and scornful of convention, had led a life in which, despite appearances, heterosexual love played no part. To her, the only daughter in a family of sons, 'every man, no matter when I met him in my life, always seemed to conceal a brother'.[2] Rée had been, and would remain, the epitome of friendship, and could never be a lover; Nietzsche's offer of marriage she had firmly declined, despite the formidable intellectual attraction. When she finally consented, in 1887, to marriage with Friedrich Carl Andreas, a professor at the Berlin Institute for Oriental Languages, under the pressure of his attempted suicide, for him too the hope of physical possession proved to be vain. She held inexorably to the view that true marriage must be on a plane higher than that of mere physical love—a 'kneeling together', as she once expressed it—and after nearly five years convinced him that this was indeed a basis for a serene and happy existence together, with each partner free still to lead an independent life. The world, inevitably, would regard such a union as simply a marriage of convenience for her; but she cared nothing for opinion, and for the rest of her life would prove capable of maintaining her ideal. Meanwhile, in what Nietzsche had bitterly called her 'animal-like egoism',[3] she used her liberty to the full, travelling wherever and whenever she liked, pursuing her own studies, writing. In Munich she was at once a presence, already known to the friends from Berlin such as Max Halbe and Frank Wedekind, and making new ones in Wassermann, Eduard Count Keyserling, Conrad, and the young architect August Endell.

René Rilke, like many before and after him, succumbed at once to her spell. It seems he had already admired her from afar, for, as she later recalled, she had received letters with poems from an unknown whose handwriting turned out to be the same as that in his letter to her the day after their first meeting. That 'twilight hour' with her, he wrote, had not been the first for him. During the winter, when he had been writing his *Visions of Christ*, Conrad had sent him her essay 'Jesus the Jew', which he had experienced as a revelation: he had rejoiced to find what he was trying to express in the *Visions* set down with such power and mastery. 'That was the singular twilight hour which came back to my thoughts yesterday.... Your essay was to my poems as reality to a dream, as fulfilment to a desire.' From that hour, when he had been alone with her, he had longed for the chance to meet face to face. Though his gratitude could not be expressed with others present, perhaps he might hope to read her some of the poems on another occasion.[4] In fact her essay, though also treating Jesus as a man, a religious genius, but not a God, explores much more deeply the transformation of his death on the cross into the symbol of the new religion, a 'compact and useful belief', by the 'historically unacceptable' device of the resurrection.[5] René's letter must therefore be read rather as a measure of the *coup de foudre* he had experienced, and its respectful flattery coming from a compelling need to make himself interesting to her.

It was by no means an unfamiliar situation for Lou, but she found herself unable to resist the tenacity of his pursuit in the weeks which followed. At the theatre the next evening he contrived to join her party, which included Endell and the Goudstikker sisters; they supped afterwards in relaxed mood at Schleich's restaurant until half-past one in the morning, and he and Endell escorted her home. Three days later he saw her alone, and read to her some of the *Visions* before taking her and Frieda to the theatre again. She received a copy of *Crowned with Dreams* with a dedicatory verse; they dined together often at the pension and he showed her his one-act plays. When he could not see her, he was disconsolate: 'I wandered around the town and into the English Garden with a few roses in my hand, in the hope of finding you. Yes, instead of handing them in at the door with the golden keys, I carried them around, fairly trembling with my determination to meet you somewhere'—much as one throwing a letter into the sea hopes that it will land on the friend's shore, and, like such a letter, his roses sank too.[6] But 'Longing' sang for him:

> I know that you from lonely shores
> Are headed for the greatest bliss . . .[7]

At the beginning of June he had to return to Bohemia for preliminary examination for military service, and before he left reached out 'with both hands for every second you will grant me'. To friends he showed none of the revulsion one might have expected at the thought of renewed contact with the military machine—his one thought was how soon he could get back to her; and he promised to telegraph her the result. His 'Songs of Longing' would still come in his letters, he wrote, but they would be different now, 'for Longing has been beside me, and I have looked into her eyes, and she leads me with a sure hand'. He could indeed be confident that his love was returned, for a day or two before he caught his train for Prague they made a sortie together to the village of Wolfratshausen, to the south of Munich, to look for a quiet retreat nearer the mountains where they might be together in suitable propriety (for all her emancipation, Lou's regard for her husband kept her within reasonable bounds of convention). There was some uncertainty over how long the military might detain him, but on 4 June he was able to telegraph 'Free and soon happy too', and was at her side again in Munich two days later.[8]

For Lou, as she looked back many years afterwards, he was the 'first true reality' in her life, 'body and soul indivisibly one . . . I could have confessed to you word for word what you said in your confession of love for me: "You alone are real". So we became man and wife even before we became friends . . .'.[9] Though she was so much older than he, and in many ways more mature, it was in fact her first such experience. But it was clear to her from the start that the relationship could not, indeed should not last. Paramount was her concern to keep undisturbed the unusual, but in both practical and emotional terms satisfactory, union with Andreas. She was a dispassionate judge of René's gifts, and to her intellectual approach to the artist there was no doubt added something of a maternal urge to help him to a full development of his powers. For all that, the experience was one she would not deny herself. She admired and was enormously attracted by the integration in him of mind and senses, his uncomplicated manliness and joyful acceptance of all that life had to offer.

René for his part was in ecstasy. 'You come to me from all that's beautiful, my breeze of spring, my summer rain, my June night with a thousand ways which none before me was blessed to tread: I am in you!' Reading his work to her, he felt it was all of the past, no longer a part of him, something left behind in an old garden. The hours he could spend with her were 'like islands enveloped in blossom', apart, as though lived in 'another, higher existence'. She was a 'clear mountain spring to the thirsting traveller', he was hers 'as the sceptre is the queen's', 'as the last small star is the night's'. He felt the 'first glimmering of a new epoch', wanting to have done with everything that had gone before and with those who had peopled his earlier days. 'If they deserve it, I will leave a faded remembrance on their grave as I pass, for I am too happy not to be thankful. But their words to me are only words on a gravestone, I can feel only cold, stiff letters. I will praise these departed in my happiness, for though they disappointed me, misunderstood, and mistreated me, they led me—to you, on the long road of suffering.'[10]

On 14 June they moved out of Munich, Lou with Frieda to a small cottage in Wolfratshausen and René for the first few days to a room in the neighbouring village of Dorfen before joining them. A little later they found a more suitable haven, in a cottage they dubbed Loufried, where, before Frieda left for Holland, August Endell often made one of the party, painting a flag for it with the name and lending his artist's touch to the interior furnishings. The summer idyll marked in every sense a 'new epoch' for René. Lou's feeling for nature, her habit of observing the animals at dawn and walking barefoot through the dew brought him for the first time down to earth from the insubstantial romanticizing of the city poet. They studied Italian Renaissance art together. Under her powerful influence he began to slough off the overheated and strained complications of his earlier work, which, for all its musical charm, she found unsympathetic, and to strive for a simpler, purer style: 'I have left the garden in which I walked so long in weariness.'[11] She refused to call him by the precious and feminine-sounding name of *René*, and used *Rainer* instead, a 'plain, fine, German'[12] name which he adopted at once. The outward sign of this sea-change was the transformation that summer of his writing, from a carelessly-formed, often almost illegible hand, into the clear Italianate German script which would in itself become an expression of his art, whether in transcripts of his poems or in his letters.

They were like the two halves of an indivisible whole, she thought later, 'like brother and sister, but from primeval times before incest became a sacrilege'.[13]

In her moments of passion she could no doubt, as she said, have formed the same thought as Rainer, in a poem he laid one day in her room:

> Tear out my eyes: I still can see you,
> Stop up my ears: I still can hear you,
> Without feet I still can walk,
> Without a mouth still plead to you.
> Break off my arms: I'll grasp you yet
> With my heart as with a hand,
> Tear out my heart, my brain will beat,
> And if you set my brain afire
> I'll carry you still in my blood.[14]

But most of his lyrical outbursts did not survive their self-censorship, for, although completely open always with her husband, she did not wish to give him gratuitous offence by leaving such effusions for him to read. Andreas in fact came down to Loufried in the last week of July, staying for a month without any disturbance to its peaceful happiness, and did not want to hear when she volunteered to tell him how things stood. Rainer discreetly absented himself in Munich from time to time, spending a few days there in August to see his father, who came over on a visit.

Lou herself was not so overwhelmed by this first surrender to a man's passion that she was willing to abandon all for Rainer. A previously-planned visit to Kufstein in July was not overlooked, nor in September did she hesitate to leave him alone in favour of an 'appointment' in Hallein with the family of Friedrich Pineles, a doctor she had known since 1895 in Vienna and who would later prove a stormier and more disturbing suitor than Rainer. As firmly as ever, she maintained in her mind the clear distinction, which she had confided to her diary only eighteen months after her union with Andreas, between friendship, physical love, and marriage: marriage, she wrote, should be 'not a binding, but a being-bound', 'something lying beyond all interests of friendship, much deeper, much loftier', a kind of pinnacle which the partners are striving to reach, 'the recognition that each belongs *in* and not just *to* the other, in an almost religious or at least ideal sense'. 'I have never been able to understand why people physically in love with one another get married.'[15]

That this was her feeling would only gradually become clear to Rainer. He himself had never before felt so all-consuming a physical attraction combined with such intellectual and artistic powers, and for the moment had not the slightest doubt that in Lou he had found the ideal woman, a mate for both soul and body. While she was away in Hallein, as he read the life and letters of an artist whose unhappy love-affair had ended in disaster, he wrote to her: 'It is not enough for two people to recognize one another, it is enormously important for them to find each other at the right time and celebrate together deep and quiet festivals in which they can grow together in their desires, if they are to be united against the storms of life. . . . Before two people can be unhappy together, they must first have been blessed with a common happiness, have a common sacred memory which brings a shared smile to their lips and a shared longing into their souls.'[16] The 'quiet festivals' of Loufried, which he now relived alone in the mists of autumn, and the 'sacred memory' of the love they had shared, made him sure that with Lou he could face whatever life might bring. From Hallein she planned to come back to Munich for a while, before returning home to Berlin in October, and he had decided to move there too.

With her at his side, and encouraged by this new-found security after the 'industrious summer' in Wolfratshausen, he felt confident that the change of scene would be for the better.[17] Ganghofer's publisher, Adolf Bonz in Stuttgart, had agreed in June to bring out the twelve 'sketches', as Rainer called them, on promising terms, and the book had taken on a considerably changed form since then, in both serious and lighter vein and with a number of newly-written stories. *Hoar-Frost* had at last been produced, in Prague, and not unfavourably noticed. His new name appeared for the first time in September, under a translation of a poem by Fernand Gregh. To his father, whose visit in August had probably been prompted by concern over his future after hearing of his decision to leave university, he had been evasive, and broke the news only later that he would not be returning to Prague, as Josef obviously hoped. He was still a long way from financial independence, but it no longer seemed an impossible dream as the Berlin scene opened before him.

Lou and her husband lived modestly at Schmargendorf, on the outskirts of Berlin, near woods and open country but only a fifteen-minute rail journey from the Potsdamer station. Rainer found comfortable rooms not far away, in Wilmersdorf. To Ganghofer he said the move was on health grounds, claiming that he had found that Munich's damp climate the previous autumn had not been good for him and that he thought a winter in the rough dryness of Brandenburg would suit him better, especially in the peace and solitude of Wilmersdorf. Reporting to his mother on the move, he told her also of his change of name. 'René sounds forced and precious in public ... There is nothing I hate more than the suspicion that I am trying to appear original.' (She was no doubt less disturbed than his father by the decision to move, for the Berlin literary world must give him more opportunity than that of Munich; but, although not displeased by the change to Rainer, she never thought of him or addressed him otherwise than as her René.) He maintained his Munich contacts—Max Halbe, Conrad, von Wolzogen, and of course Ganghofer—but was already a not unknown figure in Berlin to editors and others who could help him, notably in the theatre, for he was busy on a new two-act drama. It was to be 'a winter of work', he told Ganghofer, now he was secure in the 'strong support' of the publisher.[18]

Bonz was indeed proving most encouraging. For the novella volume, now in its final form of eleven stories, Rainer had settled on the title *The Stream of Life* (*Am Leben hin*), and it would appear in the spring. As his next prose work he promised the publisher 'a bigger book', which he hoped to have completed by the coming summer. Bonz advised him against a further volume of verse, however, until he had made more of a name. This was emphatically not Rainer's feeling: since *Crowned with Dreams*, he said, he had filled seven notebooks with things he was 'burning to express', and it must be 'now or never'. With the eighth he had now begun, he seemed to have entered an entirely new stage, and he felt he must mark each period of his lyrical development with a book. These volumes would not make money, he admitted, but they were his contact, his 'compromise' with the outside world.[19]Thus it was that *Advent*, 'Poems from Munich 1896/97 by Rainer Maria Rilke', dedicated to his father, appeared at Christmas with Friesenhahn, who had published *Crowned with Dreams*.

The selection included a few poems which had been written in Prague, but just after he had made up his mind to leave, so that it can fairly be regarded as representing the 'Munich period' now ended. The style is still largely 'pre-Wolfratshausen' (only five were actually written there) and with signs of the same straining after effects of rhyme and assonance: but the greater simplicity he was seeking begins to show. The poems are grouped into 'Gifts', 'Travels', and 'Finds', and in this first edition the 'gifts' bore names significant not only of the ideals before him in his art—Jacobsen, Maeterlinck, Hugo von Hofmannsthal—but also of the help he had received—Ganghofer, Conrad— and of friendships like that with Emil Orlik. In this way they are true Rilke, for all his life he regarded his work, like his letters, as something to be 'offered', in formal dedication on the printed page or in more personal form, but often simply to a friend or one he admired, in an impeccably drawn holograph without thought of publication. It was enough to have written and brought it as an offering, on whatever occasion it suited. But it still remained his work, painstakingly preserved in his notebooks with the date of conception—in this respect his is probably the most completely documented poetic *œuvre* ever known—and poems which first saw the light in letters or as occasional 'offerings' often took their place, revised or not, in publication. So now, in 'Travels', the Venice poems he had addressed to Nora Goudstikker. Most significant perhaps is the first of the 'Gifts', written in February in Munich, throwing out his challenge to the world:

> This is my fight:
> In longing's light
> Through all my days to wend.
> Then in broad might
> My thousand roots to send
> Down to life's depths sans end—
> And past grief's bite
> Far clear of life extend,
> Out of time's sight![20]

The sentiment was not as forced as the rhymes, and would remain his guide through many vicissitudes.

For the 'bigger book' he had been promised, Bonz wanted a novel. Instead, Rainer insisted on further novellas, more substantial in form, and planned a volume of two 'Prague Stories', the first of which, *King Bohusch* (*König Bohusch*) he completed in November. With the autobiographical *Ewald Tragy*, written the following year and, as we have seen, withheld from publication for obvious reasons, they represent his final attempt to work Prague out of his system. 'Homeland and childhood—both distant long since—are the background,' he wrote introducing the *Zwei Prager Geschichten* when Bonz's reluctance had been overcome and they finally appeared in 1899. 'Today, I would not have written them thus, indeed probably not at all. But then it was necessary to me. The book made the half-forgotten dear to me, and I was enriched by it: for from the past only that which we hold dear can we really possess.'[21] The theme of both stories (the second, *Brother and Sister* (*Die Geschwister*) he finished within a few months) was the Young Czech nationalist movement 'Omladina', which had emerged in 1893 from a semi-underground existence with the arrest of the ringleaders and the subsequent murder of the police informer responsible. Bohusch, the little hunchback, is Rilke's version of the real-life informer/*provocateur* Mrva; in the executioner, the student Rezek, who appears in both stories, he portrays the idealism of the movement. His sympathy is apparent, though the resignation he expressed in Rezek reveals a sentimental and somewhat condescending view, not surprising with his upbringing, of the Czechs as a people still in infancy, thwarted in its attempt to grow up among the serious, adult Germans. But, as before in *Larenopfer*, he does not despair of reconciliation between the two nations, and in this last offering to his household gods there is foreshadowed the genuine welcome he would give to the coming of age of the Czechs in the republic of 1918.

How close he was to Lou during this 'winter of work' is hard to judge. He was a frequent visitor at Schmargendorf, but there obviously could not be the freedom they had enjoyed at Wolfratshausen. Her entrée in Berlin literary society, however, was invaluable for him. With her he was able to join the select circle at one of Stefan George's ceremonious readings, and they were invited together to a reception at the house of the publisher Samuel Fischer, where Gerhart Hauptmann's brother Carl read his new drama. Rainer made a great impression on Fischer's wife Hedwig: they found much in common in their admiration for Peter Altenberg and Gerhart Hauptmann, and his friendship with the Fischers was to last many years, Samuel indeed, though he never published more than a few single poems of Rilke's, proving a strong support in time of need. Lou apparently also arranged for the first translation of a Rilke work, a version of one of the novellas from *The Stream of Life*, which appeared in October in a Russian journal to which she had sometimes contributed. He was able to meet for the first time Julius Hart, and the revered 'master' Richard Dehmel. And together with Lou he pursued his interest in the Italian Renaissance. Over the New Year he was deep in the art and literature of the fifteenth century, trying his hand at translation from Dante's *Vita nuova*, and resolved to travel on to Florence after seeing his mother in Arco again in the spring.

For this more funds would be needed. Bonz, having received the first of the 'Prague Stories', responded promptly in February to his request for an advance on the honorarium for the book, and made him a contract for it, no doubt encouraged by his renewed promise of a 'book-length novel', for which he said he wanted to seek the warmer climate his doctor had recommended.[22] Looming again was the possibility of a call-up for military service later in the year, and a visit to the depot at Böhmisch-Leipa was necessary: this he could combine with a lecture in Prague to the German Dilettante Society, which had invited him to follow up the success of that on Liliencron (but this time for the benefit of his own purse), before joining Phia in Arco. His talk, a wide-ranging review of 'Modern Lyric Poetry', found a most attentive audience, he reported to Dehmel, the latter's poems from *Woman and World* having figured prominently in his thesis; and in Leipa there was heartening news a few days later—he was released for good from any military service. Bonz was the first to hear: 'so all the coming years—if I stay in good health—belong to me and to my work! and you shall be pleased with me.'[23] Before leaving Prague on 11 March 1898 he sent him the second 'Prague Story'.

In Arco he found a rainy spring, and he was chilled both in and out of doors. He wrote a number of poems, a review or two, and an essay version of his 'Modern Lyric Poetry', but if he thought of the novel, there was no sign of it. When his copies of *The Stream of Life* arrived, towards the end of the month, he sent one to Liliencron with a long offering of doggerel verse: not, he feared, the spring greetings he had wanted to convey, huddled as he was round the stove, his fingers freezing as he wrote, but still a hope that 'his Detlev' would find enjoyment in this 'book of long-past stories', which were no more than the last dying notes of bells, or gardens that had already yielded their best blooms.[24] There was no doubt that the sooner he went south to Tuscany, the better; but his finances still gave him cause for some concern. Sending Julius Hart a copy of the book, and promising him the essay when published, he enquired delicately whether Hart's publisher in Florence could perhaps 'advise' him how to overcome the slight difficulty. The response is not recorded, but he was able to set off on 4 April, 'a-tremble with expectation' of the city where 'spring became eternal in name and deed'.[25]

The journey had to be spent sitting on his luggage; but his exhaustion fell away as he walked that evening through the streets of Florence, wandering by chance into Piazza della Signoria, catching his breath at the palace's 'cliff-steep fortress-like power' and the watch tower's 'sinewy neck stretching up into the twilight'. In the Loggia dei Lanzi, where Cellini's bronze Perseus and da Bologna's *Rape of a Sabine* were just visible in the dusk, he could feel the presence of the building's creator, Andrea Orcagna: 'the first Renaissance man initiates me into the secret of his time'. Turning into the Piazzale degli Uffizi towards the Arno, he seemed to see the men of the Renaissance—Orcagna, Giotto lost in thought, Michelangelo, Leonardo; Boccaccio, Petrarch, Dante—and drew strength from the stillness of the giants who had grown beyond the great palaces 'into an eternal home of ineffable splendour'.[26]

His room, in a pension on the Lungarno Serristori, was built on to the roof, which made a wide terrace for his home, from where all Florence lay spread before him 'on its knees—like the adoration of the shepherds'. 'When I first stepped out, I thought, presumptuously, "here there should be roses" [the title of a Jacobsen novella]—and as I turned, there were the outside walls of my room covered in the gentle blooms.'[27] Pansies in stone pots kept their friendly eyes on his movements: he hoped they would find in him a sort of related being 'whose faith is in a warm and radiant spring, and then, far beyond, in a heavy, beautiful fruit'. But it was nearly two weeks before he could thus put pen to paper, so overwhelming was the impact of the city—a rare experience for so compulsive a writer. On 15 April he began what he thought of as a diary for Lou, a book bound in white leather and impressed with Florentine lilies. Emerson's 'all mankind love a lover' headed a page of mottoes, and his first entries were short stanzas of evocation: the atmosphere of the 'radiant viale', the Madonnas of the galleries, evenings over the Arno valley when he 'painted God in gold' for himself, the Renaissance when men 'prayed in images and made buildings of prayers'. Whether he was 'quiet enough and ready' to begin the book he wanted to bring her, he did not know; but his joy would remain a distant thing if he did not at least try to record it for her, and it was a happy omen that just a year had passed since he had journeyed with similar longing towards a yet unknown fulfilment in her.

Fellow guests from Germany, he told her, had taken much of his time in the early days, but it was the confusion of impressions from the city spread before him that had made a consecutive account impossible, and only now could he draw breath and try to convey what had remained in his net. Florence did not reveal itself so readily as Venice to the traveller, its palaces 'presenting their silent fronts almost in hostility', but once one had gained their confidence, they readily related 'the legend of their existence in the splendid, rhythmic language of their courts'. The early Renaissance appealed most to him in the cloistered gardens of the monasteries, with the ironwork tracery round the well and wild roses along the white gravelled paths, ending in a cypress against the walls. 'The masters must have felt like me, as they created their gentle Madonnas.'[28]

He gazed, listened, and absorbed; but apart from the few summary pages of the 'diary' for Lou, what he gained found its expression in poems. Many were of his worship for her, his dreams of the 'distant woman' as he wandered 'without aim . . . until fear fell away from me and I am as a gentle lute in your hands'.[29] In his notebooks these with the earlier works began already to form a cycle which he would call *A Festival for You* (*Dir zur Feier*), but which discretion would keep from publication, many of the poems being destroyed by common consent. Others, however, notably a series of 'Maidens' Prayers to Mary', had the Madonna as their theme, and it was the Renaissance portrayals of the virgin mother* which left perhaps the deepest impression on him from the month in Florence, milestones on the artists' 'stern, dark road to the sun'.[30]

Two chance encounters were significant for his later development. Walking one day in the Boboli Gardens, he met Stefan George, and would long remember their talk: for George made a point of condemning the urge of young poets to rush too early into print, stressing instead their need for patient work at their art without regard for the outside world. Though not exactly welcome at the time, it was a lesson he eventually took to heart from this much-admired elder. On another occasion, at the end of an evening with fellow guests at the pension, he invited them up to his rooftop terrace, and was much struck by the absorption in the view, silent in large-eyed admiration, of a young painter from Bremen named Heinrich Vogeler. They did not see each other again in Florence, but they exchanged letters and met in the autumn in Berlin, and he was glad to accept the artist's invitation to spend Christmas with his family in Bremen and out at his own house, the Barkenhoff, in Worpswede. Vogeler's ideas on the place of art in life, with more than a touch of English *fin-de-siecle* aestheticism in its expression, and his decided though unobtrusive fastidiousness of conduct and dress, were very like the other's at this stage, and the few years of their friendship were to mark a turning-point in Rainer's life.

In the end, Florence proved altogether too much for him. By 11 May he had fled that 'network of singular streets' for the calm of the Ligurian shore at Viareggio, near Pisa—after the manifold beauties of man's achievements, 'the single, great, inexhaustible treasure-house of nature, deep within which still untouched works await their release'. Here he could muse on what he had seen, the glorious spring of the *quattrocento*, to which modern art could be the summer and the autumn fruit. In his 'diary' for Lou, interspersed with his thoughts of longing for her, he distilled his own theory of the artist as one who must create, not for others, but only for himself. 'Know then, that art is the road to fulfilment for the individual, for the solitary'; 'art goes from the lonely to the lonely, in a vaulting arch high above the people'; 'what becomes laughter or tears for you the artist must form with his struggling hands and raise above

---

*His apparent preoccupation at this time with the mystery of motherhood, coupled with the loss of any letters he may have written to Lou, has led to speculation that she was pregnant, possibly even by him, or at least that he hoped she was. The supposed evidence is flimsy in the extreme, and can safely be discounted.

himself . . . his material is of this world, and so he must set his works in the world. But they are not for you. Touch them not, and stand in awe.' An aristocratic approach indeed, quite opposed to his one-time idea of 'art for the people' in the free gift of poems in *Wegwarten*.[31]

The attitude is not without its significance, for in his future work Rilke would tend more and more to creation for his own sake, exploring near and beyond the borders of the expressible, whether or not it might see the light in print. The compulsion to 'mark each period of his development' with a publication would recede: and he would spend much longer over the shaping of a book, to render precisely what had been granted him in inspiration or in hard work, as an act of creation in itself—truly art to leap in a vaulting arch above the common herd. But in Viareggio he did not spend all his time over the fine chiselling of such solemn aphorisms. There were walks along the shore with his table-companion, Helene Voronin from St. Petersburg, who was holidaying there with her father and sister, and whose melancholy he was able to disperse with his joy in nature. His entries in the leather-bound book, usually his morning task on the sunlit balcony, record satisfying days when poems 'came to him', songs celebrating girlhood and its longings, and also the silent visit to the garden of a black-robed and hooded monk to collect for his order, standing amid the flowers like the figure of Death himself awaiting a victim, and his own quiet and unafraid recognition, in this contrast, of the unity of life and death. 'That is the essential: to see everything *within* life itself, even the mystical, even death.'[32] The incident was the germ of inspiration for his lyrical drama *The White Princess* (*Die weisse Fürstin*) which was written later that year, and the conception of death as simply an unseen part of life, as it were the dark side of the moon, would remain a basic element in his outlook.

Through it all there is the thought of the triumphant return to Lou, clarified by his experiences, a pilgrimage 'deep into her soul, where it becomes a temple'.[33] The news towards the end of the month of her plans to visit friends in Danzig at first dispirited him, but he rapidly recast his own to join her at Zoppot, with no fears of the colder Baltic coast after his months among the beauties of the south: he would bring her treasures enough for them to forget the people who would surround them. Lou was apparently less enthusiastic, and found it inconvenient to see him so soon. The journey to Zoppot, which he had thought to make via Innsbruck and Munich, had to be deferred, and he travelled in fact through Vienna, Prague, and Berlin. 'I had a bad pilot this time,' he wrote to Franziska Reventlow, regretting he had had to miss seeing her in her 'full-bloomed courageous happiness' with her baby Rolf, through being driven so hastily from the 'blessèd shores of my early summer solitude'.[34]

The reunion with Lou, when at last it came, towards the middle of June, proved a hard blow to the hopes of the ardent lover. She knew full well, as she had always known, that there could be no future for their relationship, and a meeting in such impersonal surroundings, far from the intimacy of Wolfrats-hausen or even of Schmargendorf, had no doubt seemed to her the right way to see it gently to an end. He was at first embittered and ashamed. '*I* wanted this time to be the rich one, the giver, the host, the master, and you were to come, guided by my care and love, to indulge in my welcome. But I became once more the merest beggar at the outermost threshold of your being, which rests on such broad, firm pillars.' He had come to her 'full of the future', but found in the flat days by this cooler sea only the unhappier memories of their past, not even recapturing its joys. Offering the journal he had made for her, he could not see her pleasure at it, but only an irritating gentleness and a provoking attempt to give him courage. He hated her even, as something altogether 'too big' for him. He did not want her comfort, and was so miserable that he felt he must escape from the toils of a kindness so humiliating.[35]

But when he came to set this down in his final entry in the journal, in a frank and extraordinarily clear analysis, he had found new heart. For she had put to him—after evidently making it clear that, however close they might remain intellectually, any physical union was ruled out—the 'inexorable question: "What will you do?"' And he had come to realize that she could still remain his ideal, not one goal but many, as he strove towards the heights. 'However far I may go, you are always before me . . . The final worth of this book is the recognition of an art which is only a road towards final fulfilment in a rich existence.'[36]

What would he in fact do, in practical terms? Lou was deeply concerned about him, and wisely began to draw him into a project she had been considering for some time. It was several years since she had seen her homeland, and she was thinking of a journey to Russia with Andreas: why should not Rainer join them? The coming autumn months back in Berlin would give time for studies of the language under her guidance. The courage of such an idea, and her cool control in suggesting it, were typical of her: no more effective way could have been found of putting Rainer at the same distance as her husband—two brothers, in fact, for her, not lovers. The prospect immediately appealed to him, and already at the end of June he was writing about it to his mother.

They stayed until the end of July in Zoppot, and in his new-found calm he thought once more of work. Writing back to Bonz, who had sent one or two notices of *The Stream of Life*, he said he might now complete the *Visions of Christ* and finally make them ready for publication: 'the other side of my lyrical vein, which so far in my books appear somewhat monotonously hesitant'.[37] In addition, he began essays on the *quattrocento* and on art in general— 'revelations I experienced in Florence'—and a new journal. To Phia he enthused over the East Prussian landscape, and even praised the 'ancient magic' of Danzig, unlike anything he had yet seen[38] (but then his letters to his mother were rarely less than enthusiastic). In his journal, his thoughts were

Frieda von Bülow, Rilke, August
Endell, and Lou Andreas-Salomé in
Wolfratshausen, 1897

Rilke and Lou Andreas-Salomé with
the Russian poet S. D. Drozhzhin,
1900

Rilke in 1897

Lou Andreas-Salomé, about the time of her first meeting with Rilke
in 1897

once more of greatness, the new beginning for every true man, for whom there is no history: 'his fathers and ancestors . . . are contemporaries of his spirit, and their influence is *in him*, not in the past'.[39]

On their return to Berlin he took a room in the Villa Waldfrieden at Schmargendorf, closer this time to the Andreas home and set in a quiet little garden bordering on the pine forest. Letting him completely share their modest everyday existence, Lou was able now to school him in the ways that suited her. It became an intellectual companionship, but in the kitchen rather than in the drawing-room, for Andreas occupied the only living-room for his study and teaching sessions. Rainer helped her with the household chores, cooking, washing-up, and splitting wood, they wandered barefoot through the woods where friendly deer nuzzled into their pockets for food, and sat quietly in the kitchen over their books of an evening. It re-created the idyll of Wolfratshausen—but the bedroom played no part. He began to lose his rather spoiled fastidiousness, which had earlier made him jib at the slightest restrictions and complain about his lack of money, and found contentment in this simpler life, with mainly vegetarian food, and no alcohol—a regime to which he kept all his life, though not, if he could help it, in such relatively unluxurious living conditions.

He found the isolation of Schmargendorf welcome. For his Munich friends he was in Berlin, but those in Berlin thought him still in Munich, and if two happened to meet, they agreed he must be away in Italy—an excellent situation to be in, 'for being nowhere has the positive side of being everywhere'.[40] His studies of Russian began in earnest; he wrote essays, and completed *Ewald Tragy*, as well as two more novellas, which he already planned for a new volume, and, towards autumn, *The White Princess*. The verse drama, which he would later remodel and dedicate to Eleanore Duse, throws an almost mystical light on the problems of love and death: a sudden outbreak of plague, in sixteenth-century Italy, strikes terror into the Princess as she waits for the lover for whom she has preserved herself inviolate in spirit through years of unhappy marriage, and with the approach of the black-masked Brothers of Mercy, administering the last rites, her lover's boat passes on without her signal. In form and theme it was in marked contrast to Rilke's earlier, and earthier, naturalistic efforts.

'An important time of hard work,' he wrote to his mother.[41] But he was by no means a hermit, and went from time to time into town, especially when there were exhibitions of modern art and interior decoration—the Impressionists, Degas, Liebermann, Van de Velde, Stoeving. Art Nouveau in particular struck a chord in him, as was clear from his report for a Vienna journal on 'New Art in Berlin'. In Heinrich Vogeler, whose work was strongly influenced by William Morris and Beardsley, and for whom art was a design for living rather than mere decoration, he found indeed 'a dreamy companion on my road'[42] when the artist came to Berlin in November: for his own work at this time (*The White Princess*, and a *Play* (*Spiel*) he wrote for the artist Ludwig von Hofmann) was thoroughly in the *Jugendstil* spirit, even down to the symmetrical typographic setting of the verses.

Before joining Vogeler for Christmas, he visited Hamburg for a few days, where he was able to meet for the first time two of the 'masters' with whom he had corresponded earlier: Gustav Falke and Liliencron. The days which followed with Vogeler's family in Bremen, in their elegant patrician house, he found of an 'indescribable beauty'.[43] On Christmas Day they moved out to the Barkenhoff in Worpswede, the country property Vogeler had bought with his inheritance and which he had been extending and furnishing to his own designs. The village was the centre of the artists' colony which already had given it some renown—Fritz Mackensen, Otto Modersohn, Fritz Overbeck, Hans am Ende—but Rilke's first impression, as he walked with his friend out to the edge of the peat-bogs in a sulphurous evening light and watched a violet cloud reaching out over them like a clawed hand, was anything but favourable. 'What a gruesome place you people have found to live in,' he exclaimed.[44] After his return, he sent Vogeler 'for the beginning of the new year and as an appendix to the old' a motto for the Barkenhoff, which is still to be seen where the artist had it carved over the door lintel:

> Radiant be its fate.
> If the Master is the heart and the hand
> In its building, with the lindens in the land
> The house too will grow shady and great.[45]

Writing to Helene Voronin in St. Petersburg about his plans for the journey to Russia, he said he felt the end of this year was also the end of a phase in his work, in which much promise from his stay in Italy had been fulfilled: 'for me that was a great beginning'.[46] The fruit would be the volume of verse *A Festival for Me* (*Mir zur Feier*)—the published counterpart to that for Lou which he kept back—to appear, after much careful selection, at the end of 1899. 'Slowly collected together,' as he said to George: 'as though I had no others behind me, a first, serious, ceremonious book.'[47] With title-page and vignettes by Vogeler, it was in fact the first he would be willing in later years to acknowledge as of any worth.

In the New Year of 1899 he began to think of resuming university study— spurred on by Lou, but no doubt also at the insistence of his family. Georg Simmel, professor of philosophy, with whom, as with Sauer in Prague, he would maintain friendly contact over many years, seems to have advised him, and he was enrolled for the summer term at the Friedrich-Wilhelm University for lectures in history of art, modern history, and classical lyric poetry. He would have liked to hear Richard Muther, professor of art at Breslau, he told Frieda von Bülow, but was loth to leave his home at Waldfrieden which had given him so many good hours for his own work—'for that comes first and foremost, and everyday duties must give way at the glance of an hour of inspiration'.[48] He was certainly reluctant to go far from Lou. But his aim, as he wrote to Frieda, was the decent minimum of university work and no more.

Whether he gave himself time even for this is doubtful. Their plans for the Russian journey were occupying them more and more. He had told his mother that this was to be the big spring trip: but he was away for almost the whole of March, spending the first two weeks with her in Arco, followed by a few days in Vienna and Prague, and was not back in Berlin until towards the end of the month, with only a few weeks left until the departure for Moscow. Arco and Prague were duty visits, to see both of his parents, and his grandmother, before embarking on that adventure. Vienna, however, offered two attractions on 18 March that he was determined not to miss: the opening of the *Sezession* exhibition, with Gustav Klimt and others and the première of Hofmannsthal's dramatic poems *The Marriage of Zobeida* and *The Adventurer and the Singer*. Since his Munich days he had admired the verse of 'Loris', and in his Prague lecture on 'Modern Lyric Poetry' had paid tribute to these gems, known to few beyond the privileged readers of George's *Blätter für die Kunst* or Flaischlen's journal *Pan*. After the première, which he attended with Arthur Schnitzler, he was at last able to meet the poet in person. The following day from Prague he sent him his deep gratitude for the unforgettable experience, from which the overwhelming excitement had lingered in him 'like a shared secret'. 'While before I had often seen you as a guide, speaking mysterious words in front of grave pictures and impressing a deeper meaning on trees and flowers as you passed, yesterday you became for me the master, the will of whose being would be my way.'[49] Perhaps under Hofmannsthal's spell, he had found Vienna this time more appealing, and, as he wrote to Phia, was glad to feel a 'spontaneous patriotism' as an Austrian, 'Heaven bless me'.[50]

He had asked Bonz to send him a copy of the *Prague Stories*, to give to his father on the latter's name-day. It was opportune to be able to show Josef that, while not neglecting his studies, he was achieving some standing as a writer. The look of the volume, now that it had at last appeared, pleased him greatly. To Bonz he sent from Prague a long list of suggestions for the review copies, spreading his net to Theodore Herzl, Karl Kraus, and Schnitzler in Vienna and Rudolf Steiner and Jacobowski in Berlin. Later, from Berlin, he asked for two copies for him to present personally, one to the Czech poet Jaroslav Vrchlický and the other to Tolstoy when, as he hoped, he saw him in Russia. Bonz for his part seemed well content with his author, for he readily sent him an advance on the next book, even though Rilke spoke still of another volume of novellas rather than the hoped for novel. The money was welcome at this point, but Rilke preferred to regard it as a loan, and in fact repaid it in the course of the summer.[51]

The April weeks were spent in preparations for the great journey: studying the *Baedeker*, assembling letters of introduction and all the necessary documents, including passports. Jews were not permitted to cross the frontier, he told Phia, and an unbelievable quantity of documentation was required to prove oneself a Christian.[52] Simmel was helpful with advice over reporting his absence from lectures. Describing his travels to von Scholz, he wrote that he had found the voice of Easter too thin for him, impotent: 'I want to hear it again to the sound of deeper bells, and let my reverent ear find a crowning joy in the peals from the churches of the Kremlin.'[53]

3

'Part of my existence is to rest on this experience of Russia'

(To Phia Rilke, 5. 12. 1899)

The long train journey through Warsaw brought them to Moscow on 27 April 1899, just before the Russian Easter. Rainer's first call, armed with letters of introduction from friends in Germany, seems to have been on the young artist Leonid Pasternak, professor at the Art Institute, with whom he established at once a warm rapport. Pasternak, at the time engaged on the illustrations for Tolstoy's *Resurrection*, was able to arrange for them to visit the Count the following day. Rainer, though impressed by Tolstoy's 'kindliness and humanity', seems to have been too intimidated to say very much, or even to present him with his book as he had planned: according to Lou's diary, the conversation turned mainly on Andreas's researches into the Babi (Bahá'i) sect in Persia, which greatly interested Tolstoy, and on her contention that the Russian people's future lay in a synthesis of Western intellect and Russian 'soul'. This Tolstoy vigorously rejected, condemning the Russian peasant's piety as pure superstition. What the *mouzhik* needed was enlightenment and practical education, not encouragement in ignorance through a mystical preoccupation with his 'soul', and he urged them not to countenance such superstition by participating in the Easter rites.[1] But this was the experience they had come for; and the 'long, extraordinary, agitated' Easter night, as they mingled with the enormous throngs in the churches, was an unforgettable event for Rainer. The cry 'Christ is risen' and the fervent response from a thousand throats 'Verily He is risen', the booming strokes of Ivan Veliki, the great Kremlin bell, made it for him an Easter once in a lifetime, enough for a lifetime.[2]

They spent only a few days in Moscow, for Lou was anxious to rejoin her mother and family in St. Petersburg. But there was time to meet, again through Pasternak, the sculptor Prince Pavel Troubetskoy. St. Petersburg, when they arrived there on 3 May, was beflagged for the Pushkin centenary celebrations, and made a Western contrast with Moscow: 'much more international and un-Russian', he found, whereas Moscow had seemed the true Russia, a 'new translation of the word beauty'. 'The melodies of the Orient played on the organ of humble thoughts—that is Moscow, that is

Russia.'[3] His rudimentary command of the language made recourse to signs necessary to make himself understood in the 'maison meublée' where he stayed in St. Petersburg—sometimes a welcome relief, he confessed, for the vocal chords—but he still found it a 'singular experience' to be among this people 'full of awe and piety'.[4] He called immediately on Helene Voronin, and saw her often on this stay, writing her several poems and dedicating to her the copy of the *Prague Stories* he had intended for Tolstoy. Sometimes with her, sometimes alone, he visited the great art collections at the Hermitage and in private hands. In the painter Ilya Repin, prominent in the Naturalist School, he found another of the 'true Russians', people who 'tell one in the dusk what others deny in daylight'.[5] Spending a few days back in Moscow at the end of May, he was able to meet other artists in Pasternak's circle.

On his return to St. Petersburg he immersed himself in Russian religious art, studying closely the varying icon styles and reading art histories with an enthusiasm which he assured Helene would be anything but a passing phase. 'The study of these Russian things I shall return to—I would even rather say, return *home* to—from all other distractions . . . they are God's innermost, most secret chamber, in which he keeps his most beautiful treasures, not lying dusty and idle, but all dedicated to that profound piety from which came works and wonders since the beginning of time. . . . I feel that they are the best images and names for my own feelings and confessions, and that with them . . . I shall express everything which in my art strives for sound and clarity'.[6]

The abrupt explosion of the Russian spring, 'with none of the faltering and disappointment of ours', was like a revelation: overnight, 'at 3 or 4 in the morning, there comes an infinite release over the land,' he wrote to Phia after returning to St. Petersburg, 'the birch trees have suddenly grown a thousand tiny green wings which they try out in the hesitant wind.'[7] His whole impression, indeed, was of a new country, one just at the beginning of its life, with all its future still before it, as though its palaces and churches had not yet fully come into being—and yet of a country that was his true homeland. 'I can hardly express what Russia was and is for me,' he wrote later: 'unknowingly, I brought with me a certain predisposition which, right from the first moment there, and absolutely completely, made it seem like home to me.'[8] Italy had been like 'a land in a dream, whereas Russia is full of deep and unexpected verities'.[9] Florence now seemed to have been a kind of preparation for Moscow: here he had been carried 'deeper into greater simplicity'.[10] Despite Tolstoy's disparagement, for him the simple folk kneeling and praying before their Madonnas were not ensnared in superstition: their worship in such wondrous surroundings was the manifestation of a creative process, that same process which he saw in art, in which God Himself was still in the forming. 'From the people's every gesture there streams out the warmth of His growth like an infinite blessing.'[11]

There is no direct evidence on the state of Rainer's relationship with Lou during this first visit to Russia. It was natural that she and Andreas should stay with her family in St. Petersburg, while Rainer lodged elsewhere. They travelled back together in the middle of June to Danzig, but Lou continued to Berlin a few days later, while Rainer stayed on alone at Oliva, near Danzig, until the end of the month, content, in spite of rain, to digest his experiences in solitude there. Summer plans had already been made before the Russian journey: Frieda von Bülow had invited them both to share with her a villa on the Bibersberg, near Meiningen on the borders of the Thuringian Forest, and Lou was no doubt relieved that, in the flood of his enthusiasm, it was now to be a working holiday devoted to Russian studies—language, literature, art, and history. He had first to put in an appearance at the University, and could not join them there until after the end of term; but while he was at Schmargendorf he continued eagerly with his study of the language, already attempting Pushkin and Lermontov, with his grammar beside him, and celebrating a 'little intimate festival' wherever a line or two came easily. In a long letter to Helene Voronin at the end of July he confessed an increasing aversion to all things German: 'as soon as I have learned and mastered the language, I shall feel myself entirely a Russian. And then I shall bow low before the Znamenskaya Chapel (which I love before all others), three times in suitable reverence'—a reverence not so much religious as in recognition of the essential identity of pride and humility which was to be experienced only in Russia. 'If I had come on this earth as a prophet, I would preach all my life that Russia was the chosen land over which lies God's massive sculptor's hand as though in a provident delaying action: *everything* it needs is to come to this land, but the fulfilment of its destiny is to be slower and clearer.'[12]

The energy with which he entered into their work together during the six weeks in Meiningen was phenomenal. Frieda was in fact somewhat put out to find her two companions had almost no time for her at all, so deep were they all day in their books, 'as though preparing for some frightful examination', and so exhausted when they came for meals that no stimulating conversation was possible.[13] 'The days were too short for us,' wrote Lou.[14] Rainer found time for a respectful letter to Tolstoy, recalling their visit by sending him a short work by Andreas on the Babi sect, Lou's latest collection of novellas, and his own *Prague Stories*, 'sprung from many dark feelings binding me to my Slav homeland'. The party broke up on 12 September, when he and Lou suddenly decided to return to Berlin upon the news from Andreas that her little dog, to whom she was devoted, was sick. Frieda, saddled with forwarding their heavier luggage and books, was perhaps not altogether sorry, having felt herself so excluded. But Rainer had rarely felt so content. He had found a 'new health and gained new courage through a definite plan of study', he wrote to her, with his thanks for all she had done and enclosing, with his usual meticulousness, his contribution towards the September costs of the villa.[15]

For he was now all Russia, and was impatient to read all he could, asking Lou to lend him something, anything, Lermontov or some prose work until his other books came up from Meiningen. Waiting for him was a reproduction he had asked Helene Voronin to send of Vasnetsov's painting *Three Knights*. He would hang it, he told her, in a simple frame above a little chest he had brought back from Moscow: 'with chest, crosses, pictures I am gradually creating a devout Russian corner in my study'.[16] Resuming the simple life at Schmargendorf, helping Lou to prepare *bortsch*, or his favourite dish of Russian groats, he now wore a blue Russian-style peasant blouse. He had read somewhere that the real artist should be able to find within four leagues of his home material enough for a lifetime: but for him, home was not necessarily one's birthplace, and indeed the search for one's true homeland might be the source of everything great in art—to find it 'open, festive, as though awaiting our return!'[17] Certainly the feeling of coming home he had experienced in Russia was the spring now of an intense creative activity. In less than two months he had written *The Prayers* (*Die Gebete*), which would later form the first part of the *Book of Hours* (*Das Stunden-Buch*); the *Cornet*, later to be called the *Lay of the Life and Death of Cornet Christoph Rilke* (*Die Weise von Liebe und Tod des Cornets Christoph Rilke*); and *Tales of God and Other Things* (*Das Buch vom lieben Gott und Anderes*)—works which were in due course to bring him a wider recognition than anything he had so far achieved, and which for many would always represent the essential Rilke.

The Prayers, the first draft of the book *Of the Monastic Life* (*Vom mönchischen Leben*), was a long cyclic poem giving expression, in the mouth of a Russian monk, to the concept of God which Rilke had evolved from his journeys to Italy and Russia. The monk, painting his icons in humble devotion in his cell, invokes God as a mystery Whose nature is to be concealed in these traditional representations, rather than to be revealed as in the overweening presumption of the *quattrocento* artists: a God of the darkness of Byzantine painting, not of the light of the Italian Renaissance. The monk sees his work— the task of the artist, the poet, indeed of all mankind—as that of *constructing* God, like the patient, apparently interminable, building of a cathedral:

> We are building Thee, with tremulous hands,
> And we pile atom upon atom.
> But who can complete Thee,
> Cathedral Thou?[18]

He sees God, not as the ultimate creator only, but also as a creature still to be formed. The impossible antithesis is repeated in a thousand invocations: the 'neighbour God' existing in all things, now a frightened little bird, now a bearded peasant, yet still 'ripening' like a tree towards an ever-distant maturity and still being created by the artist, in fact truly existing only in him:

What will you do, God, when I am dead?
I am your pitcher (what if I should break?)
I am your drink (what if I should perish?)
I am your robe, your craft,
You lose your meaning when I am no more.
When I am gone you have no home . . .

What will you do, God! I am afraid.[19]

Such a strange combination of a God immanent in all things with One who is yet to be, a kind of spiritual heir to the artists and poets who must come before and help to form him, and with no meaning outside their creative minds, has no part in any orthodox religion. As E. M. Butler observed, 'Rilke's seemingly religious monk was worshipping at the shrine of art, and seeking a God that never was'. Yet the myriad images, at once mystical and concrete, in which he expressed this paradox, in verses of soaring rhythms and a poetic mastery as yet unequalled in his work, even in the *Visions of Christ*, have such a heavenly ring to their ambiguity that countless readers and commentators, with not a few theologians among them, have found little difficulty in assimilating the concept to orthodox views. Many of the monk's prayers can quite well be read as prayers to the Christian God: but even when aware of Rilke's rejection of Christianity, the reader can still find, in the manifold images in which God is portrayed, the confirmation of almost any form of deism or theism it may suit him to seek. In fact, Rilke's belief was not in God but in his own power to create him. 'If he no longer exists, or does not yet exist, what does it matter?' he wrote later. 'It will be my prayer which will make him. . . . And if the God whom it projects from out of itself does not persist, all the better: he shall be made all over again, and he will not be used up in eternity.'[20] It was a notion which he had already begun to formulate in Italy, and which explains his feeling that Florence had been a preparation for Moscow. Despite the Russian trappings of *The Prayers*, therefore, his brief experience of the country and studies of its history and literature were not so much the poem's inspiration as its catalyst. It came to him in a rush during the stormy autumn days and nights in late September and early October, and Lou was the first to hear the Prayers.

On one particular night, however, as the moon gleamed fitfully through clouds scudding before a high wind, he was seized by a quite different subject, prompted by a reference in an old chronicle (with perhaps also in mind a tale of Liliencron's, published a few years earlier). The chronicle was one of the papers unearthed during Jaroslav's genealogical researches, and, as he now recalled it, recorded a brief note of the death in 1664 of an eighteen-year-old Otto Rilke while serving as cornet in the Austrian campaign against the Turks in Hungary. This Rilke, in fact named Christoph and not Otto, was the youngest of the three sons of the lord of Langenau in Saxony—the family whom Rainer and his uncle had tried in vain to establish as their ancestors. In that 'one night' (as he always afterwards claimed), 'without a single correction',[21] he wrote in lightly-flowing poetic prose the romantic story of the young standard-bearer's ride to his first and last experience of love and war—the night of love in his castle billet ('no yesterday, no tomorrow, for time has fallen, and they blossom from its ruins'[22]) and an heroic death at dawn, falling with his blazing standard. 'How young I was then!' Rilke recalled in 1924,[23] when the slightly revised final version, prefaced by a more accurate quotation from the chronicle, had long since proved a popular success beyond anything he had ever dreamed of, or indeed ever desired.* For those whose standard for Rilke is set by his greatest works, the *Cornet* verges on kitsch: but it deserves at least the indulgence he himself always accorded it, as the last expression of the exuberance of his youth.

Early in November he began his journal once more—still in the form of an offering for Lou, but reflecting now the change in their relationship. Though it continues his dialogue with her, sometimes developing thoughts prompted by their actual talk, the ardour of the entries in Florence and Viareggio has faded, giving place to a melancholy resignation. 'In all my happier hours I will see your smile as a city, a far-off city that gleams with life; a word from you will be to me an island with ... tranquil and stately trees; your glance I will think a spring ... I shall know that all this *exists*, that the city is accessible, that I have often seen the island, that the loneliest moment by the spring is familiar to me; but if you ask, you will see me hesitate: I don't know for certain whether the wood we walk through is not just a reflection of my own feelings ...'. Lou's sensible handling of him in this frustration is evident from the journal, for in counterpoint, as it were, there emerges a new determination to seek fulfilment in his work. 'I must learn to exploit even my weariness, even my *justified* fatigue.... Every day must and shall have its meaning—and it shall have it, not from chance, but from my own effort!' His introspection becomes less and less centred on his feelings for her, the verses are no longer her 'festival'. 'If ever there was a God-given law, it is this: Be solitary from time to time. For He can come only to one, or to a couple between whom He can no longer distinguish.'[24] The entries take on more and more the character of a diary of work attempted or done, and a number of prose pieces in fact find their first record here.

One in particular he probably owed to Lou's encouragement. The idea of a novel based on his military college experience had long been with him, and they had often talked of it, for none knew better than she the value it could have as therapy for the trauma he could not rid himself of. It may well have

---

*From its appearance as the first volume of the *Insel-Bücherei*, in July 1912 ('What a ride you have given him!' wrote Rilke to Kippenberg after 8,000 copies had been sold in three weeks: 'who would have thought it'), it had reached sales of over 300,000 before his death in 1926, and passed the million mark in 1962.

been the theme envisaged for the novel he had earlier promised to produce for Bonz. Now, during the night of 5 November, he felt a sudden impulse to make at least a start. In the colder light of day, considered alongside his other projects, it took on a less urgent aspect; and he felt uncertain whether he was capable of truly conveying the monstrous attributes of boys in the mass. 'The individual—even the most depraved—is after all still a child, but it is what emerges from the community of these children as a whole which would be the main impression: a terrifying totality which acts like a dreadful organism with a life of its own.' But he nevertheless set down in the diary a vivid scene, undoubtedly based on an actual incident at St. Pölten which had remained indelibly printed on his mind: the strange despairing effort in the gymnasium of the most backward of the class, the 'pale, moonstruck' Karl Gruber, as he climbs unbidden almost to the ceiling, applauded by his astounded fellows, then slides down in a rush, sits uncomprehendingly, and finally collapses without a word; the effect on the class as he is carried out unconscious and the regimental doctor arrives; the eerie tension until the lieutenant parades them and curtly announces Gruber's death; the mingled feelings of release and awe as they are dismissed.[25] That Rilke could sometimes still recall his youthful dreams of military glory, he had shown in the *Cornet*: but in the watches of the night it was more often the nightmare aspect of soldierly training which preoccupied him.

Set against the realism of this sketch and the exaltation of the *Cornet*, the *Tales of God and Other Things*, which he wrote shortly afterwards, are slighter and more light-hearted efforts; but they too have an autobiographical flavour in their settings (Russia; Venice and Florence; Munich) and in their glimpses of some of his experiences (the dark period period of childhood; an unmarried mother once again reminiscent of Franziska Reventlow). 'Tales told to adults for children', as they were subtitled when published at Christmas 1900, they are a frank admission of Rilke's embarrassment at talking to children himself, a trait which he never lost. 'That isn't serious in itself— but the children might think I'm confused because I'm not telling the truth, and I set great store by the truth of my story . . .'.[26] The God presented here is a sometimes quaint version of the 'being still to come', the 'unfinished God' he had apprehended in Russia: a God who, though possibly omniscient, is not in fact all-seeing, who had delegated to His hands the task of the creation of man but then could not see the result, who takes fright at finding Himself in Michelangelo's block of marble but is restored to joy and heaven without end at the knowledge that He is in the sculptor too, that they are each at work in a process of mutual creation. Although heavily engaged by this burst of productivity, he had found time to write encouragingly to Franziska Reventlow in her new quarters in Schwabing, and also to ask Ernst von Wolzogen's help over a publisher for her translations. 'I shall stay here over the whole winter,' he told her, 'with the work inspired by my visit to Russia. I can already read Russian fairly well, and am pleased with the progress each day brings.'[27] Once the *Tales of God* were finished, his language study became more intensive, and he was soon able to work his way through Dostoevsky's *Poor Folk*. Plans for another, longer tour with Lou in Russia were already being made, and he enrolled at the University in the Russian faculty, determined to attend the lectures regularly. 'It was so essential for me, with my many divergent interests, to concentrate at last on something,' he wrote to Phia the day after his twenty-fourth birthday, 'and now I've chosen Russia, I must stick with that, don't you think?'[28] Two or three hours every day were spent on Turgenev in the original, and three or four on French works about Russia, including de Vogüé's treatise on the Russian novel, a 'fine book' from which he made copious notes.

These preoccupations did not prevent him from attending to the more practical matters of publishing, for income on the side was still of paramount importance for him. To Bonz, in default of the novel still to be written, he had sent in July a selection of his novellas, and explained that, having received a subvention from a Prague foundation through the good offices of Professor Sauer, he would place his next volume of verse elsewhere: 'you told me last year that you had no plans to publish verse, and in the form I want, with H. Vogeler's drawings on each page, it would not suit your style.'[29] *A Festival for Me* (*Mir zur Feier*)—that 'first, serious, ceremonious book', as he had described it to George—accordingly made its appearance at Christmas 1899 with the Berlin firm of G. H. Meyer. Bonz's reaction is not recorded, but he was unwilling to bring out yet another series of short stories, and in the end contented himself with an undertaking from Rilke to give him first option on any future longer work—a commitment which was to give the poet much trouble later.

He was in touch as before with a wide variety of journals in Vienna, Munich, Berlin and Prague, which printed poems and stories from time to time, bringing welcome relief to his purse. A new venture, however, drew his attention now. *The Island* (*Die Insel*), a bibliophile monthly whose first number appeared in October, funded by the wealthy aesthete Alfred Walter Heymel, who edited it together with the poet Rudolf Alexander Schröder and the writer Otto Julius Bierbaum, seemed the vehicle he had once dreamed of setting in motion himself: for its aim was to create 'a meeting-point for the artistically most valuable contributions of modern German and foreign literature' and to 'participate in the new movement in applied fine art' by providing in ornamentation, type, and paper, a frame worthy only of the best.[30] Heymel and Schröder were cousins, a few years younger than Rilke, and had gravitated as young men from Bremen to Munich, where they had already dreamed, like him, of such a project; Bierbaum, thirteen years their senior, brought his journalistic experience to the venture, and for its presentation Schröder recruited Vogeler, an artist whose style ideally suited their concept. Bierbaum enthused in December over the first poem Rilke sent in, 'The Three Kings': 'a quite exceptional pleasure for us, a delightful poem. We hope Vogeler will draw something for it.'[31] The artist in fact provided the ornamentation for all three numbers of the second quarter, January to March 1900, and 'The Three Kings' appeared in that of March.

The editorial triumvirate did not hold together for long, Schröder and Heymel leaving Bierbaum alone responsible for the third year before closing the journal down. But meanwhile they pursued an even more ambitious idea: to establish their own publishing house under the 'Insel' sailing-ship symbol. This came into being already in the summer of 1899, at first under the aegis of the publishers of the journal, Schuster & Loeffler of Berlin and Leipzig, but by 1901 as an independent house based in Leipzig. One of its first publications was an edition of Vogeler's poems *For You* (*Dir*) in a facsimile of his own hand and with his own ornamentation; a copy, coloured by hand, he dedicated to his friend Rilke. The 'boundless romanticism' of Vogeler's drawing in these *Jugendstil* years—'a beautiful curtain concealing reality', as he conceded himself[32]—held great attraction for Rilke then, as we have already noted. And in the emerging Insel-Verlag, with its lofty aims for artistic production, he recognized at once a spirit more suited to his own work than the more commercial Bonz or Meyer. He was overjoyed when the *Tales of God* found ready acceptance with Bierbaum and Heymel, and their appearance with Insel in December 1900 was an event of great moment in his career.

After spending the Christmas days of 1899 in Prague, he returned via Breslau in order to call on Richard Muther, the professor of art history he had long admired, and undertook an article on Russian art for the Viennese journal *Die Zeit*, of which Muther was art editor. In the quiet Schmargendorf routine he now resumed in the New Year he concentrated more and more on preparations for the coming return to Russia. As he wrote to Leonid Pasternak in February, sending him a copy of his verse volume, the country had been more than a fleeting experience for him: since August he had devoted himself almost exclusively to the study of its history, art, culture, and not least the 'beautiful, incomparable language'. 'What a joy to read Lermontov's verse or Tolstoy's prose in the original!' He had an immense longing for Moscow, and if all went well hoped to be there by April, this time for a longer stay 'as an initiate' in Pasternak's circle. He had plans to write much more about Russia, as soon as he had gained deeper insight into the material. The Crimea and Kiev would, he hoped, figure in the itinerary. 'Before this prospect I feel like a child before Christmas.'[33] Sophia Nikolaevna Schill, a Russian writer whom he had met though Lou in Berlin over the turn of the year, sent him a number of books after her return home, and one in particular, the verses of the peasant-poet S. D. Drozhzhin, aroused in him an enthusiasm which surprised her. He translated some of these poems 'full of music and dance' at once,[34] publishing two in Prague in April, and pressed Sophia to arrange a visit to Drozhzhin for him and Lou during their stay. He longed, he told her, to be able to write verse himself in Russian. Meanwhile he asked for copies of Chekhov's *Seagull* and *Uncle Vanya* to pass on to a publisher in Munich, for he had hopes for their production in translation in Germany; his own translation of the *Seagull* (which has not survived) he had completed by the end of March.

There was no question, this year, of paying his usual visit to his mother in Arco. She heard how he was 'working like a day-labourer', writing 170 pages in two days and having even to forgo the première of Ibsen's 'dramatic epilogue' *When We Dead Awaken*.[35] Involved 'head over heels' in the preparations for the Russian journey, he wrote to Franziska Reventlow, he was only sorry that it would be the first time in four years he had not made a spring excursion to Lake Garda, at the very time when she was planning to be there with little Rolf. His efforts would bear fruit, he hoped, in a collection of monographs on Russian painters whose work he was studying, 'which I think could be significant for creativity in art as a whole, for to write about Russian artists is to talk of unusually profound (yet simple) people'.[36] 'Russian Art', the essay promised for Muther, based on the general impressions of his first journey, but dealing at some length with Vasnetsov's work, was already done, and he was eager to see more. Just as the God of the Russian people was 'unfinished', so their art was still in the making, and he felt that each would develop alongside the other in a perpetual interaction.

The excitement of the Russian Easter was over when he arrived with Lou in Moscow on 9 May 1900. From their rooms looking out at the Kremlin, one of whose windows reflected the sinking sun 'like a holy lamp', they felt in the city an atmosphere 'between prayer and jubilation', its colours melting together into 'an expression of celestial happiness'.[37] 'Little Schill' was a ready guide, taking them the following day to the History Museum, and later on repeated visits to the Tretyakov Art Gallery, a long-felt want. She recalled what a striking couple they made as they explored the alleys and side-streets of the city, hand-in-hand like eager children, oblivious of curious glances and smiles: Lou's 'tall, somewhat thickset figure, in the oddly-coloured loose-flowing dress she had made herself', Rainer 'pale of countenance like a girl', but with a very becoming reddish goatee, 'slim, of medium height, in his jacket with many pockets and a real Tyrolean hat'. They would often stop to drink tea in little eating-houses frequented by drivers and porters, listening to their talk and joining in; and Rainer was impressed by the open friendliness they encountered wherever they went. Sophia had letters of introduction for them to the writers she knew, but their search, as it seemed to her, was for 'the authentic face of Russia', the further from literature and Europe the better.[38]

Every day they used to the full, returning to their rooms only to sleep. Rainer felt himself 'indescribably at home' now that he could understand the language so well. Pasternak, to whom he appeared quite the young Russian intellectual, made two pencil sketches of him, on which he based the oil 'Rilke in Moscow' he painted after the poet's death. At his instigation, the prominent writer and art-collector Pavel Davidovich Ettinger, who knew personally most of the leading artists, called on Rilke on 15 May, and would long remember his impression of the 'pale, longish face with its full, sensual lips', the 'thick ash-blond hair' and 'watery-blue eyes'. Both Ettinger and Pasternak saw to it, during his three weeks' stay in Moscow, that he should meet as many as possible of the artists of the day, and Ettinger in particular was helpful later in sending him books and reproductions he needed for his work.[39]

'Thanks to the excellent connections I now have, every circle is open to me,' he wrote to his mother.[40] There were evenings at workers' educational classes, where Sophia Schill lectured and they could take tea afterwards with the weavers and printers who attended; an invitation from Prince Shakhovskoy to join him on a tour of the Kremlin armoury and treasury; a visit with a priest to the Tchudov Monastery. They paid another visit to Abramtsevo, the estate near Moscow which was now a centre of Russian artistic life, 'a sort of Russian Worpswede', as he described it to Phia;[41] and at Zagorsk saw the extraordinary 'monastery city' of Sergei Troitsky, walled like a fortress, its twenty churches and cathedrals interspersed with booths as in a fairground, in a strange mingling of sanctity and worldliness.[42]

At the end of the month was to come the highlight of the visit: a 2,500-mile journey through the south and east of European Russia, first to the Ukraine, with a fortnight's stay over Whitsun in the 'holy city' of Kiev, thence down the Dnieper to Kremenchug and across through Kharkhov and Voronezh to the Volga at Saratov, where they would take ship up-river as far as Yaroslavl, returning to Moscow by train. For Lou as well as Rainer it would be a voyage of discovery, to the heartland she had not yet seen. A visit to Tolstoy, on whom they had been able to pay only a brief call this time in Moscow, was a possibility *en route*, for they would pass near his country estate at Yasnaya Polyana; but up to the time of their departure on 31 May they were uncertain whether he had yet returned there. It chanced that Leonid Pasternak was taking the same train, bound with his family for Odessa (the ten-year-old Boris, looking back later on this sole encounter with the poet whose work he so admired, found his main impressions had been of a man with an unfamiliar accent in his German and of a tall woman accompanying him, 'perhaps his mother or his elder sister').[43] A friend of the Tolstoys was also travelling, and, introduced by Pasternak, held out hopes that the Count was indeed now at Yasnaya Polyana; so, after spending the night at Tula, they made their way there by a combination of local and goods trains and a hired troika.

Their arrival was clearly far from welcome, so soon after the Tolstoy's move from their winter quarters in Moscow, and amid the growing conflict between the Count and his wife. The old man, who seemed to Rainer 'smaller, more bent, whiter', though still with keen and benevolent eye, was distrait, and said he would see them later; after coffee in the great dining-room upstairs, with its ancestral portraits, and a walk in the park and through the great avenue of birches with the eldest son, they returned to find the Countess in inhospitable mood, testily sorting out books and saying her husband was indisposed. There was a banging of doors, arguments and tears could be heard in an adjoining room, with Tolstoy's voice raised in pacification; he wandered in, then left them again, but finally emerged to suggest another walk through the park while the family were at lunch, a meal which would have promised dubious pleasure for them under the circumstances and which he was obviously glad to miss. This time they could give all their attention to their host, hanging on his words as he strode along into the wind and stooped now and then to gather great handfuls from the carpet of forget-me-nots, in a sickle-like movement, as though catching a butterfly, pressed them to his face and let them fall again. Taking their leave from him at the house, 'with a feeling of child-like gratitude', as Rainer wrote the next day to Sophia Schill, 'and enriched by the gift of his being', they walked back to the nearest station and returned in the evening to Tula.[44]

Lou felt later that the encounter had been like their gateway to the country and its people on this second journey. For Rainer, the Tolstoy experience was an ambivalent one. To see him in this setting of gently rolling countryside chimed with his preconceived notion of him as the true, the 'eternal Russian': at the same time his relatively great age precluded any real understanding between them (in later years Tolstoy could not even remember their meeting). Rainer's hesitant admission that he was a poet had brought down on him an almost violent tirade against all art; but the overpowering personality of the patriarch did not prevent him from sensing the conflict in Tolstoy between art and life—succumbing to the temptation to renounce his art, the 'heart-work' he was made for, in favour of the real life of 'hand-work', at which he was a fumbling amateur, had brought, it seemed to Rainer, disillusion and an immense loneliness.[45]

First impressions of Kiev, where they arrived in the late afternoon of 3 June after a hot and uncomfortable journey, were disappointing. From their reading, they had expected to find an essentially Russian city, the ancient capital where St. Olga and St. Vladimir had first raised the standard of Christianity: but its outward aspect was entirely modern, an international veneer left by centuries of Polish and western influence. 'I try to see as little as possible of all this,' Rainer wrote to his mother, 'and turn all my attention to the ancient churches and cathedrals with their old pictures and costly relics.'[46] It was in the Vladimir Cathedral, the Vidubetsky monastery, and the church of St. Sophia that he rediscovered the essence of Russia he had glimpsed on his first visit. Wandering with lighted candle through the low narrow galleries of the Pecherskaya catacombs, past the cells where the saintly monks of a thousand years before, arrayed in costly damask, lay embalmed in open silver coffins, he was overwhelmed once more, as at Easter in Moscow, by the intense devotion of the throng of Whitsun pilgrims who had come from all over

Russia. Lou, more down to earth, was struck rather by the repulsive greed and ignorance of the present-day monks, and the whole power-oriented political system of the priests, with their insistence on maintaining their monopoly of education: though it might be dangerous to release the people from this stranglehold, to let it continue seemed to her even more dangerous.[47]

They settled in a delightful small hotel, in rooms with a balcony overlooking gardens along the Dnieper. The weather was sultry, with occasional storms, and the chance to bathe in the river was welcome. Between visits to the churches and monasteries, they wandered round the Podol market, and were often in the nearby gardens. On the Sunday after Whitsun, after a final tour of the market, they embarked on the steamer *Moguchy* (*The Mighty*) for the journey down-river to Kremenchug, which Lou found of desolate aspect, and Kresl. From there it was another train up to Poltava, where they spent two days, with a trip to nearby Korbonovka and a visit to a peasant's hut typical of Little Russia.[48]

On 21 June began the long train journey across to Saratov, third class through Kharkhov to Voronezh but in comfortable coupés the second day. In Saratov, waiting two days for the arrival of the *Alexander Nevsky* to take them up the Volga, they explored the town and the Cossack area on its eastern slopes; Lou, somewhat exhausted by now, rested on the second day, while Rainer visited the National Museum. The steamer, after a characteristic delay, finally sailed at one in the morning on 25 June, and they slept little on the thirty-six-hour run past Yekaterinenstadt with its German colony, Khralynsk and Syzran to Samara, so serene was the weather and so splendid the thrill of their progress through the expanse of the great river. A gently attractive countryside, without melancholy, noted Lou, quite the opposite to the picturesqueness of the Rhine, the churches standing rooted firmly in a true homeland.[49] For Rainer it was a re-education, seeing land, water, and sky in new dimensions, the whole of creation on the scale of God the Father. During the long halt in Samara they went shopping, and enjoyed *koumiss* with cranberries from a Tatar vendor. But the most beautiful stretch lay now before them, round the sweeping bend of the river to Stavropol, and despite a clouding over they remained on deck until midnight. It was raining when they reached Simbirsk (Ulyanovsk) early on 27 June, but the weather brightened steadily as they continued to Kazan. From there a fast steamer, the *Grand Duchess Olga Nikolaevna*, brought them to Nizhni-Novgorod (Gorky) on 30 June, and then, following up the now narrower Volga they took the *Prince Mikail Tverskoy* to Yaroslavl, arriving on 2 July.

Before returning to Moscow, they determined to try to get closer to the life of the ordinary people. In the nearby village of Kresta Bogorodskoye they found an *izba*, a peasant's cottage, newly built by a couple just married, who had had to go into service for an income and were only too pleased to find temporary tenants. There was a built-in bench, and a samovar; a palliasse was soon filled with fresh straw (broad enough for two, said their neighbour—but another was made ready for Rainer in the adjoining stable). For a few days they could share the simple life and spare meals of the friendly villagers, wandering round the flowered meadows, drinking their tea at the cottage door in the dawn light—an idyll of the primitive life, in fact far removed from its harsher realities. For Lou, the brief interlude was the symbol of her joy at seeing her homeland again: Rainer, as it seemed to her, found here the very essence of the Russian people's piety, amid a life of deepest poverty, even misery, their trust in the protection of what they called 'God'. Its echoes had come to him in fragments of verse in Poltava and Saratov, or on the Volga near Kazan, which found their way into the continuation of the *Prayers* he began to write after his return.

In Yaroslavl, where they spent the day of 5 July before taking the train back to Moscow, they saw the family church of the Shakhovskoys, where three of the Prince's ancestors, resting in bejewelled coffins, were venerated as saints by the local people. Shakhovskoy was one of the few among their new friends who had not left Moscow for the summer, and during the two weeks they now spent there was often their guide to the museums. An idea for another long journey, this time on the Ural Railway as far as Chelyabinsk, had to be abandoned for lack of funds; but Sophia Schill was able to satisfy their eargerness to see more of village life by the visit she had arranged to Drozhzhin at his home in Nisovka, on the upper reaches of the Volga. The peasant-poet, now over fifty, having made something of a name, Robert Burns fashion, in his earlier years in St. Petersburg, had long since returned to his village, where he was now the respected elder, working in the fields in the summer and writing in the winter. Impressed by Sophia's description of his distinguished admirers from Germany, his translator and the 'famous authoress', and anxious to ensure that they were properly received, he had furnished suitable quarters in a hut next to his own which he had just completed as his work room. They were given tea on arrival; 'Rainer Osipovich' presented his host with a copy of his translations; he and 'Luise Gustavovna' were then led over the fields to the Volga, and returned to hear Spiridon Dimitrievich read from his poems after the evening meal.

He was startled to find the next morning that they had risen at dawn, before he was awake, and gone wandering barefoot through the dew along the riverbank meadows—'good for the health, they told me later', but he was sceptical enough to pull on his boots before joining them on the following day's walk at sun-up.[50] The simple poet with such close ties still to the soil was the epitome of Russia and the Russian people as Rainer conceived them: 'these days have brought us a big step nearer the heart of Russia,' he wrote to Sophia Schill, the heart whose 'beating marks the just rhythm for our lives.'[51] Nikolai Alekseevich Tolstoy, a neighbouring landowner, sent his carriage over to bring them for a day to his estate at Novinki, and when they made a second visit there prevailed on them to stay the night—a glimpse of the country-gentleman life, with a family just as devout as the peasants, which Lou found an unexpected and attractive complement to the impressions of their journey. But it was the village life, here and everywhere they had been, which had most inspired her: 'the people are silent, they pray a lot, everyday life here is not continually noisy and vehement . . . one reason why these folk have depth, and seem to have no need of education.'[52] 'I could wish to stay here for ever,' she wrote in Drozhzhin's guest-book, after Rainer had inscribed in Russian a brief autobiography and expressed his deeper understanding and love of their host's poems now he had seen where they were inspired.[53]

Leaving on 24 July, they spent two days in the old Hanseatic city of Novgorod Veliky before continuing to St. Petersburg. This was effectively the end of their journey together, for Lou was to go on to Rongas in Finland, to join her eldest brother and his family, leaving Rainer alone for nearly a month until the time came for their return to Berlin. He plunged at once into study, spending long hours in the Imperial Library, where he dipped into the history of old Moscow and applied himself once more to works on art history. But he soon discovered his lack of talent for systematic work, faced with so many hundreds of thousands of books without a guide, waiting in vain for a revelatory moment in which he could 'absorb and experience their collective spirit with all their contradictions and obscure wisdoms'.[54] He was enthusiastic, in his letter of thanks to Drozhzhin, over what he was discovering: but this feeling of inadequacy at book-learning was one which would often recur. To it now was added his desolation over Lou's absence. She left him without news for a week or so, and he felt 'inexpressibly uneasy' at the sudden gap, the loss of the comfortable companionship to which he had become accustomed, the removal of this essential prop to his existence. The city they had enjoyed together the previous year took on a depressing, 'almost hostile' aspect, he wrote to her, in a letter whose tone reminded her of the 'pre-Wolfratshausen' days. He was full of contrition over this outburst of misery, so unexpected for her, as soon as he received her reply, with its details of the happy summer amid the Finnish birch-woods with her nephews and nieces; but was all the more impatient for her return. At each turn, in the bustle of the city, he could see everything only in the thought 'when you come', and from his favourite place by the Neva, looking across to the St. Isaak Cathedral, found a new comfort in the assurance that that moment would be soon.[55]

A new friend now was Aleksandr Benois, the artist, art critic, and stage-designer, and Rainer enjoyed an evening at his country house, walking through the great part of Peterhof where stood Peter the Great's 'little Dutch châteaux', with their 'avenues of leaping fountains leading right down to the calm sea'.[56] Benois was writing a history of nineteenth-century Russian art from the modern viewpoint, like Muther's for Germany, and Rainer began to plan a translation. He met Serghei Diaghilev, the editor of *Mir iskusstva* (*The*

World of Art), to which Benois was a contributor, and discussed with him the idea of a Russian art exhibition in Berlin. Feeling more and more, as he wrote to his mother, 'like one born in St. Petersburg', he even considered seriously Benois' suggestion of moving there for good, with a post as correspondent for a Russian art journal.[57]

This notion of a 'Russification' of his life, though it did not last, was another reflection of what had surprised and disturbed Lou in his letters to Finland— the symptoms, as it seemed to her, of a relapse into those 'pre-Wolfratshausen' excesses of which she had hoped their relationship had cured him. This troubled her all the more now that the journey of rediscovery of her homeland had given her new strength and zest to go forward with the life she had chosen, whereas he, after the same experience, appeared 'shaken to the depths'. 'Never was I more conscious from what primeval depths *your* mature development would be able to come.' Their ways, she was convinced, had to part—he should seek 'freedom and distance' without delay, go out into the world and among people, while she was impelled away from him, away from 'that reality of your beginnings when we had been as one'. 'For all the caring fervour of our relationship,' she wrote later, 'I stood detached, outside the bond which truly links man and woman.'[58]

She had in fact, while they were at Yaroslavl, already prepared the way, by encouraging him to accept a long-standing invitation from Heinrich Vogeler to stay at Worpswede again; and Rainer had now had confirmation that he was expected there immediately after their return to Germany, not least to deal with the first proofs of the Insel edition of the *Tales of God*. On 22 August they left for Danzig, and were back in Berlin four days later, from where Rainer went straight on to Worpswede. On the last day of the year, Lou noted in her diary: 'What I want from the coming year, what I must have, is really just quiet—more solitude, as it was four years ago. It will come, it must come again for me.'[59]

4

'My life, so remote from the everyday world ... needed for
its development the quiet peace of a house of my own, under
the broad skies of solitude'

(To Gustav Pauli, 8. 1. 1902)

'A rum-looking customer, I must say!' exclaimed Vogeler's housekeeper: 'wears his shirt outside his trousers!'[1] Rilke's Russian garb made a stir in the village when he arrived on 27 August 1900, accustomed though the Worps-weders were to artists' eccentricities. Under the white gables of the Barkenhoff his friend had made ready a quiet room, and offered surroundings 'full of the atmosphere of a creative spirit';[2] of a comfortable elegance he had rarely before experienced. The furnishing was to Vogeler's own design, his pictures and drawings decorated the walls, and the artist, Rainer thought, made a picture himself, like some distant ancestor, with his slim figure in high-necked, wide-winged collar, cravat secured with a cameo and velvet waistcoat. The countryside no longer took on the somewhat sinister aspect he had remarked on his first visit. 'It is a strangely beautiful meadowland,' he wrote to Phia, 'rich in change and movement'; 'flat, with avenues of birches, old farmhouses, rowans, the ground divided between wonderfully scented heather and singular moorland cut through with canals.' He could appreciate now its attraction for the painter—'the clarity and colour of the varying moods of the atmosphere and the splendid cloud effects'.[3]

Most satisfying of all in these surroundings was a sense of relief at having found a home. In the impulse of his passion for Lou, he had abandoned the more stable life of Munich for a nomadic existence—rich in impressions, certainly, and often intensely productive, but with its reference point in Lou alone. Even after his return from Florence he had still hoped this could continue; and in the excitement of the Russian experience, to which she had led him, imagined himself content, a satellite in orbit around her, more distant but held still by her attraction. With the sudden removal of this gravitational force, he was floating free, but lost. In the first days at Worpswede he felt he had failed in Russia to measure up to his mission in life: the transmuting of experience into poetic form. 'Everything truly seen *must* become a poem!' he had cried to Lou in Moscow—but the long journey since had produced few verses. 'Countless poems I failed to hear. I passed over a spring: no wonder there's no real summer now. Everything that came found my doors closed. And now I open them, the roads are long and empty. . . .'[4] But his reception now into the Worpswede community of like-minded people of his own age, as guest in a house which had become a centre of attraction for artists, writers, poets, and dramatists, rapidly lifted him out of this despondency. In Berlin, when he emerged from the solitude of Schmargendorf, it had often been in the wake—and in the shadow—of the 'noted authoress': here he was accepted in his own right by colleagues who wanted to hear him read his work and talk to them of Russia, its artists, Tolstoy, the ikon painters, Kramskoy, Drozhzhin.

There were frequent gatherings in Vogeler's candle-lit music room, 'white, its white doors with vases painted on them from which rose-garlands gently fall on either side',[5] on the walls old prints and graceful portraits, the furniture Empire-style. Carl Hauptmann, visiting the Worpswede painter Otto Modersohn, came to read his poems and prose and air his views on the philosophy of art, other guests played and sang Schubert, Richard Strauss, or Handel, Rilke read his *White Princess*, or from the *Tales of God*, in his 'wonderfully soft, vibrant voice'. As Modersohn recalled: 'the poets lent a rich ceremonious air to the life of our little circle'.[6] The more robust pleasures of a harvest festival in the village, with dancing in which the artists all joined, left Rilke silent and uncomfortable among the fumes of beer and tobacco: his delight was in the talk and sympathetic stillness of the white music room, the exchange of confidences with Vogeler on long walks over the heath, past the new-mown cornfields, their reds and yellows 'like costly silk', every moment fixing a sharp image of tree, house, slowly-turning windmill.[7] And there was a special attraction, among the company of artists living in and near Worpswede, in the presence of two girls, still novices, who had settled there to learn from Mackensen and Modersohn: the blonde Paula Becker, almost his own age, and the tall, dark-haired Clara Westhoff, nearly three years younger. They listened attentively and receptively when he read his poems during the music-room evenings ('delicate and full of insight,' found Paula, 'sweet and pale'),[8] or came to their studios to talk of art and life and death—a flattering contrast to the cool appraisal of Lou.

Paula Becker's life till now had run a course in some ways like his own. The daughter of a railway official in Bremen of limited means, she had been encouraged in her early talent for drawing and painting by an artistically inclined mother. The aid of relatives more comfortably off had enabled her to pursue formal studies in England and Berlin, and to spend a month in Worpswede when she was twenty-one. Although her father, forced into early retirement by a reorganization, urged her to make a career which would earn her a living, he was still indulgent towards her chosen path; and when relations once more promised an allowance sufficient for her to pursue it for three more years, made no objection to her move to Worpswede in the autumn of 1898, where Mackensen had agreed to supervise her work. The beauty of the surroundings and the feeling of acceptance and familiarity in a community of artists had proved stimulating, and she had worked assiduously under Mackensen's eye—an eye not entirely approving, though he could appreciate her gifts, for what she saw and drew was sometimes further from nature than the Worpsweders were wont to stray. Like the young Rilke in Prague, she felt instinctively that she needed a wider world for her development; and after a leading anti-modernist critic had mercilessly condemned the finished works and studies she exhibited in the Bremen Kunsthalle in December 1899, she had been glad to escape to Paris to work and study there for a few months. Like Rilke, too, she had been drawn to someone older than herself whom she could idolize as an artist and idealize as a person. To Otto Modersohn, her senior by ten years, already married and with a child, came letters from Paris which left him in no doubt of her adoration and her joy at his visit there with Vogeler and Overbeck for the Great Exhibition of 1900. The early death of his wife in June spared them what had threatened to become a highly delicate situation. When Paula returned to Worpswede soon afterwards, in indifferent health, his frequent visits to her, and when she was better the evenings at the Barkenhoff, gave her assurance that her love was returned, though with perfect discretion they kept their friends in ignorance for the time being. And Rilke, hearing her speak of the homesickness for the heathland she had felt while in Paris, had no inkling yet that more than just its natural beauty was the attraction for her in Worpswede, nor that, for all her admiration of his 'delicate lyrical talent, tender and sensitive',[9] she had already given her heart to Modersohn.

In Clara Westhoff, who had arrived at about the same time, also as a student of Mackensen's, she had found a 'sister spirit'. Clara's parents—Friedrich Westhoff, a wealthy Bremen import merchant, and his second wife Johanna—had been equally encouraging to a talent in art. Westhoff himself, though he had devoted his life to making money and succeeding in business, would have chosen under differrent circumstances to be an artist, and in his spare time showed a certain gift as a painter, while his wife was far from conventional in her way of life, fond of the outdoors and a keen cyclist; and they were in a better position than the Beckers to finance their daughter's studies. At seventeen Clara had been able to spend three years at art schools in Munich and Dachau, and had seen in 1895 the Munich *Sezession* exhibition as well as the international exhibition which had marked the Worpswede group's first success. When she came to Mackensen, who was not only a painter but also a sculptor, he recognized at once where her gift lay, and taught her the elements of modelling. Paula admired her as she worked on a bust of an old woman: 'I should like her for a friend,' she wrote in her diary in December 1898, 'tall and splendid both as a person and as an artist.'[10] They often worked from the same model, and spent much of their spare time together. Paula visited her the following year in Leipzig when she spent a few weeks there studying under Max Klinger, and followed her to Paris at the turn of the year, when Clara had decided to pursue at the Académie Julian the study of anatomy not then open to women in Germany. An introduction from Klinger gave Clara the opportunity of visiting Rodin in his studio in the rue de l'Université and of joining his school for a short time, where the master himself corrected her work occasionally. The impressions they brought back that summer from Paris, especially their discovery of Cézanne, lent a feeling of joy and harmony to their return to Worpswede. (Less harmonious was their sudden impulse, on a walk very late one evening, to ring the bells of the Zion church: this false fire alarm caused great consternation among painters and villagers alike, and as penance Clara presented the church with eight copies of an angel's head she had been working on, which are still to be seen there.)

For Rilke, the pair were like two facets of a single personality, in a charming combination of shyness and innocent bohemianism quite different from the self-assured freedom he had encountered with Lou. With their contrasting looks and temperaments, they seemed equally attractive: Paula alert, vivacious, sometimes pert, Clara more contemplative and reserved. Every detail of their lives fascinated him—the story of devotion to art, a dedication like his own, but in gentle beings whose existence was itself an inspiration for the poet:

Maidens—poets are those who learn from you
To say in words what you express by living.[11]

When the Barkenhoff company turned at midnight to wine and dancing, and
he retreated to his room, he was restored to humour as the girls in their white
dresses followed him to lean silent out into the moonlight at his open window,
'half-knowledgeably, as painters, half unknowing, as maidens ... I was
grateful to them for their beauty, framed simple and white in my big window.'
From his diary, in which he continued to address Lou, it is difficult to see to
which of the two he felt the more drawn: Clara, in her long white Empire
dress, with the Barkenhoff seeming to pay compliment and adapt itself to her
presence, 'doubly beautiful' as she listened intently to his reading; or Paula,
'gentle and slender in her white virginity, her hair of Florentine gold', her
voice 'with folds like silk'. 'How much I am learning from watching these two,
especially the blonde painter, who has such brown observant eyes! How much
closer I feel now to everything unsensed and wonderful, as in those days of my
"Maidens' Songs".... My whole life is filled with the images in which I can
talk to them ...'[12]

Why should not one—or other—of these charming spirits make the partner
he needed? Marriage was in the air: Vogeler had told him of his plans to take as
wife, in the spring, the young Martha Schröder, a girl of great beauty whom he
had worshipped since she was only a child and whom he had rescued from a
difficult family life, arranging for her education and installing her with his
brothers on the family property near Bremen. And Worpswede seemed more
and more to Rainer the ideal place for his future work, in its remoteness and
the natural beauty of its broad expanses of moorland, 'the lofty, excited
heavens beneath which so many images and gestures ... are in movement'.[13]
He was hesitant, at any rate, to give this up: and during September, so as not to
outstay his welcome with Vogeler, moved from the Barkenhoff to a place of his
own nearby. The personalities of Clara and Paula remained for him curiously
intermingled. In a four-wheeler to Bremen one Saturday, as Paula sat opposite
him in a stunning broad-brimmed Paris hat, black with dark red roses, her
lively brown eyes reflecting her feeling for the countryside, they were
overtaken by Clara bicycling to visit her parents at their summer house in
Oberneuland, and he waved long after her as she pedalled briskly ahead. With
them in the carriage was an enormous wreath of heather, which she had made
for Carl Hauptmann, but which she said ought rightfully to be his, as her
thanks for the drama he had read the previous evening. In its twined branches
he seemed to feel the 'simple, reverent power of her sculptor's hands',[14] and
the journey passed in quiet enjoyment of the strength of Clara, through his
hands, and the gentleness of Paula, through his eyes.

When the whole group met in Hamburg, for the première of Hauptmann's
new play—Vogeler and his brother Franz, Mackensen, Paula's sister Molly,

Modersohn—the first impression of a city intimidating to these 'children of the heath' was banished for him in the company of Paula and Clara, eager to see and absorb everything. With them he was truly seeing works of art for the first time, learning from them appreciation of detail. 'I feel strangely confused, yet clear, in these days,' he wrote in his diary later. 'I find a country, and a people, find them as if waiting for me.' And he began, not just a new page, but a new book—his 'Worpswede Diary'. As they returned with the mail coach, Clara pointed out the family home at Oberneuland, where for the first time she had learned to find beauty in the country in all its seasons, in decay as well as in growth. They reached Worpswede on 'a beautiful, still, starry night, so good for a homecoming. It was at that moment I decided to stay. I feel already how the solitude grows with each day that passes, how this country, as the colours and shadows leave it, becomes ever bigger, ever broader, more and more a background for trees waving in the storm. I want to remain in that storm, and feel every tremor ... have autumn, then cover myself with winter ... be snowed in for the sake of a spring to come, so that the fruit germinating in me shall not rise too soon from the furrows.' His own art could find no soil more fertile than here, among artists. He felt once more how much he had missed in Russia, 'with my immature eyes, unable to receive or to retain and yet incapable of letting go, eyes laden with troubling images, passing beauties by': here he could learn from people whose 'effect on me is like that of landscape'. As he followed Vogeler's progress in an early sketchbook his friend showed him, the Worpswede time seemed to reveal the artist's true beginning: all the impressions of this countryside were absorbed into the clean, gentle lines of his enchanted princesses, swans on dark pools, strange beasts and dragons, and contemplative naiads, his great shining angels and their good tidings for the shepherds. And, coming straight from this to Paula, he was moved to hear her deep feeling for Clara's gift for concentration on a single thing, a flower: 'I am your pupil', he told her, 'and become your teacher too now when I tell you you are good and holy.'[15]

Wandering with his friends over the hill behind the Barkenhoff, on the last Sunday in September—'the heath very dark and dull, the thin grass soft like Japanese silk, the mown buckwheat field metallic red, dark and heavy the ploughland'—he fell behind in wonder at the contrast in the colours of the girls' dresses, Clara's slim, light 'reed-green figure' so 'ineffably pure and great', as they went ahead of him two by two, the men's dress merging into the grey light, following a winding path over the slopes like the background in devotional pictures. The evening at the Barkenhoff was one of the most beautiful, with a sense of community that seemed almost sacred. And the days that followed, as he visited the girls in their studios—Clara's was in Westerwede, a few miles away—brought him closer to both, listening to their experiences, and speaking to them of his idea of God still in the making and of the artist's task to continue His building, of Christ as the 'concealer of God'.

His diary of these 'days rich in gifts' overflows with exaltation at the prospect of life in such comradeship.[16]

Yet, suddenly, at the end of the week, at dawn on 5 October, he left in the mail coach to take the train for Berlin. A visit there, to discuss a possible production of one of his dramas, in November, seems in any event to have been planned—but he did not return to Worpswede. In a brief word leaving his notebook of poems behind for Paula, he gave her no indication that his departure would be more than temporary. What made him change his mind can only be guessed at, for two pages have been torn from the diary at this point. It maybe that his choice had fallen on Paula—the book of poems, after all, came to her and not to her friend; or simply that he needed distance to make up his mind between them, and to think out how marriage, in his still precarious situation, was possible at all. And once in Berlin, contact with Lou again will certainly not have been without its influence. Though she is hardly likely to have encouraged any thought that their old relationship could be revived, her earlier concern for his stability may have been renewed when he had spoken of burying himself in the wilds of Worspswede, interrupting the studies and continuing experience of Russia which she felt important for him. She certainly did not feel he was ready for marriage.

At all events, when he replied to letters from Paula and Clara two weeks later, Russia and things Russian were his explanation. 'You know what these studies I have started alongside my most personal work mean for me,' he told Paula: 'Russia for me has become like your Worpswede countryside for you— homeland and heaven', a far-off homeland which he must not lose by giving himself to another.[17] To Clara he said the inspiration of her work had brought the conviction that he must apply himself to his own: the whole winter through he would be diligent, and perhaps go to Russia again in the New Year. But to neither was he saying farewell; and he felt less lonely when he thought of their Sundays in the white music room, when 'Beethoven spoke'—

> To know that the evening sings for you
> rests round my shoulders like a damask robe,
> and my hands I feel as if they are beringed.[18]

After his temporary withdrawal from 'things Russian', he told Frieda von Bülow, it was good now to resume quiet, daily work as in the days of Meiningen, away from the 'too powerful' influence of the colours and the artists of Worpswede.[19]

Finding new quarters—still in Schmargendorf but, perhaps significantly, not as close as before to the Andreas home—he took his usual careful pains to set the stage for work: the 'Russian corner', with a convenient samovar; a Rubens reproduction; a Turkish carpet over a settee; ample desk room; a tiny kitchen where he could prepare his porridge. He wrote often to Paula and Clara, sometimes to both on the same day, and it is hard to distinguish any difference in his feelings towards them. Full of longing for their company, half in hope they will visit him in his new home, his letters to both show that extraordinary empathy with his correspondent characteristic of him, in delicate prose carefully constructed as a work of art and sometimes already drafted in his diary. To his 'dear Clara Westhoff' there is a more serious tone; to his 'dear friend' Paula more directness and warmth, as he sends her poems or Jacobsen's novels. True, on 5 November, thanking her for returning his poem notebook, he is prompted to depressing talk of his predilection for cemeteries at All Souls, while to Clara he writes almost as a Lochinvar, dreaming of abandoning his books and wandering off without hat or coat 'until the birch avenues begin and the little huts, and I turn off the road down the darkening path and can recognize dimly, under a broad and turbulent sky, the outlines of your house'.[20] But he is with them both, on their Sunday evenings, 'with you who are like sisters of my soul', 'the pillars of my solitude' with its memories of 'the hours against the white background'.[21]

A week later, Paula broke the news of her love for Modersohn and his for her: 'it goes back a long time, before Hamburg even. I did not tell you. I thought you knew. You always know, and that is so beautiful. And today I had to put it into words for its baptism, laying it reverently in your hands, for you to stand godfather.'[22] Whether or not he had known before, or guessed, his blessing came by return, in elegantly turned verses which greatly pleased Paula. His interest in the two sister spirits, both as persons and artists, continued in frequent letters; understandably, however, those to Clara became more cordial—and longer. For her birthday in November she received a copy of *A Festival for Me*, and more of his earlier productions followed, including the *Cornet*; he asked for photographs of her work, and wrote at length in appreciation; recalled in detail what she had told him of her earlier life; spoke of a Rodin he had seen in Berlin, and the pictures of 'a remarkable Frenchman called Cézanne'. 'We ought sometime to write an essay together on [Rodin]! Yes, go to Paris, later on—I feel that would be good.'[23]

But as the end of the year approached he was sometimes overcome with deep depression, in the feeling that his life was out of joint. He had come full circle, back to the point from which he had set out on the second Russian journey: yet the studies he had resumed and the plan of further visits to Russia no longer seemed to point him in the right direction. For, now, he lacked the powerful support he had found before in Lou. Outwardly, they had taken up the earlier relationship. She introduced him to Gerhart Hauptmann, and they were privileged to attend together the dress rehearsal for the dramatist's *Michael Kramer*, with its theme of the artist in society—an unforgettable experience for him. They still walked together, occasionally, in the Schmargendorf woods; he wrote poems for her in awkward, yet to her mind 'strangely poetic' Russian. But he was only too well aware that she was lost to him in the way he needed her, that in fact she wanted him, for his own good as she saw it,

to leave. His diary—which ended with the year, and was not continued—
became increasingly fragmentary; and aside from long appreciative passages
on Hauptmann, sank sometimes into despair and morbid reflection. The
poems of happy Worpswede memories gave place to a requiem on the early
death of a friend of Clara's—a macabre image of the ivy wreath Clara had
made pressing down and into the coffin, until 'its long tendrils creep up to the
white shroud and grow together with the folded hands and the soft hair never
touched with love . . .'[24] A brief visit from Vogeler early in December lifted his
spirits for a while; but for days afterwards he felt incapable of writing to the
friends in Worpswede. On 11 December he implored Clara, in a short letter—
'really just the germ of a letter, in the dark soil of my memory'—not to stop
writing to him, to tell him of her hopes, her progress.[25] These were days in
which he felt as though buried, 'days spent in damp and decay' in some kind of
intermediate realm, a limbo like that for the inmates of Bedlam: 'what good are
the efforts one makes, ever more sluggishly, ever more laboriously . . .
overcome with disgust? The will is there—but it is like steel striking on
stone. . . . God stands above life and above death. But He has no jurisdiction
over this land between, which exists in spite of His power and His presence,
and has no space, no time, no eternity.' It was an 'infinite humiliation' to
confide this to his diary, but it had to be written, 'as a sign for myself. God help
me'.[26]

If Lou saw passages like this in the diary, and read the 'Requiem', they
could but confirm her misgivings over his mental stability. Certain it is that,
after the turn of the year, she was more than ever convinced that he should
seek new surroundings, in the interests of both. She needed solitude for
herself, to get on with her own work; and saw clearly the danger for him if he
lingered in this frustration. 'To make Rainer go,' she wrote in her diary on 17
January, 'go right away, I would be capable of real brutality. (*He must go!*)'[27]
She was fully aware of the attractions in Worpswede. 'I know he *has* at all costs
to find support, and an exclusive devotion,' she confided to Frieda von Bülow,
'if not with me, then elsewhere: better for him to lean on even the most
unsuitable object than to have none. And so he will find what he needs very
soon.'[28]

For Rainer his uncertainty was not of course all gloom and despondency.
The *Tales of God*, in an elegant production by the Insel-Verlag, appeared in
time to be sent as a Christmas gift: to Clara, together with the *Prague Stories*
for her to find the atmosphere of his childhood; to Paula and Otto Modersohn,
hoping they would read it together; to his mother 'with a part of my deep piety
and a foretaste of my future';[29] to Hugo Salus, the Prague poet he greatly
respected, trusting he would find in it 'a few seeds from which trees may later
grow'.[30] For Vogeler's birthday in December he sent him a manuscript of
poems 'In and after Worpswede', including many inspired by works of the
artist. He still considered a further visit to Russia, and continued to write to

Russian friends—Shakhovskoy, Drozhzhin, Pavel Ettinger. Paula came in the New Year to Berlin, to prepare herself with a cookery course for the housewifely duties soon to be her lot. They saw each other almost every Sunday, at her relatives' house or at Schmargendorf, the 'fine mellowness' of her presence lingering in his room, and the diary of her earlier days which she left for him to read was a vivid reminder of Worpswede when he perceived 'in joyous thankfulness the certainty of your love for life'.[31] She brought him such cherished memories, he wrote to Modersohn, that he felt once more in gratitude his nearness to the old circle of friends.

It was Clara's arrival, early in February 1901, which precipitated a decision. Joining him and Paula, she made for him 'a piece of Worpswede' in the city:[32] and when she came to his rooms in Schmargendorf, on 11 February, he sought in her embrace, almost desperately, the consolation he had been denied by Lou. It seemed the beginning of a new life. When she left Berlin on 15 February, his letter following her was full of a quiet confidence, regardless of the practical difficulties which might lie ahead. 'Behind it all, I am calm . . . so serious today, and somehow comforted in all my former anxieties. . . . Give me strength for everything that has to be done now. . . . Beginner of my joys! First one! Eternal!'[33] As though to set the seal on a final parting from Lou, he moved the next day to the hotel in Berlin Clara had just left.

In their last talk, before he went from Schmargendorf, Lou was dismayed to learn that he had decided to marry Clara. She had wanted him, at all costs, to go, to find the support he needed even from 'the most unsuitable object'; but she had found so much that was abnormal and morbid in him that such a dramatic step seemed the last thing he should contemplate. They were parting, the sharing of all their thoughts would end, they would not even write: but she could still assure him of a lifeline of last resort, in words she was too moved to utter, scribbling them instead on a scrap of his paper: 'If one day much later you feel low in spirit, there is always a refuge for you with us for the worst hour.'[34] His own emotion at this leave-taking was expressed in three poems— which he did not show her: 'standing in darkness, as though made blind, because my glance no longer finds you', he likened her to Pygmalion dreaming of a figure to be formed and clinging to him 'only as the shaping hand clings to the clay'—

> but then it tired, relaxed its hold,
> and let me fall, and I was shattered.

To him 'most motherly of women', 'the gentlest being I met', she was yet

> the hardest thing with which I wrestled.
> You were the height that gave me blessing—
> to become the abyss which swallowed me.[35]

It hardly seemed the mood in which to start the new life. But to Clara the next day he was ready to write the most fervent hopes for it. 'My life till now was something uncertain, but now all is reality around me ... everything becomes straightforward ... and I want to stay with my feet on the ground, the earth on which our home will stand.'[36] He was already planning a visit to her parents and, as though to forestall their doubts about his prospects, was casting around once again for some kind of regular journalistic work. The fact remained that money was desperately short; and when Clara asked him to come to her in Westerwede first, rather than straight to Bremen to her parents, he was obliged to borrow fifty marks from his bookseller before he could travel. 'But I don't look back,' he wrote eagerly to her: 'I run to you as a foal runs to the cool night meadow, mane flowing and neck outstretched ...'[37] Paula received an indication before he left—'Life is earnest, but full of goodness. So much lies before me. You will soon hear all about it!'[38]—and his mother a cryptic note to the effect that 'unexpected circumstances' would have to rule out another visit to Russia.[39] He stayed in Westerwede for a week, and they began to make their plans. The word of their engagement was as much a surprise to the Worpswede circle as to the Westhoffs when he finally called on them. Exactly when his father was told, and what his reaction was, has not been revealed; Phia Rilke, staying as usual over the spring in Arco, he proposed to join for a few days early in March, and would then break the news to her in person.

For Lou meanwhile there had come almost as dramatic a turning-point. She had been to Vienna, and there seen Pineles ('Zemek') again. Whether she had been drawn more by the hope that, as a doctor, he might be able to relieve her concern over Rainer, than by the expectation of a new sexual relationship with a man whose advances she had so far resisted, it is impossible to say. What is in no doubt is that she returned having found relief in both senses: a sexual experience quite new for her, and at the same time a diagnosis of the 'Rilke case' which, if she could only express it to Rainer, might be a way to save him. On 26 February, about the time of his return from Westerwede to Berlin, she penned a long letter to him, rather solemnly superscribed 'Final Salute', in which new-found euphoria overlay and to some extent distorted her view of their relationship.

Now, when nothing but sunshine and quiet surrounds me and the fruit of life has rounded into sweet ripeness, comes a final duty to you from the memory, surely dear to us both, that I came to you in Wolfratshausen like a mother. Let me therefore—like a mother—express the obligation that I shouldered some years back after a long talk with Zemek. If you roam free, then you are responsible only for yourself; but if you should contract a new tie, then you must know the reason *why* I tried continually to show you a certain road to health—

and the reason was that Pineles had diagnosed a temperament that could lead to suicide. In Rainer, as she described him, he had seen a disquieting symptom familiar in cases ending in nervous breakdown or mental disorder: the appearance from time to time of a different personality, whom Lou and Rainer called 'the Other', the being who 'fluctuated between depression and excitement, between the depths of fear and the heights of exaltation'.

'*But this need not happen!*' she wrote. He had often been quite unaffected; yet time and again she had seen him slip back into a vacillating uncertainty. Increasingly rejecting him, she had always let herself be drawn back to his side, because of Pineles' warning. 'I felt you would be healed if you only stood fast! But then there came something else—something like a tragic guilt towards you: the circumstance that, in spite of the difference in our ages, I myself had still, after Wolfratshausen, to develop and grow—more and more, until . . . strange as it may sound: I grew *into my own youth!* for it is only now that I have become young, that I can be what others are at eighteen—my own person.' Without knowing it, she had 'obeyed the great plan of life' and received with humility the 'gift surpassing all understanding and expectation' it had held for her: and she cried now to him 'Follow the same way back to your dark God! who can do for you what I can no longer do . . . bless you with the sunshine of maturity. I send you this call from far, far away, I can do nothing more for you than this to protect you against the "worst hour" Pineles spoke of. That was why I was so moved when at our parting I wrote down the last words on a scrap of paper—I could not speak them out. *I meant them all.*'[40]

The effect of such a letter on his state of mind can only be a matter of speculation. The fact remains that he was undeterred from his purpose. He went to Arco as planned on 5 March, and while there sent for official entry in his baptismal record in Prague a notification that he had left the Catholic Church—a necessary preliminary before marriage with a Protestant, and one of which his mother would certainly have disapproved. Letters came to Clara with poems which, though they might lack the almost delirious exaltation of the earlier verses to Lou, nevertheless showed clearly how complete was his confidence in their future together. No longer mere clay in another's hands, he could be his own master now, with Clara his

> fair dark lute, granted to me
> that I may test my mastery:
> Life itself I'll play upon you![41]

He called on her parents immediately after returning from Arco in the middle of March, then rejoined her in Westerwede. The plans for the marriage then went ahead with some haste, the banns being posted in Worpswede on 6 April and the ceremony arranged for 28 April in Bremen. It seems probable that Clara was pregnant, and that the parental and social pressures alike were too great for Rilke to ignore. To this extent, for all his evident attraction to her, he had been trapped, as Lou indeed thought, into a decision which he would profoundly regret. Perhaps not surprisingly, he fell ill with a fever and

Johanna Westhoff took him into their home for nursing; but there was no question of postponement. When the day came, he was barely convalescent, and a simple ceremony in the Westhoff dining-room had to be substituted for that originally planned in the nearby church of St. Jürgen. No one from the Rilke family was present.

From any practical standpoint, as Rilke conceded later, it was a rash venture. He had virtually no reserve of money, his income from the Prague allowance, which his cousins and Josef were still continuing, was anything but lavish, and he was constrained to press for an outstanding honorarium from publication of his poems. The home they planned to rent in Westerwede, part of a simple farmer's cottage with an adjoining building to serve as Clara's studio, was modest it is true: but even this was possible only with their parents' help, especially as he insisted on having most of the furniture made locally to his own and Vogeler's designs. The 'new tie' he was soon able to rationalize as a necessity: 'my life, so remote from the everyday world, was exposed in a bachelor's room to every wind that blew; unprotected, it needed for its development the quiet of a house of my own, under the broad skies of solitude.'[42] After the turbulent years in pursuit of Lou, and her final rejection of him, it made sense, certainly, to seek such stability in the company of one whose mission in life was like his own and whom he felt he could help towards its fulfilment. But already he began to conceive of marriage as a union in which each partner was the self-appointed 'guardian of the other's solitude'. 'It is an impossibility for two people to be *really together*, and if they appear so, it is a limitation, a mutual agreement by which one or both are deprived of their freedom and their development,' he wrote only a few months afterwards.[43] Whether or not Clara had had a similar notion before their marriage, she very soon adopted it under his influence. 'Each felt in the other,' she wrote later, 'an existence which needed undisturbed solitude if it was to be made resolute for a long and serious life's work. The purpose of our life together was to create this quiet seclusion.'[44] It was to prove an unattainable ideal.

5

'For the moment, all kinds of petty and ugly cares bestraddle our road into the future'

(To Arthur Holitscher, 26.8.1901)

While waiting for the Westerwede house to be ready, the couple stayed at first with Clara's parents. He was still far from well, and his later recollection was of an almost Strindbergian atmosphere there—the father 'awful', the mother 'completely broken inside'.[1] It was a relief therefore when Johanna Westhoff suggested they should go off, in default of a honeymoon, to the sanatorium of the *Weisser Hirsch* on the outskirts of Dresden, run by a Doctor Lahmann. She herself had earlier been a patient of his, and was enthusiastic over his 'modern' methods of vegetarian diet and nature cure. Rainer spent most of May 1901 there with Clara, undergoing a thorough examination and a strict 'cure'. Apart from general debility, the aftermath of the fever, he was pronounced physically sound, and when they finally moved into their new home at the end of the month seems to have entered with zest into the chores of furnishing and ordering, even to tilling the tiny garden. The front of the cottage was ivy-covered, and there was a vine-clad arbour outside the kitchen door leading to the garden and Clara's studio. Their quarters were small but adequate: two rooms and a kitchen on the ground floor, shut off from the cow-stalls by a whitewashed wall on which hung a picture from the Rilkes of St. Cecilia, with a tall dresser to Rainer's own design displaying peasant pottery and a silver bowl and ewer, his father's gift to the bride. A narrow staircase led up to the attic rooms, a broad study for Rainer flanked on either side by small chambers to serve as spare bedrooms. 'We shall not be stirring much in the immediate future,' he wrote to Wilhelm von Scholz on 10 June, 'our house needs to be warmed by being lived in before we can travel, and there is much to be arranged, stowed and built.'[2] The making of the furniture was a slow process, and during that summer neither he nor Clara could find the time and solitude they needed for their work. At the end of June they were able to journey to Prague, to meet his father and friends such as Emil Orlik; and later both Josef and Phia—separately, it seems—visited them in Westerwede.

The planning of their installation was an absorbing and pleasurable task for Rilke. He set the scene for work with his usual meticulous attention to detail, once more establishing his 'Russian corner' in the upstairs study, and ordering writing-paper for which Vogeler designed him a *Jugendstil* vignette as letterhead, its fountain motif a favourite symbol. The petty cares of practical life were not few, as he wrote to Holitscher in August;[3] but the small, insistent fear that their income would eventually be inadequate to sustain them could for the moment be ignored. Sending a photograph of Clara at the end of July to the artist Oskar Zwintscher, with a copy of the *Tales of God* to introduce himself, he invited him to come and paint her portrait. They were 'very poor', and would hardly be able to afford any fee 'in the foreseeable future': but, coming from 'a family of the ancient Carinthian nobility' from which no portraits had come down to him, he felt it was his duty to preserve for children and grandchildren his wife's 'first beauty, before the second beauty of motherhood'.[4] (In the event, Zwintscher could not come until the following March, when he stayed at the Barkenhoff and painted an outstanding portrait of Vogeler. That of Clara, seated with hands folded, in semi-profile but looking directly at the artist, captured appealingly the 'second beauty of motherhood'. He painted Rilke too, head and shoulders, highlighting the forehead and the penetrating eyes against a dark background—a faithful and expressive portrayal of the poet as he was then, though in later years Rilke looked back on it as a failure.[5])

Their euphoria lasted well into the autumn, with Clara at work on a bust of her husband. The countryside was becoming more familiar to him now, Rainer wrote to his mother, in the harmony of its dark and simple colours and the immense height of the autumn skies; and it was impressive to stand outside the house and watch the raging of the great storms as they uprooted young oaks and scattered the apple crop.[6]

The future, he realized, was obscure, and he began once again to look for some kind of regular work which would give his life, as he said to Holitscher, 'a somewhat more secure basis'.[7] Not, as his father never ceased to urge, a clerkship in the 'dark counting-house existence' he had always rejected, but perhaps as art correspondent, or 'reader in residence' at the court of the Landgrave of Hesse. He still hoped that translations from Russian could offer a fruitful sideline, and in fact continued during the summer his work on Aleksandr Benois' art history. But he remained inflexible against any form of compromise in the mission he had set himself. He would write what he felt was in him to write, and if it could be published and bring in money, so much the better; but work to order made no appeal (already at the end of May he had refused a proposal from the Fischer Verlag that he should edit the poems of Walther von der Vogelweide, pleading the prior claim of his work on the 'big translation from the Russian').

With the autumn, always a productive time, he came once more into his own, with another novella and the series of poems which would form the second part of the *Book of Hours*, the *Book of Pilgrimage*, a distillation of what he had gained from the Russian experience, with a subtle change of emphasis in the light of the new life opening before him:

> I am the same who knelt
> Before Thee in the habit of the monk
>
> . . . .
>
> Am I not all, when I weep
> And Thou alone the listener?
>
> . . . .
>
> Are any voices there but mine?
> Is there a storm? I too am one,
> And my forests greet Thee.[8]

Discreetly woven in would come the poem he had written in Wolfratshausen for Lou—'Tear out my heart, I still can see you'—but the cycle was a premonition, still unconscious perhaps, of what his life would actually bring: not the stability of home and a family, but the hard road of the pilgrim.

The last house in this village stands
As lonely as the last in all the world.

The road the little village cannot hold
Goes slowly farther out into the night.

The hamlet is but transient, a point
Between two fast expanses, frightened in its bodings,
A way past houses only, no path up.

And those who leave it wander along,
And many die, it may be, on the road.

. . . .

Deep in the night, I dig thee out, like treasure,
For all the riches I have seen
Are but poverty, poor substitute
For Thy beauty which is still to come.
But the way to Thee is fearful long,
And, long untravelled, obscured to us . . .[9]

He was in touch now with two publishers: the Insel Verlag, whose edition of
the *Tales of God* had delighted him, and Axel Juncker in Berlin. Juncker, who
was turning increasingly from bookselling to publishing and whose list would
include moderns such as Elsa Lasker-Schüler and Max Dauthendey, had
become a friend while Rilke was in Berlin—friendly enough, indeed, to have
advanced him the fifty marks for the 'emergency' journey to Bremen in
February. He was the source to which he turned for the books and journals he
wanted (in this, as always, Rilke spared little expense if he thought he needed
them), especially in Scandinavian literature, where Juncker's Danish birth
made for a shared enthusiasm. Towards the end of September he agreed to
publish as a collection three of the stories which had appeared separately in
journals earlier in the year, under the title of the third, *The Last of their Line*
(*Die Letzten*). With gratifying speed, the volume appeared at the end of
November. It was dedicated to Prince Emil von Schönaich-Carolath, one of
the potential contributors to the stillborn final number of *Wegwarten* in
Munich five years earlier, who had made Rainer and Clara welcome for a short
stay on his estate in Holstein at the end of September. The book was well
received, and Rilke was the more disposed to consider Juncker, rather than
Insel, for a new volume of verse, *The Book of Images* (*Das Buch der Bilder*),
receiving from him words of encouragement and finding a readiness to listen to
his ideas on format and typography he had so far rarely encountered with
publishers.

On 12 December 1901, as the snow lay thick around the Westerwede cottage, their daughter was born. 'An unusually big and lusty child,' he reported
to Phia, 'firm in body, a strong head with a high, serious brow, deep blond or
actually darker hair and wonderfully formed hands.' They would call her by
'the beautiful biblical name of Ruth', without adding a second.[10] Her arrival

naturally brought disturbance and disorder: but to him this Christmas, alone with their child, seemed like his first—'Life has suddenly became quite new, richer by a new future!' he wrote to Franziska Reventlow.[11] Looking back, a few years later, on the weeks of care and devotion which followed, he felt again the peace which he thought he had found then: 'like a seedling destined to become a tree, I was taken then out of my pot, carefully, the soil dropping away and light getting into my roots, and planted into my proper station, where I was to remain to full maturity, into the great, real, whole earth itself.'[12] Thus transplanted, he felt nothing could stand in the way of an uninterrupted growth. In Clara's copy of *Die Letzten* he invoked the happiness their home would bring: taking it as their right, not as alms from fate, and asking no quarter from sorrow.[13] In a letter to Gerhart Hauptmann, sending *Die Letzten* and gratefully recalling the unforgettable performance of *Michael Kramer* he had seen with Lou the previous December, he looked forward to his and Clara's return soon each to their own work, and asked if he might dedicate to him the *Book of Images* to appear in the spring. Hauptmann's acceptance, on Christmas Eve, came 'like a gentle blessing': in his simple country surroundings Rainer felt he had at last made his own the secret of the life of the Russian peasants, their sorrows and joys 'linked in some way with God, that is, with the highest needs and unfolding of their existence . . . artists, they could be, led by some hidden impulse to a wise selection of realities and finding thus their own life, released from the confusions of the world.'[14]

But the world was soon to shatter this prospect and make his hopes illusory. On 6 January 1902 he was dismayed to hear that his cousins had decided to stop the regular allowance for which, not unreasonably, they considered Uncle Jaroslav's original purpose scarcely applied now that Rainer was married and no longer a student. The payment, which had been enough, with a small subvention from the Westhoffs, to ensure the bare essentials for their existence, was to cease in the summer; and his search for an income, hitherto somewhat dilatory, became at once desperately urgent. It even seemed to him, in the first access of gloom, that unless some sort of regular employment could be found, the home he had thought 'built on granite' would have to be abandoned. In a stream of letters he sent despairing appeals for help to every friend, editor, acquaintance, or even stranger he could think of, laying bare his circumstances and often (it must be said) exaggerating his difficulties. 'I fear the day after tomorrow like an enemy . . . The future rises around me like a high tide and threatens to drown us . . . A wind is blowing here that is insupportable for me.'[15] Yet still he would not give up the great aim he had set himself, so hard to explain to others, even his father: he could not leave the road he had travelled since his youth and 'abandon the building blocks of a life which bear the traces of my chisel . . . for indifferent work with factory-made bricks on some house or other for the daily pay of an ordinary labourer.'[16] His ideas therefore centred on a position as correspondent, reviewer, or art critic for a journal (in Vienna, say, or Hamburg or Darmstadt); a post with the art-museum in Hamburg, or that in Bremen, or the chance of a series of public lectures on modern verse or Maeterlinck's drama; Russian translation work. He even seriously considered moving to Russia, if a journalistic appointment could be found there, declaring to Pavel Ettinger that he felt 'little related to Germany', where he could see no way to earn a living.[17] His frank avowal of his difficulties and modest needs brought plenty of sympathetic replies, but few concrete suggestions.

His hopes naturally concentrated on Bremen or Hamburg. If they could somehow contrive to stay on in that area, it would be easier for Clara to find commissions for her own work, and give lessons, perhaps even start a school. In Gustav Pauli, the director of the Bremen Kunsthalle, with whom he had been planning the staging of Maeterlinck's *Sister Beatrix* for the formal opening of the museum's new building in February, he found a sympathetic ear: and Pauli, alone of all those he had appealed to, was able to offer at least a temporary alleviation. Admittedly, it was work to order: a commission to write a monograph on the Worpswede artists, as one of the series being published by the firm of Velhagen & Klasing. Pauli had originally undertaken the work himself but had met with opposition from the artists. His intervention with the publishers now secured it for Rilke, who with his Worpswede associations would clearly have a better chance of success.

The idea attracted him, and he felt he must accept it, although he was hesitant, not only from repugnance at what he regarded as hack work, but also from the difficulty of form: the Worpsweders had long since grown apart and were no longer treatable as the group of kindred spirits of their first exhibition seven years earlier. He saw it as a series of five separate monographs (or six, if he could overcome Carl Vinnen's continued refusal to be discussed at all), tracing the individual development of each artist that he had been able to follow himself at close quarters, and linking them through the Worpswede countryside and atmosphere, which he proposed to set as the scene in an introduction. There would be no final judgements, for they were still developing: and he chose as his motto Jacobsen's words in *Nils Lyhne*: 'where would the best of us be, if justly judged? No, think of him as he was in the hour when your love for him was deepest.'[18] Vogeler's work of course he knew best, and was in fact just now engaged on a long essay on his friend for a Darmstadt journal; that of Modersohn, Mackensen, and Overbeck had, as he told Pauli, 'opened many interesting perspectives' for him; and he was well placed to learn more of Hans am Ende's and Vinnen's.[19] By the end of January all except Vinnen had agreed, and he had drafted his introduction. He applied himself with diligence to the task—'half enjoyment, but half drudgery[20]—and completed the manuscript by the end of May. That his subjects, with the exception of Vogeler, were no more than mediocre talents was not his fault, and he can hardly be blamed (though he has been) for taking no account of Paula

Modersohn-Becker, one day to be considered as the only artist of lasting worth to come out of Worpswede.

The honorarium would undoubtedly be of great help, and he had meanwhile, in response to a direct appeal, also received a substantial grant from the Prague 'Concordia' society. Over the first months of 1902, indeed, he was not lacking in other opportunities of earning. Papers in Bremen, Hamburg, and Berlin offered him reviewing, in which he showed himself a perceptive critic, notably in recognizing the talent in Thomas Mann's first novel *Buddenbrooks* and the significance of Ellen Key's *Century of the Child*. In February a well-attended lecture on Maeterlinck and the performance of *Sister Beatrix*, which he directed himself and for which he wrote a *Festspiel* pendant, took much time and brought in no return save the polite esteem of a select audience and a reprint of the lecture. But Juncker's enthusiastic acceptance of the *Book of Images* had been encouraging, and the publisher, although he could not meet his plea for regular work as reader, did at least hold out the prospect of fees for recommendations for his list. He also agreed to publish a volume of essays by the young Munich critic Wilhelm Michel in which that on Rilke figured prominently. Looked at dispassionately, in fact, Rilke's literary activity showed a reasonable prospect of being able to support him and his family after the allowance from Prague came to an end in the summer, even without a regular appointment, such as that of *feuilleton* editor on the Bremen Tageblatt, which was another of Pauli's suggestions. He certainly seems to have made little effort to economize on what most people in his circumstances would have regarded as luxuries. The portrait project with Zwintscher, for example, went ahead in March—even though there was to be no fee, it was presumably not without its costs to Rilke—and the threat of penury pictured in his earlier despairing letters did not rule out employing a servant-girl.

The fact was that the way he sought was not to be found in a life of domestic bliss and writing for a living as little more than a journalist. He had hoped for the patronage of a publisher who would have enough confidence in him to finance 'a year of quiet work', 'offering me the possibility of the progress I am sure I could make now'.[21] But even had such a philanthropist appeared, with the resources to spare and ready to stake them on a highly problematical return, it is clear that Rilke could never have found himself if he had remained tied to Clara in a 'normal' relationship. It was all very well to think of their marriage as the guardianship of each other's solitude. But in his first desperate appeals for help, when the financial blow fell in January, he had already foreseen the need for them to dissolve their household and separate, for each to find their own solitude if her mission and his own were ever to be fulfilled. Having thought that together they must drown as the waters rose around them, he now found that separately they could strike out for the shore—a conclusion which must have irked those friends like Pauli who were busying themselves in the search for lifebelts. His, he knew, was a solitary art. His 'literary' endeavours were belied by a deep feeling that he stood apart from any group or movement: 'I am my own circle, and a movement inward'.[22] The break-up of the home, therefore, which his correspondents had probably dismissed as a grossly exaggerated fear, was in fact the unconscious expression of a desire, his instinctive recognition that this, to ordinary people an unthinkable step, was for him the right solution. Marriage, which had seemed 'a necessity', had very quickly laid bare a problem that would remain with him throughout his life, in all his relationships with women and with the outside world: the irreconcilable conflict between the 'the great work' and a normal existence.

Though we do not know how Clara really felt about this, she had become so imbued with his ideas that she made no demur ('Is that what love demands,' Paula had written to the friend who seemed now to be lost to her, 'that you should become the same as your lover?'[23]); and already in April, while he was still at work on the Worpswede monograph, they had reached their decision. He would accept another invitation from the Schönaich-Carolaths to stay at their Haseldorf estate during June, putting the finishing touches to *Worpswede* and correcting the proofs for the *Book of Images*, while Clara with the baby visited friends in Amsterdam; the rest of the summer would be spent in winding up their affairs in Westerwede, and in the autumn they would move to separate 'working lives' in—Paris, perhaps leaving Ruth with her Westhoff grandparents.

They wanted, he told Pauli in a letter from Haseldorf, to resume their former 'bachelor' existence, if possible in the same place and in such a way 'that each could live his life according to his own work and its needs . . . That will make things much simpler, and advance us both, whereas this exhausting and anxious life together is a dangerous and hopeless standstill. I believe with all my heart that Clara Westhoff can reach the greatest heights as an artist, and it was in this conviction that I joined her, not to disturb her and turn her into a "housewife", but on the contrary to help her follow, quietly and securely, the road she had taken alone with such courage.'[24] It was a sincere enough aim, no doubt; but one cannot escape the feeling that it took second place to the overriding egoism of his own desire for the lone road. For, in the same letter, he confessed he did not know what 'Clara Westhoff's plans for this winter' were. To Pauli, moreover, who had been more than helpful to Clara, buying her bust of Vogeler for his museum and offering her premises there for a school, it was important to stress concern for her future and, while explaining why the school plan was not the right answer, to seek his further aid in obtaining her some form of bursary.

Paris, at any rate, was where *he* would go, however things might turn out for Clara. At first his ideas of what he might do there were as vague as his prospects of subsistence. 'I hope for a lot of help for my Russian work and for everything else,' he had written to Holitscher in May. 'Here I often lack the necessary aids, libraries, etc. . . . . There I shall find all I need in abundance, and solitude into the bargain.'[25] But while he was at Haseldorf a more concrete project emerged. The Breslau professor Richard Muther, who had been his guest at Westerwede after lecturing in Bremen the previous autumn, was editing a series of monographs on the arts, among which was to be one on Rodin. The chance of being near the French master had been an important factor in their decision for Paris, and Clara had already written to Rodin with photographs of her work, to seek his advice on her future. Now in June came a formal commission from Muther for Rilke to undertake the study. Though not likely to bring him immediate financial relief, it was the foundation he needed on which to build the still uncertain future. He wrote at once to Rodin, stressing the great honour of the task, its fulfilment of 'one of my most ardent desires', asking the 'honoured master' for advice on reading and where to obtain reproductions of his work, and announcing his intention of coming to Paris in the autumn to see him and steep himself in the works, especially the drawings. He did not omit to mention Clara's hopes for advice too: and was overjoyed to receive very promptly a benevolent reply, encouraging them both to come.[26]

The *Book of Images*, for which he had corresponded in great detail with Juncker over the choice of paper, binding, and typeface, appeared in July 1902. It could have been earlier, had it not been for his insistence on upper case throughout, which made great difficulties for the printer: no single word was without its significance and its ceremonial, he told the publisher, even the smallest must stand 'like a monument'.[27] He insisted too on the utmost simplicity in presentation, the only ornament to be Vogeler's vignette with the fountain motif. He was against Juncker's suggestion of prior subscription, which he felt would be lacking in taste for a book dedicated to Hauptmann; but he agreed the edition should be limited to 500, without aiming for a wider public. The selection was made with great care from poems written over the previous three years, in Meiningen, Schmargendorf, and Worpswede: 'things Russian' (a cycle on the Tsars), his songs to the maidens, the macabre requiem for Clara's friend, a poem for Paula. The overriding impression, despite the variety of images, is one of melancholy, rather than the joy of *A Festival for Me*—the melancholy of childhood, of the 'last of a line', the intense depression which had beset him at the end of the year just past—and as coda come the oft-quoted lines on Death:

> Death is great.
> We are his
> With laughing lips.
> When we think to be in the midst of life,
> He dares to shed his tears
> Deep in our hearts.[28]

It was effectively a farewell to a part of his life now to be closed—though he did not see it that way, and indeed would complement the volume, for which he always held great affection, with further verses written in Paris and Sweden, for a later edition.

The rest of the summer passed quickly, his mood transformed by the eager expectation of what awaited him in Paris, the chance of learning from a great artist and he was 'entirely taken up with Rodin, who grows and grows on me the more I hear of his work'.[29] Though he did all he could to help Clara to secure the bursary she needed, their efforts failed, and the feasibility of her coming to Paris was problematical; but his own purpose remained firm. Rodin was to be away from Paris in October, and he was determined, come what might, to see him before he left. More reviews and articles helped to provide a minimum of capital. 'I know that my pen will be strong enough to carry me: but I must not misuse it in these early days, and must give it time to develop.'[30] It was an extraordinary confidence, to be justified only after much faltering. He set off, alone, for Paris on 26 August 1902.

III

Paris, Rome, and Sweden
1902–1905

'"Il faut travailler toujours" ... can I ever do it?'

(To Clara Rilke, 18.9.1902)

I

'Paris is a heavy, heavy city, a city of anxiety ... to it all
Rodin stands as a great, peaceful, powerful contradiction'

(To Otto Modersohn, 1.1.1902)

'Je suis une seule attente: que deviendra?' Writing at once to Clara on his arrival, he said he had found a modest room with friendly and obliging folk—'three, or four, flights up, I don't dare to count'—in a small hotel in the rue Toullier, near the Sorbonne, where he could spend his evenings reading and writing notes. 'Thinking, rest, solitude, everything I longed for.'[1] He sought out the places he had long wanted to see: the Louvre, Notre Dame, the Luxembourg Museum, all for the first time, yet with a feeling of familiarity. But the overwhelming impression of this 'strange, strange city' was one of sickness and death—the place seemed to be full of hospitals. 'I see now why they figure so often in Verlaine, Baudelaire, and Mallarmé ... You suddenly feel that in this vast city there are armies of the sick, hosts of the dying, whole populations of the dead.'[2] Paris was supposed to have more vitality than any other city: but vitality did not necessarily mean life itself, it was no more than an aimless rush. Rodin, he felt, would be the key, the centre round which all would revolve, and the thought of seeing him in the next few days overcame his unease.

It was a place, he felt immediately, where he and Clara could *work*. To her hesitation over following him he was firm and optimistic. 'You must come ... all you need is a quiet studio, nothing more, with next to it somewhere, not too comfortable, to sleep. ... We must stop being weak and soft, and start our life over again.' Trying to set up home with all the fuss of a conventional installation had simply tired them out and left them sitting in the fine rooms with their sense of purpose quite lost. 'Let us now make no preparations, but just start work.' They should have no regrets for their year together, it had been an essential part of life 'and we saw the highest beauties life has to offer'; but their lofty aim remained, 'to give everything to art and nothing to life, which always made us sad and dispirited'. And art could be created out of everything, even the anxieties she felt over Paris.[3]

Rodin received him first in his studio in the rue de l'Université, interrupting his work to talk with such frank goodwill that to Rilke, despite his own still halting French, he seemed to be renewing a friendship already of long standing. He liked him at once: the impressive features, themselves like a sculpture, the youthful impression of his words, the laugh 'like that of a child with a present, half embarrassed, half delighted', and not least the hands, with gestures as though he were ever shaping and forming. The works here, even the smallest, seemed to 'extend the studio into the infinite'. How much stronger then was his impression of greatness when he came to the Meudon villa the following day. Rodin's pavilion which Clara had seen at the Great Exhibition stood now in the garden, almost completely filling it, 'all the dazzling white figures looking out through high glass doors like the denizens of an aquarium'. Marbles, plaster casts, cases with splendid fragments of the 'Gate of Hell', a veritable army of works; row upon row of studies, arms, legs, torsos, scarcely one finished, yet 'each of so supremely gripping a unity that you forget they are only parts of bodies. ... These riches, this infinite, continuous creation ... this purity and vehemence of expression, this inexhaustibility, this youth ... unparalleled in the history of man.'[4] Rodin joined him from time to time as he wandered round, but Rilke found the language barrier still too hard to overcome. The al fresco lunch which followed was a strange affair. He was not introduced to Madame Rodin, who seemed tired and *distraite*, nor to other guests who appeared; and there was an evident tension between his hosts which reminded him of the scenes at Tolstoy's, though he had as little inkling, here as there, of the circumstances which lay behind it. Madame was civil enough after lunch, however, and said he would be welcome to meals whenever he came to Meudon. This he was resolved to do, for so much had to be seen, exhausting though he had found the profusion of the white figures and the virtual snow-blindness they had induced.

So through the September days he made many more visits there, roaming through the collection, making notes from the documentation Rodin had amassed and preparing his monograph. The master often spent an hour or two with him, and it was these talks which left the most profound impression. For Rodin's obsession with his art, his unflagging observation and accumulation of tiny details from which the great work sprang, confirmed what Rilke had instinctively recognized must be his own aim. 'When people learned to despise those who do the real work, the whole concept of work was lost,' Rodin told him. 'Artists especially are no longer workers in the proper sense: in the whole of Paris there are perhaps five or six who truly work, the rest are just amusing themselves. ... And none has any patience. But that is everything: patience and work. To this I devoted my youth, and to this I devote every one of my days.'[5] And it could be achieved only in solitude—though he conceded that a wife might be a necessity. The unedifying spectacle of Tolstoy's family life, and the obvious discomfort Rodin suffered at Meudon, confirmed Rilke in the conclusion he had already reached for himself: you could not have both family happiness and art, it must be one or the other—and if art is your choice, then find your happiness there.

All this he put to Clara, in long, almost daily letters, describing how he spent his time and seeking to strengthen her resolve to follow the same path. The beauty around us, he told her, is one of atmosphere only, not of strength: it is a rival to the beauty we must create in our art, the 'beauty that awaits our hands with the longing of the water in the well for the bucket which will bring it up to the sun, and turn it from an inert element into a bright mirror of the heavens, of the light and the air.'[6] It was not of course so easy for her to make such a break, not only for lack of funds, but also because of the problem of their baby, whom she was loth to entrust to the grandparents. She had intended to appeal for advice and help to Ellen Key, in the hope that the author of *The Century of the Child* might know of someone imbued with her progressive ideas who was planning to come to Paris and could take charge of Ruth there. Rainer himself had his doubts whether it would be wise to expose the child to the insalubrious atmosphere of Paris, where to him the children in their prams seemed part of the armies of sick and dying he saw everywhere; but he nevertheless took up Clara's idea in a letter of his own, his first to the Swedish educationalist, explaining their plight and enclosing a copy of his review of her book.[7] Her sympathy was aroused, for she felt strongly that a baby should not be separated from its parents; but they could not afford the Swedish girl who proposed herself at her instigation. He also wrote again to Pauli, pressing for a decision on the bursary for Clara from the Bremen Senate and for the balance she was due for the Vogeler bust. Regardless of the difficulties, Clara meanwhile went ahead with the task of selling up the Westerwede home, over which she was glad of Vogeler's help, especially for his ready agreement to store for them the more precious items not destined to go under the hammer. And finally, with some limited 'private support' (from Pauli and a group of art-lovers in Bremen, and from her father, who, whatever he may have thought about Rainer's apparent fecklessness, never failed to help her, and now agreed to look after Ruth), she was able to reach Paris in the early days of October. By then, Rainer had found suitable quarters, with a studio for her, in the rue de l'Abbé de l'Epée, between the Boulevard St. Michel and the rue St. Jacques—separate quarters, as they had agreed, where they planned 'to work as we have never worked before', scarcely even seeing each other except at weekends.[8] On 10 October they visited Meudon together, in Rodin's absence.

What the Master made of his remarkable disciple is far from clear. He had no German, so could not gain any idea of Rilke's capabilities from the copy of the *Book of Images* with which he was presented; and Rilke's stumbling French could scarcely have helped understanding. Now sixty-two, he was over twice the other's age, and as always was entirely ruthless in seeing to it that his own work was not disturbed. Nevertheless, he seems to have been indulgent and well disposed, making available the material Rilke needed and giving him an introduction to Eugène Carrière. But he will have been surprised to find that his straightforward approach to his art—'il faut travailler toujours, rien que travailler'—which to him was probably no more than a glimpse of the obvious, had had such a profound effect on the other. Despairing of expressing himself adequately in the spoken word, Rilke had written him a long letter on 11 September, in 'gratitude and joy' at this revelation of the secret of life for the artist: 'travailler, c'est vivre sans mourir'. Till that moment, the work he loved had been a rare festival only, awaiting the inspiration of the creative hour: now he realized that steady application could summon up inspiration, indeed was the only way to preserve it. 'You have given me rebirth of my life and hopes.' And he would try to stay on in Paris, with nothing but that aim in view, both for himself and for his wife, for whom it would equally be the watchword.[9]

But could he ever do it? he had written to Clara: could he find the way to work like that? The sculptor could continue steadily, patiently shaping the clay or the marble until it reached the image he had conceived: how could the poet apply himself in the same way? The diligence required for a task to order was one thing, and he had spent long hours in the Louvre and the Bibliothèque Nationale by way of preparation for the prose of the Rodin monograph. But to *work* at verse? To compel, to harness inspiration? And especially in surroundings which, contrary to his expectations, he found harsh and inhospitable. The Paris where he had dreamed of 'working as he had never worked before' remained 'infinitely strange and hostile', a lost city 'rushing like a star out of orbit towards some fearful collision'.[10] Not to speak of the ever-present and pressing need to augment his funds. That, over a path strewn with such difficulties, he could still keep before him the ideal Rodin had shown—the aim as a poet to convert experience into an objectively represented 'thing' which could stand as a work of art, independent in space like a sculpture—reflected once more the almost monomaniac dedication which had characterized him from his earliest days. Most of the verses written that autumn were 'mood-images' still: the contrast of the city streets, an abyss 'deeper than the bottom of the sea', with the distant moorland he had left; the leaves falling as though from 'far-off fading gardens in the heavens'; the end of the summer when 'he with no house will never build one now, / And if he is alone will long remain so'.[11] And these he would keep where they belonged, for a later enlarged edition of the *Book of Images*. But in November came the first-fruit of his new ambition, the first of the finely-chiselled works which he would rightly call *New Poems*: the panther pacing his cage in the Jardin des Plantes, the bars gliding past his weary eye till he feels there are a thousand of them and, beyond them, nothing.

Soft padding steps of supple strength,
turning and turning in so small a space,
are like a dance of power round a centre
where a strong will lies benumbed.

But now and then the curtain of the eyelid
lifts soundlessly—. An image enters then,
runs through the quiet tension of the limbs,
reaches the heart—and ceases to exist.[12]

The marvellous rendering of observation is justly regarded as one of the finest of the *Dinggedichte* ('thing-poems') which sprang from the conception of the poet as 'hand-worker' he had taken from Rodin.

In his study of the Master, which he finished early in December and which was published, dedicated to Clara, the following spring, he saw him as once more fulfilling the age-old longing of the human soul for the art 'which gives more than word and picture, more than simile or appearance: the simple presentation of its longings or fears as things',[13] as in the sculpture of the ancient world, the Middle Ages and the Renaissance. He showed Rodin's progress from commissioned decoration of buildings, the Bourse in Brussels or a memorial in the park at Loos, like the work of his predecessors on the great Gothic cathedrals, to the realization of things which could stand alone, complete, visible in their three dimensions; his abandonment of the traditional ideas of sculpture (posed beauty, grouping, 'composition') for the single aim of reproducing the surface relief, 'le modelé', of his subjects in its infinitely variable forms, which Rilke felt had become the very stuff of his art. The patience, the unremitting application of a life which was 'passing like a single working day'[14]—the ideal which Rilke sought for himself—form the essential theme of a study which also shows his acute receptiveness for the visual arts. But it remains a poet's idealization, lacking a truly profound appreciation of the struggle Rodin had been through and of the controversies his work had aroused.

His finances continued to be a nagging problem. The monograph would bring him a derisory fee of 150 marks—even with his vegetarian and wine-free diet, sufficient only for about a month's food. He kept on with his reviewing, for Bremen and Berlin papers, and *Die Zeit* in Vienna carried in November another essay on trends in modern Russian art. Towards the end of the year Juncker offered him the job of revising a translation from the Danish, and other similar commissions, including work as reader, followed from the publisher in the New Year. Protesting strongly in January 1903 over the unauthorized inclusion of ten of his poems, some with arbitrarily chosen titles, in an anthology published in Stuttgart, he did not omit to demand the minimum honorarium due of 50 pfennig a line.[15] With such small aids, he could keep his head above water, just; and although a long stay in Paris seemed out of the question and the future was still uncertain, he planned to remain, he told Juncker, at least until the spring. If he and Clara did not visit Oberneuland to spend Christmas with Ruth, as might have been expected, this was probably due as much to his aversion to a resumption of family life (especially with his parents-in-law) as to shortage of money: for they managed to spend a few days together in Brittany during January. And, as always, he did not spare expense when moved to a generous gesture with his work. Juncker was bidden to send a copy of the *Book of Images* to the Swedish girl whom Ellen Key had recommended for them and who was now off to America ('I would like my verses to go with her'[16]), as well as to Ellen Key herself, with *Die Letzten*, after she had written him enthusiastically over the *Tales of God*. Here however he may have had more of an eye to business, for the interest she was taking in his work held perhaps a promise of more material assistance.

For all his determination to work like Rodin, he was unable to force himself to write. 'The very feeling that there is a connection between my writing and the needs of the day is enough to make work impossible for me. I have to wait quietly for the call, and I know if I press for it, it will never come.'[17] Clara at least had the tools he lacked, and was working steadily, with even an occasional commission; but her pleasure too was clouded by his depression, which was accentuated by severe influenza during February and made Paris increasingly unbearable for him. Paula Modersohn, in näive delight at the chance of revisiting the city, could not understand their 'joylessness' in such surroundings. A year earlier, she had not concealed from them her disappointment at the way Rainer had imposed his personality on Clara, who she felt had laid down her old self 'like a cloak for her king to walk over'. The resulting estrangement had been painful for them all, and they were glad when, after a long letter of justification from Rainer had prepared the way, she arrived in Paris and their friendship could be restored. But she saw clearly the oppressive anxieties the city induced in them both. They seemed fated never to be happy, she wrote to her husband.[18]

> Still waiting to be done
> Is what life demands of me

ran a verse which Rainer wrote now; and again

> Would I could lift up my voice
> out of the world in which it fades confused:
> my life cleaves still to things long lost,
> my time I know is running out.
>
> Rising up from dire uncertainty
> I feel my final judge draw near:
> alas, my hand is torn from off me
> for that it lived with nothing done.[19]

Yet he held fast still, through this depression, to his ideal. In a long and careful letter to Franz Kappus, a young cadet at the Wiener Neustadt Academy who had sought his advice on his poems, he insisted on the vocation, the solitary dedication essential to the true poet: 'go into yourself, look into the depths from which your life springs—there you will find the answer to the question whether you *have* to create. Take the answer as it comes, without trying to explain it. It may be that you are called to be an artist. Then accept upon yourself this lot, and bear it, in its burden and greatness, without ever asking what reward may come from outside. For he who creates must be a world for himself, and find everything within himself . . .'[20]

With the Rodin study finished, he felt he had to escape the pressures of Paris, at least for a while, and restore his health in some warmer southern climate. He thought of Spain, and even wrote to the artist Ignacio Zuloaga, whose works he had admired in Bremen and Paris, for advice: but settled instead for the cheaper and more familiar Italy. Leaving Clara still at work on a commission, he went first to Genoa, then to Santa Margherita, in a vain attempt to escape the flood of German tourists, and finally reached Viareggio which had offered him such peaceful solitude five years earlier. His misgivings over whether it might have changed were quickly dispelled in the sunshine of a Sunday morning: the same girls walked arm-in-arm, the fishermen sang in front of the *osteria*, the ocean murmured the same conforting background to words and silences. His former Hotel de Florence, true, had moved, but Signora Malfatti, recognizing him, made him welcome in the new one, closer to the sea. Although at first still plagued by obtrusive conversationalists, this time English, he was able to escape to a beach hut he hired at the end of the line and enjoy at last the undisturbed peace he had come for, stretching his bare feet on the smooth clear sand and even bathing nude if no one came by.

Escape from the oppressive atmosphere of the city was enough immediately to restore him. The stay of a couple of weeks he had originally planned drew out to well over four, despite more changeable and occasionally stormy weather, and he had no compunction at asking his father for funds to tide him over. His frequent letters to Clara showed a lighter heart, and sometimes a humour which had been long absent. Though he could not yet see what his next work would be—a study on Carrière, perhaps, or after a visit to Spain one on Zuloaga—he felt that it was still in the solitude of Paris, with all its drawbacks, that he would find it: a solitude in the middle of the city as complete as he had found here, but first to be made 'firm and secure again like an untrodden wood which fears no footfall'.[21]

Before leaving for the south he had returned to Juncker some of the manuscripts the publisher had asked him to look over. In the first few days in Viareggio he conscientiously completed this task, and once duty was discharged, found once more the inspiration for his own work. In the space of a week during April he set down more 'prayers', the *Book of Poverty and Death*, to form the third cycle of the *Book of Hours*. In the feeling of being buried deep under the crushing weight of mountains (an image prompted by his claustrophobia in the train tunnels to Genoa) he cries

> am I in the basalt
> Like a still undiscovered ore?
> In reverence I feel Thy folds of rock,
> Thy hardness everywhere.
>
> Or is this the anxious fear assailing me?
> The deep terror of the sprawling cities
> Wherein Thou plunged me to the neck?

The prayers are for redemption from the cities, where all is false and where man's unnatural life brings him an unnatural death:

> O Lord, grant each his own, his death indeed,
> the dying which out of that same life evolves
> in which he once had meaning, love, and need.
>
> For we are but the leaf and just the skin.
> But that great death which each one has within,
> that is the fruit around which all revolves.

And they continue as a hymn in praise of poverty, 'a great inward splendour', lauding 'the poor man's house like an altar-shrine' and Francis of Assisi, 'great evening-star of poverty'.[22]

Like the first 'prayers', these themes show for many readers an affinity with Christianity—indeed, in the glorification of poverty, Rilke comes as close as he would ever reach to the orthodox faith he had long since denied—and when the *Book of Hours* was eventually published entire, in 1905, the three parts of the cycle seemed to form an organic whole. Yet, despite the evocative power of the verse, the essential ambiguity of the message remains. As he wrote to Ellen Key in 1904, when she asked for his views on immortality, he was not prepared to commit himself: 'for there is in every such definite statement something conclusive, and I do not feel myself at all as final and definite, on the contrary, I am sheer transformation. I would like one day to find my own personal expression for all these things.'[23] A great part of his later work was to consist of variations on the attempt. It may well be, as Lou thought, that the concept of 'one's own death', taken from Jacobsen (whose novels, as always, were with him in Viareggio), represented 'a reaction to the fear of death', and was 'a faded hope of immortality'. But he never gave up the search for the meaning of life and death, believing always in their essential unity as two sides of the same coin, even though in the end—again in Lou's words—he may have died 'without hope'.[24]

As the books of the *Monastic Life* and *Pilgrimage* had come, in a rush, under the stimulus of the Russian and Worpswede/Westerwede experiences, so now that of *Poverty and Death* in the bitter taste of Paris and the horror of its poverty and 'armies of the dying'. In that sense it was recidivistic: far from creating the 'thing of art' in the example of Rodin, life observed and reproduced in words, here he was still the instrument of an inspiration born of his inner impressions and flowing out in a style whose fatal facility, as he said later, could have let him continue like this indefinitely. But the ideal remained before him; and although he would return to Paris, less terrifying for him now, he was already thinking of Italy again for the autumn and winter, perhaps even Rome. To his reading of Jacobsen and the Bible he now added Pater's *Imaginary Portraits* and a work on Leonardo: and, as he had written to Rodin on the appearance of his monograph, the Master's work had never ceased to occupy him—the book had been 'the little door through which it entered my life, from that moment on to be in every work, every book it may be vouchsafed to me to finish'.[25]

Ellen Key's letters had followed him to Viareggio. Since his first appeal to her she had taken a lively interest in his life and his work, and he had turned more and more frequently, like a son as he said, to one whose influence he felt could somehow bring him aid. She had asked for copies of his books and all the details of his background and aspirations; and early in April he was able to send the *Rodin*, with an extra copy for her to forward to Georg Brandes in Copenhagen. With them went an immensely long letter, much in the tradition of that to Vally nearly a decade earlier, and to Ganghofer: the same story of a gloomy childhood and the five years in the penitentiary of the military college, and his determination to pursue the path he had chosen despite the hand-to-mouth existence it seemed to have condemned him to. What concrete help he could hope for from Ellen Key was not clear: but the self-analysis in his letter undoubtedly aided the therapy of the break from the city, and as he returned through Avignon and Dijon at the end of the month he had the feeling of a new-found peace.

But Paris would not be overcome so readily. Within a few days the oppressive sensation had returned of being back in a 'vast screaming prison'. Even the spring had seemed to turn almost at once to an 'unnatural, ugly autumn'.[26] The 1903 Salon for him was saved from mediocrity only by Zuloaga's works, and the Spanish painter's presence in Paris was the only brightness in his gloom. In June he and Clara resolved, as soon as her current commission could be completed, to move back to Germany, but could not decide where—family relationships, as he wrote to Gerhart Hauptmann, were not encouraging for a return to Oberneuland and Ruth, and they thought the Weisser Hirsch sanatorium at Dresden might once again be a salutary change. A stipend for her from the Bremen Senate was again in the offing, with which a period in Rome might be possible in the autumn, and he importuned Rodin for a visit to her studio and a supporting testimonial. Towards the end of June they settled on Worpswede, where Vogeler with his usual good humour was prepared to put them up, as a temporary refuge for the summer.

How deep the Paris neurosis went may be measured from the fact that he was impelled, after over two years' silence, to write again to Lou, recalling the promise in her 'last salute' and clearly feeling himself close to the crisis Pineles had foreseen. 'For weeks I have wanted to write these words, and dared not, for fear it could be much too early: but who knows if I can come in the worst hour?' When they returned to Germany, could he come to see them? But if not, could she tell him Pineles' address? She replied, briefly but comfortingly: he would be welcome any time, in bad hours as in good, but she suggested their meeting should first be by correspondence. 'For two old scribblers like us there is nothing artificial about that, and whatever you want to tell me will come straight to me, as it once did to—Lou.' On 30 June, the eve of departure from Paris, he poured out his deep trouble to her—the only person he felt could understand, explain what it meant and tell him what he must do. There was so much to tell, his life seemed to have put on many more years than the two which had passed—'yet I have not grown older, or better at dealing with everyday life, or more diligent: I am still a beginner in life, and I have it hard.'[27]

This letter, and those which followed from Worpswede during the summer, are among the most remarkable he ever wrote. To Lou, who knew him so well, there was no need of the self-conscious stylization that overlay his 'confessions' to others like Ellen Key; and in the relief at her readiness to listen he sent her his detailed anamnesis of an unusual case, trying to describe the interplay of psychological and physical tensions which had brought him to this pass. 'I wrote a book on Rodin, a good one. And then I made quiet and stern efforts to keep on at my work, efforts which have left me in great dismay when I feel I have not succeeded. The city was against me, standing in opposition to my life, like an examination that I did not pass.' He described the 'interminable nights of fever and great anxiety', the retreat to Viareggio and slow recovery, which was followed by peculiar symptoms he at first thought imagined only, strange vagaries of his body which for a time he overcame by strength of will. 'But then came something so full of dread, came and came again, never really leaving me since': like the great, indescribable fears in the feverish nights of his childhood illnesses, except that now they came by day, when he felt well, 'and took hold of my heart and held it over the void. . . . Everything changes, falls away from my senses, and I feel myself cast out of this world . . . into another, uncertain environment full of nameless fear. . . . I felt as though I would not recognize anyone coming in and as though I too was strange to everyone, like one dying in a foreign land, alone, superfluous, a fragment from another context.' And he had feared that the 'worst hour' she had spoken of might come to him in that other world from which he could never return.[28]

No need for fear, replied Lou: his influenza was probably at the root of such intensely depressive states. But she encouraged him to go on writing—that would of itself be of some aid, especially when his letters were coming to one whose 'home is in joy', 'for I never had any power, Rainer, but that which is born in joy'. He would try to follow her advice, he told her after the first two weeks at Worpswede, and conquer his fear: but the physical symptoms had been worse than before, with migraines, severe toothache, pain in the eyes, and finally a sore throat and feverishness. Some irregularity in his circulation, he felt, might be behind the unusual condition of both body and mind. Though a quiet room to himself had eventually brought him some relief, the Barkenhoff was no longer the peaceful haven of old, with Vogeler's wife expecting her second child soon and the first, about Ruth's age, 'twittering' in the garden. A week with the Westhoffs was planned as soon as he was better, but he dreaded the disturbance of the inevitable family differences at Oberneuland, much as they longed for the chance to get to know their Ruth a little. 'I would not like to leave again without this meeting, even though it will be practically another farewell. I need a joy, and this joy I will grasp and keep, for where else could I find a joy which truly belongs to me.'[29]

Meanwhile, he told Lou, he would try to work, perhaps continue the translation he had begun of the Russian *Lay of the Band of Igor*. But it was in his next letter a few days later that the true source of his troubles was revealed: the overwhelming horrors of Paris life, every detail of which he had absorbed, and his inability to follow Rodin in the 'presentation of longings and fears as things'[30] and convert what he had observed into objective works of art—'to make things out of fears'. He recalled for Lou, in vivid precision, the 'comfortless, discoloured mimesis' of the excessively big city under which its people suffered, people who were 'the ruined remains of caryatids', 'the whole great edifice of suffering, under which they dragged a slow existence, like tortoises': the armies of sick and dying, the old women with heavy baskets or pitiful trash for sale, their eyes 'drying up like puddles', the folk hurrying by, in some transitional state, 'perhaps from madness to health, or the other way round', and the feeling of his own total isolation among them, the vehicles running straight through him, over him, 'contemptuously, as over a pothole full of water'. 'Oh Lou, I suffered so much, day after day. For I understood all these people . . . I was torn out of myself and into their lives, right through all their lives.' Transfixed by the compulsive movements of a man afflicted with St. Vitus's Dance, whose progress along the street he could not resist following, he had felt as though used up, 'as though the *Angst* of another had fed upon me and drained me'. 'If only I could have *made* something out of the fears, could have formed things out of them . . . but these fears, coming upon me every day, stirred up a hundred others.'[31]

Lou recognized at once that the very act of *writing* this had put him on the road to salvation, that to impart these impressions to another was in itself to turn them into the 'things' he wanted, no different from the creation of a poem. The poet, she wrote, had begun to create from the fears of the man. The reality he sought was already in him: 'you have become like a plot of earth, and everything that falls into it—be it broken, or miscarried, or repulsive, or mere refuse—must combine into nourishment for the seed which has been sown. No matter if at first it looks as though a rubbish-heap has been cast over the soul, it all turns to humus, becomes you. Never were you so close to health as now!'[32] He, too, if unconsciously, must have had this feeling, for his long letter with the sharp impressions of Paris found its way almost verbatim into the 'thing' he was eventually to make of this shattering experience—the *Notebooks of Malte Laurids Brigge*. But it would be long before he could thus finally overcome the crisis.

For the moment, as it seemed to him, 'whatever I receive falls too deep into me, falls and falls year after year, and in the end I lack the strength to lift it out of myself, and I go around uneasily, nursing my heavily-laden depths without ever reaching them'.[33] As he had foreseen, the visit to Oberneuland at the end of July did not help, the querulous outbursts of his father-in-law ruining the pleasure of their reunion with Ruth. The imminent birth of Vogeler's second child drove them back there early in August, however. Money had to be saved if the plan for winter in Rome was to succeed; the Worpswede countryside in any case, once wide and beckoning, seemed small now, and the Barkenhoff itself to grow more everyday in its self-satisfaction as Vogeler sank into domesticity and his art began to lose its edge. Rainer realized now, he told Lou, what a mistake it had been to tie himself to family and home: 'what was my house, then, except a foreign thing for which I had to work, what more my family than visitors who refused to leave? . . . To whom can I mean anything, when I have no calling to people and no right to them?' After Rodin, he knew that there could be no reality for him outside his work—that was his home, 'there the figures who are truly near to me, the women I need and the children who will grow and live long'. But how was he to find the way to it? how concentrate his flow into a single great river instead of dispersing into a thousand separate channels?[34]

Somehow he had to learn how to work, to find the tool that would correspond to Rodin's, 'my own hammer that can become the master'. Lou, having now read his *Rodin*, was right to see that the encounter had been, along with Paris itself, the prime cause of his trouble: the impossibility for his art to take the same solid form had given rise to both bodily and spiritual disorder. 'But I must follow him, not by transforming my creative process into sculpture, but by learning to order it from within', learning patience in observation and a continual, steady, day-by-day application to its transformation into art.[35] Italy could perhaps show the way—to see the antiquities of Rome, and then, leaving Clara there to spend the winter, to move to some quieter refuge, find some 'vessel in which I can collect myself'.[36]

What he sought was still beyond his reach, and the practical problems of his life remained unsolved, but Lou's forthright and sensible analysis had removed the fear that his case was hopeless. Now, spurred on by the growing discomfort in his relations with the Westhoffs, he determined to set off earlier and take a more circuitous route to Italy. His parents were holidaying, separately as usual, in the spas of western Bohemia: after calling on them, he and Clara would stop in Munich and Venice, where there were Zuloaga pictures to be seen, and go on through Florence to Rome. Before they left on 21 August, Rainer sent Lou the third book of the *Prayers*, to be laid with the others she had in manuscript: 'my thoughts dwell on the time after this journey, on the return when I may come to you and read from these Prayers which have long belonged to you'.[37] How they financed their journey, and what they hoped to live on in Rome, is far from clear, although support for Clara from the Bremen friends and from her father still continued, so that at least her stay in Italy over the winter was provided for. Josef Rilke wrote in some anxiety from Marienbad to ask them to avoid any eccentricity in dress when they arrived, and offered to pay for a tailor in Prague for Rainer if need be, so he too may once more have lent his aid. They reached Rome on 10 September 1903.

2

'I am still completely a beginner at what I must become'

(To Ellen Key, 14.2.1904)

The first weeks in Rome were not encouraging for his hopes of 'salvation through work' in the new surroundings. Their rooms to begin with were in the Via del Campidoglio, overlooking the Forum, but he was depressed to find Rome's splendid past preserved in apparently disconnected fragments, in 'the dead atmosphere of a dreary museum',[1] in spite of the beauties of the living city around him: the fountains, the gardens and glorious terraces, and the steps built like waterfalls. After a long search, Clara was able to move to a lodging at the Villa Strohl-Fern, outside the Porta del Popolo. In a vast overgrown park here, once part of the Borghese Gardens, Alfred Strohl-Fern, a wealthy Alsatian dilettante, had established a number of separate studios which he let at modest rents to artists. Another of these studios, an isolated summer-house built over a bridge, Rainer decided might be the place for him: it had one room, with a high window, and a flat roof affording extensive views of the surrounding country. But until it was possible to take this over, on 1 December, he passed 'bad days', as he wrote to Ellen Key. It was the same story: not illness, but the inhibiting effect, the 'psychological defeat', of his inability to apply himself to steady work.[2] It would be better, he hoped, when he could retreat to his hermitage there, prepare his simple meals himself 'and be quite alone with my hands'.[3] In quiet patience, cutting himself off from the outside world, he would try to 'build a winter' of solitude, to re-create his life on the pattern of the days in Schmargendorf, that 'good, expectant, joyous time' which he recalled now in his letters to Lou.[4]

There was meanwhile heartening news from Juncker, now established in Stuttgart. The publisher had already reported a good demand for the *Book of Images*, for which he hoped a 'slow but sure success',[5] and the growing enthusiasm for Rilke's work in Scandinavia, thanks to Ellen Key and Georg Brandes. Now he offered him a monthly fee of 50 marks for continuing the work as reader for him on a regular basis, and began at once to send more manuscripts for his opinion. It was an offer which Rainer gladly accepted, taking characteristic pains over his duties. The task played its part over the next few months in directing him towards the more settled tenor of life he was seeking, as well as deepening his interest in Scandinavian literature, as manuscripts of translations passed through his hands. The news that there were still poems of Jacobsen's untranslated inspired him to thoughts of learning Danish.

He was encouraged too to hear again from the rival publishers. The Insel was now formally reconstituted as the Insel-Verlag in Leipzig, and the new Director, von Poellnitz, wrote him in the New Year to say they planned a second edition in new format of the *Tales of God*. This came at a good moment, he replied, as the book was Ellen Key's favourite among his works and she was planning a Swedish version as well as featuring it prominently in the essay she was writing on him.[6] In his enthusiasm for this new edition, for which he sent detailed suggestions and made some revisions, he secured her agreement to using part of her essay as a foreword: but later, having seen it, he was uneasy at her too revealing use of personal information from his letters, and in particular her praise for his early work when he felt himself now still 'a beginner at what I must become'.[7] After a diplomatic evasion, therefore, the book appeared, in June 1904, without it, but a fulsome dedication made amends.

The New Year brought some progress at last. Amid the antiquities of Rome, 'dreary museum' though they might be, he succeeded with three poems in creating works nearer his ideal, which might stand alone like sculptures— 'Orpheus. Eurydice. Hermes', 'The Birth of Venus' and 'Courtesans' Graves'—and which would find a place later in the *New Poems*.[8] And a prose work was begun. Envisaged at first as a 'sort of Part 2 to the *Tales of God*', it was in fact to turn out quite differently, and, in contrast to its forerunners, would be many more years in the gestation: the *Notebooks of Malte Laurids Brigge*. This 'bigger work' he started in February, after finishing his translation of the *Igor*—with no clear idea, as he wrote to Lou, 'if, or indeed when and in what direction, it will continue',[9] and finding that his way of working was no longer as of old, when he could dash off a book in ten days. For a while the poems, and the composition of 'firm consecutive prose',[10] gave him the feeling that he had made the first step towards his ideal: but the fear that he lacked the strength for sustained effort still inhibited him.

Disturbances there were in plenty, notwithstanding the isolation of his little house. Strohl-Fern, for one thing, though amiable enough, was afflicted with an insatiable curiosity about his guests' work, and was not easily eluded. By April, Rome's spring, whose first signs he had welcomed from his window as early as February, had suddenly burgeoned into high summer, and the tourists began to flock to the city, some even penetrating to his park and their chatter driving him to take cover: 'Rome began to swell, became thoroughly fat and Germanic and enraptured'. He had trouble avoiding the intrusion of visitors who arrived with letters of introduction. Most unsettling of all was the arrival of his mother in Rome: knowing she was due had been enough to set it as a date when his work would stop. 'I see her only occasionally,' he wrote to Lou, 'but—as you know well—every encounter is a sort of relapse'.[11] The result was that, having scarcely begun, he found himself falling back into the old accidie. There was a recurrence of the symptoms he had remarked in Paris, with severe migraines and intensely painful toothache, the same irregularity in his circulation which seemed to concentrate the blood at the affected part in daily and nightly torture. One cause, he realized, was his effort in the new work to bring to paper the dire impressions of Paris, with the inevitable stress the memories brought.

The little house had at first seemed ideal, and he had in fact rented it for almost a year, up to October, but it was increasingly clear that he would not be able to withstand the oppressive climate that long. This was not the Italy of Tuscany, where 'Botticelli, the Robbias, the white of marble and the blue of the skies, the gardens, villas, roses, bells and unknown girls' had spoken once so directly to him—and even that Italy, he felt now, was not the influence which could bring him progress. It had called him, once, but was now 'a closed episode'. Lou, as before, was the confidante of his doubts and fears, and the source to which he turned in May for advice on where he should settle next. Clara, he told her, would return to the Bremen area, where she had the best prospects for commissions and students: for himself, though money was short, he was more convinced than ever that 'from my work, some day, my bread must come . . . it must be possible (or become possible) to do that work and to live from it, if only it is well done'.[12]

So many projects were in his mind: the *Prayers*, which he wanted to continue; the new book he had started, which he felt was a necessary step forward in the preparation for 'everything else' he would one day write (perhaps even the 'military novel' of his school-days); a drama; monographs on Jacobsen and Zuloaga, for which he would some time have to travel to Denmark and Spain. Copenhagen, indeed, might well be his next 'station': he had started learning Danish, and the lecture on his work Ellen Key had given there after her talks in Sweden seemed to have aroused great interest. What

troubled him, however, was the feeling that he needed a more solid grounding
both in his own language and in essential knowledge of the physical world: he
lacked a true understanding of what he observed and the means to express it,
not just in native woodnotes wild but with the full range of the language. Stars,
flowers, the animal world, 'how life arises, the form it takes in the smallest
living things, how it branches and broadens out, how it blossoms and bears—
all that I am burning to know ... to *be*, not only with feeling but also with
knowledge'. He wanted to stop being 'an outsider of life; one who cannot read
in depth the journal of his time': not to study the sciences, or history, or art
history, as such, but somehow to acquire 'a few large and simple truths', to
have his questions answered like those of a child.[13] The tool of language he
could sharpen on his own, and in fact he was continuing a habit he had started
in Paris—browsing through Grimm's Dictionary. But he needed guidance and
help if he was to deepen his true knowledge, and perhaps one of the smaller
German universities, or Zurich, might now be the answer.

All this he poured out at enormous length to Lou, in pathetic trust in her
human and practical wisdom. She was now established, in a new Loufried, in
Göttingen, where her husband had accepted a chair at the university, and he
felt that she and Andreas must be able to suggest a solution to his problem. His
letter crossed with a card from her—from Venice, where she was spending a
short holiday with none other than Pineles. 'So near!' he wrote again at once. 'I
had a feeling all the time that you would be coming to Italy, and when I saw
your writing and the Italian stamp—for a moment my hopes rose, too much
...'[14] But he had news for her for now which cut across all the foregoing. The
interest in Ellen Key's talks had produced invitations for him to Scandinavia,
and he had accepted at once one to Skåne, in southern Sweden, where a quiet
room in a country house awaited him. He was expected there by 20 June, for a
stay which was happily indefinite and which he hoped would let him get down
to work. Lou was doubtless not sorry to find the two letters together on her
return, relieving her of the necessity of worrying out detailed suggestions for
him, for she was soon off to Russia again. It was best, she wrote, to wait and see
what this change of plan and the new impressions in Sweden would bring.

It was a most fortunate turn, one of the many which would come,
unexpectedly but well timed, in his life. Ellen Key, convinced of his genius,
had taken immense pains to help him, not only through her lectures, but also
by enquiring in Denmark and Sweden for a suitable refuge both for him and
for Clara. Though she was clearly not very happy over the effect on the child of
the couple's insistence on 'separate development', concern for their art
overcame the scruples of the educationalist. She had made a number of
suggestions, on the assumption that it was a question of finding the right place
rather than of direct support. Rainer's delicate hints about his weak finances,
however, were followed finally, on 10 May, by a direct appeal from Clara: she
was worried about his deteriorating health, and asked outright whether
someone in Scandinavia, perhaps Ellen herself, could offer him a 'quiet corner'

where he could resume his interrupted work.[15] Within a week Ellen Key had organized just that. The Swedish poet Anders Österling, a close friend of the artist and writer Ernst Norlind, put her in touch with Hanna Larsson, Norlind's fiancée, the chatelaine of a large country house at Borgeby Gård, north of Malmö, who said at once that Rilke would be welcome. Norlind, who was also living at Borgeby, was leaving for a visit to Russia on 1 July, so Rilke should arrive well before that, but he could stay on in July if it appealed to him. Both she and Norlind wrote him sympathetic letters—in French and German respectively, sparing him the trouble of deciphering Swedish. He was overjoyed, he told Ellen, all his fears and worries over the immediate future were banished in the feeling that he was going to people who would understand him: 'I feel it must be a turning-point for me', more especially with her assurance that there were further invitations in the offing for later. 'We know that no one else in the world could have done this for us. But we are like children, who do not give thanks and whose only promise is that they want to grow and develop and become good and strong.'[16]

With a light heart he quickly made his dispositions. Returning some of the manuscripts he had had from Juncker, with his careful assessments, he tactfully avoided mention that Sweden, not Denmark, was his destination; the remainder of the scripts he dispatched from Viareggio, on 14 June, where he broke the hot and tiring journey for a day or two. Milan gave the opportunity to see Leonardo's *Last Supper*, 'immeasurably splendid, like the wall-paintings of antiquity, incomparable'.[17] From Viareggio he had warned Norlind that he might be something of a nuisance as a house guest—vegetarian diet, need for a room away from the ground floor, penchant for going barefoot—and was relieved to find a letter when he reached Düsseldorf brushing aside his worries.[18] They spent four days there—Rodin's works like 'a wild quarry', Zuloaga's 'a great garden', amid the orderly surroundings[19]—and travelled on together as far as Bremen, where he left Clara. At Kiel he took his first ocean ship and arrived in Copenhagen on 23 June, exploring this 'strangely uncommunicative city' which dissolved like its language 'in nuances', and feeling himself surrounded by Jacobsen's characters.[20] A whole afternoon was spent in the Ny-Carlsberg collection, which housed Rodin's *Calais* group, before he crossed the Öresund to Malmö, on 25 June 1904, where Norlind was to meet him.

3

'I feel this must be a turning-point, and a new beginning of
much that's good'

(To Ellen Key, 30.5.1904)

Despite high winds and heavy rain, he was on deck for the whole crossing, arriving so drenched that Norlind had to take him to a hotel to change before they boarded the afternoon train from Malmö to Flädie, to the west of Lund. From there they travelled the few kilometres to Borgeby in an old landau which awaited them at the station—still in 'such rain that I saw neither horse nor coachman, but felt that we were well taken care of on the drive'.[1] It was through flat meadowland, grazed by fat cows and dotted with farms, until the big trees of Borgeby Gård rose into view and they drove past its farm buildings through the central gate of the centuries-old château, under a tower. Rilke was shown up to a room which Norlind had vacated for him and which appealed at once, with its big window looking out towards park and orchard. It was isolated from the main rooms, and the only noise was from the farmyard chickens and the birds in the trees. Work must be possible here, he thought: and when he had seen the alternative semi-basement chamber to which Norlind had temporarily banished himself he was thankful he had made clear to his hosts what he needed. The food too was entirely to his taste, with ample milk from the farm, vegetables and fruit from orchard and kitchen garden, including summer delicacies like asparagus and strawberries, and home-baked bread. With such plenty there was no difficulty in keeping to the regime he preferred.

The house and estate were extensive. Hanna Larsson, from a farming family and some few years older than her fiancé and Rilke, had only recently acquired it, and gave most of her attention to the farm, for which she had a manager and a few hands. There was one servant only in the house itself. Rilke found himself left largely to his own devices, therefore, apart from long talks with Norlind when he felt like it: and the peace and closeness to nature he had missed since Westerwede were once more his. He could wander barefoot again of a morning through the grass, and admire the prosperous cattle, of which there were two hundred head, the bull in his stall—'a mountain with thunder inside'[2]—and the many horses. He was drawing breath and resting, after the long journey, he wrote to Ellen Key in reply to her letter of welcome, 'in this quiet and beautiful house you have opened for me . . . how much good your country is doing me . . . the countryside, the sky, and the language which has something in it of the ring and echo of great bells'.[3] To Ellen Bojer, wife of the Norwegian novelist to whom Ellen Key had introduced him in Paris, he enthused similarly: 'my longing to get to these Nordic lands finds now a thousand new experiences and reasons to justify it'.[4]

Clara received rather more objective accounts, in great detail, of his new life. 'I keep thinking what you would see here, and what you would say about it all, and I miss that. . . . But we have to strike out now each for himself, we know that is the essential thing.'[5] With Norlind, he told her, he had found at once an affinity. The somewhat monkish impression the other gave at their first meeting was quickly belied in the animation of his talk—he had a good command of German from his studies in Munich and Dachau; and Rilke learned much more about the Scandinavian cultural scene than his work for

Juncker had so far revealed, from this painter with wide literary and philosophical interests, whose style and lively demeanour reminded him of his Worpswede friends. Norlind for his part found his guest 'delightful', though he had realized as soon as they met that he had to change his tone to a minor key to suit that of the poet of the *Book of Images*. Rilke seemed to him almost childlike in his love of flowers and nature—but at a loss in dealing with animals, horses or dogs, who sensed how disconcerted he was by their approach. Every now and then he would go off on his own for the whole day, making for the coast at Bjärred or into the country, and returning late in the evening, 'wind-blown, sun-drenched, and full of that simple happiness accorded only to great souls', noted Norlind: 'he explained that he needed such "white days" in which to give his bodily mechanism a complete rest. He eats and drinks nothing, and spends the time immersed in thought . . . days of fasting and prayer. In his whole way of life there is something of the Catholic Middle Ages.' Watching him walking alone through the park, bare-headed, lost in dreams, Norlind thought he looked like a slim page-boy from those times, raising his eyes only when he stopped, as if he were following an invisible procession behind an image of the Madonna.[6]

'We have the same outlook,' Norlind told Ellen Key, 'we found immediately we were like brothers.'[7] This was true in another sense too, for like Rilke he had suffered from periods of deep depression—so much so, that Hanna Larsson had been dubious whether the two would get on. Probably for that reason, though she had made Rilke very welcome, the length of his stay was at first left open.

Communication with her Rilke found more difficult, for their only common language was French. She was a short and energetic body, yet somewhat diffident, 'simple, like a housekeeper',[8] and of uncertain taste in the still rather sparse furnishing of the house, where the guest was disappointed not to find pieces more suited to such a stately home. He was impressed however by her efficient handling of the estate, which he learned had almost always been run by women, the inheritance passing in the female line; and he felt at home with her and Norlind, solid folk, 'both with a firm foundation of generations of farming people'.[9]

After Norlind had left on his long-planned trip to Russia, on 8 July, Rilke's solitude was thus even more pronounced: but this was by no means unwelcome to him. Indeed, as time passed and there proved no difficulty over extending his stay more or less indefinitely, he excused himself from the evening meal, which was anyway 'one too many' for him and where the inevitable efforts at social converse tended to break up the day's impressions. Alone, he could absorb and digest them to the full, enjoying his walks through the park, even a bathe one very hot day in the rather muddy stream which ran past it, under the fascinated scrutiny of the grazing calves on the far bank. There was an occasional visit to Lund, 'standing respectfully around its pride, the university'. He was far from idle, he told Clara: but although his activity was no more than writing letters, or reading and checking a Kierkegaard translation for Juncker, he felt he was 'building', 'preparing the ground for something that will rise one day'.[10] It was a time of recovery, a point of departure, 'an examination of my own I am passing'. Summer had never been his 'high season', and he greeted with joy and expectation the autumn heralded by the high winds and rain which came in August. 'I am avoiding . . . all my summer paths now, for I want autumn! . . . the only creative time . . . when it comes with its drive for change, and destroys the self-satisfied, almost bourgeois stagnation of summer . . .'[11]

Lying fallow thus, he found no verse within himself, though early in August he made a faint beginning with the continuation of the *Prayers*, and later that month a revised version of the *Cornet* for publication in the journal of the Prague society which had given him a grant. It was in his long letters to Clara that the poetry of his surroundings found expression. They are strewn with delicate vignettes, reminiscent sometimes of Hokusai sketches he had seen in Munich: the new-born foal he discovered with its mother in the fields one early morning, the young storks gravely trying out their wings on the thatched roof, the autumn overgrowth of an unkempt path in the park.

In such a renewal of hope, the *Angst* that had assailed him in Paris, and pursued him to Worpswede and Rome, began to be dispelled. For the troubled Kappus, on 12 August, he could find reassuring words, from his own experience, as he said, of a life of 'many troubles and much grief': 'we have no reason to harbour mistrust of our world, for it is not against us. If it holds terrors, those are *our* terrors, its abysses belong to us, and if there are dangers, we must try to love them.'[12] 'Vivre et travailler dane votre grand exemple,' he wrote to Rodin the same day, remained his aim;[13] and the experience of Scandinavia seemed to be bringing him closer towards it.

The visit one day of Torsten Holmström, a young zoology student from Lund, gave him particular pleasure. The lad was so attentive to the movement of nature—the flight of a wild swan or a skein of duck, the swoop of a bird of prey over the trees—and so versed in its every detail, yet was so open to the delights of books and paintings, that he seemed the epitome of the special appeal for Rilke of Nordic people. He had come over for a day's duck shooting only, but his very light pack included a book—Jacobsen's *Niels Lyhne*, no less, in the same Danish edition that Rilke knew. Acquaintance a little later with his sister Tora, a talented artist who was equally wide-ranging in her interests, played its part in convincing Rilke that his immediate future must be linked with Scandinavia.

He had not given up the idea of university study in Germany, he wrote to Lou, but had the feeling that he wanted first to try a winter in Copenhagen: 'I should like to have achieved something before that next plan comes into operation'.[14] It was early in July that he had heard of the award of the grant

from Prague, thanks largely to Ellen Key's essay, as he gratefully acknowledged to her: with a thousand Austrian crowns, his finances looked now a little
healthier, and a stay in Copenhagen was conceivable. It would give him the
opportunity at least of preparation for the Jacobsen study he still had in mind.
Clara, who had set up in Worpswede again after only a short stay in
Oberneuland with her parents, was also turning her thoughts to Denmark,
where design work for a porcelain manufacturer might be better than teaching
as a complement to her earnings from commissions. Hearing from Juncker
that he would be visiting Copenhagen in August, Rilke said he would meet
him there, as a reconnaissance and to have the chance of introduction to
individuals important to him, like Brandes and the novelists Hermann Bang
and Karin Michaëlis—so long as he did not have to attend any larger
gathering, he stressed, which was always an inhibiting experience for one
accustomed to solitude and an abstemious regime. As it happened, Juncker's
letter proposing a rendezvous on 20 August arrived almost simultaneously, to
his great surprise, with a card from Lou from Copenhagen, dated 17 August
and showing her hotel, but with no message (a meeting was perhaps not
exactly what she wanted at this point). He took the next available train, but
found her gone when he arrived on the 19th, to his intense disappointment.
She had taken a Russian ship there, it turned out later, and was on her way to
visit her homeland—probably with Pineles, he gloomily surmised.

When he returned to Borgeby the following evening, he found a letter from
Ellen Key announcing her long-awaited visit for 26 August. Clara had
meanwhile been invited there too. It would be a joyous occasion for them both,
he assured the good Ellen, who with her customary helpfulness had already
been active in seeking out suitable quarters in Denmark, which remained their
goal after a short stay at Borgeby. She arrived like a whirlwind, embracing
everybody, including the dog, rushing through all the rooms to inspect the
pictures, then changing quickly for a swim in the stream, plunging in 'like a
young girl and splashing around like one of Böcklin's sea-monsters', while the
others (and the calves) looked on from the bank. Both Norlind, who had now
returned, and Rilke found her week's stay somewhat exhausting, as they
listened to long lectures on 'life, love, sin and death, marriage, economics and
Goethe'. 'It is impossible not to like her, but you become uneasy after listening
to her for hours on end,' wrote Norlind afterwards: 'Rilke, who has such need
of inner peace just now, is not the right object for her solicitude. . . . Almost
everything she says is sensible, often right to the point, and yet you don't
believe it. She hasn't really experienced it.' Taking him on one side, Rilke
confided his fright at the thought that she might write something more about
him: 'she is so kind, but . . .'[15]

The contrast with Clara was striking, Norlind found. 'Her appearance was
perhaps the most beautiful I have ever seen—that of an Aryan type with a
straight nose and most expressive black eyes. . . . Silent, discreet, natural in

every respect, she immediately won all our sympathies.' She even succeeded in calming Ellen, whose loquaciousness seemed if anything to be lessened by Clara's serious attention to everything she said.[16]

When Ellen left, she took the Rilkes with her to stay for a few days with friends at Jonsered, outside Gothenburg, James (Jimmy) Gibson and his wife Lizzie. Gibson, a civil engineer who owned a textile mill at Jonsered, was a man of wide cultural interests, and the welcome for the poet and his wife was warm: Rilke had the feeling that, if he had found a mother in Ellen—with the drawbacks that entailed—Jimmy and Lizzie were like a brother and sister, and their home, Furuborg, a safe haven. Like Ellen, they gave him introductions for Copenhagen, and Lizzie's letters followed him when he and Clara arrived there on 12 September.

Copenhagen however brought them nothing positive. None of the contacts suggested by Ellen were to be found; the Director of the porcelain factory, to whom Clara was to propose designs, was also away; their search for suitable accommodation for the winter proved fruitless. 'The city and all the turmoil, and our worries over the future . . . have tired us out,' he wrote to Lizzie on 23 September; the thought of the peace of Furuborg and of their 'dear friends' there aroused a great longing to enjoy the 'protection of their love and understanding' once more. And he asked outright whether they might return to Furuborg, just for a week or ten days. 'I know you will tell us quite honestly whether you can stand us, and whether you will mind if we are a bit quiet and sad: in Furuborg we shall surely cheer up again and regain the inner joy we had with you and which we need for the start of our work.'[17] The Gibsons responded at once to this appeal, and they were back with them before the end of the month.

There had been some good days in Copenhagen, of course, particularly with Karin Michaëlis and her husband Sophus, and they had been able to see Georg Brandes (though Rilke found him 'old, and more a place of entertainment than a person'[18]). But Clara's drawings had found little favour with the porcelain manufacturer when he returned: and after increasingly depressing results from their constant financial calculations it had become evident that she would have to return to Oberneuland, while he continued his search in Copenhagen. After the welcome short break in Furuborg, therefore, he accompanied her back there and saw her off on 6 October, with even less confidence that he would find what he wanted in Denmark. The autumn to which he had looked forward so eagerly, and which always brought his 'best days for work', was slipping by fast. Fortunately the Gibsons had offered him their lifeline again: 'it is an immeasurable comfort for me, dear people, that I may come back to you, to think things over and collect myself. To have found you seems the best step forward I could have made: all the future seems nearer to me.'[19]

What had really unsettled him was not so much the failure to find any prospects in Copenhagen, as the knowledge that Lou had been near without their being able to meet. More postcards had followed from her, from Christiania and Bergen, and she had also called at Stockholm, he found when she finally wrote more fully from St. Petersburg. She had no suggestions to make for his winter plans: Göttingen itself was still unfamiliar to her, and he could not stay with them at Loufried 'because I shall probably (if Zemek [Pineles] gets his way) have to take to my bed for two months'. She excused herself for her 'stupidity' over Copenhagen. But her letter shows a lack of feeling for his predicament that would be surprising, were it not typical of her ruthlessness. She undoubtedly realized that his general talk of some quiet university town for his studies in fact meant Göttingen; and she was not prepared, in spite of having at first said he could come 'at any time', to have such a disturbance at close quarters. When he eventually brought himself to write to her, on 17 October from Furuborg, he confessed that for weeks his only thought had been of her nearness: all his resolution had depended on *talking* to her, since that first desperate appeal from Paris—and now it would be impossible, at least for the time being.[20]

He told her of his barefoot walks in the autumn woods near Furuborg, on paths like some of those at Schmargendorf, 'even to the noise the single leaves make as they fall'. 'I have a nice room here and a big window looking out to the burning, glowing, blazing trees and the pines. But I can't be alone enough, cannot get natural food, and the customs of the house deny me my evenings: we eat at seven and stay together after the meal.' He had found he lacked the courage to take up again the book he had started in Rome. 'I am trying to get into work again. But if only it were in my room at Waldfrieden, with its good long evenings, if only I could have such a time again . . . I am still thinking of study somewhere—if I can't find the road to work from within me, it will have to come from outside, I suppose.' And he asked again for her advice— Göttingen, or Zurich?—after she had reread his long letter from Rome. 'For the wider expanses (the Volga world, which I often long for) I am probably not yet strong enough . . . And yet something must still be made of my life. Dear Lou: help me to it!'[21]

In a letter two days later, however, he was less plaintive. What was wrong with his life these past few years, he had realized, was bad conscience and inadequate physical strength: 'everything I touch floats and steams ahead just for a brief while, and then scrapes the bottom and runs aground'. The strength he lacked would have to await a cure: but at least he could do something about the conscience, which stemmed from his failure to learn how to work, to find a few simple ways to handle what experience and living brought him, and was all the worse when others had faith in him. He had made a plan at last. First, he would profit for a few more weeks from this welcome hospitality; return then for some weeks to Copenhagen; spend Christmas, a 'long Christmas', at 'home' in Oberneuland with Ruth; follow this with a cure, in Skodsborg, or

Dresden again, over February and March, the time when influenza usually attacked him; come to see Lou, wherever she was then; and finally enter for the summer semester at a university, for the study of history and the natural sciences—'physiology, biology, experimental psychology, some anatomy etc.' Here he would need to find a teacher who could give him the personal attention his inexperience and helplessness required—such as Georg Simmel in Berlin, perhaps, or at least someone who could help with advice, such as Ricarda Huch in Zurich. Zurich, indeed, seemed to him the best choice, as he had thought before, with country living possible, vegetarian diet, and above all a university that was not German and where he would find himself among people (including Russians) rather than just students.[22]

'If I am not mistaken,' he wrote the same day to Ellen Key, 'I shall make a great step forward in this happy time here . . . lead a more laborious and more directed life than hitherto, and leave here another man. . . . I feel that many benevolent influences are at work on me. The true kindness and immense helpfulness of these people, the strength and clarity of their sunny temperaments; the majesty and melancholy and grave happiness of the autumn—all this is working on me and transforming me. I am a horse-shoe that will soon be brought to red heat. And then the hammer-blows will begin to fall.'[23] He had sent a copy of her essay, which had at last appeared in a Swedish journal, to his father, who had been particularly troubled about him, and was touched by his evident pleasure at it.

The hospitality at Furuborg, though it brought distractions, gave him many a stimulus too. The evenings lost to solitary work were often the occasions for readings organized by his hosts—a new play by Bjørnson, or Verner von Heidenstam's novel *Karolinerna* just out, which Rilke at once recommended to Juncker for translation and publication in German. He had been particularly interested by visits, when Clara was still at Furuborg, to the Samskola, a new school in Gothenburg, of which Jimmy Gibson was on the governing board. 'Comprehensive' in the best sense, it was run on thoroughly modern lines of free development, with children, teachers, and parents in happy co-operation, and without the oppressive atmosphere he remembered from his own school-days. He was so taken by the 'waves of encouragement'[24] for the future which emanated from this experiment that he began an essay on the Samskola, which Jimmy, looking in on him one day, was delighted to notice on his desk. When he read it to him and Lizzie, they insisted that it deserved a wider audience, and to his surprise they assembled no fewer than forty people one evening at Furuborg—teachers, parents, and supporters of the school—to hear his words, which he followed with one or two of his poems from the *Book of Images* and 'The Panther'. He was pressed too to give a reading from his works in Gothenburg itself. For this he suggested the school as venue, with the two upper forms and invited guests as audience. The evening, held on 17 November, was a heartening experience for him. A gathering of over a

Heinrich Vogeler in the 'Barkenhoff',
c. 1900

Clara Westhoff at the time of her marriage to Rilke

Paula Becker and Clara Westhoff

Rilke and Clara at the time of their marriage in 1901

hundred and fifty listened with obvious appreciation to one of the *Tales of God*, 'Orpheus. Eurydice. Hermes', 'The Panther', his 'Autumn' poem written in Paris, some from the *Book of Images* and *A Festival for Me*, and one just written, 'Evening in Skåne'. There were several positive comments in the following day's press, one comparing this 'high priest of the new mysticism', as Ellen Key had done, with the Norwegian poet Sigbjörn Obstfelder,[25] with whom in fact he had felt a close affinity and whose 'Pilgrimages' he had himself just reviewed.

When Ellen Key had earlier suggested he should give such a reading, knowing from her own experience that a good response awaited him, he had been hesitant. He still felt that publicity for the person, as opposed to publication of the work, was premature, almost presumptuous when the writer was as unformed as he was and still finding the way to himself. A public reading, at any rate to a limited audience like that arranged in Gothenburg, was perhaps an acceptable extension of the printed word; but he remained strongly against accompanying the German translation of her essay with all the paraphernalia of photographs, facsimiles of his manuscripts, earlier Vogeler illustrations, and so forth. 'I find all that painful, and less appropriate than ever at a time when I have nothing new and good to offer. . . . I am so glad at the prospect of it in German, and I know what it will mean for me—but I feel that it would have the right look *without* all these conspicuous and pretentious trappings.'[26] He asked her to return the long letters he had written her from Rome: he had taken another look at the beginnings of the *Malte* book, and thought the letters, so 'hastily dashed off' at the time, would be a valuable help in the formulation of the Paris experience. What he did not tell her was that, grateful though he was for her interest, he felt she had made too free a use of their revelations.

Though the real 'work' he wanted still eluded him, he was well occupied during this month with what lay to hand: 'daily work, as best I can—bad or good, but work at all costs'. In addition to the new *Cornet* already done, which Juncker was keen to republish in book form, he revised *The White Princess*, giving it 'a new form, much broader in sweep . . . something with *modelé*'.[27] He wrote a number of reviews, finished his essay on the Samskola for publication, sent Fischer the three Rome poems for the *Neue Rundschau*, and continued with his jobs for Juncker, completing the revision of the Kierkegaard translation and writing notices for new additions to the publisher's list. The days passed thus in a quiet routine. He rarely missed his barefoot walks in the woods, sometimes, as Johnny Gibson, the elder son, recalled, even going nude. The congenial surroundings of his 'golden room' at Furuborg semed 'more and more like the shell in which I am the fruit', he wrote to Clara.[28] There had been encouraging words too from Lou, at last, on his plans for the immediate future. 'So I am astride the steed of my new resolve,' he told her, 'holding fast to its neck and hanging on to the mane—probably not the ideal picture of a horseman, but the main thing is we are getting along. And if I should come off (memories of my riding lessons!) then I am determined to run after it as long as my breath will allow.' Whether the spring would see him in Göttingen or Zurich could be decided later. He longed to see her again, but that too would come. 'I am confident I could be quiet, just another person on the outskirts of Göttingen, who doesn't claim to know more of "Loufried" than that it contains vast quantities of apples and a white, inquisitive, uncommonly clever dog.'[29]

A visit to Ellen Key at her home in Oby, in Småland, south of Alvesta, had long been planned, and over the last weekend in November 1904, after the first snows had fallen, he was finally able to make the long journey. She lived in one of the wings of her brother's country house, the main body of which, Rilke knew, had burned down many years before. But as the sleigh brought him up the snow-laden drive he had an uncanny feeling that the central portion still stood, behind the steps and terrace which led up, that 'the air behind the terrace was not yet part of the rest, was still divided into corridors and rooms and in the middle still formed a great hall, an empty, deserted, twilit hall'. In her old-fashioned room, 'on a red sofa of her grandmother's, [Ellen] sits at work on the second part of her "Lines of Life" and answering the countless letters from young girls and young women and young men who want to know from her where life begins'.[30] The Sunday he spent there, he wrote on his return, was 'like a book bound in the covers of two white journeys, its pages filled with pictures and words, with simple and charming things, and matter weighty and expansive . . . As when someone takes a beautiful old family jewel out of a soft white case and then lays it gently back on the velvet, so this long and abundant Sunday was lifted out of the snow and then laid carefully back. But between were the hours during which one could hold the jewel in one's hand, observe and admire the pure and costly workmanship, thinking on how it carries so much within it of feeling and festivity, and how, like a brooch bedewed with tears, it links past wearers with those to come'.[31] Not many hostesses can have received so elegantly-turned a letter of thanks, and in fact he delayed its dispatch so that the Gibsons might admire the work of art. But the sharpest memory of the visit was his arrival in the Saturday dusk, driving up to a house that was no longer there but yet could be felt, and the weird impression would find its way into *Malte*. Ellen herself found her confidence in him confirmed, and wrote to Axel Juncker shortly afterwards: 'Our friend Rilke will bring you joy: his star is rising, slowly but surely, over Germany! In Sweden he already has many friends.'[32]

He left the haven of Furuborg soon after. He put up at first in Charlottenlund, just outside Copenhagen, and spent his thirtieth birthday quietly amid beech woods near the sea. He had had in mind to discover where material on Jacobsen was to be found, and to meet the painter Hammershøj, on whom he thought of writing; and there were friends of Ellen Key's to visit. But he was too unsettled, and too homesick for Furuborg, he told the Gibsons; and the brief stay brought him little. Travelling on to Hamburg, he arrived in Oberneuland on 11 December to join Clara and Ruth for Christmas.

4

'There is a distant murmur within me, and a movement as of
a coming flood'

(To Gertrud Eysoldt, July 1905)

Clara had been able to find independent quarters soon after her own return, and was now lodged not far from her parents' home, with a good friend whose house was large enough to give both her and Rainer separate work-rooms and who conveniently left for Egypt a week after his arrival. To little Ruth, the traveller with hat, coat, and bag who got out of the train was a stranger, but she rediscovered the father she remembered when she was brought over from her grandparents to see him later. He found the reunion difficult: 'she already seems a complicated little personality of her own, and I shall have to go a long way, with great attention, to find her ... I can't say I find it a joy (it is too difficult)—but it is life that speaks to me with her small and strangely melodic voice, and as always I am a learner, and patient. And she looks just like I was as a child. It's all a very remarkable experience.'[1]

With the change to Germany, to surroundings which he found uncongenial, even 'tormenting',[2] he quickly lost control of the 'steed of his resolve'. The influenza he had expected later attacked him well before Christmas, and money was once more running short. Juncker had continued the monthly fee for his work up to December, but said he would be unable to carry on the arrangement thereafter. Rilke did not hesitate to turn to his 'brother' Jimmy, who had evidently promised his help if it were ever needed. He had, he confessed, been 'rather thoughtless' on the journey: in Copenhagen, while buying on Lizzie's behalf some collars of old lace for Clara, he had been tempted also to get her a lace jacket, and some shoes for Ruth, and then in Hamburg a doll, and a felt cow which could moo. 'And now I have lost the small monthly allowance of 50 marks just when I could really have used it. I ought to draw 200 crowns from my account in Lund' [presumably what he had saved from the Prague grant] 'but I would be happier not to have to touch that: knowing it's there gives me such a good feeling of security. .... If you can let me have something now, I will take it thankfully, and not think of my troubles.'[3] Gibson did not fail him, and within a few days 200 marks had arrived at the bank for him. These were good friends indeed, who also sent gifts for Christmas; and they received a painting from Clara and long letters from Rilke, appropriately lyrical, with much sympathy too when he heard of the serious illness of their handicapped younger son Bertil.

To them, and to Ellen Key, he wrote frankly about the turn for the worse in his health, and on 6 January 1905 stressed the contrast between the petty cares that now beset them in Oberneuland and the peace of Furuborg, such that 'neither Clara nor I have had a single quiet moment for work'. 'All this saps my strength, I pay it out in small change for the chores of everyday life, moving far, far away from myself, from my work, from what I *can* do, and struggling sadly and helplessly with things that are beyond me.' He sent them copies of the 'Samskola' essay when it appeared in the New Year, and transcribed for the Gibsons some encouraging letters from readers who wanted to see a similar progressive system in Germany.[4] At the root of his trouble, however—and this he could not tell them—was not simply the economic struggle, but family life itself, the reunion with those who, as he had bitterly remarked earlier to Lou, were nothing more than visitors outstaying their welcome. He could write with apparent pleasure of Ruth's simple joys, and of a new portrait commission for Clara: but he knew his own salvation could only be found away from them. It was significant that, as he came to check the German translation of Ellen Key's essay, he insisted on the deletion of all references to his marriage and to the time in Paris and Rome.[5]

It was Lou, as always, who heard the truth. 'Christmas is over, and a New Year has begun,' he wrote her: 'I hardly noticed it, scarcely had any festive feeling, and no rest. The circumstances I found here were unfinished, temporary. . . . It was hard to love, to summon up all the attention, the strength, the kindness, and the devotion which love consists of. Helpless, that's all I was, incapable, in all the outward turmoil, of being someone, of being the one I am to become. . . . It was the same story again: as soon as life touches me with one of its realities . . . makes demands on me, I am disturbed. Where others feel themselves welcomed and in good hands, I feel as though prematurely dragged out from some hiding-place. . . .' He wanted desperately to see her, tell her about the Samskola and his new version of *The White Princess*, and read to her the whole cycle of the *Prayers*—'and there is an infinity of things for me to do by your side. I have felt for years now that my next steps forward are in your hands. . . . You must write and tell me if I should better come now or later . . . this time I *must* not miss you: seeing you again is the only bridge to my future'.[6]

Though Lou's reply has not survived, it seems clear that she once more discouraged him from a visit; and his plans for departure, somewhere, to be alone, were in fact abandoned, probably simply for want of funds. Later in January he wrote again to Jimmy Gibson for his advice on how to escape from the impasse. 'I confess, not without shame, that a certain degree of hopeless poverty which . . . spurs others into activity completely paralyses me, seems to take everything out of my hands. My mind wanders helplessly among the figures, and I'm totally confused if I have to decide between buying a book or a pair of shoes.' He felt that both he and Clara were at a point where, if only they could be assured of, say, a year's undisturbed life and work, they could prove themselves. But there was the rub. He had lost the link with Juncker, his books brought in no money, 'and I am more and more depressed at the thought of the ungrudging help from my none too well-off father, who is deferring his retirement only to be able to come to my aid.' Unless she could perhaps teach drawing at the Samskola, Clara would have to return to Worpswede, and he must try to make up at a university for his uncompleted higher education: but how could this be assured? He would be ready to borrow, but had not the first idea how to go about this. Could there be some other way? some wealthy patron perhaps, who might be ready to buy the manuscript of *The White Princess* and others to come. Even this he would consider—anything to secure a year of quiet work. 'My centre must be my work . . . but how money gets into the world, and what it is for, passes my understanding, and I am not up to that struggle.'[7]

Gibson, though he could not introduce him to a suitable Maecenas, was nevertheless once again a tower of strength, and in February sent him 300 marks, more than enough to remove the most pressing problems. The cure at the Weisser Hirsch sanatorium, which he and Clara had always planned when the time came to leave Oberneuland, but which had begun to look financially out of their reach, was a first call on this new wealth; and it gave the opportunity of seeing Ellen Key again after her lecture in Dresden at the end of February. Meanwhile, thinking over the university problem, he was reminded again of Georg Simmel, the philosophy professor in Berlin. Simmel responded very positively when he wrote to explain what he wanted; and he decided to place himself entirely in his hands for a summer semester in Berlin. The Rilke household was packed up once more, and on 1 March, while Clara went to Worpswede to re-install her studio, he preceded her to Dresden, in order to meet Ellen Key before their cure began on 6 March.

In her zeal to help him, Ellen had arranged for lectures not only in Dresden but also in Prague, aiming to interest the German public in his work after her essay and the talks in Scandinavia. He was not surprised to find she encountered a chillier, even hostile reception from her Dresden audience, in contrast to the more open Scandinavians: but, for all his gratitude for her efforts, he was greatly troubled, as he had been before, over what he still felt was premature publicity for one who had scarcely begun. On the night of 1 March, in his room only a few steps from her hotel, he set out his misgivings in a long letter. It was not only his unreadiness, the need for a long, long period in the dark earth before the seed could sprout: he also felt that his art could not reach the mass, that it was destined only for a few, who must come to him of themselves. Showing it forth to a multitude must lead to misunderstandings. 'To keep myself to a certain extent unknown is more necessary to me almost than my daily bread . . . I am still so far from a real work, still have to learn to work . . . A beginning is there, certainly, and that can be indicated . . . but it should not be pressed upon people: it cannot mean anything to those who do not thirst after it.' In Prague, he told her, she could speak freely about her 'child', but there should be caution with 'the others', giving them only what had really been achieved. Such diffidence was clearly beyond the good Ellen's comprehension, but at least she had his blessing for Prague, where he saw her going 'like a generous angel' to bring his long-suffering father the tidings of recognition at last for his only son.[8]

His father was unable to attend her lecture, but she made a point of calling on him, and from his letters Rilke could see the pleasure her visit had given him. 'What I have striven for so hopelessly—to convince my father that the way I've chosen is essential—you have finally achieved with your great confidence in me.'[9] This relief, the ordered life of assured accommodation in the sanatorium, and the comforting thought of enough money for the immediate future, combined to produce a euphoria he had not felt for a long time. A letter from Eva Solmitz, a young admirer of Ellen's, came 'like the voice of the blackbirds who wake me here, in the morning,' he told Eva, 'there was a distant prospect in it, of days and nights in their brightness and transitions.' And he pictured Ellen in her progress through Vienna and Germany as 'a wind carrying the scent of unknown distant regions, waking voice upon voice, a hundred beginnings of a hundred songs of life . . .'[10] Her generosity in remitting to him the net takings from her Prague lecture was of course a more practical contribution to his well-being, and he was suitably grateful.

Meanwhile he turned his thoughts to the possible publication of something already done: the *Prayers*. Lou, in whose hands they had been 'laid', readily agreed to return them for the purpose; and on 13 April he wrote to the Insel Verlag, recalling his promise of a year earlier to submit a new work for them. The prose continuation of the *Tales of God* he had not yet completed, but the other work he had mentioned was ready: 'a long, extensively rounded cycle of poems which encompasses all the progress I have made and the best of all I have written since the publication of my last volume of verse over two years ago.' He proposed to entitle it *The Book of Hours* (*Das Stunden-Buch*), 'First, second, and third books of the Prayers'.[11] The former director, von Poellnitz, having recently died, the proposal was accepted by Carl Poeschel, who now shared the post with Anton Kippenberg, and Rilke promised the manuscript ready for the press by May after he had moved to Berlin.

Altogether his future began to look brighter. Ellen Key had meanwhile been in Vienna, and, ever practical, had the idea of approaching the Education Minister with a view to securing him a stipend. She suggested he should send his application in draft to Marie Herzfeld there, the translator of Jacobsen and other Scandinavian writers, who could advise him on the correct form. His last few days at the sanatorium were taken up with this, and the application was sent off before he left for Berlin on 19 April. The chance of such security for his planned studies was not to be missed. He had had an encouraging word also from August Sauer, his former teacher in Prague. And another stimulating sign for the future came in proposals for him to give lectures in the autumn, which he at once accepted, in Dresden and Prague. They would of course be on Rodin. Simmel, as it happened, had told him he proposed shortly to visit Rodin, to whose work he had earlier devoted an essay; and Rilke took the opportunity, when writing to the master to announce this visit, of telling him his own plans.

He and Clara had followed the cure with diligence, and there had been few distractions. Among their fellow patients, however, were some they could spend quiet hours with: Anna Schewitz-Hellmann, an artist from Riga, who made a striking charcoal sketch of Rilke, and her friend Alice Dimitrieva; and an older lady, Luise Countess von Schwerin, née Nordeck zur Rabenau, who during her short week at the Weisser Hirsch took a great interest in the young couple. It would be ungenerous to suggest that Rilke scented in her another possible patron, but her aristocratic background certainly appealed to him, and with his ever-eager interest in the histories of old-established families he found out all about her. 'She knew about us, and surrounds us with kindness,' he told Ellen Key. He did not fail to send the Countess a letter with their thoughts of 'thanks and love—no, only love' to await her return home to Friedelhausen, the family castle near Giessen.[12]

Just before they themselves left, Clara for Worpswede and he for Berlin, he was surprised to receive a card from Lou and Ellen, who was visiting her at Göttingen. From the station he wrote to Lou that he hoped she had been able to 'correct' Ellen's 'undiscriminating kindliness' towards him. For better or worse, he was on the way now, even though Simmel would not be back from Paris for a while; and he asked her to send the *Prayers* manuscript to him in Berlin without delay, so that the typescript could be prepared.[13]

With all these, at it were, extra-curricular excitements, it would have been surprising if he could have succeeded in sticking to his resolve and settling into city life and an academic routine, even had Simmel been there when he arrived. He found himself, after the energetic cure, extraordinarily tired, falling asleep in the middle of the day: and in fact held out for only a few days 'on the frayed edges of the great city'.[14] On a sudden impulse, he decided to take himself off again just before Easter, to rejoin Clara at Worpswede, an 'unexpected guest', with the idea still of returning when he felt better.

The fact of the matter was that, until he had been able to see Lou again, the way would not be clear. Over four years had passed since he had gone out of her world, unsettled by the warning of her 'Last Salute', and nearly two since he had begged, in vain, for the aid of her presence. In the 'grey cell' of his Worpswede room now, as he held once again the old black album in which he had inscribed the first 'Prayers', he relived their time together, in a mingling of 'joy, recognition, longing and gratitude, submission and uplift'—a foretaste of the meeting which, more than ever now, he needed with the 'only person I could really talk to'. Until that could come, he was powerless to regain his confidence. Preparing the book for publication, to which he devoted the first weeks in Worpswede, seemed like a ceremony of anticipation, for the poems belonged to her 'like some distant inheritance'.[15]

On 19 May, after the transcripts had gone off to the Insel, with his detailed ideas on the format of the book, he was able to return the manuscripts to her: and his letter rehearsed once again his despair. 'All these attempts to find a more natural life . . . a healthier way of living, whose only purpose is simply to make life lighter and more industrious, have over the years, God knows how, become a job in themselves, a duty, full-time expenditure of strength and time, a profession. . . . It's like continually dressing and preparing for a part in a play while already on the stage with the curtain up. Is there only one thing left to do: play the part as one is?' His 'confused and stupid letter', he felt sure, was hardly likely to make her want ever to call him to her side. When a brief note came to say why not come in Whitsun week, he could scarcely believe his good fortune. It would be a year of blessing after all, 'full of goodness, now it is really to bring this *one* event'. All else was forgotten. Berlin he put now 'in brackets', could think of nothing beyond Göttingen and Loufried. He might hear a few lectures, by way of preparation for the autumn, when he would start in earnest; but two or three days with her would clear his mind and bring the right decision.[16] The stay in Göttingen 'will sort out and make firm my plans in every direction. My friends have to be very patient with me, don't they? But I hope to improve.'[17]

Whatever Clara may have thought of his impatience to see Lou, her ideas of the overriding importance of the 'work' for the artist were so exactly his—her letters read as if he had written them—that she saw nothing unnatural in the separation of their lives. He had taken a room elsewhere for his writing while in Worpswede, otherwise sharing the quarters she had rented; but, as he had written to Lou, it was no 'home' for him, and there was nothing to hold him there now she called him.[18] He saw Ruth twice, briefly, during his stay; but although he would remind her later of their happy hunt for the Easter hare's eggs, the joys of fatherhood meant little to him. He was considerate, and ready to help Clara when he could: but he did not delay his departure for Göttingen on 13 June.

Luise von Schwerin had been a frequent correspondent since her return to Friedelhausen, and from her kindly letters, which she often accompanied with a book, or a Rodin publication for Clara, he began to feel already a part of the circle of her family: her daughter Gudrun, wife of the biologist Jacob von Uexküll, her stepmother Julie von Nordeck, and her sister Alice Faehndrich, who had a villa in Capri where the Countess would be spending part of the summer. She was interested in all his plans, and indicated that he would be welcome to visit Friedelhausen later, if it fitted in. He promised to keep her informed after his consultation with 'an experienced and dear friend' in Göttingen. He was still uncertain about Berlin, and it seemed, from all she had told him, that Uexküll, if they could meet during the summer, might be the adviser and helper he needed.[19]

The reunion with Lou gave him all he expected in strength and encouragement. She was far from well, and unable to get out very much, and he took long walks alone in the woods behind the house on the Hainberg above the town. The change of scene and the stimulus of her presence transformed him. 'We often wish you were with us,' he wrote to Clara, 'as we sit in the garden and read, or talk over all the things with which I often troubled you and which now seem so much lighter, or at least more bearable in their weight . . . How good . . . it was, that I came. It is so much more beautiful than I could ever have dreamed, because the need was greater than I thought.'[20] All his gloom, and the lassitude which had troubled him since leaving Dresden, had been dispelled by the time he moved on. What Lou's advice had been, in practical terms, is not clear: but at all events he headed now for the capital, saw Simmel at last, presumably discussing with him his plans as well as their impressions of Rodin, and listened to some of his lectures during the three remaining weeks of term. A winter of study lay ahead of him, he felt. During the vacation he had arranged to meet Lou again, when she visited a friend at Treseburg in the Harz mountains; and in August he was expected at Friedelhausen. He seemed to be drifting, as though awaiting a sign, some dispensation from an unknown hand which would settle his direction for him.

The turn came with an unexpected letter which reached him in Treseburg on 19 July, just when he was wondering, after Lou had left, how he could hold out there in the overcrowded tourist season. Gertrud Eysoldt, an actress whom he knew well, had visited Rodin with greetings from him: and the master wrote to his 'bien cher ami' to express the admiration he felt for the writer 'who has so much influence everywhere through his work and his talent. I feel I must send you these words of friendship and support for your spirit as a worker.' Rainer and Clara were among his cherished memories. 'Travail, courage, intelligence modérée, pour que ces biens ne se surmènent pas . . . A vous de cœur . . .'[21] Rodin had been much in Rilke's thoughts, not only through the many works he had seen again in Copenhagen and Berlin, but also because his mastery of work remained the ideal he was still striving to attain: and the effect of such an encouraging message just at this moment can be imagined. He resolved to visit Paris briefly in September, before buckling down to his studies: 'to see you again after all this time, and to breathe the sublime air and creative wind which blows from the mountains of your Work'.[22]

The rest of the summer passed quickly in the anticipation of this visit. On the way to Friedelhausen he stayed briefly in Kassel at the end of July, where apart from the Rembrandts in the picture gallery he found little to attract him, and in Marburg, exploring the Gothic splendours of the castle and the

Elisabethkirche. Clara joined him at Friedelhausen for the first half of August, until the sudden death of her father called her back to Bremen. Their welcome in the castle was warm, in the atmosphere of aristocratic patronage which was always so congenial to him: and the sojourn there, coming after his meeting with Lou, was like the completion of the cure he had looked for in vain in Worpswede. 'My life, everything that I am,' he wrote with his gratitude to Luise von Schwerin, 'went through Friedelhausen as a full river goes through the warmth of a sunny countryside, spreading out and broader, and glistening with all its waves.'[23] During his stay there was detailed correspondence with the Insel over the format and decoration of his *Book of Hours*, a motif from an old Venetian print being finally decided on for the cover: a fountain with a threefold jet, to represent the three books of the cycle. Before he left he had already corrected the proofs.

Among the house guests for a time were Karl von der Heydt—banker, writer, and art-lover—and his wife Elisabeth, who invited him to stay with them at Godesberg on his way through to Paris. Rodin, to whom he now proposed a date, telegraphed he would be glad to expect him from 7 September, and this was followed by a letter from the secretary suggesting he should stay at Meudon: 'M. Rodin tient à ce que vous restiez chez lui pour pouvoir parler.'[24] This was more than he had dared expect, and he hastened to accept, at least for part of his stay. 'He means it, it's just what he wants, and it will be good,' he wrote to Clara. 'I said just for a few days, fearing to be too much trouble for Madame Rodin: but we shall easily see how long I can make it . . . I feel a deep joy at the prospect of the close intimacy of his daily life, and the little Villa des Brillants and the garden with the distant view.'[25] After a few days with the von der Heydts, who asked him to choose for them a Rodin work for their already substantial collection, he arrived in Paris on 12 September 1905.

IV

France, Italy and North Africa
1905–1911

—◦⟩⟨◦—

'He who has had these disturbing thoughts, must begin to do
some of the neglected things ... will have to sit down in his
room ... and write, day and night.'

(*Malte Laurids Brigge*)

I

'Perhaps here I shall learn everything I lack'

(To Lou Andreas-Salomé, 14.11.1905)

Rilke put up at first in a hotel, to acclimatize himself to Paris before
announcing himself for 15 September 1905 at Meudon. Three years for this
city had passed like a day: it was the same, 'as sure of itself as ever'[1]—but for
him, in his new confidence, it no longer held its former terrors. As he revisited
his vegetarian restaurant, sat again in the Luxembourg Gardens, or watched
from the high balcony of his room the evening grey descend over the river, he
seemed back at the beginning of his first stay, but this time in even keener
anticipation of what Rodin would mean for him. He was not disappointed. 'It
means nothing when I say he received me warmly,' he wrote to Clara on the
first evening at Meudon: 'rather it was like the reception one finds returning,
on paths grown difficult, to a loved place, a spring which has sung and lived
and given back reflections day and night while one has been away.' Rodin had
recently seen a translation of Rilke's book, 'and has paid me the greatest
compliment possible: he has placed it among his own works'.[2]

Since his admiration for the master had first been awakened, Rilke's letters
had contained many a hymn to Rodin, but none to equal the dithyrambs which
poured now from his pen to Clara, Ellen Key, Gudrun Uexküll, Luise von
Schwerin, von der Heydt. 'He moves like a star, he is beyond all measuring ...
his example is incomparable, his greatness rises up before one like a tower
close at hand, yet his kindness ... is like a white bird circling one in glistening
flight till it settles confidingly on the shoulder[3] ... One often has the feeling
that it is he alone for whom God makes the sun to come and go ... that he is
the only one of whom God knows, for like none other he takes and loves
everything, surrenders himself in a humility that is transformed naturally into
greatness, nobility, majesty—that is, into harmony ...'[4]

There had been changes at Meudon. Rodin had built a number of smaller houses below the museum, one of which Rilke found was allocated entirely for him—three rooms with every comfort and a magnificent view over the Sèvres valley. The crowd of 'things' was denser than before: houses, corridors, studios, and gardens were full of the wonders of antiquity alongside Rodin's own works, greeting each other like members of one family. The old man spent long hours in talk with him, spoke of his earlier days in Brussels, how in sketching outdoors he had learned to observe nature and become one with the landscape. He took him to Versailles, and once to lunch in town with Carrière and the writer Charles Morice. In these first few days Rilke was entirely absorbed, 'always with him or with his works'. In the evenings, after Rodin's return from the rue de l'Université, they would sit watching the swans on the pool in the garden, 'talking of serious, essential things, like friends ... an evening hour of such repose and depth (through which the swans glide slowly, like veins in a beautiful stone) that I often have a feeling of the next world, of blessed transfiguration ...' Before his window, as he looked out to the blue starry night, a gravel path led up to a little eminence on which, 'in fanatical silence', stood a Buddha: 'c'est le centre du monde,' he exclaimed to Rodin.[5]

The other clearly set great store by his judgement and critical appreciation. Taking him one day among his works in the museum, he asked for his impressions of one and another of them, and wrote on the base the names they evoked for Rilke. He spoke too of his loneliness, and how he lacked a secretary capable not only of relieving him of the burden of correspondence but of really helping him in the realization of his work. It was natural that he should see in Rilke the person he needed, and towards the end of September he proposed that he should stay on as his private secretary—boarded and lodged as before, but with a stipend of 200 francs a month. The correspondence would take up only a few hours of the day, and the rest of his time would be free for his own work. It was a generous gesture; and Rilke, after some hesitation (for he could foresee how long the letter-drafting would in fact take him), was very glad to accept. It relieved him at a stroke of day-to-day cares, and there could be no better opportunity for him, at last, to 'learn how to work'. The plans for his lectures had meanwhile progressed: he was due in Dresden on 23 October and Prague on 25 October, and Rodin made no objection to his absence. To prepare the talk in these new conditions was of course ideal; and already he began to feel how beneficial Rodin's presence was for his own work.

When he left for Dresden he was pleased with his draft, which he felt had gained in maturity over his Rodin book. And he had good reason to be pleased with the success of his talk there, with a hushed and attentive audience of over six hundred—except that they were mostly older people, rather than the young who he felt needed the Rodin message of patience and unremitting application.[6] In Prague, there was a much smaller attendance—mostly old women, some dozing off, as he reported to Rodin, some managing through curiosity to keep their eyes open; and a few clerks 'tired from their interminable days dominated by their bad digestion'. But he had spoken well, he thought, and two or three younger persons came to press his hand in silence afterwards. 'I feel I have done good work, and one day I shall find ... the public who will need my words: for I know, more than ever, that all who live need you, the good news of your existence is the Gospel with which our days touch eternity.'[7] Most of his few days in Prague were of course spent with his father. Josef, still weak after an illness, could not attend the talk, but was understandably delighted at his son's material progress and new-found independence. It was indeed something of a triumphal return. After a brief visit to Leipzig to discuss the *Book of Hours* with the Insel, Rilke returned to Meudon in the first days of November.

Rodin's benevolence had meanwhile extended also to Clara. She had earlier sent him some of her work, and he had been sufficiently impressed to telegraph his congratulations and ask her to come to Meudon. 'There are few sculptors who can achieve something like this,' he said to Rilke.[8] She stayed altogether about a month, and was able to work in one of his studios. For her and Rainer, the fortunes were now reversed: he had found a measure of security, whereas she, after the death of her father, had lost the financial support which had been regularly, if not always ungrudgingly, given and had sufficed her for essentials. Rainer was concerned about her—though not to the extent of himself making any contribution yet to her income: 'I must first get myself properly organized,' he told Ellen Key, 'there are many pressing purchases, and I feel I must finally start putting something aside.'[9] To Ellen, and to the Gibsons, who had written hoping he could come to stay with them again, he explained his new situation and his hopes from it. His place must be with the master, 'whose friendship means as much to me as yours,' he wrote to Lizzie. But if Clara could take his place in the 'golden room' in Furuborg, this would give her a quiet time in which to work and save in preparation for the following summer in Worpswede—perhaps even to earn, if Jimmy and Lizzie could find her some commissions. A study of Ellen Key would surely find support. Christmas they would spend together with Ruth: perhaps afterwards he could accompany Clara back to Jonsered, if, as he hoped, they could arrange for him to give the lecture on Rodin and a reading from his own works in Gothenburg. But everything would of course depend on Rodin's demands on him.[10] (None of these ideas for helping Clara, in the event, could be realized: though the Gibbons acquired for themselves her bust of Rilke reading, which she had modelled at Friedelhausen, they were unable for various reasons to have her to stay at Furuborg, and Ellen Key, he learned, was loth to sit for her.)

He gained greatly in self-confidence as the end of the year approached, after the lecture tour and in the security of his new position, casting off the diffidence over self-publicity he had expressed so recently to Ellen. The three Rome poems which appeared in Fischer's *Neue Rundschau* in November brought him warm appreciation from Hofmannsthal, Wassermann, and others whose opinions he valued. Though lectures or readings in Scandinavia did not materialize, he had already been invited by Herwarth Walden to Berlin for a reading from his own work early in March; Harry Graf Kessler, whose own short essay on Rodin had given him many new insights, wanted him to talk in Weimar; and he had hopes of extending the tour to take in Elberfeld, Hamburg, Bremen, perhaps Vienna as well. It would primarily be for further propagation of the Rodin gospel, and that might be possible in Berlin too. The bad conscience which had troubled him was being eased at last, and the faith in his mission justified: he was proving it posible to be nothing but a poet, and yet to survive. From Rodin, in his 'magnificent ripeness of age', emanated 'happiness, and greatness, and capacity for work which enhances every day and makes every hour a solace'.[11] 'Only the truly great *are* artists in that strict sense, the only true one—that art has become a way of living for them.'[12]

How far-reaching the change in him was, can be seen from his letters to Lou in November—the first he had written to her since the summer. Gone is the agonizing self-analysis, the preoccupation with his bodily condition, the desperate grasping at straws, the multiplicity of plans impossible of fulfilment, and in their place a factual, almost sober summary of the surprising events since August and his life at Meudon and Paris, with all the stimulating contacts it was bringing, notably the Belgian poet Emile Verhaeren and Ignacio Zuloaga. 'Perhaps here I shall learn everything I lack . . . My shout of joy has come: but I will measure it out in small fragments over a long time, so that it becomes just an occasional drawing of breath. And then it shall be transformed, if I can do it, into the real and the visible, and not be merely empty utterance.'[13]

At last he could hope to attain the ideal Rodin had inspired: to work, steadily and without impatience, at fashioning experience into things which could have an existence of their own, and to turn his back on the mere expression of subjective mood or vague longing at the caprice of inspiration. His letter-writing for Rodin (in a French for which there must be a special purgatory somewhere, he told Lou) took, as he had foreseen, a great deal more of his day than the few hours the master had suggested. Yet, during these winter months, he began to succeed in his aim, and a number of the 'New Poems', of which 'The Panther' had been the forerunner, took shape. There were classical and biblical themes: but perhaps the Buddha before his door provides the best illustration of the new departure:

Buddha
He seems to listen. Stillness, things remote . . .
We stop, and they no longer reach our ear.
He is a star. And others of great note,
unseen by us, are ranged about him near.

Oh, he is all. In truth, are we in wait
for him to see us? Can such a need he feel?
Were we to bow down here before him, kneel,
he'd stay withdrawn, indifferent to our fate.

For that which casts us at his feet
in him for long millennia has turned.
He who forgets what we have learned,
and learns, where we can but admit defeat.[14]

The standing he had eagerly, too brazenly, sought in Prague and Munich was beginning to come to him. As the secretary of Rodin, he was in contact with a circle beyond the purely literary—when a letter had to be written to Eleanore Duse, for example, the master encouraged him to add one of his own to tell her something of himself and his work. And he was achieving wider literary recognition, not only in letters like Hofmannsthal's and in serious studies, as they began to appear in Germany and Austria, of his work, but also from admirers as yet unknown to him. For Stefan Zweig he seemed the poet *par excellence*, 'linking with the eternal' through the very tenor of his existence, 'aloof from people and yet the inheritor of the great figures of our time like Rodin, Tolstoy ... an enviable picture.'[15]

There was a new assurance too in his relations with his publishers. Ellen Key had long been urging him to see that he got proper contracts to ensure an adequate reward for himself from the successes she was convinced were to come; and he was at pains now to remind both Juncker and the Insel of this. He had been quite open with Juncker about his agreements with the other house for the new edition of the *Tales of God* and for the *Book of Hours*. To Poeschel he wrote that he had decided that all his future works should be under the one imprint: 'but it must be with the publisher who can offer me ... a certain reasonable monetary recompense, which in my circumstances unfortunately I cannot do without.'[16] It was clearly his hope that this publisher should be the Insel, for with Juncker, to whom he wrote soon afterwards, he concerned himself only with 'old' works—a new edition of *The Last of their Line*, the *Cornet* in separate book form, and a revised and enlarged edition of the *Book of Images*. But to him also he insisted on contracts. As he said to both, he had little idea of business, and was in their hands. But he had made his point and both met his wishes.

To live from his books, as he had written to Juncker,[17] was, truth to tell, never really his objective. He wanted to live for his art alone: and to this end he felt that, somehow, the means to create it should be given to him—the right surroundings, and a modest, though not minimal, income. 'One cannot create beauty,' he had said in his lecture on Rodin, 'one can only create circumstances favourable for it.'[18] But what he might create, the books themselves, once brought out in the form he thought fitting, he did not regard as articles of commerce from whose sale he was to live; and he was less and less inclined to read the reviews on which their sales depended: 'they seem to me ... like letters addressed to another, the contents not intended for my eyes'.[19] On the contrary, his books became part of himself, offered for those who could appreciate them and given freely to friends and colleagues like the 'Gifts' in his *Advent* poems. (There are probably more signed and dedicated copies extant of Rilke works than of any other comparable author's.) When the *Book of Hours* came out in December, he at once ordered, from the first printing of 500, thirty or so copies for his own account to distribute to his friends, and followed this later with further orders—which must have made a considerable inroad into the half-share of the net profits from the book which he had agreed to accept instead of royalties.

The arrangement with Rodin was the best that had yet fallen to his lot, but with it came the obligation of daily drudgery in the service of another, however admired. He knew he needed a less demanding patronage, making it possible for him to create, but without necessarily seeking a return. Whether it would come from a private benefactor, or from the State, or from a publisher, made no matter. In the event, he succeeded in enlisting all three at various times to his support—though only at the cost of unremitting pressure, sometimes direct but more often through an admirable diplomacy, none the less effective for being innocent of any baser calculation.

Thus now, over the winter and spring of 1905/6—with all the stimulation he was finding from the daily contact with Rodin, but under the steadily increasing burden of his secretarial duties—his feelers were out in all the directions from which help of the right kind might be expected. The earlier application to the Ministry in Vienna for a grant had been turned down; but, encouraged by Ellen Key and Marie Herzfeld, he tried again in February, listing his books, enclosing a copy of Ellen's essay and carefully drafting a letter which he hoped would make him look 'thoroughly poor and worthy of compassion'.[20] In reply to an enquiry from Juncker, he said he was willing to resume work for him as reader, on the same terms as before, if the publisher felt this would be of service. With Karl von der Heydt, for whom he had arranged the acquisition of Rodin's 'Brother and Sister', and who wrote a perceptive review of the *Book of Hours*, placing Rilke 'on the heights of German lyric poetry',[21] he corresponded regularly, in well-turned letters with his views on art and life, and what he needed for both: and by the end of April von der Heydt was offering him the possibility of an alternative refuge. He had also not forgotten Luise von Schwerin: her appreciation for the *Cornet* partly accounted for his plan to republish it in book form—characteristically, in a limited edition, without regard for its commercial potential and garnished with the Rilke coat of arms of which he was so proud—and the knowledge that she was there 'had represented a protection, a haven, an aid for the coming years', as he wrote after her unexpected death in January.[22] But his cultivation of her family ensured that Friedelhausen remained open to him if he wanted. His adopted relations in Scandinavia, the Gibsons and Ellen Key, received regular reports of his hopes and plans, so that Furuborg too made a fall-back position should the need arise, and Ellen was receptive to his suggestion that she might make over to Clara the honorarium from the publication of her essay in a Prague review.

Clara now had Ruth with her, at last, in Worpswede, and was at work on a child's head, with her as model, when Rainer came for his stay over Christmas and the New Year. It had to be brief, as Rodin could not spare him for long, but that was probably no hardship for him. 'There is no sadness in being alone,' he wrote to his mother from there, 'if the roads to the loved ones remain open.'[23] Worpswede he found the 'same remote place' as ever, 'with its slow mail-coach', a singular contrast with the countryside of Meudon. His most striking impression was that from Paula Modersohn's work: she was painting 'things which are very Worpswede-ish, yet which no one has ever seen or painted', following a path he thought strangely close to that of Van Gogh.[24] Once he was back amid Rodin's art, their image faded; but when he heard she was coming to Paris again he made a point of seeing her in her rooms in the rue Cassette, just before he left on his tour, much delighted 'at being taken with her' into the new life she planned apart from Modersohn[25] (another case of separate development of which he obviously thoroughly approved).

Much work awaited him meanwhile in Meudon. For the shoal of New Year's cards which had to be sent, temporary help was at hand, to his relief; but to him fell the letters to the distinguished and the princely correspondents, and the difficult drafting and re-drafting of Rodin's speech and a letter in connection with his forthcoming exhibition in London. What was left of the day was devoted to his own correspondence, also substantial in the preparation for his own lecture tour. 'A hundred letters a day,' he told Clara, 'and gladly done, I would add—in the mornings for the Master and in the afternoons for myself; and if there is any time left before night, I listen again to the poems which want to go into the *Book of Images*'—the poems from the earlier pre-Rodin time, which did not take the new direction of 'The Panther'. He did not find it easy to insert them into what he now saw was a homogeneous whole, 'full of inner feeling'. 'Only a few will pass the test ... some will take a different form, some be left only a fragment until one day perhaps something gets added to it.' And some of the earlier, already included, needed changing, carefully, to bring out more clearly what he had meant, but did not well express, seven years earlier. For the *Cornet* there was little to be revised, the main changes being in the introduction, which he planned to limit to the dry quotation from the original document, and of course in the hero's name. 'A pity, one had become so accustomed to Otto Rilke ... whose death in his late years is not recorded. But I feel the truth must prevail and we must call the Cornet by his right name.'[26]

'My time is too limited all round,' he wrote to Hugo Salus early in February, 'and my health won't permit me to add the nights to it.'[27] Rodin, a *monstre paperassier* as one earlier secretary had called him, was a demanding taskmaster over the vast archive he was accumulating: but there were nevertheless welcome days of relaxation in his company. The old man would call him down from his desk to the garden 'pour me montrer le paysage', or take him off to Versailles or Chartres. The indifferently restored Cathedral there saddened him, but he held in memory the first impression of it rising up before him 'as in a great cloak'; the first detail of 'a slim weathered angel holding a sundial ... the deep smile of his acolyte's countenance as though mirroring heaven'; and around the mass of the building the great wind in which they 'stood like the damned' while the angel 'held so blessedly his dial towards the sun he could still see'. There were visits too to Troubetskoy, now settled in Boulogne-sur-Seine, whom he had not seen since St. Petersburg, and to the Jardin d'acclimatation in the Bois de Boulogne, with its monkeys and flamingoes, and precious Chinese pheasants 'as though made of enamel', so carefully fashioned that it came as a surprise to see among them a seemingly unfinished head of dull grey.[28]

Rodin left for London on 20 February 1906, and Rilke had only a few days to himself before starting on his own tour. After the work on the new *Book of Images*, he felt himself on the verge at last of a new start: he longed for the complete solitude which he had known in Rome and which the garden in Meudon sometimes reminded him of. 'The mornings, and the afternoons with the Bible on my desk, and limitless evenings, and nights as though rising out of one's own heart—and all mine.' 'I ought to be bringing you bread with this letter,' he wrote to Clara, 'but my fields are not yet in cultivation again. ... I could transcribe all your long letters, with their questions about what life intends for us, and they would be *my own*, word for word. ... Practical problems ... everything wanting thinking out and dealing with, and alongside all that the other, which longs for a sea, wants to sing day and night.'[29] But, quite clearly, worry of this kind was a far cry from the *Angst* that had assailed him in the early days in Paris: his letter to Lou the day before, telling her of his itinerary and looking forward to meeting her, however briefly, in Berlin, was entirely serene and matter-of-fact.

His plan was for Clara to join him for part of the tour and in particular for the few days in the capital. She arrived there in fact the day before he came on from his first Rodin lecture in Elberfeld, and stayed in the same pension as Lou, who gave her a friendly welcome at this their first meeting. Two talks had been planned for Berlin: the first a reading from his own works, on 2 March, for the 'Art Society', and the second on Rodin a week later, with appearances in Hamburg and Bremen between. Vienna, in default of the hoped for invitation from the *Sezession*, had been abandoned, Stefan Zweig's efforts to arrange an alternative having also failed. For various reasons, there were postponements in the latter part of this programme, and the Weimar talk was in the end cancelled, so that after Hamburg he went with Clara for a few days' rest in Worpswede. From there he reported to Rodin the successful outcome so far, as he saw it, notably the lively interest in his work among young people; and asked his indulgence for a slightly longer absence than foreseen—not only because of the postponements, but also because his father had fallen gravely ill in Prague.

The very day after he had written this, on 14 March, his father died. Putting off the second Berlin appearance until 20 March, he left at once with Clara on the sad mission of winding up the affairs of one who had been 'kindness itself to me, the most loyal aid and the most touching friend, ever closer to me in his devoted affection as the years went by'.[30] Phia, who was on her annual spring visit to Arco, did not see fit to join him. It was significant that he telegraphed the news, not only to Rodin, but also to his surrogate mother Ellen Key. For one usually so helpless in dealing with practical matters, he was surprisingly efficient over what had to be done: in a few days his father's apartment was cleared up and his papers looked through, and he was laid to rest, with violets at his head and a heather wreath from Ruth, in the family grave in Olšany. After these 'saddest labours' he wrote to Phia from Berlin on 20 March: 'I don't know how I could have done it all without Clara's loyal and self-sacrificing support. . . . To you . . . he was, many years ago, a friend, an austere friend who later left you, under the pressures of your relationships, to bring you much pain and despair: but life should not be the avoidance of all that or not going through it—it must be to rise above it . . .'[31]

Rodin was kindness itself when he finally reached Meudon again on 31 March, 'tired and confused after all the rush and relentlessness' of the days he had been through;[32] and there was time to rest before he was immersed once more in his duties. But the feeling was stronger than ever within him that he was ready for work of his own, and he began to long to be free for it. 'Every day I have to exert all my good sense to keep myself from boarding a train down to Viareggio,' he wrote to Karl von der Heydt, 'diverted from myself by the continual qui-vive of my job, by the impossibility of ever being inwardly alone'. When the other asked in some concern what he could do to help him, he told him what he needed: one or two years in circumstances like those in Rome, where—quite alone but with Clara working nearby so that they could help each other—he had been able to start the Malte book 'to which I have not yet returned'. The stay in Sweden and in Friedelhausen, and now in its different way Meudon, for all his friends' kindness, could not offer the same 'unlimited solitude, where each day seems like a whole life . . . the space whose bounds one cannot see, in the midst of which one stands surrounded by the illimitable'.[33] But his conscience would not allow him to leave Rodin at this point. His time would come, and he would meanwhile be patient, relieved at any rate to express his longing to a sympathetic ear. To Clara also, as the spring began to draw into summer, he recalled their time in Rome, and bade her be of good heart: 'these things do not happen twice, but perhaps life may yet come back on itself and let us work alongside one another again . . .'[34]

Possessing his soul thus in patience, through the April days, he had much to absorb him in what life offered at Meudon. Rodin was hard at work on a bust of Bernard Shaw, and Rilke was privileged to watch him during the first sittings, the remarkable 'compression of hours into minutes' in the rapid transformation of the clay rough into the profile seen from all angles.[35] Shaw, a conscientious model and immobile, seemed to concentrate his whole being in his face, 'so that trait after trait sprang across to the bust like a series of electrical discharges'.[36] Rilke, who had read *The Man of Destiny* in Trebitsch's translation, found the dramatist 'not unsympathetic',[37] and sent to Fischer, Shaw's publisher in German, for other works, not only because he thought of possibly writing something on him but also so that he could tell Rodin something about them, no French version being available. During a visit from William Rothenstein there was much talk of Gerhart Hauptmann, for whom Rothenstein had a great admiration, and Rilke was impelled to write to Hauptmann, about whom he had just had news from Lou, to urge him too to sit for Rodin. He attended the unveiling of *The Thinker* at the Panthéon on 21 April, sitting among the crowd with Mrs Shaw, Maillol, and Paula Modersohn—'at last a place for a work of Rodin's in his home city'.[38]

Among the many letters he had to write, was one to Baroness Amalie Nádherný von Borutin, to arrange her visit to Meudon with her daughter Sidonie. The family had their country seat at Janowitz, not far from Prague, and it was indirectly from Amalie's grandfather that Johann Joseph Rilke had bought the Kamenitz estate in 1806. His great-grandson was pleased now to act as guide for the ladies through Rodin's collection, and his letter to Sidonie after their visit was the beginning of a correspondence which lasted the rest of his life.

Towards the end of the month a certain unease set in at the Villa des Brillants. Rodin was unwell again, the house seemed suddenly full of visitors, interviewers, and art dealers waiting to see him, and Rilke found himself caught up in the confusion. A letter arrived just now from von der Heydt, offering him a lodging on his estate: but this chance of one or two years of quiet life for work seemed to him an impossible dream, and he could only refuse, rather wistfully, the generous gesture. 'If I might one day really live there, I would have Clara to share it, and little Ruth too from time to time. (How wonderful that would be for them!) But I'm only dreaming . . .'[39]

Within a few days, however, he was to be jolted into a harsher reality. Rodin took great exception to the way he had answered two letters without consulting him first: and in an outburst of irritation told the poet he could leave at once. Rilke felt his action had been quite in order—one answer had already been drafted as Rodin wanted, and he had merely added a postscript in reply to a subsequent letter from the same correspondent which he had felt not worth troubling the master with: the second was his own reply to a letter from Rothenstein addressed to himself as Rodin's friend rather than secretary. But he submitted at once without question to the decree, even though he was being dismissed as if he were 'a thieving servant'.[40] The circumstance was distasteful: but the event was in fact what he had been longing for, and needed. 'I am packing up and moving out of my little house,' he wrote to Clara on 10 May, 'out into the old freedom, with all its cares and all its possibilities . . . I am full of expectation, and light of heart. How it came about would not take many words, and I do not care to write them. It had to come, I suppose, and it came of itself.' He was arranging to take a room in the small hotel in the rue Cassette, where Paula was already installed—'no commitment, just from week to week'. There he would think over his future, 'be alone for a while with what is in me', and finish preparing the *Cornet* and the new *Book of Images*. 'Don't be anxious about the future, roads are there and we will surely find them . . .'[41]

2

'I am in work like the kernel in the fruit'

(To Manon zu Solms-Laubach, 3.8.1907)

It was almost a relief to be back in Paris. His room, only a few steps from the Luxembourg, was small, 'but not too small, not very airy, but not stifling', its furniture shabby but 'not obtrusive in its memories'; and above the wall opposite his window, and all around, 'Paris, the bright, the silken . . . Paris in May . . . I think on Malte Laurids Brigge, who would have loved all this as I do if he had survived the time of his great fear'.[1] His first act was to write to Rodin: explaining but not excusing, expressing his deep hurt at this dismissal after he had given so much of himself, but with comprehension for the higher law of the 'wise organism' of the master's life which made it reject anything which might appear harmful. 'I am convinced that there is no one of my age, in France or elsewhere, who is as gifted through temperament and work as I am to understand you, to understand your work and to admire it with such conscience.' His only regret was that Clara, innocent of any offence, should have to share his disgrace. 'I shall see you no more—but like the apostles left saddened and alone, for me too life begins, life which will celebrate your high example and find in you its consolation, its right and its strength. We were of the same mind: that in life there is an inherent justice which fulfils itself slowly but unerringly. In this justice I place all my hope: it will one day put right the wrong it pleased you to do to one who no longer has the chance or the right to show you his heart.'[2]

His first week he passed entirely idle, writing nothing, neglecting his correspondence even, content just to look and enjoy the relief of 'not being on call, of being alone'. Like the girls in their white confirmation dresses, he too felt himself at a turning-point, with all his life before him.[3] There was good news from Vienna: a grant of 600 crowns was to come to him, 'not a lot, but anyway something, and doubly welcome just now,' he wrote to Marie Herzfeld with his thanks for her aid. 'As you see, I have left Rodin to devote myself entirely to my own work . . . I might have held out a while longer, but I have to believe it is for the best.'[4]

Ellen Key was due in Paris shortly, and he told her how much he had longed to introduce her to Rodin, show her round the works and let her see his little house. 'Now it has turned out differently. But don't conclude that I have lost the admiration and love I always felt for him, my inner relationship to him is unchanged, but for the moment I can't give it any outward expression.'[5] Verhaeren would perhaps be able to take her to Rodin—Verhaeren whose verses accompanied him now on his walks through the Luxembourg Gardens, as he wrote to the Belgian poet, and whose *Rembrandt*, 'admirable in its strength and understanding', he had just read.[6]

Ellen's visit, despite his regard for her, was a disappointment. A lifetime of straitened circumstances had made her thrifty to the point of miserliness; and Rilke, devoting much of his time to her during her three weeks' stay, found himself reduced to 'quite unknown poverty', for she saw to it that for once he should live within his means. He was constrained to take her sightseeing at the Louvre or out to visit Verhaeren at Batignolles by unfamiliar omnibuses, eating almost furtively in cheap chain restaurants and watching her follow every franc as she spent it with the anxiety of a skittle-player his ball, 'expecting each throw to make nine'. He admired her for having made a happy life for herself out of joyless beginnings, but could not overlook the school-marmish limitations of her art appreciation, and the over-serious approach to life which had made her into a slightly ridiculous universal aunt, distributing sweets to all and sundry but unable to satisfy anyone's hunger. Stina Frisell, Lizzie Gibson's cousin, whom he had met in Gothenburg, chanced to be in Paris, and in her simple charm and loyalty was a striking contrast with Ellen, who seemed to him 'gnawed and eaten away by all these rat-like souls who hang on to her'. To give real aid to someone is a rare thing which cannot be made into a profession, he wrote to Clara telling her of his changed outlook towards Ellen: and only someone like her, looking so indirectly on the human condition, could fall with such conviction into the error. Somehow he had lost contact with her, the words spoken, however honestly, seemed to turn away and disappear before they arrived. And she was inattentive, her talk just a monologue which any attempt to join only disturbed.[7] When he saw her off on 17 June at Fontainebleau, it seemed symbolic that they waited on separate platforms for the trains that would take them in opposite directions. It was a strangely detached judgement on this 'old maid' who had done so much to help him, and after he had been not the least troublesome of those 'hanging on to her'.[8]

His objectivity reflected in fact the equilibrium he had achieved with his freedom. For, even while Ellen was taking up so much time, he was at last hard at work, putting the finishing touches to the *Cornet* and completing the composition of the new version of the *Book of Images* with a large number of additional poems. These tasks had to be out of the way before he could turn to the new road, to *Malte* and the *New Poems*. Sending both manuscripts to Juncker on 12 June, he looked forward to 'a winter of work' if his resources would stretch to it.[9] He was 'still a long way from Malte', he had told Clara in May:[10] but almost a flood of 'New Poems' now began—the fruit at last of the Rodin experience. He had found time for Paula Modersohn too, who had joined him and Ellen on a visit to Chantilly and started his portrait: but in June he broke off the sittings.

It was a Paris of joy for him now, no longer of terror. While with Rodin he had mingled with the cream of the artistic establishment: free, he could meet younger artists struggling to make their way—Mathilde Vollmoeller, a painter he had known from his early days in Berlin; Augustus John's sister Gwen, who had often posed for Rodin; Elisabeth Taubmann, another painter; the English-born Dora Herxheimer, a sculptress—and, still faithful to Rodin, bring them the master's message. Dora Herxheimer arranged a small gathering on 12 June at which he read them his Rodin lecture: a joy for him, he wrote her, 'one cannot give pleasure without finding it oneself, life takes care of that so justly'.[11] He would stay on for the time being, he told Clara, for his room, even in the hotter summer days, was so congenial and his diet so exactly what he needed—one vegetarian meal a day, at noon, fruit mornings and evenings, two glasses of milk at night, made an excellent regime, 'nourishing me as lightly and self-evidently as the sap the tree'. Later in the summer there could be invitations for them both, perhaps with Ruth, to stay with the von der Heydt families at Elberfeld and Godesberg, but for the moment, as he told Paula, he was 'in love with the regularity of my days'.[12] And through July the 'New Poems' continued to flow. Day followed day with the absorption of new impressions—in the galleries, or the Louvre, or looking at the 'Lady with the Unicorn' tapestries in the Cluny Museum; studying the animals in the Jardin des Plantes, for which he later obtained an 'autorisation d'artiste' for the non-public visiting hours—and learning not just to wait until 'the things in their power made something of one, but to forestall them'.[13] Dora Herxheimer recalled his pleasure of an evening in reading to her his work of the day, absorbed in the words, eyes closed like one in prayer. 'Prayer and work were one for him.'[14]

Under Clara's gentle pressure, however, he made plans to meet her in August somewhere near the sea—in Brittany, perhaps, where Mathilde Vollmoeller had already gone, or in Belgium, of which he had heard so much from Verhaeren. Karl von der Heydt was generous, not only in inviting them both to Godesberg for the last fortnight of August, but also in sending him funds to make the earlier journey possible. He settled finally for Belgium, and arranged to arrive in Furnes in time to see the traditional annual procession of the penitents on the last Sunday in July and the *kermesse* which followed it. Waiting there for Clara, he wrote to Dora Herxheimer that it was not exactly the quiet little town he had expected: rather as though he had been plunged into the midst of one of the pictures of the Flemish painter Teniers. 'I know now what they *sound* like!', with the unceasing tolling of the bells and the turmoil of the fair, the enormous town square 'quite filled with noise and booths, swings and the mad whirl of roundabouts, and a great press of people pushing to and fro amid the heat, in a smell of beer, honey-cakes, and dust, until far into the night'.[15]

Clara was looking forward to the break. Stoutly though she had maintained the same philosophy as her husband's; that her work, no less than his, demanded solitude—she longed in fact to be with him again; and it was her hope, as she wrote to Georg Brandes just before leaving, that somehow, somewhere it would be possible after these summer holidays for them to stay together. 'Worpswede is too remote from intellectual developments to make a permanent work-place, and as far as models are concerned I have exhausted its possibilities.'[16] For Rainer the reunion with his family was more duty than pleasure. In Oostduinkerke, which had seemed the quietest among the resorts he reconnoitred before Clara and Ruth joined him at Furnes on 1 July, and where they spent ten days, it was somehow inhibiting to find himself alongside a child's existence, self-absorbed and seeming like 'the next life, almost denying ours in continually consuming it'. And the whole mood of a crowded seaside resort was repellent, with everything oriented towards idleness and time-wasting, 'not a trace of real life and experience and existence, as if one were the first in an impossible world'.[17]

It was a relief, in every sense, when they left for Bruges and Ghent, on their way to the von der Heydts at Godesberg. Bruges, in spite of the tourist throng, he found 'incomparably beautiful' with its churches and museums.[18] Ruth went everywhere with them, asking in the churches for a little prayer stool and finding it quite natural to kneel quietly, or playing on the floor with her shells in the museums while they looked at the pictures. And there was an unexpected encounter: as they walked up the nave of the cathedral, Rainer whispered, 'There's Rodin'. The master was visibly pleased to see them, drew Ruth to him and kissed her on the brow. 'You have the most beautiful model there you can imagine,' he said to Clara, 'a model for an angel.'[19] It was a brief meeting, but gave hope of reconciliation.

Uncertainty for the future hung over the rest of their summer. Although Friedelhausen stood once more open to them in September, at the invitation of Alice Faehndrich, they could not yet see further than that. For all the generosity of their hosts there, and during August in Godesberg, the comfort of such patrician houses and the new impressions he gained from Belgium and Hesse, Rilke felt later that he had been ill advised to let himself be diverted from the routine of work which had begun to prosper in Paris. And, lacking as he was in any sense of economy, their journeyings cost more than was prudent. Greatly though he longed to return to Paris, that now seemed financially impossible. Of two things he was certain. He needed to be alone to find his work again—there was no question of re-creating somewhere the conditions he and Clara had known in Rome; and it must be anywhere but in Germany. Clara had no option but to fall in with this, and while they were at Friedelhausen they considered a number of different possibilities. As always, he hesitated long—his friends had indeed to be patient with him—but the hesitation no longer sprang from inner uncertainty: he knew now, after Paris, that once he could find the right conditions the work would come.

They lingered on at Friedelhausen, enjoying a boat trip on the Lahn, or a visit to Marburg, where Rilke was particularly impressed by the fifteenth-century tapestry in the Elisabeth Church depicting with 'such convincing expression' the parable of the Prodigal Son.[20] Ruth played for hours among the treasures of the family doll collection, and was delighted with the doll in Hessian costume which Alice Faehndrich gave her. By the middle of the month a decision had been reached at least for Clara: she would try her luck in Berlin as a work-place, while he was thinking of Greece for himself, he told von der Heydt. This was in fact more than a passing idea, for he wrote asking for details of climate and cost to the dramatist Ernst Hardt,[21] who knew Greece well and, according to Mathilde Vollmoeller, was planning to spend the winter in Athens. The solution came of itself, with the welcome suggestion from Alice Faehndrich that he should join her at her villa in Capri for the winter months. She could offer him a separate cottage at the end of the garden, where he would find all the quiet he needed. He still toyed for a while with the notion of Greece first, where he thought he might prepare a second volume for the *Rodin* book, based on his lecture, before going on to Capri: but at least there was now an assured haven for the winter.

They left Friedelhausen on 3 October. Clara first took Ruth back to her grandmother at Oberneuland, and then went on to Berlin, while he went to Wiesbaden for a brief call on Princess Madeleine de Broglie, an admirer from Paris who was staying nearby and with whom he had kept in regular correspondence. On 5 October he joined Clara in Berlin, where with the help of their many friends, not least some of Ellen Key's, she was soon able to set up her studio, provisionally, in Halensee, with what promised to be good prospects both for commissions and for students. Staying on himself until the end of November, he had the chance of renewing old acquaintances, like the Fischers, and of making new ones, like the Swedish novelist Gustaf af Geijerstam or Ellen Key's young friend Eva Solmitz; and there was time for Ibsen evenings at the theatre, with the Duse in *Rosmersholm* and Moissi in *Ghosts*. The idea of personally presenting to the Duse a copy of his *White Princess*, which he had dedicated to her, had to be abandoned for lack of an introduction.

He was alarmed to be reminded once again of Ellen Key's essay when Samuel Fischer asked him for photographs to accompany it ('unfortunately not her masterpiece') in the planned German edition of her collected essays.[22] This prompted him—after having neglected her shamefully since their leave-taking in Fontainebleau—to write at last and once more plead with her not to place it in 'this very prominent and exposed position'. 'As it is based so largely on what I wrote in letters, for which there is so far no justification in my books, the essay outdistances me, so to speak, while at the same time fixing the development of my religious ideas at a stage from which they have in some respects moved on.' He asked her at least to defer publication until he had produced something which could speak for itself.[23] (He got his way, since the essay volume, in which it appeared with the subtitle 'A Seeker after God', was not in fact published by Fischer until 1911.) He tempered the annoyance his plea might cause by extending a warm invitation from Alice Faehndrich for her to visit them in Capri.

In Berlin too he was able to see Axel Juncker. In their, for him, too sparse correspondence during the summer about the forthcoming new editions, he had been highly critical over the way the choice of typeface had turned out, finding it far too big and spread out, giving a page which looked like the text of an eye test card. Both *Cornet* and *Book of Images* were slow in preparation, and in spite of his pressure Juncker could not send him copies until Christmas, in Capri. But it was heartening meanwhile to find the Insel Verlag taking increasing interest in his future works. The *Book of Hours*, which was selling well, had been largely the concern there of Poeschel: but Anton Kippenberg, who had now assumed sole charge of the firm, began to make it his personal affair to deal with the poet who, as he correctly estimated, would prove a valuable asset. Rilke set right his misapprehension that Juncker was publishing something new, and made clear that it was his firm intention to entrust to the Insel every new work he should complete. 'At the moment there is a great deal forming and growing, but the beginning of next year is the earliest I expect to have a completed work ready for the press.' He added, to avoid any further misunderstanding, that in the mean time the only thing destined for other hands would probably be the second volume of the *Rodin*.[24] Kippenberg wrote at once to express his satisfaction that nothing stood in the way of their future collaboration; and the 1907 *Insel-Almanach*, issued during November, featured long extracts from the *Book of Hours* and reproduced Walter Tiemann's cover design of the threefold fountain.

Journeying south at last, Rilke arrived in Naples on 28 November 1906, and before crossing to Capri spent a few days there. In the terrace garden of the Hotel Hassler—his demands for accommodation were never modest, however short his funds—he found the scene refreshingly strange, 'so comfortingly unusual ... down to the cracking of the acorns under my feet in the little garden', and took delight in this feeling of truly foreign surroundings after the unwelcome familiarity of Berlin's 'insistent confusion'.[25] Opposite, in the distance, he could make out the contours of Capri. Taking a boat to Sorrento, he saw the island closer, its outline 'like a signature I have often read':[26] and finally made the crossing from Naples the day before his birthday — with some reluctance, as he confessed to Clara, at leaving behind a solitude he had not known since Paris. For him, hospitality, however good-willed, always seemed a threat to such solitude, for a minimum of social contact could not be avoided and he still longed for the anonymity of his room in the rue Cassette.

But he need not have worried. Alice Faehndrich, with perfect understanding, had arranged for him to occupy the tiny Rose Cottage at the end of the garden of her Villa Discopoli. He found it was not unlike his little house in Rome: a south-west-facing room in yellowish-white wash, with a vaulted ceiling, some simple dark-brown cupboards, blue-grey chairs, a divan and a writing-desk with all he needed. A standing-desk, which he always preferred, was immediately ordered to be made to his measurements. A separate little gate led through the wall at the side, and a path up a narrow garden terrace the thirty paces or so to the villa. Here he could be entirely to himself, as long as he wanted, joining the others in the evenings when he felt inclined. For the moment he was the only guest, but 'Frau Alla' was to be joined just before Christmas by her stepmother Julie von Nordeck ('Frau Nonna') and the young Countess Manon zu Solms-Laubach.

He still regretted Paris, he wrote to his mother — 'it had become for me like a school where I was making sensible progress, and not being able to go there is a kind of inhibition for me'.[27] And his first impressions of the island itself were far from favourable: it was 'a monstrosity', 'created from the misunderstandings of German admiration', an organized 'landscape exhibition', a 'concert of beauty in which everything is a programme item, rehearsed and designed and selected'.[28] Others in self-imposed exile there were the subject of somewhat disparaging comment. The German painter Diefenbach 'is now and then to be seen, grey in grey, the weathered grey of old wooden palings', 'everyone has become accustomed to his caprices, as they are becoming used to Gorki, who allows himself to be celebrated as an anarchist, but for the moment, agreeably enough, scatters money instead of bombs among the people'.[29] But as the days passed he grew more and more to appreciate the good fortune of his surroundings, and later he realized how they had somehow given him strength for years ahead.

Complete solitude, the total invisibility which he had 'carried around like a jewel' during the days in Naples, seemed once more his, 'like a kind of spiritual plaster-cast in which something is healing. . . . There is perhaps no profession as jealous as mine; the life of a monk, completely shut off, would not be for me, but I must still try myself to grow into a monastery, with walls around me and within me God and the saints, most beautiful pictures and equipment, quadrangles round which pillars dance, orchards, vineyards, and wells of unplumbed depths.'[30] It seemed to him he should emulate the aged Hokusai and take a new name to suit new work, beginning with it a 'new existence in which I have no friends, nothing but this work which is one with me, is my world and my home, beyond which all else fades into oblivion'.[31]

His preparation for it—in what had now become his habit—was a vastly extended correspondence, clearing his desk of long-unanswered letters and clarifying for himself his thoughts and hopes by pouring them out at length, not only to Clara and to friends such as von der Heydt or Dora Herxheimer, but also to those who heard from him more rarely—Leonid Pasternak, Hedwig Fischer, Sidie Nádherńy—or new acquaintances such as Countess Mary Gneisenau, or Geijerstam. This, far from being a waste of time, was for him the essential prelude to the distillation of experience in prose or lyric form. Some letters were of course of a more practical nature. With the approach of Christmas, he pressed Juncker to hasten his copies of the new *Cornet* and *Book of Images*, and ordered from Kippenberg more of the *Book of Hours*; and he did not omit, somewhat belatedly, to thank Ernst Hardt for his detailed suggestions on Greece, explaining how the wind had now changed and carried him elsewhere. But most sprang from the imperative need to leave none of those who were part of the circle of his life uninformed on how he hoped to justify their faith in him and fulfil his own expectations. And none seems to have been forgotten, not even his cousins in Prague, or the Gibsons, who had not heard from him for nearly a year. As he said himself, part of the productivity of his nature lay in his letters: and their flow always came in spate at times like the present, when he felt himself on the verge of creativity and wanted the decks cleared for action.

For Lou in particular there was a longish gap in their contact to be made good. He brought her summarily up to date, the calm tone again in great contrast to his earlier anguished cries for help: told her how he planned now to 'hold out and work . . . (though I've still not yet reached that point) until the next wave carries me back to Paris, which is definitely the place for me for another stretch'.[32] Thinking her in Göttingen, he was surprised to learn from Clara that she was in Berlin and had called on her. He was possibly even more surprised to hear that in their talks Lou, of all people, had been highly critical of what she saw as his selfish neglect of wife and child. Such reproaches, he told Clara when she relayed all this, he had many times made to himself. He wanted to respond to all the calls of life, without exception:

But at the same time I am determined not to abandon my post, exposed and often irresponsible as it is, determined not to exchange it for a more understandable position of resignation, before the final, the ultimate, the decisive voice has spoken to me . . . If I were to acquiesce, prematurely, in that which seeks, as 'duty', to overcome me and make me serviceable, I might well eliminate from my life some insecurity and avoid the impression of constant evasion: but I feel that, if I did so, I would also shut out the aid of the great and wonderful powers that take hold of me in almost rhythmic succession.

... Lou says one has no right to choose between duties and avoid those which lie nearest and are natural: but what I have now has always, since my boyhood, represented my nearest and natural duty —

a higher responsibility he had never shirked and for which he had taken the harder, lonely path. Though he and Clara were no longer together, living many days' journey apart and trying to do what their heart commanded, was there not in fact a real house around them, invisible only to the outside world? 'As I hold out, up there where I have spent most of my maturer years, am I not in the true, the arduous, am I not submitting to "duties"?'[33]

He had not forgotten their first Christmas together, and writing to her again two days later tenderly recalled their Westerwede home, the hall 'so large and shadowy right up to the tall radiant tree', seeing again how she stepped up to it, with the uncertainty of a young girl, 'the tiny head held against your lovely face towards the light which neither of you could see, for each of you was so full of her own life and that of the other'.[34] But the sentiment was firmly put behind him. 'My family is not a home, and is not to be one,' as he wrote later to Geijerstam: 'even Ruth is already a world to herself, a solitary little world.' For him there could be no 'home' in the accepted sense: 'thus it is ordained, it is part of my destiny, and I must create something good out of it.'[35] His long letter to Clara was a clear confession of the faith in which he lived his whole life — and which he could have expected Lou, 'the first to help me to my work',[36] to be the readiest to understand. Only later did he come to realize that Clara, who had seemed so whole-heartedly of the same exalted view, was not in fact capable of sustaining such ruthless dedication.

For the present, however, she certainly shared his outlook. Even without a husband, her own action in leaving Ruth once more with her grandmother while she went her way in Berlin was no less open to condemnation by the conventional. And, with the same belief as his in the overriding importance of her art, she was equally ready to accept, as of right, the aid and hospitality of friends or patrons. Thus now she planned to travel, in January, to Egypt, at the invitation of her close friend May Knoop, who with her husband ran the 200-room Al Hayat Hotel and its attached sanatorium in Helwan over the winter months. Her ship would leave from Naples, and it was arranged that Rainer would bring her over to Capri for a brief visit before seeing her off.

That he could, as so often before, 'build a Christmas' for his friends by sending or giving them his books was a particular pleasure. Juncker's packet arrived on 23 December, and he found both books a satisfactory outcome to their efforts. The *Book of Images* especially was a great improvement on the first edition, 'in content a new and highly characteristic unity, a truly new book and I may say, without making too high a claim, one that is justified'.[37] In the December days, as the backlog of correspondence dwindled, a few poems had started to come to him, and some made dedications for the copies of his books for the Capri friends:

> Who can have lived his life in solitude
> and not have marvelled how the angels there
> will visit him at times and let him share
> what can't be given to the multitude . . .[38]

With some of these 'Improvisations in a Capri Winter', as he later called them, he felt that 'something like a new Book of Hours was starting':[39]

> Daily before my heart you uptower
> mountain, stone,
> wilderness, waylessness: God, in whom I alone
> climb and fall and stray . . . daily back to my own
> yesterday's traverse by ways unknown
> circulating.[40]

But they could not be placed with the 'New Poems', and remained unpublished.

After listening in the Piazza to the strokes of midnight on New Year's Eve, the moon, just past the full and still high, creating 'a world of moonlight and moon shadows', he returned to stand on the roof of his little house 'to find a good beginning in myself': to believe in 'a long year granted to us, new, untouched, full of things that have never been and work never yet done'.[41] 'I must hold myself back from letter-writing,' he told Eva Solmitz in Berlin: 'my task from now on must be to take what would have gone into letters to my friends and weave it into contexts of more permanence, so that it may one day come to them from me in another form, less recognized yet more candid.'[42] And through January and February he began: more 'Improvisations', some in prose form, after Clara's visit, on the museum and the fish-market in Naples, the Certosa and the road down through the vineyards to the Piccola Marina in Capri; but, above all, poems which continued the flow begun in Paris — 'The Rose Bowl', 'Alcestis', 'Song of the Sea', and on 24 January, the anniversary of Luise von Schwerin's passing, the verses entitled 'Death Experienced' which he transcribed for her sister.[43] Kippenberg sent him good news: the first edition of the *Book of Hours* had sold out, in a little more than a year, bringing him some 300 marks, and a second printing, this time of 1100, was in preparation. It was a success he had never known for any of his earlier books — and not least welcome in that the money due to him was paid at once: and it was highly encouraging for his future with the Insel Verlag. Kippenberg indeed was already looking forward to his next work, and he undertook to try to have the verse collection ready during the summer, though his prose (the *Malte*) was progressing much more slowly.

Following Clara's progress from afar, he tried to picture what the Nile would be like. Its course on the atlas climbed up 'like a Rodin contour, containing a wealth of transmuted movement', its deviations and twists looking to him like a human coronal suture. For the first time he could feel the reality of a river, its essence, 'on the verge of personification', 'as if it had a destiny, a dark birth and a great, extensive death, and between the two a life, a long, enormous, princely life . . .' And then the contrast of the desert, 'without end and without beginning', and the head of the Sphinx, 'as if the universe had a countenance, and this countenance projected images out beyond, right out to the outermost stars, where no images had ever been . . . Tell me . . . is it not like that? I feel it must be so, infinite space, space which extends beyond the stars, must have grown round this figure.' His eyes would be in hers as she saw all this.[44]

He looked forward eagerly to her detailed letters and shared them with his 'three ladies'. But he urged her above all to concentrate on absorbing impressions, even the most fleeting, even the apparently unimportant. 'Looking is such a marvellous thing, of which we know little; as we look, we are directed wholly outside ourselves—but, even when we are at our most outward, things seem to happen within us which have been waiting longingly for the moment when they should be unobserved, and while they take their course, intact and strangely anonymous, their significance grows in the object outside, a more convincing, more powerful name, their only possible name, in which we happily and reverently recognize the happenings within us.' Such experience through observation signified for him the very root of all art—for the painter and sculptor, but no less, as he had tried to learn from Rodin, for the poet. Clara must 'look, look, look,' note and sketch on the instant of impression rather than save it for considered narrative in her letters, and accumulate as much material as possible in this way so that on her return they could 'shake it all out'.[45] The vicarious experience of Egypt he gained through Clara made a remarkable foundation on which to build when he went there himself later.

His resolve to cut back on his own letter-writing proved hard to maintain. Capri was the goal or staging-post for friends, who naturally sought his advice and help: Geijerstam, seeking a warmer work-place than Sweden; Siegfried Trebitsch, on his way through Naples to Tunis and eager at least to see him again if not to take him along; Ellen Key, of course, planning to take up Alice Faehndrich's invitation and call at Capri on her return journey from Sicily. Others more distant could not be neglected. To Gudrun Uexküll, who had written in gratitude for his dedication to her of the *Cornet*, he not only wrote at length but added a charming postscript to the *Tales of God* for her little daughter Damajanti; to Stefan Zweig he sent a delicately expressed appreciation of his verse volume *Early Garlands* (*Die frühen Kränze*), comparing its unevenness with that of his own beginnings, and his thanks for an invitation Zweig had arranged for a reading evening in Vienna later in the year. Lizzie Gibson received an introduction to his doctor at the Weisser Hirsch in Dresden, where she sought treatment for young Bertil. All this could not be a distraction from the work he had hoped for. Although his tactful stress the drawbacks to Capri life succeeded in turning Geijerstam back from Rome, Trebitsch had to be seen and dined; and Ellen Key's visit over a few days in March, even though she did not stay at the Villa Discopoli, was something of a trial (his three ladies were no little surprised, he told Clara, to find the much-heralded New Age breaking in on them in the shape of such an old maid[46]).

Lucky the man who could be alone, he had sighed in a letter to Ellen in Syracuse.[47] For life in his Rose Cottage was itself not all he had dreamed of. The stillness of approaching evening, as he stood at his door, a stillness 'made of nothing but tiny sounds, beginnings of verses from little bird-songs', reminded him of the Villa Strohl-Fern in Rome, and he had the feeling that he had progressed, matured, since then. There were experiences he would not have missed: long walks with the charming Manon zu Solms, exploring Anacapri, climbing Monte Solaro, or visiting Migliera and the little church of Santa Maria a Cetrella, revealed a countryside like Greece itself—'without the works of art of the Greek world but almost like the time which went before them'.[48] Of an evening the ladies offered an appreciative audience, as they sat over their needlework or peeled him an apple, ready to hear his work of the day, to join in reading aloud from Ibsen, Hesse, or Geijerstam, or to share with him Clara's letters from Egypt. 'Our little circle is the most delightful imaginable,' he told Ellen, 'but for me it is so fearfully hard to combine real work with sociability, no matter how pleasant the company ... With people ... I am so easily tempted to talk and to give out from myself all kinds of things which I then lack for my work.' He was achieving a certain amount, 'some of it good', he reported to the von der Heydts. 'But I have once more laid in such a vast store of longing for complete solitude, the complete solitude of Paris.'[49] By March he was already planning his return there, and asking Paula Modersohn and Dora Herxheimer to look out for suitable quarters for him—a studio this time, with furniture, 'to settle down seriously to all the work that is to be done ... in the vast solitude I long for'.[50] Only there could his undertaking to Kippenberg to have the verse volume ready for Christmas publication be met, and only there his ideas for the *Malte* book crystallize: in the city which made such immense demands on the artist, which was in itself a labour, but to which he owed the best he had yet achieved.

In Capri meanwhile, both in fact made progress, and even the distractions of social intercourse were sometimes positive. With the aid of Alice Faehndrich, who was the daughter of an English mother, he continued an attempt, begun earlier in Paris with Dora Herxheimer,[51] at translating Elizabeth Barrett Browning's *Sonnets from the Portuguese*, and completed the whole cycle during March and April. He conceded that, as translations, his versions were very far from perfect, but considered that as poems in their own right these 'very personal renderings' deserved a place with his own work,[52] and he found ready acceptance with Kippenberg for their publication. During this time too he thought much on a theme which would permeate *Malte* and run like a

Rilke in Adiek an der Oste,
18 Sept. 1900

Rilke and Clara with her
parents and Phia Rilke
after the wedding, April
1901

Mimi Romanelli

Princess Marie von Thurn und Taxis
as a young woman

Anna de Noailles

Marthe Hennebert

thread through later work—the nature of love between man and woman, the ability of some exceptional women to rise above humiliation and betrayal by their lovers, the ideal of 'love without possession'. The case of the seventeenth-century Marianna Alcoforado, who had entered a nunnery after her lover Count Chamilly had deserted her, had occupied him since reading the Insel publication a year or two earlier of her letters. Though the nun had certainly existed, the expression of her passion in letters was actually a work of fiction: but Rilke refused to believe this, for they represented for him a perfect example of the love which finds its true fulfilment only in abnegation. He wrote a short notice of the book for Kippenberg, as a contribution to the forthcoming *Insel Almanach* for 1908, and also sent him three of the 'New Poems', written earlier—'The Merry-Go-Round', 'Abisag', 'The Panther'.

Clara's ship was due in Naples on 19 April, and he planned to bring her over for a while to Capri, before beginning the journey north, in May, on their separate roads to Berlin and Paris. In the weeks before her arrival the social obligations began to increase, as the Discopoli house party grew. Rilke paid a visit to Gorki, who impressed him as a man, and in his appreciation for Verhaeren and Hofmannsthal, but whose revolutionary spirit seemed to him quite inappropriate in a Russian and an artist: for both, 'nothing is so important as patience, nothing so natural for the one as for the other'.[53] He gained much more from Axel Munthe when he called at San Michele a few days later, finding in him great wisdom about life and a nature of 'strangely sympathetic goodness', surrounded with beautiful works of art but making of them a real home and not a museum.[54]

Though holding fast to the idea of following his path alone in Paris, he was concerned about Clara's future. In a letter to Geijerstam he explored the possibility of her coming with Ruth to them during the summer—which she could only do, he stressed, if she could find commissions there. The proposition brought a warm invitation from Geijerstam, who said he would be delighted to have Clara stay at their summer home and model him: but in the event it proved out of the question.[55] Clara landed in Naples exhausted, having overstretched herself in the heat of Helwan: and it was a cruel disappointment when a study of a group of African gazelles she had completed there, on a commission from London friends of the Knoops, was ruined by an incompetent workman making the cast in Naples. It would have to be redone in Berlin, and other work still awaited her there. To recover she stayed on in Capri with Rainer until 16 May, and they then spent a further ten days in Naples, where Alice Faehndrich and Manon zu Solms joined them for a while. By the end of the month she was back in Berlin, and Rainer in Paris.

He spent the first few days in an hotel. The so-called 'furnished' studios Dora Herxheimer had looked at for him proved unappealing, and requiring too big an outlay if he was really to install himself as he wanted. There seemed no alternative to a return once more to the rue Cassette, depressing though such rooms were in their 'emphasized homelessness'.[56] After some haggling to get the price reduced, he was able to move on 6 June 1907 to one on the second floor, above that which Paula had just vacated. His standing-desk arrived, the hydrangea Dora had tended in his absence was in promising bud: the longed for solitude was once more his. Friends were there if he wanted them—Tora Holmström, Madeleine de Broglie, Mathilde Vollmoeller, Dora—but it was splendid to be left in peace. In the vegetarian restaurant, or the creamery where he took his evening milk, it was as though he had never been away.

In these first few days he followed his earlier advice to Tora Holmström, as she came to Paris for the first time: taking the city 'like a bath, without making too much effort oneself, beyond feeling it and letting it take its course'.[52] But the acclimatization was not easy. 'The Paris I marvel at so much, which I know I must go through as one goes through a school . . . just as one begins to feel its greatness, its boundlessness almost, chooses that moment to show its ruthless side, reducing one so completely to nothing that one has to start the attempt to live all over again.' The fear the city once instilled in him was still there, he wrote to Clara, it was still 'the Paris that devoured Malte Laurids'. In his room at night there came an incessant sound from his neighbour's as of some tin lid thrown down again and again and rolling across the floor: the noise seemed to gnaw at him, for he could feel instinctively the suffering and despair which underlay the senseless act, the rhythm in the madness, even before he discovered its cause. The student in the next room, whose long-prepared examination was approaching, had been afflicted with a lazy eyelid which needed an operation to make it open at all, and was in an agony of restlessness.

'His mother came when he was at his worst,' Rainer wrote to Clara. 'Just to hear her step outside, ah, she had no idea how much support that step gave me. . . . You could hear it: a mother had a sick son—hear it, as plain as if you saw it pictured in relief in ten episodes . . .' The torment would be added to the others suffered by Malte Laurids Brigge as the notebooks took shape. To Arthur Holitscher, who had criticized the 'verse-infected' prose style of the *Cornet*, he recalled that it dated from 1898: 'what I am working on now looks very different.'[58]

First priority however was to complete the manuscript of the verse volume for Kippenberg. By the end of June he was able to report it was more or less ready, but kept it by him a while longer, and continued in July to add to it. He favoured simply 'Poems' for the title, being less and less inclined to invent fanciful names for his volumes. After Clara had seen the manuscript (for he valued her opinion) it reached the publisher early in August. Rilke was pleased with his final suggestion of 'New Poems' as the title, for this conveyed the change the book represented, his lesson from Rodin. They agreed on a larger format than that of the *Book of Hours*, in an entirely plain cover but with poem titles in green. He could, he told Kippenberg, already look forward to a second volume, for during the following months he was truly 'in work' once more.

These were indeed 'new' poems, compared to the *Book of Hours* or the *Book of Images*: created in the spirit of Rodin, they were no longer the direct expression of inner mood, but its reflection in 'things' observed, in the way he had urged on Clara in Egypt, which became a symbol, a 'more convincing, more powerful name', for the 'happening' within the poet's soul. Apart from 'The Panther', the best known is probably 'The Merry-Go-Round' ('Das Karussell'), inspired by the roundabout for small children he had often seen in the Luxembourg Gardens—a marvellous evocation of the simple world of childhood with its make-believe soon to be ended in the dawn of sexual awareness:

> Complete with roof and shadow it rotates
> a little while, bearing its gallant band
> of gaily coloured horses from the land
> that lingers long, ere it capitulates.
> Though yoked to carriages some of them pant,
> they one and all have courage in their faces;
> with them a lion, red and savage, paces,
> and now and then, all white, an elephant.
>
> Even a stag, as in the forest, too,
> but with a saddle, solemnly advances,
> strapped on its back a litle girl in blue.
>
> And on the fearful lion, grasping tight
> its teeth and lolling tongue with tiny hand,
> intrepid rides a little boy in white.
>
> And now and then, all white, an elephant.
>
> And as the horses gallop by, it chances
> a girl, too big almost for such pretending,
> out of the cavalcade, with charm unending,
> lets stray this way one of her random glances—
>
> And now and then, all white, an elephant.
>
> And it pursues its purposeless careering,
> revolving only, eager to be done,
> a red, a green, a grey receding, nearing,
> a little profile, hardly yet begun.
> And sometimes, this way turned, a smile appearing,
> a blissful smile, too dazzling, too endearing
> to waste on breathless make-believe and fun.[59]

Many others were the fruit of such observation—the gazelle or the flamingos seen in the Jardin des Plantes, the Paris parks, a rose-window, a beggar, islands remembered from the North Sea; many too of observation once removed, so to say—Christ pictured in the garden of Gethsemane, in the same

despair of abandonment as in the earlier 'Visions'; the departure of the
Prodigal Son, recalling Rilke's own feelings as he left Prague; classical and
other biblical themes seen in a new light. But all were characterized by his
endeavour to follow Rodin in forming a 'thing of art' more definite than its
model, lifting it 'up out of time' and giving it to space to make it 'capable of
eternity'.[60] How he saw this endeavour was well expressed in a letter to Clara,
written as he was putting the final touches to the first volume:

Works of art are always the result of having been at risk, of having pursued an
experience to the very end, beyond which no one can go. And the further on this road,
the more personal, the more unique does this experience become, till in the end the
work of art is the necessary, the insuppressible, the most final expression possible of
this uniqueness . . . This is the secret of the immense aid given by the work of art to
him who must create it—that it is his summation, the bead on the rosary at which his
life speaks a prayer, the ever-recurring proof given to him of his unity and verity . . .[61]

He was thankful that, in spite of the difficult first days back, his resolution
had not faltered. Telling Clara early in July that he had refused May Knoop's
invitation to visit England, he said that, although he felt somehow oppressed
by Paris, and every carriage he saw on its way to the station stirred a certain
emotion, he was nevertheless firmly convinced that this solitude was absolutely
essential for him, after 'talking the whole winter'.[62] For weeks now, through
July and into August, he exchanged scarcely a word with another, as work-day
followed work-day, 'unreeling in monotonous regularity'. He stuck to his last,
making 'now and then a little silent progress at my standing-desk, from which
I haven't moved all week', in a kind of 'health regime of work'.[63] 'I feel how
good for me it was, having to stand and write day after day,' he told Dora
Herxheimer on 14 July with the *New Poems* and the *Rodin* in book form
completed. 'Writing is after all my handicraft, and one must love not only the
work itself, the splendid intellectual work, but also the manual labour that goes
with it, in all its hidden and unrewarded tediousness.'[64] Even an invitation to
join Karl von der Heydt in Reims, and later to revisit Bad Godesberg, was
refused—the 'smallest break' in his 'continuous path of days' would 'make
fragments of the rest (and such fragmentation is the greatest danger for me)'.[65]
But he was glad to see his friend when he passed through Paris, and resolved to
dedicate the *New Poems* to him.

Prompted by Stefan Zweig's earlier suggestion of a reading evening in
Vienna, and encouraged by Hofmannsthal, who assured him that an appreciative audience awaited him there, he planned for November another tour, this
time mainly for readings from his own work. What would follow was still
uncertain: though loth to move from Paris, he lacked the courage for a winter
there, fearing a recurrence of his previous malaise, and began to toy with the
idea of a return, in spite of all he had said, to Capri when he heard that Alice

Faehndrich and Julie von Nordeck were counting on him. For the time being, as usual, he let the future take care of itself.

The present was meanwhile productive indeed. In August alone he completed no fewer than forty further 'new poems'—well over a third of the eventual second volume—and there was progress too with *Malte*, as the fifth anniversary of his first arrival in the rue Toullier came round, with all its memories of the dismaying impact of this city of hospitals and festering, anonymous poverty. In spite of the achievements of the summer, however, something of the old despair crept over him, the feeling that, unlike Rodin, or Van Gogh, he was still far from his ideal of being 'always in work'. He found, suddenly, the 'right eyes' for Cézanne's work in the Salon d'automne, precisely because he now knew the monomaniacal dedication that lay behind them, the furious devotion of a man who would not abandon his daily stint 'sur le motif' even for his mother's funeral, 'making his "saints"' out of his winebottles and apples 'and forcing them, *forcing* them to be beautiful, to mean the whole world'.[66] Under the spell of the Salon, with repeated visits, he wrote a series of long letters to Clara which in themselves, though unshaped, form a monograph on Cézanne comparable with that on Rodin.

It was Clara who put into words for him what he had instinctively recognized without at first realizing it—that here was a turning-point in painting which paralleled that he had just reached, or at least approached, in his own work, with the *New Poems*. For that reason, he told her, he must resist the temptation to write on Cézanne—no one viewing paintings from such a 'private standpoint' was justified in writing about them—but he knew that 'this unexpected encounter' had become a part of his life.[67]

3

'Je suis descendu dans mon travail plus loin que jamais'

At the end of October 1907, when the time came for his tour, he still had no certain idea of where he would go afterwards. Clara was now back with her mother and Ruth in Oberneuland, the few commissions she had obtained having been insufficient to maintain the Berlin studio. During the summer she had still hoped to be able to go to Sweden: and he had asked the Gibsons to secure for her a post teaching drawing at the Samskola, which would have given her a measure of security and made it possible for her mother to join her and for Ruth to enter the school they so much admired. He pressed this plan even in the face of Ellen Key's vigorous arguments against it; Gothenburg's winter climate was unfavourable, and the Samskola itself no longer the same, she considered. But Jimmy's application to the Director was unsuccessful, and for Clara a firm base of her own had to remain for the time being a dream. Rainer therefore could not well avoid another visit some time to Oberneuland, perhaps over Christmas. He was inclined after that to accept the Capri invitation: without any illusions over what it would mean in loss of solitude, he told Clara, but determined to get something done in the Rose Cottage before being drawn into the 'long conversations' of the Villa Discopoli.[1] And he would return earlier this time to Paris, for another summer of work.

His tour was to take him first to Prague, then to Breslau, and finally to Vienna. Even the most modest way of life in Paris had left him virtually without resources; an honorarium for an extract from his Rodin volume, on which he had been counting, turned out to be only half what he had expected. After Prague, howeve, the cost of the tour would be more or less assured, and he might be able to revisit Venice after it was finished. 'Never have I felt so clearly how contrary to our nature it is to think beyond the present,' he had written during October:[2] he would rely on something turning up in the fullness of time, and further invitations would surely not be lacking—Sidie Nádherný was already looking forward to welcoming him as Schloss Janowitz while he was in Prague. His things in the rue Cassette were packed and stored, Mathilde Vollmoeller taking care of his desk and books; and before leaving he was able to send off to Kippenberg the corrected proofs of the *New Poems*, with a few final revisions to the selection.

As he arrived in Prague on 1 November, the sight of the 'stubborn old city' of his childhood was immeasurably depressing. The buildings, once so overpowering in their great bulk, still seemed even now, reduced to normal, to weigh him down, with a presence he could not comprehend. 'My aversion was never so great as on this visit (probably because I have developed so much my disposition to see and take everything in relation to my work).'[3] With his mother he experienced the same guilty sense of his own unfairness towards her: but he felt that her idea of him was so completely false, that he would never be able to bring to her even the smallest part of what was real to him. She seemed like a doll's house whose painted doors and windows could never be opened and entered. On All Souls he contrived to visit his father's grave without her, its inscription now weathered into the stone 'as if it had stood in an old park undisturbed for a century'. His mother and all the old acquaintances fussed about him, 'all wanted to have me as if I were something to eat— but when they got me, I found they weren't hungry, as if they were on a diet'.[4]

But there were some rays of light, before his appearance in the Concordia Society on 3 November: the visit to Janowitz to take tea with Sidie Nádherný and her brothers, and, most gratifying of all, a letter from Rodin. Dictated to the new secretary, it was no more than a polite enquiry about the reliability of Hugo Heller, whose bookshop in Vienna was proposed for an exhibition of some of Rodin's drawings, and where Rilke himself was shortly to read: but it also mentioned that Rodin had had translated the extract just published from Rilke's lecture volume. He was delighted to find the ice thus broken; and replied at once, equally factually but expressing his joy at being permitted to resume contact and his enthusiasm for such an exhibition in Vienna, for which he confirmed no finer venue could be found than Heller's.

The audience for his reading was admiring but unresponsive: the same old ladies, the same handful of self-satisfied literati. He gave them some poems from the *Book of Images*, an extract from his draft of *Malte* and a few of the *New Poems*, but with the exception of 'The Merry-Go-Round' his words fell like stones. He felt it an inauspicious start. But there was encouragement afterwards from August Sauer and his wife, and from Rosa Schobloch, an industrialist's wife, who apparently expressed her admiration in more concrete form. 'My road is long, and leads far,' he wrote to her in gratitude from Breslau: 'and I know how to appreciate every aid which makes it possible for me. Many think the development of a poet can be a secondary thing, alongside some normal career; but the further I go the more I discover what enormous effort this art demands, how even an undivided, concentrated strength directed solely to this one aim often seems inadequate . . .'[5] The performance in Breslau went better than he had expected, making up for Prague, with a large audience who wanted, and he felt got, their money's worth. 'They sat still, coughed at sensible intervals, and behaved as the better among them had learned.'[6]

The real success of the tour was reserved for Vienna, where he arrived on 7 November. Two evenings had been arranged, one at Heller's for readings from his own work, on 8 November, and the second elsewhere a few days later for the Rodin lecture. As Hofmannsthal had promised, he found here the audience he needed, and the music of the *New Poems* and some of the *Malte* prose, in a skilful *mise-en-scène* of darkened room and green-shaded lectern light, held them spellbound. The Viennese poet Felix Braun, ten years his junior and an enthusiast for the *Book of Hours*, long recalled the effect as this slim, youthful-looking, elegantly dressed man emerged from a side door, paused a moment, then threw back his head to break into a veritable song of verse.[7] It was the first time such an occasion had given him the feeling of true contact with those for whom his work was destined, especially those of the younger generation such as Felix Braun, or Herbert Steiner, still a schoolboy, who hurried forward with the throng to shake his hand. His hotel room that night he found full of flowers. In the days that followed he had the opportunity of making new friends—Rudolf Kassner, the cultural philosopher, Franz Servaes, the *feuilleton* editor of the *Neue Freie Presse*, and the actress Lia Rosen—and of seeing many with whom he already felt an affinity, in particular Richard Beer-Hofmann, the lyric poet and prose-writer whose work he had long admired, and of course Hofmannsthal, with whom he lunched at his house in Rodaun. Their natural and spontaneous welcome was an experience in itself. 'I felt as if I had been working for them, these last years, so much did they seem to need what I had to bring them.'[8]

Best of all was another letter from Rodin, written as if the unpleasantness had never been. It talked of his work and his ideas, praised the extract he had seen from Rilke's lecture, and at the end left him in no doubt that all was well again between them: 'come and see me when you are in Paris. . . . We have both of us a need for truth and for poetry, a need for friendship.'[9] The letter gave him new strength for the lecture on 13 November. Though it was well attended, and received with applause, he doubted whether he had succeeded in imbuing all his audience with his own enthusiasm for the Master. But it seemed to him a sign from fate that his words should coincide with the reconciliation he had longed for, with the publication of the lecture just now in Berlin in the second volume on Rodin, and with Heller's preparations for showing the drawings, on which he was able to advise—altogether one of those providential dispositions which he often thought to discern in his otherwise unplanned existence. 'I have an infinite need of you and your friendship,' he had replied to Rodin, 'and I am proud that I have advanced sufficiently in my work to be able to share your glorious and simple desire for truth.'[10]

The lionization in Vienna was exhausting to one so used to being alone. He decided that, before joining Clara in Oberneuland, he could afford a brief rest after all in Venice, where he had earlier been recommended a quiet pension run by the sisters of Pietro Romanelli, an art dealer in Paris. For ten days he was able to enjoy the stillness there, a 'vibrating stillness' like that in a glass cabinet, the city overlaid with the grey, cold pallor of autumn, 'pale as though from great excitement', 'magnificent but hard': not a Venice for beginners, and needing to be learned anew.[11] In one of the private palazzi, once the property of Doges, he marvelled at the play of the afternoon light on the Flanders tapestries and the enormous mirrors, the long galleries with tall pictures of 'violet cardinals, purple procurators, and stiff iron generals astride a sturdy high-stepping white horse'.[12] He told Clara of the Bellinis and Carpaccios he had seen, and the *Descent from the Cross*, Titian's last painting which had had to be finished by another hand: 'great, unforgettable, tragic . . . as if he too in his extremity had felt what was coming—and had snatched at what could still be grasped—such is the movement and colour . . .'[13]

The Romanelli sisters had known nothing of him when he arrived—indeed they had understood their guest was to be a woman. Adelmina (Mimi, as she was known), a beautiful and talented pianist, alone when he stepped from the gondola, was fascinated by the eyes of this stranger who seemed as though endowed with magical powers. The first evening he sat beside her after dinner and whispered: 'You must have so much to tell me, and I am sure that one day you will tell me it all.' He asked her for a photograph, saying that no sooner had he entered his room than he had kneeled before a Madonna on the wall and exclaimed: 'C'est elle, c'est Mimi que je devais rencontrer un jour.'[14] It was small wonder that she fell frankly in love with him, the three weeks of his stay passing for her like a dream; and it was hard for her to understand that when he spoke and wrote of love, in the ethereal style which ran so well in

French, his concept was of the most platonic. 'Belle et admirable,' he addressed her while still there, 'il est bien naturel que je vous aime . . . ce mot . . . je le prononce: de loin, parce que j'ai pris sur moi toute ma solitude; de près, parce que ceux que j'aime m'aident infiniment à la supporter.'[15] She knew he was married, and when he left sent with him presents for Clara and Ruth; but though she maintained later that their relationship had been a purely spiritual one, it is clear that at the time she hoped there might be a place for her in his life, however much he insisted that his work must come first.

How near he came to succumbing to the temptation was revealed in his letter to Sidie Nádherný a little later, in which he spoke of 'unexpected turns' in Venice which had led him to happiness and yet to a 'strangely real suffering'. These few days, he wrote, had come to represent the unity of a whole existence, 'which might have endured, but which (being human) was bounded and cut off by birth and death, and appears to me, as I look back, in a powerful, confusing foreshortening, like the action in a Michelangelo painting'.[16] Yet he could not resist adding Mimi to the list of the correspondents to whom he had to pour out his hopes and fears, his troubles and joys. Scarcely back with Clara again, early in December, he was expressing to his 'chère, infiniment chère' Mimi his dismay at this oppressive country and 'all this other life which is not mine', difficult and intimidating 'because it is not my work which holds me here'.[17] More letters followed: saying how happy he was, amid his depression, that he had had the privilege of just knowing her beauty existed; developing to her his idea that death is an integral part of life, to be prepared intensively as its crowning masterpiece; telling her to take solace in Verhaeren and the Bible. Such effusions could have been but cold comfort. Her need was for more than fine words, and it was hardly surprising that over the following year she came close to a breakdown. Her brother, seeking some sort of intervention from Rilke, found no help there: 'You overrate me . . . I am no support, I'm sorry to say,' he wrote him in January 1909, 'I'm only a voice. And this voice I must always devote to my work.'[18] Mimi Romanelli would not be the last to suffer from his inability to find in himself the complete ruthlessness, the utter dedication of the artist he had seen in Rodin and Cézanne. Time and time again he would reach out for a new relationship, only to find that it could never be reconciled with his work, and that he must remain alone.

The family was of course a stronger tie, but he chafed under it as the obligatory Christmas preparations got under way. Reading again the letters he had written to Clara about Cézanne, he even began to feel it had been a mistake to leave Paris for the lecture tour, and to regret the interruptions of Vienna and Venice. 'It is my old inadequacy: I have only a single energy, which cannot be dispersed.'[19] Yet he thought of accepting further lecture invitations, in Oldenburg and Hanover, before going back to Paris, or perhaps to Capri, later in the winter. And there was every reason for encouragement in the news from Kippenberg during December: the edition of the *New Poems*, which came out that month, would be even bigger than planned, in a first printing of 2000 copies, and the royalties from this and the earlier books, now reaching more substantial figures, came in promptly before the end of the year. To be able to send dedicated copies to his friends and colleagues was, as always, the best pleasure of the Christmas and New Year period: to Hofmannsthal, Lia Rosen, Richard Beer-Hofmann, Manon zu Solms, the Sauers in Prague, and, breaking a long silence, to Lou in Göttingen. Sidie Nádherný had sent a small Christmas tree, and a doll which delighted Ruth: he could write her charmingly of the joy from her gifts, but confessed he found it increasingly hard, as the years passed, to celebrate these 'outward festivals', 'so much do I long for all celebration to come from within'.[20]

Rodin of course received a copy of the *New Poems*. 'I hope people will see in them how much your Work and your example have impelled me on to definitive progress—for if one day I am counted among those who have worthily followed nature, it will be because I was whole-heartedly your faithful and determined pupil.'[21] A copy went to Emile Verhaeren too, in 'friendship and admiration', and asking for some lines in his hand to forward to the Belgian poet's equally fervent admirer Hofmannsthal. Away from Paris, he told him, he felt as though exiled from the solitude so dear to him.[22]

Much as he longed to return there, the memory of his previous experience of its winter chill and damp was enough to make him finally decide for Capri again. Meanwhile the proofs for the translations of the *Sonnets from the Portuguese* were sent off and the contract for the book agreed. Finally, on 19 February 1908, he started on the first stage of his journey—to Berlin. Samuel and Hedwig Fischer had written warmly about the *New Poems*, and the publisher had suggested further contributions from Rilke for his *Neue Rundschau* (he had himself no particular appreciation for lyric poetry, but his commercial instinct was no less acute than Kippenberg's, and he had besides a genuine sense of his responsibility to help struggling writers of talent). Rilke had not offered him any early prospect of this, pleading his slow production and the need first to complete the second volume of *New Poems*; but the idea made great appeal, for it would not cut across his undertakings to Kippenberg, and he was glad of the opportunity of talking it over personally with Fischer.

A cordial welcome awaited him during his few days in Berlin. Hedwig Fischer in particular had gradually learned to appreciate the genius of the modest poet Lou Andreas-Salomé had brought to her house ten years earlier. And in Samuel he found perfect understanding for his position and his commitment to the Insel: not only was he content to accept whatever individual poems or prose pieces Rilke felt could appear in his journal, he was even prepared to consider, as a quite separate issue, some sort of financial assistance for him. Immediately on arrival in Capri, on 29 February, Rilke wrote his thanks and his hope that this would make possible for him 'a quiet year of work in Paris'.[23] For his situation, still very much hand-to-mouth, had been giving him increasing concern while he was at Oberneuland, not least because of his responsibility for making provision for Clara and for Ruth, whose education, now that she had turned six, was becoming a pressing problem for her rootless parents. Fischer's offer was generous, but at best could be only a temporary palliative. He needed, if not long-term security, at least some assurance that the coming few years could be spent in the work he knew he was ready for, without having to rely on intermittent hospitality from friends. At the Villa Discopoli, even though he once more had the Rose Cottage to himself, he resolved to make his stay much shorter than before, devoting most of his time to correspondence, and much of that in the search for a solution to his problem.

His journey through Germany had in fact originally been intended as an effort in this direction, but, apart from the meeting with Fischer, circumstances had been against him. Eva Solmitz, now a teacher in Berlin, had been away and he had been unable to consult her as he had planned over Ruth's education, and the meeting with Kippenberg had been impossible to arrange. To them both he now wrote, in terms reminiscent of his cries for aid six years earlier in Westerwede. Eva at once declared herself ready to join Clara at Oberneuland and take charge of Ruth personally: although this selfless gesture was not practicable at the time, she proved a tower of strength over the years to come in devising ways to help. Kippenberg he asked outright whether the Insel could see its way to making him a regular allowance in anticipation of the books to come—the second volume of *New Poems*, to be followed by a selection from the earlier verse collections; the prose work, whose title would be *The Notebooks of Malte Laurids Brigge*; a possible study on Cézanne; and a revised, definitive version of *The White Princess*. He explained the difficulties that could arise with his previous publishers and enclosed such contracts as he had had, underlining in particular the regrettable undertaking to Bonz to give him first option on any future long prose work, and the necessity of Juncker's agreement for any republication of the early poems. As he waited for Kippenberg's reaction, increasingly worried whether he had not perhaps presumed too much, he had heartening news from Fischer. It had long been his hope, the Berlin publisher wrote, to help him in his art, and he had a concrete proposal now to make: he was placing at his disposal for the year the sum of 3000 marks, on which he could draw as and when he wished. 'It will give me great pleasure if thereby I can ease your position a little.'[24]

It was a delicate situation, for although Fischer attached no strings to this munificent offer, it seemed likely that he would be looking for rather more return than a few contributions to the *Rundschau*. Rilke felt obliged, for all his deep gratitude for it, to explain quite frankly what he was seeking from the Insel, and how this would inevitably limit what he could promise to Fischer. It was just as well, for soon afterwards Kippenberg sent his own proposal:

advances, payable quarterly, on the coming books, and an undertaking to try not only to acquire Juncker's rights in the earlier verse volumes, but also if necessary to buy out Bonz's option on the prose work, to make sure that *Malte* came to the Insel. The agreement would be renewable each year in the light of progress. It was the security he had wanted, and he was only too pleased to accept. To Fischer he made quite clear what he was doing, trusting that he would understand, and saying that he would no doubt wish to reconsider his offer as a result—though perhaps the circumstance of annual renewal of the Insel agreement might nevertheless allow him one day to place a book with him. Fischer, confessing that he hoped for a similar arrangement to that with Hofmannsthal, who published both with him and with the Insel, nevertheless replied that he was more than delighted to hear Rilke had secured such a sound economic basis, and confirmed that his offer still stood.[25]

'Life is taking shape,' Rainer had written to Clara as he dispatched his first letter to Kippenberg.[26] He was jubilant now: Paris lay before him, for as long as he might need for the work he planned—'the only city which does not suppress the spring, but picks it up and reflects it in a thousand images, as if in nothing but bright mirrors';[27] the only possible conditions for him. Capri was a brief interlude only, a much needed rest. 'I put out my light early, need a lot of sleep, in fact must keep my eyes closed for much of the time.' He refused all outside invitations, and when he was compelled to talk with the Discopoli friends he tried to make a mental note of what he said, 'so that it doesn't just turn into band music in a Kurpark, a background for a mental stroll'.[28]

Early in April he began to see about his accommodation in Paris. Rodin had cordially invited him to Meudon to begin with, and he hoped to be there by the middle of the month, but it was essential to find somewhere more isolated and more permanent. Fortunately Mathilde Vollmoeller, about to leave to spend the summer in Italy, suggested he should take over her studio in the rue Campagne-Première, where of course his desk and books awaited him, until the end of August. Accepting with alacrity, he arranged to leave on 15 April. Lizzie Gibson, who was convalescing in Sicily after an illness and wanted to visit him in Capri, was delicately put off until all this was firm: and the relative whirl of the Villa Discopoli (all a bit much, he confessed to Clara) came to an end for him on 14 April when Lizzie and her sister Florence Waern, an accomplished pianist, came over for his last day.[29] He was all impatience to get to Paris, and even Rodin's invitation was not taken up. 'I must shut myself up with my work, all alone,' he wrote to him after his arrival in the rue Campagne-Première.[30]

He had received Kippenberg's first advance, for the April/June quarter, even before leaving Capri, but in his new-found security did not forget his family responsibilities. It was possible now for Clara too to come to Paris, leaving Ruth at Oberneuland with a suitable girl to take charge of her first lessons. Through the good offices of Edith von Bonin, a painter, stepsister of

Karl von der Heydt, an ideal studio was found for her towards the end of May. The Hôtel Biron, once the residence of the Duchesse de Maine, then of Louis XIV's Marshal Biron, until recently a nunnery, and now in an advanced state of decay, was being let off where possible in individual apartments, the temporary home of a number of artists and writers (including later Isadora Duncan and Jean Cocteau), the high-ceilinged rooms giving on to a terrace and a neglected garden. On the corner of the rue de Varenne and the Boulevard des Invalides, it was not far from Rodin's studio in the rue de l'Université, where Clara was welcomed by the Master when she wanted to work there—but (as in Rome) far enough from Rainer's for him to maintain the solitude he craved. A few days later he drew the first half of Fischer's grant, and set aside 300 of the 1500 marks for Clara. Meanwhile he spent much time over organizing for her young brother Helmuth a summer stay with the Gibsons in Furuborg.

With all this, the 'summer of work' took its time to develop. As usual, it was necessary for him to prepare it by clearing his desk of correspondence, and thereby to clear his own thoughts, to let 'the abundance of insights' break through like a river 'into the *one* bed'.[31] In one form or another, all his friends heard how he planned now to work—'at the same spot, as a tree works, which cannot stir but can only go down into the depths, into the darkest of the dark'.[32] His pleasure in the *Sonnets from the Portuguese*, when they came out in May, was overshadowed by the news soon afterwards of the sudden death in Capri of Alice Faehndrich, for whom the original dedication had now to be changed to an 'In memoriam'.

He was wont to stress to others the 'heavy load' his calling laid upon him— thus now, to his mother, describing how 'completely alone' he was and compelled to reject any well-meant helping hands: this was part of his life and his profession 'and one may not avoid or deny it'.[33] But the early summer in Paris, as he readied himself for the allotted task, was unmingled pleasure. The breeze in Paris 'lifts the heart', he wrote to Sidie Nádherný, with something of the eighteenth century about it, Watteau-ish, as though it were in the frame of a picture.[34] Fischer and Kippenberg supplied him with books he wanted, and he was well enough off now to launch into more extravagant purchases of his own. A 170-volume encyclopaedia which had tempted him was delivered, and he and the concierge toiled up with the monster, in relays, 'like the Egyptians building the temples. I had to wash all over afterwards—but how wonderful any work is. You start awkwardly, but with each go you gain in experience, and finally, when it's all done, feel you are on the point of making something of yourself'.[35]

By early July he was ready to turn to his own labour. During that month, and into August, in a flow even more productive than that of the summer before, he wrote the rest of the 'New Poems' for the second volume promised to Kippenberg: weeks of work, 'as though under water ... with such an attentive heart that the external was scarcely to be distinguished from the internal'.[36] Ordering and revising the whole, which was substantially longer than the first, he sent it off to the publisher on 17 August, with the feeling that it made a fitting sequel—as it seemed to him, with greater depth. If there should one day be a third, he wrote, 'then there will again have to be a similar increase in the ever more factual grasp of that reality wherein lies the further significance and clearer validity of all things. But first, perhaps, I shall be able to devote to my prose what I have learned from these poems: this is exactly the progress it must turn to its use.'[37] The July days had fortunately been cooler and rainy, for in a sense he had been working against a deadline—the end of August, when he would have to move from Mathilde Vollmoeller's studio. In no other place had he felt so well and suitably installed, he wrote her. His achievement showed how well he had learned Rodin's lesson of unremitting application. With the 'New Poems' nearly done, he was able at last to accept the Master's renewed and cordial invitation to visit Meudon, still with deference but now as a 'dear friend'.

When it came to the search for new accommodation money was no longer a problem. Not only had Kippenberg's next quarterly payment arrived punctually, but he also received a settlement from Juncker for his royalties from the *Cornet* at the end of July, and drew the second half of Fischer's allowance during August. 'You cannot imagine what it means for me to have now an undisturbed autumn and winter ahead,' he wrote with his thanks to Fischer, 'more indeed, a whole year of peace. I need it so, and will not waste it.'[38] He had been greatly attracted by the surroundings Clara had found in the Hôtel Biron. As it happened, she planned to go to Hanover towards the end of August, to complete a commission already started there, and he arranged to take over her room in the hope that another would be free for him during September before her return. In this Louis-Quatorze mansion, the atmosphere of the past was a delight, however faded the glory: it would be a relief not to have to return to the rue Cassette, or even the studio ambience of the rue Campagne-Première. As soon as he was installed, on 31 August, he wrote enthusiastically to Rodin of the beauty of the building and of the prospect from Clara's three bay windows over the tangled and overgrown garden, 'where now and then rabbits are to be seen hopping innocently through the trellises, like in an old tapestry'.[39]

It was satisfying to be able to receive Rodin here, on his own ground, when the old man came to call two days later. Their earlier breach now totally forgotten, they could talk almost on equal terms; and what was more, he shared Rilke's enthusiasm for the place. So much so, indeed, that within twenty-four hours he had decided to rent a great part of the ground floor, having seen at once that the lofty rooms would provide the ideal home for his sculptures which he had sought in vain to create at Meudon, and a seclusion he could enjoy from time to time as a welcome retreat from the turmoil of the

Villa des Brillants. (No. 77 rue de Varenne would one day in fact become the Museé Rodin.) Rilke was so delighted with the news that he rushed out to buy for him a little sixteenth-century wood carving he had seen, of St. Christopher carrying a child with a globe in its hand—a good omen, he said, for here is Rodin himself bearing his Work, ever heavier, but work which holds the world. With the prospect of such a neighbour, he did not hesitate to speak for a more expensive apartment for himself than the one originally in mind, also on the ground floor and with a round corner room opening directly on to the terrace—much too dear for his circumstances, he told Clara, but after all he was resolved to stay put and work through the winter and it ought to be possible somehow to make good the extra outlay.

The reconciliation with Rodin had meant much. It seemed to him that his lonely path, in danger of losing itself in confusion, had now taken shape, rounded itself to full circle in the knowledge that the Master needed him, even if only to a thousandth part of his own need for him. His view of Rodin had gained in distance since the days in Meudon, and he was not blind to the god's feet of clay: for him, women were simply sex objects, requiring only to be satisfied, nourishment for a man 'like a drink coursing through him from time to time, like wine'.[40] The difference in outlook here could not have been more profound. But, as Rilke wrote to him, each could be right, in his allotted sphere, if he could find there a 'radiance' like Rodin's. 'You were born a conqueror, for you have a thousand and one strengths. I have only the one, with which I must shut myself up (like the stone in the fruit).'[41] The second volume of the *New Poems* would be dedicated 'A mon grand ami Auguste Rodin'.

Clara was not to return for another few weeks, so that he was well able to wait out the time required to get his new rooms ready, a task which, with the work on Rodin's, was causing the manager of the Hôtel Biron, dilapidated as it was, no little concern. For Rilke it was bliss to know that for the first time the year of security he had always wanted now lay ahead. 'I am so happy with my installation here,' he wrote to Hedwig Fischer, 'in the feeling that I can be still for a while and have time in a great stretch before me!'[42] His wants were modest—of necessity, for the rent alone would make a bigger inroad into his resources than before. There was not much available for extra furniture, and he was glad to accept Rodin's loan of a table. But such limitations were in keeping with his dedication to his work, and with a certain nomadic outlook which he was never to lose. To Dora Herxheimer, who had written from Rome of her progress and offered him one of her sculptures, he said he felt himself too unstable a home for possessions: 'every time I move I tell myself (and not just out of convenience) that I have no right to own more, my whole life long, than the standing-desk you know of. Even the books I shall give away one day, or place them somewhere where they can be of profit to many, to people who can use them better than I do . . .'[43]

Fischer's allowance would pay his rent, but the income on which he had to subsist was to come from the Insel, and for that he now had to fulfil a solid commitment—the long-nursed project, in embryo since Rome, of the prose work, a book based not only on the experiences and recollections of childhood and adolescence, but also on those of maturity, reflecting the ideas he had formed on life and death, on the human condition, on love. Under the influence of his Scandinavian reading he had imagined a young Danish poet, Malte Laurids Brigge, last scion of an aristocratic family, living in Paris, as he himself had done, in wretched circumstances, and perishing (as he had not) under the oppressive horrors of the city. But he had begun to conceive the book, not as a connected narrative in conventional novel style, but as a series of apparently random jottings in Malte's notebook, which would provide only glimpses of his outward life but a deep insight into his soul.

While staying with the Gibsons at Jonsered, in November 1904, he had reviewed an edition of the posthumous papers of the Norwegian poet Sigbjörn Obstfelder. In his wandering life Obstfelder too had lived for a while in Paris, and in the one completed manuscript he had left at his death, *The Diary of a Priest*, Rilke recognized much of his own, and Malte's, experience of that city. But most striking for him was the fact that the rest of the papers were only a mass of undated, unarranged, corrected, and rewritten material, mere jottings, 'not books, but the beginnings of books ... everything in the process of formation ... a jumble that was at bottom just movement, a world of moods and voices that trembled and revolved around the singular silence left behind by one who has died'. The editor had had, as it were, to bring this circling movement to a halt, 'as if someone had entered a ballroom and bidden the dancers stop ... But we must believe that that was the end of the dance, that it was a dance ... which had to stop just at this point. For we cannot hear it said too often: every life is a *complete* life'.[44] From this may have come the idea of giving his Malte a complete life in just such fragmentary and shapeless style, as he looked over the beginning he had made in Rome. From an artistic point of view, as he said later, the result might lack unity in the conventional sense; 'but humanly it is possible, and what becomes visible behind it is at least the outline of an existence and a shadowy pattern of interacting forces'.[45]

The notion suited the way he worked. The diary he had once kept for Lou had already, in his last days at Schmargendorf, tended to become a vehicle for random reflections: he had since abandoned even this semi-formal record. Instead, his habit was to carry always with him a pocket notebook in which he would pencil what came to him, in verse or prose, on his walks; while at his desk at home, he would set down impressions from his reading or from what he had seen in street or country, in museum or art gallery, and his ideas on the human condition. His papers tended thus to be just such a jumble as Obstfelder's, but more meticulously kept, and usually dated. In this sense, Rilke was indeed Malte, and many passages which would appear in Malte's notebooks already existed by this time in notes or drafts, in copies of letters, or in his mind in the memories of his own childhood fears and hopes. Some he had in fact already made public at his readings.

The imaginary figure had grown more and more real to him since he had made a beginning in Rome and continued the work in Sweden, and even more when he was alone in Paris again. Friends had heard about Malte in his letters, and often, especially to Clara, he had related his own feelings and experiences in terms of the young Dane. The stay in Sweden, his reading of Jacobsen, Kierkegaard, and more modern Scandinavian authors, the visits to Copenhagen, had all combined gradually to create a Brigge background. Now, four years later, Rilke felt that it was high time to write Malte out of his system, that until he had done so he could make no further progress himself. 'Only through him can I get on, he stands in my way.' He had survived, where Malte had gone under; but his survival could not be assured until he had portrayed their deep existential crisis. 'I should really have written it last year,' he told Clara, 'after those letters on Cézanne, which touched so directly and strongly on Malte: for Cézanne is nothing more than the first primitive, arid victory of which Malte was not yet capable. What was the death of Brigge, was Cézanne's life, the life of his last thirty years. ... Help me to a quiet time, to make my Malte ... I will not stir, will strike roots and do the long overdue work this winter, through until spring; I feel I must stay healthy over it and for it, and not least through it ...'[46]

At the end of August 1908, just before moving into the Hôtel Biron, Rilke had written to Mimi Romanelli: 'You know I have long had in mind a book with some portraits of women who, after unhappy love-affairs, found the accomplishment, the fulfilment of their hearts' mission, beyond the overwhelming initial passion, by finally rendering them up to God—fulfilling it in spite of everything, and more gloriously than any earthly lover could have supported' women like Marianna Alcoforado, but also those who had found this sublime consummation in art: Sappho, Eleanore Duse, Anna de Noailles, and the sixteenth-century poetess Gaspara Stampa. With a singular lack of tact, but perhaps in the hope that Mimi would take the shining example to heart, he suggested they might one day study together the works of Gaspara Stampa.[47] Such women, he felt, were the truly 'great lovers', for they had risen above the need to be loved in return. As he prepared now for the writing of *Malte*, in which this would indeed be an important, if not dominant theme, he found yet another to add to his gallery. Reading the correspondence between the young Bettina von Arnim and the much older Goethe, he thought to see in her that ineffable '*sensualité de l'âme*' which since Sappho has been one of the great transformations, through which the world slowly grows more real.'[48] He was appalled by Goethe's awkward and conventional responses to her love: whereas Bettina herself, like the other 'great lovers' among women, had, he felt, unconsciously transcended the need for her love to be returned, and like them had passed on the message of 'solitary love, in all its suffering and bliss, the only love worthy of the name'. Letters were inadequate to express all this, he wrote to Sidie Nádherný, 'it must become a work, made a clear and most inward reality. (Give me your good wishes, that I may achieve it.)' As he thought, almost obsessively, on Bettina, on Héloïse, and the Portuguese nun, and Gaspara Stampa, he felt more and more the true 'infinite splendour of love, of honest, independent love'.[49]

'A life difficult and full of danger do those lead who are loved,' he finally wrote as Malte: 'Ah, that they might conquer themselves and become lovers.' And in the margin of this notional notebook: 'To be loved means to be consumed. To love means to radiate with inexhaustible light. To be loved is to pass away, to love is to endure.' For Malte, the Prodigal Son resolved 'never to love, in order not to put anyone in the terrible position of being loved', gave away all he had to avoid having that experience himself, 'wounded women with his gross payments, fearing from day to day lest they try to respond to his love'. And when he returned, it was an indescribable relief to find his family did not understand him, knew nothing of him and did not realize that he had now become 'terribly difficult to love'.[50]

This strange philosophy was a reflection of Rilke's make-up, a rationalization of his constant drawing back from the conventional relationship between man and woman, in which two are made one. He himself had effectively renounced wife and child in favour of his solitude and his art. It was scarcely a parallel with the unhappy experiences of his 'great lovers' among women, but he could still think of his lonely road as leading the same way as theirs, to a transcendent state which might be called God. Two should not be made one, but at most be the 'guardians of each other's solitude'. While he was pondering this, he thought of the sad fate of Paula Modersohn. She too had followed this road, leaving her husband, as Rainer had left Clara, to devote herself to her art alone in Paris. But to his mind, she had weakened, 'slipped back from the first beginnings of great artistic achievement into family life and then into the fate of an impersonal death that she had not prepared for herself'—for in November 1907, back in Worpswede with Modersohn, she had died at only thirty-one, giving birth to a daughter. With the approach of this melancholy anniversary, in an 'unexpected, powerful flow'[51] of inspiration, he wrote a long 'Requiem for a Friend' which brought out, even more strongly than in Malte's notes, how unforgivable for him was the pressure of 'normal' life against the full development of the individual, 'the tortuous suffering of spurious love':

> For this is guilt, if anything be guilt,
> not to enlarge the freedom of a love
> with all the freedom in one's own possession.
> All we can offer where we love is this:
> to loose each other; for to hold each other
> comes easy to us and requires no learning.[52]

'I have my dead,' he had begun this requiem to Paula: and in the flow came to mind another who had recently died, Wolf von Kalckreuth, a poet of great promise who had succumbed under the burden of art and taken his own life at the age of only nineteen. Rilke had never known him personally, but had been greatly moved by yet another instance of a death not fitting and unprepared. Only a few days after completing the requiem for Paula he wrote another for Kalckreuth, in lament for his decision to slam the door for ever at the moment when it might have been opening wide for him, without waiting for that

> own death
> Which has such need of us because we live it.
>
> . . . .
>
> O ancient curse of poets!
> Being sorry for themselves instead of saying,
> for ever passing judgement on their feeling
> instead of shaping it . . .
>   . . . instead of sternly
> transmuting into words those selves of theirs,
> as imperturbable cathedral carvers
> transpose themselves into the constant stone.
> That would have been salvation . . .

Yet he does not reproach him.

> The big words from those ages, when as yet
> happening was visible, are not for us.
> Who talks of victory? To endure is all.[53]

With the poem, he told Kalckreuth's mother later, he had wanted to mark 'the greatest and richest experience of death' that had ever been vouchsafed to his inward being.[54]

He was indeed 'deep in work' in the closing months of 1908, undisturbed by outside commitments which, at other times and in other surroundings, he might have found distracting. By October Clara was back in her room, while he was installed and more than content in his; Edith von Bonin, also a neighbour in the Hôtel Biron, came to call, and they talked of Rudolf Kassner, for Rilke 'a writer of rare talent and a dear friend';[55] Mimi Romanelli came to Paris to join her brother for the winter, and although a frequent visitor was successfully kept at the right distance. He did not miss the autumn Salon, where El Greco's *Toledo* made a deep impression on him; there was correspondence with Jessie Lemont, an American writer preparing lectures on Rodin and later to be a translator of Rilke's own work into English. Rodin often looked in on him when at the Hôtel Biron, and their relationship was relaxed and satisfying: they occasionally lunched together, 'leaving each other in peace and enjoying each other's company'.[56] Kippenberg heard often from him, and was particularly interested in following up his suggestion of tracking down the fate of the long out-of-print volume *A Festival for Me*, of which Rilke had been reminded when he turned up among his papers some verse manuscripts dating from 1899. The idea of a revised edition of these early poems appealed to the publisher, and he also responded at once to the idea of presenting the two Requiems as a separate volume.

As he wrestled with *Malte*, Rilke was somewhat nettled to receive from Ellen Key, who was visiting Lou, a letter rather critical of the *New Poems*. They both felt, she said, that these poems smacked too much of the study, were not always the fruit of 'strong experiences': they failed to sing in him, spontaneously, as they should. 'Your friends among the critics . . . say the same thing! . . . We wish for you some great love (preferably unhappy!) and a thousand other beautiful things!'[57] He replied at once that his next book but one (*Malte* after the second volume of *New Poems*) would amply set their minds at rest. His conscience was clear: the *New Poems* had been a school for him,

I have to know that I can grasp the whole world, no matter what form it takes . . . to make myself capable of working continuously, that is, to see in everything I encounter a challenge, a task, a claim to artistic transformation. . . . That is what I am trying to do now, and you will see it was not in vain if I can manage it. . . . As for love, there's no lack of that, both happy and unhappy . . .

He took their criticism seriously, he said, but was just as serious in his reply, and in his determination to finish the book that would 'justify a development which must be right, unless I have been wrong in everything through my whole life'.[58] It was not the only reproach he had received on these lines, he confessed to Sidie Nádherný, 'but I can't tell you how comforted I am to feel I am in the middle of . . . the difficult task which is truly *mine*.'[59]

He plunged ever deeper into it, until he was 'as though at the bottom of the sea', with 'the pressure of all the waters and all the heavens' upon him, but happily relieved from time to time by the passage of 'phosphorescent ideas'.[60] It needed all the patience he had learned from Rodin: for, as he told him, verse is aided by the rhythm of outside things, the lyrical cadence of nature, whereas prose needs to find its rhythm inside, 'the anonymous and multiple rhythm of the blood'; it has to be constructed like a cathedral, and at the work one is alone on the scaffolding. 'And just think, in this prose I know now how to create men and women, children and old men. Women especially I have delineated by carefully drawing in everything around them, leaving a blank space which would be empty but for the tender and detailed outline, within which it becomes vibrant and luminous, like one of your marbles.'[61] Clara returned to Oberneuland to spend Christmas with Ruth, leaving him alone. His mother had grieved to hear that he planned to work even on Christmas Eve: but he hastened to assure her that his work was more and more his 'one single unqualified festival', and that the evening could not be better spent than in quiet and serious concentration.[62]

He had successful and solid progress to report, he told Kippenberg in his end-of-year letter, and although he could not yet see when *Malte* would be finished, it might possibly be by the end of the summer. *A Festival for Me* in its revised form he would send by the middle of January, and he suggested they might entitle it *Early Poems*, so as to leave the way clear one day for a reissue of the even earlier verse collections as *First Poems*. In his concentration, however, he had neglected his accounts; and he found to his dismay that he had overspent by a thousand francs or so in setting up in the Hôtel Biron, with further expenses still to come. So he once more appealed to Kippenberg for aid: with their financial agreement due for renewal with the new year, it seemed hardly the moment to increase his demands, but perhaps the Insel could provide some additional work for him to justify them, such as a translation. He would be loth to give up the ideal conditions he had now found, in which the work was coming on so well. And in another letter in the New Year, even before the other could reply, he stressed again how all important it was for him to have the security in which to finish this work, the 'massive, lasting prose' he was training himself to produce, the 'fullness' he was attaining, which seemed to be approaching such finality that he sometimes felt he could die when it was done.[63] Kippenberg in fact needed no further prompting: his letter was already on the way with a cheque for the thousand francs deficit and confirming that the agreement was to continue for another year, with quarterly payments this time of 500 marks.

Rilke had every reason to be grateful for the relationship which had developed in 'so indescribably timely a way' and which he could not now imagine his life without.[64] In Kippenberg he had not only found the source of security he had always sought, and a man of business to whom he could turn over the enquiries which were coming in more and more frequently as his fame increased—proposals for translations of his work, or for inclusion of his poems in anthologies: he had also found a friend and father confessor who, as time would show, could give him sound advice and lend support beyond the call of interest. The publisher's generosity was certainly not without an eye to the return he hoped to earn on his investment, for which the sales so far of the *Book of Hours* and the *New Poems* had shown encouraging prospects. But it was greatly to his credit that at all times he was prepared to do more for Rilke than would have been warranted by purely commercial considerations. It is indeed highly unlikely that, if a comprehensive balance sheet could be drawn up for the period of Rilke's lifetime it would show much net profit for the Insel Verlag, however favourable its results thereafter.

During 1909 he was indefatigable in the pursuit of the rights for Rilke's earlier works, already with the aim of eventually producing a collected edition. Although Juncker had bought up the remainders of *Advent* and *Crowned with Dreams*, in the days when he too had thought of republishing them, it was established by the end of January that he was not in a position to contest their transfer to the Insel. The prose stories *The Last of their Line* were similarly free. The *Cornet* was just out of print, and Juncker was proposing a new edition; but Rilke was able to refer to the contract stipulation of one edition only, and so this work too could go to the Insel. By the end of February Kippenberg had purchased from Bonz the rights in *Two Prague Stories* and *The Stream of Life* and consequently annulled Bonz's option on *Malte*. On the other hand, Juncker was most unwilling to release the *Book of Images*, which was one of the most successful in his list, and for which he proposed yet a third edition later in the year, and Kippenberg had to let that lie until a more favourable opportunity for an offer should arise. He was making substantial progress towards his goal, however, and, while waiting for *Malte*, was keeping his author before the public eye with the *Early Poems* (to which Rilke had now added 'The White Princess' in the revised form he had prepared in 1904 in Sweden) and the *Requiem* volume, both of which appeared in May. Readings in Berlin from Rilke's verse by the well-known actor Josef Kainz could be expected to stimulate demand, and he planned a third edition of the *Book of Hours*.

Paradoxically, however, the security he had guaranteed for his poet was failing to have the desired result. Already in January, Rilke found his work going more slowly than he wished, and by February he fell victim once more to the influenza to which he was always prone during winter months in the north European climate. Distractions he had hitherto been able to take in his stride began to prove too much. Clara was back, and a certain tension seems to have developed between them. Mathilde Vollmoeller returned, and the spring brought many more visitors—Karl von der Heydt, who wanted to meet Rodin; Stefan Zweig, after his Far East tour; Georg Brandes; the Fischers, with the Austrian writer Felix Salten; and finally, in May, Lou and Ellen Key. There was a report too that the Hôtel Biron was to be sold. It seems clear, however, that it was rather his own inner uncertainty that gave him these 'almost entirely bad months':[65] the failure of health, as often before, the result rather than the cause. Lou recalled how, as they sat together in the Hôtel Biron, he spoke of the 'intoxication of production' that had held him in its spell, to the point of identification with Malte and an inextricable mingling of fiction and reality in the episodes of his life: and then of the unbearable pressure this had built up, making him feel he was taking the wrong path in substituting a work of fiction for what should have been true autobiography.[66]

He had in fact got no further with it since January. In his discouragement, he told Kippenberg in May that he could not see when he would be able to take it up again: it certainly would not be done by August as he had once hoped. He must first regain his health; he might once more have to move; and in any case he would probably need to spend a while in the discipline of verse, to let observation of nature restore 'the inner world from which I draw that book'.[67] To Mimi Romanelli, he compared his condition with that of a broken twig, still attached by a scrap of bark to its tree but no longer responding inside to the sap coursing happily through all the other branches.[68] He realized that he must rely on himself alone, on his own efforts and not those of doctors, to 'overcome this complicated interaction of bodily and mental depressions', for he alone knew 'their cause and the laws underlying their confusion': he must follow the example of Münchhausen and pull himself out of the marsh by his own pigtail.[69]

A week at the end of May spent in the south made a good beginning—Saintes-Maries-de-la-mer, where he attended the pilgrimage and night-long vigil in the little church, full of 'pilgrims, dogs and gypsies';[70] Arles; Aix-en-Provence. It was just travelling, without really 'looking', as he wrote to Clara from Aix; but at least it was a start on the way back to himself. She returned to Germany early in June, having made considerable progress in her work and with the prospect of more commissions. It turned out that the sale of the Biron was not yet imminent, so that he was able to stay on there through the summer months, at his desk but, as he had foreseen, working only at occasional verse when not at his correspondence or sending copies of the *Requiem* to selected friends. And he was not yet ready to resume the *Malte*. In August he learned from Vienna that he had been awarded the Bauernfeld Prize for lyric poetry. It was a distinction which of itself made little appeal to one who always claimed indifference to public recognition, but it came very appositely now, for (distrusting in the end his ability to restore himself unaided) he had in fact taken medical advice, and the extra cash from the prize made it possible to undertake the cure he was recommended. Without further delay, he travelled to Strasburg on 1 September and on to the spa of Bad Rippoldsau, in the Black Forest.

Paris had been like a protracted siege, he wrote to Mathilde Vollmoeller, where in the end 'my spirit had only rats for nourishment. What a capitulation. I am ashamed: but perhaps I held out long enough to have earned a certain right to honourable retreat with all weapons.'[71] Writing to Tora Holmström in Sweden, he said he had toyed for a moment with the wild idea of going instead to Norrland, to seek solace among its waterfalls and perhaps see a real bear 'instead of the *inner* bear I have taken on without being able to defeat him, and who stands there so threateningly that I'm not strong enough to do more than lie pretending to be dead.'[72]

It was his hope that two weeks in Rippoldsau would be sufficient to restore him. Once in the hands of the doctor, however, he found that even so short a stay would be costlier than he had thought. His appeal to Kippenberg for an advance payment to tide him over crossed with a proposal to this very end from the thoughtful publisher, who had realized, as soon as he had heard where he was, how essential it was to get him over this hump if ever *Malte* was to materialize. Rilke was enormously grateful for the extra help, and immediately began to plan his next move: to Avignon. It was not the place for a long stay or for work, as he soon discovered: but the journey proved one of his most memorable, he wrote later to Lou. Almost daily, during a stay of over two weeks, he saw the 'hermetically sealed palace' where the papacy, 'feeling itself decaying at the edges, had thought to preserve itself ... However often one views this desperate house, it stands on a rock of improbability, and one finds the way into it only by a leap over everything unbelievable that has gone before'.[73] He was impressed by the 'unheard-of mystery' of this *chateau-fort*, with its 'admirable frescoes', and was sure that one day, somewhere among the countless dilapidated rooms, there would be discovered 'the most impossible unicorn ever painted'.[74] He visited Orange, with its Roman triumphal arch and its amphitheatre; Carpentras; Beaucaire. All this would set scenes for Malte's reflections.

Perhaps his most remarkable day of all, however, was that spent at Les Baux. 'As you come from St. Rémi, where the Provence soil bears nothing but fields of flowers, everything suddenly turns to stone. A completely barren valley opens and then closes in behind the rocky road, three mountains in echelon rear themselves, like three spring-boards from which three last angels soared up in a terrified leap. And opposite, etched against the sky like stone on stone, rise the edges of the most singular settlement, the way to it passing through such immense ruins (whether fragments of mountains, or of towers, you cannot tell) that you feel you too must fly up to carry a soul to the open space aloft.' He learned the history of the Les Baux family, descended according to legend from the Magus Balthasar, and, as he reported in some excitement to Lou, that of the banishment of the Protestants from Les Baux in 1621, among whom was a family of Salomés. Instead of staying with the guide, however, he preferred to wander round with a taciturn shepherd: 'we just stood beside one another and gazed at the place. The sheep were scattered wide, seeking the little grazing there was. But now and then, as they found some, the scent of thyme arose and stayed awhile around us.'[75] It was in Provence that he later pictured the Prodigal Son in *Malte*, as a shepherd seeing 'the petrified age outlast the lofty race' of the Les Baux, or leaning against the triumphal arch of Orange, or in 'the spirit-haunted shade of Aliscamps'.[76]

Though he was not yet fully out of his Slough of Despond, the experience of Provence had done more than the cure to give him back the courage he needed. Returning to Paris on 8 October, he told Kippenberg he had given up the idea of going further south, and had determined now to make the best of the circumstances. He would have to leave the rue de Varenne anyway on 1 January 1910, and then would be the time to make a new plan. He had to confess that the Malte manuscript was little more than half completed, and at that, in a rough form which he had not the strength to transcribe. Kippenberg's offer soon after, to provide a stenographer for his dictation if he would come to Leipzig in January with his draft, spurred him on, however, and he resolved to make that journey his next stage before starting to look for a new home. The deadline thus set seems to have acted as a catalyst, like that of the year before, when he had to hand over Mathilde Vollmoeller's studio; and by early December he could report that he had been for some time once more 'on the hob, boiling with work'.[77] Not only that, but he had even begun to negotiate for reading engagements in Elberfeld and Jena to help finance his journey.

His correspondence began to grow again, in more cheerful vein now that he was at work once more. He had always found time to reply to admirers who wrote to him; but he spread himself now to a young nurse at the Charité hospital in Berlin, encouraging her to set down her impressions of her life and hoping one day with her help to take up again a theme he had once made some notes for, on the life and experiences of a night-nurse. Already the images began to form in his mind: 'the creaking of the linen-baskets in the cellar; the lying there awake, hyper-wakeful, awake in pain and looking up at the lamp . . .'[78] The plan never materialized, but they corresponded for some years.

He was delighted to receive from Hedwig Fischer a photograph of the bust of her little daughter Brigitte (Tutti) which Clara had now completed, and to learn that Gerhart Hauptmann had so admired it that he had commissioned her to do his own, instead of going to Rodin. ('Rodin does nothing now but portraits of American money-men,' Rilke had written to Clara, 'helpless mortals who can't even make the effort to trim their moustaches, so that they all look like Nietzsche.'[79]) Birthdays were not forgotten: Clara received an amusing account of Paris as she would remember it, Ruth a delightful picture-book which he thought she would be able now to read. And he contributed to a *Festschrift* for Ellen Key's sixtieth birthday, due in December, celebrating 'not her goodness and readiness to help, but the pure strength of her existence; not what she has achieved, but her unseen, inner heroism. This will be the lasting beauty of Ellen Key.'[80]

It had turned out a hard year, he reflected as its end approached, 'like a constant trial', a perpetual struggle with his health, with the *Malte* book, against visible and invisible opponents. 'Never was there such resistance all around me. Would to God it were that of a dragon, but it is of phantoms only, an army of scarecrows.'[81] When Lizzie Gibson wrote that his 'golden room' at Furuborg stood always ready for him if he wanted, he explained that the complete solitude he needed for the work was possible only in Paris.[82] He confessed to Sidie Nádherný that *Malte* was giving him 'strange insights': 'on the one hand it seems to set the seal once and for all on my solitude, but on the other I simply can't see how I shall be able to complete all that remains to be done, without the peaceful companionship, the warmth and protection of someone near and dear'.[83]

In December, as his deadline approached, there came a welcome break in the solitary routine. He received an invitation from Princess Marie von Thurn and Taxis-Hohenlohe, who was visiting Paris, to call on her at her hotel on 13 December: she was eager to make his acquaintance, she said, for she had long admired his verse and had heard much about him from Rudolf Kassner. Countess Matthieu de Noailles would also be there and looked forward to meeting him. Whether or not he had been forewarned by Kassner of the Princess's interest, this was the sort of distraction he could never resist, no matter how demanding his work, and he hastened to accept. He was already familiar with the poems of Anna de Noailles, and during his second stay in Capri had sent her his *New Poems* and the *Rodin* with a fulsome letter of admiration: the uninhibited passion she revealed in her verse seemed to him to qualify her for inclusion in his collection of 'great women lovers', and while in Capri he had devoted an essay, 'Books of a Lover', to her work. In Paris later they had corresponded, but he had not ventured to approach her himself. The invitation was therefore doubly attractive.

In background and upbringing Princess Marie was a typical product of the supranational aristocracy of pre-war central Europe, and in her taste and aesthetic appreciation representative of all that was best in that now vanished society. Almost exactly twenty years older than Rilke, she had been born in Venice, where her father, Prince Egon Hohenlohe-Waldenburg-Schillings- fürst, scion of a German reigning house, was serving in the Austrian army; her mother, Countess Therese Thurn-Hofer-Valassina, came from the ancient Italian family of the Torriani. Marie had spent much of her childhood in Venice, at the Palazzo Contarini-Fasan, known as the house of Desdemona, where her father had died when she was only nine, but with long stays at their grand country house at Sagrado and at the castle of Duino, near Trieste, which belonged to her mother. In 1875 she had married a distant cousin, Prince Alexander von Thurn und Taxis, from a family also of Italian origin—Princes of the Holy Roman Empire, its first postmasters general in the eighteenth century, and lords of the castle of Lautschin in Bohemia. She had had three sons, but had lost the second through pneumonia in 1903; the eldest, Erich, was about Rilke's age, and the youngest, Alexander, known as 'Pascha', a few years younger. As fluent in German and French as in Italian, a voracious reader, a writer herself of novels and poetry, and talented in music and painting, she lived a very active and full life, with extended house parties at Lautschin and Duino, much entertaining at the Thurn und Taxis apartment in the Victorgasse in Vienna, and constant travel in the grand manner through Germany, France, England, or Italy. But she was a dilettante in the best sense. Her devotion to the arts was not the superficial enthusiasm of a society hostess, and the writers, poets, actresses, and musicians she gathered round her found an unaffected appreciation beyond mere lionizing. Although with her invi- tation Rilke may at first have felt that the prospect of meeting Anna de Noailles outweighed even that of taking tea with a Princess, he was soon to discover how much more important to him was the entry into his life of a figure of such wide-ranging culture, allied to a healthy common sense.

Punctual, as was his habit, he was the first to arrive. The Princess was surprised to find the author of the *New Poems* much younger than she had expected, looking almost like a child: 'very ugly, yet very *sympathique*, extremely shy, but with excellent manners and a rare quality of distinction'. Their rapport was immediate, and they talked at once as if they were old friends. He was full of his *Malte*, speaking as though of a real person and not of a book, and telling her dejectedly that he felt he had said there everything he had to say, there was nothing left—a confession which left her somewhat baffled, since she could not yet understand what the work meant to him.[84]

The appearance on this quiet scene of Anna de Noailles—late, for effect—was enough to dumbfound the shy poet. 'At that time,' the Princess recalled in her memoirs, 'women wore enormous hats and long, very narrow skirts. The Countess's huge, dark, feather-laden hat could hardly get through the door, and in the tight-fitting sheath that enveloped her from head to foot she looked almost like an Egyptian statuette. But the poet, I'm sure, saw only her great, imperious black eyes. She came one step nearer, stopped again and exclaimed: "Monsieur Rilke, what do you hold of love, what do you think about death?" It was only with difficulty I managed to keep a straight face: Rilke for his part was disconcerted and quite speechless.'[85] But once they relaxed over tea around the fire, the Countess abandoned this pretentious tone; and Princess Marie listened with increasing interest to the conversation between the two poets.

Rilke, there seems no doubt, came under the spell of the Countess's commanding presence; but he showed an instinctive wisdom in avoiding further entanglement. He pleaded the weeks of work that still lay before him, and although when he wrote to her the following day he begged to be allowed to call on her when it was done, there was in fact no further meeting then. His 'great lovers' were best viewed from afar, and preferably at a distance of centuries. In the toils of the de Noailles salon that 'beast of prey', as Cocteau called her, would have simply devoured him. In Princess Marie, by contrast, he could recognize the motherly support he always seemed to need. On 8 January 1910, as he prepared to leave on his journey to Germany, he wrote to her his feeling that their meeting had been 'one of those things which one later realizes had to come'. She had, of course, invited him to come to Duino in the spring, and already he could picture their talks in her 'castle by the sea', how he would be able to tell her what a marvellous concatenation this had been. 'More and more I shall come to understand what a wonderful protective spirit I felt on that evening ... my anxious aloneness had suddenly—I can hardly grasp how—become once more the solitude I have loved since I was a child, which transcends me but which is never my enemy.'[86] It was the beginning of a correspondence and a relationship which would last the rest of his life.

4

'Now everything can really begin'
(To Anton Kippenberg, 25.3.1910)

Once he was on his way from Paris in the New Year, second thoughts began to creep in about the wisdom of leaving it. Writing to Mathilde Vollmoeller from Elberfeld, the first stage of his journey, where he held a successful reading from his works on 9 January 1910, he said he had deferred his departure to the last moment in order not to miss a Cézanne exhibition, which had revealed much that was new to him. Rodin had seemed genuinely sad that he was going, and had presented him with one of his drawings of a Cambodian dancer which he treasured greatly. 'What a nonsense it is, to leave Paris . . . Once things have been arranged in Leipzig, I feel I should go straight back.'[1]

At all events he would certainly do so in due course. He had been able to store his things at the Hôtel Biron, the future of which was still not settled. Its tenants had been given notice partly because of the unseemly, not to say rowdy, behaviour of some of their number (notably Cocteau and the actor De Max, whose nocturnal parties in the garden had occasionally disturbed Rilke), but mainly to prepare the way for a projected redevelopment of the site. This had aroused furious opposition from the conservationists, and Rodin himself had refused to budge. He continued to wage a determined campaign against the administration, which in the end compromised with an agreement for him to occupy the mansion for his lifetime in return for the bequest of all his works to the State. From Elberfeld Rilke wrote to ask if the table he had lent him might remain part of his furniture for the time being, unless the Master needed it himself: it had been an inspiration to him, 'I have nowhere worked with such perseverance and faith.'[2]

He had not told Kippenberg exactly when he would arrive in Leipzig, and on 11 January put up first in an hotel there, in order not to disturb him. The publisher, however, lost no time in collecting him, eager as he was to meet his author for the first time and to see the *Malte* put into shape after this long gestation. His house in the Richterstrasse had a turret on one side in which a room had been made ready for Rilke. Both he and his wife Katharina were of an age with the poet, whose innate modesty and tact made him an ideal guest. Katharina Kippenberg, already captivated by the verse, developed a lasting affection now for the man which, like that of Marie Taxis, would give him much strength in the years to come. She was happily married, with a four-year-old daughter, and her admiration, though barely this side idolatry, fortunately made no demand on him stronger than friendship, an effective complement to the steadfast support offered him by her husband.

The turret room made an ideal setting for the dictation, which began at once and was completed during Rilke's two weeks' stay, interrupted only by his second reading engagement at Jena. The result was remarkable by any standard. The contrast with the *New Poems* could not have been more marked, and surprised and bewildered many of his admirers. In the *New Poems* he had striven to create works of art which could be regarded and comprehended like sculptures or paintings, and even this had seemed to some a loss in poetic effect compared with the *Book of Hours*. With *Malte Laurids Brigge*, in the form he had chosen of heterogeneous and disconnected passages in a notebook, he had gone to another extreme, with an esoteric composition as difficult for the reader to follow in its allusiveness as that of Joyce would be— an anti-novel before its time.

Much was autobiography: Malte heads his first entry with Rilke's 1902 address in Paris, the rue Toullier, and is the age Rilke was then; his descriptions of the horrors of everyday life in the Paris streets, the sick, the armies of the dying, the poor, are Rilke's, often in the actual words of his letters of the time; the hypersensitiveness to his room-neighbours, the nameless absolute fear that grips him, the recollection of his anxieties as a child, the mother's game of treating him as a girl, are all Rilke's experiences. And some even of what is imagined is Rilke as he wished he might have been: Malte as the last of a noble line, his mother loving and understanding as Rilke's own had never been. Malte reads and muses on the books and the episodes from French and Russian history that Rilke absorbed. In theme after theme—on life, death, poverty, on non-possessive love, and finally on the Prodigal Son, 'who did not want to be loved' and whose gesture on returning was not repentance but an imploring of his family 'not to love him'[3]— Malte is expressing Rilke. But, in truth, this intensely personal portrayal of the crisis he had himself gone through, making Malte 'partly out of my own dangers', was for Rilke not autobiography, but autotherapy: Malte must die, that Rilke might live. He had to 'make a thing out of his fears', so as to overcome them at last and be able to move on. and it surprised him later that what he had made might be interpreted as a gospel of nihilism, of unmitigated despair. It must be read 'against the current', he always insisted.

Vital to him was the cathartic effect of writing the work, the purification on which, he was convinced, any further progress depended. Whether what he had produced was valid as a work of art, or even saleable as a book, was a matter of indifference, and it was fortunate that he had behind him a publisher prepared to invest thus in his future. Opinions have been sharply divided on the aesthetic value of *Malte*. 'Not great art', says one critic, a style of 'laboured irony, mannered prose and purple patches', a failure 'to convince the reader of Malte's separate reality';[4] another finds the 'spiritual organism disclosed by the terrible vivisection inflicted upon Malte' so 'amazingly and movingly beautiful', 'the intensity of the expression so irradiating the most repulsive objects, that a secret, paradoxical jubilation emanates ... from the work in its entirety'.[5] But many readers now, turning these pages for the first time, will blench, like one before them, in an unsettling sense of identification with Malte in his torment, the feeling that 'res mea agitur'.

It was a huge relief for Rilke to have finished it at last. The 'year of work' made possible by Fischer's generosity had spread into a second, which Kippenberg had seen him through: but with *Finis* under the manuscript—'a new book done, separated out from me'[6]—and the proofs expected in a month or so, he could relax. There was no more talk of returning at once to Paris. He would go first to Berlin, to spend some time with Clara, who had started work on the Hauptmann bust, and with Ruth; to see the Fischers; and to attend the première of Hofmannsthal's new comedy *Christina's Homecoming*, with between times another stay with the Kippenbergs in Leipzig. After that, southwards once again, to Rome, 'in solitude and sun',[7] and to Duino, where Marie Taxis hoped to see him in April, before making his way back to Paris. He could afford it, or at least thought he could (in the event, Kippenberg had often to come to his rescue); and although he found Berlin, as before, a 'violent and aggressive city'[8] and suffered under its restless social pressures, he was able to enjoy his stay in the feeling of calm and security the Kippenbergs' hospitality had given him, and the sense of a task well done.

All the same, it was an abrupt contrast with Paris, where he could select and plan his company in quiet surroundings: Berlin was a place where 'you have to go without the people you want to see and are always tracked down by those you don't'.[9] It proved, for instance, impossible to see Hofmannsthal before the première on 11 February; and, although his colleague sent him and Clara tickets for the occasion, for which the Kippenbergs came up to Berlin, their first meeting with Clara, the Rilkes could not face the gathering afterwards in the Hotel de Rome. The Fischers invited them to an evening party two days later, which they also at first refused: he was so useless in a large company, he wrote to Hedwig, and neither he nor Clara had evening dress with them. But they were persuaded, nevertheless, and were to be found after supper, in one of the back rooms of the vast Grunewald villa, far from the dancing and occupied with their own thoughts. Hertha Koenig, granddaughter of a wealthy German sugar-beet producer in the Ukraine and herself a writer and poet of talent, recalled long afterwards the quiet oasis of this room as Hedwig Fischer brought her to meet them: Rilke slowly lifting his gaze as they came in, and behind him Clara, tall, her penetrating dark eyes 'like those in the angular face of a horse'.[10] He would not forget Hertha Koenig though it was three years before they met again.

Other new friendships offered themselves. After his reading at Jena he had received a letter of gratitude from Helene von Nostitz, who had come over for it from Weimar. A beautiful woman, of partly Russian origin, she was a devoted admirer of Rodin, and Rilke had already heard her artistic gifts praised by Kessler and Hofmannsthal. Though after the death of her elder son she could not come to the première in Berlin as she had hoped, she pressed him to visit her and her husband in Weimar when he was in Leipzig again, and he heard Hofmannsthal read there from his first draft of the *Rosenkavalier*.

On his first stay in Berlin he had already spent more than he could afford, but Kippenberg, with 'splendid precision', stood ready to tide him over with extra money, almost before he could ask, and readily agreed to his retention of the royalty from the third edition of *Worpswede*. The first part of *Malte*, which was to be published in two volumes, was already in proof, for him to correct when he went back to Berlin for the first fortnight of March, and the rest would follow him to Rome. Confirming to Marie Taxis that he would come to Duino on about 20 April, he said he looked forward in Rome to the proof-reading of his book, and hoped it might be in her hands by May: 'I have an affection for it, and feel I shall myself read nothing else for a long time.'[11]

The month he spent there was more restful for him than Berlin, closer to his solitude of Paris, with company he could choose when he did not feel in 'misanthropic' mood. The Fischers with their little daughter were fellow guests for three weeks in his Hotel de Russie, on the Piazza del Popolo, and he could enjoy occasional visits with them to the museums or a chat on the terrace without being tied to an evening meal, which he usually made of milk alone in his room. In was a disappointment that Sidie Nádherný, whom he expected to find, had had to return to Vienna with a broken arm, but she came back to Rome later for a few days while he was there. Eva Solmitz, however, married since the previous October to Kurt Cassirer, who lived in Rome, he was able to see often. With Leopold von Schlözer, writer and translator of Maeterlinck, who had been one of the guests at the Villa Discopoli, he visited the elderly Nadezhda Helbig, née Princess Shakhovskoy, one of the 'characters' of Rome; but this was probably his only really social evening. He spent much of his time on the *Malte* proofs. The galleys he had found in some way depressing to read through, but with the page proofs, which he now completed, his pleasure in the book was renewed. 'I feel there will be much coming to me now,' he wrote to Kippenberg, 'these notes are something like a basis, everything is reaching upwards, has more space around it . . . Now everything can really begin. . . . After [Malte] almost any songs are possible.' The beginning was not yet, however, and only a few fragments of verse found their way into his pocket-book. Paris was the only place, he felt, where he could be and work—or else some really far-off city or country, among thoroughly foreign objects, no longer constrained to say the same things in the same way but confronted with the 'constant task, the active stimulation' of trying to express himself through something completely different.[12]

He felt himself in a state of transition, after the intensive struggle over *Malte*: 'like Raskolnikov after the deed, I don't know what is to come next'.[13] And there came once again now the urge to reach out from his solitude for human contact. In spite of all he had said about the beauty of solitary love, 'the only love worthy of the name',[14] he could not deny his own need for something

more, a relationship nearer the conventional. He had not found this with wife
and family, would not indeed impose himself on Clara for fear of diminishing
in her the artistic mastery he was sure she was capable of. Yet there was no one
else who came close to what he was seeking. There were women enough at his
feet, or ready to throw themselves there if encouraged—and it is difficult to
believe that many of those who had received his letters full of the philosophy,
if not the reality, of love did not feel a certain encouragement. There were
Hertha Koenig, and the artists Mathilde Vollmoeller, Dora Herxheimer, and
Edith von Bonin; Sidie Nádherný, beautiful and still unattached, had become
a close confidante through his regular letters; Helene von Nostitz, though
married, was rapidly becoming another; while—not far from Duino—Mimi
Romanelli was still eating her heart out for him as he continued to write to her.
He showed a remarkable capacity to convert them all, with the exception of
Mimi, into selfless and undemanding friends, like Katharina Kippenberg, and
Lizzie Gibson, ready to lend their aid when the need arose: but his longing
remained unstilled 'for someone who would be there for me', the longing 'to
shelter my solitude with someone, put it under their protection'.[15]

In this mood, he found the prospect of Duino somewhat daunting, with the
'extensive household' of Princess Marie's 'siblings, sons, daughters-in-law
(among them a very *difficile* Princess, neé de Ligne), grandchildren etc.,
people, guests'. He could look forward to Marie Taxis herself—'protective,
full of the joy of living as she ages'—and felt instinctively what her friendship
and patronage would mean for him; but at the moment it was not the kind of
'protection' he was looking for.[16] It turned out as he had feared, and he stayed
only a week. He was made welcome, of course, but it is clear that Princess
Marie could not devote much time to him, and he was at a loss in a house party
of this size. Kassner was there only for his first few days, and Rilke found him
a trifle forbidding, 'like an examination, and this was not the time for me to
pass it'. Still, there was something 'secure and true' about him, something
'basically very earnest', and he was glad to know they would meet again in
Paris.[17]

He had been under such a strange pressure when he arrived, he wrote with
his thanks to the Princess, 'I don't know how you managed to bear with me.
But I hope you could feel how you slowly made me less useless. . . . I have to
come from work, be still immersed in it, if I am to be really myself: this time I
had so much disjointed time behind me.'[18] His letter came from Venice. He
had gone there from Duino for a short stay, in order to follow up in the library
the story of the fourteenth-century Venetian admiral Carlo Zeno. The history
of Venice held a fascination for him, and he had a vague notion of writing the
life of this saviour of the Republic at the battle of Chioggia against the
Genoese. Introductions from Marie Taxis opened every facility to him: but he
soon had to admit himself defeated, as he had been in earlier years, by his total
incompetence in handling the materials of book-learning. 'They treat me like a

scholar, lay out everything for me, but I just crouch over the folios as a cat might, concealing what is in them and at most taking a pleasure in the novelty of its situation. And when the lagoon down below laps and laps again at the old marble foundations my attention concentrates completely on the noise, as if there were more to be learned from that than from the old prints.'[19] The Zeno story was more than a passing idea, for he took it up again on a later visit, but for the moment he could make no progress.

Though he stayed this time at an hotel (Kippenberg once more helping with funds), and not at the Romanelli pension, he could not resist seeing Mimi again. The encounter was evidently distressing, to judge from his letter to her of 11 May, the day of his departure:

For the first time I think of you only in bitterness . . . instead of profiting from my strength, you rely on my weakness, and yourself destroy what I would give you, by doing me violence. The one mortal wrong we can do to each other is to link ourselves together, be it only for an instant. . . . How different my life would have been these last days, if you had undertaken to protect my solitude, protection I stood in such need of. I am leaving distracted and tired. Never forget that solitude is my lot, that I must not have a need for anyone, that all my strength in fact comes from this detachment. . . . I *implore* those who love me to love my solitude . . .

'Burn these lines,' he begged her in a postscript: 'preserved, they become less true.'[20] She did not do so, of course, incomprehensible though they must have seemed to her—for how could she truly love him and yet leave him alone? She was no Gaspara Stampa, nor yet a Marianna Alcoforado.

His journeyings had afforded but 'sparse experiences', he had written to Clara from Venice, by way of excusing his longer than usual silences. But he hoped he might find, once back in Paris, that something had worked within him, unbeknownst.[21] The first problem when he arrived there was to find a new home, and nearly two weeks went by before he discovered that it was possible after all to return to the rue de Varenne. On 24 May he took over a three-room apartment there—simple, conducive to work as it seemed, and half the rent of his previous abode. It was on the third floor off a side courtyard of the Hôtel Biron, and the full-length window of the study looked out on the tips of the lime trees in the garden. Anyone seeing such a room would say it was his own fault if he did not do good work there, he told Kippenberg; and he was firmly resolved to set to, after his unsatisfactory travels, 'to be alone, at last, and get down to productive labour'.[22]

On the face of it, there was every reason for hope. Financial worries were a thing of the past: his regular income from the Insel was assured, and in addition he had just received word from Vienna of a special grant of 600 crowns, 'for outstanding poetic achievement', from the Ministry of Culture and Education, the result of an application on his behalf by his good friend August Sauer in Prague.[23] *Malte* was to come out at the end of the month, with no fewer than five printings of 1100 copies each, and his account would benefit immediately from the royalties on the first three. So confident was Kippenberg in its success that he did not even ask for repayment of the extra advances made for the Italian journey. They could both take pride in what had been produced, wrote Rilke, and he was particularly pleased to hear that fifty copies were to be specially bound in leather. All in all, the circumstances could not have been more favourable. Yet still he could not overcome the feeling of transition, and the new beginning he sought eluded him. By early July he had grown so impatient with himself and, though not actually ill, so physically run down, that he felt he had to get away, with no very clear idea of what he would do. 'I abandoned everything this summer was to bring me,' he wrote later to Kippenberg; 'Paris was against me.'[24] He had realized more and more clearly what a decisive demarcation line *Malte* represented: one could not simply go on writing after that, a completely new start was needed—perhaps, as he said to Marie Taxis, he should even give up writing altogether, start a new life, become a doctor, anything.

Surprisingly enough, it was to Oberneuland that he headed first, spending in the end a full month there with Clara and Ruth. In a letter to Marie Taxis, who was at Lautschin for the summer, he confessed how ashamed he was at the failure of his good resolutions in the empty weeks in Paris: he longed now for the country somewhere, but for the moment did not feel up to accepting her invitation to Lautschin. A consultation with a doctor in Hamburg revealed nothing really wrong, and once more confirmed his conviction that he must be his own healer. Finally he made up his mind, and after a brief meeting with Kippenberg in Leipzig arrived on 11 August in Bohemia, to spend two days with his mother at the little spa of Franzensbad before going on to Lautschin. His stay could be only for a week, as his hosts were due to leave for Munich and Duino on 20 August; but fortunately Sidie Nádherný, in reply to his letter of sympathy on the death of her mother, invited him to join her and her brothers at Janowitz. 'Lautschin amid its forests helped me a lot,' he reported to Katharina Kippenberg from Prague, where he spent the intervening days. 'If the country place I am to go to now is half as splendid . . . the Bohemian castles will justify themselves and outweigh all else.' 'When I read your letter I felt at once I should be able to work when I came to you,' he told Sidie.[25]

For the first time since Rome, in fact, one or two drafts of poems appeared in his notebook, as he relaxed in the softer, almost sentimental countryside round Janowitz, walking on 'rarely-trod paths' and 'learning to become a little human again':

> The insistent quiet of humming insects
> makes nothing of your being there.
> Where are the challenges that once so terrified?
> Your heart holds meeting in the undiscovered
> and in the future lies the song.[26]

The castle too, still in mourning, was quieter than Lautschin, though just as grand: to his mother he reported on 'the real silver and beautiful porcelain' that graced the dinners in the great hall. The elder brother (Sidie and the younger were twins) he liked especially, 'much travelled and well read';[27] and the renewed encounter with Sidie undoubtedly made great appeal. He read to her from the *Book of Hours* in the chapel, she played the piano for him, they went for drives or on long walks in the park, and read Kleist or Jacobsen together. Did she love him? she asked herself in her diary—but had to confess that, for all her regard for him, she did not.

He was three weeks there. The simple friendliness and unpretentiousness of the Bohemian countryside seemed true, good-hearted, 'like a domestic animal'.[28] But he was no further forward; and his indecision may be measured from the fact that he went next to Riva to join his mother again. Writing to Sidie on the way, from Innsbruck, he thanked her for the 'beautiful, rich, happy days' he had spent at Janowitz. 'The life of the three of you is close to me now—my own seems often distant and hard to fathom'.[29] At the end of September he wandered on to Munich, attracted by the announcement of an exhibition with Oriental manuscripts and Islamic art.

Of all the cities of Germany, Munich was that which came closest to Paris in his estimation, and he was tempted, briefly, to settle there. Hofmannsthal, who happened to be in the same hotel, sent him a ticket for the première on 29 September of his adaptation of the *Oedipus Rex* of Sophocles; he saw Moissi in *Hamlet*; and it was a pleasure to meet again friends from earlier days, like Elsa Bruckmann, whose husband was the publisher of the art journal now preparing another issue devoted to Rodin, on which his advice had been sought. The highlight of his stay was undoubtedly the Islamic exhibition, especially the display of materials and carpets, which he found 'quite incomparable'. These had been 'true marvels', he wrote to Rodin: but the weeks of nomadic life were coming to a close and he would be back in Paris shortly.[30]

Still drifting, and in danger of sinking unless he found the new beginning he needed, he clutched now at a straw which seemed to offer hope. In Munich he chanced to meet the wife of a wealthy fur dealer, Jenny Oltersdorf: neglected by her husband, she was planning a journey over the winter with friends to North Africa, and, attracted by the melancholy poet, suggested he might join them—not without some expectation, clearly, that a more intimate relationship might develop. The foretaste of the Eastern world he had gained from the exhibition lent glamour to the idea, as he recalled Clara's journey to Egypt and imagined what new impressions in such exotic surroundings could do for him: and he began at once to work out how he could manage it. His new friend was apparently quite prepared to treat him as her guest, but he was not anxious to be thus beholden, and felt it important to pay his own way. From Cologne, therefore, where he stopped for a few days on the way back to Paris, he turned once again to Kippenberg, to ask whether the Insel could possibly make him a special advance for the coming year. A quick decision had to be made if he was not to miss this opportunity. Although he proposed to give up his rooms at the rue de Varenne and raise as much cash as he could, there would not be enough to cover such a tour, which might stretch over several months. He realized it was a lot to ask, but the prospect seemed to fit so marvellously with his present situation that he felt he must not fail to 'put this question to destiny'. There was a limit however even to Kippenberg's generosity. The most he could do, he replied, would be to pay him now the quarterly allowance due in January. He greatly regretted being compelled, for the first time, to disappoint his hopes, and trusted that the journey, which held out such promise, would nevertheless be possible.[31]

Rilke had not really expected better than this, and went ahead with his plans, confident that somehow he would manage at least part of the tour. Already from Cologne he had written to André Gide, whose *Porte étroite* he had long admired and and whom he had met earlier in Paris, to ask his advice on travel in Algeria and Tunisia. He felt on the threshold of a truly new departure, the sense of adventure enhanced perhaps by the knowledge that he would be with a new and attractive companion. It was symptomatic that, accepting Kippenberg's offer, he said he did not feel capable of undertaking a task the publisher had suggested some time earlier, which in former times he would have been only too delighted to embark on, and which would have helped even further financially—the revision of a translation of Jacobsen's works. He had been through a sort of crisis, he wrote to Marie Taxis: circumstances had shown him a way out into the world now, however, and he hoped that, with her protective influence still reaching over him, he could return with something achieved.[32]

Jenny Oltersdorf joined him in Paris in November. The plan was to sail from Marseille to Algiers on the 19th, spend six weeks in Algeria and Tunisia, and return to Naples at the end of the year: after that perhaps Egypt, but this was not yet certain. Kassner, who was now in Paris for a while and with whom Rilke felt this time more at ease, had once been to Biskra, and from him and from Gide he gleaned useful hints for the European traveller in North Africa. The day before his departure, writing to Clara to tell her what was afoot—but making no mention of Jenny—he confessed he did not find it easy to leave Paris: 'yet I feel so plainly that I must be on my way again, travel as far as ever I can'.[33] He had decided after all not to give up his rooms, and it was a comforting thought that they would stand ready for his return. The previous day he had taken Jenny to call on Rodin, and had learned from him something which overshadowed his pleasant expectations of the journey: the report— premature, but to become fact shortly afterwards—of Tolstoy's death. 'It becomes ever harder to find the outward expression for the activity of the soul: Ibsen achieved it, obstinately, through his art; Tolstoy, avid for truth and namelessly alone, forced life time and again to be the thermometer of his soul's condition. The enormous pressure under which this final act was played drove the mercury up far beyond the scale of conscience, till no reading was possible—yet he fulfilled himself as a poet . . .'[34]

Not much evidence has survived—or at any rate been revealed—of the progress of this journey, which after Russia was the most extensive he ever undertook. For so compulsive a letter-writer he seems to have put pen to paper comparatively rarely, and with few exceptions only to Clara and his mother. The party spent a week or so in Algiers before going inland to Biskra. The climate he found invigorating, and the startling suddenness of the rising of the sun, 'smooth and ready-made', over the Atlas a remarkable experience. The native quarter was straight out of *A Thousand and One Nights*, 'beggars and porters go around as though in destinies, Allah is great and there is no power but His in the air'.[35] From the balcony of his room at Biskra he could look down on an enclosure where the caravans spent the night. 'The village is small, but stands in a vast countryside of palm groves and mountains . . . a market, coffee-houses, domino players squatting on mats, two streets full of dancers, now and then the sound of a reed pipe . . .'[36] They made an excursion to the gorge of El Kantara, impressive gateway to the desert.

By the middle of December they had reached Tunis, where the souks could at moments give almost an impression of Christmas, with their gaily-coloured stuffs and hangings and glittering gold, and where in the light of the evening lanterns the Thousand and One Nights were transformed into 'everything one ever anticipated and wished for'. Even by day he was astonished at the play of the sunlight there, through the gaps in the roof, on the variegated colours. 'In the perfume souk we already have a friend . . . I asked him for geranium essence (which is often sold for attar of roses); it pleased him I should ask for that, and not attar of roses, he initiated me in it and thus we became friends.'[37] On Christmas Eve the party planned to attend a mass to be held in a former mosque. The mosques themselves, he wrote to Phia, were 'houses of God, of another faith but of the same God, you can feel that from the religious fervour in which life here concentrates its effort. It is a land of great and passionate belief, and you only have to recall that it was here early Christianity struck strong roots, Carthage or nearby was the native soil of Saint Augustine'.[38] Visiting Kairouan, 'after Mecca the great centre of pilgrimage for Islam', there was borne in on him 'the simplicity and living quality of this religion, the Prophet is but from yesterday, and the city his own like an empire'—or 'like a vision . . . with nothing but flat plain and graves around it, as though besieged by its dead'. For the first time he saw columns, isolated, surviving on abandonment, 'standing quietly over against far distant horizons'.[39] They sailed for Naples on 29 December, with brief calls at Trapani and Palermo, and from there the decision would be taken whether or not to go on to Egypt.

Though by more modern standards it was a leisurely enough tour, it would be a long time before he could find words for these new impressions, he had written to Clara from Algiers. He had gazed with the eye, not of the artist, but of a mere beginner, 'trying himself, hesitatingly and awkwardly enough, against some wise and immeasurably superior existence'.[40] Much later, he realized that he had gained more than he thought at the time: 'in spite of the "foreignness", the Arabian character was, after the Russian, the closest to my own'.[41] He had even made a start on learning Arabic, and decided in Naples to continue with the party when they finally made up their minds to go to Egypt. It was with some hesitation, however, and this was mainly for financial reasons, for the trip so far had been far from inexpensive, in the best hotels in Algiers and Tunis; he was in the Hassler once more at Naples, and in Cairo it was to be Shepheards. Kippenberg was prevailed upon to send yet another quarter's payment in advance.

It was almost a year now since his work in the turret room at the Richterstrasse, Rilke wrote to Katharina the same day. Since then he had quite lost the ability to write; after *Malte* there had been a kind of crisis, in which the old habits had died and new ones failed to grow; his life had 'gone into chrysalis form', following Heaven knew what strange law. Even the long journey was not giving him a new outlook, merely shaping a further cocoon around this chrysalid existence, but he was determined to press on to the new horizons ahead: the Oriental world had begun to open up for him, and his expectations had not been disappointed.[42]

They arrived at Alexandria on 8 January 1911, went on immediately to Cairo and on the 10th began a journey up the Nile aboard the *Rameses the Great*. The first stop was opposite Helwan, and they landed and rode out towards Sakkhara, near ancient Memphis, to the palm grove where the colossus of Rameses II lay, 'as only world, alone with itself, can lie under the fullness of space'. The following day they sailed on past the minarets of Beni Souef, past villages under the palms, little Coptic monasteries, quarries: 'we can see all the life on the banks, from that of the birds to the simple routine of the villages, brown and monochrome as they descend to the blessèd waters: groups of shepherds and merchants, funeral processions pressing hastily by, the single figures of the women carrying water ...' As the day clouded over, the colours changed to variations on a brown 'which has the secret of looking pink ... and you get more and more accustomed to savouring the black or blue of the figures as colours and treating the rare spot of red as a jewel'.[43] And so further, until they reached Luxor: landing occasionally on the way, riding through the desert or to the 'gigantic tombs hewn in the rock where paintings and columns are preserved'—though sometimes he jibbed at being herded along the tourist circuit, and stayed aboard with his Arabic grammar and dictionary, savouring the wonderful evenings, 'the nights when the vastness of space handles you like a rose petal'. In some ways, he was reminded, he wrote to Phia, of the splendid voyage up the Volga.[44]

His few letters were brief jottings of immediate impressions, just as he had urged Clara to write when she was in Egypt, recorded as they came, to be sorted and digested later. Luxor and Karnak, though they could spend only three days there, were the most memorable and striking experiences. 'This incredible temple world of Karnak which on the very first evening, and again yesterday, under the moon just starting to wane, I gazed—gazed—gazed—my God! one gathers one's strength, looks with both engaged in a desperate will to believe—and yet it begins above them, reaches everywhere beyond them (only a god can command such a field of view)—and there stands a lotus-bud column, solitary, surviving, one cannot grasp it, so remote does it stand, out beyond one's life . . .' Crossing the Nile, they rode through the great Valley where the Kings lay, 'each resting under the weight of a whole mountain, on which the very sun itself is halted, as if it were out of its power to keep kings in check'.[45] The voyage continued upstream as far as Aswan, where there were visits to the island of Philae and the dam installations.

By the end of the month they were back in Cairo, of which he had great expectations, he wrote to Clara while still on the ship, especially of the Museum.[46] In the event, in this 'threefold world' of vast metropolis, teeming life, and monumental artefacts he found himself overwhelmed. Writing to Kippenberg after ten days there, he said he could not see how one could cope with it all. He hinted too that the journey had not been without its contretemps—'but fortunately I foresaw most of them and took them calmly'.[47] Whatever he may have meant by this obscure allusion, we know as fact only that during February in Cairo he decided to separate from his companions and, pleading illness, sought sanctuary on the 24th in Helwan with Clara's former hosts the Knoops, at the Hotel Hayat. Jenny Oltendorf was one of the few women in his life who never recorded what passed between them, and gossip from third parties has revealed little that is reliable. Rilke himself took some trouble over a present for her birthday in the May after they parted, asking Kippenberg for a specially-bound copy of Dostoevsky's *Idiot* to be tooled with her initials;[48] but he made only one further reference, many years later, to this 'enigmatic friend', as he called her, when he came across her letters—'even now still full of fire and flame'[49]—which, with for him exceptional discretion, he apparently destroyed.

But everything points to the conclusion that she had pressed him to make it a closer relationship, and that he had refused. Insouciant in money matters he might be, but he was hardly likely to have embarked on such a costly tour, still less to continue it to Egypt, had there not been a stronger attraction than that of a mere change of scene: and when the affair threatened to make demands on him his reaction was to draw back and break it off. Jenny was certainly not cast for the role of 'guardian of his solitude'. The only letter of his that has come to light lends support to this interpretation. In the summer of 1911, from Lucerne, she had evidently announced a radical turn in her life—possibly a plan to leave her husband. In his reply, from Lautschin where he was once again a guest, he chatted about what he himself had been doing, his travels, and the contrast between Bohemia and the mountains around her: 'their nearness and steep rise will surely develop in you the feeling of bird-like freedom you are going to need. I'm not surprised, my dear, the plan stands in honourable relation to the great courage in you, your heart already flew with the birds in Heliopolis, no, not "with" them, quite on its own it soared up and described its curves in the wide open heavens where there was so much space.'[50] No doubt he would have happily continued a correspondence on this cordial though distant plane, as he had with Mimi Romanelli; but their contacts evidently lapsed before long, for by September of the following year he admitted he did not even know if she was alive.[51]

The Knoops' hospitality at Helwan had been a stroke of fortune, for his funds were fast running out. Worse, even though he could just manage the return journey to Paris, he could see that he would have virtually nothing left with which to start even the most modest life there again. Alarm signals therefore went out to all who might be able to help, both now and later—Kippenberg, the Princess and her husband, Sauer in Prague, and possibly others. The 'contretemps' of the journey now became 'all kinds of misfortune';[52] his illness (which does not seem to have been worse than a heavy catarrh and a natural fatigue after the tour) was stressed; he could see no future unless he could somehow get back to his 'fallow writing-desk'. Kippenberg of course was his main hope. He ought not to complain, he wrote at the end of February, for he had gained what he wanted, a definitive break between 'yesterday and today'. But the fact was he had got himself into serious straits, largely through his own fecklessness. His books seemed to be going well, but he had no idea what this really represented for his account. At all events, unless his friend could not only continue the regular payments but also let him have a certain sum in addition, he feared he would never be able to return to the self-contained life in Paris that was really his own, to *his* world 'that must be willed and conquered', but would have to fall back on friends' hospitality, which in the end, however well-intentioned, could only frustrate. To Marie Taxis and the Prince, who were in Vienna, he hinted delicately that Duino, should they be going there at the end of March, would be a welcome staging-post on the journey to Paris. He wanted in any case, he told Kippenberg, to take his time getting back, so as to get rid of his catarrh and arrive in Paris in warmer weather. But if it was not possible—and always provided that the publisher could somehow assure his future in Paris—he would go direct: 'after all, only one thing is important for me—to be there.'[53]

Not without some misgivings, Kippenberg yielded once again to the pleas of his problem child. On 4 March he telegraphed his agreement to provide 500 marks extra for each of the months of March and April. 'I trust,' he wrote in his follow-up letter, 'that this will suffice to get you to some extent out of your troubles.'[54] Rilke immediately relaxed, and asked for the funds to be remitted direct to Paris. Arriving in Venice on 29 March, he found that Princess Marie was spending a short time there and not in Duino: a hotel stay was therefore unavoidable, and he had to dun the long-suffering Kippenberg for yet another remittance (this time as a loan) to see him through. On 6 April 1911 he was finally back in the rue de Varenne—full circle in every sense, for he was no nearer to finding his new start.

V

Duino and Spain
1911–1913
—⊶❦⊷—

'A man's own observation, what he findes good of, and what
he findes hurt of, is the best physicke to preserve health'

(Francis Bacon)

I

'I've still not achieved the turning my life must have'

(To Rudolf Kassner, 16.6.1911)

'In spite of all, one is a northerner at heart,' Rilke had written to Clara from
Venice: 'as I stood up forward on the ship, I should have liked to see a channel
open up through Europe, and let me sail right on to Norway.'[1] Paris, where
there were snow flurries as he arrived, was the next best thing; taking up the
old threads in expectation of the spring, he could still hope for the new
beginning. He had come close to frittering away the chance of returning there,
but all had turned out well, thanks to Kippenberg's help. As he resumed his
neglected correspondence and his friends heard the reason for his long silence,
the North African tour became now a venture into which he had been dragged
almost against his will, and no one would have guessed how eager he had been
in fact to go. 'I let myself be taken along by acquaintances who were on the
point of leaving—and really the only purpose was to put an abrupt end to a
hostile and gloomy time, and to try to bring about the change I needed from
the outside, since it would not come from within.'[2] In reality it had been his
hope that a new and exciting relationship would somehow get him over the
barrier, a stimulating episode after which he could return to his solitude
refreshed and ready for a new start. In the moonlight at Karnak, it might have
seemed still possible—but as soon as it became a threat to his solitude he
promptly abandoned it. For he had to remain the hermit 'in my theory'.[3] He
looked back now on the whole affair as nothing more than 'an evasion':
crossing the 'watershed' of *Malte*, he had found on the other side only sterile
country, a dry river bed as it were, to which the flood waters might or might
not return. Which was the more arrogant, he asked: 'to give up the work, step
down, as if something had already been achieved—or to stand firm through all
the drought, because what has been done is no more than the beginning of
what one has felt a boundless duty to strive for?'[4]

He stood firm, because he had no alternative. Paris was a hard assignment—'the beginning here is always a judgement';[5] but as the lilac and chestnut blooms began to appear, and the spring exhibitions opened their doors, it was a good feeling to be back, even though he still lay fallow. 'Paris is more nourishing than ever,' he wrote to Clara after seeing a splendid El Greco in an art dealer's window. Yet somehow the familiar surroundings of the Hôtel Biron did not seem to help his acclimatization. His rooms were not a real home, he felt, 'the concept of this Monsieur Rilke, 77 rue de Varenne, seems to me too unequivocal, too definite'.[6] Recollections of the journey lay 'in bundles inside', but instead of trying to put them in order he found himself longing for the Luxembourg Gardens 'like a sentimental dog for its first master',[7] and constantly returned to the glories of the red and white may blossom over its balustrades.

With an effort to accustom himself again to work, he began with some translations: *The Centaur*, a prose work by the Romantic poet Maurice de Guérin, published in 1840 after his death, and an anonymous sermon that had recently come to light in St. Petersburg, 'The Love of Mary Magdalene'. He had also discovered the sonnets of Louize Labé, sixteenth-century poetess of Lyon, 'la belle cordière', and in May sent a translation of one for a Vienna almanach. The obsession with 'intransitive love' he had made so much of in *Malte* found its echo here and in the 'Mary Magdalene'. All this was a sort of beginning, he said to Princess Marie, sending her the original of the sermon and a transcript of his translation of *The Centaur*, but the 'long drought' was really bringing him close to starvation: 'it is as though I had completely lost the capacity to create the conditions which could help me.' He needed somehow to reach a turning-point, but still sought it in vain. Should one invent a grotesque character, he asked her, just in order to introduce the sentence 'he has spent the last six or seven years fastening a coat-button that obstinately refuses to stay done up'?[8]

In this mood he did not find unwelcome the many distractions Paris had to offer or the inevitable spring tide of visitors. Gerhart Hauptmann's son Ivo, developing as a painter, was back, with Erica von Scheel, later to become his wife, and they had taken studios in the Biron, so that Rilke saw a great deal of the young couple before they left in May for the south. He would visit Erica almost every day for tea, share with her his enthusiasms, lend her books, and together with the sculptor Hans Arp they visited Aristide Maillol's exhibition in Marly-le-roi. The Kippenbergs were expected in the middle of May, their first time in Paris, and Rilke took much trouble over reconnoitring a suitable hotel and in advising and guiding them during their three weeks' stay in the city they had so far glimpsed only through the pages of *Malte*. In his room they heard his translation of *The Centaur*, and on Katharina's birthday, on 1 June, he welcomed them with a cake and read the *Mary Magdalene* he had just completed. (For the publisher, these were some signs at least of productivity,

and he put *The Centaur* in hand immediately on his return. It appeared in
July, dedicated to May Knoop.) Katharina found Rilke the ideal cicerone: 'he
would leave you a long time alone with a work of art, and then, just when you
began to feel the need to formulate what you saw, would offer you his own
profound experience of it.'[9] He took them too to Maillol, finding a cordial
reception with the sculptor and coming away, as he wrote afterwards to Erica
von Scheel, with a sense of having been in contact with a creativity constantly
renewing itself, like the water in a spring. 'When he is in his work it comes to
him as pure joy.'[10]

He missed few art exhibitions, and went with Harry Graf Kessler to the last
night of the Russian ballet season, with Nijinsky in *Sheherazade* and the
spellbinding new *mise-en-scène* for the *Spectre of the Rose*, 'dance in his every
vein'.[11] Kippenberg obtained for him an advance copy of Kassner's new book
The Elements of Human Greatness as soon as it was ready early in June, and he
devoured it eagerly, overnight and again at leisure in the Luxembourg
Gardens, 'as of old the place where I bury my best bones': 'a beautiful, strong,
helpful book ... unique, far ahead of the afflictions in which we live and
sending messages back from the next turning-point or the one after'.[12] 'Among
all of us who write and express, is not this man perhaps the most important?'[13]
Sending his appreciation to Kassner in Russia, he said he had not yet reached
his own turning-point: but while he was in Egypt he had written out, from
memory, one of the other's aphorisms—'the way from inwardness to greatness
lies through sacrifice'. It was a statement, as he said later, which spoke in a way
both for and against himself.[14]

While Kippenberg was still there, Rilke wrote to Gide suggesting a call if he
would care to meet the publisher. 'For myself, despite the long and varied
journey, I am still in the depths of that apathy of the spirit in which you saw
me leave'. Gide, one of the rare French writers with a command of German,
had been greatly impressed with *Malte*, and unknown to Rilke had just
completed a translation of two extracts, including the powerful description of
the bared wall of a demolished house still bearing the traces of its 'stubborn
life'. When he read these in the *Nouvelle Revue Française* in July, Rilke wrote
how moved he had been by such an 'inspired transposition, giving me back
two important fragments of my book more definitively, so to speak, than I
conceived them myself ... I never thought it possible to get so close to my
somewhat esoteric prose'.[15]

Thus, despite his indecision and inner uncertainty, there was much to
occupy him—as there always is for one who cannot settle to his own work. His
correspondence was active and varied, the pile of incoming letters sometimes
reaching unmanageable proportions. The steady reduction of such an accumulation usually made a kind of preparation for work to come, but now there was
little sign of that. The *Magdalene* translation was done, he wrote to Mathilde
Vollmoeller: 'I hope the good Lord will soon have some more work for me,

otherwise I shall pitch a stall across some niche in the street and start up as a cobbler, that seems a highly durable sort of occupation, and full of continuing inspiration'. The old longing for real solitude often returned, he told Erica von Scheel, who had suggested he might join them in St. Tropez; he must forget any idea of travelling again, and felt an 'indescribable need' to stick it out at his desk.[16] Unluckily, towards the end of June, the céiling directly above it developed alarming cracks, which threatened to break over him 'like a storm', and he was displaced by the repair work, with dust and plaster penetrating everywhere. Such resolution as he could summon up evidently weakened under this onslaught, for he seems to have escaped for a few days to Mont St. Michel. More travel too lay ahead, for Princess Marie had invited him again to Lautschin some time in July—although this he looked forward to now as a lifeline rather than a disturbance.

He was not entirely barren of ideas and impulses. His enthusiasm for Nijinsky was such that he felt he must 'make something' for him, he told the Princess: 'a poem which could so to say be swallowed and then expressed in dance'[17]—but it did not get beyond a fragment, 'Figurines for a Ballet', never published. Translations from Petrarch and the *Confessions* of St. Augustine were seriously considered. He had a sudden urge to discover Shakespeare, and Katharina Kippenberg sent him the new Insel edition, just out, of the Schlegel–Tieck version, delighted to give him her detailed advice on where to begin his voyage on this vast ocean. But all this was in a sense mere temporizing. He was able neither to resume the steady application to work he thought he had learned from Rodin, nor to find a new direction. His outward circumstances left nothing lacking: it was the inner need that remained unsatisfied, the need for that perfect partner who could be the complement to his solitude.

> Like a door that will not stay closed,
> so time and again as I sleep
> the embrace looses hold. O nights of trouble . . .[18]

Three years earlier, musing in a letter to Sidie Nádherný on how little he knew of his daughter, under the compulsion of his solitary vocation, and how he hoped that one day Ruth would understand what he had tried to do, he had imagined that, as she grew up, she might come to help him. 'Perhaps she is the person I need, more and more urgently, in my work . . . another hand to add to mine, two more eyes and a heart on which I can hear, as on a bell, what escapes me in the murmur of my blood . . .'[19] In Paris now he found someone who, it seemed, might be the one to bring such 'another heart' into his life. In the street one day he chanced across a young girl, pale and listless, so obviously at the limit of endurance that he felt he must do something for her. Marthe Hennebert, just eighteen, came from a very poor family, and had been earning her bread since she was eight; she was out of work now, and hungry. As they talked and he learned her circumstances—a beautiful and innocent being, only outwardly hardened by misery—he was more than ever convinced she must be 'saved'. He saw her often during June, and was increasingly amazed at her quick mind and eagerness to learn, despite the dark and uncontrollable side to her nature. He wrote poems to her, to the 'soul arisen with me': seeing himself as fanning into flame the dormant embers of her life, as an angel even, leading her to the gates of an undiscovered paradise:

> A rose to show you, this one, over there,
> too far for us and yet in fullest bloom,
> a hundred more, though faded, to rehearse
> in your now reawakened spirit.[20]

How much he himself was able immediately to do for her is not clear; but later he persuaded an artist he knew, Hedwig Woermann, living in Paris with her sculptor husband Johann Jaenichen, to take the girl under her wing and make a start with her education. He asked Sidie Nádherný too for some financial aid, to give the child 'a moment to draw breath, win friends for her and ... bring her life up to the level her nature deserves, have her learn something which can bring satisfaction to her and in which she can find herself and use her talents'. It was his dream, as he said later, that Marthe might develop to become that complement and protective influence he needed in his life.[21] The dream would prove unrealizable, of course; and it is difficult to understand quite how, concerned for her half as lover and half as father, he could imagine such a creature adapting herself to an existence in his shadow. But he continued over the years to do what he could to help her, through many vicissitudes and disappointments.

It was a preoccupation which undoubtedly made inroads into his funds as well as his time. 'Life here at the moment has really crowded in on me,' he had told Kippenberg at the end of June, excusing his delay in sending the promised foreword for the Guérin translation: financially he was fairly well covered for the summer, but he would probably need some extra help for the coming autumn and winter. The only possible sources for such aid, he wrote, seemed to be God, or the Schiller Foundation (where he was thinking of applying for a grant)—and God seemed the more worthy and richer hope, albeit more difficult to reach.[22] Kippenberg was able to calm his worries: 'you are forgetting that, between these two courts of appeal, there is a third, namely that of your friends.'[23] And in fact he did not only mean himself. The news in Rilke's despairing letters from Cairo, when he had felt Paris might be lost to him, had reached many ears. At the end of March Hofmannsthal too had heard about his plight from Kassner—*Malte* had perhaps contributed to the picture of the poet starving in a garret—and had written to Helene von Nostitz: 'some circumstance or other has landed him in a highly awkward situation, such that when he returns from Algiers [sic] he has no idea what he can live on for the summer and autumn. . . . We want now to turn to a few friends, like yourself, like Marie Taxis and Harry Kessler, who truly have much human sympathy for him and from whom a little help will surely come with friendly feelings. It is of course not a question of a *big* sum from each, that's the last thing we want, for the total we have in mind is no more than two to three thousand francs.'[24] Helene von Nostitz, and doubtless the others, had been only too pleased to contribute. Whatever was raised presumably found its way to Rilke anonymously through Kippenberg, for he never seems to have known about the generosity of these friends.

At all events he was relieved to hear from the faithful publisher that he need not rely on an uncertain Providence, nor go cap in hand to the Schiller Foundation. 'Just in time,' he wrote: 'looking at my bank account, it seemed as though by the end of August all exits would be walled up. If we can only put together the means to make a breach through which my heart can pass—if the worst comes to the worst, and if I live, I shall just throw it over the wall, let it fall where it may . . .'[25] 'Professional procrastinator'[26] that he was, he had anyway hesitated long over his plans for the summer. Lautschin with Princess Marie beckoned, Kippenberg wanted to see him in Leipzig again, Helene von Nostitz in Auerbach, in the Saxony Vogtland, where her husband had recently been transferred; and some time he must go to Munich, where Clara was planning to investigate proper schooling for Ruth.

On 19 July, finally, he set off for Prague, calling briefly on the Kippenbergs *en route*. His mother, unexpectedly, was there, instead of at Franzensbad, and he learned that his cousin Irene von Kutschera had just died. On 22 July he reached Lautschin—ready, as he told the Princess, to be made into the 'Dottor Serafico' she had decided to call him 'or into anything else really serviceable'. (She had wanted to find a special name, her own private name, for him— 'Rainer Maria Rilke' was too long, 'Rilke' too short, and 'Rainer Maria' wanting in respect; and he had been delighted with her idea. 'Perhaps it will be my real name, the secret name that belongs to me alone.'[27] 'Doctor Seraphicus' had been a sudden inspiration: whether or not she knew of that St. Bonaventure who had earned the sobriquet as reformer of the Franciscan Order in the thirteenth century and intrepid defender of human and divine truth, the hint of sublime wisdom seemed to her ideal now for the poet of the *Book of Hours* and, as she thought later, of the *Elegies*.)

Though he had met her only three times, his correspondence with Princess Marie had lent them such a close understanding that coming to Lautschin was like coming home, to 'familiar and dear relationships'.[28] The house party was more congenial than in Duino, and he could lead a quiet country existence, strolling through the park or the woods or seeking refuge, if it was too hot, in the book-lined rooms of the castle. Among the guests was an Italian writer, Carlo Placci, a good deal older than himself and one of the few men with whom he could feel at ease. These were 'long, slow days', hot enough to be almost a persecution for the farmer, but for him giving a comfortable feeling of having found at last a real summer, 'humming with insects and fluttering with butterflies'[29] (sentiments hardly likely to interest Jenny Oltersdorf as a reply to her letters).

His peace was short-lived, however. In the first days of August Princess Marie's four-year-old grandson Raymond developed an alarming temperature, which the doctor thought might signal scarlet fever or diphtheria, and the company rapidly dispersed for fear of infection. Rilke went back to the 'insupportable' Prague, to await the outcome, in the hope of returning to Lautschin—himself not well and nursing boils which had unaccountably come to plague him, unable even 'to read the Book of Job'.[30] Raymond's illness fortunately proved to be minor; and after a short visit to Janowitz, staying with Sidie Nádherný's brother and then meeting her in Prague on her return from England, Rilke was able to spend a few more days at Lautschin. Leipzig and the Kippenbergs remained his next port of call, and Princess Marie had an attractive suggestion: to join her in a drive there by motor car, and visit Weimar before he moved to the Kippenbergs.

They left on 20 August, and he enjoyed to the full this first experience on a long journey by automobile, 'the whole day map in hand like a General Staff officer, eating somewhere as in battle, sleeping somewhere as on a campaign'[31] (in fact, of course, in comfortable hotels in Leipzig and Weimar). 'It is as though you are travelling on the map itself, like a cheerful index finger, the villages don't go past disconnected, like sudden notions, but one develops naturally from the other and you combine them all easily into a whole, you never cease to be part of life, whereas in a train there are always neutral periods to be simply waited out.'[32] The Prince was to meet them in Leipzig, so Princess Marie had her poet to herself, declaiming from his verse as they made a halt under the oaks of the forests of Saxony, and continually delighting her with his receptiveness to new impressions and flashes of humour. They could spend only one day together in Weimar, for the Taxis were to travel on to London, but Rilke stayed on a while there after they had left.

In earlier years he had felt a strong antipathy towards Goethe, to the point of refusing to read him—an instinctive reaction, perhaps, against a poet who had not disdained the pursuit of worldly success, and a reaction intensified as he had observed Goethe's behaviour, to his mind almost monstrous, towards Bettina von Arnim. Kippenberg, however, an ardent Goethe admirer, with an already extensive collection of Goetheana, had given him a more open mind, even enthusiasm; and he was ready now for Weimar. In Goethe's house he was absorbed for hours with the tangible remains of an earlier existence, 'the small objects which unwittingly bear witness'[33] and which always fascinated him, the manuscripts and portraits. And during his stay with the Kippenbergs in Leipzig, where he arrived on 23 August, he began to find his way for the first time to the marvels of Goethe's verse, as well as paying another visit, under the collector's expert guidance, to Weimar, to see the archive. 'Goethe looked with favour on me for the first time,' he wrote later to Hedda Sauer: 'you know he had no altar in my temple, but reading the letters to Gustchen Stolberg I suddenly felt an inclination towards him, I was keen to find him and take some trouble—then came Weimar, and it was an annunciation, a revelation.'[34]

A more practical matter, however, was also occupying the publisher's mind. He had not given up his aim of acquiring from Axel Juncker the rights in the *Book of Images*, and it was agreed that Rilke should go for a few days to Berlin in an attempt to smooth the way for this. He failed to see Juncker, however, and was obliged to leave empty-handed on 12 September for Munich, where Clara was awaiting him.

She had been there for some time, and her work was flourishing, with a bust of Dehmel finished and an entry for a competition with a substantial prize. She planned to stay, and bring Ruth to join her from Oberneuland, to start a more settled school life now that she was nearly ten: this would mean taking an apartment, and the crucial factor was money, for which Clara had to turn to her husband. The decision was pressing with the school year just beginning. An unexpected source of relief to his purse had fortunately just been revealed, which might help to meet these immediate demands. His cousin Irene von Kutschera had left him a sizeable sum in her will, which would not be available for some months yet, but on the strength of which he could ask her sister Paula for a loan, to cover Ruth's transfer and the initial school fees. After some correspondence with Josef Stark, the lawyer who had succeeded to Uncle Jaroslav's practice in Prague, he was able eventually to secure the advances they needed from Irene's estate, thanks to the consent of her son Oswald, and Clara received them direct in October and January.

It is doubtful whether, without Clara's pressure, Rilke would have got even this far in the discharge of his responsibilities to his family, conscious though he was of them. His mind was elsewhere: he longed to be alone, to get back to Paris, to be 'deep down on the bedrock of work' again, even though he still had no clear idea of how to find it in a life that seemed to be 'avoided by the Muses', and was still irresolute.[35] Princess Marie had been well aware of this when she left him in Weimar, and had worried about how to help him. In London it occurred to her that Duino would be standing empty after her usual autumn house party, except for her English housekeeper Miss Greenham and the old butler Carlo, and it might be just what he needed. She wrote at once, on the impulse, to suggest they should meet in Paris and drive there together through Provence and northern Italy. He grasped eagerly at the chance, though he feared he would be a poor companion on the drive in his present mood: 'I can't tell you adequately how my need for solitude increases daily . . . What a blessing that you want to hide me in Duino: I shall stay there like a refugee, as if under another name, and only you will know it is I.' He would return to Paris as soon as he could, and wait there until they could drive off early in October. Perhaps, while she was in Duino, they could embark together on a translation of Dante's 'Vita nuova'—he knew that from childhood she had the *Divine Comedy* almost by heart.

She heard meanwhile how he had met Hofmannsthal again in Munich, and of the letters Marthe was writing him. 'The fire of her nature, now it has awakened to freedom, will be inextinguishable: a Shakespearean world.' Hedwig Woermann, he could see, had played the role of the sorcerer's apprentice, the girl had been released to a glorious independence, and the magic word to bring her under control again would be hard to find: 'poor "Dottor Serafico", never was he less the master . . .'[36] He could confide to Princess Marie his concern for Marthe; but he made no mention of a situation which had just arisen and which, on the face of it, was more important—the formalization of his separate life from Clara in a divorce.

According to his own account, when he wrote later from Paris to Stark to set the wheels of the law in motion, the initiative for this had come from Clara herself. Reluctant though she must have been to admit it, she could no longer be under any illusion that Rainer would ever attempt to re-establish their life together, even as the 'guardian of each other's solitude'. Since the spring she had been undergoing psychoanalysis, which had probably crystallized her decision. To settle in Munich with Ruth gave the opportunity for the fresh start which would one day have to be faced, and which was better made now, in her thirty-third year, than later. He himself had long been clear that they were better apart. As he wrote later to Sidie Nádherný, his presence was propitious neither to the artist in Clara nor to her life as a woman: 'the further and the more completely I withdraw from her life, the better it must be for her; I fully understood that she should propose the divorce.' But he realized how much harder it was for her than for himself. 'Everyone finds out, in due time, that work in art at some point is incompatible with the demands of life, it must be one or the other—but for a woman it may admittedly mean an anguish and a parting without parallel.'[37] He had not yet solved this problem himself, was indeed still on his quest for the being who could help him reconcile the conflicting demands, and in his present uncertainty the prospect of the formal freedom of divorce was probably far from unwelcome.

From both their viewpoints, therefore, it was a solution that made sense: but it was easier said than done. Though he had been formally registered in Prague as having left the Catholic church, he had unaccountably omitted to record this on the marriage certificate. In addition, his Austrian nationality, according to Clara's Bremen lawyer, was a bar to a divorce in Germany, and would first have to be renounced—a step which, in spite of all his criticism of Austria, he felt somehow reluctant to take. It was also difficult for two such nomads to produce the full documentation required by the bureaucracies; and Rilke, who never allowed the matter to interfere with his travel plans, found the correspondence with the lawyers, as it dragged out over the following two years, becoming more and more irksome. None of the obstacles was insurmountable, but both he and Clara began to have second thoughts, especially as they reflected on the distress this action might cause their mothers (the shock to Phia Rilke, believing him still a Catholic, would be profound). In the end, although from time to time in the years that followed they returned to the idea, the decisive step was never taken.

Though the Muses might now have temporarily deserted him, Rilke was as single-minded as ever in his search for the right conditions for their return, and determined to make sure that whatever arrangements he and Clara came to would acknowledge this priority as absolute. As he wrote frankly to his lawyer, 'my profession is of the kind that cannot be turned to useful account without doing it great harm, and like every artistic activity it has the peculiarity of demanding for itself unconditional attention and utter concentration . . . so that right from the start I have been able to make progress only by totally neglecting everything else, with a ruthlessness that is actually foreign to my nature.'[38] For Clara, of course, whether or not the divorce went through, it was vital to know to what extent he would provide support, if not for her, then for Ruth's education. Over the past year he had been making over for Ruth a small monthly sum which his mother allowed him from her pension; but apart from this his help had been sporadic and hand-to-mouth. And so, essentially, it remained. A windfall like Irene's legacy he was ready to share, and over half of this went to Clara, until it was used up in the course of the following year: but there was no question of his allotting a regular amount from his Insel income. Even after he learned, on his return to Paris at the end of September, that this would henceforth be raised to 500 marks a month, he was capable of assuring his lawyer that he could reckon 'with absolute certainty' on a monthly income of only 200 francs,* and for the moment could do no more for Ruth than he was already doing. (Such poverty, which made it impossible for him to support wife and child, must surely of itself be grounds for divorce, he told Stark.[39])

He was unaware, at the time, that the renewed sign of Kippenberg's 'loyal and powerful support'[40] had been made possible by guarantees from other friends: Kassner, von der Heydt, and Harry Graf Kessler had undertaken to join with Kippenberg in making up the income from the Insel to the new level for the coming three years, after which the publisher was confident that his author's sales would suffice. But even if he had known, he would probably have regarded their generosity as no more than was due to his 'mission'. What might seem ruthlessness was for him simply a matter of giving absolute priority to securing the conditions in which he could fulfil his task, and for which, even in his present sterility, he must at all costs plan. He had great hopes of his solitary stay at Duino; but he dreamed also of Spain, of Toledo, after seeing El Greco's *Laocoön* in Munich—who could tell where new

*At this time the franc and the mark were, very roughly, at parity.

inspiration might be found?—and he knew only too well how hard he found it to husband his resources. He was made even more cautious by a further complication which awaited him on his return to Paris. All the occupants of the Hôtel Biron, including Rodin, were given notice to vacate by the end of the year, which meant that after Duino the search for a home would have to begin once again. He had vague ideas of a return to Munich, perhaps to hear some lectures at the university on Egyptology and medicine, at any rate to programme his life a little until his 'work' returned. But for the moment he was content to look forward to Duino, and leave the future to itself.

When the Princess arrived from England on 10 October, she found she would after all have to travel to Vienna before being able to come to Duino. But she was anxious not to disappoint Rilke's anticipation of the journey, and so left her car with the chauffeur Piero for him to make his way in his own time. He left two days later, and took it in leisurely stages, through Avallon and Lyons to Avignon, where he had a day's 'rest' in the Hôtel d'Europe, to the coast at Juan-les-Pins, and then on through Ventimiglia to Piacenza and Bologna and finally to Duino, arriving there on 21 October. 'Not always easy,' he wrote to Kippenberg, 'at each night's stop to recover from the tempo and find myself again. The machine is in control, you are its property, at night you lie in bed like a sort of spare part, your dreams and ideas those of a nut and bolt. All the same, it was quite an experience—impressions in sheaves, one's whole face still tingling from the rubbing-in of so many different landscapes. . . . Whether I stay on here will be decided in the course of the next few days.'[41]

2

'Now I'm alone again, I hope for a long time. I need nothing
else, for me that's the fundamental material'
                                    (To Katharina Kippenberg, 13.1.1912)

It was his hope, after the restlessness of the past two years, to find repose in Duino—'that is, outward repose and inner movement'. He could scarcely ask for more favourable surroundings than this huge castle 'towering against the sea, like foothills of human existence, with many of its windows (including mine) looking out to the vast open expanse of ocean, directly into the universe one might say'.[1] Princess Marie wanted him to do entirely as he pleased, and had been more restrained than usual with invitations to other guests. Her elder son Erich was there, with his family, when he arrived; Kassner came to stay for a week on 5 November directly from his long tour of Russia; a little later they were joined by the Scottish landowner Horatio Brown, friend and literary executor of John Addington Symonds and an authority on the history of Venice, where he had lived for many years. Of course, no hospitality of this kind, with such an active hostess—excursions to Aquileia, pigeon shoots, concerts by the Trieste Quartet on the terrace—could ever allow the guest the total solitude Rilke always needed. But he was not really ready yet for that: and in the knowledge that towards the end of the year he might be able to stay on after the others had gone, he seems to have enjoyed to the full their company while they were there.

'Rilke was particularly happy to have Kassner there,' recalled the Princess in her memoirs. 'In the early morning they would take long walks . . . and from the terrace I would watch them return, deep in conversation: Kassner with his glittering, commanding eyes, violent in gesture, talking loudly, and beside him the gentle Serafico, leaning forward a little, turned towards him and listening earnestly, smiling occasionally but then again with an alarmed look in his eye as the other damned the world and all its works.'[2] Kassner had been eight months in Russia, travelling extensively, as far as Tiflis, Tashkent, and Bokhara, and his lively account brought home to Rilke how far back now his own memories of the vast land lay. 'I shall soon be like the little boy pulling along just a string, while the horse that was tied to it has long since come off and is lying overturned somewhere far behind.'[3]

Contrary to Princess Marie's first thought, he had been quite serious in his suggestion that they translate Dante together. Many years earlier, before his first visit to Florence, when he was deep in studies of the *quattrocento*, he had found in the Dante of the 'Vita nuova' the first poet, as it seemed to him, of true self-expression—'is anything more "modern" than this tireless, pitiless self-preoccupation?'—and had tried his hand at a translation of one of the sonnets, that on Beatrice's death.[4] To take up the 'Vita nuova' again might be a step on the road back to his own lost productivity, and the idea appealed to the dilettante in the Princess. During November they began a regular evening routine. He would join her punctually at six in her little low-ceilinged drawing-room (by the sound of it, not unlike that of Lady Marchmain at Brideshead), bringing his own oil lamp to supplement hers and settling into a favourite armchair. Each had a copy of the work: the Princess would read aloud one sonnet and the commentary, they would discuss it, and then Rilke would translate it word for word into simple German prose. This in turn they went through in detail, and finally he would make an attempt at a rendering in verse form, often astonishing her with his virtuosity, though he maintained his efforts were no more than preliminary sketches. Regrettably, none of the versions thus made has survived.

This was work, of a sort, and served to some extent to bring his hand once more into practice. He still spoke of his earlier plan to write on Admiral Zeno, and also developed at length to Princess Marie his favourite theme of the great 'unhappy lovers' of the past, which he said he must one day treat more fully. When she happened, turning out a drawer one day, to find a diary, written in a tiny book, of a close friend of her mother's, Thérésine Rayson, who had lived as one of the family and carried the burden of a tragic love affair which was

never revealed to the children, he was greatly moved to discover this link with
a modest sister of his 'great lovers'. His obsession with such destinies, and
what he believed was the positive power of spurned or unrequited love, found
many reflections in his later poems, but was never developed into the
philosophical prose of which he spoke to Marie Taxis. Instead, it was almost as
though he was impelled to demonstrate its validity in his own life, by himself
playing the part of the spurner. Thus now, when he spent a few days in Venice
at the end of November with Marie and Erich Taxis, he was not averse to
calling once more on Mimi Romanelli, in connection with the purchase by
Marie Taxis of some pictures from Pietro Romanelli—reawakening her love
only to leave her again, and then indoctrinating her into the role she was to fill
by sending her his copy of the original sermon on 'L'amour de Madeleine': 'a
work which I envy, for I could have written it myself, ought in fact to have
written it . . . but only its translation was left for me.'[5]

After their return from Venice Erich and his family departed, and the
Princess planned to leave towards the middle of December. Rilke was hesitant
at committing himself to the total isolation which stood ready for him: but the
foreclosing on his home in the rue de Varenne, due in the New Year, left him
no practical alternative. He had left provisional instructions with a firm of
packers in Paris to collect and store his furniture, books, and papers, and he
wrote now to ask Erica von Scheel, with whom he had left a key, to oversee the
work for him. She was to send him two copies of the *Book of Images* before
they were packed, and of course take or borrow for herself any books she
wanted—'books don't like being in boxes'. He asked her too to send him the
measurements of his standing-desk: 'I am thinking of having one made here, if
it should really come to the point of holding out for a longer time.' She was not
to be surprised if she met Marthe in his rooms, though the girl was not likely to
be there often, as Hedwig Woermann was keeping her days well occupied with
a cookery course. (When she went in, she did in fact find Marthe, not best
pleased, it seemed, at her intervention, and claiming that Rilke had promised
to give her his looking-glass. But he reassured Erica when she reported this: 'I
would let Marthe have anything rather than deprive her of the smallest item,
for it is so hard in her life to acquire the things we have almost as our
birthright.'[6])

Having finally decided to stay, he horrified the Princess and her Miss
Greenham with a proposition to isolate himself still further by taking up his
quarters, not in the castle itself, but in a dilapidated pavilion which stood some
distance away, in the woods of the so-called 'Tiergarten', a sacred grove indeed
but with no water and no means of seeing to his creature comforts, simple
though he claimed these would be. He even began to rummage through the
castle for odd items of furniture which he might use. But in the end he had to
admit it would not do, and the Princess was relieved, when she left on 12
December, to have him more suitably installed in Erich's corner room, which

looked out on the sea both eastwards towards Trieste and south-west to Grado. 'I shall have to try and climb over the hump of the year here, . . . inside these old walls; outside, the sea, the karst, rain, maybe tomorrow storm: now we shall see what the inner self offers as a counterweight to such prodigious elemental forces. So—unless something quite unexpected turns up—I shall stay here, hold out, keep still, in a sort of curiosity about myself . . . Hearts, like medicine bottles, bear the words "Shake well before taking", and I've been continually shaken up these past years but never taken, so it's better I should aim now in quietness for clarity and productivity. . . . The old castle sports a very stout skin, but inside there is a fair amount of fruit in which the living is juicy, though not without demanding some adaptation and trouble.'[7]

His solitude seemed empty at first, he wrote to Marie Taxis in Vienna. 'But I shall gradually get the taste for it . . . nothing in the world could be more necessary for me now.' He ordered the new standing-desk, tangible sign of his resolve; walked in the Tiergarten when the weather allowed; but otherwise spent much time in his room, relaxing in the care of Miss Greenham, who kept the hum of household activity away from him. Carlo agreed to serve his meals in the adjoining room, 'with the infinite benevolence of a big old dog who allows some puppy to eat out of his bowl. The cook was bewildered the first day, faced with my vegetarian demands, but we have gone some way to meet each other and she is recovering her skill, today she was really inventive. . . . At 7 I have a supper worthy of a child, and am ready for bed just after 9, Lord preserve my simplicity.'[8]

It must be possible, he had told Sidie Nádherný earlier, to use the old walls like an iron mask, with only very few knowing who was hidden inside.[9] In fact, the outside world knew very well where he was, and since his arrival business correspondence had given him little respite. Kippenberg was as active as ever in his interest, with further editions planned for the *New Poems*, and sent him a contract for the *Cornet*, the rights for which he had finally succeeded in wresting from Juncker, though the *Book of Images* was still outstanding. The *Magdalene* was in final proof, and sending it back in December Rilke urged him to produce it in as cheap an edition as possible: 'how many women need this, how many will it support and comfort . . . this is where woman's suffering is transformed into greatness . . . Let us make sure this vademecum comes into many, many hands (hands of women and girls, it's no concern of man, *cet animal . . .*)'[10] Kippenberg also wrote to suggest a translation of Verhaeren's monograph on Rembrandt, which he was keen to publish. Rilke was glad to see again this 'passionately conceived testimony', but felt he would be unable to find the right tone for its rendering into German, apart from being insufficiently familiar with Rembrandt's works. Stefan Zweig, he wrote, perceptively, had come much closer to Verhaeren, and would be a better choice for the task.[11]

The publisher had wisely realized that the more he could relieve his poet of

the correspondence inevitably generated by his increasing renown, the sooner
he would find his way to renewed productivity: and it was becoming routine
now for Rilke to treat him as his general man of business, sending on letters for
him to deal with, as well as making all kinds of requests as they occurred to
him—to find a librarian for the Taxis' collection, consider the publication of
the memoirs of the Prince's grandfather, or search for second-hand books.

Business on which his friend could not help him, of course, was the divorce
procedure. For the moment the lawyers were not plaguing him with too many
questions. But it is clear that Clara's proposal, no matter how minor its
practical effect on his situation, weighed on his mind. Coming as it did when
he was still languishing in sterility of inspiration, it reinforced his sense of
hopeless blockage, paralleling in his sentimental life the dead end he seemed to
have reached in his work. For, even if his separation from Clara were
formalized, he was no nearer to finding the right companion to replace her,
someone who could support his solitude in the way he needed.

While still in Munich, when he had grasped at the Princess's offer of Duino
as a refuge, he had heard something of Lou, in a context which made his
thoughts turn once again to her. Victor Erich von Gebsattel, later to qualify as
a doctor, deeply interested in Freud's doctrine, and already trying his hand as
a psychoanalyst (it was he who had been treating Clara), had just returned
from Weimar, where both he and Lou had attended, as lay persons, the Third
Congress of Psychoanalysts. Rilke had first met him in Paris, during the winter
of 1908/9, the 'gloomy and laborious period'[12] of the gestation of *Malte*, and at
that time had often discussed with him these new theories, perhaps even the
possibility that analysis might resolve the problems besetting him—the
malaise, both mental and physical, he had talked over with Lou when she came
to the rue de Varenne just afterwards, in May 1909. The Weimar Congress
now marked an important milestone in the advance to practical application of
the theory of analysis, and it was natural that Gebsattel should have considered
it with Lou as therapy for the depression their friend was in, deeper still now
that *Malte* was behind him: though both had their doubts of its advisability in
his case.[13] As Rilke pondered the idea once more, in the lonely fastness of
Duino, his instinctive feeling—just as it had always been over his bodily
illnesses, real or imagined—was that he must be his own healer. On the other
hand, he desperately needed someone's help to find the way: and the news that
Lou also was, as it were, entering the field made recourse to her almost self-
evident.

The bitter feeling left at their parting, just before his marriage—that she
had shaped him and then let him fall, 'the height that gave me blessing, to
become the abyss that swallowed me'—had long since mellowed. In poems
written to her now—the only verse he succeeded in achieving in the closing
months of 1912, apart from an 'Evening Song' for Ruth's birthday—he looked
back on a relationship which had offered them both fulfilment:

As one will hold a handkerchief before
accumulated breath—no, as one presses it
against a wound from which in one spurt life's
trying to escape, I held you to me, saw
that you were red with me. Who can express
what happened to us? We made up everything
for which there'd been no time. I ripened rarely
in every impulse of omitted youth,
and you yourself, above my heart, beloved,
entered upon a kind of wildest childhood.[14]

Lou had been his 'doorway to the open air',[15] through her he had found maturity 'in every impulse of omitted youth', while she through him had discovered and grown into her own youth (the echo of the 'Final Salute' is unmistakable). 'Recalling won't suffice here,' he wrote,

from those moments
there must remain a layer of pure existence
upon my being's floor, a sediment
of measurelessly overflowing solution.
For I'm not *recollecting*—all I *am*
bestirs me now because of you. I'm not
discovering you at sadly cold-grown spots
you've left: the very fact that you're not there
is warm with you and realer and more
than a privation.[16]

Analysis, as he understood it from the little he had heard, would be a turning inside out, a complete emptying, of his being: a prospect he found 'hair-raising', and which could well leave him even more purposeless than before.[17] What need had he of that when Lou was there?

Why should I eject myself,
while, it may be, your influence falls upon me,
lightly, like moonlight on a window-seat?[18]

He did not show these poems to her until many years later. But after his solitary Christmas, he wrote her his first letter for over a year, 'another of my confessions', taking it for granted that she would still find interest in the 'subject of Rilke' and would be willing to hear him out. At great length he described the hopelessness he had felt since *Malte* was completed. 'Perhaps that book should have been written as one sets off a mine—perhaps I should have jumped right away from it when it was ready. . . . It was presumptuous of me to invest my whole capital in a forlorn hope: but on the other hand only in the loss could its value become apparent.' Nearly two years, wasted and wretched, had gone by since then: patience was needed, he had told himself, but the patience he had thought to possess had worn increasingly thin as

everything he saw and touched seemed to turn to ashes. He had seen Rodin at
seventy faltering in the toils of a ridiculous affair: if even the supreme master of
work could not prevail, how could he expect anything of his own poor efforts?

What on earth *is* this work, if one cannot experience and learn everything from it, if one
stands around outside it and allows oneself to be pushed and shoved, grasped and
dropped, entangled in happiness and injustice, and can never understand anything.—
Dear Lou, it goes ill with me when I want others, need others and look around for
them: it only drives me into deeper gloom and makes me guilty; they cannot know how
little trouble really I take over them and what ruthlessness I'm capable of. So it is a bad
sign that since *Malte* I have often hoped to find someone who would be there for me—
how does that happen? I had an inexpressible longing then to shelter my solitude with
someone, to place it under their protection . . . With a kind of shame I think back to my
best Paris time, the time of the *New Poems*, when I looked for nothing and nobody,
the world itself was all before me simply as a task or duty, and I replied, clear and sure
of myself, with pure achievement. . . . I awake each morning feeling my shoulder cold
just where the hand should grasp to shake me. How can it be that now, prepared and
readied for expression, I am without the call, superfluous?

What was he to do, he asked her. A doctor could not help, still less a
psychoanalyst, whose treatment would be a once-for-all purge leaving him
probably more hopeless than in his present disorder. Was all this just the
symptom of 'the long convalescence' that was his life? Or did it mean some
new illness? It was perhaps a good thing that for the time being he was safely
tucked away, imprisoned almost, within the immense walls of Duino.[19]

Lou was certainly not averse to taking up the subject of Rilke again. His
'case', indeed, which she knew so intimately, was one of the determining
factors in her resolve to embark on a serious study of Freud's theories, and
remained a key example in her later work in psychoanalysis after her schooling
by the master. She replied at once, and more letters passed between them in
rapid succession over the first few months of 1912. Though hers, regrettably,
have not survived, it is clear from his that it did him immense good to be able
to unburden himself to her. He spent whole days during January, pouring out
all his feelings and fears, analysing his thoughts and actions and hesitations—
like a mole, as he said, throwing up dark earth across her path.

On 14 January he also wrote to Gebsattel to ask him whether he thought
psychoanalysis might yet be the answer: but to him, as to Lou, he maintained
his own serious reservations. He was loth to undergo a 'correction' that was
artificial, like red ink on the page of a school exercise-book.[20] Gebsattel was
apparently not encouraging in his reply, although ready to lend his services if
his friend insisted. Rilke sent his letter on to Lou, repeating his own doubts,
but still undecided, more especially as he felt himself more and more ill at ease
physically, sometimes unbearably so. 'The hypersensitivity of the muscles, for
example, is such that any slight exercise . . . produces swellings, aches etc., and
then, as if they were waiting for this, come all kinds of fears, interpretations,

and torments; I am ashamed to admit how, often for weeks on end, this fatal circle encloses me, with one misery feeding on another.' The immense effort of art demanded the support of a body which did not imitate its excesses, and in his case his body was in danger of becoming the caricature of his mental processes. 'Dear Lou, if it's not too much for you, send me a few words to help me decide. . . . You see how it is with me, up and down, now this way, now that: what should I do?'[21]

If these long missives were our only evidence, the picture of Rilke in Duino would be a dark one indeed, a state of almost pathological introspection and exaggerated hypochondria. And yet we know that he passed his Christmas and New Year much as he had passed others when alone: happy to be able to send copies of the *Centaur* translation to a few of his friends, and reminding many others of his existence in letters which, although not without complaint over his inability to work, were still in the old tone and attuned to each correspondent. Mathilde Vollmoeller heard his enthusiasm for El Greco's *Laocoön* and his congratulations on her marriage, Julie von Nordeck and Manon zu Solms his nostalgia for Capri; Erica von Scheel his memory of Chartres Cathedral with Rodin, Rodin himself his hopes that the Master would find an alternative to the Hôtel Biron he too was about to have to leave. He spent much time over the negotiations with the Romanellis for the pictures Marie Taxis wanted, and was delighted to be able to tell her, on Christmas Day, of Pietro Romanelli's final acceptance of her offer: 'I'm very proud of this, my *début* as intermediary.'[22] Ilse Sadee, a young admirer in Krefeld, received a long and thoughtful comment on the poems of her fiancé which she had sent. Gide heard from him, seeking his help in obtaining Pascal's death-mask for a doctor friend in Munich; to the Fischers he sent belated good wishes on the house's jubilee, with his views on Hofmannsthal's *Everyman* and a request for a separate copy of the *Neue Rundschau*. And, as always, he was reading voraciously: St. Augustine, Ribadaneira's *Legends of the Saints*, Balzac's letters to Madame Hanska, the work of the Dane Johannes Jensen.

In short, alongside the conscious unburdening in his letters to Lou, he was already 'in work', and finding the way to being his own healer. Writing to a friend was not simply a conscientious discharge of an obligation, ticking off a reply in his carefully maintained letter-book: it was also the groundwork of that self-analysis which would eventually free him of his troubles. To Lou he could make his full 'confessions'; his letters to the others, each in their different way, were all part of the same process. Merely to write, out of the blue, to Tora Holmström, who had not heard from him for many months: 'I'm a worked-out field, there must at least be some weed that can flourish on me when I see myself so completely arid',[23] or to Marie Taxis: 'I creep around the whole day in the thickets of my life and cry out like a savage and clap my hands, you won't believe what hair-raising creatures fly out', was in itself a relief and a step forward. Beneath the complaints there was increasing confidence in the efficacy of his own treatment. 'Every day I become a little sharper, if anyone were to come it could be dangerous for him, I may bite any minute.'[24] Even as he hesitated whether to take the plunge into psychoanalysis, the subconscious decision was already taken, for he was curing himself, of his non-productivity at least.

Over Christmas Heinrich Vogeler had proposed to Kippenberg the publication, with his illustrations, of Rilke's poems on the Virgin Mary—a project which they had considered long ago in Worpswede and which Rilke had thought abandoned, more especially since their ways had diverged. He could not in fact recall having ever written enough for a full 'Life of Mary', and was doubtful: but his undiminished friendship and respect for Vogeler made him take up the idea seriously. During January, even while he was writing in such apparent desperation to Lou and Gebsattel, he produced thirteen poems to form *The Life of Mary*—inadequate sketches, as he later thought, and put together 'second or even third hand, adopting rather than inventing'. But, as it turned out, the work was 'a little mill' driven by the flood of a greater stream, for as he wrote it he was suddenly seized by the concept of the *Elegies*, 'perhaps the greatest and purest work of my heart'.[25]

To the Princess, he later claimed that the germ of the First Elegy had sprung from nothing less than the divine afflatus, an unlooked for inspiration. One morning he had received a tedious business letter, he told her, which required immediate attention. Outside a strong *bora* was blowing, but the sun was shining and the sea a radiant blue, shot over with silver. He climbed down to the narrow path connecting the two bastions to east and west at the castle's foot, from where there was a sheer drop of two hundred feet to the sea. As he walked up and down, lost in thought over his answer to the letter, he suddenly stopped dead—for he seemed to hear a voice call through the roar of the wind:

> And if I cried, who'd listen to me in those angelic
> orders?

As Marie Taxis related it, 'he stood still and listened. "What is that?" he whispered. "What is coming?" Taking out the notebook he always carried, he wrote down these words and several more verses that formed themselves without any conscious effort on his part. Who had come? He knew now: the god. Then he went up to his room quite calmly, laid the notebook away and dealt with the letter. Yet by that same evening the entire First Elegy had been written down.'[26] What was more, within the next few weeks he had written a second and formed a clear picture in his mind of the structure of the whole work, writing down fragments of three more Elegies and, more firmly, the first fifteen lines of what he saw as the last.

'The fearful thing about art is that the further one advances in it, the more it commits one to the ultimate, to the almost impossible,' he had written to Lou, when still uncertain whether he could endure the test.[27] The Elegies were to be his commitment to his art, the celebration of the mission he had embraced in all its terror—

> Because beauty's nothing
> but the start of terror we can hardly bear,
> and we adore it because of the serene scorn
> it could kill us with. Every angel's terrifying—

and to culminate, if he could stay the course, in its jubilant praise:

> One day, when this terrifying vision's vanished,
> let me sing ecstatic praises to angels saying yes!
> Let my heart's clear-struck keys ring and not one
> fail because of a doubting, slack, or breaking string.
> Let my streaming face make me more radiant,
> my tiny tears bloom. And then how dear
> you'll be to me, you nights of anguish.[28]

The end he could already see, but not yet what had to lead up to it. It was beginning, the first two Elegies, which came fast: the distillation, dense and elliptical in its allusions, of his experience of the conflict between the poet's mission and the demands of life.

> All that was your charge.
> But could you live up to it? Weren't you always
> distracted by hope, as if all this promised
> you a lover?

Despite his longing for such another, some 'future beloved', someone who would be there for him in his solitude, he felt profoundly that this should not be:

> Isn't it time our loving freed
> us from the one we love and we, trembling, endured:
> as the arrow endures the string, and in that gathering momentum
> becomes more than itself. Because to stay is to be nowhere.[29]

In singing to the Angels, 'almost deadly birds of my soul', he was hymning the perfection for which the poet must strive:

> spaces of being, force fields of ecstasy, storms
> of unchecked rapture, and suddenly, separate,
> *mirrors*: each drawing its own widespread
> streaming beauty back into its face—

the perfection of giving and receiving in supreme non-dependence, without loss; in human terms seemingly attainable only by those who die young, or by the great lovers like Marianna Alcoforado or Gaspara Stampa, whose love no longer depends on its object; but still a goal he spent his life trying to attain.

> But we: we vanish in our feelings. Oh, we breathe
> ourselves out, and out; our smell dissolves
> from ember to ember.
>
> .   .   .   .
>
>   Like dew on new grass,
> like heat from a steaming dish, everything we are rises
> away from us.
>
> .   .   .   .
>
> Didn't the caution of human gestures on Attic steles
> amaze you? Weren't love and separation placed
> on those shoulders so lightly they seemed made
> of other stuff than we are?
>
> .   .   .   .
>
> The self-controlled knew this: we can only go this far.
> All we can do is touch one another like this. The gods
> can press down harder on us, but that's the gods' affair.
> If only we could find something pure, contained,
> narrow, human—our own small strip of orchard
> between river and rock. For our heart rises
> out of us as it did out of the others. And we can't
> follow it any longer into figures that tame it, or
> into godlike bodies where it finds a greater mastery.[30]

The First Elegy he sent immediately to Marie Taxis, transcribed into an old leather-bound book they had bought together in Weimar: 'the first Duino work (and the first for a long time!)' for which he felt the book had been expressly made.[31]

These monologues came to him naturally in the rhymeless verses, with mainly dactylic rhythms, of the antique elegy which had become a tradition in German literature since Klopstock and of which he had recently been reminded when he read Goethe's 'Euphrosyne'. They were as though 'dictated' to him, he always averred. To say the god had spoken is one way of putting it: more realistically, we can regard this sudden inspiration as the result of his instinctive determination, after the long preoccupation with his troubles, to heal himself. The 'voice' that had come now found one already prepared to begin. As Hermann Hesse wrote, a few years later, a poet, however attracted by the new approach of psychoanalysis, could not do otherwise than 'carry on dreaming and following the call of his unconscious'.[32] The Elegies were a remarkable instance, Simenauer has noted, of the elemental break-through of the poet's unconscious:[33] the words welled up, just as words would have emerged—though in a very different way—had Rilke laid himself on Gebsattel's couch. It seems highly likely that the day of this onset was 20 January 1912. That day he certainly received a business letter from his lawyer about the divorce proceedings, but more significantly it was also the day he received Gebsattel's reply to his question about the advisability of psychoanalytic treatment, and sent it on to Lou.

The decision for Lou, greatly exercised by his situation, was, as she later recalled, one of the most difficult of her life.[34] In a telegram, followed with a letter, she advised him finally against analysis. '*Dear* Lou, *good* Lou,' he wrote on 24 January,

> you *speak* to me when you write . . . and I am so prepared for what you say through my own feeling, the feeling I had at first and which you agree with, that I cannot fail to be convinced. . . . I know now that analysis would make sense for me only if that strange idea of *never writing again*, which was often in the back of my mind as a sort of relief while I was finishing *Malte*, were to become really serious. In that case, one could let the devils be cast out, for in ordinary life they are only disturbing and tiresome: and if the angels were to go with them, that too one could regard as a simplification and tell oneself that in the new profession (which?) they would surely be superfluous.[35]

Sending her two of the poems of the *Life of Mary*, he did not tell her yet about the Elegy just completed; but later in the month she received a 'shout of joy' with the good news. 'Daj Bog zhisn!' ('May God give life!') she responded, relieved to hear the crisis was past. For his part, he knew that this was only a beginning. 'The worst of it is,' he wrote on 7 February, 'that, purely physically, I am affected almost as badly by conception as I was before by sterility. An old coach, alas, once so finely sprung, and now—if the miracle rides in me a while I wonder why it doesn't get out again: I bump and rattle like the most miserable *telega** and practically fall to pieces.'[36] He had waited more than two years for this moment, had deliberately prepared for it in the solitude of Duino; but, just as the patient on the analyst's couch cannot expect a cure in one session, so he too would find the road to final expression of what was in him a long and hard one, though even now he could perceive the eventual shape of his elegiac symphony.

While the flow lasted, he made a regular routine of his days, which he was unwilling to interrupt. For Marthe's birthday in March, rather than look in Trieste for a present, he asked Marie Taxis' help in Vienna, and was delighted when she was able to find an antique silver locket exactly corresponding to the meticulous description he had sent her. He was still wrestling with his solitude like Jacob with the angel, he wrote to Sidie Nádherný: 'it is of course stronger than I, but that won't do me any harm.'[37] The Princess had meanwhile sent him her praise for the First Elegy, whose power had greatly moved her and which she had shared with Hofmannsthal and Kassner. 'I fully agree the nightingale is a marvellous bird,' he told her, 'would to Heaven all my thorny thickets were the right bush for it.' Any admiration for the poem should rightly fall to her, he added, 'for what would it have become without you,

*A Russian farm cart.

without our talks, without Thérésine, without Duino, without my retreat here for which I daily find more courage?'[38]

But in fact his courage was already slipping from him, and the changeable climate taking its toll, though he manfully stamped barefoot through the snow when it came. As February wore on he began to think of a move to Venice, and asked Kippenberg for earlier payment of the funds due; he had a longing to lay his hands once more on some 'warm old wall' in Italy. Remembering his first visit to Venice with Nathan Sulzberger, sixteen years earlier, he looked up Goethe again, and found himself reading the whole of the *Italian Journey*, lost in admiration at the serious, often pedantic, application to the gathering of new impressions on a tour which seemed to mark a turning-point in Goethe's life. 'I find it astonishing how everything comes at its due time, it can't be forced but when it does come it is inevitable,' he told Lou.[39] His plans for after Duino were for the moment only rough notes, as he had said to Kippenberg in January—loose sheets still unnumbered, whose order would have to emerge of itself in the fullness of time—but it was unthinkable, after living so long just outside the door to Italy, not to take the opportunity of going in.[40] His moods were as changeable as the weather, however, and he made no move until 'Pascha' Taxis came and took him off for a short stay in Venice during the last days of March.

While he was there, May Knoop passed through briefly from Helwan, accompanied by Algernon Blackwood, to whom she introduced him, and the two spent several hours together in a gondola. Blackwood, who had been at school in Germany, had little difficulty in following the conversation, but was unequal to contributing much himself, and in later years his main recollection of the encounter was of Rilke's incongruous dress—a black tail-coat and a billycock hat.[41] Rilke, however, as he wrote to Marie Taxis, felt they had 'made good contact in the short time, that is, we were full of honest admiration the one for the other',[42] and found they had much in common. Apart from Shaw, Blackwood was the only English writer he ever met.

He continued to write often to Lou during these still difficult weeks, grateful for the support of her letters, and wishing, as he said, that he had appealed to her sooner, immediately after *Malte* was finished. Knowing she had heard from Gebsattel of Clara's wish for the divorce, he spread himself in a dispassionate analysis of his relationship with his wife: Clara had been totally subordinated to him, taking on his very character, writing letters that could have been his, yet she had shown deep antipathy towards him when it came over her from time to time how much she had thereby accepted which was alien to her nature. 'If one tries, behind this, to find *her*, find what she has become since her girlhood, there is nothing there (aside from her role as a mother), nothing but this alternating function of ingesting me and eliminating me again.' If, as he hoped, the psychoanalytic treatment succeeded in casting him out alto- gether from her, she would probably have to start over again at the point where

Rilke in the Hôtel Biron, Paris

Rilke's dedication to Rodin of the *New Poems* 1908

The 'Rose Cottage', Capri

The castle of Duino

he had come to interrupt her life. He could see now why nothing real could come from their union. 'Either she *was* me, with all her strength, and thus too much for me, or she was a *counter-me*, a devil's advocate.' Even her work was a puzzle for him, for he could not conceive how true art could come without inner compulsion: work for her was simply there, diligently pursued and steadily improved—'rather like a well-kept annex where the cooking is done for the house'—and he could see no sign of that inner call to plunge head first, cost what it might, into true creation. He confessed he was worried what would become of her—perhaps life together with Ruth would be more beneficial for her than the pursuit of her art.

Only indirectly did he acknowledge any responsibility of his own. 'As a woman she should of course have been loved, for being loved brings the woman to fulfilment, and it's true that sometimes she went around with an expression that hit me like a reproach'—reminding him of Madame Rodin, on whom a shocked young girl had once remarked to him: 'For God's sake, did it have to be that she should take on such an *unloved* look?'[43] This had been, in fact, the rock on which their ship had run aground. Whatever the first careless rapture, it had soon dissolved in his realization that conventional union was not for him; and while she had tried for a time to be convinced by the lofty philosophy of 'guardianship of one another's solitude', it could not be in her nature to accept such a role permanently. He, however, was in earnest, and was in less doubt now than ever of the companion he needed: not a wife, but a silent helpmeet, making no demands but simply there to 'protect his solitude'.

Clara, he seems to have felt, would have to fend for herself. He was more concerned about Ruth, whose schooling had still not been arranged and for whom his responsibility was obviously more closely defined. This was a problem he could, and did, air with many other friends not yet privy to the divorce plans. Offers of advice, as usual, were not lacking from motherly and sisterly sympathizers anxious to relieve their poet from such worldly worries. Princess Marie's suggestion of a Catholic nunnery school did not appeal, when he recalled his own youth in similar repressive circumstances; his hopes for Ruth were for something on the more progressive lines of the Swedish Samskola. In this sense Eva Cassirer's idea was much more attractive. She had now returned from Rome, and her husband was on the directing staff of a new boarding school, the Odenwaldschule; more important, she wrote that they were prepared to set aside 10,000 marks towards Ruth's education there. To him this seemed an ideal solution, and he began optimistically to work out how he could complement the sum from his own resources. Clara, however, was adamant that Ruth should remain with her in Munich. Nevertheless the Cassirers (in what was becoming almost a tradition among Rilke well-wishers) maintained their offer of the funds, regardless of where Ruth went to school. 'A miracle,' he wrote in gratitude to Eva in April, hoping that she would be able to devise some suitably diplomatic system of supervision over the disbursement ('my wife is as unskilled as I in money matters'), and suggesting that she visit Clara as soon as possible to break the good news.[44] 'Our little girl does not have an easy time with her parents, and I'm amazed at her generosity and patience ... Letting her grow up thus over ten years was not a bad start, but it's all the more necessary that the next ten should be well considered and planned.'[45]

His brief visit to Venice at the end of March had done him much good, not only through the milder weather but also with the break it had made in his solitude—always welcome, whatever he might say: and now that Ruth's future was to some extent settled, he determined to return there as his next staging-post. The Princess came back to Duino in April, and Kassner too for a while, and they were treated to a reading of the Second Elegy. The flow of guests she never seemed to be able to do without began, and on 9 May Rilke was glad to exchange the bustle of this society for the quiet of a modest room in Venice where he could be alone when he wanted.

3

'Is there nothing to follow?
Does nothing remain but remaining?'

(Ronda, February 1913)

He had made no firm plans yet, he told Kippenberg soon after his arrival, but would stay a while at least to see what Venice had to offer him, 'for each time we never seem to finish with one another, and it would be good to see what it is we expect each from the other'. Over these last few months he had received a succession of good tidings from the publisher: the forthcoming edition of the *Cornet* as Number 1 of the new series of cheap but elegantly produced volumes of the Insel-Bücherei, and the appearance at last of the *Mary Magdalene* translation, the format exactly as he had wished, in a very appropriate binding of humble sackcloth.[1] The first letter to reach him now in Venice contained the news of Kippenberg's acquisition of the rights to the *Rodin* monograph and a proposal for a new edition with illustrations chosen by Kessler. On a recent visit to Vienna Kippenberg had been shown the First Elegy by Princess Marie, and was understandably eager to keep Rilke in the public eye by publishing an extract in the next *Insel Almanach*. Rilke was pleased that he should know of it, and told him there was now a Second, which the Princess and Kassner felt was even better; but he was against any premature revelation of the work. It would need, he knew, a long time for its development, like the *Book of Hours*, whose first part had remained 'for years and years in the hands of a friend before it was put together as a book ... I should like to do the same with the Elegies ... and I'm sure you will let me have my way and not see this just as a whim'.[2]

He had taken a room on the Zattere, but the Princess had said he was welcome to occupy her own *pied-à-terre*, a small but elegantly-furnished mezzanine apartment in the Palazzo Valmarana just off the Grand Canal, while she was away on a tour of Bosnia. His inclination at first was to avoid the social obligations this would bring, and to remain in his more austere surroundings; but after calling on the Valmaranas, and with a week or two's experience of the room he had chosen, which though cheap was rather hot, he decided to take up her offer. (The presence in the house of Countess Valmarana's daughter Agapia, a beautiful woman of thirty, still single, already an admirer of his work and another of those ready listeners he liked to have about him, was probably not without its influence on his change of mind.) 'The rent I'm paying here is actually very low,' he told Princess Marie, 'but over there I would spend it on filling the place with roses.' A friend of hers, Prince Volkov-Muromzov, had also offered his own house, much grander, but he preferred to take refuge in the *mezzanino* against this temptation to pretentiousness: 'I feel like a dog who almost desperately gobbles up the plateful already in front of him, in distrust of the big new one he is being enticed to.'3

The apartment suited him admirably. When he moved in, on 1 June, he took some trouble to adapt it to his needs: a little writing-table he found in the ghetto was added, and yet another standing-desk made by a local carpenter ('the most beautiful of all my European desks'); he set hydrangeas and trailing ivy on the balcony, and stood vases of roses everywhere. Even the din of the children playing on the Campo San Vio and the twittering of the myriad sparrows grew less and less disturbing, becoming in the end a background of 'a kind of exaggerated silence'.4 In spite of all these preparations for work, however, little was achieved, apart from a few fragmentary concomitants to the Elegies: and although his stay lasted into September, it gave him a feeling of more than usual temporariness. 'How slow the future is in coming—and then, once it's here, will I be up to it? I'm losing, waiting, not preparing myself for anything.'5 It was in fact not easy to shake off the effects of the singular winter in Duino, and at first the feeling would recur that he ought to return to the 'hermetic loneliness' of the castle.6

As June wore on he began to think that after all Venice had little to offer him, and was turning over ideas of going back to Germany, when an unexpected stroke of fortune came to quicken his spirit. Carlo Placci came to spend a few weeks in Venice, and was instrumental in arranging an introduction to Eleonora Duse. He had long wanted to meet the great actress, dreamed even of seeing her one day in the dramatic poem *The White Princess* he had dedicated to her: but although opportunities could have been made, he had not pressed himself forward, and had continued to admire her from afar, not least, from the well-known story of her affair with D'Annunzio, as another in his *Malte* gallery of great women lovers. Now, on 1 July, he was able to call on her in her apartment on the Zattere. 'What can I tell you?' he wrote to Placci. 'It would always have been beautiful—but what I could never have foreseen was the incomparable gentleness of our encounter ... How right I was to do nothing about my great desire through so many years. It should not be an act of will to seek one another out, one must follow the course of the orbit, like the stars, then everything happens in accordance with the eternal law, in the fullness of the universe.'[7] To meet her had been perhaps the most burning wish of his life, he told Princess Marie: and although he had for some time lost the precision necessary for successful wishing ('that's target-shooting, and I'm in the middle of a great fire-fight against an invisible enemy'), its fulfilment without effort on his part seemed to him one further proof that, in spite of everything, he was on the right road.[8]

There followed many afternoons in the exchange of visits or excursions together to the islands. For a while he surrendered completely to her spell, held himself every day at her disposal, not shying back as he had at the encounter with Anna de Noailles, though still with slight misgivings, as he recalled his experience with Rodin, over the danger such dominant personalities represented for his work and for himself. The Duse, now fifty-one, had left the stage for health reasons three years earlier. In her unsatisfied longing for a return, she had become a creature of moods, and a trial to the few friends of her seclusion, not least to Signora Poletti, a devoted young companion whose over-ambitious attempts to write the vehicle which would restore her glory were, as Rilke saw immediately, not likely to prove successful, and to whom she felt an obligation even as they prepared to separate. 'What splendour and what a waste! No poet for her in the whole world, and she is passing.'[9] He wanted desperately to help, discussed ideas with them separately or together, but could never find the right words, and knew himself to be a bruised reed in such a crisis. *The White Princess*, written for her so long ago, was too immature, an anachronism almost: and although she was greatly taken with the notion and pressed him for a translation, he could not but agree with Marie Taxis, who knew the ageing actress well, that this dream-like fantasy was not what she needed now. 'I'm afraid you are spending your substance once again,' the Princess warned him, 'you want to help—but is help possible for her?'[10] It was a relief when early in August the Duse and Signora Poletti finally went their separate ways from Venice. But from time to time thereafter he returned to the idea of somehow creating for her a way back to the stage.

The impulse to do something for her had sprung from his feeling that he too was at a critical point in his life. The future of wife and child without him was to some extent assured, and he was free to walk his own road, the road to an achievement of which the first Elegies had given him a glimpse. Yet something more was still needed: the love of someone who would be ready, undemandingly, to support him in the effort. In the few poems and fragments of verse which came to him now in Venice, even through the tantrums of the Duse, this longing was a recurring theme, longing curving on an orbit through the cosmos 'through the once existent future',[11] the expectation of some 'future beloved' who must surely come to him.

Pearls come unstrung. Alas, if one of the string were lost?
Yet what would it boot me to string them again, for you,
Belovèd, strong clasp to hold them together, are lacking.
Was it not time? As the hour before dawn for the sunrise,
so I'm waiting for you, pale with the night achieved

. . . .
       as a desert river-bed
longs for the yet heavenly rains from the mountains to beflood it:

. . . .
as one who throws aside
his crutches warm that they be hung upon an altar,
and lies there and cannot stand without a miracle:
so must I turn and writhe, if you come not, until I die.
For you alone I yearn. Must not the crack in the pavement
when, despondent, it feels the springing of the grass, must it not
crave the whole of the spring, the very springtime of earth?

. . . .
How can the least thing come to pass if the future's fullness,
the sum and absolute of time, does not move toward us?

Are you not of it at last, ineffable one? A little while
and I shall not be equal to the test. I shall grow old,
or be brushed aside by children . . .'[12]

Chance—or fate, as he preferred to call it—would undoubtedly lead him to her, just as it had to the Duse, in 'one of those dispensations which are infinitely right and which do everything for you, because from the beginning you felt they were too big for you to make the slightest effort towards them.'[13] But of course it left him as undecided as ever where to await the revelation, more especially as there was no longer any financial pressure, his income from the Insel Verlag being still supplemented by drawings on the Prague legacy. In Kippenberg's hands his earlier work was taking on new life, the *Cornet* in particular being 'given a ride' never experienced with Axel Juncker; and in August came the news that Juncker had finally parted with the rights not only to the prose stories *The Last of their Line* but also to the *Book of Images*. This was a real joy for him, he wrote to Kippenberg, a crossroads of his journey: 'perhaps one day I must go back to it and strike out again in the opposite direction, or in no direction, on the trail of the unicorn, the eternal unicorn . . .'[14]

His indecision lent him a melancholy air, which Pia Valmarana remarked on. 'I've used Venice as I've used all my surroundings these last few years,' he told her, 'asking more of them than they can give . . . trying to terrify things by aiming at them point-blank this pistol loaded with expectation.'[15] He had made Venice difficult for himself, he wrote to Sidie Nádherný, it had really been much more Malte's than his: he must put it behind him and move on—somewhere. He began to think once more of Spain: Toledo with El Greco seemed more than ever to beckon, a late autumn spent there, not as a visitor but really living 'in as Toledan a fashion as possible', might offer him visual and spiritual relief.[16] When the Princess announced her return to Duino he joined her there again on 11 September for nearly a month, enjoying excursions to Grado, to Saonara near Padua, to Petrarch's tomb in Arqua, and to Verona: but Spain more and more took shape as his next goal, and to steep himself in El Greco became almost a call of duty.

Perhaps because he had unconsciously already decided, an unusual experience in Duino took on a deeper significance. 'Pascha' Taxis was a keen experimenter with the planchette, and Rilke took part in three seances, sitting apart from the others and writing down his questions silently for the spirits to answer through the intermediary of the board. Though, as he said later, he had himself no talent as a medium, he was in no doubt that in his own way he was open to the influence of such forces as might exist beyond human perception. The responses emerging on these occasions were Delphic, to say the least: but those from someone wishing to be called 'the unknown woman', and whose grave, according to another 'voice' which gave her a name, was in Bayonne, seemed to confirm that he was to go to Spain. 'The bridge, the bridge with towers at each end ... When you get there, go under the bridge where the great rocks are, and sing, sing ...' It was Toledo, he was convinced, and he hesitated no longer. 'Perhaps I'm exaggerating,' he wrote to Kippenberg telling him of his plans, 'but it seems to me that this journey could be as significant for my progress as that to Russia was once ... the state of expectancy I'm still in since the last great effort may also be a factor in my desire to try this new direction, in which I suspect the most varied lines of my work will converge.'[17]

His idea was to pay a short visit first to Munich, to see Clara and Ruth, and be off as soon as possible, but circumstances combined to keep him much longer. There were many friends, old and new, to see there—Annette Kolb, Elsa Bruckmann, Placci again, Sidie Nádherný, who came through for a few days, Jakob Wassermann, whom he had not seen for many years, Hofmannsthal, even Princess Marie on her way to the Stuttgart première of Strauss's *Ariadne auf Naxos*. His mother arrived unexpectedly, and extended her stay; and there was much correspondence with Kippenberg, in particular over an Insel-Bücherei edition of the *Life of Mary* and proof corrections for a special new edition of the *Book of Images*. News of Marthe gave him concern for a while—she had suddenly left Paris, it seemed, abandoning the security he had tried to find for her, and might be looking for him: but it would not help to tell her of his plans. He spent much time with Ruth, and arranged for the first year's instalment of Eva Cassirer's generous funding to be allocated to her and Clara jointly.[18] Clara was obviously finding their life together in Munich a joy, and was not short of commissions after her success with the busts of Dehmel and Hauptmann, but the money would make their situation more assured.

It was not until the end of October that he was finally able to get away: but delving into El Greco literature, and repeatedly revisiting the *Laocoön*, which he never tired of seeing and showing to his friends, served to still his impatience, and he was not deflected from his purpose by the frequent advice against going to Spain which he heard on all sides. He had originally thought of extending the journey even further south, perhaps to Sicily, but felt now he must not defer any longer finding his own independent quarters for work. When he heard, just before leaving, that a studio in Paris was available, he decided to reserve it from the New Year. It was in the house in the rue Campagne-Première, and he could think of no better solution than a return to the memories there of the 'industrious summer' of the New Poems.[19]

He made as directly as he could for Toledo, pausing only for a day in Bayonne. Changing trains in Madrid—as repellent, he thought, as Trieste— he hurried on, to arrive in the city on the Tagus at ten in the morning of All Souls' Day, and be lost at once in wonder. To describe it, he wrote to the Princess that night, would need the tongues of angels: he could understand the legend that God, when He created the sun, set it directly above Toledo. 'I've already been all round, impressed everything on me as if from tomorrow I have to know it for ever ... the two bridges, this river, and over above it this open profusion of countryside, to be viewed like something that's still in the making.'[20] From the Hotel Castilla he wandered through the narrow streets, in an incredible feeling of certainty, as though taken by the hand by an unseen guide, through a day as long as a day out of Genesis. All his journeys before now seemed like a foretaste merely of this, Avignon, Les Baux, Cairo, even the desert only 'the mirages of my desire to see Toledo'. 'How many things have I loved because they tried to be something of this, because there was a drop of this blood in their hearts—and now the whole itself is upon me ...'[21]

It was strange, he wrote to Pia Valmarana, that in Spanish you did not take a walk, but *gave* it—'dar un paseo': 'not at all my case, for I have given nothing, but simply received, both eyes filled.'[22] Of an evening he would often walk out to the desolate contrast outside the city, where the rocky landscape stood 'like a lion before each gate': 'I go up and down out there, where prophets might walk, and turn now and then away from the spectacle before me, close my eyes and say: now I'll try to picture it within me, and so I do, indescribably, but when I look again, it is so much more, so completely surpassing, that I despair of ever taking its image with me.' The city was not history, but only legend. 'A saint and a lion must have been at work here to bring it into being.'[23]

He was practically living in the Cathedral, as he wrote to his mother;[24] yet there seemed something elemental in the manifestations of the Christian religion in this land where dogs were allowed in church—perhaps the most Christian of beings, even if their faith was directed only towards their human masters.[25] Here, where the Christian, Jewish, and Arabic cultures were so closely intermingled, he could fancy that the journey Leonardo da Vinci was supposed to have taken to Arabia might in fact have brought him to Toledo, to investigate the Arabic script and the 'tangled growths of its ancient secrets'. For him, the only possible reading here was the Old Testament, to open the Bible and then read on in the landscape, itself a prophecy.[26]

He had come prepared to find the El Greco of Toledo, but instead had found the Toledo of El Greco: a Toledo into which the artist merged, like 'a great gem set in this terrible and sublime reliquary',[27] the works, especially the *Assumption of the Virgin* in the church of San Vincente, gaining in power in this ambience. Hope had been his watchword on the first day—the hope that these biblical surroundings would restore the flow that had stopped in Duino. It was not yet to be: the experience was too overwhelming to find any immediate expression, except in letters. He felt it to be one of the most decisive of his life, 'one of the greatest things that ever happened to me',[28] but he was not ready, either physically or spiritually, to absorb it. For one thing, the intensifying cold ruled out his original idea of spending the winter in Toledo, and towards the end of November he realized he would have to seek warmth further south; for another, he was still beset by the longing for the lover to come, a longing which was expressed in a fragment of verse, the only product of these weeks:

> come when it's time. All this will have been passing
> through me and through me but for you to breathe.
> I've gazed at it, for your sake, endlessly
> with the gaze of poverty, and, as though
> you had begun to drink it in, have loved it. . . .[29]

Heading southward, without any clear idea of a destination, he stopped for two days in Cordoba, then from 3 December for nearly a week in Seville. From that city, as he told the Princess, he had expected nothing, apart from the sun, and was not disappointed. Cordoba however held something of the elemental Spain he had seen in Toledo, and that despite the shameful way the great mosque had been converted to Christian use: the chapels tangled in the darkness made him want to 'comb them out like knots in beautiful hair'. 'Quite insupportable to hear the organ and the choir's responses in this great space (qui est comme le moule d'une montagne de silence); the thought came, spontaneously, that Christianity is continually slicing God up like a splendid pie, while Allah is whole . . .'[30] In Seville a chance recommendation led him on to Ronda, in the mountains between Gibraltar and Malaga, and on 9 December he was installed in the English-built Hotel Reina Victoria there— not exactly fitting amid the spectacle of this 'heroic' landscape, he wrote to 'Pascha' Taxis, but its well-run comfort particularly welcome at this time of year.[31]

Welcome too because he had really not been feeling at all well. There had been days when he felt 'sick and blemished, like a page of a school-book where blots have been rubbed through to holes, and I can't even fathom whether the trouble is of the body or of the mind: for I fear I actually do have a hole where the two sides of existence should be exactly in contact'.[32] Ronda, he knew at once, had much to give him. Toledo remained an incomparable experience, but his wonderment at Spain was renewed here at the sight of the ancient town perched, 'heaped-up' almost, on twin rocky eminences joined by a fantastic bridge over the deep gorge of the Guadalevin, as though offering itself up on an immense altar; the houses encrusted with whitewash, but each with a coloured portal, and overtopped by a few reddish churches; the whole raised high in the clear air and 'exposed to the eternal judgement of a vast circle of mountains, each older than the other', mountains which stood open like a psalm book ready for the service.[33] Even stronger than in Toledo was the feeling of familiarity: not just that the town seemed to correspond to one 'Pascha' Taxis had described from a dream just before he left Duino, but more particularly that it was unmistakably the original of an unnamed sketch he had once seen in Russia, in the journal of a long-past Grand Tour undertaken by a young nobleman. It was always uncommonly satisfying to him to come thus full circle. More than ever he felt El Greco was *in* this landscape, where 'I know not what truth of the human spirit has found its final expression, has reached an existence, a visibility which one feels must be the same for a goatherd as for God's angels.'[34]

Here would be a place to stay—were it not for winter. Spring was needed, and above all the capacity to absorb, to adapt oneself, and he still could not overcome his restlessness. The sense of full circle at the sight of Ronda was also a sense of an aimless circle; a new direction eluded him. He happened to turn up, in the *Instructions* of Angela da Foligno, a passage he had marked earlier which exactly described his own situation: that all the blessings of the wise, of the saints, of God Himself would be of no avail if they did not cause within her 'une nouvelle opération', a change of heart; without that, 'instead of doing me good the wise men, the saints, and God would aggravate beyond expression my despair, my rage, my sadness and my blindness.' Turning to Lou, as Christmas approached—she had not heard from his since the crisis of a year earlier—he told her how the promise of Duino and Venice had failed to give him the help he had hoped for: how Toledo, which might have been the stimulus to that 'nouvelle opération', had proved too cold to endure, and had brought on once again the old bodily troubles: and how even the 'pure high air' of Ronda and the magnificence of his surroundings could not restore the pleasure of earlier days in what he saw. 'Four, five years ago even, a sunrise ... could transform me to pure joy from head to foot ... now I sit and gaze and gaze till my eyes hurt, point it out to myself and say it aloud as if I have to learn it by heart, and still do not possess it.' Sometimes he felt that he tried too hard: 'au lieu de me pénétrer, les impressions me percent'.[35]

He felt a 'real thirst for reading, a certain dryness where the eyes swallow', and the many books Kippenberg sent him—among them Ricarda Huch and Jacobsen, but especially Stifter—served him well.[36] But what he longed for, he told Lou, was an environment like that of Schmargendorf: 'long walks in the forest, barefoot . . . a lamp in the evening, a warm room, the moon when it likes to appear, the stars if they come out, otherwise just to sit and listen to the rain or hear the storm as if it were God Himself.' The Black Forest, perhaps; a place in Sweden like Ellen Key's (but preferably not 'with' anyone); or a small university town in Germany where he could read and learn something. He was often deep now in the Koran, and felt attracted to Arabic—perhaps Andreas could help him there? 'I'm rambling on, as you see, and there are no limits.'[37]

Lou's sympathetic reply—though she confessed she could not fully understand his complaints—did not reach him till early in January. She was away in Vienna, already involved in the circle round Freud, and planned to stay there for some months, so she could see no possibility of their meeting before the summer, by which time she hoped he would have clarified his ideas. She sensibly compared his condition to the stubble field after the harvest, for after all the two Elegies, which Kassner praised so highly to her, had been achieved, and she felt sure more was to follow. As before, it had been enough for him to have put his fears and worries on paper to her: by the time her letter arrived he was already beginning to prove them needless. Verse began to flow, which showed that the impressions of Spain he thought himself unable to absorb were in fact at work within him—the almond trees in blossom, the Assumption of the Virgin in El Greco's painting, the shepherds with whom he often stood silently on his long walks, all found their reflection. The Elegies were only 'a tiny, snapped-off fragment of what had been given into my power':[38] but what he was producing now, he realized, was not yet the continuation he had hoped for:

> Out of that cloud, look, that so wildly hides
> the star that peered this instant—(and myself),
> out of that mountain-land beyond, possessing
> night and her winds awhile now—(and myself),
> out of this river in the vale, that catches
> the gleam of torn-sky clearings—(and myself);
>
> out of myself, Lord, and all that, to make
> one single thing . . .
>
> .   .   .   .
>
> Let me, though, having once more the thronging of towns
> and tangled skein of sounds and chaos
> of vehicles around me, uncompanioned,—
> let me, above the enveloping whirl,
> remember sky and that earthy brim of the vale
> where the homeward-faring flock emerged from beyond.

Let me feel stony, and let
the shepherd's daily task seem possible to me,
as he moves about, sun-tans and with measuring sling-shot
mends the hem of his flock where it grows ragged.
His slow, laborious walk, his pensive body,
but glorious when he stands.[39]

This 'Spanish Trilogy' was more the expression of his longing to create than creation itself: but it was a step out of the aimlessness he had been prey to. The 'Assumption of the Virgin', the poems 'The Raising of Lazarus' and 'The Spirit Ariel (After reading Shakespeare's "Tempest")' were still in the line of the *New Poems*, directly the result of experience.

His conception of Creation, of the universe, was one of three levels: that of inanimate things and the lower orders of plants and animals, that of Man, and, beyond and above, that of the invisible and mysterious Whole, what he called the realm of the angels, where life and death were made one. The task of the artist and the poet was to interpret that higher domain—had he read Milton, he might have said 'to justify the ways of God to Man': not to rest content, as he had in the *New Poems*, with observation and factual description of what was visible on 'this side', but to go beyond, as he had begun to do in the Elegies, to the expression of the invisible, the realm in which all that existed here was subsumed and for which the Angel was the symbol both of its reality and of the inspiration he needed to convey it. As he wrote in his notebook at this time: 'Through *things* I have become so accustomed to this world—but certain it is (and that is what I have found so hard these last years) that I must get beyond Man and pass over (as a novice) to the angels.'[40] What kept him earth-bound, unheard still by the Angel, was the unfulfilled need for a companion, the continuing conflict between life this side and the 'great work'.

At moments in Ronda, though, he could feel closer to his goal. In Spain he had found the land of the prophets, an Old Testament and Koranic wilderness; Toledo a city reaching beyond man up to the stars 'through all the dimensions of visibility, a vision from the gaze of animals up to the contemplation of the Angel', and Ronda an 'heroic' landscape in direct communion with the Whole.[41] He was reminded of earlier occasions when he had had the sensation of such communion, in the garden at Duino, and once in Capri: the feeling of 'passing through to the other side of nature' and, while still in full and benign awareness of his surroundings, of looking back on them as though over his shoulder. These 'Experiences' he also set down in his notebook, writing in the third person: 'He recalled too how important it was for him . . . to observe the star-studded heavens through the gentle branches of an olive tree, how the universe presented itself to him like a countenance in this mask, or how, if he bore it long enough, everything was so completely taken up in the clear solvent of his heart that the taste of all Creation was in his being.'[42]

And he began to rediscover, if only briefly, the 'inwardness' of the Elegies, to feel the presence of the angel, 'strong, still light upon the verge of Being',[43] the angel of inspiration. He took up once more the lines he had roughed out in Duino, on a theme then dimly seen, and brought them to final form as part of what would become the Sixth Elegy: the celebration of the Hero, whose death, like that of those who die young, is not as we conceive it, the opposite of life, but the very fruit of life, the dark side, unseen, of a single Whole.

> Survival
> doesn't concern him. His rising is his Being . . .
> But we linger:
> oh, we glory in our flowering, and so we come to
> the retarded core of our last fruit already betrayed.
> In a few the surge of action rises so strongly that,
> when the temptation to bloom touches the youth
> of their mouths, of their eyelids, like gentle night air,
> they're already standing and glowing with full hearts;
> only in heroes, perhaps, and in those destined to die young,
> those in whom death the gardener has twisted the veins
> differently. They plunge ahead of their own laughter
> like the team of horses in front of the lovingly
> chiselled reliefs of the conquering king at Karnak.[44]

To prolong his stay in Ronda beyond the time he had planned to return to Paris seemed worth while with these slight signs of progress. He was still going through a process of 'complete ploughing-up of the soil' of his being, he had written to Kippenberg early in January: 'the advent of the Elegies last year gave me a slight confidence in what may come, in unutterable slowness, from this devastating effort.'[45] The process was something he *had* to go through, he told Placci. 'I feel these are only interminable peripeteias of a great transformation taking place within me, body and soul completely changing, molecule by molecule . . . if I can succeed in supporting it, eternity will come afterwards, no matter where I find myself.'[46] It was dawning on him, however, that he had taken too little account of his finances. He had arranged while in Spain to draw the balance of the Prague legacy, and from that had settled in advance the first quarter's rent for the Paris studio: but the relatively costly stay at the Reina Victoria and his return fare were clearly going to leave him with no reserve in hand for the inevitable installation expenses he would face on arrival in the rue Campagne-Première. Kippenberg once more came to his aid, doubling his January allowance of 500 marks and promising him the same in March.[47]

Now that he was relieved of the immediate economic pressure he was in no hurry to get to Paris. It was not until 19 February that he finally left Ronda, to spend a week in Madrid on the way—still an unprepossessing city, 'like a mouth the dentist is working on, gaping and thoroughly uncomfortable',[48] but with the El Grecos and the Goyas in the Prado to offer him. He had some bad weeks behind him, he wrote to Sidie Nádherný from the Palace Hotel: 'a brief prospect of work set in, before that, and started me into inward movement, but then abandoned me, and since nothing but bad times, spiritually and physically . . . I feel somehow it's not a fulfilling end to my journey . . . I long for work and peace, it's fortunate I have a studio in Paris to look forward to, but it's empty and will first have to be organized (horrible thought).'[49]

A World at War
1913–1919

——◦❧ ❦◦——

'I have paid my price to live with myself on the terms that I
willed'

(Rudyard Kipling)

I

'Au moment où un trés fort courant intérieur commençait à
surgir en moi ... j'avais le tort de partir et de m'exposer'

(To Pri Valmarana, 15.6.1914)

Arriving on 25 February 1913, he put up for a few days at the Hotel Lutetia on
the Boulevard Raspail until his furniture could be brought from store and the
studio made habitable. Paris, as it had often been, was a restoration of
harmony, giving him 'moments of indescribable hope': and despite a vague
feeling that he had somehow missed something vital in Spain, the eighteen
months' absence seemed no more than a patina on an unbroken surface, so
exactly did this new beginning fit where he had left off and so powerfully did
the city's influence overlay even the experiences of Duino and Toledo.[1] After
the foreign land that was Spain, he wrote to his mother, he felt 'infinitely at
home' again.[2] It was an 'incomparable reunion', wandering once more through
the streets, passing familiar figures, a little older perhaps but otherwise
unchanged, finding the beggars at their same posts. 'What a joy to see again
someone I've seen go by for years, weighed down by his daily cares, to
recognize him from afar and find he has put on some weight, is wearing a
cleaner overcoat, might even buy a flower—to find in fact that he has
survived.'[3]

His second day was mid-Lent, a holiday on which nothing could be done
about his rooms, and he decided to seek out Marthe in Sceaux, where he knew
she was now living with a Russian sculptor. In a studio of the wildest disorder,
she appeared from behind a curtain, wide-eyed like a startled fawn at the
sound of his name, a gold fillet round her forehead and robed in white like a
Tanagra figurine. She had spent the day preparing herself for the dancing in
Paris, but with a presentiment of something more—and now nothing would do
but Rilke must escort her. He could not resist, for he wanted to hear all about

her life; but it proved a depressing night for him. They missed the last train back to Sceaux, and he could see no alternative but to roam the streets with her till morning, drifting from one cabaret to another through the crowds of merry-makers, an incongruous couple. In her tunic and sandals, among the girls of doubtful repute, she looked like 'a little one about to die who will be canonized a few years afterwards'. That she got little dancing did not seem to worry her, so long as she could talk and eat, for she was famished and devoured everything with desperate eagerness, 'like a ghost materializing'.[4]

He was inexpressibly saddened to find her in such a sordid Bohemian existence instead of the security he had hoped to provide. With Erzia, the sculptor, she was living like a sister, she assured him, and relieved not to be in love, for this good-hearted giant, a Mordvinian, would have been as brutal as a caveman to any lover. Such money as he made went fast through his hands, there was little ever to eat in their disorganized and irregular life, and Rilke sensed she was finding her path difficult 'through the mud of liberty'. Erzia spoke of leaving for Italy, and she would not go with him. Still only twenty, she could see nothing ahead of her. Recounting all this to Princess Marie, Rilke said he felt powerless, and could only let things take their course. 'I've neither the experience which could help in a detached way, nor the love which can find inspiration in the heart. I can never be the lover, this touches me only from without, perhaps because no one has ever truly overwhelmed me, perhaps because I do not love my mother. . . . For me all love is an effort, a task, *surmenage*; only towards God have I a certain facility in loving . . .'[5] A few weeks later Marthe in fact left Erzia, on a sudden impulse, and he had no idea what she would do. 'Perhaps both she and I will have need of your aid,' he wrote to Sidie Nádherný, who was planning to come to Paris after a tour in North Africa.[6]

Marthe was one care on his shoulders in these first days back. The other—as usual was lack of money. Reclaiming his furniture, moving and buying the necessities for a solitary existence were rapidly exhausting what he had in hand, and he was obliged to try Kippenberg's patience once again, this time with a telegram 'like a fog-signal from a ship at sea'.[7] The publisher fortunately sent further remittances; and by the middle of March he was settled in and looking forward to re-establishing the 'unbroken regularity of my days'[8] he had once enjoyed in that very house in the rue Campagne-Première. It was splendid to be back in this quarter again, a few steps from the Luxembourg Gardens which were already taking on a spring-like air: 'more than ever I perceive what a foreign body the rue de Varenne was in the tenor of my ways.'[9] He was making a new start in Paris, he told Dora Herxheimer: the transition from the prose of *Malte* had dragged out longer than even he had foreseen, the only answer seemed to be to 'give my heart once more such a simple, open beginning, the kind that is possible more than anywhere else, and see if the onset of spring cannot carry me on its flow'.[10]   While still in Spain he had promised Kippenberg to settle seriously, once he was back in Paris, to the translation of the Maria Alcoforado letters, and he took an early opportunity to write to Gide whose advice he thought would be invaluable. Besides representing an instalment on his debt to the publisher, it was work on which he himself set great store, following the *Mary Magdalene* and the *Centaur*, to prepare the ground for whatever work of his own might come. From Spain too he had been in touch with Rodin, following up an earlier proposal for the Mannheim Museum to acquire one of his works and in particular expressing his gratitude for his consent to model for a bust by Clara for the same museum. Rodin was therefore also on his list for a call, though it was not until the end of March that the Master's health permitted a meeting in the rue de Varenne, where he was now re-installed. (Clara's hopes were in the end disappointed: Rodin received her cordially enough when she came to Paris in May, and gave her free run of his studio in the rue de l'Université, where she created one of her most delightful works, a bust of Sidie Nádherný; but he was unwilling finally to allow her to make his likeness for a German museum when there was still none in France.)

Apart from Gide and Rodin, the only person Rilke thought now of seeing was Emile Verhaeren. His aim was to return to the solitary routine and simple regime of former times, sticking to his desk and going out as little as possible, 'comme un jeune étudiant qui commence,' as he wrote to Rodin.[11] But the routine was scarcely established, Rodin's writing-table and the standing-desk hardly installed, when he was already compelled to break his good resolutions. Stefan Zweig, who had also just arrived in Paris, brought the news on 15 March that Verhaeren would be leaving in a few days. He went at once out to Saint-Cloud and spent an afternoon and evening with the Belgian poet, strengthened as always by the other's serene goodness and their deep affinity of spirit despite their infrequent meetings; and he did not hesitate to accept Zweig's invitation to join them at lunch on 17 March, in the company of Romain Rolland and Léon Bazalgette, the translator of Walt Whitman, exchanging the modest surroundings of his usual vegetarian restaurant for the elegant Boeuf à la mode. He was saddened by the prospect of Verhaeren's departure, he replied to Zweig: 'I had been quietly counting on him, so great and spontaneously helpful, when I finally returned, in the thought of seeing him often.'[12]

It was an exception he did not regret. Verhaeren was as splendid as ever: but his most striking impression was of Rolland, long a near neighbour, in the Boulevard Montparnasse, but never till now encountered. He had not yet read *Jean Christophe* (and later, ploughing through the pages of that monument to Franco-German understanding, found its *longueurs* frustrating): its author however was at once sympathetic, his delicate, drawn features those of an indefatigable scholar, pale from the reflection of books open before him, but the tired eyes ever renewed, by some divine dispensation, 'with the purest blue of his childhood'. 'The assurance, wealth of experience and mature modesty, the goodness . . . the immense purity of all his purposes emanate from him like the fragrance from a baby's body, and with just such intensive innocence.'[13] No artist, no poet—but how much more was it, he thought later, to be something so solid, so consciously developed by an act of will, than to suffer the intermittent onslaughts of the artist's daimon, or his angel.

Zweig, highly gratified at having been able to bring together the three personalities he most admired, found an almost sensuous pleasure in the contrast they offered, as the animated talk continued through the afternoon in his hotel room overlooking the garden of the Palais-Royal: Rolland, pale, reminding him of a portrait of Jens Peter Jacobsen, his limpid French entirely free of affectation; Rilke bronzed by the southern sun, slim and boyish, bringing vividly to life each character in his account of the meetings with Tolstoy; Verhaeren four-square and vigorous, full of lively anecdote and discoursing eloquently on the development of French art. All shared Rilke's enthusiasm for Spain, and Rolland's ideal of the moral and intellectual unification of Europe, though Rilke and Zweig felt that France was more in need than Germany of education to this aim. For the host these were 'unforgettable hours, touching life at all its points'.[14]

For Rilke too, as he wrote to Princess Marie, it had been time well spent, and he was glad to follow it with an exchange of books and visits with Rolland. The narrow book-lined study high above the Boulevard Montparnasse he found a touch spinsterish, contrasting with the light airiness of his own studio, and Rolland's tight-buttoned fastidious dress 'like an allegory of winter in the provinces, so thoroughly frock-coated': but their understanding was immediate.[15] Rolland's impression was of anything but the withdrawn hermit he had expected from Zweig's description, as he listened to Rilke talk at length of his unhappy upbringing, of Gide and the translation of *Malte*, of Rodin and cathedrals and their opposing views of El Greco, or watched him sit in quiet enjoyment of his piano transcripts of Gregorian or ancient Greek melodies. Though they met rarely after this, Rilke felt he had gained a generous and indulgent friend.

During the remaining few weeks of Zweig's stay in Paris, Rilke devoted more time to him than was his wont with such visitors, returning his lunch invitation, walking with him through the city they loved, even showing him some of his latest verse and presenting for his collection the manuscript of the second (1904) version of the *Cornet*. Zweig felt himself privileged indeed to have had such glimpses into the workshop of a poet who to his mind stood head and shoulders above even George and Hofmannsthal. He heard how for Rilke his writing was like an act of prayer, for which the right devotion was not always there: 'big works' had been begun in Duino, but he was struggling now for a renewal which would not come.[16]

In their wide-ranging talk the other's calm courtesy and unobtrusive manner gave Zweig no inkling of how deep this trouble went. In a letter to Sidie Nádherný, on 30 March, Rilke had likened his inner life to a tangled skein—one perhaps from which something surprising might now and then be unravelled, but which made him long for 'separate strands to work on day by day at the fixed loom'.

People are bad for me ... I find they all mean well, but it doesn't work, on the contrary, what finally happens is that I give, and give, without ever possessing ... I'm only saying all this ... because you will be seeing me and won't otherwise understand what is making me so infinitely sad and depressed and fearful. Look: Marthe, who (so I dreamed two years ago) was to be educated to be an integrator, a complement, a protection for my existence—now nothing but a hopeless worry and distraction for me, and for her not a step forward in the deep sand of her life. .... I'm stuck in the pressure of the new beginning, which I want to do *well*, *well* (it can so easily be ruined), what I want is a pure, spiritual life, every day the same, no distractions, no claims on me, *all expectation turned inward* toward the heart where my next task must emerge.[17]

'No matter how I try to stay in hiding, people find me, and once found, I'm devoured like a hot brioche,' he complained to Rodin the same day.[18]

Yet it was not simply the demands of 'people', the dissipation in sociability of what he should keep for his work, that lay at the root of his trouble. Visiting Rolland, asking Zweig to call, diverting Marthe with a book when she dropped in unexpectedly, even the arrival in Paris of Mimi Romanelli—none of this was keeping him in fact unduly from his desk: notwithstanding his words to Zweig, some work was being done, even some drafts on the themes of the Elegies, and during April at least he felt the 'turning inward' was imminent. What unsettled him was the growing realization that all through his life the claims of others had been laid not so much on his time as on his inner stores of regard and love. His need, if he was finally to achieve the 'great work', was to find someone whom he could love *without being loved in return*, to reach that apotheosis of love in which the Portuguese nun, or his Prodigal Son in *Malte*, had found their happiness. He had already elevated the experience in abnegation of his 'great lovers' to the level of a philosophy, and indeed extended it now to the love of God Himself, arguing in a draft for a possible lecture that the true love of God should have no need of reciprocity. But, as he continued with the translation of the Alcoforado letters, and went on to that of the Sonnets of Louize Labé, he was more and more clear that it was a philosophy he must apply to his own life.

It seems likely that he managed to avoid seeing Mimi Romanelli during her stay: but the mere presence of one who had been so eager for his love cannot have been without its influence on a remarkable diary entry he made about this time. Written, like the account of that 'Experience' at Duino, in the third person, it analysed his 'oldest and most fatal error', the too ready response to the love of others:

Had he passed all the years of his life without being hard? He resolved to become so in this his thirty-eighth year—to change, he told himself, to change. At the time when his whole being felt an immeasurable longing to love, he came to the painful conclusion that he would never find the object of his love as long as he was receptive and yielding to those who thought they loved him. The faces that crowded in on him, opened towards him, masked any view of the shy, cast-down countenance of the distant beloved. The presentiment of her features faded for him before the all-too-clear outlines of those who had come to love him.[19]

The vision of the undemanding 'future beloved' still hung like a mirage before him. Until he could find her, the change would not come; and meanwhile his depression was unrelieved. 'How many spectres get into me, thinking they are at home ... my Angel rose, but I slipped back and have long lagged behind him ... Everyone else has worked at his life, I alone, it seems, have spent the time gnawing away at mine with my very capabilities. . . . When I see the good Verhaeren, in the assurance of his simple heart, I'm ashamed to be where I am.'[20]

As April drew into May the pressure of visitors increased, and his resolution to close his door against them sank without trace. 'So many people, meetings, demands, questions, influences both sincere and hostile':[21] he seemed to do nothing but talk. Whether Clara stayed with him when she came, is not clear, but they certainly saw much of each other, visiting Rodin together at Meudon and at the end of May making an excursion to Senlis and Fleurines. Siegfried Trebitsch, whose stay was mercifully short, he managed to keep at arm's length; others in fact were far from unwelcome. He spent a good deal of time with Sidie Nádherný, eagerly expected after her journey to Tunis, and was glad to have as his guests on several occasions the poet Otto von Taube and his cousin Rolf von Ungern-Stenberg, whom he had long looked forward to meeting. It was good to see Kippenberg too, who came for a few days during May, mainly to secure from Rodin a fresh series of illustrations for the new edition of the monograph he was planning. When the publisher left he was able to take with him the Alcoforado and Louize Labé translations, and Rilke received soon afterwards his copies of the Insel-Bücherei *Life of Mary*, dedicated to Vogeler, and the first Insel publication of the *Book of Images* in a special limited edition.

With these, and with the translations, the new *Rodin* and a republication of a selection of *First Poems* in the offing, Kippenberg had every reason to feel satisfied with his author. The purchase now of the rights to the early drama *Daily Life* finally completed his assembly of all the works under the Insel imprint; and Rilke's Paris establishment, with the continuing income from himself and the other friends and the possibility of an additional grant from Prague, seemed to augur well for the future. He had left Rilke apparently in good spirits, and had no idea of how difficult he was finding the new beginning, or how disturbing for him was the constant coming and going. It came as a surprise therefore to hear, on his return to Leipzig, that something of a crisis had arisen. When the flood of visitors abated, Rilke wrote on 3 June, he had felt so physically and spiritually exhausted that he was not far from breakdown. A sudden hot spell had made Paris as intolerable as in August; a neighbour's piano was getting increasingly on his nerves; and Rodin had shown an abrupt change of humour, as unexpected as his dismissal of Rilke eight years earlier, not only withdrawing his permission to use the photographs agreed on with Kippenberg but apparently bent on breaking their relations for good. When this was followed by the news of the suicide of Johannes Nádherný, Sidie's elder brother, to whom he had felt very close, it all seemed more than he could bear. A quiet retreat alone somewhere was needed to restore him, and he thought of going once again for a few weeks' cure among the forests at Bad Rippoldsau—if, as he hoped, Kippenberg could see his way to helping with the cost.

Kippenberg sent him a reassuring telegram, and by 6 June he was in Rippoldsau, his whole being drinking the peace for which he had thirsted, enjoying to the full, after the mental stress of Paris, the physical fatigue induced by the cure and the change of air, walking through the pine woods, reading quietly in Goethe or Martin Buber. 'I must yield, and behave for a time like a tree—it can't write, but it can surely think out through the whole of space, up to God Himself, undisturbed.' This was well and good: but the weeks passed without relieving his inner uncertainty. 'Me voilà, me dictant le repos, l'insouciance chaque jour, mais ayant je ne sais quelle incertitude d'esprit.'[22]

Among the relatively few guests in the hotel was a young actress, Hedwig Bernhard, a welcome confidante to whom he became greatly attached, spending many hours with her on the terrace or on walks. She was captivated by the stories of his journeys, to Russia and Spain, to Venice, Capri and Duino, his soft voice 'speaking the words like melodies', the Italian names gaining an 'incomparable magic' on his lips.[23] 'How I miss you,' he wrote the day after her departure, early in July: 'did we really *walk*? was it not *flying*, flowing, rushing? Did we not fill the whole space with the strength of your heart? ... May my aspiration to the greatest grow stronger in your feeling for me ... Today I will do nothing but think of you, and so begin the work—the work in which I devote to my beloved solitude you, my love, and all the beauty and fullness with which you came to me.'[24]

Despite his confident words, this brief flowering of love was not enough to bring him to 'the work', and his uncertainty remained. His choice had fallen on Rippoldsau because it was not too far from Paris, but he could not bring himself yet to return to his desk. He felt he needed to maintain the change of air: and, as he cast around for further temporary refuges in Germany—at Friedelhausen, if 'Frau Nonna' could have him, or with the Kippenbergs in Leipzig—it was not surprising that he should have been drawn once more to

Göttingen and Lou Salomé. There was a practical reason for seeking her out, for Kippenberg was anxious to finalize with him the selection for the *First Poems*, and on this there could be no better adviser; but most of all he hoped for the relief of the wise counsel she had always been able to offer him. As soon as his July allowance had arrived he was on his way there, to spend nearly two weeks near Lou.

He had told Hedwig that he would be visiting 'old friends' in Göttingen. Writing to her as he left there again, on 21 July, he said it had seemed almost a homecoming: the time had passed 'like a single day', with people who knew him best because they had known him 'at the beginning, when one was still quite in the dark about oneself . . . almost, surely, as if they had taken one with them in their progress, and one had simply to slip into the place alongside them kept free for the prodigal . . . so I experienced it, my dear, let myself go in all the glory that had flourished around them in simplicity, like the harvest home.'[25] Once again Lou's presence seemed to have shown him, if only dimly, the way. 'At moments, I feel that, with all that you know and are, I am slowly beginning a new life,' he wrote to her the day after he left: though he could not say over again all she had told him, or explain how thoroughly right it seemed, he cherished its circulation 'day and night in my blood'.[26]

For Lou, fresh from her studies with Freud, their talks were as much a case-study as the resumption of an old and dear relationship. It had been four years since their last meeting, when he had been deep in depression over his struggle with *Malte*: now, as she confided to her diary, she was seeing the real Rainer again, no longer the schizophrenic being who had once been constantly disturbed by 'the other' within him.[27] The danger which his continued self-preoccupation presented will have been brought home to her by the poem 'Narcissus', written lately in Paris, which he transcribed now for her:

> For when I gaze until I disappear
> in my own gaze, I seem to carry death.[28]

Yet she felt that somewhere behind there was a quiet progress toward fulfilment for him, 'even though he to whom it is happening is full of suffering and must be plagued by doubt. Each day I felt happy, and less worried about Rainer than scarcely ever before.' What he was going through, she thought, came from this reunification of the personality, for which the body seemed to be taking its revenge, 'no longer, as before, in isolated attacks, or in individual, specific symptoms, but as a whole—a body for which illness can be foreseen, and which moreover shows no sign of ageing, as if the maturing process were replaced by an infirm hesitation and inability to keep step with the passage and development of time. . . . The body itself has become "the other" for him.'[29]

It was an acute observation. She may or may not have put it in these terms to him: but, as he wrote later to Princess Marie, there was no one with such insight, no one who 'had life so firmly on her side'. In the eight years that had passed since he was last in Göttingen, nothing seemed to have changed, or rather everything was more enhanced, he told Ellen Key: 'how many conversations, and how much innovation and happiness they bring, when Lou is one's partner.'[30]

While there he had seriously considered taking Lou's advice to follow up the good beginning made at Rippoldsau with a further cure, at a well-known sanatorium at Krummhübel, in the Riesengebirge. He could not in any case stay with the Kippenbergs in Leipzig, as Katharina was away. There was a tempting alternative, however: Helene von Nostitz had written enthusiastically from Heiligendamm of the bracing air of this quiet resort set in beech woods on the Baltic coast, where she was spending July with her husband, and he had hardly set foot in Leipzig before he had decided to follow them there. The sanatorium could come later: now he felt a sudden need for the sea. So in Leipzig it was a few days only, but full of interest—visiting Weimar again with Kippenberg, meeting at the Insel Verlag Professor Steindorff, an Egyptologist, with whom he could talk of the Nile and Assiut, and discovering the work of his young fellow countryman Franz Werfel, 'great poet, I cannot call him less'.[31] A surprise was Kippenberg's revelation of the other friends' contribution to his monthly allowance, and he felt no little remorse at the poor return he seemed to be making for such generosity, dissipating it all 'to right and left like a parrot with his beak'. (Kippenberg may have intended the disclosure as a spur to his unproductive poet; and in fact Rilke, writing to Lou, asked her to look over the manuscript he had left with her of the *Visions of Christ*, perhaps thinking that this long-forgotten cycle might now find its turn. She found them far removed in tone from the Elegies, of course, but was nevertheless struck by the essentially unified progress shown by all he had created 'between these past visions of Christ and the coming visions of the angel'.)[32]

By 28 July he was in Heiligendamm—to see, as he wrote to Princess Marie, whether his instinct was right and sea air would bring him what he needed, whether indeed he could give up altogether the idea of the cure at Krummhübel, or at least cut it short. 'With doctors after all you find only the other half of your own perplexity.'[33] When he called on Helene von Nostitz, she thought he looked grey, 'extinguished', as though he had drawn over himself a cloak of invisibility as protection against an uncongenial environment.[34] Hesitant at first, he was won over by the peace of the woods, and the chance presence of a Countess Ross, whom he had last met in Capri and with whom he could renew his memories of Alice Faehndrich and their other friends of those distant days. After the Nostitzes had gone, he stayed on until the middle of August: and there is no doubt that his spiritual depression was beginning to clear. He was less preoccupied with himself, and his letters revealed a lighter heart and a new keenness. 'As the unexpected seems so rightly the law of my existence, so here, quite unprepared, I have found myself again,' he wrote to Hedwig Bernhard;[35] and to Pia Valmarana: 'I've begun perhaps to acquire a new life, in many ways, partly because I've got to the bottom of the defect which has lain so heavy on my spirit these last few years, at least I think I have; partly thanks to certain very surprising illuminations on psychoanalysis which I owe to a knowledge-able friend . . . a miracle, Pia, hope, joy, I've glimpsed a completely new remedy, the Art of life and of death which will make us . . . the possessors of the true values . . .'[36]

For the first time since leaving Paris in May, he could bring pen to paper in verse—not yet the renewal of the 'divine afflatus' of the Elegies, but still in the new tone which these had initiated, the striving for expression at the very limit of the expressible:

> Behind the guilt-free trees
> old Fate is slowly forming
> her taciturn face.
> Wrinkles travel thither . . .
> Here a bird screams, and there
> a furrow of pain
> shoots from the hard sooth-saying mouth.
>
> Oh, and the almost lovers,
> with their unvaledictory smiles!—
> their destiny setting and rising above them,
> constellational,
> night-enraptured.
> Not yet proffering itself to their experience,
> it still remains,
> hovering in heaven's paths,
> an airy form.[37]

His reading was now almost exclusively Werfel, for whose work his admiration was boundless. 'Never before have I thus experienced and gazed on the figure of the poet', he wrote to him: 'those before us, and our contemporaries, were so to speak always there, and we ourselves seemed pressing forward as though in a cloud, confusedly, towards the god trying his hand with us—and now, how splendid for those long since matured to see you rise so purely, casting over the world all the rays of your ascent and bringing it to the dawn.'[38] His enthusiasm led him shortly afterwards to draft an essay 'On the Young Poet'—for through Werfel he had regained the confidence in his own mission which he had begun to lose after the flow of the Elegies had seemingly run into the sand. 'In the end, what can change the circumstances of one who is destined from his earliest days to arouse in his heart that ultimate of feeling which others suppress and control in theirs?'[39]

Another symptom of renewal was his reawakened interest in things Egyptian. In Leipzig Steindorff had shown him from his collection a cast of the newly-discovered head of Amenhotep IV, and on his way through Berlin he had been able to see the original, noting on the spot in his pocket-book his impressions of its splendour:

As the acorn in its cup, so the crown bedded down on this cup-like containing head: it was a part of the head, together they formed a single piece of sovereign authority, the king-fruit which Heaven had ripened to sweetness. (A face laid so lightly upon its core, scarcely more than the distribution of the sundial over massive, oblique stone. Face, flowing soundlessly down, O vineyard, from the slant of the skeleton . . . The Bacchus of an interior wine. Face whose structural parameters were one with its application, so that of themselves, without any addition, they found the purest expression . . .)

The distillation of these impressions in the short poem which a little later sprang from the experience gave a sign that his progress was not irretrievably halted:

> As young and flowery meadows through a lightly
> spread covering of growth will give a slope
> a share in the sensations of the season,
> wind-wise, perceptive, gentle, almost happy
> along the mountain's perilous abruptness:
> so, bloom-expending, mildly transient, face
> rests on this skull's anteriors, which, descending
> with something like the slope of terraced vineyards,
> outreach into the All, confront the shining.[40]

Amenhotep and Werfel, he wrote to Marie Taxis, 'are the two centres of my somewhat mournfully elongated spiritual ellipse'.[41]

Meanwhile Heiligendamm offered restful pleasure. The cure at Krummhübel remained vaguely on his programme, and as he wrote to Lou he was not yet feeling fully recovered: but he gave all credit to the instinct that had drawn him to the sea. His confidence was returning, but was not yet firm enough for him to face a return to Paris, and more and more reasons for staying longer in Germany began to suggest themselves. On 7 September the Fourth Psychoanalytical Congress, to which Lou would be coming, was due in Munich, and Clara was about move into a new apartment there with Ruth that month, so that for both reasons he felt he should be there; later in the autumn would be the première of Claudel's *L'Annonce faite à Marie*, at Hellerau near Dresden, and he might have the opportunity of meeting Werfel there or in Leipzig.

It was clear however that all this, and Krummhübel if he went, would cost more than could be available from his friends' generosity. Just before leaving the coast, therefore, he wrote in some anxiety to Kippenberg, outlining these plans at length, and asking whether he should try for additional funds from some other source, such as the Schiller Foundation—and followed up his letter with another the same day in rueful apology for his apparent fecklessness: 'the irregularity of these last years is coming home to roost, a delayed effect—and whenever I try to make the damage good from my monthly allowance, there's nothing but inadequacy, deficits, and holes, never an end to it. If one day you were to feel you must tell me I've dangerously overburdened my budget, well then I'd have to sit down and write something which could count directly as repayment—or else, if nothing offered, accept some hospitality over the winter and do without the allowance to straighten up my account . . .'[42]

Kippenberg replied that the past year had indeed marked a considerable overspending, and he was becoming concerned about the future. There was no immediate cause for alarm, but the contribution from the others would cease at the end of 1914, and then Rilke would be back on 250 marks a month, which, even allowing for the royalties expected from the *Rodin* and the Alcoforado letters, would make more stringent calculations essential. But he submitted to the gentle blackmail—for he knew it would be fatal to condemn the poet to mere hack work to balance the account—and, having delivered himself of the warning, told him that an additional 750 marks would be forthcoming for September.[43] His admonition was, of course, of little avail. Rilke was incapable of modifying his life-style to forestall the 'deficits and holes' that inevitably appeared in his finances: and within a few weeks, even while this generous bonus was being paid, he was asking Eva Cassirer for advances of 2,000 marks for himself—as a loan, naturally, but with scant prospect of its repayment—from the fund originally set aside for Ruth's education (but actually going in quarterly instalments as a general allowance to Clara).[44]

In Paris, only six months before, it had been brought sharply home to him how pernicious a busy social life could be, and he had longed for a daily routine of work in utter solitude. Yet now, in Berlin, where he spent nearly three weeks, and then in Munich, he seemed to be deliberately deferring his return to the one place where this might be found, and—to outward appearance—thoroughly enjoying both the planned and unplanned encounters which crowded in. 'Time passes and overtakes me every day . . . I travel—my surroundings are continually changing, and I change with them, people I've not seen for years turn up unexpectedly, and show me the past which does not fade . . .'[45]

His road from Heiligendamm had taken him through Hamburg, to call on the Woermanns nearby, where Clara and Ruth were spending a few days, and on Ivo and Erica Hauptmann, now living at Blankenese. Berlin brought a welcome reunion with Hedwig Bernhard, and with Princess Marie, whom of course he led at once to see the Amenhotep head; afternoons with the actress Lia Rosen; evenings at the theatre. In Munich he arrived just in time to attend some of the sessions of the Congress with Lou, and she was active in introducing him to prominent participants, including Freud, with whom they spent an evening, and the Swedish doctor Poul Bjerre—'men important and remarkable for me, the whole trend and application they represent is definitely part of the most significant movements of medical science, of that *human* science which has really not yet come into being'.[46] They met Gebsattel again, and the Dutch writer Fredrik Van Eeden.

He helped Clara with her move, and spent some time with her and Ruth, who was delighted to have her own room at last. But there were so many other people to see—'as though in a parade, almost all the people I knew came by'.[47] His days were so full in fact, as he wrote to Sidie Nádherný, that a week after his arrival he had not even been to see El Greco's *Laocoön* again. Hofmanns-thal, as in the previous year, was staying at the same hotel, and they met occasionally, comparing their impressions of Werfel, whom the other had already met in Prague and in whose praise he was rather more circumspect than Rilke. One meeting he had particularly looked forward to was with Regina Ullmann. She had sent him in 1909 the manuscript of her first work, a dramatic poem in prose, which he had warmly recommended to Kippenberg, recognizing in it unusual gifts; and since then he had written an introduction to another for which she had found a publisher in her Swiss homeland. When they met now for the first time, he was able to offer hopes that the Insel would publish the first. In her strange, withdrawn personality, and from her first attempts at verse which she showed him, he felt a power almost of the occult, which, as Lou noted, was now once more occupying him (to the point of consulting a clairvoyante and experimenting again with the planchette—both essays which he quickly recognized were absurd. 'Et pourtant je voudrais bien que l'Inconnue me parle').[48] It was a frame of mind in which he could find beauty in the somewhat macabre wax dolls which he saw in Lotte Pritzel's exhibition in Munich—'grown-up' dolls which, unlike the ordinary toys of childhood, seemed to possess a definite soul of their own.[49]

The Claudel première was set for 5 October, and he planned to travel to Dresden for it with Lou. Reading Claudel's play, he could not find it appealing: but the occasion promised a reunion with so many friends—Sidie Nádherný, Helene von Nostitz, Annette Kolb, Lou's young actress protégée Ellen Delp, the Kippenbergs themselves—apart from the eagerly anticipated meeting with Werfel—that it was not to be missed. It proved indeed more a social than an aesthetic pleasure, and with Claudel after the performance he felt embarrassed at not being able honestly to reciprocate the other's compliments on his own work.

Werfel too was a disappointment. 'I was all ready to open my arms to this adolescent—and instead of doing so, kept them behind my back like an indifferent stroller.' He kept telling himself that this was the author of the marvels he had so admired, but face to face with him he felt ill at ease. Not that this all too Jewish-looking young man was antipathetic: but he seemed too intelligent perhaps for his poetry, which might be considered contrived, 'réfléchie finement, rusément par un esprit juif qui connaît par trop la marchandise'.[50] It was an impression which Hofmannsthal shared, as he had learned: but when Rilke read more of Werfel's poems, published the following

January, he was quick to concede that his judgement of the person had been gratuitous when set against the warmth of his approval for the work, and he continued to expect from him the highest attainments. For Werfel himself, as he recalled many years later, the first encounter with the idol of his generation, the man who was in his eyes *the* great poet, was also somehow disappointing. His praise of the *Life of Mary* or the *Book of Hours* found only deprecation, and the *Cornet* was dismissed as a product of immaturity. He felt he could not come close to Rilke: there seemed 'a tension between his inner and his outward life', he had the 'blank, immobile exterior of a blind man', the neat clothes sitting ill upon an ethereal body like those on a shop-window model, as though he had been dressed by other hands. 'I have never known anyone with a more affecting dissociation between the spiritual life and everyday existence.' Only later, as he sat through an unattractive vegetarian meal as Rilke's guest in Dresden, and they talked of their birthplace, did he feel he was beginning to understand him.[51]

Rilke stayed a few more days in Dresden, and then set off on 10 October with Lou for the Riesengebirge, where they spent nearly a week. He got as far as the doctor's consulting room in the Krummhübel sanatorium, but as Lou said was unable to explain to him where exactly his troubles lay, and firmly set his face against staying for any treatment. The help he still needed he found in Lou. On their journey back to Dresden she attempted an analysis of his dreams, current and remembered, continuing for her own benefit the case-study of one she knew so intimately; and although we need not dwell on the somewhat esoteric interpretations that found their record in her diary, there is no doubt that the process brought him a good step forward. He decided to abandon the visit to the Kippenbergs and return immediately to Paris, to start once again where he had left off, and by 18 October was back in his rooms in the rue Campagne-Première. 'You showed me that I'm still somehow the same,' he wrote to her, 'that in fact none of my former advantages has been dispersed or lost, maybe they are all still there, and it's only that I don't know for the time being how to use them. . . . Somehow you have been of infinite help to me, the Other is now there for me and for the Angel, if we only stick together: he and I, and you far away.'[52]

It was high time to exchange the social whirl for solitude again. 'I had been through so many stages, arrivals, departures, meetings, separations, feelings, sentiments, hands, cordialities, rooms and corridors, hotel porters and maids, that all at once I could take no more, and simply rushed to the place whose door I can slam behind me; the place . . . which is more a reproach than a blessing for me, but which is still where I can feel myself in some way at home.' 'If it would only become once more the hiding-place that it was for years on end, then I would still be content with Paris, and have an idea of what I am up to here.'[53]

Yet another new beginning, and hard, as always. His room, 'full of last

June', seemed almost threatening in its expectancy, and his very first impulse was to leave it for a day or two for a relaxing glimpse of French provincial life, in Rouen with a 'whole cathedral' to drown out his misgivings, and in Beauvais. Under the powerful impact of Paris he felt like an over-exposed photographic plate, the ordeal to be faced only if he could pretend it was for a passing visit, without responsibility.[54]

The urge to be back here, among his own things, had seemed in itself a kind of therapy, he wrote to Eva Cassirer soon after his arrival: 'to what extent I shall be able to make anything of myself, and how long I can last into the winter, will not worry me for the moment, I'll simply try each day to create something, settle to a daily stint which will slowly work towards the future.' To her, his letter was something more than the general situation report his friends usually received, for it was necessary also to broach again the delicate question of the 'Ruth fund' she and her husband had established. He had already borrowed from it for himself—but, as he told her now, 'a matter affecting both Clara and me, which had become of less urgency, has come up again in the last few weeks'. After he had left Munich, Clara had written to him to press once again for the completion of the divorce proceedings; and, as it happened, he had received at the same time the Viennese lawyer's account and request for his further instructions, if any. Seeing Clara and Ruth in their new home, he too had felt it was right now to go ahead, as the only way to encourage her to a really independent existence. The problem of course was how to meet the costs of the legal process, and it was his hope that the Cassirers' fund might be used. To Eva therefore, who was now offering to treat her loan to him as a gift, independent of the fund, he followed up the warning signal with a letter on 29 October revealing their wish for a divorce, and setting out at great length his relationship with Clara, much as he had done earlier to Lou: the paradox in their early years together of a wife proving totally incompatible while yet striving to be as like her husband as possible, in profound conflict with her real character, dissipating its strength in the devotion of a weak disciple.[55]

The divorce, he was convinced, would give her the spur to make a life of her own. His proposal to Eva was that the fund should continue the quarterly allowance to Clara through 1914—3,600 marks in total—but that the balance, whatever it might then be, should come to him towards the legal costs. Under the divorce agreement he would then undertake provision for her, from his hoped-for improved Insel income, but only for 1915: after that she would have to have learned to cope alone for herself and Ruth. The proposal, assuming the 2,000 marks remained a loan from the fund, as he protested it should, would actually have left a further balance of only 500 marks for the lawyers. But Eva's sympathy for the couple, and her eagerness to do all she could both for them and for Ruth, was such that she insisted on making over to him the full 2,500 marks. Like Kippenberg and the other friends, she felt more than repaid—

even when in the event the divorce was dropped and the money was simply absorbed into Rilke's own income—by the satisfaction of having helped a genius to survive; and this was not to be the last demonstration of the Cassirers' generosity. He was undoubtedly grateful, but never felt in any way contrite for what turned out a misapplication of the funds. To him, it was simply one more instance of what was due to him and to his mission. Nevertheless, subject always to this overriding priority, he never failed in his readiness to help Clara as far as he could.

With the divorce costs thus off his mind, and his finances healthier than they had been for a long time, he could try to 'spin himself into his cocoon',[56] seeing virtually no one except Gide, whose *Enfant prodigue* he now hoped to translate. To Marie Taxis, who was inviting him to join her and the Prince on another journey up the Nile, he was firm: such 'great enterprises' had brought him so little, had left such a bitter after-taste at having squandered matchless opportunities, that he dare not run the risk again.[57] The winter months were free of time-consuming visitors, apart from Kippenberg who came for a few days at the end of November—and even he was told he must adapt himself to the hermit's routine. There were occasional evenings at the newly-established Théâtre du Vieux-Colombier, where he could hear and see some of the new French writers, among them Jacques Rivière, Valéry Larbaud, and Jules Romains. But it was music, strangely enough, that seemed to restore him most, 'putting back in place some of the condensed fragments of my scattered being'—Mozart's Requiem, or Sunday high mass in Notre Dame.[58]

Imitating, 'as far as is possible in this unprotected state, the days in Duino', he gradually found his way towards something approaching the old productivity. A number of poems and fragments still showed the tentative search for a new form and tone; but it was significant that he took up again the Third Elegy he had begun there, and brought it to completion. For, as in Duino, he had determined 'to be once more my own severest doctor: alone and quiet'.[59] Lou had confirmed in him the notion that his salvation must lay in the self-analysis of work, not in medical treatment or on the analyst's couch (not even hers): and after her almost exclusively sexual interpretations of his dreams, especially those in the fears of childhood, and with the closer knowledge he had gained of Freud's theories, the themes of the Third Elegy already in his mind came naturally now to the fore.

> To sing about someone you love is one thing; but, oh,
> the blood's hidden guilty river-god is something else.
> Known to her only from a distance, what can her lover,
> even, say about the lord of passion, who often out of
> loneliness, before she could comfort him, often as if
> she didn't exist, raised his godhead, oh, who knows from
> what depths, came streaming, and incited the night to riot.
> Oh that Neptune of the blood and his terrible trident!
> .   .   .   .

And lying there, relieved, mingling the sweetness
of your slight body with the first taste
of approaching sleep under his heavy lids,
he seemed protected ... But inside: who could
stop or turn the floods of Origin in him?

.   .   .   .

Look, we don't love like flowers
with only one season behind us; when we love
a sap older than memory rises in our arms. O girl,
it's like this: inside us we haven't loved just some one
in the future, but a fermenting tribe; not just one
child, but fathers, cradled inside us like ruins
of mountains, the dry riverbed
of former mothers, yes, and all that
soundless landscape under its clouded
or clear destiny—girl, all this came before you.[60]

The final lines of the Sixth Elegy, on its theme of the Hero, also came to him—

For whenever the Hero stormed through love's stops,
each heartbeat meant for him carried him farther:
turning away, he'd stand at the end of the smiles, another—[61]

and in December a version of the last, the Tenth, continuing the start made in
Duino (a version which he would radically change when the work as a whole
took shape).

He was leading an outwardly normal literary life, as day succeeded day—
reading much in an unsystematic way, with great enthusiasm for Kleist, and
the poems of Rabindranath Tagore in Gide's translation; maintaining his
correspondence; producing a little, some completed poems and many more
fragments, and a few pages of translation; sending his essay 'On the Young
Poet' to Sidie with the suggestion that it might be published in Karl Kraus's
journal *Die Fackel*, and to Rolland a dedicated copy of the new *Rodin*. The
Alcoforado letters appeared in November, and in December the *First Poems*.
Yet as the year drew to a close he was obliged to admit that the treatment
under his own prescription lacked the effect he had hoped for. He could almost
wish for a 'sort of blindness, in order to turn completely inward'; to be 'a
curled-up hedgehog who only unrolls himself in the ditch in the evening and
cautiously emerges and lifts his grey snout to the stars'—but this happy state
eluded him.

I don't think of work, only of gradually regaining my health through reading,
rereading, reflecting ... Nothing was so harmful for me as the constant society this
summer of others, for whom one had to collect oneself, he prepared and seasoned to be
set before them. But I'm no dish, I'm quite unready to be served up, I'm like a
Cézanne still life—a couple of uneatable apples and a bottle, haphazardly arranged on
an old table-cloth, and the lot in constant danger of falling off.—And now here, with

no one to ask or see, I'm like an ant with a far too long piece of straw, losing it, finding it again unexpectedly, then losing it once more, running around in terror and amazed that in all this disorder no one treads on me. And yet—is that not life?[62]

Ideas of exchanging this aimless existence for the discipline of a university course somewhere, perhaps in Leipzig, came to his mind, but—as so often before—were rejected. He was in his chrysalis, he told Princess Marie, and she must await the emerging butterfly: 'you saw in Berlin how melancholy and detestable the caterpillar was.'[63] His discontent with Paris mounted, as though it were at fault rather than his own failure to find his way—not only to the Angel, but also to the companion he so needed in his life.

> You who never arrived
> in my arms, Beloved, who were lost
> from the start,
> I don't even know what songs
> would please you. I have given up trying
> to recognize you in the surging wave of the next
> moment. All the immense
> images in me—the far-off, deeply-felt landscape,
> cities, towers, and bridges, and un-
> suspected turns in the path,
> and those powerful lands that were once
> pulsing with the life of the gods—
> all rise within me to mean
> you, who forever elude me.
>
> You, Beloved, who are all
> the gardens I have ever gazed at,
> longing. An open window
> in a country house—, and you almost
> stepped up, pensive, to my side. Streets that I chanced upon,
> you had just walked down them and vanished.
> And sometimes, in a shop, the mirrors
> were still dizzy with your presence and, startled, gave back
> my too-sudden image. Who knows? perhaps the same
> bird echoed through both of us
> yesterday, separate, in the evening.[64]

'If God has understanding, He will let me find a couple of rooms in the country, where I can rave in my own way and where my Elegies can howl at the moon as they will ... long, lonely walks, and just the one person, that sisterly being (alas, alas!) who would take care of the house and have no love at all—or so much love that she would ask nothing except to be allowed to be there, active and protective, on the borders of the invisible. That's the sum total of my wishes for 1914, 15, 16, 17 etc.'[65] Until such a providential dispensation came his way, he must stay in Paris, burrowing deep into the solitude 'that since the immeasurably fruitful pains of childhood has given me all that is greatest'. He must 'dig over all the soil of the heart', turning under 'everything that has already grown there', and no longer seeking to find love— for that, in the accepted sense, was beyond his capacity, making demands that were an interruption to his true task. Strange to feel that he would perhaps never experience the love he wanted and needed, the love which could stand *behind* his work, making it 'purer, clearer, more transparent', needing no effort from him.[66]

He had hardly commited these thoughts to his pocket-book, during January 1914, when he received a letter which gave a sudden lift to the heart he was trying to 'dig over'. It was from one Magda von Hattingberg, in Vienna, who had been impelled to write, to the 'dear friend' she had come to know only recently through a copy of the *Tales of God*, her thanks for what he had given to her music. If only she could have been Ellen Key, just for a short while, she wrote, and the book dedicated to her, so that he might know that she too loved these stories 'as no one before'. A letter like this could not suffice to express her gratitude: but 'perhaps, if life is kind and allows me to find you somewhere, sometime', she could tell him through the medium of Beethoven, or 'something great by our Sebastian Bach'—for she was sure he loved music.[67]

Seizing the block of squared paper he used for his work, for his usual letter-paper had run out, he replied at once, taking up the same tone as hers in his joy at her letter: thankful, as he said, that she had *not* been transformed into the Ellen Key whose way had diverged so far from his since the *Tales of God*, and keeping her words for himself instead of passing them on to the callow author of those fables. 'I have at least the advantage over him . . . that he will never hear your music, as I will I hope.' Had she but happened to have come to Spain, to Ronda, while he was there—what fulfilment her music could have given him, when he had reached the limit of the purely visual. 'There I sat, at the end of my eyes, as if I should go blind through the images I'd absorbed': only the quite different sense of the ear could have taken him further. He had heard someone play, in the hotel there, and had experienced then 'how, in that wonderful element (I scarcely knew it, and it had always been too powerful for me), the world transcends into a more detached form, my cup ran over in the almost effortless joy at feeling it enter into me, for my ear is as new as the sole of the foot of a babe in arms . . . Your music is before me like some season one day to come . . . Farewell, good friend . . . do not let this new welcome fire die out, even if I can only once in a while throw into it a small grain of the heart's resin to give it perfume for you. I am devoted and grateful to you.'[68]

He had never failed to respond to approaches of this kind, entering into the hopes and problems of his unknown correspondents, but always from the distance of the poet-philosopher. Magda's letter in itself was little different, but it had come at a moment of particular despondency. Only the day before it arrived, he had written to Carlo Placci of the darkness and 'tristesses infinies'

William Ashton, *The Island of Philae*

Ronda

Sidonie Nádherný   Mary Dobržensky

Magda von Hattingberg ('Benvenuta')   Loulou Albert-Lazard

that seemed still to stretch out before him: 'I'd had plenty of such mountains on my road before, but then I climbed them . . . and sometimes . . . the distant prospect lit up for me a clear vision of the future. This time I feel rather as if I'm going through the rock itself.'[69] Magda's words now gave him sudden hope: he felt instinctively that the music she mentioned opened that distant prospect of a clear, new world, and that she herself must be the sisterly being he had begun to despair of ever finding.

Magda Richling, Vienna-born and eight years younger than he, was a concert pianist, a student of Ferruccio Busoni's and already of some considerable repute. Her early marriage to von Hattingberg had ended in divorce, so that, like Rilke, she was alone and searching for someone who could bring the fulfilment her life needed. That the letter she had dispatched into the blue should receive a reply at all, let alone in such terms, gave her indescribable joy. She told him at once of her plans to go now for some weeks to Berlin, then to Munich: of her hope that they might meet then somewhere in Germany, or even in Paris, which she had long planned also to visit.

For Rilke, the floodgates seemed to open. In a stream of letters, writing almost daily and scarcely waiting for her replies, he began to pour out his heart to her as he had done to no one before, save only Lou. He grasped eagerly at the idea of this 'wonderful future' she offered him, a future 'with the power of bringing down on me storms, tempests, and clarifications, the purest convulsions of the universe, at its sweet will'. 'Friend, sister', 'blessèd, joyous, bright one'—he longed for her to come to him, yet hesitated over his lack of understanding, his incapacity, for music, and hesitated too because she could not know how different he was now from the young author of the *Tales of God*. Writing *Malte* had been like going deep into a mountain, so deep that he had seemed to become pure rock himself: he had cried out then for someone to come and free him, to 'chisel him out', but each attempt had been unavailing. 'I'm not practised with people . . . my spirit went beyond them, I wanted to stay where I was, or at most be saved by the Angel, for with *him* I was sure to find the right note of intimacy.'[70]

'I would have to write to you day and night just to express everything which wells up and sinks again under these contradictions, and God knows if I can make myself understood when I do not understand it all myself.' For months, he told her, he had been playing at hide-and-seek: and now, when her bright joy had suddenly sought him out, he was like the little boy who cries out 'Not yet!' and wants to find a better hiding-place so as to put off the moment of terror and pleasure when he's found—or like the countryside which seems to beg the sun not to rise. 'Who are you, dear friend?—this garden of mine fears the sun, for it's so dug up and turned over that it no longer looks like a garden . . . in no state to receive you, radiant one, and the god or demigod who is with you.' Paris, the city 'I've so desperately lived and suffered through', could not be the place for her music to come to him—for 'your music (so I allow myself to dream) should come not only to bring a new order to my inner world, but also to make the context for entirely new outward relationships'.[71]

At the receiving end of these long letters—'light, beautiful, rushing from the heart,' he recalled later, 'I can scarcely remember ever having written such letters'[72]—it was not surprising that Magda should feel herself destined to be the lover he sought, the one to free the prisoner of the rock. She assured him that she did indeed know *Malte* and the man he had become: that he must have no fear of the new world she could offer him, but only trust in the bright future before them. For him, these 'inexhaustible confessions' seemed to restore his very being, confident that here at last he had found the soul-mate he had longed for. Always before, he had felt swept along passively into relationships that proved only fruitless entanglements: this must be different. She was 'Benvenuta', his welcome one, 'dear heart', 'loving sister', to whom he could speak 'as though to the clouds and the deeps of my heaven'.[73]

He sent her the only photographs of himself he had (ironically enough, taken by Hedwig Bernhard in Rippoldsau), and begged for one of her as he tried to picture her 'dear, distant, distant figure'. Others had come to love him through his work, but for them, his books were like telescopes in which they could see all kinds of things, a kaleidoscope which they might find beautiful: she alone could see into his heart. 'Look closely into the directed telescope— over there, that tiny tiny point of light—have you got it?—that's my heart, scarcely recognizable. Ah my sister, is it a house? or just a bright, rigid spot in the rock, blinking blindly out from the happy green of busy nature around it?'[74] As he rambled on, in a kind of diary, such as Malte might have written had he been happy, sometimes for several days on end before sending off the closely-written pages, he rehearsed little by little for her his whole life—René's childhood, that had seemed without love, the military college; the *Cornet*, Paris, Rome, Capri, Venice, the Duse; the marriage that 'should never, never have happened',[75] Ruth, the divorce that was now in preparation—but all of this directed now to his 'dear girl', 'an inconceivable journal of my will to live in your heart'. 'It seems to me as if this were my *work*, my definitive task, to make myself true for you . . . as if in your heart I could for the first time make myself recognizable to God.'[76]

Through the February weeks, these extraordinary outpourings were work indeed, a flow of poetic prose he had not known since the night of the *Cornet* in Schmargendorf. Almost a stream of consciousness, they were yet creativity, a composition overlapping and intermingling with that of verse or pocket-book, where he would occasionally even draft or copy some of the passages. It was not chance that, even when new stocks of his letter-paper were to hand, he should choose to continue on that of his working block. In the mounting euphoria his life seemed to have taken a new turn: the intensive self-analysis of these letters was the cure he had sought for his ills, he felt, all previous failures to find the right relationship with a loved one were forgotten in this 'pure and transparent' act of communication. Lou noticed a change in his handwriting, though she did not yet know the reason: his 's' suddenly carefree, like a banner waving or a surge heavenwards.[77] New life breathed in what had been his 'work' before, as he completed his translation of Gide's *Enfant prodigue* and sent it off to Kippenberg, wrote his essay on Lotte Pritzel's dolls, began translations of Michelangelo's sonnets. The enthusiasms that had tended to wane with the old year—Werfel's latest poems, Proust's *Du côté de chez Swann*—were reawakened, and new interests flooded in. His reading widened; he was full of suggestions for new Insel publications, received with joy Kippenberg's news of translations in hand of the *Cornet* into other languages; welcomed Gide's proposal to attempt it in French; put forward impassioned arguments to a potential patron for a come-back for the Duse.

Benvenuta wrote to him almost as often, responding increasingly as the sisterly lover he saw in her. They exchanged ideas on where their longed-for meeting could be—Vienna, Munich or Würzburg, Geneva—anywhere, he cried, but best of all in a city he did not yet know, 'I want to be with you first only in places that are quite new for me, as radiantly new as all this, until the old familiar ones gradually, as though resurrected, pass over into *our, our* glory without looking back'.[78] Paris becoming more and more insupportable, he began to think of Perugia or Assisi, and asked Pia Valmarana whether she could suggest somewhere for him, not a hotel but perhaps a small furnished house—adding in confidence that it would not just be for himself, but also for the friend 'who wishes to devote herself to me', who might be persuaded to come and play her music for him.[79] Even Paris, however, when Magda mentioned possible engagements there later, was transformed for him, and he at once asked Gide where suitable rooms might be found for his 'dearest friend'. 'You send me a couple of ready dates, shining in their newness, dear heart, all the red-letter days—Easter, Whitsun, or whatever—cannot compete ... a glorious calendar, far fairer than Pope Gregory's, a year of the heart ...' But they could not wait, and when she pressed him to come to Berlin, his heart leapt towards her in impatience. As the few days passed before he could set off on 25 February, he still wrote and wrote, 'letter after letter, none could have waited even an hour in my drawer, dearest one, all rushed to you.' In the train he continued them with verses to her—

> Can you imagine how for years
> I've travelled thus, strange among strangers?
> And now at last you take me in, to home—

and was still writing when her knock came on his door.[80]

For a few brief weeks all his hopes seemed to be fulfilled. The day after his arrival he took a room near hers, in Grunewald, where she arranged at once to have a piano delivered, for his introduction to her world of music—a gentle introduction to overcome his apprehensions, with Händel, a Bach aria, a

Scarlatti pastorale. Grunewald was just as it used to be; 'as if I were still young,' he wrote enthusiastically to Lou, on 9 March: 'the most singular dispositions here, and music—magnificent through Busoni. And the Egyptian Museum. All kinds of unexpected, good things brought me here . . .'[81] He attended a concert of Busoni's who later invited them to his house, and there were many other social occasions: but Magda's commitments—practice, rehearsals, performances—left him much to his own devices, and this was indeed what he had sought. Here was freedom to dream, work, stroll, write, interspersed with afternoons or evenings with his Benvenuta: at last, the undemanding love he had dreamed of, the love which could stand protective behind his work.

> Oh how you peel from my heart the hulls of misery.
> What betrayed you the core in so sorry a shell?
> Core sweet as the stars, world-sweet, within me.
> Ah, as I suffered, sleepy growth overcame it,
> as suffering silently shattered my limbs
> in my heart slept a heart, a future one, guiltless.
> One heart, oh see: I know not yet which, nor can guess,
> this conjectural heart. Its were the stars
> I gave the more troubled one. Oh come to it
> through my anxious being. Be understanding. Know it
> and call. Astounding one, call. Give a small
> smile first, that it may stir with the rays;
> bow your fair face to it: the space of awakening,
> that it may wonder in you, grow used to the dawn.[82]

An untroubled future seemed to stretch before him while she could be with him. They would travel a while together, prolonging the idyll which their letters had so ardently imagined—to Munich first, through the Tyrol, her homeland, to Zürich, Basle, the cities he had not yet known, then to Paris where with her support he could see renewed hope for work.

Apart from Pia Valmarana, no one had heard of his new relationship. Even Lou he had told only of the 'beautiful correspondence, somehow full of hope' which had kept him busy,[83] and for Kippenberg the Egyptian Museum had been sufficient excuse for his sudden departure to Berlin. In Marie Taxis, however, he felt a need to confide, and from Munich asked her when he might bring to Duino 'a dear person . . . I know she will be sympathetic to you, and music lies in her in a great and wonderful way such as I would never have believed possible: I feel that through her I can develop with music, raise myself up as I once did with Rodin's sculpture.' Although he had hoped they might even come to Duino before going on to Paris, there was no reply from the Princess and so, after the 'slight detour' through Switzerland, as he called it to Kippenberg, they arrived in Paris on 26 March.[84]

Magda had realized—as who would not have, after those letters?—that she was to meet a poet who was not as other men; but the delicate reserve she found in the lover who had been so ardent on paper must all the same have come as a surprise. In the first days in Berlin, she thought him truly 'a being from another world': that he should be married, with a child, was as unbelievable as that an archangel should be subject to human destiny.[85] During their week in Munich, where the presence of Clara in any case demanded discretion, she stayed with her sister out at Nymphenburg and he at his usual Hotel Marienbad, so that they met only occasionally; while on the rest of the circuitous journey to Paris they travelled less as lovers than as brother and sister—or once as patient and nurse, when she ministered to his acute suffering under the effects of the föhn in Innsbruck. It was the role for which his letters had prepared her, in fact, and which, in her admiration for him, she was ready to accept. But in Paris, as he guided her through the scenes he knew so well, and she gave for him each afternoon a private recital in her room in the Hôtel du Quai Voltaire, it became clear that he needed something more than sisterly devotion. He asked her if she would be ready to share his life 'for ever'—but insisted that she should not answer him at once. She was to follow the dictates of her own nature, and if she should feel the task beyond her of bearing and sharing a life such as his, then she must return, 'simply and bravely', to her own, without promises and without thinking of him.

Writing to her sister of this, she reflected whether she loved him as a woman loves a man, '*the* man to whom she wants to belong all her life—do I love him so, that I want to be the mother of his children? And there I must say to myself, no. For me he is the voice of God, the immortal soul, Fra Angelico, all that is unearthly, good, high, and holy—but not a human being!' And she could not avoid thinking of the wife and child he had left: however much he had loosed these bonds, they should be respected.[86]

She did not tell him yet, but he sensed what her reply would be, and his health worsened, in sympathy with his pessimism. When he read her a cycle of seven poems, apparently just written, she could not at first believe they were his, so different was the tone;[87] and her reaction obviously depressed him, with the thought that he might indeed have lost all capacity for renewed achievement. He agreed when she suggested they should each return for a while to their work: but it was a resolution he found impossible to keep, and he would come and sit for hours listening to her practise. Princess Marie's letter with the news that they would be welcome at Duino after 18 April came as a release for them both, and to Rilke as a flicker of hope, which the visit however was to reveal as illusory.

The house party, with Kassner and Horatio Brown among the guests and 'Pascha' and his family there, went its usual course. It was a new and exciting scene for Magda, their hostess in the romantic setting of the castle truly a Renaissance princess, eager to hear her on the piano where Liszt had once played, and on one occasion sending for the Trieste Quartet to join her (as

Kassner later noted, Marie Taxis' appetite for music was 'insatiable'[88]). Rilke gradually recovered his health, but his gloom increased. Unburdening himself to the Princess, he realized that his had been a hopeless dream; he did not really need her to tell him that, if ever he was to find the right 'guardian of his solitude', it could no more be Magda than Clara. Magda herself knew in her heart that if she joined herself to him as he had asked, she could never give him what he needed. Not for nothing had she heard him quote Kassner's aphorism, 'the road from inwardness to greatness lies through sacrifice': his goal, she could see, demanded the sacrifice of their dream, while she herself must seek someone strong enough to lead her 'into the protective security of an *undivided world*'—not an ethereal Fra Angelico who could be no more than a distant voice of comfort.[89] It had been arranged that they would accompany the Princess to Venice early in May, and before they left Duino, the die had been cast: in Venice their ways would part for ever.

Troubled times lay behind him and more were ahead, he wrote to Kippenberg on 27 April 'from the memorable shore of the Duino Elegies', confessing that he was yet again in need of his friend's support (on which he had in fact already been calling through these lost months). 'I have had a whole succession of unexpected expenses during March and April . . . whether I go back to Paris now, or stay a while here in the country (I'm thinking of Assisi, which I haven't yet seen), I can't afford either without a little help, for I haven't a penny left.'[90] He asked for nearly double his monthly allowance, and Kippenberg, resigned to the continual frustration of his hopes for more careful budgeting, responded with his wonted generosity. The separation from Magda in Venice was painful, but they both remained resolute. Princess Marie was full of understanding, rightly convinced that it was for the best, and made Rilke free of her *mezzanino* in the Palazzo Valmarana if he wished to stay on after her return to Duino and Magda's departure to join her sister in the Tyrol. But he decided, in an 'immense need for solitude', to escape to Assisi, for the solace of a completely unknown place which 'like a virgin page will bring not the slightest memory'.[91]

'Beloved, lost from the start . . .'—perhaps he had always known that he would not find his undemanding lover in Benvenuta. Even in the midst of those letters to her, 'rushing from the heart', he had felt it incumbent on him to warn Sidie Nádherný against too deep an involvement with Karl Kraus when she told him of the satirist's ardent wooing. 'I'm thinking here of a painful experience that has been my lot several times in life, again and again even though I should have been able to guard against it: three or four times, in an intellectual way (or by an intellectual detour if you like) I've unwittingly drawn a person more intimately into my life than I really intended—as if one forgot that, in absorbing the spiritual existence of the other, one is also continually taking in something which may be alien to one's nature—and can end up awakening, as it were, to feel a foreign body in all one's limbs.'[92] With the realization now that he had made the same mistake again, even if not quite in these terms, he began to overcome the dull feeling of emptiness left by the parting from Magda, and after a fortnight in Assisi was back once more in Paris, resolved to draw a firm line under the experience.

'Don't think this is yet another sudden reversal,' he wrote from there to Kippenberg on 26 May: 'on the contrary, I hope it will bring everything back to its proper element. ... The unexpected, unquiet months could have brought indescribable good—perhaps—but it's time to face honestly and turn to good account the fact that they haven't, and in the end a purer benefit will result than could ever have come from all the foolish hopes.' He had felt a real homesickness for Paris, but hoped to come to Leipzig whenever his friends could have him, for it was time to try and bring some order into his affairs. 'Looking back is sad, looking forward far from joyful,' he wrote to the Princess. 'On reste cloué sur place et on voudrait fermer les yeux par une centaine de paupières l'une sur l'autre.'[93] Magda received a letter early in June, 'to tell you where I am, and am remaining', with news of mutual friends, in the tone more normal for him—and, significantly, on his regular letterhead. He was sending her Francis Jammes's poems—but their watchword now must be 'silence, and let time do its work'.[94]

It was to Lou that he drew up an unsentimental balance sheet of these months in which once again 'a kind of future' had gone by. His previous failures he had been able to put down to the others' lack of understanding: this time he had come to realize, he told her, that no one else, but no one, could help him, no matter how understanding.

One will finally have learned much from it all—but for the moment I can see only this: that once more I've proved unequal to a pure and joyous task, when life offered itself to me again, innocent and forgiving. ... Now it's clear that this time I've failed the exam, that I'm not to be promoted and have to stay one more year in the same class of sorrow and start over again with the same words written up on the blackboard, whose dreary turn I thought I already had by heart. ... You realize that what I am describing to you is now long past and lost for me; three months of reality (which I couldn't face up to) have placed something like a stout, cold glass over it, and it becomes unpossessable, as in a glass case in a museum. The glass reflects, and I can see nothing in it but my own face, the old, earlier face, the face of long ago that you know so well.

He had come back from Italy hoping to plunge into work, but felt so petrified that he could do little more than sleep. For the future he could imagine only a different kind of work, something disciplined from outside and as remote as possible from productivity. 'For I no longer have any doubt about it, I am sick, my sickness has greatly increased and lies also in what I've hitherto called my work, so that there's no refuge there ...'

Lou was moved to tears by his letter, she wrote, for she had thought to see, in the lyrical flourish of his handwriting during February, the signs of renewed productivity, under the stimulus of a new relationship. Yet the 'unpossessable' exhibit in the glass case was still 'a proof of the greatness of your possessions', would still 'have sides to turn to you as yet unsuspected, perhaps separated from your view by a partition even thinner than glass'. For once, however, she felt at a loss: 'now the only thing you'll feel is that something, be it thin or massive, is separating you from life, and *every* word is stupid and powerless against that.'[95]

All the same, he was deeply grateful for her comfort. Although he was convinced that his 'sickness' would demand medical aid, and contemplated seeing his doctor friend Wilhelm von Stauffenberg in Munich when the time came for his visit to Kippenberg, he began to take heart in finding poetic expression for the problem of his life. Helene von Nostitz had written of her plans to revisit Heiligendamm in June, and the memory of the forest pool they had walked to together a year earlier called up a sudden image for his dilemma—the sharp contrast of its unruffled stillness with the agitation of the mountainous seas beyond the woods, two worlds,

> and I, that know the two,
> back in unresponsive room
>
> .   .   .   .
>
> Could but one thing utterly possess me!
> Shudderingly I bow my head,
> for I know it: love would overpress me.
>
> Who's equal to what love should be?
>
> .   .   .   .
>
> Have I been recklessly rapacious,
> circumscribing those capacious
> things within my narrow heart?
> Have I embraced them only in the way
> this room, this unrelated room, embraces
> my soul and me?
>   Oh, has my breast no places
> with gently murmuring woods, no spaces
> for silence, light as breath and mild as May?
>
> Image, symbol, gleaned with such insistence,
> are you sorry to have been within me?
>
> .   .   .   .
>
> Oh, the world's no link with my existence,
> unless out there that splendid vision,
> as if with lightly preconceived decision,
> gleam from afar with joy right into me.[96]

He felt himself at the turning-point of which he had spoken earlier to Kassner. He had found no relation with the outside world, least of all in love, all his attempts to grasp it, all this 'gazing outward from myself', had 'eaten him empty', and must be replaced by 'a devoted effort to achieve inner intensity'.[97] The day after the verses on the forest pool, on 20 June, he sent to Lou 'a remarkable poem, written this morning ... which I instinctively entitled "Turning-point", because it portrays the turn which must come if I am to live, and you will understand what it signifies':

> For a long time he attained it in looking.
> Stars would fall to their knees
> beneath his compelling vision.
> Or as he looked on, kneeling,
> his urgency's fragrance
> tired out a god until
> it smiled at him in its sleep.
>
> Towers he would gaze at so
> that they were terrified:
> building them up again, suddenly, in an instant!
> But how often the landscape,
> overburdened by day,
> came to rest in his silent awareness, at nightfall.
> .   .   .   .
>
> Looking how long?
> For how long now, deeply deprived,
> beseeching in the depths of his glance?
>
> When he, whose vocation was Waiting, sat far from home —
> the hotel's distracted unnoticing bedroom
> moody around him, and in the avoided mirror
> once more the room, and later
> from the tormenting bed
> once more:
> then in the air the voices
> discussed, beyond comprehension,
> his heart, which could still be felt;
> debated what through the painfully buried body
> could somehow be felt — his heart;
> debated and passed their judgement:
> that it did not have love.
>
> (And denied him further communions.)
>
> For there is a boundary to looking.
> And the world that is looked at so deeply
> wants to flourish in love.
>
> Work of the eyes is done, now
> go and do heart-work
> on all the images imprisoned within you; for you
> overpowered them: but even now you don't know them.

> Learn, inner man, to look on your inner woman,
> the one attained from a thousand
> natures, the merely attained but
> not yet beloved form.[98]

Oblivious of the more drastic turning-point for Europe that was imminent, Rilke continued intensely preoccupied with his personal problem. To Lou again, a few days later (only two days before the Sarajevo assassination) he said that he still lagged far behind the change foreshadowed in his poem, and God alone knew whether he could in fact achieve it. 'That was why I had such indescribable hopes from having at last found the right relationship to another, because then all the distances would have been set to rights: that to the world equated to infinity, that to my body to zero, and in between all other numbers in harmless order'. His travels, the changes of scene had been nothing more than 'a continual desperate exposure of face and body, exhausting and overloading it, while the soul, turned away, preoccupied, withdrawn, cannot relieve my tensions'. 'My spirit is the bell-metal, and God brings it time and again to white heat and prepares for the solemn moment of casting: but I remain still in the old shape, that of the previous bell, obstinate in its achievement and unwilling to be replaced—and so it stays uncast. Is it possible to see all this, and still not help oneself? all these years.'

Meanwhile his door stayed closed, he needed an inordinate amount of sleep, and 'work' would not come: faced with a sheet of paper or a book, he felt as restricted as a tethered goat. He badly needed to talk to Lou, and when Kippenberg said he would be welcome in Leipzig towards the end of July, he decided to try and see her in Göttingen first. After Leipzig, however, he must see a doctor, if he was ever to resolve the paralysing conflict between body and spirit: 'not a psychoanalyst, who starts from original sin (for it's my overriding, most inward calling, the whole basis of the artist's view of life, to set up a counter-magic to that), but a doctor who, starting from the body, can follow up into the mind'—and Stauffenberg had said he would have time for him in Munich during August.[99] After further hesitations—quite unconnected with the march of events in Europe, of which he remained unaware—he left Paris on 19 July 1914 for Göttingen.

2

> 'Now the war has long since become invisible for me, a
> spectre of affliction'
>
> (To Karl and Elisabeth von der Heydt, 6.11.1914)

His hopes for a long consultation with Lou were disappointed, for she had to leave Göttingen a few days after his arrival, to keep an appointment with Gebsattel in Munich. He was himself in any case anxious to get to Leipzig without delay, for he had been unsettled by a hint in Kippenberg's letters of a 'most painful' development, which could only concern money, and it was high time to clarify his situation (he would not have been able to travel at all, had not Kippenberg sent yet another remittance to cover his Paris rent).

In fact, he had a suspicion of what was worrying the publisher. Princess Mechtilde Lichnowsky, the wife of the German ambassador in London and author of a book on Egypt which had found an enthusiastic reception with Rilke on its appearance in 1912, had been in occasional correspondence with him since then, hearing not only of his Egyptological discussions with Steindorff and his rapture over the Amenhotep head, but also of the difficulties, both spiritual and material, in his life. In June she had had the generous idea of launching an appeal for his support, with a circular letter which she had asked her publisher, Kurt Wolff, to handle in Germany on her behalf: and she had told Rilke of her plan. He could imagine only too well that for Kippenberg this well-meant action would come as a 'painful surprise',[1] nothing less than a poaching on his preserve, especially since it involved a rival publisher whose promotion of the progressive and expressionist avant-garde, including Werfel and Kafka, found little favour with the more conservative director of the Insel (Kippenberg had already taken Rilke severely to task for 'endangering his reputation' by publishing his 'Dolls' essay in the March issue of *Die Weissen Blätter*, a journal appearing under Wolff's aegis[2]). Arriving in Leipzig on 23 July, he found that this was indeed the case. Kippenberg's ruffled feelings were somewhat smoothed when the Princess, at Rilke's urgent request, expressed her readiness to consolidate her appeal with what she now knew had been Kippenberg's similar action over many years to support the poet. The outbreak of the war shortly afterwards put great difficulties in the way of their plans, but Kippenberg was able later to report some benefit to Rilke's account from these new sources, even though in the end this 'tactless action', as he continued to regard it, ran into the sand.[3]

From today's standpoint it is little short of astounding to find among such people, on the very eve of the First World War, no evident sign of any realization of its imminence. The wife of Prince Lichnowsky, whose vain efforts for peace during his London mission were later to be gratefully recalled by the British Foreign Secretary, could scarcely have been unaware of the crisis: yet her letters in the Rilke affair reveal no concern, any more than those of the two publishers. As for Rilke himself, still taken up with his own problems and making as usual a point of never reading the daily papers, except for a glance through the *feuilleton*, it is less surprising that he should have had no appreciation of the situation until 1 August, three days after Austria-Hungary's declaration of war against Serbia and the Russian and German mobilizations, and the day of Germany's ultimatum to Belgium. Interrupting his quiet discussions with Kippenberg about his future, he hastened that day to Munich, hoping to find Lou there—but she was at the same moment returning to Göttingen, assuming he would not now be able to travel.

Putting up at his usual hotel, he held to his original plan of consulting

Stauffenberg—though what was to come after that was more uncertain than ever in the turmoil. He was now cut off from the only place, through the many years of wandering, he could have called home, and all his possessions, except for the scanty luggage he thought necessary for the visit to Germany, had been left behind in Paris. For the first time therefore really homeless, and with Germany and Austria, for neither of which he had ever held a trace of patriotic feeling, at war with Russia and France—the one his spiritual motherland, the other his country of adoption—he might have been expected to succumb to the deepest of depressions, or at least to remain deaf to the shouts of jingoistic fervour around him. Not so: in the first days of August even his 'inexpressibly solitary' spirit felt at one with the herd.[4] His own problems seemed suddenly trivial under the glare of these awesome events, and it was his duty now, he thought, to serve the common cause, as a clerk perhaps, or a medical orderly. In an access of exaltation, his mind filled with Hölderlin's visionary apostrophes to the gods of Greece which he had just been reading, 'with extraordinary feeling and devotion',[5] he began 'Five Hymns' to the god of battles, 'rumoured, remotest, incredible war-god', whose terrible figure had risen so suddenly, 'a god at last'.

> For three days, is it true? Am I really hymning the horror,
> really that god whom as one of the olden times,
> distant and only remembering, I was wont to believe and admire?
> Like a volcanic peak he lay to the westward. Sometimes
> flaming. Sometimes a-smoke. Sorrowing, godlike.
> Only perhaps some district near to his borders
> would quake. But we raised aloft our undamaged lyres
> to others: to which of the future gods?
> And now he uprose. He stands. Higher
> than standing towers. Higher
> than the inbreathed air of our days just past
> he stands. He transcends. And we? We merge into one together,
> into a new kind of being, mortally animate through him.
> So too *am* I no more. Out of the general heart
> my heart is beating in tune; and the general mouth
> is forcing my lips apart.
> .   .   .   .
> For we have been altered, changed to resemble each other.
> Each one has received of a sudden
> into no longer a breast of his own, meteoric, a heart,
> hot, an iron-clad heart from an iron-clad cosmos. . . .

He felt himself part of a sublime spectacle, and for the first time the verse of this intensely individual poet expressed a profound shared emotion—though without a trace of the purely nationalist spirit which filled the 'war poetry' of his contemporaries. But the ecstatic moment was brief indeed. Even as he wrote these hymns, the inspiration seemed to fade, and the fifth sounded a less rhapsodic note.

> Up, and frighten this frightening war-god
> .   .   .   .
>
> Now you're confined once more to what is your own. Though now
> it has grown far greater. And though it be far from world,
> accept it as world! Make use of it like a mirror,
> catching the sun and casting the sun it has caught
> upon those that have erred and strayed. (May your own error
> burn itself out in the painful, terrible heart).[6]

He knew that his own heart was not made to 'beat in tune' with the general, could not join in surrender to the mighty power that had seized mankind: and he almost came to envy those for whom the call to the colours had been a call to drown out all others. Even before the first month of the war was out, as news came of the many friends already in the field and he waited to see what the 'inscrutable future' might hold, his jubilation gave place to horror and he began to 'encapsulate' himself against the immense outside force that at first had seemed so glorious.[7]

Stauffenberg, in spite of the new demands on his time, spent many hours in a thorough examination. He rightly recognized the psychosomatic roots of the malaise, but Rilke firmly resisted any attempt to explore beyond the purely physical, overcome by a kind of 'spiritual nausea' at the thought of anything approaching psychoanalysis: 'to vomit up scraps of childhood would be terrible for one whose call is not to resolve these problems within himself but essentially to exploit them, in fiction and feeling, through things, animals — through everything, in fact, if necessary through the supernatural.'[8] After Stauffenberg had finally discovered a slight lesion of the lung, though long healed and harmless enough, he was almost relieved to be able to cling to this insignificant but after all concrete symptom, and at the end of August gladly took his advice to retreat from Munich for a while to the clear air of Irschenhausen, in the foothills of the Bavarian Alps.

Undisturbed enjoyment of the late summer days in these peaceful surroundings was not easy while 'the world of man sprouted up in conflict over the fearful acres'. He tried to shut himself off in Hölderlin's 'nocturnal landscape', reading again the last odes and the *Hyperion*, and thought on that 'turning-point' which outside events seemed now to have turned into a mirage:

> O house, O sloping field, O setting sun!
> Your features form into a face, you run,
> you cling to us, returning our embrace.
>
> *One* space spreads through all creatures equally —
> inner-world-space. Birds quietly flying go
> flying through us. Oh, I that want to grow,
> the tree I look outside at grows *in* me!

It stands in me, that house I look for still,
in me that shelter I have not possessed.
Belovèd that I became: now on my breast
this fair world's image clings and weeps her fill.[9]

Irresolute, after a week or two he was already preparing to return to Munich, when a new guest arrived at the pension where he was staying—and suddenly the seeker after salvation within himself was faced once more with temptation from outside, the hope he had thought for ever abandoned with Benvenuta rekindled. For opposite him at the lunch table sat a figure he had already admired from afar in Paris, a strikingly beautiful young woman who had been among the artist friends of Edith von Bonin. They had never met, but it seemed to him providential that just at this moment his path should cross that of someone from Paris, and he decided at once to stay on.

Loulou Lazard, born in 1891 in Lorraine, the province of long-standing contest between France and Germany, had been married four years to the much older Eugen Albert, a research chemist and joint owner of a chemicals firm in Munich, and had a three-year-old daughter. For all his kindness, her husband was buried so deeply in his work that he found little time for her, and she had been relieved when, in the year before the war, he had willingly agreed to her moving to Paris, to pursue the painting at which she had already made a name in Metz and Munich. In Brittany in July she had managed to take one of the last trains back to Germany, horrified both by the war fever she saw in Paris and by the transfigured look of dedication on the faces of the German troops advancing towards Belgium. A senseless war between the two countries she reckoned equally as home, a war in which there could be no place for art, was nothing short of torture for her, and she had sought refuge in Irschenhausen to try to recover from this shattering blow to her hopes for the future. She knew and loved Rilke's work, and had heard Edith von Bonin speak of him in Paris, but had never thought to meet him like this, at a time when her only wish was for solitude.

Full of understanding, he asked if he might nevertheless sit by her—without speaking—as she rested out on the lawn. Over the next few days her reserve was overcome under his spell, and they were soon talking like friends of long standing. On their walks she heard, like Benvenuta before her, the story of Rilke, the perennial conflict between the demands of life and love and those of his work, the conflict she herself knew only too well. Their meeting was predestined, he assured her—'have I not long since been on the way to you?'[10] As September went by he pursued his wooing—for, regardless of his past disappointments, it was nothing less—with a stream of verses, some as dedications in copies of his books, others inscribed in a little volume he bought specially for the purpose, yet all expressing the predicament both he and she found themselves in, of simultaneous outgoing and withdrawal:

> Let me never at your lips be drinking
> for from mouths I drank despondency.
> Let me not into your arms be sinking,
> for arms can't encompass me.[11]

Like her, he longed for, yet feared, the exposure 'on the mountains of the heart' to which their relationship beckoned:

> Look, how tiny down there,
> look: the last village of words and, higher,
> (but how tiny) still one last
> farmhouse of feeling. Can you see it?
> Exposed on the cliffs of the heart. Stoneground
> under your hands. Even here, though,
> something can bloom; on a silent cliff-edge
> an unknowing plant blooms, singing, into the air.
> But the one who knows? Ah, he began to know
> and is quiet now, exposed on the cliffs of the heart.
> While, with their full awareness,
> many sure-footed mountain animals pass
> or linger. And the great sheltered bird flies, slowly
> circling, around the peak's pure denial.—But
> without a shelter, here on the cliffs of the heart. . . .[12]

Yet his first thought, when he returned to Munich in the last week of September, was to find a way to bring Loulou into his life: and he proposed that she should take rooms alongside his in the pension where he settled, in the Finkenstrasse.

Here they found they had almost a whole floor to themselves, their creature comforts assured with a maid to look after them, and a restaurant nearby for their meals. Her husband had raised no objection: with the war he was more engrossed than ever in his own activities, and he realized that this unconventional arrangement would give her the outlet she needed and freedom to resume her work in tranquillity. He himself greatly admired Rilke, and apparently anticipated no real rivalry from him for her affection—though he could not overlook the omen of their choice of lodging, for the pension was the very place where she had stayed before their marriage. For her, this was one of life's mysterious circles that Rilke always spoke of, and the very symbol of a new beginning. Life here—extraordinarily quiet although near the city's centre—seemed suddenly 'free from all earthly ties', the sombre backdrop of the war quite removed.[13] Painting again, she discovered a close affinity between her sense of colour and its expression in Rilke's *New Poems*. She heard him tell of his friends—the Princess, Kassner, the Kippenbergs, Gide, Rolland—so vividly that she felt she already knew them. The October days passed for her in an unclouded idyll.

Rilke, it is plain, felt that at last his search was over, the elusive 'future beloved' found. Here was a perfect understanding, a lover with whom there was no tie, yet who could offer him the feeling of 'protection' for his work he had looked for in vain till now. He could fill her rooms with flowers, read her his own or others' poems, share his thoughts—but always withdraw to his solitude when he wanted. He transcribed for her from his diary his earlier words of despair at ever satisfying his 'immeasurable longing for love ... as long as he was receptive and yielding to those who thought they loved him': 'that was how I was before I found you,' he told her, 'but now you have come everything shall be different, and new.'[14] (That this had been written eighteen months earlier, he preferred to gloss over; and though she knew of Magda von Hattingberg, she never heard of her as his 'Benvenuta'.) 'Do you not feel that a miracle like ours, a joy like ours, can only happen once in a lifetime, only once?'[15]

He loved to give, and was a master in the art. From his daily walk he would always return with some surprise for her: a vase or statuette, or a piece of old jewellery rummaged out from an antique shop, or books—Montaigne, Flaubert, Dostoevsky—or, for her greatest delight, a poem that had come to him.

> No more than birds with nesting-places
> on the ponderously hanging
> bells in belfries, whom a clanging
> burst of unpent feeling chases
> out in crowded morning flight
> to indite
> their invading
> fears' initials round the towers:
> can we, amid such cannonading,
> keep within these hearts of ours.[16]

He had written to Kippenberg, who was now serving with the army, to reassure him that he was husbanding his resources in modest accommodation; but since then there had come an unexpected windfall which made him even more than usually carefree with his money. In a letter at the end of September from Ludwig von Ficker, editor of the early expressionist journal *Der Brenner* in Innsbruck, he had been informed than an anonymous donor, about to be called to the colours, had made over to him 20,000 Austrian crowns. He could scarcely credit this unlooked for generosity, until Kippenberg on a visit to Leipzig confirmed it a few days later and proposed he invest the sum for him in gilt-edged stocks, leaving to him only the income from it. This cautious approach he agreed to, but with the proviso that he should retain a portion of the capital—2,000 or 3,000 crowns—as a small emergency reserve and also, as he put it, to enable him to settle his current debts and replace the deficiencies in his wardrobe, of which so much had been left behind in Paris.

The benefactor, whose identity neither Rilke nor Kippenberg ever learned, was none other than Ludwig Wittgenstein. In July, from a village in southern Norway where he was engaged on his *Tractatus logico-philosophicus*, the Austrian philosopher had asked Ficker, of whom he had heard through Karl Kraus, to suggest suitable recipients among needy writers and artists for a large sum he had just inherited, which he felt it his duty to use for charitable purposes. Ficker's proposal of the poets Rilke and George Trakl, among others, met with his enthusiastic approval, and he left the administrative details to the editor now that he was about to be called up. He felt more than repaid when in February 1915, on garrison duties in Cracow, he received through Ficker Rilke's letter of thanks with transcripts of some unpublished poems: and in his reply to Ficker wrote: 'The affection of every noble being is a support in the precarious equilibrium of my existence. I am quite unworthy of this marvellous gift, which I will carry in my heart as sign and memory of this affection.'[17]

The windfall—as unbelievable for Rilke as the existence of the unicorn, he told Kippenberg—was timely for another reason. Clara, who had been on holiday with Ruth in north Germany at the outbreak of war, was also in some difficulty, with payment for her work for the Knoops in England naturally interrupted and other settlements outstanding. Sidie Nádherný, on his request, paid up promptly for the marble version of her portrait-bust: but from now on he had to divert part of his income to Clara to supplement the stipend from the Cassirers, which they too, it seems, were not finding it easy to maintain, and which in any case would cease at the end of the year. Nevertheless, his comparative wealth now, and the company of Loulou, promised him the stability he needed, as he waited on developments in the increasingly oppressive atmosphere of war. He was not to be able to relax for long, however. 'Everything seemed to form itself into a strangely happy restfulness,' he wrote later to Marie Taxis, 'such as to insulate me against the indescribable times; two good rooms I found most congenial, a dear companion whose society lent this temporary lodging a warm feeling of home—but at the last minute, just when all this, after delays and all kinds of difficulties, was in my grasp, it collapsed in the face of obstacles and complications from outside.'[18]

The euphemism stood for objections from Loulou's husband. Rilke had discovered another room on their floor which he felt, impulsively, would make the ideal studio for her, and she had asked Albert's permission to take it. While he was still thinking this over, a letter arrived from Rilke stressing how vital it was for them to be able to pursue their work together: 'I realize my request is an unusual one, but I also know from Loulou that it is addressed to an unusual person; even if her love for you is childlike, it is as if God were taken as father. And so in the fullest confidence we leave the whole decision in your hands.'[19] Albert could hardly be expected to take such innocence at its face value: it was clear to him now that the relationship with Rilke went deeper than he had at first imagined, and he was not so far unusual as to continue his complaisant attitude in the affair. In November he announced his intention of divorcing her, and even Rilke recognized that it would be better for them to separate, at least for a while, though he still hoped a *modus vivendi* could be found.

On 16 November he set off, without any clear idea of how or where he might find refuge. In Frankfurt first, he called on Philipp von Schey-Rothschild, an Austrian officer between postings in Galicia and the German Western GHQ, with whom, knowing him a patron of the arts, he had corresponded earlier in his attempt to rally support for the Duse's return to the stage. From him, and other officers he met here, he learned more of outside events than had reached him in the isolation of the Munich pension. He also took the opportunity of visiting Loulou's banker father, Leopold Lazard, in Wiesbaden, and then moved on to Würzburg in the hope of seeing the poet Maximilian Dauthendey, only to find he had been trapped in the East Indies by the outbreak of war. News from Schey that Alfred Heymel had been invalided home from the cavalry on the Western front, and was dying of tuberculosis in Berlin, decided him to go on to the capital, where he was able to take farewell of this admired poet and friend from the early days of the Insel. Heymel's untimely death, and the suicide of Trakl while serving on the Eastern front, though not exactly war casualties, deepened his horror at these 'indescribable times', and friends found him as though 'shattered by events'.[20] 'Who could ever express what we are experiencing,' he had written earlier to Helene von Nostitz, 'or tell what sort of people the survivors of these years will later prove to be. It is inexpressibly painful for me, and . . . I have understood and envied those who died before and did not have to go through all this'; and to Pia Valmarana, 'on a écrit tant de paroles, moi je me tais . . . je ne sais rien, je ne prévois rien, je crois en Dieu qui a survécu tant de batailles.' The war-god he had hymned had long since dissolved into 'a spectre of affliction, no longer a god but a spirit let loose to scourge the nations'.[21]

Offers of a haven were not lacking. Marie Taxis in Lautschin and Sidie Nádherný in Janowitz had both said he would be welcome there, and the Kippenbergs, who came to Berlin for Heymel's funeral, renewed their invitation to his turret room in their Leipzig home. If he could not be with Loulou, however, he preferred to be alone. Berlin seemed as good a place as any at the moment, and as he cast around for something more suitable than his room in the Hotel Esplanade, Providence intervened once again, through the intermediary, it need hardly be said, of yet another beautiful young woman. 'Imagine,' he wrote on 8 December to Loulou, 'I am to have a fine apartment . . . in the Bendlerstrasse . . . a charming friend (Mrs Mitford, daughter of Friedländer-Fuld) offered me this chance, insisted and would not be talked out of it. So the dice have fallen for Berlin, at least as an experiment.'[22]

If the name of Mrs Mitford was new to Loulou, she would have been familiar with that of the father. Friedländer-Fuld was a prominent coal magnate, one of the rare Jewish entrepreneurs who could be counted among the creators of German heavy industry, and his palatial residence on the Pariser Platz was one of the leading centres of Berlin's social life. His wife, and their twenty-two-year-old daughter Marianne, Rilke had met for the first time at the Heymel obsequies: an invitation to tea followed, and he was soon a regular visitor at the house where many of his acquaintances, such as Harry Kessler and Annette Kolb, had already been frequent guests. Marianne, or 'Baby Friedländer' as her friends like to call her, was indeed at this time Mrs Mitford; but her marriage early in 1914 to the Hon. John Freeman-Mitford, fourth son of the first Baron Redesdale, had lasted only a few months (for reasons which remain obscure), and she was now back with her parents, while Mitford, a reserve officer of the 1st Life Guards, was already serving with the BEF in France. (The marriage appears to have been annulled in 1915.[23]) The small house destined for the couple in the Bendlerstrasse had been opened for refugees from East Prussia, but when she heard of Rilke's plight her immediate impulse was to offer him rooms there, and by the middle of December he had moved in. 'She is a marvellously beautiful creature,' he wrote a little later to Marie Taxis, 'who, emerging from childhood of which she still bears the dark traces, had suddenly been transformed by a touch of fate into an independent, limpid personality, transparent through and through . . .'[24] He was struck by this rather spoiled young woman's taste for modern art, in particular for Picasso, some of whose works he had just seen in Munich. She was to become through the war years yet another of the confidantes to whom he could air his ideas in the long letters which never failed to delight, even though the faint hint of the erotic was always overlaid by his didacticism and self-preoccupation, and in Marianne's case by his increasing revulsion at the continuing slaughter.

His new quarters he found congenial, with all the writing-paper he needed, and even a new standing-desk ordered specially by Marianne: but the separation from Loulou left him unsettled, for he still clung to the hope of finding his happiness with her. Financially at least, he could be carefree, with the comfortable feeling that the miraculous 'bequest' was there to be drawn on, however anxious Kippenberg might be to conserve the main portion of the capital; and the publisher, whose military duties had not yet fully removed him from affairs, was asked to send him a sizeable sum before Christmas. A telegram brought 'Lal', as he called Loulou, to Berlin on 23 December, and their few days together seemed to her the most beautiful Christmas of her life, not least for the gifts he showered on her: a blue glass vase of curious design, a leather handbag with a gold clasp inscribed 'Christmas 1914' in his hand, a special edition of the *Cornet*, and another volume bound in leather in which he wrote out for her the essay 'On the Young Poet'. In the Egyptian Museum the curator was prevailed upon to take the Amenhotep head out of its case, for her to draw for Rilke. Her gift to him was the portrait she had just finished of

Regina Ullmann, who had been one of their first visitors in Munich and had since become a firm friend.

Their reunion could only be brief: they must stay apart for the time being, she felt, if he was to be spared unpleasantness and their dream one day restored. 'Time and again,' he wrote while she was with him,

> however well we know the landscape of love,
> and the little churchyard with lamenting names,
> and the frightfully silent ravine wherein all the others
> end: time and again we go out two together,
> under the old trees, lie down again and again
> between the flowers, face to face with the sky.[25]

She returned to Munich before the New Year, leaving him more depressed than ever: his outward circumstances all he could ask, as he told Marie Taxis, but inwardly so heavy of heart that he must seek complete seclusion, try to collect himself again. 'Duino days, that's what would be needed.'[26]

He had been worried about his belongings in Paris. On leaving, he had paid the rent for his rooms up to the end of September, and now, hearing that the property of 'enemy aliens' had not so far been touched, he was anxious to protect his own by settling the rent for the rest of the year and the first quarter of 1915, which he was told could be done through intermediaries in Holland. Kippenberg was disturbed to receive over the New Year yet another call, this time for 2,000 marks—part to cover the rent, the rest as 'the reserve which will assure me a certain freedom of movement in any unforeseen emergencies'.[27] The invested capital was already down to 10,000 marks, and the publisher's prudent business sense was offended by this further inroad into what would surely be needed to see Rilke through the difficult years of the war, especially as nothing further would be forthcoming from the other friends and supporters, and royalties in such times were problematical. He begged his friend to make do, apart from the rent payment, with an allowance of 800 marks a month for himself and Clara, which should be ample for the 'freedom of movement' he wanted. Both by telegram and letter, however, Rilke insisted that he have the full 2,000 now—for 'so many personal reasons'—after which, he promised, he would keep strictly to his budget, spending only 'what I can answer for to my most stringent conscience'. He could see no risk, since at that monthly rate the 10,000 marks would more than cover this year, the most difficult.[28] (Kippenberg, in despair at this confused attitude, must have given him his head, for by November 1915 there was nothing left of the 'bequest'— with a corresponding saving, of course, in the Insel accounts.)

The 'personal reasons', naturally, concerned Loulou, for he hoped, still, though with less and less confidence, that somehow they could be united again. On a sudden impulse, he returned to Munich on 7 January, intending to stay only a few days. Loulou was away for the time being in Irschenhausen, leaving her little daughter and the nurse in the Finkenstrasse rooms, which she had been able to retain after the demise of the Pension, so that he could move back there a little later without causing any stir. Once away from Berlin, even though he had left most of his things behind and often spoke of returning, he was won over once more by Munich, and his few days drew out into almost the rest of the year.

It was not only that he felt freer here, less hemmed in by social pressures: the voices which were beginning to be raised in Munich against the war— Annette Kolb, Wilhelm Herzog, the editor of the pacifist journal *Forum*, and others—were an echo of his own feelings. The dove of peace had disappeared into the clouds, he had written from Berlin: 'I can't bring myself to read the evasions of the papers, and everything people tell me, no matter what its tone, brings me suffering.'[29] Particularly welcome was to hear from Annette Kolb herself about her campaign for a review dedicated to international understanding, to which Rolland, Shaw, and Van Eeden had already promised their support and which was to begin publication in Zurich in May. Like René Schickele, the editor of *Die Weissen Blätter*, she was of Franco-German parentage: as Rilke wrote to Marianne, 'she stands organically between the nations, just as *we* all do in our spiritual make-up—and this mental attitude, which can never be eradicated, must conquer the madness of war, must survive.'[30]

One of his first calls was at Hertha Koenig's house in the Widenmayerstrasse: for there hung Picasso's *La famille des Saltimbanques*, a picture which had 'all at once' revealed to him the stature of the artist. He had met her in Munich in September, for the first time since the Fischers' soirée in Berlin in 1910, hearing only later that she already possessed a Picasso, and when in November he discovered the *Saltimbanques* in a Munich gallery he had written to her at once: 'this is certainly one of the decisive pictures of our art—can you not rescue it and make it yours?'[31] Now it was accessible, and he came again and again. Hertha recalled how he brought Regina Ullmann to see it, leading her up to it like a child, and how each time for him there was some new delight to be discovered: 'the child's black velvet jacket over the washed-out pink dress and its gentle hand on the flower-basket, the immeasurably desolate yet colourful grey of the Spanish desert behind the great figures, the clay pot beside the seated young woman.'[32] 'You must see it,' he wrote to Marianne: 'it wouldn't have done for your rooms, for it is an ungracious guest, a world in itself which will tolerate no surroundings.'[33]

Through January he remained alone, avoiding invitations, reading much— Strindberg, Dostoevsky—but rather as a drinker seeks alcohol, to take him out of himself, and sinking more and more into a condition of 'depressed watching and waiting'.[34] Promising Ficker a contribution for his journal, he could produce nothing new, and sent him verses written earlier in Paris. The situation with 'Lal' was not the least of the causes of his depression. Her husband had said he would defer the divorce action until after the war; but although Rilke spent much time during February with her in Irschenhausen, and they were often together in Munich too (among other occasions, for a patriotic lecture by Thomas Mann), they both seemed to draw back from living together permanently. As he confessed to Marie Taxis, he had realized that this renewed attempt at life with another was turning out no better than the others. 'God knows what is to happen ... I shall have to escape again, but I don't want to leave a trail of destruction and disaster behind me.'[35]

This brought down on the head of her 'Dottor Serafico' a veritable storm of motherly scolding—well merited, as he admitted. '*Every* person is alone, and *must* remain so, and stick it out ... Why are you always looking to rescue some silly goose, who ought to save herself—or let the devil take her, he'll certainly bring her back (don't get angry, I don't know any names ...) It seems to me, D. S., that the late Don Juan was a babe in arms compared to you—and you must always be seeking out such weeping willows, who are by no means so weepy in reality, believe me—*you* find your *own* reflection in those eyes ...' What could he do—'incorrigible as I am'—but agree? 'As soon as all this is over, there will be no more such attempts,' he promised her, 'then I'll keep my heart to myself once and for all—and if it turns out inconsolable, be glad that so much inconsolability enters in, and stick it out.'[36]

For the moment he must stay in Munich. Report had it that Austria would be calling up all men up to the age of forty-two, so there was no point in making any plans until the call came for him—a prospect scarcely inviting, after his early experience of the military, but (as must surely have crossed his mind) one which would bring him convenient and honourable extrication from the relationship with 'Lal'. In the mean time there was a more immediate prospect, of support and advice from a quarter which had never failed him in the past: Lou Salomé. She had now been for some time in Berlin, and in a letter at the end of January he had given her an idea of his dilemma and how he wished he had seen her there to talk it over. When at the beginning of March she spoke of making her long-deferred visit to Munich, he telegraphed at once to offer her one of the rooms in the Finkenstrasse. Her arrival was delayed, but he wrote to say how much both he and Loulou looked forward to having her stay with them.

If it's possible for you to grow fond of her, then her life will once more enjoy a happy season. *I* have on the whole brought her little good, after a few first happy weeks of giving and hoping I have taken back most of it ... and now it is clear between us that I cannot help and that I myself am not to be helped. But she still needs me for a while, as you will quickly understand. ... The call-up for my year is between 6 April and 6 May—and as they seem to be taking everybody, it's possible I may be dragged off. So we should certainly meet before that.[37]

Yet it would be wrong to picture Rilke, during these months of waiting, as overwhelmed by his personal problems and seeking seclusion in silence from a world more and more repellent to such a sensitive spirit. The painter and writer Hermann Burte, who met him now for the first time, recalled how much more down-to-earth, rational and orderly a person he was than he has often been depicted.[38] His work, certainly, was broken off. Apart from a piece 'to order' for Sidie Nádherný's wedding in Florence, no verses would come, not even 'the sound with which a piece of silence crumbles off from the great mass of dumbness within me';[39] his correspondence, always an essential form of self-expression, was necessarily more restricted, and reflected the despair he felt at being compelled to suffer the 'horrible insomnia' of 'this night of conflagration and slaughter'.[40] Far from retiring into his shell, however, he enjoyed the company not only of Loulou but also of the many other friends here—Regina Ullmann, Wilhelm Hausenstein, art historian and diplomat, the dancer Clotilde von Derp, Hans Carossa, doctor and poet, Hertha Koenig, the Bruckmanns, the astronomer Erwein von Aretin, Paul Klee. He was to be seen at some of the functions which the wartime cultural life of Munich had to offer: Norbert von Hellingrath's lectures on Hölderlin, the fantastic projections of ancient Rome by Alfred Schuler; and he continued to canvass his friends for support for the *International Review* (though he realized that for the moment this could be no more than a probing of 'Europe's vast wound from edge to edge and sounding its depth'[41]). When Lou Salomé arrived on 19 March, he was drawn even more actively into the social and cultural life of the city. 'Our days were fully programmed with her activities,' wrote Loulou later: 'in the mornings a spiritualist séance, in the afternoons historians and astronomers, the evenings taken up with psychoanalysts, writers, or doctors'— each in themselves interesting enough, but such a whirlwind succession making her head reel, and after a while she felt she had to take flight again to the peace of Irschenhausen. She found Lou a woman of penetrating understanding and powerful temperament, but too exclusively intellectual, in spite of her strong sensuality.[42]

Rilke, remarkably enough, seemed almost to welcome this whirl. The presence at last of the friend who had followed his vicissitudes through almost twenty years was 'singularly comforting', he wrote to Princess Marie in Duino, and he looked forward with equanimity to the medical examination for his call-up, to be undergone on 6 May in Munich (though he also wrote to the Prince for advice, should he be accepted, on how to go about seeking a post, preferably in Vienna, which would suit his inadequate physique and unmilitary temperament[43]). In the event, Austria's manpower needs were not, it appears, desperate enough yet for her to call on him, and his case was deferred.

Lou stayed until nearly the end of May. Among the host of people she sought out, she made it her business to include Clara. She had heard something from Gebsattel of Clara's more recent analysis with him, and had been apprehensive of the effect on Rainer of her presence in Munich during the affair with Loulou: but he had told her that, following further purely medical treatment, Clara was on the contrary serenity and friendliness itself, 'quite changed'.[44] So in fact she found her; and she clearly felt that it could do nothing but good for all the parties, and for Rainer in particular in the interests of extricating him from his difficult position, if they could be brought together in an open and candid way. Without her forceful influence it is not likely that he would have thought of making a party with Clara, Ruth, and 'Lal' for a Whitsun excursion to Chiemsee—a happy day of which thirteen-year-old Ruth's clearest recollection later was, of all things, a discussion on education, prompted by Lou's fox-terrier puppy 'Druschok' and his incessant barking at all the passers-by: her father maintained, and she solemnly agreed, that both children and dogs benefited from occasional punishment, an opinion which neither Lou nor 'Lal' shared.[45]

It is clear that by the time she left Munich Lou had gained the younger woman's affection, and convinced her that Rainer's path must remain a solitary one. 'It is senseless to sit down to write, at a time when even the spoken word dies on my lips,' Loulou wrote to her on 9 June. 'I do so only to tell you that your advice has done me good, and to send you my thanks. I wish so much that sometime in my life I may stand before you not quite so needy, and make more than just a negative impression.' In a short postscript, Rainer added that he would write more as soon as he found 'rest' again, and 'solitude finds me. Would it were now!'[46]

His only poem of this summer had been for Loulou, in delicate nostalgia for 'Love's Beginning':

> O smile, inaugurating smile, our smile!
> How one it was!—Breathing the scent of lime-trees,
> hearing park-stillness, suddenly looking up,
> each in the other, wondering, till we smiled.
>
> Within that smile was mutual reminiscence
> of a young hare that we had just been watching
> out on the lawn at play; such was its childhood,
> that smile of ours.
>
> .   .   .   .
>
>   —And the tree tops, outlined
> against the pure, free sky, already teeming
> with future nights, had described outlines for it
> against the ecstatic future in our faces.[47]

But, although heavy of heart at the memory of those first days in Irschenhausen, she was as strong a character as Magda von Hattingberg, and like her, with her art to fall back on, determined to make her own life. In a final separation from her husband, she put in hand alterations to the Finkenstrasse apartment to accommodate the rest of her own furniture; and it was decided that Rilke would leave as soon as an alternative could be found. A possibility she reconnoitred for him was a villa on the Ammersee, not far from Munich, but the proposition turned out to be impracticable. Finally, he turned to Hertha Koenig, who was about to leave for the family estate in Westphalia, to ask—'probably a quite absurd idea'—whether she might allow him to stay a while in the Widenmayerstrasse flat in her absence, just occupying a minimum of the rooms for himself and a housekeeper and with permission only to use her desk and to sit now and then before the 'great Picasso'.[48] 'If he has nowhere to stay, why not?' thought Hertha's mother: and so it was arranged. On 14 June he moved in, and was able to stay in fact until October in this quiet third-floor apartment looking out over the river.

'The peace around me is perfect,' he wrote to Hertha: 'no day passes without my blessing and thanks in spirit to you for this beautiful refuge.' With him was the manuscript of a sonnet sequence she had written, which had greatly impressed him and which, by way of gratitude, he recommended for publication by the Insel to Katharina Kippenberg, who was now handling much of the business for her husband. This was the kind of hospitality he always preferred, and which he had not been able to enjoy since Duino: to be a guest without a host, with assured nourishment in elegant surroundings, and freedom to fashion his solitude as he wished, in the knowledge that he did not have to look further, at least for the time being. Admittedly, Rosa Arnold, the housekeeper, never really mastered the art of pleasing his vegetarian palate: for the first few days, what she served up took on a 'somewhat ghostly look', the asparagus had the air of having 'just sighed and fainted away (and tasted as if it had given up hope)', and in the end he was taking most of his meals in a nearby vegetarian restaurant.[49]

Clara and Ruth were among the first to be invited to share the results of her early experiments, and in fact in the months that followed his life was far from that of a hermit. For what he sought was not so much to *be* alone, as to be able to *live* alone, choosing his company rather than having it thrust upon him. Human relationships, however casual, quite literally 'took it out of him', for he was incapable of taking any lightly. 'Only months of not expending myself in social contact can bring forth in me that tension which leads, inexorably, to my work.'[50] In his whole way of life, as Hermann Burte rightly noted, he strove to keep himself fit for his poetic mission, to conserve his strength for the decisive moment when it came.[51] He was more than content now that the general run of his acquaintance should for as long as possible be left in ignorance of where he was hiding, while he could select for company those whose presence he felt could bring something for his work: Norbert von Hellingrath, Thankmar von Münchhausen on convalescent leave from the front, Regina Ullmann; Clotilde von Derp invited to look at the *Saltimbanques*; Stauffenberg, Aretin, Lotte Pritzel; von der Heydt and Katharina Kippenberg when they visited Munich; and not seldom, 'Lal' herself, and Clara and Ruth. Paradoxically, he was more busily engaged by this social round than he had ever been when together with Loulou, quite apart from evening functions such as Heinrich

Mann's lecture on Zola, and renderings of Bellman's songs by Inga Jung-hanns, or the theatre for Büchner's *Woyzeck* and Strindberg's *Ghost Sonata* and *Dance of Death*. His diary between July and October records only one day 'alone—letters written'.[52] Such prodigal 'self-expenditure' was bound to make any work impossible. He even proposed himself to succeed Hellingrath and Schuler at the lectern, for a reading from the *Book of Hours* at one of Elsa Bruckmann's war charity evenings, but thought better of it when he realized that his introductory words, however remote from actuality, must inevitably run up against the censor.

Italy's entry into the war against the Central Powers at the end of May had increased his feeling of being shut off from the world he had known. 'Those who never saw it before will from now on have a world of only one room, God forgive me, the German front parlour: and we who used to travel are faced with indescribable privations.'[53] A letter before Easter from Ellen Key, with greetings from the Gibsons too, had roused in him such longing for Scandinavia's freedom that he could not bear to write to them for months.[54] At one moment he had even thought of joining Rolland's Red Cross work in Geneva, for the chance of serving the universal rather than the merely patriotic cause. He dutifully contributed, through Marie Taxis, to an anthology published in Vienna for war charities—a poem written years earlier, and oddly enough on England's patron saint, though this probably escaped him: but his true sentiments could never be 'German'.

Even though I cannot be strange to the German spirit, rooted as I am so firmly in the language, yet its manifestation today, its current aggressive conviction has brought me nothing but loathing and mortification; and still more the Austrian ... that I should ever feel at home in that is quite unthinkable for me ... How should I, whose heart has been formed by Russia, France, Italy, Spain, the desert, and the Bible, how should I be able to feel with those whose boastful words surround me here?[55]

He grew steadily more disgusted with the press, including the French and Danish which he occasionally saw: 'over-eager lies give birth to brand-new facts, and now that a press has developed which goes beyond all bounds, one has the impression that a war once started can never end, for these vile sheets continually anticipate its actual course.'[56]

When an opportunity came, early in July, to communicate through Switzerland with France, his first thought was to write to Marthe: 'for a year now I have been going forward, step by step, in a desert of bewilderment and suffering ... the slightest consolation of action is denied me, for I could only fight *for* all and *against* no one.'[57] The Picasso seemed to incarnate Paris, and for moments he could forget the present, feel again how, when he returned there from Spain, the city lent 'a unity to life'.[58] Others might find uplift in these momentous times: for him, all that was greatest and most stirring was buried and lost in that other world of yesterday. He looked back on a Paris that (unlike Munich now) had offered him 'a presence of life which as it were filled and overfilled every breath I took, without drawing me into the slightest bodily participation in its life. I could treat myself almost as though I were invisible, or at least my visibility was no more than that of a thing comforted and sustained by the companionship of all the other visible things.'[59]

Then, early in September, came a blow which drove in the last nail, as it seemed. He learned that his Paris studio had been requisitioned and everything he had left behind there auctioned off in April, on the pretext of recovering the outstanding rent. His books, his notes, many of his manuscripts and many of the letters he had received, including those from Rodin and the Duse, the few family mementoes he had, all were gone. He had already given these possessions up for lost, had told himself that they were no more than the posthumous papers and effects of Malte Laurids Brigge: and he tried now to see their disappearance as the extirpation of an obsession he had long wished to be rid of. Yet, now he knew all was really gone, there was a sharp sense of loss: something there, a scrap of paper or a letter, might suddenly seem quite indispensable, something that had been linked to the centre of his life by a fine thread that was now broken. He felt denuded, 'and the wind of these days of autumn blows particularly hard through my soul'. 'For someone a little more diligent, it would be an excellent reason to start all over again, courageously, overweeningly even—I agree, but will I have what it takes, strength, youth, determination?' 'Since the *Malte* closed behind me, I have been standing here like a beginner, a beginner who does not begin . . .'[60]

Whether he had succeeded in his earlier plan, to remit his rent at least for the period up to April, is not clear. At all events writing to Kippenberg in October to tell him of the disaster, he gave vent, for the first time, to a reproach to his friend, for having handled the 'bequest' so excessively carefully, and to himself for having concurred in his caution. Had he been allowed to dispose of the money freely, he maintained, he would surely have found a way to pay the rent and secure his possessions, and perhaps also other decisions in his life this past year might have been different. It had been a grave error on his part, to yield to the authority of his mentor and friend and allow such an 'extraordinary dispensation, a miracle, that had come to me like a dream in the night, to be dissipated in businesslike consideration and bourgeois calculation . . . That was wrong, my friend, wrong in that inner sense, that foolhardy, fantastic sense if you will, in which I have all my life accepted the unexpected and the incomprehensible, believe me, such things cannot be weighed and ordered in a merely business way.' This stroke of fortune, like so many others in his life, could have borne him up, refreshed and renewed him, had it been his to use as he thought fit, instead of being reckoned as just a contribution to his monthly allowance. With all that he had heard of the success of his books—the *Cornet* in particular, of which already over 85,000 copies had been sold—he found it hard to believe that the Insel could not have continued his normal support without calling on this extra windfall.[61]

From Rilke's point of view, the reproach was not unjustified, for Kippenberg, faced with the poet's increasing demands, had undoubtedly decided to use the new capital for his regular funding, deferring the Insel contribution for his inevitable needs later. Knowing him as he did, however, and in the uncertainties of the war years, with no prospect yet of any new book to boost the income from royalties, his decision cannot really be faulted: to have given Rilke an entirely free hand with the capital would simply have exhausted both sources all the sooner. He was obviously hurt by the tone of the letter, which reached him in Belgium, where he had been posted as editor of an army newspaper and had other preoccupations; and he did not immediately reply. It was only in November, after Rilke had accepted the situation, with a graceful apology for his *naïveté*, that their earlier good relationship could be restored— and, of course, the customary demands for extra money began once again.

A year had gone by in Munich, and he had nothing to show for it. The attempt at life alone here was proving no more successful than life with Loulou, and he would gladly have moved on, if he could but think of somewhere better to go, and were it not for the shadow of the call-up which now loomed again. A visit from his mother—it was the last time they would meet—did nothing to disperse his gloom. Hertha Koenig, briefly returning to Munich and invited to meet her over lunch, found a different Rilke before Phia's somewhat forbidding figure: not the man whose modest charm so captivated, but 'exclusively the son of this dark mother', his sad, discouraged look that of a boy who has just been reproved.[62] On 11 October came the time for him to vacate the Koenig apartment; until he could find an alternative he returned to the Finkenstrasse, Loulou being away, and while there wrote a remarkable poem for her, knowing that her relationship to her own father was not unlike his to Phia:

> Alas, my mother will demolish me!
> Stone after stone upon myself I'd lay,
> and stood already like a little house round which the day
> rolls boundlessly.
> Now mother's coming to demolish me:
>
> demolish me by simply being there.
> That building's going on she's unaware.
>
> ·   ·   ·   ·   ·   ·   ·   ·   ·   ·
>
> In lighter flight the birds encircle me.
> The strange dogs know already: this is *he*.
> It's hidden only from my mother's glance
>
> ·   ·   ·   ·   ·   ·   ·   ·   ·   ·
>
> No warm wind ever blew to me from her.
> She's not at home where breezes are astir.
> In some heart-attic she is tucked away,
> and Christ comes there to wash her every day.[63]

His bitter despair over the war grew ever stronger. The monstrous god he had thought to see rising, in those first days of August 1914, had soon become a monster only, with 'heads, claws, a body swallowing all', and was now nothing but 'the evil effluent from the swamp of humanity'.[64] 'Why are there not a few people,' he cried, 'three, five, ten, to stand together and shout on the square "Enough!", and be shot, and at least have given their lives to make it enough, while those out there can only die to keep the horror going ...'[65] Munich life was a continual round of talk on the one subject, inexhaustible and necessarily vague, and yet, equally necessarily, with the accents of violence: 'and is there any greater torture, for one trained in the discipline of artistic work, than the combination of the vague and the violent?'[66]

It was not long before he found new quarters, this time in what was almost a country house on the edge of the English Garden, in the Keferstrasse. The wife of the owner, a diplomat now in The Hague, rented him from 21 October a comfortable three-room apartment on the first floor, and proved a charming hostess. Here he tried in earnest to find the solitude that had escaped him, begging Elsa Bruckmann not to tell anyone his address, and especially not to reveal that he was on the telephone ('a connection which, even in my hide-out with Frau Koenig, bid fair to be fatal for me').[67] He would shun the outside world for long enough to feel and find the words to express all his experiences, 'from Moscow to Toledo', 'to grasp everything, and the measure of everything, into its innermost being, through my work'.[68]

The good resolution was not easy to keep. But, almost as though against the deadline of the next army medical examination, due on 24 November, he found the way at last: the thoughts on God, love, and death that had long been with him crystallized in letters and poems, and made these few weeks, surprisingly, among his most productive. Nature knows nothing, he wrote, of man's urge to make abstract ideas of God and death, separate from life: in Nature, death is everywhere present, 'at home all around us, looking out at us from the cracks in things, and a rusty nail sticking out of a plank somewhere does nothing day and night but look forward to it'. Lovers make no such separation: 'God comes true for them, and death does not harm them, for they are full of death while they are full of life.' Tolstoy knew this unity—and he also knew the fear of 'pure death'; yet his fear built itself into a veritable tower, and the strength with which he experienced it suddenly turned the tower into 'firm ground, earth and heaven, and the wind and a flight of birds were around him ...'[69]

His memory of a shooting star seen from the bridge in Toledo seemed to symbolize for Rilke this concept of Death as part of life:

> There stands death, a bluish distillate
> in a cup without a saucer. Such a strange
> place to find a cup: standing on
> the back of a hand. One recognizes clearly
> the line along the glazed curve, where the handle
> snapped. Covered with dust. And HOPE is written
> across the side, in faded Gothic letters.

The man who was to drink out of that cup
read it aloud at breakfast, long ago.

What kind of beings are they then,
who finally must be scared away by poison?
Otherwise would they stay here? Would they keep
chewing so foolishly on their own frustration?
The hard present moment must be pulled
out of them, like a set of false teeth. Then
they mumble. They go on mumbling, mumbling . . .
.   .   .   .

O shooting star
that fell into my eyes and through my body—:
Not to forget you. To endure.[70]

'As rest is not just a cessation of movement . . . so Death is not a lessening or loss of life; to me, it seems certain that for us this singular name signifies life as a whole, the completeness of life, all life in one.'[71]

   No resignation, however, nor any renunciation of life on earth. The demand that Death makes on us, on the contrary, is 'to understand our earthly existence as simply one side of being, and drain it passionately to the dregs'.[72] Interspersed in his notebook with the poem on Death, with extracts from his own letters he thought memorable, and with other fragments of verse, there came a cycle of seven frankly erotic poems, begun even before his move, hymning the phallus as God and the sexual act as one of rebirth: love, procreation, God, and Death in one.

(I)
All unexpectedly, while gathering roses,
she clasps the full bud of his vital part,
and, at that sudden difference, with a start
vanish the gentle gardens she encloses.
.   .   .   .

(IV)
Swooner, you don't know how towers can rise.
Now you're going to perceive a tower
through that power
of space within you. Close your eyes.
It has been upraised by you,
unforeseen, with glance and nod and sweetness.
Suddenly it stiffens with completeness,
and blest I may enter thereinto.
.   .   .   .

(VI)
What are we near to? Death, or that whose day
has not yet dawned? For what were clay to clay
unless the god himself formed feelingly
the figure growing between us? For just see:

this is my body, that has risen again.
Now help it from the burning grave into
that heavenliness which I possess in you . . .[73]

The concept of these poems went back to October 1913 and his discussions with Lou Salomé. Fresh from her schooling with Freud, she was ever intent on sexual interpretations of his dreams, and, diagnosing in him a fundamental bisexuality, had felt that his idea of 'phallic hymns' was 'wonderful'. 'He is of course trying thereby to compensate his inadequacies in the erotic relation to the sex-object,' she noted in her diary at the time, before the poems had even been written, and adding that here, 'as always', poetry for him was 'self-transfiguration'—a judgement on Rilke as poet somewhat wide of the mark, and in the present case particularly so.[74] As Jacob Steiner has remarked, the 'Seven Poems' were nothing less than a continuation and intensification of Rilke's hymn to the 'hidden guilty river-god of the blood' in his Third Elegy, bringing the mythical directly into the realm of the body, the 'terrible trident' of the 'Neptune of the blood', 'inciting the night to riot', expressed now in precise anatomical terms.[75] Not self-transfiguration; sublimation rather, in that continuing self-analysis through work in which he knew his salvation must lie.

Significant too, as Siegfried Unseld noted, are the five lines which also appear interspersed with the 'Seven Poems':

Now I'll speak, no longer be an awed
pupil facing their Examinerships.
Now I'll say 'Blue sky', I'll say 'Greensward',
and may the spirit taking it from my lips
turn it to eternity's account.[76]

He had gained a new freedom in the poetic expression of the human condition, turning 'to eternity's account' the symbols of sky, meadow, bridge, tree, tower, doll, bird, and beast; and at last, continuing this 'good, powerful rush of work', could take up again the great cycle of the Elegies.[77] Not surprisingly, against the background of war and a world 'fallen into the hands of men', his theme now, in what would become the Fourth, was bitter and negative: man's dividedness of mind and awareness of his transitoriness, which prevent him from surrendering to the unseen forces whose instrument he is, and whose purposes alone can give meaning to his life.

O trees of life, when does your winter come?
We are not in harmony, our blood does not forewarn us
like migratory birds'. Late, overtaken,
we force ourselves abruptly onto the wind
and fall to earth at some iced-over lake.
Flowering and fading come to us both at once.
.   .   .   .

Conflict
is second nature to us. Aren't lovers
always arriving at each other's boundaries?—
although they promised vastness, hunting, home....

. . . .

we never know
the actual, vital contour of our own
emotions—just what forms them from outside.

A puppet is better than 'these half-filled human masks': 'it at least is full'.

I'll put up with the stuffed skin, the wire, the face
that is nothing but appearance. Here, I'm waiting.
Even if the lights go out ...
I'll sit here anyway. One can always watch.

Am I not right? You, to whom life tasted
so bitter after you took a sip of mine,
the first, gritty infusion of my will,
Father—who, as I grew up, kept on tasting
and, troubled by the aftertaste of so
strange a future, searched my unfocused gaze ...
        ... And you, dear women
who must have loved me for my small beginning
of love toward you, which I always turned away from ...
        ... am I not right
to feel as if I *must* stay seated, must
wait before the puppet stage, or, rather,
gaze at it so intensely that at last,
to balance my gaze, an angel has to come and
make the stuffed skins startle into life.
Angel and puppet, a real play, finally.
Then what we separate by our very presence
can come together. And only then, the whole
cycle of transformation will arise ...

But the end is a praise of childhood: if we could regain the child's open and undivided consciousness, we should be able to play our parts

in the infinite, blissful space between world and toy.

. . . .

        ... Murderers are easy
to understand. But this: that one can contain
death, the whole of death, even before
life has begun, can hold it to one's heart
gently, and not refuse to go on living,
is inexpressible.[78]

He was to be brought sharply down to earth from these flights into 'glorious work', in which he had also continued his translations of Michelangelo. At the medical examination on 24 November he was this time found fit for combatant duty and, pending a second examination two days later, ordered to report on 4 January 1916 at Turnau, in north Bohemia, for service with the *Landsturm* (territorial Home Guard). It had been his hope that Stauffenberg's letter certifying a nervous condition, aggravated by the earlier lung lesion, if not enough to keep him out of the army, would at least ensure him some form of more appropriate non-combatant service; but it was not even opened at the second examination, and the order was maintained. He turned at once to friends who might be able to influence his posting—Philipp Schey, now in Berlin, and Alexander Taxis in Vienna—and himself spent the first ten days of December in Berlin to explore with Schey the various possible interventions in the workings of the military machine.

One was to invoke the agreement whereby Austrian citizens resident in Germany could seek exemption, and this he tried both through von der Heydt and through the adjutant of Prince Ludwig Ferdinand of Bavaria; another, failing exemption, was to obtain a posting, like other writers such as Stefan Zweig, Anton Wildgans, and Rudolf Hans Bartsch, with the War Archive in Vienna. Returning to Munich for Ruth's birthday on 12 December—for which he had not forgotten to order a book she wanted—he went on immediately to Vienna, where with Alexander Taxis' support he took his case to ministerial level. All that was achieved, however, was a change of station from Turnau to Vienna: and on 4 January, as ordered, Private Rilke reported to a barracks near Hütteldorf, greatly cast down at this renewed encroachment of the military in his life, for him 'no less incomprehensible and terrifying than that first time as a boy'.[79]

3

'Quiet and work have not yet returned to me, since the
Vienna rupture'

(To Lou Andreas-Salomé, 5.1.1917)

'Both by our comrades and by the officers, we "older gentlemen" (among whom I had to reckon myself, for there were eighteen and nineteen-year-olds in the platoon) were treated with the utmost consideration,' he wrote later in January to his mother, 'it was really touching to find such sympathy for my awkwardness. There was a fine spirit of mutual support—plenty of less pleasant surprises, of course, but among them some heart-warming experiences.'[1] The calming of Phia's worries glossed over what was in fact a more than painful episode for him. 'My life has already been ruined once by this,' he told Stefan Zweig, calling on him one Sunday morning, 'I thought I had recovered, and now I'm back again in its clutches.' Unsuited both mentally and physically for the exertions demanded, he seemed to Zweig quite annihilated by them[2] (on one exercise, indeed, he actually collapsed). The fact that he was known to enjoy, and to be trying to exploit, protection in high places proved counter-productive at company and battalion level, and did not encourage any indulgent treatment, quite the reverse. In his ill-fitting uniform, which had seen damaging front-line service, he cut a pathetic figure; and the many friends aware of his plight were determined to find a way of rescuing him. Their efforts finally succeeded in getting him transferred to the War Archive after only three weeks of 'torture' with the infantry.

If it came to military service for a writer or poet, no more congenial niche could have been devised. Literature enjoyed high standing in the Austro-Hungarian Empire, and whatever faults the authorities may have shown in their prosecution of the war, they had at least taken care to enlist their literary men in the service where they could be best employed, namely propaganda for the sustaining of morale. Rilke found himself in a section whose job was to write up from field reports a series of anecdotes of daring and heroism, or longer articles on various aspects of service life, which were then assembled in volumes published for the edification and encouragement of the home front. 'For form's sake,' smiled Colonel Veltzé, who was in charge, 'we'll have to give him something to do—but it won't be particularly burdensome.' His immediate superior, Franz Carl Ginzkey, poet and regular lieutenant, led him to a remote room where, among leather-bound archives of the times of Maria Theresia and the Napoleonic Wars, he was left more or less to himself.[3] With comfortable office hours from 9 till 3, and living a virtually civilian life, most of his colleagues had overcome their distaste for the hack work: for Rilke it proved quite impossible to write to order like this, and he was soon relegated to the simple routine tasks of ruling up registers and card-indexing reports. What was worse, the mere feeling of being forced into the service he had always hated, and the oppressive background of war, were enough to inhibit him completely from any creative effort of his own, either in his office or in the hotel room out at Hietzing, near Schönbrunn, which he had taken after a short stay in the Taxis apartment in the Victorgasse.

Even the news from Stefan Zweig that there was a prospect of saving at least the papers among his Paris possessions seemed of little consequence in his misery. Zweig, on learning of the affair when Rilke first arrived in Vienna at the end of December, had written immediately to Rolland in neutral Switzerland, in the hope that he could ask the friends in Paris to try to save something from the wreck. During January, in response to Rolland's urgent appeal to both friendship and 'the honour of France',[4] Gide and Jacques Copeau had hastened to see what could be done. The sequestration, they found, though perfectly legal, had been a hole-and-corner affair, and the 'auction' in fact nothing more than direct disposal of the effects, to some dubious and elusive dealers, for the ludicrous sum of 538 francs. The concierge, however, in tears now as she spoke of it, had been able to put aside two cases of papers, which Gide was hopeful of removing to a place of safety. After much effort he was eventually successful, and stored them with the publishers Gallimard; but although Rilke was able to fetch them, long after the war, it seems doubtful whether they contained all the documents and letters he had left. At the moment, he was too depressed to do more than send Rolland a melancholy telegram of gratitude on the occasion of his fiftieth birthday at the end of January.

Vienna itself he found a 'torment, as it must be to anybody with a tidy and precise mind: it is inexactitude personified, and the sloppy enjoyment everyone takes in this hopeless slovenliness gives the city's spirit its own particular sad bloom'.[5] He felt he must at all costs regain his freedom, and after barely a fortnight in his new assignment contrived a short 'duty visit' to Munich, from where he hoped to arrange to re-submit his earlier application for exemption, on which his eligibility had been acknowledged but which had reached Vienna too late to affect his original posting. He would need as much support as possible from prominent people, and, hearing that Kippenberg was home on leave, he turned to him to arrange this. Dependable as always, the energetic publisher had a circular letter out within a week to all who could conceivably subscribe the renewed application: 'if it is backed by the best names in intellectual Germany and Austria-Hungary, it will be possible to free this physically so poorly equipped poet from military service.' Pointing out how, while he remained in the army, he had no hope of completing his promising works, and stressing the fact that he and his family had to live from his books, the submission itself added: 'we need not say what the loss would be to humanity if these works should be stifled by the unpropitious times.'[6]

Rilke fully expected that this action, given the 'thoughtless, forgetful, and *ineffably* slow' Austrian manner, would take months to achieve a result:[7] and so it proved. Typically, after his return from Munich on 17 February, he sought to interest everyone he could in his case—the industrialist Richard Weininger and his wife Marianne ('Mieze'), with whom he made firm friends, Hofmanns-thal, Sidie Nádherný, and Karl Kraus; and it was fortunate that all these efforts did not create an even worse tangle in the already complicated procedures. Colonel Veltzé was indulgence itself, and promised to release him as soon as the right papers got to the right place. The demobilization order ('for an indefinite period') was finally issued on 9 June, and his last day in the War Archive was 27 June.

The months of waiting for that day he passed as though buried alive, as far as any work of his own was concerned. After duty, an early evening meal in town and the tram ride out to Hietzing, he had not the energy to do more than read, and his fatigue was such that even reading was impossible after eight. 'I'm lucky to have been all my life a practised and dedicated sleeper.'[8] The short stay in Munich, looking out from his desk there to the trees with their breath of Spring, had brought home to him how impossible his present condition was, and made him more impatient than ever to escape. 'It wasn't Paris, but compared with the insanity here, a great deal,' he wrote to Marie Taxis, who was still in Vienna, describing the joy her present of a bracelet had given to Ruth. 'I've brought nothing back with me, no Elegies, nothing shall be with me here, "il faut séparer les pleurs et les ris" as Leonardo has it.'[9]

He was by no means buried alive socially, however, even if his work was in 'unconcerned suspended animation'.[10] Vienna, though he regretted he had so little feeling for its temperament, had much to offer, and there were many friends to see. He enjoyed a Schoenberg concert, attended a reading by Karl Kraus, and was particularly taken up with Kokoschka, whom he saw often during this time and whose work, of which so far little had come his way, greatly appealed to him. He could even find it in him one evening to read aloud, to Kokoschka and some young friends, from the New Poems, a book he had long not opened: it seemed now like the work of another, something with an existence of its own, and delighted him as much as his audience.[11]

During April he was able to return to Princess Marie's hospitality, but in May the Victorgasse apartment was to be remodelled, and she herself planned to visit Trieste, where 'Pascha' was serving, after duty on the Serbian front. Loulou had just arrived in Vienna, and was staying at Stelzer's Hotel in Rodaun, near the Hofmannsthals, so Rilke took up his quarters there too on 22 May. Her company stimulated him to an even busier social round, though mostly with visitors to Rodaun rather than in the city; and he sat for her portrait of him, for which Hofmannsthal made available a pavilion opposite his house and his wife Gerty provided some yellow and lilac brocade hangings as background. The garden of the pavilion, and the company of the Hofmanns-thals, gave relief from the tedium of immobility, which for him aggravated the fatigue and sleepiness already induced by the change of air. 'If only I were more sprightly,' he wrote to Helene von Nostitz who was about to visit Vienna: 'I fear my expression is that of a last year's apple, and if the memory of my livelier and more ardent times does not spring up in Loulou Albert, this will turn out a still life, or a nature demi-morte at least . . .'[12] The result in fact did not entirely displease him, though it seemed 'more like an enquiry for me, a search for information', and later he would refer to it disparagingly as 'never more than a kind of improvisation'.[13] Inviting the poet Felix Braun, and Franz Theodor Csokor, a colleague in the Archive, to see it one evening, he stood it in a niche in the wall of the Stelzer garden, flanked by candles, and they were struck by the pleasure their approval gave him. Kokoschka told Loulou he had not been best pleased that Rilke should have sat for her after refusing him, but now he had seen the result he could no longer be angry with her.[14]

By the time the portrait was finished, his final release had come through. Loulou left for Munich early in July, while he stayed on in Vienna for another two weeks, before himself taking the train to Munich. His finances were once again in a deplorable state. Kippenberg had been maintaining his monthly payments, but had to be asked for an additional advance to cover the journey, which in fact also needed some help from the Weiningers; and it had been only thanks to Sidie Nádherný, who knew Reneé Alberti, his hostess, that he had been able to retain the apartment in the Keferstrasse. 'That I find myself now really back at more or less my own writing-table, in the surroundings I left so hastily seven months ago—how much I owe this to you,' he wrote her on 20 July. Though he was still 'inwardly buried', he hoped he might now, in this familiar background, regain some sort of balance, 'reach the places where mere outward effort is transformed into inner feeling, for which I have an indescribable yearning'.[15]

To strip off the slightest trace of Vienna he found still about him, and breathe again in freedom, was not difficult: but the road was long back to his inner self, 'especially for me, ever slower in the essential'.[16] Munich was empty of the friends he had hoped to see again; he was alone in the house after Renée Alberti left for Sweden to join her husband in his new post; and although he thought of travel, his means would not allow it. 'Like an insect, I climb up every grass stalk of my deserted meadow, and keep falling down again on my back.'[17] For some weeks through August, as though in reflection of his spiritual condition, an obstinate inflammation of the right hand almost prevented him from writing at all—yet a mountain of letters awaited attention, as they had on his earlier visit in February, and until his desk was cleared he would be incapable of progress.

Too often the fame that had attracted them was that of a Rilke whom for the most part he preferred to forget. There would come an enquiry about his early dramas, or enthusiastic words about the *Tales of God* (though when these were from a Prince, he was prepared to concede his pleasure that this work had not 'abandoned its past and its youth', even though he himself had outgrown it).[18] To hear that the *Cornet* in the Insel 'field edition' was in every soldier's pack, with its 'chance superficial resonance for a war in our times',[19] had not been unwelcome, if only because it helped his income and kept the publisher happy. But he had been greatly irked at the readings of the poem to Paszthory's musical accompaniment, of which none other than Magda von Hattingberg had been an enthusiastic exponent during the first years of the war in Munich, Leipzig, and Vienna, and which bid fair to continue like a variety performance 'in response to popular demand', as he had noted, with some bitterness, on the Vienna posters. Katharina Kippenberg had regretfully reported that there was no legal way for him or for the Insel to stop this (or to prevent the royalties from the performances from going all to the composer). When he heard in October that not only was the Insel preparing an illustrated edition, but also had no objection to a separate publication by Paszthory of text and music, his instinct was to refuse, but in the end he was resigned. 'The moths have got into the *Cornet*, artistic moths and musical moths: the old fur will have to be jettisoned.

... I had agreed to *one* single trial performance by Frau v. Hattingberg, as a courtesy, but through that chink the moth population crowded in, and now I'm punished for it. C'est plus fort que nous.'[20] Poetry for him contained its own music, and should stand in no need of the composer's aid.

After their separation in Venice he had continued a friendly occasional correspondence with Magda, grateful for her attention to Regina Ullmann, sending her from Irschenhausen a copy of his 'Hymns' to the war god and sharing with her the desolation which had overtaken him so soon after they had been written. Their paths too had often crossed since then, in Munich, Berlin, and Vienna. She had been well aware of his relationship with Loulou: and the fact that in Munich, before his call-up, with the presence there of both, not to mention Clara, he had been able to steer a course without unpleasantness, and without leaving a 'trail of destruction' behind him when he regained his solitary life, says much for the sympathy he could arouse in those for whom his 'small beginnings of love' had so quickly faded. After her persistence with the *Cornet* performances, however, he was disinclined to keep up with her, and the connection seems to have been broken.

Kippenberg, home again on leave during September, was faced with the all-too-familiar litany from his protégé, but this time his response did not follow the book. No only was a further largish sum demanded, as the 'reserve' Rilke had never yet succeeded in maintaining (with the usual protestations of a search for cheaper lodging): he was also asked whether, since the Insel had secured his release and was therefore in a sense responsible for him, it might find it possible to arrange a spell abroad, in Sweden or Switzerland, or failing that, to employ him in Leipzig.[21] This was too much for the publisher's patience. Rilke, he replied somewhat shortly, had had more than 25,000 marks over the past two years, and his Insel account was overdrawn by 2,000 into the bargain. There could be no question of a German house helping him, an Austrian, to a journey abroad in wartime. After it was over, he would try to re-establish a small society of supporters, like that of pre-war days, he promised, but for the moment Rilke would have to be content with his allowance.[22] Unperturbed, and as unashamedly single-minded as ever in his pursuit of what he felt was due to his art, Rilke set about finding other sources of aid, writing directly to Philipp Schey for a loan, which he promised to repay 'gradually' after the war, and telling Kessler and other friends like Sidie Nádherný of his predicament. By the end of the year he had received through Schey altogether 5,500 marks, as a gift rather than a loan, the result of a collection among a number of friends unknown to him in Vienna, for which Sidie, in addition to helping him further with his rent, had also lent her support.[23]

In his thanks to Schey, he spoke of the work which would be furthered by their generosity—his translations (the Michelangelo sonnets were still on his desk) and in particular the preparation for publication of Paula Modersohn-

Becker's papers, which her mother had sent him (but for which finally he did not feel himself the right editor). In fact, he still lacked congenial surroundings for true work of his own, and was indeed, as he had said to Kippenberg, searching for an alternative to the Keferstrasse house, since there was talk now of its being put on the market. Regina Ullmann had settled with her mother in Burghausen on the Salzach, east of Munich on the border with Austria; and in November he visited them there, with the thought of taking, like them, one of the towers in the old castle which were going at an absurdly cheap rent—a refuge perhaps where the 'broken threads' might be joined again. He hesitated long, but eventually abandoned the idea; and, although renewing his complaints at the 'demands' of people and the lack of a place of his own designed exclusively for his work, he stayed where he was through the whole winter. Perhaps one day, he told Sidie in a letter on her birthday in December, he would find it, and the right woman to help him 'take the measure of my work', organize 'space, surroundings, and food only for that and nothing else—then, no more people or letters, only the one, regular, goodwilled, simple work-day which fits exactly into it'.[24]

Meanwhile there were people, and letters, in plenty, and much in the Munich artistic and literary scene to attract him. Thankmar von Münchhausen came through on leave, and the Weiningers from Vienna; Van de Velde and Richard von Kühlmann called on him. There were readings by Alfred Wolfenstein and Theodor Däubler, and the posthumous Franz Marc exhibition during September, which he visited with Karl Wolfskehl and Kassner, was a delight he urged Marianne Mitford (in vain) to come from Berlin to share: 'at last an *œuvre* once more, a life's unity attained and wrestled out of work.'[25] A great event for him, he wrote to Loulou, who was now in Switzerland: 'that as well as Cézanne I should be granted this man may well remain my sole claim to distinction in art appreciation.'[26] He saw a good deal of Clara, and of Ruth as her fifteenth birthday approached.

The war was ever-present, as he talked with Walther Rathenau, on a brief earlier visit, or with Annette Kolb and Wilhelm Herzog; and added to the news of its casualties, that of the tragic death of Verhaeren in Rouen in November came as a painful reminder of his Paris days. The Belgian poet had been one of the few men he felt close to, one who had sensed and appreciated his aspirations, he wrote to Sidie, and with his loss 'this world becomes a desolate place'.[27] He tried to see it in a better light now he was freed of his immediate financial worries by the discreet donation Schey had arranged, but the times did not make this easy. 'Happiness is an inexpressibly misleading and temporary thing, decides nothing: the true stations of joy are on the road which lies through simple endurance.'[28] All the same, during December and January he found temporary happiness through a 'quite unexpected experience (not work, alas)'—acquaintance with a most beautiful young girl, Mia Mattauch, whose company brought him 'almost a new life', even if not '*the* new life' he wanted. 'Youth is in the right, even now, and is so incredibly much, so wonderful.'[29] He had not yet recovered from the 'Vienna rupture', he told Lou in January, but at least, through Mia's presence, 'the unrest of these last months was like that of restless angels'. Two lindens he arranged to be planted at Burghausen were to make a living memorial to the brief but clearly heartening episode. It was fortunate for his peace of mind perhaps that, 'monster of uncommunicativeness' that he had become, he did not tell Princess Marie of it, when he wrote her his hopes that the new year would not prove 'the third bad one, but once again a first of better days'.[30]

For him the better days were not to come until the war was over, and 1917 would prove a year of vain effort to repair the broken threads. There seemed a 'great dumbness' in his world, Munich was 'like the bed to a sick man':[31] the surfaces of the jagged break in his work had 'grown hard and cold, without the heat of innocent joyousness to weld them together again'. The war for which no end was in sight pressed down ever harder upon him, especially after the news of Hellingrath's death in action, and America's declaration of war against Germany in April. Even the patriots, he wrote, must surely by now admit that this 'world catastrophe', to which only Barbusse's *Le Feu* did justice, was horribly unlike the chivalrous contest they had expected in August 1914.[32] His earlier life, with its travels and events, a life which had been commitment to a specific task and not merely existence, was lost without trace in the 'corrosive sorrows' of the present. 'To what purpose to have known Toledo, the Volga, the desert, only to be pinned down now in the most stringent disavowal of the world, and be full of memories suddenly unusable?'[33] The publication at last by the Insel of his translations of the Louize Labé sonnets, which he had begun in Toledo, served only to underline his melancholy.

Ideas for relief in a change of scene flickered briefly early in the year—to stay with Katharina Kippenberg in Leipzig, or even to take up Richard von Kühlmann's invitation to Constantinople—but were impracticable. His efforts to keep himself remote from Munich's social and artistic life were half-hearted only, when he could find no spirit for work in solitude, even though he still refused invitations to give public readings. He continued the Michelangelo translations, some of which had now been published in the 1917 *Insel Almanach* and elsewhere, and was busy enough with correspondence, devoting much time not only to trying to help Clara to additional income from commissions or a teaching post, but also to promoting with publishers poets such as Max Pulver or Hertha Koenig whom he thought deserving. When the need seemed likely to arise of justifying his continued exemption from service, Katharina Kippenberg took up his suggestion of appointing him officially as adviser to the Insel, writing him letters which could be produced to show him actively engaged in its projects—a task which in fact he carried out conscientiously. But all this was surface activity only. Real letters, in which he could give of himself, came with difficulty from a pen grown heavy, in times which were 'as though cast in lead' around him. Even when he heard in April from Inga Junghanns, now in Switzerland with her artist husband, that she was translating *Malte* into Danish, it was a month before he felt able to express his pleasure at such an 'event for this book, [to be] lifted into its imaginary homeland'.[34]

During April, while Clara was at work in Travemünde, he had seen to Ruth's boarding with a family in Dachau. For the Whitsun holiday, after Clara's return, they set off for another visit to Chiemsee, but he was deterred by the crowds at the station and left them to go on alone, himself coming later for a day or two with the Weiningers, who were again visiting from Vienna. The surroundings seemed to promise him some relief, and after the crowds had departed he went back again, to stay until the end of June, this time on the Herreninsel. To Hausenstein, who was there at the time, it seemed as though the presence of the poet left its mark on the island, as he sat under the plane trees set like columns before the old castle, or wandered out to the nunnery at Seeon: 'the world spread a gentle radiance around the head of this man, but even more beautiful was the way his inner spirit shone softly out of the countenance of the world.'[35] What did most for Rilke was acquaintance with Sophie (Sonia) Liebknecht, the Russian-born wife of the socialist leader then serving a four-year jail sentence for a pacifist demonstration. He felt her companionship like a renewal: 'I have been myself again during these days,' he wrote after she had left, 'and even though I know it was *your* strength, Sophie Borisovna, your pure vitality and the power of your joy through which I could prove equal to the moment of revival, all the same I have been able to take possession of myself once again, of my wonderful memories and the feelings of my heart so penned in and denied by the times. It is so good to know that all that is still there, beneath the petrified state in which I live.' The unexpected encounter had, at least briefly, shaken him out of his lethargy. 'I have gradually come to realize that what at most I can have in common with others are just fleeting moments: meetings—but who can complain, when granted such encounters, that he is denied true contact . . .' The poems he read to her affected her deeply; but when she wrote later than she was convinced his road back to productivity lay, not in isolation, but rather in relating more to the outside world, however repellent he might find it—'you would then not find yourself again, but be standing on firm ground'—she touched a chord to which he remained, and by his nature must remain, unresponsive.[36] He did take her advice, at least, to follow events in the papers; but, as he told Kippenberg, what was happening outside continued to press on his spirit and distort what was inside him.[37]

'I remarked in Chiemsee how beneficial for me now a change of surroundings can be,' he wrote on 2 July to Hertha Koenig, who had been pressing him for some time to come to stay on her estate at Böckel: 'I've given notice here as from 1 August.'[38] He began to pack up his things, to store them in Clara's apartment while she and Ruth were away in Fischerhude, near Worpswede, for the rest of the summer. The further submission to the Austrian Consulate, seeking to justify his indefinite exemption, had not yet elicited a decision (though he was encouraged to hear that even 'Bandmaster Lehar' and the minor Viennese writer Hans Müller had secured release for the duration on the grounds of their 'artistic work'[39]), so that he would have to return in any case to Munich in due course. On 18 July he set off for Berlin, as the first stage on his journey to Gut Böckel.

4

'In every city of every land you can hear the passing bell;
In every heart there's a single plaint,
I hear it more clearly every day'

(Ivan Goll)

He had thought of only two or three days in Berlin, but stayed a full week, in order not to miss a visit from Elisabeth Taubmann, the artist he had first met in 1906 at Meudon. He was able to see Marianne Mitford only briefly, at the memorial service for her father, who had died suddenly the week before; but the stay was rewarding in the renewed companionship of Elisabeth Taubmann, with whom he could share nostalgia for Paris, of his old friend Emil Orlik, and of Sophie Liebknecht. In the Kaiser-Friedrich Museum with Sophie he enjoyed a few hours of 'more alert receptivity and observation (something on which I can hardly count now, in my dense apathy)'.[1] There was an exhibition of Max Liebermann's works, and he went with Gerhart Hauptmann to the artist's seventieth birthday celebration; he saw some admirable work in the 'Free Secession' by the sculptors Georg Kolbe and Renée Sintenis. Good days for him, on the whole, he wrote to Mieze Weininger as he left on 24 July for Böckel.

He had been glad to accept Hertha Koenig's invitation, though what he had heard of her moated grange—low-lying, damp, and shrouded in high trees—had not filled him with enthusiasm. His first impressions of the area in the rain were indeed not encouraging, and although Hertha made him comfortable in rooms in the original seventeenth-century wing of the house, the noise of the farm activity in the courtyard over which he looked was not much less than that of the children outside his Munich apartment. With improving weather, however, he could find quiet out in the park; and on occasions, as he wrote to Inga Junghanns returning her long questionnaire on *Malte* translation problems, almost felt he was back in a Nordic landscape, the wind coming as though from the sea. Picking raspberries and gooseberries, warm or still wet with dew, in the productive kitchen garden was a pleasure which his spirit could summon just enough energy to enjoy.

Waiting and waiting 'until the world should come to its senses',[2] he spent his time on letters, many long overdue, and often transcribing poems for friends such as Eva Cassirer or Sophie Liebknecht. He had taken out a subscription to the *Münchner Post*, he told Sophie, in order not to remain a 'complete illiterate of the times'—but this was not the way to recover his lost productivity. 'I've been all my life concerned with words which can be believed, and ... I fear that the certainty of my own words, precise and brought to glowing heat, would suffer a bewildering set-back if I were to choose my subjects out of the crowd of those other words of dubious credibility.' More contact with active and knowledgeable people might perhaps bring him closer to the present, even make his anguish productive, but never the press. 'Perhaps my indescribable suffering at being unable to produce is my most accurate response to the present situation, and I would sooner submit to that suffering than make any concession in the essential.' The world, and life, might well be beautiful, he agreed, but 'alas, not humanity ... its madness is a prison for us, and the fact of being human has set us outside the whole of nature in its unity'.[3] Yet, following events now more closely, he felt he was gaining a clearer understanding of the war. Writing to Katharina Kippenberg at the end of August, and influenced no doubt by the change in Russia after the March revolution, he saw the conflict as the final struggle between two great contenders: one, short-sighted, bent on petty gains, the other a 'party of humanity', dedicated to the irrevocable reshaping of society. 'Never in all history has mankind been so radically transformable as in this most fearful furnace—if only the pure sculptor's hands were here, it would be as wax in them.'[4]

A preoccupation during his stay was Ruth's schooling. Clara was anxious for her to remain in North Germany with her grandmother, where her health would benefit from the better and more ample food than was available in Munich, and spoke of private tuition there to get her through the final two school years in one—at a cost, of course, which neither she nor Rainer, in their improvidence, had any hope of meeting themselves. He turned as usual to his friends: to Hedwig Jaenichen-Woermann first, who had been so helpful with Marthe in Paris and was now in Dresden, and then to Marie-Anne Friedländer-Fuld (as she now preferred to be called). Hedwig responded at once, promising 2,000 marks, which was enough for the tutor to be engaged from October, but was only just over half what was required. 'Baby Friedländer' was apparently not forthcoming, and the remaining funds had to be sought elsewhere. Fortunately, Eva Cassirer did not seem to mind being appealed to once more, and contributed a further 500 marks towards the end of the year. How the remainder was found, is not clear. One can but marvel at the readiness of Rilke's friends, not only to help, but to be positively overjoyed to have their help taken for granted in his innocent but quite ruthless attitude.

More surprising still is that such appeals should be necessary at all at this time. He and Clara were after all receiving a reasonable monthly income from the Insel, to which had been added his Army pay for the first six months of 1916, which cannot have been negligible even for his lowly rank, and the fees from such commissions as Clara had been able to obtain. There was the rental of their apartments, but both had enjoyed free hospitality for sometimes long periods—Clara's summer holiday in Fischerhude, his stay now with Hertha Koenig for over two months. A modicum of good housekeeping should therefore have seen them both not only solvent but able to cope with extra expenses like Ruth's education. Neither led the sort of life, however, to foster such caution. Rilke was anything but bohemian in his ways—always faultlessly dressed, fastidious in taste, and pedantically tidy—and his bodily wants were modest in the extreme: but he set the utmost store on the right surroundings, stayed only in the best hotels, saw to it that even rented rooms were furnished as he liked, sent all his letters registered, and never stinted on books he thought of interest, even in expensive editions, or on gifts for his friends. On all this he spent his money as it came; when it began to run out, he simply appealed for more, as a right due to his mission—and one way or another, as if in a charmed existence, he never failed to get it.

For the moment, thanks to Hertha Koenig's hospitality, he had cash enough in hand to be able to consider a visit to Berlin, putting off his return to Munich and the renewed search for lodging there—the first step into 'an unimaginable winter' which he was not yet ready to face.[5] Towards the end of September the Consulate in Munich sent him official notification that his exemption was maintained 'till further notice', and there was thus no actual call for his presence there. Ideas of visiting the exhibition of Paula Modersohn-Becker's work in Hanover, and seeing Clara and Ruth in Fischerhude, were abandoned after he arrived in Berlin on 3 October: for once in the capital, as though with Sophie Liebknecht's advice in mind, he plunged into an energetic programme of contacts and discussions with active participants in the events which hitherto had left him entirely bewildered and apathetic.

It was an attempt to understand the war, to distinguish more clearly for himself 'the entanglements into which so much well-meant human effort gets drawn again and again, and ties itself into tighter knots the more it tries to get free'.[6] He attended a session of the Reichstag, and dined with von Kühlmann, recently returned from the Constantinople Embassy to be appointed State Secretary for Foreign Affairs, and concerned in efforts for peace. He was to be seen in clubs, and talked with people 'of every opinion and from all camps': Karl von der Heydt, Wilhelm Herzog; von Moltke, the Kaiser's ADC; Jacob von Uexküll, Walter Rathenau; Fritz Wichert, now von Kühlmann's private secretary. 'I would so like to learn, but the lesson would be a long one, and the student is sad'—and he found it impossible to form any clear opinion.

Most people here consider the assurance of peace mere empty phrases, and I admire the instinct of the French, lumping together all the results of the Vatican's note under the amusing term *le Saint-Piège*. People take on the whole a curious view here:

knowing that politics by its nature can't always be honest, they immediately come to the harsh conclusion that dishonesty is the best policy. If we realize that peace can only take root in a completely changed world, one that had readjusted its ideas, then, my God, it's clearly not yet time for peace. Berlin does not give the impression that anyone is ready or willing to change.[7]

An occasional quiet morning in the museums gave little relief from the almost feverish activity of his October days, as he rushed from appointment to appointment, often late into the night, in the vain effort to make some kind of sense of the power-political scene. It was not surprising that the unaccustomed tempo left him exhausted and unwell. 'I'm probably not more tired than most of those who crowd into the Underground, but I'm less inclined than they to make a permanent stimulus of their fatigue. God, what a pressing and pushing, and ... the spaces between people are filled with news-sheets, as if the whole lot was packed and ready for long-distance shipment. Where to? to what future?'[8] Yet he stayed on, much longer than he had first intended, in the fascination of being near the hub of affairs, 'right next to the German dial',[9] and in spite of the feeling that he was further away than ever from grasping any 'thread of orientation'.[10] Writing to Clara early in November, he said that people were as though transfixed, when all should have been agreed that any price would be worth paying to get out of the predicament. 'Victories', however great, led nowhere, there was no inner will for the great changes that would be needed to save the world. 'Kühlmann ... is certainly the only far-seeing man among the "rulers" ... but even he will hardly be able to take the decisive step.'[11]

It was in long talks with Harry Kessler, during the first weeks of November, that he felt at last some hope of finding out where he belonged amid the cataclysm. Kessler, who after two years' service at the front had been given a post with the Embassy in Berne, was the friend who had known better than any other 'our earlier life (I mean Paris and the whole splendid open world)',[12] and whose transfer back to it, in some sense, after his active experience of war, could perhaps show Rilke how to reconcile the apparently irreconcilable, how it was possible to remain 'the same knowing and feeling person' in the one and the other. His letters from the field, which Rilke was able now to read, were 'the most powerful and surest description of that unimaginable life that have ever come my way, ranking with the great example of Tolstoy's "War and Peace", and carried along with a composure, presence of mind and narrative calm that seems inconceivable under such fearful conditions'.[13] But he was deeply shaken to hear Kessler say that his time in the field had brought moments far more moving, in human terms, than anything in his earlier life: the war as such might be condemned as senseless and brutish, but in its detailed manifestations he found it held spiritual beauties and revelations comparable only to those of love. The very fact that millions had learned the lesson of self-sacrifice was impressive.

Rilke, who considered that he himself, in peacetime, had already sacrificed his life to his work, found it inconceivable that anything could be more overwhelming than the moments he had experienced before a Rodin statue, the lofty regularity of a Michelangelo work, or an evening prospect at Duino. He felt that the nature in the raw revealed in the great conflict was in fact *un*natural, foreign to man's true being and with no spark of the 'divine': he recognized that the monstrous event might be somehow necessary, its seeds perhaps already within us, yet he was incapable of assimilating it. If it was in truth a natural process, 'then every line I've written is flawed and false'. The Elegies, two of which he read to Kessler, were his 'confession', he said, which he had thought to express in *Malte* but which had begun to crystallize, when the war broke out, in a way which had surprised himself: if he could only finish them, he would be ready to die. Kessler in his diary judged him, shrewdly, as an aesthete who was ready for any adventure of the spirit or of form, but who lacked the simultaneous capacity for adventures of brutal reality which others like Dante, Shakespeare, or Byron had shown in such times of upheaval. His only salvation would be 'if he could transform the war into an adventure purely of the mind'.[14]

That was a road to salvation which Rilke could not find while the war lasted. It was not in him, as he saw it was in Fritz von Unruh, to turn 'the gigantic material churned through with black' into a work—'to make things out of fears', as he had once cried to Lou. Kessler had seen von Unruh in Switzerland, under treatment for a painful disease of the hands contracted at Verdun—making enormous white fists of his bandaged hands and holding forth blazingly, 'all revolutionary and yet all officer . . . soldierly enthusiasm and conviction and at the same time the deepest revolt against the inhumanity of man'—and Rilke could appreciate the significance of his expressionist drama *A Family*, just produced in Berlin, 'a fearful book, as fearful as the times'. He himself could only continue, as the great events in Russia and Italy succeeded each other, in the ignorance he shared with the great mass of 'those in the thick of it' ('no one can complain at a lack of developments—but to see their true *face* . . . who can do that?'), and pursue the life of the aesthete unable to assimilate the reality around him.[15]

In his busy programme, in fact, there had been many occasions for relief from preoccupation with politics and war. In the 'Sturm' gallery, standing before Chagall's *Moi et le village* (and quizzing it, thought Walter Mehring, for all the world like a marquis in a rococo novel[16]), he discovered a 'dawning appreciation' for the modernist's work, in contrast to the 'brutality' of the other exhibits. With Gerhart Hauptmann he attended the dress rehearsal of the dramatist's *Winter Ballad*, and spent many an evening with the Hauptmanns during November. The work of the then little-known sculptor Renée Sintenis filled him with enthusiasm, and taking friends like Hertha Koenig to her studio at Wannsee became almost a routine. Berlin seemed indeed full of friends, both resident and visiting, whom he would have been sorry to have missed, and who could be presented with copies of the Louize Labé sonnets, just out. Thankmar von Münchhausen made a devoted 'adjutant', organizing his programme and presenting him to the various notables as though conferring a decoration.

A memorable evening in October was when Otto von Taube took him to a gathering in the imposing residence of the Brandenburg provincial governor Joachim von Winterfeldt, who had been proud to add his name to the submission freeing Rilke from military service. The talk centred on the artist Götz von Seckendorff, killed in action in 1914, whose works, which he now saw for the first time, had been strongly influenced by El Greco and showed a striking affinity with his own poems. Among the company was the artist's young friend Bernhard von der Marwitz, who was to suffer the same fate the following year and on whom Rilke's reading of his 'Lazarus', 'Christ's Descent into Hell', 'The Shepherd', and the 'Ode to Bellmann' made a profound impression. Long after midnight, von der Marwitz recorded in his diary, Rilke related the epic of Gilgamesh, 'conjuring up in wonderful words the images of that old poem . . . It was like a wind blowing high above the earth. How few sense it, because they see only the green of the trees and not the spirit which moves them high in the branches.'[17] Though they met only this once, and exchanged but a few letters until von der Marwitz's death in September 1918, his loss was one of the severest blows of the war for Rilke: in the young poet, as he wrote to von Winterfeldt then, he had thought to gain a truly close friend, and he had been denied a privilege which he had looked forward to all the more 'because men who have sought a close relationship with me have been few . . . If there is a future for German youth, then it must lie in an outlook very like his'.[18]

Now and then he could call on Wanda Landowska, the harpsichord virtuoso he had known in Paris, and feel her music conjure up that 'earlier, other world' in which 'the roots and growths of all my works' had remained.[19] A sharper reminder was the report of Rodin's death on 17 November. He did not know what effect this would have had on him in normal circumstances, he wrote to Clara, perhaps it would have come like a reconciliation: 'now, I feel mostly a bewildering confusion, that . . . behind the unnatural, fearful wall of war these figures we knew in their purity should disappear from view, who knows whither—Verhaeren, Rodin, the friends great in wisdom . . . all I can feel is that when the frightful smoke blows away, they will no longer be there, will no longer be able to support those whose task it will be to restore the world . . .'[20] To Sidie, who wrote towards the end of the month, with her sympathy and reminding him of their first meeting at Meudon in April 1906, he replied: 'Who like you could know and tell what the news meant for me . . . to all the reasons for my silence comes now the death of this dear, wise friend, as one more dumbness . . . I close my eyes ever tighter in order not to lose that inner centre from which everything found true and wonderful justification.'[21]

In her letter, Sidie had been solicitous for his material welfare, rightly surmising that he would be as hard up as ever. He told her that he would shortly be returning to Munich, and trying to find a dwelling which would give him seclusion after the pressures of the social round in Berlin: if she could manage to let him have a monthly contribution, that would be an immense relief for the worst winter months. But he also said he had been looking into the possibility of an escape to Switzerland. The Austrian Ministry of Foreign Affairs was sponsoring lecture tours by prominent writers to present its viewpoint in the neutral countries: Hofmannsthal had been both to Sweden and to Switzerland, Stefan Zweig had just left for Berne, and Rilke himself, as he told Zweig in September, had been approached for similar work, but had learned that 'in my position' (while, that is, still awaiting his definitive release) it was preferable not to 'put forward any proposals for travel'.[22] In Berlin, now that he was free, the idea had returned, and he had discussed Switzerland with Kessler and Hofmannsthal. Had he been prepared to lend himself to the sort of propaganda task required, there is little doubt that he would have been welcomed as a recruit: but he was not willing to pay such a price for his freedom, much as he longed to exchange the suffocation of the German 'front parlour' for the wide world he used to know. To a letter from an admirer of the *Book of Hours* he replied bitterly, on 3 December: 'I'm not living my own life . . . I feel refuted, abandoned, and above all threatened by a world which was ready to dissolve entire in such senseless disorder: for these should, must have been *my* years, even more than the earlier ones, years of achievement . . .'. In 1914, he said, he had thought of returning to Sweden after ten years' absence: 'If only I had gone, and seen through the worst of this world sorrow there.'[23]

Munich it must be, then—although if he could not find what he wanted there he did not rule out a serious try for Switzerland, and indeed continued his informal enquiries to that end. Almost all the savings he had made through Hertha Koenig's hospitality had been consumed by the long weeks in the Hotel Esplanade, but his purse was not yet empty enough to prevent him reserving a sleeper on 9 December, or selecting the Hotel Continental, when he arrived, as his base for the search for quarters. Fortunately Kippenberg, who was home again on leave, had good news to report on sales, and not only provided him with a Christmas bonus but also proposed to raise his monthly allowance by a hundred marks from January. Hertha Koenig, who had sensibly given him money as his birthday present and was eager to help further, said (after some hesitation) that he would be welcome to share the apartment she had recently taken in the Leopoldstrasse: but he needed, he said, a small place to himself, which he was sure could be found in spite of the overcrowding in Munich, and he made bold to suggest that her contribution might take the form of a monthly subsidy, and help with furniture in due course, instead of actual hospitality. He assured her it was not through fussy self-indulgence that he preferred to wait in the Continental instead of taking a cheap room in a pension: he simply could not cope with cold, discomfort, and intrusive new neighbours, 'and my depression, which is already deep enough, would crush me completely if I were exposed to petty disagreeableness. . . . In the worst case, and if Switzerland too proves impossible, I would have to ask you to take me at Böckel again.'[24]

It took another four months before even a provisional solution could be found, months which did nothing to relieve his depression. His endeavours in Berlin to instruct himself in politics and the war had left him 'empty', and as ignorant as ever, he maintained:[25] but in fact he continued to follow events closely in the newspapers, even though his conclusions relied on instinct and a blind desire for peace, rather than on cool and logical appraisal.

The reports of the October Revolution in Russia he had welcomed as a ray of light in the darkness. 'Russia, with its infinite sacrifices, will perhaps be the only State to make them for truly human ends, while the sacrifices of the others have been only for their mad designs and ambitions—the only State ready to change itself completely, which is what would be needed. . . . What a people this must be, to prevail against a world which will not yet admit humanity as a principle of life.'[26] Christmas in his hotel room would be no festival, he told Katharina Kippenberg, were it not for the thought of 'splendid Russia',[27] the land he could now recognize again in Trotsky's manifesto to the 'tired, oppressed and bleeding peoples of Europe'. In the Brest-Litovsk peace negotiations, however, despite his confidence in von Kühlmann, he began to suspect frustration of these hopes by 'continual errors' on the German side. It was encouraging from time to time to see the 'considered judgement of an experienced observer' like Prince Alexander Hohenlohe, in his articles for the *Neue Zürcher Zeitung*, 'corresponding exactly to my blindly felt convictions'— but such voices seemed without influence.[28]

He was more than ready to help with humanitarian efforts—contributing himself and through the Insel to Hermann Hesse's appeal for books for German prisoners in France, and actively supporting Hertha Koenig's idea for direct food issues to the Munich poor from her and others' country estates— but his pessimism deepened at the prospect of a future 'surrendered to the hands of men, a future which is like a melted-down bell never to ring again in the joy of the high morning air'.[29] The death of von Stauffenberg, at the end of February, came as a reminder of the unfinished Elegies which his friend had admired: and his longing grew to find a complete retreat in which they could be completed.

On 10 March, a week after the signature of the Brest-Litovsk treaty, he wrote on a sudden impulse to Walther Rathenau, asking straight out whether he could find such a place for him at Schloss Freienwalde, his estate in Brandenburg, 'to take me away for a few months from people, newspapers, all the paraphernalia of the times, into rural solitude where I can stay hidden from view'. Conditions, in other words, like those he had once enjoyed in Duino, 'which then proved so wonderfully fruitful for me'. For him it was vital, as he said in a later letter, to find the way back into contact with his 'earlier, joyful security, across four so negative years. ... For one who cannot usefully participate in the measureless events, the task should be to fight for that spiritual continuity which in the end everyone will once more seek'.[30] But Rathenau, though sympathetic, was unable to accommodate such a demand. It was to be a long time before Rilke could find a haven to his specifications, which, simple enough in theory, were more than difficult to satisfy in practice.

In April, however, at least a place of his own in Munich came his way. At a chance meeting he learned that the Austrian consul, after his marriage, was vacating his three-room apartment in the Ainmillerstrasse, and with it would be leaving an Austrian cook-housekeeper. On the fourth floor, its outlook over roof-tops to the St. Ursula church had a slightly Italianate air, 'not unlike the marble mosaics travellers used to bring back from Florence',[31] and although nearer the city centre than the Keferstrasse it promised to be quieter. At any rate, it would put four walls around him at last, even if he had only a few sticks of furniture. Here Hertha Koenig's aid was invaluable, not only in paying for some items to be left by the consul, but in providing others of her own. He was kept busy during April by a long-awaited visit from Katharina Kippenberg— she too was helpful with advice over his installation, and sent later what she could spare in linen and kitchen gear—but he was finally able to take possession of his new quarters on 7 May.

If not his ideal of seclusion, it was still a 'small step forward, outwardly' and, as he told Katharina, would not find him lacking in 'grateful resolve': the Michelangelo translations already stood open and ready on his desk.[32] That he should be settled at last, after the long winter of his complaints of homelessness, was a signal relief to the Kippenbergs, bringing the hope that he might now recover his productivity; and they were glad to continue material support. A parcel of rice, flour, and other provisions—increasingly rare commodities now in Germany—arrived early in July, and the publisher also made him an extra grant of a thousand marks towards setting up house. But Katharina had seen, as she recalled later, his downcast look, during apparently lively talk with their friends, and realized, perhaps more clearly than her husband, that he was still no nearer the longed for fusion of the 'broken-off surfaces' of his poetic existence. While he remained in Germany, shut off from the wider world once his, it was not likely that even the advantages of the new apartment could restore him. He was still living as though with a tourniquet applied to his arteries, he wrote to a friend at the end of May, to excuse a long silence: 'all communication is circulation, and (for so long now!) nothing has been circulating in me, nothing circulating out of me'. The St. Ursula church without its bells—melted down for munitions—reflected the utter emptiness of his spirit.[33]

The change was no small one for him, he wrote to Phia in May, but it had come at the right moment.[34] As was his habit, he took endless trouble in selecting and arranging the furnishings, and found a naïve pleasure in showing off the result to his friends (though this would not be conducive to the seclusion he claimed to seek). The range of his acquaintance in wartime Munich was in fact extraordinarily wide, and it was mainly for this reason that Hertha Koenig had been reluctant to share her quiet apartment with him. She had been no little surprised in January when, in his enthusiasm for her charity project, he introduced her to the independent socialist Kurt Eisner, the fiery revolutionary who was shortly afterwards jailed for his part in the strikes for 'peace without annexations'. 'For Rilke, *every* person had a side, a trait, something, which seemed to him important or at least remarkable. They were all human beings, and equal in his eyes.'[35]

No matter who turned to him, he seemed always ready to help: reading for hours on end to a sick friend, introducing Mia Mattauch to a job with his bookseller, or arranging readings to a select company from the work of little-known poets such as Alfred Wolfenstein or Richard Scheid, for which Hertha Koenig was glad to make her 'Picasso room' available. His contact with Eisner and Sophie Liebknecht, as with those of the more liberal persuasion like Annette Kolb, Wilhelm Herzog, or Friedrich Wilhelm Förster, and his receptivity for the expressionists' verse, were reflections perhaps of the instinctive feeling that nothing short of a radical transformation of society was needed now. But, as he had said to Rathenau, there was no role for him in the direction of events: awaiting the return of the right conditions to resume his own mission, he could be no more than an observer.

At the end of May a telegram arrived from Phia in Vienna congratulating him on his 'decoration'—mystifying intelligence which was explained only when Count Hartenau, of the Austrian mission in Munich, happened on him at the barber's and told him he had been awarded the Knight's Cross of the Order of Franz Joseph. 'I don't know what sort of face I made,' he replied to Ruth's delighted enquiry, 'for the barber scraped my expression off with the soap ... From her emotion, you would think Grandmamma Phia had received the award herself.'[36] Not untypically for Austria (and understandably in the present case, when vastly more urgent business pressed), it was not until a month after the end of the war that he received official word, and the order itself arrived. In his carefully drafted reply returning it, he said that his immediate reaction at the news had been to refuse, for it had 'always been his resolve to avoid any kind of decoration', but while still technically under the orders of the army he had not the right: now that he was free to act according to his convictions, he wished formally to do so. 'The undersigned' stressed that his decision by no means implied any lack of respect: 'his refusal derives solely from the preservation of his personal privacy, which for him, by the very reason of his artistic work, is an inescapable obligation'.[37] A genuine enough stand, no doubt; but underlying it was also the aversion he had long felt for

Austria as State and institution and for the Austrian way of life, not least because of his boyhood experiences and their revival in his brief military service in 1916.

Through the summer he led an outwardly busy life, but was quite unable to find his real work, and even correspondence required an immense effort to put pen in motion. Tiring often of the Munich round, he longed for a change of scene, for, as he told Marie-Anne, that had always been the most effective aid to a 'sensual nature' such as his in relieving an inner blockage.[38] In apprehension that domesticity might harden even further his 'petrification', he dreamed still of some country retreat. Even if another Duino was impossible, surely some quiet villa could be found. The early onset of autumn, the season that in the past had often proved a stimulus, brought no change for him. 'My mill is at a standstill,' he wrote on 6 September to Marie Taxis: 'the fair river that coursed over it has turned to ice.'[39]

If he could no longer be the poet, he could at least act the part. Towards the end of the month he received an anonymous letter from a young student and budding actress, Else Hotop, who had long admired him from a distance, for her parents' home was also in the Keferstrasse, and who, having discovered where he now lived, ventured to impart to the saintly author of the *Book of Hours* her sadness that his soul should be 'captive behind the walls of external things'. She signed it 'Elya' only: but he knew very well who she was, having seen her as the princess of that name in performances of a medieval play of St. George, which her company had given earlier in the summer. Within a week she had overcome her shyness sufficiently to accept his invitation, and they were soon going together to concerts and meeting regularly in his apartment, where she asked nothing more than to sit at his feet and drink in his words, and occasionally share his frugal evening meal. In her undemanding simplicity, and notwithstanding the sentimentality of her letters, Elya Nevar—for this was the name she adopted for her stage career—was, of all the women in his life, the one who perhaps brought him the greatest consolation—like a tame bird gladdening the days of a prisoner. 'When I think of you,' he wrote her on 4 October, 'I see us, as in a dream, kneeling beside each other.'[40]

Thoughts of escape from his incarceration continued to occupy him. Though no official word from Vienna had yet come, it seemed likely that his exit to Switzerland would be approved, and he saw salvation in the prospect of 'a real journey, different air, another countryside, some new relationships outside'.[41] Kippenberg, now away for good from occupied Belgium, had called to see him towards the end of August, *en route* himself to Switzerland on a brief duty visit, and on his return urged him to set off just as soon as he could get his passport, perhaps to Ouchy or Morges on Lake Geneva: he was prepared to make 1,000 marks a month available for the trip. Though Rilke would rather have devoted such unexpected wealth to setting up a 'sheltered and more durable refuge' better suited to his needs, as he frankly confessed to his friend, he conceded that Switzerland might in fact be the best thing for the moment, and promised to set about overcoming the bureaucratic hurdles.[42]

These should have been little more than a formality. The well-known literary society in Hottingen, near Zurich, had invited him to give a reading; Sidie Nádherný, already in Switzerland, had offered him hospitality for as long as he wanted; Kippenberg for his part let him have the first thousand marks by the end of September. But minor matters like a travel permit took low priority under the pressure of events, and as he waited, he himself became hesitant. To Axel Juncker, who invited him to read in the art gallery he had opened next to his Berlin bookshop, he replied on 13 October: 'it seems to me that this autumn and winter, while everything hangs so fearfully in the balance ... I ought not to think at all of travelling, at any rate not to Berlin.'[43]

The war had reached a crucial phase, after the setbacks to the German summer offensive and the Allied advances on the Western front, the collapse of Bulgaria in September, and Italy's pressure on the Piave against Austria. Though Germany's appeal on 3 October for an armistice, after Prince Max of Baden had assumed the chancellorship, had not been publicly announced, it was strongly rumoured, and Rilke was sensitive to the mounting evidence of the decay of the home front in both Germany and Austria. Even if he remained one who could not 'usefully participate' in events, the growing excitement in Munich by no means left him unmoved. In the closing days of October, as unrest grew elsewhere in Germany and the Austro-Hungarian Empire began to disintegrate, he was to be seen at many of the meetings and demonstrations which succeeded each other in the beer-halls and hotels and on the open space of the Theresienwiese, normally the venue of the annual beer festival, and at which a clear revolutionary trend began to emerge in spite of the confusion of opinions—the independent socialists Eisner, recently freed after his jail sentence, and Edgar Jaffé, also known personally to Rilke; the anarchist Erich Mühsam; Professor Max Weber, philosopher and sociologist from Heidelberg; the official socialist Erhard Auer following the moderate line of Friedrich Ebert, shortly to take over the German chancellorship from Prince Max.

Rilke's independent and uncommitted position attracted many individuals of different persuasions to his apartment, to hear the words of one whose abhorrence of the war was well known; and there is no doubt that, in the turbulence of these early days, his sympathy lay with revolution, though he had his reservations over the effect of the rough Bavarian temperament on such an ideal. After four years in the glare of the world conflagration, he wrote, 'all the lights have been so darkened that the extinction of the war will leave us in the most fearful blackness, unless the people in their distress whip up another powerful blaze, whose sparks are already here and there catching fire to the hem of the masses'.[44] At a meeting in the Hotel Wagner on 4 November, he heard Jaffé, Weber, and Mühsam speak to a vast audience, including ex-soldiers and students.

Although there was such a tight-packed mass round and in between the tables that the waitresses had to eat their way through it like woodworms, the atmosphere was by no means oppressive: one was hardly aware of the alcohol and tobacco fumes and the stench of humanity, so important was it, so blindingly clear, that those things for which the hour has struck could at last be spoken out and that the simplest and most valid of them were grasped with massive approval of the great crowd. Suddenly a pale young workman mounted the rostrum and said quite simply: 'Have you, or you, or you, made the appeal for the armistice? ... Let us seize a wireless station, let us ordinary folk address the ordinary folk on the other side—right away there'll be peace.' I can't hope to reproduce this so well as he expressed it—and suddenly, as he finished, a problem occurred to him, and with a touching gesture towards Weber, Quidde, and the other academics on the platform he went on: 'Here, these professors, they know French! They'll help us to put it the way we mean it.' Such moments are magnificent—and how they have been lacking in Germany.[45]

For Rilke, these were days of 'watching, listening, and above all of hope'[46]— hope for an irruption of truth at last through the institutionalized falsehood of the war years. This was the ideal that seems to have inspired Eisner too: and even as Rilke was writing to Clara in Fischerhude his account of the Hotel Wagner meeting, the great peace demonstration assembled at the Theresien-wiese on 7 November, after the departure of Auer's SPD group, was rallying round Eisner to press for direct action. By the evening, after an attack on the Maximilian II barracks, the crowd had moved into the city and the constituted authority had been deposed. Eisner—somewhat to his own surprise—found himself installed in the Diet building as the head of the provisional govern-ment, based on workers', soldiers', and peasants' councils, of the republic of Bavaria, while other public buildings and the newspaper offices were occupied, the red flag fluttered over the twin towers of the Frauenkirche, and Ludwig III and the rest of the Wittelsbach royal family slipped out of the capital under the cover of darkness.

Everything seemed quiet so far, Rilke added in a postscript to Clara early the following morning, 'and one cannot help but admit that the times are right to attempt great steps forward ... Now we can only hope that this unusual state of revolt will bring sense and not a fatal intoxication'. 'Each one of us,' he had written the day before to Anni Mewes, an actress friend,

certainly stands with those who desire the most honest and radical changes: but I have my doubts that these can be achieved *gently*, so late in the day, and against such obstinate resistance—if they come with violence, then further destruction will be added to all the rest, and especially for us much will be smashed. Art is always a promise of the most distant future, or at least that of the day after tomorrow, and so a mob eager to get to grips with the immediate will always be iconoclastic.[47]

These doubts were later to be justified, as far as he was concerned; but for the moment they were outweighed by his hope that humanity might be able to 'turn a completely new page of the future, on to which the whole debit of the fateful past does not have to be carried forward'.[48]

Just before the storm broke, he had received word from the Austrian Consul that he could be granted his exit permit whenever he wanted. The journey to Switzerland, despite the now uncertain conditions, could doubtless have been undertaken, but he put it off from week to week in his absorption in events: still on the sidelines, but holding endless 'discussions with excited people'[49] and in close contact with the members of the revolutionary government, in which Jaffé was finance minister. He interested himself in such matters as educational reforms under the new regime, and was active in the discussions for the reception and welfare of the returning troops. Recalling the concern he had often felt, while abroad before the war, at Germany's aggressive outlook, he felt relieved that it was now lifted from him following 'that mighty night of revolution': he stood now with the young people 'who hold as of right their confidence in this new beginning'.[50] At the bizarre 'revolutionary festival'— half concert, half rally—held in the National Theatre on 17 November, where the sounds of Beethoven's 'Leonora' overture were hailed by Eisner as the signals for 'a new earth, a new mankind, a new future', Rilke's face seemed transformed as he joined in the 'Hymn of the Peoples' Eisner had specially written for the occasion.[51]

Through the November days he still spared time for the adoring Elya, their innocent association sanctioned by calls on her parents from time to time. But the day before the festival he received a note which was to bring into his life a whirlwind love-affair in the sharpest contrast to this delicately paternal relationship. Claire Studer, a beautiful and tempestuous Bavarian, had been divorced in her early twenties by her Swiss husband, within a few years of their 'shotgun' marriage in Germany in 1911, her baby daughter being taken by his parents; during the war she had published pacifist articles, and in 1916 left Germany for Switzerland, where she was active among the anti-war émigrés, notably of the left wing; since 1917 she had been living with the poet Ivan Goll in Lausanne and Ascona. Immediately after the armistice, resisting Goll's pleas for marriage, she decided to visit Germany again to see at first hand the results of the revolution. She had recently published her first book, a volume of verse, which she had sent to Rilke: Munich, capital of the new republic and Rilke's temporary home, was her first goal, and the note to him her first action on arriving. His polite reply, excusing his silence over the poems, which he said he had much admired, and looking forward to meeting her, brought her to his apartment the next afternoon.

The studio seemed to 'float like an iridescent bubble' above the turmoil of Munich: as sparsely furnished as a hermit's cell, and in it Rilke writing at a standing-desk which looked more suited to an archivist than a poet.[52] He was very slim, almost ethereal, she remembered later: 'from a distance he could be taken for a cadet in mufti, but the nearer he approached, the more lofty became his brow, and from his eyes, filled with a gleam not of this world, darted the ray of genius.' Conscious of the sixteen years' difference in their ages, she was not a little in awe of 'this archangel in a jacket. But the gentle smile from his full and sensuous lips relieved my great emotion. . . . It seemed like a vision of Rilke before me, not a Rilke of flesh and blood.'[53] Only after she had left did she realize it had not been a dream, for in her hands were two gifts—a small Russian altar-piece and a poem. She responded the following day with a black statuette of a Madonna, was invited again, received him then in her hotel room, and within a few days they were lovers.

Quite uninhibited sexually—though probably not to the point of nympho-mania depicted in the memoirs she published at eighty-five—Claire Studer was a determined seducer of men, with a particular predilection for the writer or the poet. In love with Ivan Goll, she wanted her freedom still, and in the heady atmosphere of 'liberated' Bavaria, Rilke, recognized as one of the greatest poets and known for his anti-war sentiments, was an irresistible target. He for his part will have needed but little encouragement after the long abstinence since his separation from Loulou, more especially as he knew this could be only a fleeting affair. 'Yesterday,' he wrote her on 25 November, 'yesterday I made uncommon efforts to resist—yet was so glad when your voice (which sounded close and undistorted over the telephone) broke the silence. So tomorrow let us belong to each other the whole day, from 11.30 on so that you have lunch here—yes? . . . What flowers I would have liked to send you! but there is no choice.—He whom you do not name.'[54] She lodged for a while with the Wolfensteins, but for the last days of her stay, before going on to Berlin, moved into his apartment. His 'Liliane', as he called her, was a continual delight, as he heaped her with attentions: to her, their nights of love were like the tales of Sheherezade, and she could listen for hours as he read his poems. For once in his life, he could experience the transports of physical love without bitterness—though even here, in one of the poems he transcribed for her (written before the war, for he was not inspired to new), there was an undertone of melancholy:

> In the dark sweet ecstasy let us not
> distinguish the direction of our tears.
> Are you sure that it's delight we suffer,
> and not the cup of sorrow which makes us shine?[55]

After she left for Berlin at the end of December, where she planned to share rooms with the young actress Elisabeth Bergner, he wrote that he could not sit before a blank page without the 'light of her fire' falling across it.

Have I then kindled such flames in you? such a conflagration of the heart? Beloved child, and now . . . you're with your indescribably beautiful friend, full as you are of me. I feel a numinous awe that I should be there with you; just tell her that I make myself light in you, that she may be touched only with my divine essence when you embrace. . . . Evenings, in the dark, as I stretch out my arms and open my hands flat, there comes the feeling on them of your Spanish shawl. And I believe, more and more, that the shawl is nothing other than a spell, through which a contact between your body and a night was suddenly preserved by magic, as a mournful and tender fabric.[56]*

As far as Liliane was concerned, she never seemed to see him at any kind of work, yet his time when he was not with her was as fully occupied as ever, with his correspondence and with visits from friends such as Thankmar von Münchhausen or the faithful Elya. He followed political events too with the same keen interest, though the days on which one appointment succeeded another with scarcely a break made him impatient to resume his own real work. To Phia, now apparently contentedly settled in the new state of Czechoslovakia, he wrote early in December that the coming Christmas brought a more hopeful outlook: 'however widely opinions and efforts may diverge—they have become free; and were the fatigue, the sheer exhaustion not pushed to such an extreme, one could see the determination standing in a million hearts like winter wheat awaiting the first snow . . . that which is to shoot up, some day, in the next and better season for mankind, will be nothing but pure good will.'[57]

But as the coalition which Eisner's idealism had called into being began to disintegrate in December, in the run-up to the Diet elections, with on the one hand an increasing radicalization of the Left and calls for a 'Red Army', and on the other, signs of a drift to the right in permitting the return of the Life Guards under von Epp, Rilke's dismay grew—not over the political differences as such, but over the 'dilettantism' manifested by 'individuals and committees'. A new beginning could only come, he felt, 'if each could do what he had really learned to do, and can do, and do it joyfully, with the most capable standing as overseers, and at the top someone experienced, a wise man. But we're a long, long way from that'.[58] His own inclination, more than ever, was to turn back to what *he* could really do, quite contrary 'to the call of the time, which seeks to divert everyone from his proper and particular capabilities'.[59] Everyone should stick to his last: 'if you're troubled by the election problem,' he wrote to Katharina Kippenberg, 'then my cry would be: vote for the Insel, and no one else!' The reminder of Switzerland in the shape of Liliane had reawakened his longing to break out from the sterility of Munich, and when a telegram came from the Hottingen society, confirming their invitation, he considered once again making the postponed journey. The books and household gear he had accumulated, the many Christmas presents which

---

*'Liliane', in her (ghosted) memoirs, alleged that a pregnancy after this liaison was terminated on the insistence of both Rilke and Ivan Goll, who took the precaution of destroying all their correspondence about the affair (Claire Goll, *La poursuite du vent*, Paris, 1976, p. 104). The lack of any other evidence, and the lurid sensationalism of the book as a whole, must incline us to disbelief. Elisabeth Bergner wrote in a letter to the author (26 May 1983) that Claire certainly never told her about a pregnancy. 'I suspect she did not write a lot of truth, because . . . she did not speak a lot of truth either.'

had arrived, made him feel that he should still give Ainmillerstrasse the chance to prove itself: yet there was always the thought that all this would have to be 'moved somewhere else, away from Munich, before it can give me protection and support ... The only question is: where?' He badly needed to get away from 'all this approximation, all this adaptation to what is never exact, never my own'.[60]

Hesitating, he stayed put: and in the New Year resolved to keep to himself, seeing no one but Kassner and two or three other friends, to try to bring on the 'flood and flow' he had hoped the end of the war would bring.[61] He rearranged his furniture, setting the desks squarely in the middle of the studio and banishing the 'chimney corner' settee and chairs in which too many visitors had been making themselves comfortable. 'It is really good *dans mes meubles*,' he wrote to Marie Taxis, regretfully declining her offer of refuge in Lautschin: 'knowing myself, to leave here ... would be ... not so much an interruption, as a complete break—I think (between ourselves) I would never then return to Munich.' He must stay: and, while waiting for that elusive, definitive home, wherever it might be, would set himself a strict timetable, to force himself to 'a few weeks of quiet and regular achievement'.[62]

Financially, he had never stood better. Kippenberg, who had sent him at Christmas a bonus of a thousand marks and an encouraging report of new editions of his works, admittedly announced that his Insel account was over six thousand in the red. 'But never fear!' wrote the publisher cheerfully, 'the sales of your books have never been so healthy': and in February he raised the monthly allowance to 1,000 marks, as well as offering a further bonus of a thousand if needed. This Rilke accepted with alacrity, asking for half to be sent to Clara, to help with the expenses of setting up a new home in Fischerhude and also with Ruth's outfit.[63] The girl was provisionally enrolled at an agricultural college in Dachau from the spring, and had decided meanwhile to get some practical experience with a farmer near Fischerhude—the combined effect, he thought, of the revolution and of reading Knut Hamsun's 'wonderful *Growth of the Soil*', and he spoke with admiration of her courage.[64]

In a 'most stringent retreat', through the first months of the year, he manfully refused invitations,[65] while to the Ainmillerstrasse came only those who (Kassner perhaps excepted) were gentle and undemanding in engagement—Regina Ullmann, or Elya Nevar. As he had put it to Sidie Nádherný, his purpose was 'to work up the most pressing things' before him: 'good books are here asking to be read, hundreds of letters are unanswered, and as far as I may think of work, torn as I am inside, I would like at least to get some of my translations into a certain shape.'[66] In the *Insel Almanach* for 1919, which made a convenient accompaniment to many a long-overdue letter, had appeared not only his poems 'Death' and 'Narcissus', but also the entry from his Ronda notebook on that singular 'Experience' in Duino when, leaning in the fork of a tree, he had felt transported to the 'other side' of life. All these, each in their way, 'were approaches to perceptions of the outermost limits of existence', and leading him, as he sent the *Almanach* to Stauffenberg's widow, to the reflection: 'in the general fog and lack of counsel which besets humanity . . . if I see a task before me, clearly set and quite independent, it is this alone: out of the deepest joys and splendours of life itself, to strengthen our confident familiarity with death.'[67] The task, in other words, of finishing what he had begun in the Elegies, if only he could find his way back.

Translation—continuing the Michelangelo sonnets, picking up a Lermontov poem that had waited many years in his notebook, trying his hand at other Italians, and, later, Mallarmé—formed with his letters the daily stint through which he hoped a new beginning would come. Most beneficial of all, however, was his evening reading, for among the books waiting was Verhaeren's last volume of verse, *Les flammes hautes*: poems which he read again and again, reviving for him the memory of 'the great friend' and stimulating his yearning to return to 'the thoughts and hopes from which one was snatched away in the summer of nineteen hundred and fourteen'.[68] In Verhaeren, he wrote to Bernhard von der Marwitz's sister, he had lost the one who had known how to encourage him to his task: 'even if he could not read a line of my work, he believed in it with an overwhelming confidence, and I know he expected from me exactly what my inmost jubilation would lie in producing.'[69]

How far he still felt himself from his goal was apparent when he wrote in January to Lou, after nearly a year of silence. Sending her the *Almanach*, he transcribed for her from his Ronda notebook the second 'Experience' too—the garden in Capri when he had had 'the taste of all Creation in his being'[70]—and told also of the star seen from the bridge in Toledo 'falling unhurriedly through the night space and through my inmost existence': all seeming to come together 'like a first sketch of inner *being*', but all lying in a past which he was unable to recapture across the gulf of the war years. 'Now one sits here again, picking out one's own existence, pondering and planning and holding it up against the sombre background. And everything one was, lies . . . six years and more in the past. The disaster has handled us with prodigious waste.' He badly needed to see and talk to her again: and when she wrote that she might come in March to Munich, he put aside once more the idea of going to Switzerland, which still hovered before him in spite of his efforts to restore himself behind closed doors. Her stay must be at his expense, he insisted: the heaven-sent bonus from the Insel could not be better used.[71]

His doors remained closed to the uproar and political confusion which followed the assassination of Eisner on 21 February. The violent act was 'particularly painful' for him,[72] deepening his disillusion over the November revolution which at first had given him hope; and in spite of his friendship with the poet Ernst Toller, another Independent Socialist who became the

Chairman of the 'Soviet' Republic proclaimed (without the communists) on 7 April, he kept aloof from contact with those conducting the increasingly chaotic affairs of the Bavarian Free State.

Lou arrived at the end of March, staying at a pension nearby, and for them the intellectual and artistic life of Munich seemed to continue untroubled by the turmoil around them, as they talked to Kassner, welcomed Freud's son Ernst, or visited the sex-changed artist Walburga (Walt) Laurent in his studio. Lou found Rilke indeed far more balanced, his outlook once more that of their early days together. 'The Other' was still present in him, she thought, but now as an integrated part of his personality and no longer a menace to his spiritual and bodily health.[73] She stayed on through April and May, and they looked down as from an ivory tower on the wild succession of events beneath them: the second 'Soviet' Republic, this time communist, supplanting the first on 13 April, the assembly of the *Freikorps* and *Reichswehr* counter-revolutionary forces, the shooting of hostages in Munich, and the 'White' terror which followed even more bloodily after the occupation of the city on 1 May. As an intellectual considered sympathetic, Rilke was provided by the Soviet Republic with a plaque for his apartment certifying its 'protection': when he omitted to take it down on the arrival of the 'Whites', he was subjected twice to a house search, the suspicion of Leftist sympathies being strengthened by the discovery among his papers of a photograph of Toller. Unlike others under similar suspicion, however, such as the writer Oskar Maria Graf, he was not arrested; and he was courageous enough actually to give shelter for a night to Toller, on the run before his capture and imprisonment in May. He added his signature to Thomas Mann's 'Appeal against Arrogance', published on 8 May, urging an end to recrimination and pressing for sincere co-operation between bourgeoisie and working class in the task of reconstruction:[74] but looking back, towards the end of the month, on the 'poison and antidote' of recent events, he felt that nowhere was 'the true, deeper-acting medicine' being applied.[75]

Escape to Switzerland, put off in anticipation of Lou's visit, seemed more attractive now than ever, but to arrange it was, perversely, even more difficult than before, the Swiss authorities being much more cautious over granting entry permits for those from countries torn by revolution and civil war. He now had a firm invitation from Hottingen, and Sidie Nádherný had also arranged for him to be invited to stay in Nyon, on Lake Geneva, with her friend Countess Mary Dobřzensky. Kippenberg told him that sales were now good enough to carry as extended a journey as he might wish, and he was making 6,000 marks extra available immediately. Though the mark was weak on the foreign exchange, Rilke was sufficiently confident to ask him to send a third of this sum to Clara, who needed more now that she was having a house built in Bredenau, near Fischerhude, as a permanent home for herself and Ruth. The passport and visa formalities were finally resolved, by dint of much queueing and correspondence, and by the second week of June he was ready to leave.

Many others, disgusted by the events, were also leaving Munich, and some even emigrating. For him, the city had long since ceased to mean anything, 'like a book I had read through in prison twenty times from beginning to end'.[76] Yet his escape was by no means an emigration, and they were wrong who later saw him as hounded out by the 'White terror'. To Lou, and to Kippenberg, he spoke of returning to Germany after spending the summer in Switzerland, even if it might be to Leipzig rather than Munich. With Elya's devoted aid, he carefully packed all his books, notes, and correspondence, and left the keys in her care. The apartment remained his: Lou, who had left Munich on 2 June, returned to occupy it for a while after his departure, and it was sublet to a distant relation of hers from July. When he finally took the train to Lindau for the crossing to Romanshorn on 11 June, he fully intended to come back to Germany in due course.

VII

Prelude in Switzerland
1919–1921

'They do best who, if they cannot but admit love, yet make it
keepe quarter, and sever it wholly from their serious affairs
and actions of life: for if it checke once with business, it . . .
maketh men that they can no wayes be true to their own
ends'

(Francis Bacon)

I

'I praise and praise the instinct that has led me here'

(To Rudolf Junghanns, 11.8.1919)

The feeling of freedom at last, as he entered Switzerland and made his way to
Zurich, was tempered by uncertainty over his stay, for in spite of all his efforts
he had not succeeded in obtaining a permit for more than ten days. Since his
Hottingen society engagement would not be until the autumn, the first
priority was to seek a prolongation. After a few days in Zurich, therefore, he
repaired on 16 June to Nyon, and on the advice of Mary Dobržensky and Sidie
obtained a suitable medical certificate to the effect that he needed two or three
months' rest before being able to commence the 'lecture tour' marked on his
passport. With this support his application was sent on its way to Berne. He
did not feel guilty of entirely false pretences, for in fact the change of scene had
brought a surprising fatigue, and he made an uneasy guest in Mary's lakeside
chalet, the Ermitage, cramped, full of people, and with constant callers. Sidie,
about to return home, did her best to smooth his path amid the social
obligations, but, glad as he was to see her again, after only a few days he moved
on to nearby Geneva. Such an abrupt departure was small thanks for his
hostess's welcome, but he somehow contrived it without forfeiting her
goodwill.

Geneva, where he spent a week, brought Paris immediately to mind, 'in the
atmosphere, the street scenes, the set of the houses',[1] and not least in the
person of a pre-war acquaintance, the artist Baladine Klossowska. He had
exchanged visits with her and her husband, the art historian Erich Klossowski,
during his days in Paris after the break with Rodin, and had met her again
casually a few years later, but had not pursued the acquaintanceship. In

Geneva now she was living apart from her husband, with her two young sons Pierre and Baltusz. They met several times before he left for Berne, his next port of call, and Baladine's was the first entry in the new address book he had started for Switzerland, as if to mark that chance had once again brought him together with someone who would be of vital importance in his life.

For Berne, where the decision over his permit would be taken, he had already telegraphed to Yvonne von Wattenwyl, whom he knew through a friend to be an admirer of his work and whose connections would undoubtedly be useful. So it proved. To be introduced to a new scene by a member of one of its old-established patrician families—in contrast to the more cosmopolitan Mary Dobržensky—was a delight. It was partly from snobbery, of course, but also from the feeling that this was the way to the history and to the heart of a city hidden otherwise by its outward face. Switzerland had often been the butt of his irony, and travelling through to Italy he had been wont to draw the blinds of the carriage against the too-contrived *mise-en-scène* of mountains and lakes, God as stage-manager 'directing the spotlight of sunset on to the mountains'. Now, under Yvonne's guidance, he was grateful to escape this 'dismissal by generalities' and to feel he was penetrating to the native core.* He stayed in Berne until 9 July, received everywhere as the celebrated author of *Rodin* and beset with enquiries about the *New Poems*. He was quite dazed, he told Kippenberg, by the fuss over his books.[2]

His movements as yet unrestricted, he returned to Zurich. The city's bustle was trying, after Berne; but it was a pleasure to find the Busonis again there, and to see a performance by the dancer Clotilde von Derp, whom he had known and admired in Munich, and her partner Alexander Sakharoff. There was news too of Marthe, after his letters had failed to reach her: a young French artist Jean Lurçat, who knew her, was in Zurich, and told him she was soon coming herself to Switzerland. Hearing from Inga Junghanns that she was still in Sils-Baselgia, he thought a visit there to see her progress with the Danish translation of *Malte* would be as good a next stage as any, with the hope too that somewhere in the Grisons he might find the quieter spot he needed. When he learned from a traveller just returned from there of the beauty and isolation of Soglio, high above the Bregaglia valley, and near the warmth of Italy, his mind was made up. Claire Studer, he knew, was now in Zurich, but as she was living again with Ivan Goll, he tactfully deterred calling on her until the day before his departure, and it was a reunion necessarily more muted than their parting in Munich in December.

The Junghanns had reserved him a room at a hotel in Sils for 24 July, but were a trifle nervous over receiving him to a meal in their simple attic rooms,

---

*Switzerland was a joy too in the availability of many a material comfort he had missed in wartime Germany. The *coiffeur* in the Hotel Bellevue in Berne, who later opened his own salon and perfumery, produced a particular toilet-water for which Rilke henceforth remained a regular customer, and among the more curious of his letters to be preserved is a series of 21 to Herr Schönauer with his orders.

used as he was, they thought, to greater luxury: and they wondered too, knowing his depression over the war, in what kind of mind they would find him. 'Do you think Rilke can still laugh?' Inga asked her husband. 'I doubt it,' replied Rudolf, 'but he has such a wonderful smile that if he only gives us that we can't complain.' They need not have worried. In spite of rain on the journey to St. Moritz, where Rudolf met him with a waggon, his spirits had lifted and his bodily unease seemed to fall away: and Inga felt she had never had a guest at her table who could so immediately find the right note and mood.

I knew he preferred light food: but that he should so enjoy fried eggs on toast with a madeira sauce I'd concocted myself, and find they reminded him at once of Copenhagen, was a lucky chance. And that the last jar of olives I had just managed to get in the Sils Maria shop should stimulate a boyish appetite and awaken all his happy memories of Paris, was more than a housewife has a right to expect. 'May I eat them with my fingers? We used to do that in Paris when we bought them in the street and ate them straight from the bag!' And he began to talk of Paris before the war, of his friends there, Rodin, André Gide, Troubetskoy, and many others.

When the talk turned to Scandinavia and the sea, and Junghanns began with anecdotes of the Frisian islands, Rilke joined in with his own about the fisher folk he had known in North Germany, they were soon trying their Platt-Deutsch, and there was more laughter in that one evening in Sils than they had known through all the dark years of the war. So delighted was he with this prologue to the promised land of Soglio, that instead of simply overnighting he spent four days in Sils, walking in the sun and enjoying the Alpine flowers, and visiting the Nietzsche memorial. One evening he told them of his sojourn in Duino, and read them the Elegies, his slight figure seeming to Inga to gain in stature in the light of the single candle, and himself, as he read, to grow into 'his own inner format'. It was a solemn and inspiring moment, coming after so much gaiety together; but both were an essential part of Rilke as she saw him then. 'He himself was the most sensitive of instruments: where he felt a resonance, he gave of himself completely and readily, always generous, ever open to new stimulation, and ever receptive to what others had to tell.'[3] When, finally, on 29 July, he boarded the mail coach which was to take him over the Maloja pass to Soglio, he felt lighter of heart than he had been for years.

Soglio, he had heard someone say, was 'la soglia', the threshold of Paradise: and indeed he had high hopes of this remote mountain village, most of all from what he had been told of the Casa Battista, the de Salis palazzo which, under the curious name of 'Pension Willy', served as the only inn. The magnificent setting was as nothing for him: these overweening, 'stupid' mountains were simply 'imposing barriers, as senseless as some barred door', the desert of eternal snow looking down on the green slopes a banal tourist attraction.[4] He had eyes only for the immediate surroundings—the glorious chestnut trees,

Rudolf Kassner

Ludwig von Wittgenstein, 1919

Rilke during his army service, 1916

Claire Studer, 1921

Nanny Wunderly-Volkart, 1927   Yvonne von Wattenwyl, about 1920

Muzot before 1900

the French-style terraced garden behind the house, half-wild but with box hedges in traditional trim—and all his sensibility turned inward to the seventeenth-century palazzo itself. Though an inn for over thirty years now, it still held the atmosphere of its history in the panelling, the stucco work, the four-poster beds, the old tables and chairs. The de Salis library, not usually open to guests, was put at his disposal by the accommodating host, and he turned eagerly to the history of this distinguished family whose branches had spread into many lands (the then owner of the Casa Battista, Count John, was British Ambassador to the Holy See). To have old things about him, as he said once, was not mere aesthetic pretension: in the sense of the past they gave him, he could seek true contact with human life when, as now, the contemporary was repugnant. 'Everywhere I have to be able . . . to imagine that in this place, or that, if only I can gain its confidence, infinite pasts have unrolled, of which fragments at least want to grow to me and in me, as if they were my own or those of my own family.'[5] Switzerland, he still thought, was no land for him; but here, as in Berne, he could indulge his absorption in its history, with the added sense of 'protection' for his work which had eluded him since Duino. 'To have *such* a house one day all to *myself* for a year, for a whole year to see *absolutely no one*, to have only what comes from the old things . . . voilà ce qu'il faudrait pour me refaire.'[6]

It could be only a temporary taste of his ideal, however. Even had he been assured of longer residence in Switzerland, a winter at the altitude of Soglio would be untenable. He was now expected in Zurich at the end of October for the first evening of the Hottingen society's autumn season, so that he could reasonably hope for permission to stay till after that; but the worsening exchange for the income from Germany he was increasingly relying on meant that he would have to fall back on hospitality, for which the only hope was Mary Dobržensky in Nyon. She assured him he would always be welcome, and was even ready, pending better times, to tide him over with loans. While Soglio lasted, however, enclosing him like Tannhäuser in the Venusberg, 'with books glittering like tantalizing gems in the dark mine', it was so beautiful that he took no thought for the morrow, and through August and September began the slow process of reading and writing himself back into productivity, at least in the prose of innumerable letters. 'Here I sit, and ponder over my life— which always reaches its purest essence where it can find the support of tangibly traditional surroundings.'[7] With that support he had recovered, it seemed, from the great 'dumbness' to which the war had condemned him, and, if only a step nearer the inner reflection of poetic creation, had at least regained the ability to communicate, in the letters which flowed now from his pen in the seclusion of the library.

In these surroundings too his imagination could once more roam free, even if not yet in verse, to explore the regions at the limits of human perception which had seemed close to him in Spain as he recorded the Duino and Capri

'Experiences'. In an essay now, he suggested an experiment to discover what he imagined as 'primal sound': if one could treat the coronal suture of the skull like the zigzag sound-track of the primitive phonograph he had once as a boy helped to make in a physics lesson, might it not reveal that unknown sound, some strange music which could bring us closer to the mysteries of life? might not other such apparently random lines occurring in nature be similarly tried, leading us into the realm of some yet unknown sense? Somewhere there should exist an 'inmost language', as he wrote later, a language of 'word-cores', not the flowers we pluck above the soil but the very seed below. 'My prose in the "Experiment Proposal" lies deeper, a touch nearer the fundament than that of the *Malte*, but one can reach only minimally deeper, to the next layer below, and is left to imagine what expression would be like at the point of silence.'[8]

For a brief while he could pretend the protection of Soglio was for ever, 'rather like a dog learning to play dead': but outside reality could not be denied, the permit application had to be renewed and he had to return to be near Nyon, the place of his registration. 'It's like when, as a child, you take a clean page and start to write a list of things you want,' he wrote to Yvonne von Wattenwyl on 9 September, 'and you suddenly find it's never big enough and the list gets more and more cramped—so now, I'm writing smaller and smaller from day to day and there's no help for it, the page has to come to an end. I haven't got much further towards the "recollection" of myself.'[9] Having obtained a new medical certificate to support his application and sent it off to Nyon, he set off back in that direction on 21 September.

Before taking his chances with Mary Dobržensky again he had promised himself a reunion at last with Marthe, who was now in Switzerland: a first contact again with Paris, 'the Paris of my work and my hopes'.[10] She joined him for a few days at the end of the month in a little pension in Begnins, not far from Nyon. He could admire the artistic skill she had developed in the tapestry work she was engaged on, but it was in some ways a melancholy experience, 'somewhat faded at the edges', and in spite of her vivacity and her evident devotion to him still, he could not recapture the relationship they had once had.[11]

Good news on two fronts awaited him when he arrived in Nyon on 2 October. His permit had been extended to the end of the year, and Countess Mary persuaded him to accept a monthly allowance of seven to nine hundred francs a month, as a loan to be repaid at his leisure if and when the mark regained a reasonable exchange rate. Greatly relieved on both counts, he could enjoy two weeks with her, even though his room was little more than a cupboard under the stairs and there was the usual steady stream of guests. He learned that following his appearance in Zurich there were plans for further readings in other cities, and it was his hope, he wrote to Kippenberg, that such a tour, if successful, could together with Mary's funds see him through to the end of the year without need of further remittances from the Insel. After that, perhaps a return to Germany, though he was still, he confessed, curious to find out whether Switzerland could offer him, somewhere, surroundings like Soglio. 'Everything there was a promise of the future, like a sample of material from which one later gets a complete dress, a cloak with a hood to make one invisible.'[12] It could not be planned, and would have to be another of those providential dispensations he had come almost to expect in his life. But winter was approaching, and he would have to prompt Providence if he was to find what he wanted.

He went to Geneva, calling again on Baladine Klossowska, and enjoying greatly an evening at the theatre of the actor-manager Georges Pitoëff, 'a young Russian of genius ... who puts on everything that meets his vision, plays from all countries and in all languages, and each one staged from this vision, not to please the audience ... theatre as I conceive it'.[13] With Countess Mary he had looked at several possible houses near Nyon, but the *bise* was already penetrating, and the whole Geneva area he felt was highly unpromising. A few days in Brissago, in the Tessin, at least were warm, but here too he found no prospects before it was time to report for his engagement in Zurich on 25 October.

2

'Quiet, and the particular care I need, nature, solitude, *no* people for half a year! When will this come? and where?'

(To Marie Taxis, 18.1.1920)

Had he had any choice, the last thing Rilke would have sought at this time was a public appearance. What he needed was just the opposite—'quiet contemplation, for which the weeks at Soglio were only a small introduction'.[1] He held that for the full appreciation of a poem, it must be read aloud: but over the ten years that had passed since he had last stood at the public lectern, he had limited such reading to the intimate circle of his friends and had become increasingly averse to offering his work in this way to an unknown wider audience. Conscientious as he was, however, he had been preparing himself during his peregrinations for the ordeal which circumstances had imposed. He felt a double gulf here, not merely that between himself and an audience of strangers, but also that between a people emerging from the experience of war and one which had remained in an island of peace; and in his introductory words at the first appearance in Zurich, on 27 October, before an impressive attendance of six hundred, he explained the dilemma he had felt and his decision nevertheless to offer works which might appear irrelevant or a mere 'poésie de luxe'.

It had not needed the 'fearful years' of the war, he said, to put him to the test of justification of his work. Twenty years earlier, as he wandered with

Tolstoy over the meadows of forget-me-nots in Yasnaya Polyana, he had been faced with that challenge; since then, at every turn of his road, he had examined his conscience—and 'the responsible inner voice has always given me its approval'. The work he would read now came from the conviction that his mission lay in 'bringing forth a pure witness to the breadth of the world, its diversity, its fullness'.

It was to that witness that I hoped to develop the poem, in which I would strive to comprehend in lyric form every manifestation, not only that of feeling—to represent, in its specific context of feeling, an animal, a plant, every occurrence, *a thing*. Do not be led astray by my inclusion, often, of images of the past. For what has once been, exists still in the plenitude of events, if one can seize it, not according to its content, but through its intensity: and we ... should address ourselves to that superior visibility of the past if we wish to gain an image in metaphor of the splendour which still surrounds us today.[2]

Rilke, as all agree who heard him either in private or on occasions such as this, was an outstanding interpreter of his own verse, his 'warm, masculine baritone' delivering the lines with 'strong emphasis and a plastic clarity'.[3] With his natural talent for presentation, and sense of ceremony, he could hold audiences, whether of one or many hundred as now, spellbound. But the extraordinary success of this first evening was due in no small measure also to the care he took to introduce each poem or translation with a brief comment— a mention of Rodin's influence in 'The Panther', or a word in memory of his 'great friend' Verhaeren before he read his translation of 'Les morts'—and the long applause at the end showed that he had indeed established the communion he sought. That there were many friends in the hall, whom he could feel he was addressing personally, helped him to command the attention of the 'impenetrable mass of those harder to move',[4] and the highly favourable review which followed in the *Neue Zürcher Zeitung* left in no doubt how well he had succeeded.

He was persuaded to give in Zurich a second performance, this time to Hottingen society members only, on 1 November, for which he included a reading of the 'primal sound' essay. There followed a triumphal tour through the cities of German Switzerland—St. Gallen first, then Lucerne, Basle, Berne, and finally, on 28 November, Winterthur. Though at first the prospect had seemed daunting, his confidence increased as the tour progressed, and this concession to fame he would normally have shunned clearly gave him much satisfaction. His approach on each occasion was the same as in Zurich, but he varied his selection of poems and improvised their introduction to suit the locality: an appreciation of Regina Ullmann in St. Gallen, her birthplace, a reference to Bachofen in Basle, and in Winterthur, home of the wealthy family of art lovers and collectors, the Reinharts, focusing on Cézanne. Each time, therefore, an empathy was achieved with his audience which, as he reported to Kippenberg, attained even for the highly personal and 'difficult' poems a resonance beyond the usual, and it was a sure touch, with a mostly multilingual audience, to precede his translations from French or Italian with a reading of the original version. It was almost a disappointment when this 'curious public display' had to come to an end.[5]

'A hard and dense material', the Swiss, he thought, and he was not a little proud of his achievement in penetrating it.[6] The greatest pleasure from these crowded weeks, however, came once again, as it had earlier in Berne, from the entrée he gained to Switzerland's established families and the new friendships he made among them, some of which were to prove of lasting importance for him. In Basle he was made especially welcome by the Burckhardts, and in the atmosphere of the city's eighteenth-century architecture he seemed to be returning to the familiar world of Paris. As he took tea, before his performance there, with Carl Burckhardt's sister Theodora von der Mühll, her chimney-piece reminded him of his rooms in the Hôtel Biron, and he began to talk of Paris, the occasional shadow of bitterness at what he had lost always overlaid, she recalled, by his infectious laughter and sunny humour, unforgettable for all who had the privilege of knowing him.[7] In Winterthur he stayed with Hans Reinhart, litterateur and playwright, member of the literary society organizing his reading evening, and his younger brother Werner, patron of music and a performer himself of mark; and he visited the home of the eldest of the brothers, Georg, art connoisseur and owner of an imposing and growing collection. The Reinharts were business men of substance, part owners of the big textile import firm of Volkarts with extensive interests in the Far East: each, in his different way, more than a dilettante, and a Maecenas of a different breed from the aristocrats Rilke had encountered up to now.

Of the people he met, however, there was one, at the very outset of his tour in Zurich, to whom he felt immediately drawn, 'at once real and directly close, a woman, mother of a grown-up son . . . but small, attractive, young'.[8] Nanny Wunderly, actually only three years younger than Rilke, wife of the owner of a tannery in Meilen, near Zurich, granddaughter of one of the founders of the Volkart firm, and a cousin of the Reinhart brothers, was an energetic and vivacious housewife and mother, *petite*, almost elfin in figure: no bluestocking, but with decided views on what she liked in literature and art. She was devoted to her garden and home, the 'Lower Mill' at Meilen, in which she showed a considerable flair for interior decoration, and where she pursued her hobby of bookbinding. The fourth of November, Rilke's first visit there, was marked in his diary as a red-letter day, 'timelessly good',[9] for he recognized in her open and responsive nature the support he needed. Here at last, he felt, was the entirely selfless protection he had dreamed of: a 'miracle-working' friend at a distance, always ready to help but making not the slightest demands on him — the epitome of unpossessive love. 'All my life I have never felt so convinced of someone's nearness,' he wrote her that Christmas, 'and I feel, tender one, how light this nearness is.'[10]

In his hundreds of letters to her — every line of which she carefully preserved—there is a unique spontaneity. With Nanny Wunderly he was a Rilke *en pantoufles*, interspersing the trivia of his day-to-day life with his ideas and reflections, views on what he had read and uninhibited gossip about other people, with little of the stylization that was second nature to him even when he wrote to lovers like Benvenuta. But he was also the Rilke of self-analysis, not with the careful, almost detached recording of 'symptoms' that character-ized his letters to Lou, but as if he were indeed on the analyst's couch, pouring out recollections and associations, the fears of the child and the hopes of the man. Her endless patience in reading and responding to it all would be matched by a material support he had never before known, fulfilling his every request almost before he could express it, from bedsocks, spats, and linen to special soap and toiletries, and tirelessly shopping for him for clothes, often changing them if necessary to meet his exacting specifications. With a sure instinct he called her from the first his 'little Nikê', for it was to her that he would owe his final victory—not only over the forces which threatened his poetic achievement, but also over the pervading sense of a lack of identity, springing from his early antipathy to his homeland and later to the German environment itself, which had made his so rootless a life, and now reinforced by the disintegration of the Austro-Hungarian state system.

At this point, indeed, he was no more than a stateless refugee, unless he decided to obtain a passport in his new Czechoslovak nationality, and even a return to Munich, now he rated as a foreigner there, looked problematical. For all his tendency to disparage the Swiss and the artificial beauties of their country, he was learning to appreciate the virtues of a solid and regulated bourgeois existence he had never yet known; and it was dawning on him that this multinational and multilingual society might offer the lifeline he needed, perhaps with a permanent home in the sort of surroundings he had glimpsed at Soglio. It was a thought which he aired during his tour to all who would listen, and in Basle, with Dory von der Mühll as guide, he had viewed a number of possible houses, without finding what he wanted. In desperation now to secure at least a temporary refuge for the winter, he had 'provoked, practically ordered' an invitation from a wealthy admirer from many years earlier, who he knew had a property in Ascona.[11] It was a shot in the dark he realized at once had failed, when early in December he came to see the small, primitive, and inadequately heated outhouse quarters proposed by the hostess, willing but with little idea of her guest's stringent requirements. The right place would not come to order, he reflected, and it was a mistake to try.

He had prudently gone first to the Grand Hotel in Locarno: and having extricated himself, frankly but tactfully, from the predicament, decided upon two rooms in the nearby Pension Muralto—not much bigger, in fact, but at least warm and with proprietors eager to meet all his wants. It was scarcely what he had hoped for—'disappointment, insecurity, and care are all I breathe here, in spite of all the clarity and sunshine,' he wrote to Werner Reinhart as he moved in[12]—but it became tolerably habitable as a succession of parcels and crates, with candlesticks, crockery, a tea-kettle, extra blankets, began to arrive from Nanny Wunderly. 'I'll have to stay in this repulsive pension for ever!' he wrote her just before Christmas, 'for who'll be able to pack up again what I've just unpacked?'[13] A lonely and introspective season was redeemed by the thought of her presence with him in spirit, and in gratitude he sent her transcripts of three of the Elegies.

It was lightened too by a letter from Dory von der Mühll with an invitation from her mother for him to stay at her country house Schönenberg, at Pratteln, just south of Basle. He could be assured there of the solitude he wanted and (an essential he had impressed upon Dory) enough room to walk up and down as he worked. This he would store up in gratitude for the future, he told her, giving his present quarters the chance for a while to show what they could do for him, but it was a prospect which could not be more heartening: 'it is there I should let myself be housed, just like that time at Duino, misanthropic and quiet, wordless, turned inward.'[14]

Disturbing, on the other hand, was the question of money. The honorariums from his tour—the literary societies, apart from Zurich, being small and ill-funded—had barely sufficed to see him from one stage to the next; Mary Dobržensky had been away in England; and with the mark sinking to nearly ten to the Swiss franc, Kippenberg had thought it inadvisable to answer his call for a remittance—indeed, had strongly urged him to return to Germany. As a result, notwithstanding his healthy balance with the Insel, by Christmas he was virtually penniless in Switzerland. Relief came, however, with Mary's return before the end of the year. 'Everything is smoothed over,' he wrote to Yvonne von Wattenwyl, 'my loans (foolish though it may be to continue thus) will go on, the little pension here is getting used to me . . . and the best thing is, it will not be for long, after it there come new possibilities of hospitality, perhaps this time . . . the right, favourable ones.'[15]

Once assured, the money ran through his fingers as it had always done: New Year's gifts, books of all types ordered as they took his fancy—Jules Romains, Mardrus's *History of the Queen of Sheba*, Pierre Loti, a reprint of an eighteenth-century Paris diary—and purchases of even more things for his overcrowded rooms, including an irresistible Louis-Quinze escritoire, which he described in minute and loving detail to Nanny Wunderly and destined for her home in Meilen when he moved. The effort to create an ambience for work was vain, however, against the background of his insecurity: he was still out on a limb, 'une branche bien séche'.[16] On 10 January came notification that his stay could not be prolonged beyond the end of March, so that even the Burckhardt refuge at Schönenberg, which he was looking forward to, could not last, and an end to his homelessness seemed as far away as ever.

While strict solitude could not be hoped for in such surroundings, he had only himself to blame for an additional involvement which, through January

and February, absorbed an inordinate amount of his time and—not unlike that
with Marthe in Paris—threatened to exhaust his emotional resources. Angela
Guttmann, a young Austrian woman, had lived in great poverty in Russia in an
unhappy first marriage, and later in Berlin with her second husband. Now sick
and alone in Locarno, and dependent on totally inadequate mark funds from
Germany, she reached out eagerly for Rilke's sympathy and aid after they had
chanced to meet. His interest in her sad story was enhanced when he
discovered her aspirations as a writer and poet, especially as he saw so much
that was Russian in her temperament: perhaps even more, when he learned of
her conversion to the Jewish faith, which for him—like Islam—had always
seemed closer to God than Christianity, in a people whose Old Testament had
'created a mighty God ... the beginning of a God'.[17]

He recognized at the outset the danger in laying himself open once again to
the demands of other people. Their readiness to reveal themselves to him, and
his *understanding* of their situation, he told Nanny Wunderly, tempted him
into a feeling of divine superiority, yet at the same time he knew himself all too
human for this to be more than mere semblance. But his almost clairvoyant
power to see the other's fate provoked an urge to help which could not be
resisted. It had so often proved a trap for him: but he always hoped it could
remain impersonal, his aid merely that of 'an observer who passes by, not
without loving, but still not dallying'.[18] Even for the professional counsellor,
the analyst or doctor, such distance is sometimes difficult to maintain: for Rilke
it was impossible. Before long, he was enmeshed, listening to Angela for hours,
arranging a new doctor, and spending whole afternoons and evenings by her
side when her illness kept her abed. It was partly the fascination of her early
poverty, with which nothing he had himself known, or depicted in *Malte*,
could compare, but also a genuine admiration for her work, in which he made
great efforts to interest journals and publishers. Such was his enthusiasm that
Georg Reinhart, on his recommendation, agreed to send money for her, and
Nanny Wunderly too organized a collection among her friends.

Whether he could have used to better purpose the time and energy thus
squandered, is questionable. He had longed to put an end to the purely verbal
communication that, except at Soglio, had occupied him ever since arriving in
Switzerland, to be able to sit alone and write: but a desk now, and attractive
notebooks from Nanny Wunderly's bindery, were not enough to help him
surmount the hill which blocked his path, and during early January day
followed day in self-doubt. He had begun a sort of diary, noting some of his
impressions, and held fast to the lifeline of Meilen, writing to his 'dear one'
there, sometimes more than once a day, everything that happened and every
thought that occurred to him—but none of this was 'work'. His desk was piled
high with outstanding correspondence, but at first even this came hard. 'God
knows why I maintain so many connections, sometimes I think it's a substitute

for my homeland, as if this wide-ranging network of influences provides a sort of finely-spread "being-somewhere",' he told Nanny; but he recognized that his letters had to be written for himself as much as for others. They were for 'the "cause", for that which is my work, in the end all my letters impart a vibration, a trace of its intensity'.[19]

By the middle of January he had roused himself to this essential preliminary. When he sent his Nikê a copy of his meticulously-kept list for the month, to earn her 'good mark' for his industry, it showed no fewer than eighty letters (not including seventeen of his diary-like missives to her, or those purely of business): most of at least four pages, many a good deal longer, and not a few his careful responses to those young women who sought encouragement for their own efforts, or solace in their unhappiness, from the admired poet.[20] Altogether, perhaps, hardly less exhausting than his daily ministrations for Angela Guttmann, but with the advantage of distance for the 'observer passing by'.

He wrote several times to Ruth, who was occupying his apartment while on a short visit to Munich, and arranged a remittance for her there from the Insel; but no letters to Clara appeared on this list. Their relationship was as friendly as ever, and he had entirely welcomed the promise of greater independence for her as the project for the house in Bredenau took shape, in spite of doubts over its financing. It had been disturbing, however, to hear at the end of October, not only that she needed a subsidy of some 3,000 marks, which he was happy to authorize from his Insel account, but also that she wanted him to take over the mortgage. Here he drew the line. 'I regard myself, as far as any aid is concerned which exceeds the agreed allowance, purely as "friend" of Clara Rilke and in no wise "duty-bound",' he told Kippenberg, sending him her letter, 'and feel this view not unjustified in a relationship that has been based for so many years on a precise and honest separation. But I see from this latest letter that it will soon be necessary, in all friendship, to make clearer the limits this defines.'[21] In Locarno, over Christmas, he had settled to this difficult task, in a letter to Clara which, as he told Nanny Wunderly, was essential to complete his own solitary existence, by removing the last trace of 'a tie long since dissolved'.[22] Clara was now so much more secured and independent that he felt the more formal separation would be welcome to her too. At the same time, however, he arranged with Kippenberg for her monthly allowance to be raised to 600 marks from February 1920.

Dory von der Mühll had sent him a sketch of Schönenberg, and by February he was looking forward to its solitude, even if it was only to be temporary. The responsibility he had shouldered for Angela Guttmann, however, was not easily to be abandoned, for she clung to him as her only friend. Day by day he put off his departure until he could feel she was provided for, taking endless trouble to find the most suitable sanatorium for her, and as he prepared to pack passing on to her many of the comforts Nanny Wunderly had provided. It was not until 27 February that he finally made up his mind to leave for Basle and Schönenberg.

3

'Suis-je donc condamné à vous faire tant, tant souffrir?'

(To Baladine Klossowska, 17.9.1920)

His new home was a moderately large country seat, built in the eighteenth century on to the home farm and serving now mainly as a summer retreat for the Burckhardt family. One wing was taken up by a long saloon facing north, furnished in succession as music room, dining-room, study, and drawing-room, and these, with a bedroom reached through a lobby at one corner, were to be Rilke's quarters—nineteen paces in all, he was delighted to find on arrival. It was reached from Basle within an hour, by train to Pratteln and then on foot. The surrounding rolling countryside, though not of great beauty and fast becoming industrialized, offered a prospect towards the Rhine valley, his first feeling of distance in Switzerland, with the mountains no longer 'importunate'.[1] Servants were there for him, but except when the von der Mühlls came to visit he would be alone as long as he chose. Old furniture, books and pictures, an ancestral desk at which to write, a gentle old Alsatian dog to trot with him on his walks, and the only cost what he might spend on himself—he could hardly have asked for better. As he wrote to Werner Reinhart after moving in, it would be his own fault if he remained unproductive at Schönenberg.[2]

He was still on too shifting a ground, however, for this to be more than a pious hope. With less than a month to go to the expiry of his permit, and a return to Germany apparently inevitable after that, it was hardly likely that he would find inspiration under conditions which, however favourable, looked to be so temporary. Before many days had passed the uncertainty began to make itself felt in an inordinate lassitude, and he suffered from the sudden return of wintry conditions, with which the small stoves in a house geared rather to summer occupation could not cope. The physical unease was reflected in an inability to settle even to letter-writing, and a growing dissatisfaction with the surroundings he had at first thought ideal (incredible, he felt, to own a house for decades without making any garden round it[3]).

In the middle of March, with the von der Mühlls' support, he obtained from the cantonal authorities an extension of his stay until 17 May, the expiry date of his Austrian passport. The reprieve, however, and the arrival at last of spring, brought no relief: for news came from Munich that residence was henceforth barred to all foreigners who had not lived there before August 1914, and there was a risk even that his apartment might be taken over. The only way out of the impasse seemed to be to apply for a passport in his new nationality, with which there would be a good chance of obtaining a full year's stay in Switzerland, perhaps also of revisiting the old scenes, Venice, or Paris even. With the mediation of a helpful journalist with Czech Legation contacts, he spent much time in April and May over the irritating bureaucratic requirements for this, which a flattering letter from the Minister did nothing to obviate ('Austria is dead, but her pedantry seems to live on in the new countries,' he told Nanny Wunderly).[4]

To this major concern was added a feeling of remorse over his desertion of Angela Guttmann, and his apprehension that he was not far enough away to be free of her importunity. He sent her the money Nanny had collected, interviewed a Basle publisher on her behalf, and hoped that short, more distant letters would keep her at bay: but she was not to be discarded so easily. She came in April to Basle, as he had feared, and there was nothing for it but to spend whole days there with her, arranging a doctor's help, introducing her to museum and library directors for a work she was planning on negro art, and trying gently to convince her of his own imperative need to be alone. 'My sick protégée has given me sublime joys, but also caused me very great worries,' he had written to Dory von der Mühll before leaving Locarno.[5] Though he succeeded at last in distancing himself, her troubles remained for a long time on his mind. In some ways it was one of the most difficult of his disengagements from the toils into which he was constantly allowing himself to be drawn. He had left Clara, even broken the deeper emotional ties with Benvenuta and Loulou Albert-Lazard, without compunction, in the certainty that his mission demanded a solitary life. Here, however, though that certainty remained, abandoning a 'protégée' made him conscious for the first time of guilt; for the pretext of solitude was in fact something of a fraud at Schönenberg. (Angela was to die two years later in Davos.)

Basle was all too accessible, and when he was not tempted there for one reason or another, there were visitors to the house he could not refuse. In Basle, with the von der Mühlls, or on visits he made during May to Nanny at Meilen, he seemed positively eager for the social life he had planned to avoid, and Schönenberg became more and more simply a way-station on the road to a still unknown destination. Towards the end of May he was in any case displaced to other quarters in the house, when the von der Mühlls moved out there for the summer and began to receive their own visitors. Among these were the Hofmannsthals, old friends whom they had been endeavouring to help over the sale of some *objets d'art* (it was Rilke himself who succeeded in securing Werner Reinhart as the buyer for a small Rodin bronze—characteristically concealing from Hofmannsthal his part as intermediary).

In his dilemma over the future he adopted an essentially passive attitude. He took such minimum insurance as was necessary to keep the options open— applying for the new passport, arranging for Hans Feist, a writer, to occupy his

Munich apartment to prevent its being taken over, and then making an official submission there to establish his right to return, in which he was eventually successful—but still held fast to the belief that somehow Providence would come to his aid and that chance, not planning, would be his salvation. Claire Studer, now with Ivan Goll in Paris, wrote enthusiastically of the possibilities of living there, even with the bad exchange: but much as he longed to return, he told her, it could not be just of his own volition—'it would have to be in my stars'.[6]

Schönenberg, at all events, was clearly no longer the place in which to wait. When he heard from the von der Mühlls, on their return from a short visit to Venice at the end of April, that there seemed few difficulties in the way of such a journey, he grasped at the thought of joining Marie Taxis there. She had urged him to come while she was there during June, and her *mezzanino* in the Palazzo Valmarana could be at his disposal after she left. 'It can't really be the ideal for you, but for the moment I really think it's the most practical.'[7] His Czech passport finally arrived early in May. With it in his hand he obtained a temporary extension of stay until 11 June, and immediately applied for a full year's permit, after which there was no problem in securing the visa for Italy, and in fact a re-entry valid till the end of the month. It would be his first step into real freedom, he thought, for which Switzerland had seemed no more than a waiting-room—and most of all, a step towards restoring the lost continuity of his life.

When he arrived in Venice on 10 June, it was almost uncanny, after eight years, to find it so unchanged—as in a dream, or like the exact fulfilment of a mortal's wish in a fairy story. The Princess, the Valmaranas, the familiar *mezzanino* with the Louis-Seize writing-desk he had left there and forgotten; the city (practically undamaged by the little bombing it had suffered during the war) just as he remembered it, perhaps even improved by the strike of *vaporetto* crews which left the silent gondolas as the only transport; the 'warm marble of Venetian bridges' as comforting as ever to the touch.[8] With Pia Valmarana and her mother he found himself talking of their time together in 1912 as if it were only the previous year. One appreciable change was the greatly increased cost of living, but his few Swiss francs and a cabled remittance from Kippenberg were enough to allow him a longer stay than he had at first envisaged.

What was unsettling, however, was to find that he himself had not changed either, and that the return to Venice seemed not so much a continuity as a repetition, such as he had experienced nowhere before, and in which there could be only a 'hopeless sterility'.[9] Holding his breath, as it were, through the war years, he had been preserved—but preserved unchanged, without having achieved the inner progress which alone could have given Venice's too faithful reproduction of the past a rhythm. He realized this with a feeling almost of revulsion; and the last straw was to learn that the Duse was on her way back to Venice. 'The thought that this too was to repeat itself seemed to me so frightful, that overnight I decided to set off back to Switzerland.'[10]

As an attempt to mend his links with the past it was a failure. 'Aussi ce voyage ne m'a-t-il avancé en rien,' he wrote to Marthe later—any more than his stay in Switzerland, for that matter, which was not without its charm, but unrelated 'either to my past, or to the future, inscrutable still and all the more uncertain when I cannot see the place where I am to wait for it'.[11] Ideas were not lacking from his ever indulgent friends—Princess Marie offered him a small house on the Lautschin estate, the Valmaranas suggested one near Padua, there was talk of a converted monastery in Taormina—but none of these could be more than a temporary asylum, and he was more certain now than ever that only a settled existence could bring a return of inspiration. As he left Venice, on 13 July, to remain any longer in Switzerland seemed out of the question, if only because Mary Dobržensky's loans were at an end now that she herself had had to return home to Bohemia; he would have to go on temporizing through the summer in Germany, then perhaps in Lautschin, which he had half accepted.

Inevitable though that seemed, however, he could not in the event bring himself to leave the stability of Switzerland for the uneasy and disorderly conditions which reigned, as he heard, in Germany and his own homeland. After a visit to Meilen, he returned to Schönenberg for the rest of July: but instead of packing for final departure, as he had intended, he could not resist a brief tour of farewell to Geneva and Berne—and the few days became weeks, as he put off again and again 'le retour pénible'. Geneva had never appeared so beautiful, 'so radiant and blowing and open', and he regretted not having spent his winter there, in spite of the *bise*, instead of in Locarno.[12] His room in the Hotel des Bergues looked out across the Ile de Rousseau; the city, the lake, the 'graduated tiara' of the Salève and the Savoy Alps beyond were bathed in a clear light through which Paris and France seemed to wait over to him; and he gave himself up to unashamed enjoyment of days 'wrested arbitrarily and somewhat foolishly from an uncertain future'.[13] Georges Pitoëff, just back from a successful tour in Paris, he saw almost daily, experiencing for the first time the actor as true artist, independent in the Rodin sense, as he listened to him going through a play script and conjuring up the whole scene in word and vivid gesture. 'That is *theatre*,' he wrote to Marie Taxis. 'If I could arrange it, I would work a whole year near Pitoëff, attend all his rehearsals—for genius is the only thing which really grips and concerns us.'[14]

He was borrowing time, in the hope that the 'miracle' might yet come to pass. For a brief moment he was tempted by the offer of a new friend, the architect Guido von Salis, to let him occupy his chalet at Petit-Saconnex during his absence, set in quiet park-like surroundings reminiscent of

Aleksandr Benois' dacha near St. Petersburg, twenty years before. It was not miracle enough, for it could only last a few weeks, and with regret he had to decide against. Still he stayed on, delighting in the bookshops and little cafés of the rue de Carouge, and thinking 'Paris thoughts'. 'When I see over a house the sign "Bonnetterie", it somehow makes me happy,' he wrote to Nanny Wunderly, 'and much that is German is liberated in me at the sight of the big French inscription. Ah Chère, ce ne sera vraiment qu'à Paris que je me sentirai capable de continuer ma vie, mais il faut avoir patience . . .'[15]

One of his first calls, on arriving, had been in the rue due Pré-Jérôme, just off the rue de Carouge, where that other exile from Paris, Baladine Klossowska, was living with her two young sons. They had corresponded occasionally since the previous year, and he had sent her a copy of the Louize Labé sonnets, and roses after his visit in October. With few other acquaintances in Geneva, and so much to remind him of Paris, it was natural he should seek the company of an artist like those he had known there before the war: and they met often in the few days before she had to leave for a stay arranged with friends at Beatenberg, near Lake Thun.

She knew little of his work, so that their relationship had none of the overtones of admiration for the poet which had attracted so many women to him. It rested rather on shared reminiscences of Paris and the common bond of refugees who longed to return there. On the afternoon before her departure, however, as they lingered on her balcony, something seemed to happen: though nothing was said, he surprised a tenderness in her glance that spoke of a stronger bond than friendship, and in that charged moment there was an awakening of passion which they would both look back on with emotion. Geneva seemed empty without her, and although she had not given him an address in Beatenberg, he wrote at once in the hope his letter would reach her. Her thoughts were full of him, as she read for the first time his *Book of Hours*. When he telegraphed that he would be in Berne on 21 August, she came down immediately to join him for two days, and they were together there again at the end of the month—brief, idyllic days in which they wandered as lovers through the old city.

'Merline', as she liked to be called, or sometimes 'Mouky', was eleven years younger than he, tall and dark, a striking rather than beautiful figure, with little of the immediate appeal of Loulou or Benvenuta, or the sensual allure of Claire Studer—if anything, more like Clara, though of a much more demonstrative and passionate character. Not that such comparisons will have entered his head: the strongest element in her attraction for him was probably her embodiment of Paris, and with it the sense of a restoration of the continuity he was seeking in his life. Though German was for both the mother tongue, it was almost entirely in French that they talked and corresponded, in French that he wrote his first verse for her, when they met in Berne, and visited Fribourg together.

Qui nous dit que tout disparaisse?
de l'Oiseau que tu blesses,
qui sait, s'il ne reste que le vol,
et peut-être les fleurs des caresses
survivent à nous, à leur sol. . . .[16]

It was symbolic that for her he should become 'René' again: with her love, he seemed a step nearer Paris, and he even began now to think of a visit there before obeying the call back to Germany, which for the moment he was still contriving to evade thanks to subventions from Nanny Wunderly and other friends.

The shadow of eventual parting lay across their path from the start: even if he could stay on in Switzerland, as he hoped, he knew only too well his need to be alone if he was ever to complete the Elegies. When she wrote that he had given her an 'almost unknown happiness' which she could not reconcile with her life as it was, he tried to convince her that while together, if only for an instant, they lived in a dimension quite outside reality, and that whatever might happen, her heart must be calm in that knowledge—a delicate hint of the distance he must keep. Belied though this was by the passionate intensity of his letters and his outward attentions—the flowers he sent, the copies of his books, his return to join her again in Geneva early in September—she bravely maintained that the knowledge of their love would content her: 'Je t'aime tant que je peux te quitter'. In her copy of *Malte* he had written:

Fullness is not merely there to fret us,-
all have had but inklings, none possess.
Let us not fear suffering, but let us
exercise pure hearts upon excess.[17]

For her, it was a resolution that would prove hard to keep; and he did not make it easier by writing of the 'miracle' of their communion, or describing his hotel room in Berne, as he left for Zurich at the end of August, as his 'garden of love—nowhere, save in the lonely ecstasies of my work, was my heart more fulfilled!'[18] or by coming then to Geneva for twenty-four hours and staying a week. Past experience should have taught him that to surrender thus to 'this dream' was to store up trouble for the future. But, as he confided to Nanny Wunderly, he felt a sublime freedom: 'I believe I am needed, and this time when I leave I must not be pursued by the slightest regret at not having granted, to a heart that has opened to me, everything in me worthy of it.'[19]

His zig-zag course across Switzerland, to Geneva, Ragaz, Meilen, and Zurich, he still looked on as a tour of farewell—short of the miracle he hoped for. Just outside Berne he had gazed with longing through a park gate at a majestic avenue of chestnuts leading up to the little château of Holligen: 'an avenue, a house like that for a year, and I would be saved,' he wrote that night to Nikê. 'I felt if I could walk up and into a lofty study awaiting me there, I would be working this very evening! (Am I making excuses? I'm sure I am fooling myself, even then I'd discover deficiencies, barriers, interruptions, difficulties ...) But still, why should I be moved by such avenues ... protective, dark, ceremonious ... in the old trees an evening bird sang, just one, as though asking whether the stillness was deep enough for the feel of his sound ... it was—'[20]

Merline found unbearable the renewed separation after his September visit to Geneva, and implored him at least to stay in Switzerland. 'Am I then condemned to make you suffer so much?' he wrote from Zurich on 17 September, as he tried to give her strength. 'I still carry with me the little handkerchief that was wet with your weeping—as a symbol that your tears will always dry on my heart, all your tears—and let me believe, my love, that I support you day and night, that I do not abandon you for an instant.' 'But we are human beings, René,' she cried—and could not believe that with him she could be a danger to his work: if he thought that, he must tell her, and she would be strong enough to give him up. He did think so, of course; but would not have it that their love should be renounced, no matter what it cost them if he found the place for his work in solitude.

Among the fundamental promises of our love was that nothing should be forced ... to take into our own hands, as it were, this beginning of happiness would make us perhaps the first to destroy it; it must remain on the anvil of its Creator, under the hammer blows of the great Artisan ... Let us place our poor confidence in Him, Merline: it's true we shall always feel the shock of the hammer ... but we shall also be called from time to time to admire this favourite work of His which He will bring to final perfection ...

He knew that the sacrifice demanded more of her, as a woman, than of him, but begged her to find the courage to support the 'deferment of love that seems to lie in this task', as he put it.[21]

He had hunted through the Zurich bookshops for a copy of Bettina's correspondence with Goethe—'the same edition I've always read, how many times!'—and sent it with rose petals marking the 'sublime passages' she would discover:

> Malte
> l'envoie à M—
> qui de son admirable cœur
> immensément
> confirme la gloire de
> Bettine.[22]

But for Merline the example of heroic renunciation was impossible to follow, and in the face of her despairing appeals his own resolution wavered, just at the moment when there seemed a chance of a haven in Switzerland which might suit his purpose to perfection.

Richard and Lily Ziegler, friends of Nanny Wunderly's, said they were ready to install him for the winter in their property Schloss Berg am Irchel, a seventeenth-century manor house north of Zurich towards the Rhine, which they occupied only during the summer months. If the problems of his subsistence and of his Swiss permit could be solved (six months only had been granted, expiring in November), he had no doubt that this retreat, which he had in fact visited with Nanny early in August, could be just what he needed: but now he agonized over leaving Merline. 'Your letters, your letters—it's like the sea, I plunge in from the highest cliff, from the topmost summit of my heart beyond which there is only the infinite . . . If you could but succeed in removing from me this last vestige of fear of love . . . perhaps I would slowly begin to understand why God wanted me to survive that poor Malte . . .'[23] Unable to resist the call, he returned without warning to Geneva on 3 October: and for a while, in her company, persuaded himself that there need be no conflict between life and work. Geneva, so like Paris, could after all offer him a retreat, in the shape of a small apartment in the old city which Guido von Salis suggested for him and which, impulsively, he reserved from 1 November (how he was to meet even this modest rent, he left in the lap of the gods), and Merline's love would surely be a support rather than a disturbance.

Meantime, as he began to plan his visit to Paris, they abandoned care in a journey to the Valais—to Sion and Sierre, along the valley of the Rhône which linked him in spirit to France. Merline's husband, Erich Klossowski, who lived in Zurich, was holidaying in Sierre with his friend Jean Strohl, a zoology professor, and Strohl's wife Frida: long separated from Merline, Klossowski made no demur at their joining them, and the five made a congenial party of tourists, Rilke on excellent terms with both the husband and the Strohls. The Valais he found outstandingly beautiful, a countryside strangely reminiscent of Provence and of Spain but 'a little less fanatical, a little more conciliatory'.[24] It seemed the beginning of the continuity which Paris could restore, and which he felt he must regain before his work could resume: and already he began to have doubts about his over-hasty decision to winter in Geneva.

In Berne on 16 October, to collect his passport, validated for France by the Czech Legation, he found a letter from Nikê, enclosing photographs and details of Schloss Berg, with something of an ultimatum from the Zieglers: they wanted him to make up his mind without delay, as they would be vacating it shortly. It was clear that he must accept: not only would the conditions be as favourable as he could wish, with Nikê ready to arrange a housekeeper to care for him, but also it was the only solution his means could afford. 'I foresee my stay in Paris will reinforce still further my desire for complete and long solitude,' he wrote to Merline, breaking the news that he had cancelled the Geneva apartment. 'When I touch again my former life that was cruelly interrupted, I shall find myself committed to making great efforts for continuity, and I believe I can do it in the lonely surroundings afforded by this old house better than anywhere else.' Still in the euphoria of their unforgettable days together, she was ready for the sacrifice, and in Basle the next day he received her reply, 'consentante et heureuse'.[25]

If he showed more than his usual vacillation over the decision, it was because never yet had separation from a mistress caused him such anguish. Yet there was an underlying tenacity of purpose. The solitary conditions he wanted were at hand at Berg, and he knew that the essential first step towards healing the breach in his life, and preparing himself for fruitful exploitation of this fortunate turn, was to see Paris again, no matter that it could be only a brief visit. It seemed a sign that this instinct was right, when he received just before leaving Basle a warmly dedicated copy from Gide of his *Symphonie pastorale*—apart from one of Charles Vildrac's books, sent similarly earlier in the year, his first real contact with France since the war. What he sought in Paris, however, was not its people, but its things and places—the renewal of contact with scenes which were irreplaceable settings for his inner life and which, if anything could, would revive it. It was enough to walk the familiar streets again and into the Luxembourg Gardens, discovering 'la même plénitude de vie, la même intensité, la même justesse même dans le mal'. 'If I could remain here, I would have my life back, all its dangers, all its happinesses: my whole life, as it always was ...' In the Odéon Arcade he bought a new notebook, entering in it the words 'Ici commence l'indicible'— and writing no more, surrendering himself totally to the 'living contact' Paris offered, wandering around without aim, 'for every step is an arrival'. Six days only, but they were 'an inexpressible healing' for his spirit.[26] He recognized the shopkeepers, the people in the newspaper kiosks, the displays of the *bouquinistes*; even the blind man, whose life had so occupied him in 1902, still stood at his post on the Pont du Carrousel. It was Malte's Paris, but for the first time now it seemed to compensate him for his suffering under it.

'I bring you back a heart quite liberated by these splendours of a Paris autumn,' he wrote to Merline on 29 October, announcing his arrival in Geneva the following day: 'it was not a dream, it was the most penetrating reality, and I belonged to it, but without ceasing to belong to you, my darling.'[27] No sterile repetition, as in Venice, but a marvellous completion of a circle: the "broken-off surfaces' had been re-joined, and he was ready, as he wrote to Georg Reinhart from Geneva, 'to plunge, blindly, into the winter of work'.[28] To Kippenberg, who had not heard from him since August and thought him long since back in Munich, he reported the change in his fortunes and his hopes of the retreat in Berg: much like the hospitality in Duino, 'less grand, but with similar quiet and security ... with which my extended time in Switzerland shall be rounded off ... Now only one important thing is lacking for this start of winter, good friend: your approval'.[29]

4

'Et si je penche enfin du côté de ma gloire,
Crois qu'il m'en a coûté, pour vaincre tant d'amour,
Des combats dont mon cœur saignera plus d'un jour.'

(Racine, *Bérénice*)

No poet ever had so smooth a path to ideal conditions for his work as Rilke's to Berg. While he lingered in Geneva, preoccupied only with the coming parting from Merline, the Zieglers, and especially Nanny Wunderly, took infinite trouble to prepare for his arrival. The housekeeper was duly recruited from the neighbouring village of Flaach, and Nikê was often up at the house during the first days of November to see to the arrangements. Every detail of practical life was settled without his having to lift a finger, even to a supply of wine, cigars, and cigarettes which Ziegler, a bluff colonel in charge of the Federal Remount Depot, evidently considered essential to any guest's well-being, as well as assuring him support for the application for extension of the permit, which would be needed by 17 November. Nikê's selfless devotion even moved her to write a letter to Merline, an 'inspiration of the heart' for which Rilke was profoundly grateful.[1] All he had to do was to come to Zurich and let himself be driven with her up to Berg. Everything, it seemed to him, was fitting into place like the cogs in a smooth-running machine.

Entering into his new domain, on 12 November, he felt it was a miracle indeed to find provided for him so exactly the conditions he had dreamed of since Soglio: solitude among old things, a few books (Goethe, Molière, Stendhal) to hand, a silence which seemed only intensified by the quiet chiming of the clocks and the rustle of the fountain into the small lake in the park extending before his window; the ministrations of Leni Gisler, the housekeeper, as unobtrusive as 'a favourable climate'. 'Everything is right, down to the smallest detail.'[2] As if to underline his seclusion, a recent outbreak of foot and mouth disease in the area confined his movements to the park, so that, apart from Leni, his only contact was with the pastor Rudolf Zimmermann, who acted as the village messenger while the restrictions lasted, even bringing up his modest milk supplies. Over his door, he felt, should stand Thomas à Kempis's words 'Cella continuata dulcescit': here, if anywhere, he must be able to find the way back to himself, 'the overgrown path to the inmost centre of work'.[3]

He was under no illusion that his progress could be anything but painfully slow. Five years had gone by since the call-up had dammed the stream of the Elegies, years of outward preoccupation in which he had brought forth little but an occasional dedicatory verse. Ground so long fallow would require laborious preparation to become productive again; and, as always for him, the first turn of the spade, the preliminary digging over to prepare for the deep trenching, must be the resumption of his correspondence. Though shut away, he was anything but incommunicado, and the village postmaster and his wife never worked so hard in their lives as in the handling of the flood of registered letters that came now from Schloss Berg. Friends far and wide—including many, such as Hertha Koenig and Eva Cassirer, for whom his overlong silences must have seemed a poor return for their help—heard his jubilant cry of hope, in sharp contrast to the litany of despair of the war years, and his deliverance at having found at last the surroundings he needed.

For them too the news was an uncommon relief. Princess Marie and the Kippenbergs were only too ready to forgive his interminable hesitations when they learned he had settled into a hermit-like existence which held such promise. He constantly stressed his need to 'spin himself into his cocoon', and firmly resisted all invitations: from Jean Strohl to Zurich, where he would have met Albert Schweitzer, from Hans Reinhart to the première of his play with Pitoëff in Geneva, or from Nanny Wunderly to Klossowski's lecture on Daumier in Winterthur, which he had himself suggested to Georg Reinhart. 'As soon ask the pupa in the chrysalis to take an occasional walk, as expect me to make the slightest movement.'[4] Though he hoped and planned for a visit from the Kippenbergs, now that he was so near the frontier, he made it clear that they would be welcome only for a short time; and he discouraged Ruth from her idea of joining them, any twinge of conscience he may have had allayed by asking that the long Christmas list she had sent him and the small regular allowance she wanted should be met generously from his Insel funds. He had rarely guarded his isolation so jealously.

Over literally hundreds of pages, through November and December, he spread himself in endless variations on the theme of hope from seclusion, and in carefully constructed replies to the many correspondents who continued to seek his advice on their lives or their work—letters which, as he put it to Lily Ziegler, had the effect of a 'a clearing-out of the depths of the spirit', gave practice to 'the long-neglected pen', and acted as 'a kind of transition from the verbal and communicative to the written word of work that is no longer addressed to any individual'.[5] It was a transition that would be long and arduous. 'Since this solitude closed around me (and it was total, right from the first day),' he wrote to Merline, 'I sense once again the fearful, inconceivable polarity of life and the supreme task. How far off it is, that work, how distant the Angels. I shall progress but slowly, advancing only half a step each day and often falling back.' But he must at all costs sustain this act of 'devotion and obedience', he told her, and resist the temptation to slip away and join her over Christmas. He had to retreat into himself, try to recapture emotions which lay eight years back, and complete the task laid upon him—the Elegies which she did not yet know.[6]

Aside from the reams of letters, his first 'work' in Berg, 'if it can be taken thus seriously',[7] came as a sort of recompense to Merline for her patience.

While with her in Geneva, he had been greatly taken with a series of drawings by her younger son, Baltusz, made the previous year when he was only eleven and already showing signs of the creative talent later to bring him world fame. They were of 'Mitsou', a foundling kitten—the story in pictures of its life with him and the family until the sad day when it was lost again. Rilke, who was beginning to feel he was himself part of the family, and was held in great affection both by Baltusz and the elder boy Pierre, was so enthusiastic over the work that he had found a publisher for it in Zurich, and proposed to write a short preface himself. On 26 November, walking his hundred and twenty paces in the park, he composed the preface in his mind, and that evening wrote it down, gratified at having produced something which had been thought in French without a word of translation.

Merline, and Baltusz especially, were delighted: and Rilke was pleased enough with the trifle to send copies to other friends. Who really knows cats? he wrote. For himself, he confessed that 'their existence was never more than a rather doubtful hypothesis'. Animals must enter into our life a little if they are to be part of it: dogs seem to have given up their canine traditions 'to adore our habits and even our errors', living on the border of their nature and constantly crossing it with 'their humanized look and their nostalgic muzzles'. But cats— they are a world to themselves. 'Do we ever know if they deign for an instant to register our futile image on the depths of their retina? . . . Was man ever their contemporary? I doubt it. And I assure you that sometimes, at twilight, the neighbour's cat jumps over my body, ignoring me, or as though to prove to the stupefied material world that I do not exist.' But—after seeing Baltusz's story—the reader may be reassured: 'I am. Baltusz exists. There are no cats.'[8]

It was a charming effort, but in every sense a diversion, scarcely the practice needed for his 'long-neglected pen': and a day or two after completing it, a singular experience seemed to emphasize that the emotions which had begun the Elegies, still dormant, were not yet ready to be revived. One evening some strange verses 'came' to him, which he could not feel were his own:

> These mountains rest, by higher stars out-splendoured—
> yet twinkling there is time again no less.
> Oh, to my wild heart comes the re-engendered,
> always unhoused imperishableness.[9]

He heard, rather than thought them, he told Kippenberg afterwards, and described how, as he sat by the fireside later, there seemed to materialize in the chair opposite a gentleman in eighteenth-century dress, who read from an old, faded manuscript a series of poems, in which these verses also appeared and which Rilke transcribed. As title for the cycle, ten poems almost entirely in similar rhyming quatrains, he put 'From the literary remains of Count C. W.'—for he maintained always that they were not his own work, and he bolstered the fiction by an occasional 'Transcriber's Note', much as he had done for Malte's notebooks.

He had no illusions that this 'dictation' by an imagined revenant, though it made a good story, could be compared with the compulsive inspiration of Duino. So much is clear from his light-hearted words to Nanny Wunderly on this 'stimulating game', when on the night it was finished he promised her a copy he was making, like the 'Mitsou' preface, in one of the little brochures of special paper of her own binding, with which she kept him supplied.

I felt a longing for some trace of a predecessor at Berg, a manuscript perhaps that I might discover in a bookcase one evening. . . . I started to picture to myself, quite superficially, such a figure . . . but I could not find the manuscript, so what else could I do but write it myself? . . . (the whole thing took scarcely three days, done I should think rather like knitting)—and only now do I realize how . . .: not yet properly fit and prepared, it seems, for production of my own, I had to have this figure as a kind of pretext, a personality which could be responsible for what was taking shape at this highly inadequate stage of concentration: and that was Count C. W.[10]

Oddly enough, it did not end there. A few months later, while he was still at Berg, the 'Count' 'dictated' a further cycle of eleven poems. Rilke made copies of the first group for the Kippenbergs, as well as for Nikê, and of the whole later for Princess Marie, but persisted in disclaiming responsibility for verses which did not measure up to his exacting standards. Their smooth rhyming and facile imagery were indeed remote from the dense style of the Elegies it was his aim to recapture. He had invented a character from the past, but in a much more shadowy form than Malte, and linked with his own experience only in rare snatches. The only one of the poems he allowed to be published (and that anonymously), in the *Insel Almanach* for 1923, was an evocation of Karnak as he had seen it in 1911, with the great column and the avenue of sphinxes—the 'Count' and his 'Hélène' like himself and Jenny Oltersdorf:

> Why could it not help us more helpfully?
> That we endured it was enough indeed:
> you in your travelling dress, the invalid,
> and I the hermit in my theory.[11]

In a curious way, however, it had been a beginning, a step towards concentration, and in December, as he approached the end of the list of letters he had set himself to write, his 'letter-pen' began to yield place to that reserved for work proper. Though he liked to draw this distinction to many of his correspondents, if only by way of preparing them for further silence, the two pens were virtually one: for with meticulous care he would make a copy of whole letters, or extracts, which he felt had expressed in prose what must be distilled into lyric form, or were in other ways significant for the development of his ideas. At Berg, in truly settled conditions at last, remote from all verbal intercourse, and feeling himself in transition to the universal communication he saw as his mission, his urge to this self-documentation was stronger than ever before, while for the first time he had to hand the means to systematize it, in his craftsmanlike way, making another of Nikê's bound brochures into a commonplace book.

This too was work, in an interactive process from which there now began to glimmer the results he longed for. In one letter on his list, to which a reply had been long outstanding, was a voice from the distant past—that of his German teacher at the St. Pölten military college, now a Major-General, naïvely expressing his joy at having been privileged to meet 'in the golden age of his youth' the 'noble poet who has bestowed on us so rich a treasury of true poetry'.[12] This sincere effusion had called up for Rilke again all the 'horrors' of a time he had always tried to forget; and while he still pondered whether to reply at all, in the first days on December an elegy on the theme of childhood began to take shape, linked in his mind perhaps with the final passages of that completed in 1915:

> Don't let the fact that Childhood has been, that nameless
> bond between Heaven and us, be revoked by fate.
> Even the prisoner, gloomily dying in a dungeon,
> it has sat by and secretly nursed to the end, with its timeless
> hold on the heart. For the sufferer,
> when he staringly understands, and his room has ceased to reply,
> because, like all the other possessions around him,
> feverish, fellow-suffering, it's curable,—even for him
> Childhood avails, for purely
> its cordial bed blooms among nature's decay.
>
> Not that it's harmless.
>
> . . . .
>
> It is no more certain than we and never more shielded;
> no god can counterbalance its weight. Defenceless
> as we ourselves, defenceless as beasts in winter.
> . . . Defenceless
> as fire, giants, poison, as goings-on
> at night in suspect houses with bolted doors. . . .[13]

'How unsuspecting a creature is a child,' he wrote to Mieze Weininger on 2 December: 'it grows up and out from the anxious and unhealthy conditions of its family, builds for itself . . . on new ground outside its own values—and yet, in its most active years, is overtaken by every conceivable misfortune and plunged into a martyrdom whose deepest point, if it is not bottomless, lies a thousand leagues below the endurable!'[14]

> For who can fail to see that the guardian hands
> lie, while trying to defend it,—themselves in danger? Who *may*, then?
> 'I!'
> —What I?
> 'I, mother, I *may*. I was fore-world. . . .'
>
> . . . .

But anxiety!—Learnt all at once in that disconnexion
formed by us, by insolid humanity: draughtily
jerks itself in through the cracks: glides up from behind,
over its play, to the child, and hisses
dissension into its blood,—the swift suspicions that later,
always, only a part will be comprehensible, always
some single piece of existence, five pieces, perhaps, but never
combinable all together, and all of them fragile.
And forthwith splits in the spine the twig of the will,
for it to grow into a forked doubting branch,
grafted on to the Judas-tree of selection.[15]

While he was still working on the draft of this poem, on 9 December, he wrote a long reply to the General, copying it in full into the commonplace book—for, as he told Nikê, it was his first pronouncement on that 'distant and suppressed time in my life' and of great importance to him.[16] No golden age of youth, in those five years of military college, his former teacher learned: for the boy René, they had been nothing but a ruthless visitation, an 'abyss of undeserved misery', an 'inscrutable calamity', which he had been as incapable of understanding as 'the miracle which finally . . . delivered me'. He could not have lived his life, had he not denied and repressed all memory of an experience which for a ten-year-old was comparable with the Siberian prison for Dostoevsky. Only later, in Russia, had he realized that, like Dostoevsky enduring the unendurable, he had come to achieve free play for his soul, 'a fourth dimension of existence where true liberty can be found, however oppressive the outward conditions'—and so, with the years, had attained a 'certain reconciliation' with that earlier destiny. It had not destroyed him, so it had to be seen as a weight in the scales of his life which only the 'purest achievement' could outbalance; and that, since Russia, had been his resolve.[17]

Though he had often confided to others the 'tortures' he had gone through in his military schooling, this was indeed his first attempt to set down fully what those years had really meant. The repression, which had inhibited him from ever writing his 'military novel', was finally released in this cool self-analysis, and he could turn it at last to positive account. He even began now to feel he could be fairer towards the oppressive Prague of his boyhood, and to hope that that 'secret and noble city' could be absorbed into his experience like Moscow, Toledo, or 'Paris the incomparable'.[18] The interplay between letter and poem is unmistakable, even if we did not know they were being conceived at the same time. It is clear that he felt he had found the starting-point for continuing the Elegies; and towards the turn of the year he made a fair copy, destined for the Princess, of the four so far completed.

Could he have been as hermetically sealed off as he had wished, the breakthrough would have been assured: but the weeks till the end of the year brought distractions, and the new elegy obstinately remained a fragment.

Letters, forwarded in packets from Munich, arrived to restart the correspondence list he had managed to strike through; Christmas presents had to be prepared, even if shopping expeditions were unnecessary thanks to the aid of Nikê and Lily Ziegler; and while he could hope to be alone over the festive season, he was quite unreasonably worried by the prospect of visitors around the New Year. Nikê of course was welcome, but Colonel Ziegler had also announced himself, and the Kippenbergs were now expected in the early days of January. He could not imagine how he and his quiet household would be able to cope with these 'two life-sized people, with their thoughts, feelings, habits, where mine, it seems to me, already fill every last corner here'. Good and loyal friends though they were, he quailed at the thought of all that talk, and wished he had never thought of asking them.[19]

These were minor, if cumulative, encroachments of 'life' upon 'work': the real problem was Merline. With her, he had thought that for the first time the conflict between love and work was resolved: surrendering totally to her love for him, she had yet shown the fortitude to respect his need to be alone at Berg. The temptation to break out from his cell and visit her was powerful, and he had in fact asked, and received, from Nikê the funds needed for the journey. But he had resisted: and while he waited for new inspiration he had experienced an uncommon liberation of spirit, freedom to indulge his passion on paper in the assurance that she understood.

'Ce n'est pas de l'écriture, c'est de la respiration par la plume': not even to Benvenuta had he launched into such a glorification of love—a love which should stand beyond time, and in whose strength he could be confident of success.

Merline, yes, my darling, help me in this heroic way, join yourself to this quiet countryside, to these peaceful walls protecting me, protect me with them ... and if, as I descend to the depths of my work, a dark miner disappearing from the light, I send you only a rare, brief word, as a hunter lying in wait signals instead of speaking, for fear of disturbing the approaching game—do not be sad, my tender beloved, do not feel abandoned, forlorn, forgotten. Think rather that where I am buried I am drawing near to the other side of your heart, in silence—for how near our exalted moments were to this sublime core at which my ardour in work takes fire!

My dearest, dearest one, I have such longing to fold my arms about you, they open constantly without my knowing, and if your love is personified when I am with you ... my own, I swear, fills all the distance between us, everything around you to the limit of your view, everything you breathe, Merline, *is my love*, be sure of that.[20]

She was a correspondent worthy of such flights—'I carry you in me, I am your shrine, for you are holy ... you are my creator'[21]—but as Christmas approached it was becoming evident, despite her brave words, that dithyrambs from afar were not enough to reconcile her to the separation. Still protesting that her only wish was for him to 'disappear' into his work, she made no secret of her longing for his presence; and he was shaken to hear that at Christmas she was in crippling pain from lumbago, as well as having Baltusz in bed with a fever.

Urging her to send for her sister from Germany, he was himself still determined to stay where he was, and in his many end-of-year letters to others he was full of hope that the breakthrough was at hand. He was resigned by now, however, to a dead period at least until after the Kippenbergs' visit. When he heard on 4 January, not without some relief, that Katharina was too ill to make the journey and her husband's arrival was delayed, and by the same mail that Merline's condition had worsened, he resisted no longer, and two nights later was back in the Hôtel des Bergues in Geneva. It was apparent that Merline must have nursing at once, and until her sister could arrive this was arranged with a friend from Berne. Georg Reinhart, on Rilke's urgent request, came to their aid with a badly needed loan, and for a few days Merline was able to take a room in the hotel until, leaving the boys in her sister's capable hands, she departed with Rilke to Berg for a week's recuperation.

They arrived on 23 January, just in time for him to welcome Kippenberg, whose stay—perhaps mercifully—would be only until the following day. What the publisher made of the presence of 'Mouky' went unrecorded: but finding Rilke in such obviously congenial surroundings, and hearing the story of 'Count C. W.', left him less insistent on a return to Germany, and he undertook to arrange storage with the Insel of the books and more important of the other possessions still in the Munich apartment, against the day when, as Rilke hoped, a more permanent 'Berg' could be discovered in Switzerland. He was expansive enough also to agree to Rilke's plea for a monthly allowance for Regina Ullmann, whose latest story recently published seemed to hold the highest promise, and—best of all—promised a remittance to Rilke of 2,000 Swiss francs. Though it was so brief, the visit had made Berg complete for the first time, Rilke wrote after his friend's departure, and in every sense ready for a more confident exploitation.

His hopes were to prove illusory, and the distractions he had thought would be only temporary found no end in the months that followed. Merline's health was somewhat restored by her stay, but when he accompanied her to Zurich on 1 February for her train back to Geneva, there was now a greater concern to occupy them. Like him, the Klossowskis had had to abandon most of their possessions in Paris upon the outbreak of war, and the exchange problem in Switzerland had brought both Merline and her husband to the point where a move to Germany seemed inevitable, much as they loathed the prospect, especially for its effect on the hitherto entirely French education of Pierre and Baltusz. Klossowski was in fact already in Munich, on a temporary assignment with the National Theatre, and planned to stay on if he could find somewhere to live and work; Merline, though far from resigned to the move, thought of sending the boys with her sister when she returned in February to Berlin, joining them later when she was fully recovered herself. Rilke could not bring himself to withdraw into his work and leave them to find their own salvation, and took much trouble to seek help for them—which, isolated as he was in Berg, meant endless correspondence.

His first idea of offering his Munich apartment proved impracticable: Feist's tenancy had raised difficulties with the housing authorities, but in the end, after Rilke had organized the collection by the Insel of his own things, he was able to take the apartment over officially. Merline became more and more desperate at having to leave, kept the boys with her after her sister's departure, and hoped against hope for some miracle—but she was equally despairing of ever holding René for herself. He cast around for financial help for her—paying for the shipment to Berlin of two pictures, including a Delacroix, she had rescued from Paris, for her brother to try to sell, and arranging for Mary Dobržensky to buy some of her water-colours—but his passionate protestations of love were coupled with the insistence that he must remain alone and try, in the few months left to him at Berg, to organize his life. He implored her not to speak of the Elegies as if they were just the resumption of an interrupted task. Such a work (or whatever might one day be 'granted' him) could result only from an inner condition, an inner progress towards the restoration of a spirit broken and buried by the war years. 'At certain times your love has been an infinite source of strength for me ... but the decisive moments can come only in solitude.' The bitter truth was brought home to her that their love, for all its 'splendour', for him must take second place. 'Vous n'avez pas besoin de moi pour votre vie,' she wrote: 'c'est cela qui est la vérité—tandis que pour moi, *vous êtes toute ma vie*'; he loved her, but could yet hold her at arm's length like a bunch of flowers. 'Must I leave you for ever? My soul will not oppress you, and the body, my darling, God knows is a little enough thing—must I carry it elsewhere?'[22] He held firm against meeting her on her way through, when early in April she finally left with Pierre and Baltusz for Berlin, and she found small comfort in the hope that they might be together some time during the summer.

For Rilke, it was as though fate nursed a 'secret hostility' towards his work. The winter at Berg which had held such promise had been wasted and lost: the involvement with Merline's troubles, just when he had been on the point of descending into his 'mine', was as disastrous as the break inflicted by his call-up in 1915. 'In the end, there is always that one conflict—in my experience, irreconcilable—the conflict between life and work,' he had written to Princess Marie in February. 'I go through it time and again, in ever new forms, and barely survive.'[23] Though he had hoped to stay on at Berg until June, the Zieglers announced new tenants for May, and there was no putting off his departure; in any case, his peace there was ruined early in April by the installation of a sawmill nearby, the 'great stupid Gillette blade' buzzing like a big blowfly or a dentist's drill.[24] Since December, he had accomplished little but the second 'manuscript' of 'Count C. W.' and the scaling of an even bigger mountain of letters. 'Every letter a thrust, an attack which threatened to overturn everything, a deep intrusion which transformed the blood—day after day, at a time which should have become that of my purest equanimity.'[25] Wielding the letter-pen had lost the sense of preparation for work.

For that, the only gleam of light had come from his encounter, in February, with Paul Valéry's 'Cimetière marin'. He felt for the work of this poet an enthusiasm paralleled only by his admiration for Rodin, and at once made a translation of the poem, for himself and Merline. Coming in such perfection of form from one who, like himself, had 'lived long with his poems' before making them public,[26] the 'Cimetière marin'—celebration of the rebirth of inspiration and joyous affirmation of life—seemed to offer hope that he too might yet succeed in resolving the conflict between life and work, and learn to subordinate life's dangers 'like St. Hieronymus with the lion sleeping beside his desk'.[27]

'I was alone, and waiting: my whole work waited,' he would write later; 'one day I read Valéry, and I knew my waiting was over.'[28] This was not how it seemed at the time, however. On the contrary, as the last weeks at Berg slipped away, he began to despair of ever finding what he had waited so long for. To all outward appearances, he showed the same good-humoured resignation as ever, in the face of a situation which after all was only too familiar—yet another move, destination unknown—and the same trust in Providence to rescue him. Princess Marie was coming soon to Switzerland, and although not now able to welcome her in his hermitage, he looked forward to hearing her ideas on where he might go: but he still avowed himself ready to let things take their course. Nanny Wunderly, on holiday in Sicily, received gaily-written letters from an apparently contented inhabitant of Berg—a vivid cameo of the frogs serenading in the lake, Count C. W.'s likely reactions to the new tenants, Leni's perfect service—with no hint that he had reached the point of admitting, for the first time, that he had failed in the supreme task.

How deep his depression went, is shown in the record he set down at the end of April, one of the strangest and most moving witnesses ever to come from his pen. It was a collection of fragmentary reflections and extracts from draft letters, prefaced by an introduction written in the third person and omitting all direct reference to persons and places. 'The writer', this said, had been granted every possible favour from Providence: the perfect haven in which to repair the ravaging break of the war years, the chance beforehand to revisit two places which were 'inseparable components of the story of his past', and above all the 'inexhaustible grace' of that 'vast emotion which overwhelms a heart when, under the impact of being loved anew, it decides itself to love'. For one so 'fortunately endowed', the solitude granted him could have been confidently expected to be fruitful. But his reflections, the impersonal introduction continued, bear witness to 'a miscarriage, a terrible, bewildering loss'.

The writer . . . has put these random leaves together under the title of *The Testament* — probably because in these insights into his singular fate a will is expressed which will remain his *last*, even though the task of many years yet still lies ahead for his spirit.[29]

The burden of the *Testament* itself was the recognition that solitude must be his only love—the solitude that had smiled on him from his earliest days, tested him out and thrown him 'like a javelin'. No ordinary love could ever compete with the joy of being chosen for such a throw and the ecstatic quivering in the target. It was not in moments like these that the trial came for the artist, but in those between, when normal life distracted him and normal love was a temptation. The hope had proved vain that at last the one was found who could understand and accept his need for this freedom. 'As long as it stands thus between us, I know not how to live'—life was just as impossible for him when he knew her unhappy through his fault, as when he made her happy by being at her side.[30]

In the final pages, from the draft of a letter, he bowed finally to the fate that had frustrated his efforts—not in reproach to Merline, but recognizing it simply as a failure for them both. His work had ended with the 'abortion' of the Elegy begun in December; 'the violent emotions were endless, you could not prevent them'; and ever since then he had been unable to recapture the solitary existence 'out of which alone I can become master of myself. My heart has been forced out from the centre of its circles, out to the periphery where it was nearest to you—it may be great there, sensitive, jubilant, or disturbed but it is not in *its own* constellation, it is not the heart my life demands.' She had assured him once that she was capable now of every kind of love for him:

Steel yourself now to the love, whatever its name, which can grant me *my* life. . . . For, if I were to give up all that is mine, and, as I often long to do, fall blindly into your arms and lose myself in them, then you would be holding one who has sacrificed himself: not me, not me. . . . I cannot dissemble, and cannot change myself. . . I kneel in the world and implore forbearance from those who love me. May they spare me! not use me up for their own happiness, but help me to the unfolding of that solitary happiness but for whose great signs they would not have loved me.[31]

This had been his constant theme in the letters he did actually send to Merline, though never so directly expressed, and always interwoven with such ecstatic songs of praise for their love and concern for her well-being that it was little wonder that she could not bring herself to believe it. Writing to her later in May, after he had left Berg, he said their only comfort, if comfort there could be, was that they had encountered something altogether 'too powerful' for them. 'I cannot share it, nor talk about it—one day the notes I wrote in the next to last week at Berg will tell you something of it, but the final word is not even in those, God forbid it should ever be expressed in words, I would not be able to bear it.'[32]

The *Testament*, presented in such an impersonal framework, was an attempt to gain distance from the experience, and a penetrating analysis for himself of the place of love in his life and work. 'The guiding principle of my work is a passionate subordination to the object occupying me, that to which in other words my love belongs', turning then suddenly, 'unexpectedly even to myself', into the 'creative act'. 'For a spirit which finds fulfilment in such conditions, the state of *being loved* will perhaps always turn out a misfortune'—for then the creative act will spend itself in the reciprocation of that love, and its true mission be lost. 'Thus the love-experience appears like a stunted, unfit subsidiary form of the creative experience, almost its degradation—and remains incapable of achievement, unmastered, and, measured against the higher order of successful creativity, impermissible.'[33]

He had long known this, of course. His confession now was that he had betrayed even what Berg had offered him, shown himself unready for 'the javelin-thrower solitude', and come to the realization that the final conflict was not that between love and work, but a schism within his work itself—'for my work is love'.[34] The final word he could not bear to record was the knowledge that he would continue unable to resist the call of love: and in this sense what he had written was indeed a last will, testament of the fear that the supreme creative act of the Elegies would never be achieved.

It was too private and revealing a document to be committed to the commonplace book, and the only transcript he made he sent to Kippenberg for safe keeping, the original being entrusted to the discretion of Nanny Wunderly. If his fear should be realized, then at least for posterity an account would be there which spared nothing of what he had gone through, his 'non-achievement' relentlessly delineated and exposed to the light. He had made, if not *the* work, *a* work, a 'thing out of fear'—and, as with *Malte*, succeeded in this detached form in drawing a line under a harrowing experience.

It was as though the act of releasing his agonies thus had cleared all doubts from his mind. In the summer ahead, another Berg must be found—not, as he wrote to Merline, 'to start the winter to come, but to begin *over again*, with a firmer resolve, that which I spent between anguish and happiness'[35]— and a way yet to the integration of his work and his love for her. In this new mood, the impending arrival of Marie Taxis in Switzerland seemed important to him. She was to visit her grandchildren, Pascha's sons, who were at school in Rolle, on the lake between Lausanne and Geneva; and when the time came for him to leave Berg, on 10 May, he took a room at Etoy, not far from Rolle, in a pension converted from an old priory.[36] He could guess what her motherly advice would be—but he felt a need to talk things over with her, even if he had no intention of following her counsel.

Merline was languishing in the separation: a crippling sciatica had returned, the news that he was at the lake brought an infinite nostalgia for her, and her one thought was somehow to rejoin him for the summer, perhaps in the Tessin, where she had the possibility of renting a villa from a friend. For his part he seemed only too eager to have her at his side, even in the Tessin: though the pleasure at being back in a French environment in Etoy, and the memory of their visit together to Sierre, turned his thoughts rather to the Valais, and he would not lose sight of the overriding priority, to find the right place for work.

The problem of course was money, and once again he put his confidence in Kippenberg. All his friends, he wrote at the end of May, were busy trying to help him find a 'successor to Berg'—Bohemia, Württemberg, even Carinthia, 'the ancient homeland of the Rilkes' were all possibilities—but it might be important for him, 'in the interest of certain connections', to be able to stay on in Switzerland till the end of July: and he asked his friend to say in all frankness how much could be available and what his limit must be. But he was sensible enough, he said, 'to realize that I must give *absolute* priority to securing the "establishment" of that second Berg and making certain that my life as a whole through the coming years finds a form that is favourable for me'.[37]

Though he had not yet had a reply when the Princess finally reached Rolle, on 7 June, he had every hope it would be favourable; and she found a very different Rilke from the gloomy poet she had welcomed at Duino in April 1914. After Benvenuta, she was no less worried now by what he told her of Merline, but it was clear to her that this time he could not be brought to give up the dream, so anxious was he to convince her that he had found the right guardian of his solitude, the loving being 'ready to withdraw at the moment when he receives the call'. 'Poor Serafico,' she noted afterwards, 'will he never be left in peace, never find the woman who loves him enough to understand what he needs—and to live only for him without a thought for her own insignificant little life? ... If there is such a woman, how is he to find her? ... I can see no way out.'

What she did energetically oppose, however, was his resignation over the Elegies. She would not hear of his idea of publishing the fragments as they now stood: they *must* be finished, she told him, 'and they will be: only wait, I know it will come.'[38] He was astounded at her confidence, and it gave him new heart for the quest for a 'second Berg', especially when at almost the same moment he received a most encouraging letter from Kippenberg. Thoroughly approving of his plans, the publisher saw no difficulty over finding the money to see them realized: the account with the Insel was healthier than ever, and a further remittance of 2,000 Swiss francs was on the way. Merline had already decided to take the villa in the Tessin, and Rilke had almost settled on joining her there even though all his instincts pointed to Sierre; but now that funds were assured, he telegraphed her to come straight to him at Etoy. She asked nothing better, and on 17 June they were reunited there.

She had been consumed by a 'désir infini' to be with him again, her bodily ills had disappeared as though by magic, and in her passion she gave no thought to the longer-term future. Life together in the rose-covered priory was delightful, and they revisited old haunts: but it soon became apparent to her that for him this was a summer holiday only, and that his sights were indeed set on another Berg—in which there would be no permanent place for her. Contrary to his earlier conviction that what he sought would be found only by chance, and must not be searched for, he was not content now to leave things to his friends, but was actively on the hunt himself in the traditional way, through an estate agent in Lausanne. Merline, instead of using the water-colours she had brought with her, found herself joining him on a tour of inspection of the few properties which looked to answer his rather precise requirements. The Canton de Vaud offering nothing suitable, his hopes concentrated once again on the Valais, and on 28 June they arrived in Sierre, putting up in the same Hotel Bellevue they had found so welcoming in October and feeling at once, as he reported to Nanny Wunderly, that 'this remarkable Valais' was as admirable and significant for them as when they had first discovered it.[39]

After some disappointments, they were preparing to give up and return— but then came the 'miracle'. Strolling out on their last evening, they saw, in the window of the nearby hairdresser's, a photograph of a thirteenth-century tower, or small château, with the inscription 'For Sale or Rent'. It turned out to be owned by the hairdresser's mother, and lay a mile or two above Sierre, on the way up to Montana. Inspection the next day revealed a property which, with all its obvious drawbacks—water only from the well outside, no electricity and somewhat primitive sanitation—seemed to offer all he desired. Negotiations over the rent were left in the hands of the agent, and they left for Lausanne and Geneva with Rilke convinced, or nearly convinced, that his search was over. 'Chère,' he wrote to Nikê, 'c'est peut-être mon Château en Suisse, peut-être!'[40]

Elisabeth Bergner in Strindberg's *Miss Julie*

Jenny de Margerie

Jeanne de Sépibus

Nimet Elwi Bey

Rilke and Baladine Klossowska ('Merline')
at Muzot

Rilke in Sierre, 1924

Rilke with Paul Valéry, Anthy sur Thonon, 13 Sept. 1926

VIII

Muzot and Valmont
1921–1926

—∘❧❧∘—

'. . . the quality of life as of death and of light
As of darkness is one, one beauty, the rhythm of that Wheel,
and who can behold it is happy and will praise it to the
people'

ROBINSON JEFFERS, *Point Pinos and Point Lobos*

I

'*This* is the time for what can be said. *Here*
is its country. Speak and testify'

(*Ninth Elegy*)

The immediate attraction for Rilke of the little Château de Muzot (final 't'
pronounced, he noted), a square, step-gabled tower set in a small garden, was
not only its antiquity—he dug at once into the history of the families the
manor had housed since the thirteenth century, and learned with delight that
one earlier chatelaine was supposed still to haunt it—but also the surroundings
of 'La noble contrée', as this part of the Valais was called, and the outlook to a
landscape of remarkable beauty. He was once again vividly reminded of
Provence and of Spain, and this link with his own past seemed underlined
when he heard that certain species of flowers, birds, and butterflies were to be
found nowhere but here and in those two areas. There was a neglected little
chapel nearby, dedicated to St. Anne; two arches of roses in full bloom in the
garden, with a small orchard, added to the charm; downhill a little were
vineyards, and by the road junction stood a magnificent poplar, 'like a symbol
and an exclamation mark, as if to say, and to confirm: this is it!' His whole
instinct replied that it was, even though he quailed before the evident practical
difficulties of making it liveable. The remainder of the summer there with
Merline might be possible at the rent the agent expected to negotiate, and
would show whether Muzot could suit the 'severe winter' alone he planned—
always providing that the 'right Leni' could be found, and there the
receptionist at the Hotel Bellevue foresaw no difficulty.[1]

There followed some anxious weeks of hesitation. As it happened, their
rooms at the Etoy priory had to be given up, and on 8 July they moved out to

the Bellevue, with the intention of staying on in Sierre, possibly in another pension, if the Muzot negotiations failed. Rilke unburdened himself in long letters to Nanny Wunderly, endlessly permutating the possibilities but unable to bring himself to a decision and unwilling to take any step without her advice. He felt guilty at having diverted Merline from the Tessin villa, where they could have lived more cheaply and she would have had a more settled summer than this somewhat nomadic existence in the Valais offered; word came of a possibility on the Wörthersee in Carinthia which he felt he ought to go and inspect; Muzot still remained immensely attractive, but with the illness of the owner, Mme Raunier, a firm answer could not be extracted to the agent's proposals for an initial short-term let. Rilke was particularly anxious to hear from Nanny what Werner Reinhart thought—Reinhart had in fact seen a picture of the place some years earlier, and Rilke's idea was that he might consider renting it for him. 'It is possible that this marvellous Spanish-Provençal Valais could be the environment for an Elegy winter, Muzot's future might be to offer me the protection for it—I don't know . . .'[2]

It was a blessing that his friends were more decisive than he. On 17 July came an express letter from Nanny with Reinhart's proposal to rent Muzot for six months, with an option to renew. An interview that evening with Mme Raunier found her in a lucid moment and agreeable, subject to suitable notice if she should decide to sell; and in the next few days active preparation for his installation began almost over his head and regardless of his persisting doubts. Merline, with her artist's eye and some experience of dealing with old dwellings, had seen from the first what could be made of Muzot, and was soon on her knees alongside the cleaning women. Some decoration would be needed, but no really radical alterations; the furniture, including some attractive seventeenth-century pieces, was adequate; and by the end of that week Merline had already moved in, while Rilke still nerved himself in the hotel for the test.

He was deeply grateful, he wrote to Reinhart, for his confidence in allowing him to be installed as the 'steward of the castle': but hoped he would understand it must still be in the nature of a trial. 'The difficulty and uncertainty of my position is so great that I don't know if I can keep this permanent shelter, I might still be compelled to move away . . . and I can't yet see whether this stout old house may not be harder to occupy than Berg, and whether it can prove as favourable for my work.' Nevertheless, the chance to try it out, if he might do so without commitment, was a great boon: 'the inner voice which urges me to this Valais environment is as strong as my desire to spend one more winter in Switzerland, while I wait for the disturbance in my condition to abate (perhaps too for the return one day to Paris)—and, who knows, for the completion in this protective refuge of the works interrupted by the disorders of the war . . .! If that were to succeed, how I would bless our old tower!'[3] Reinhart was content to take the risk of his 'steward' moving out, for the place interested him anyway: he urged him to go ahead with any decorations and repairs he thought necessary without worrying about the cost, and offered any help needed over carpets, cutlery, and the like.[4] 'It is singularly moving,' wrote Rilke to Nanny, 'that Werner, the one person we would have been glad to welcome at Berg, is now taking over the Ziegler role, and you, my dear, remain in yours: to make this new Berg possible and habitable for me.'[5]

Though still insisting it was an experiment, he nevertheless asked her to have letter-paper printed for him with the Muzot address, and finally on 27 July moved up there himself. It was in a torrid heat ('which has certainly helped to ripen the grapes for the "crû d'Enfer", the pride of this summer country'), and he confessed that Merline was a good deal more courageous than he: Muzot was cleaner and airier now that it had been 'de-Rauniered', looked so enticing and happy from the road below by the poplar—but entering it was 'still hard, hard, as if one were putting on a suit of heavy armour'.[6]

He determined at least to reduce the repairs, decoration, and additional furnishings to the minimum, until it could be seen whether his trial run proved favourable; and his requests to Nanny were limited to what seemed essentials—candlesticks, pillows, a storm lantern (though of course she was thoughtful enough to send a host of other things equally necessary which he had not thought of). Werner Reinhart came early in August with his brother Hans, and was well pleased with his new domain, sending after his return further items to fill it out, and proposing to establish a fund for his steward for future outgoings. Merline's energy and enterprise were phenomenal, she was adept at improvisation and obtaining local advice and help, and the old house gradually took on a liveable air Rilke would not have credited. She was steadfastly determined that the experiment should be a success, and as the weeks went by he began to share her confidence, even though the image of Muzot as a suit of armour—and a rusty one at that—was often in his mind. Only after a visit with Nanny to another possibility, a mansion in Kaiserstuhl which he found unappealing, and much further heart-searching, did he finally make up his mind, at the end of September, to stay on amid 'these solid old walls' and settle to his winter of work.[7]

In itself, the disposition of the four-square tower was certainly well suited. The ground floor, reached through a verandah-porch, had a spacious dining-room with a traditional Valais stone stove and a fine seventeenth-century oak table; a tiny salon alongside opened to a balcony with a view across the Rhône valley; and there was one small bedroom, and a kitchen built on more recently to replace the original cellar-kitchen. For the moment, until a housekeeper could be found, these were Merline's quarters. On the first floor was a square room which he took as his study; the ceiling beams bore the date MDCXVII, and although it was not over-generous towards his habit of walking up and down while he worked, it had a comfortable atmosphere reminiscent of Nanny

Wunderly's 'Stübli' in Meilen. Its windows looked to south and west to the
distant majesty of the Valais Alps. Adjoining it was a bedroom for him, tiny,
with an archway door on to a small balcony, and off that again a small
whitewashed chamber, the so-called 'chapel', entered also from the landing
through a low medieval doorway above which stood in relief, not a cross, but a
swastika. There were further attic rooms above, with loophole windows only.
Thus his isolation could be ensured, 'independent of the comings and goings
and the running of the household'.[8]

His wants were simple, but not to the point of being satisfied with the
primitive; and the living conditions at Muzot, 'demeure un peu héroïque et
rude',[9] were in sharp contrast with those of the well-established Schloss Berg.
The furnishings were tolerable, candles and lamps were well enough; but the
lack of running water and the rudimentary sanitation were serious drawbacks.
What chiefly gave him pause at the prospect of a winter there alone was the
apprehension that, even with some improvements, and assuming a housekeeper half as competent as Leni could be found, it was an establishment that
would not run of itself and would require more of his own attention than he
could give if he was really to work, although Nanny Wunderly had undertaken
to meet the housekeeping costs. By early October, however, he could send to
Reinhart his written request to be confirmed in his office of steward for the
duration of the winter, and make his suggestions for the use of the float fund
his 'liege lord' had proposed: a new tiled stove in the study, the stopping of the
many rat and mouse holes, and minor carpentry work on the balcony and
windows.[10] Mme Raunier having meanwhile succumbed to her illness, her
daughter had proposed the sale of Muzot to Reinhart, and Rilke promised to
get for him an exact survey and independent valuation.

He may or may not by this time have shown Merline his Berg *Testament*. At
all events, from her devotion to the task of seeing him settled for a solitary
winter at Muzot, it was clear she had accepted his conditions, and was resolved
that the disaster of Berg should never be repeated through any fault of hers.
She was indefatigable in the search for the right housekeeper, which proved no
easy task, and had decided she would return to Berlin as soon as the post could
be filled. Meanwhile, although continuing to toil at the kitchen stove, she had
engaged a local girl for the housework, and so was able to enjoy to the full their
final weeks together, as the summer, the hottest for decades, faded into
autumn and her portfolio of sketches of Muzot and water-colours of 'La noble
contrée' began to grow. On one of the sketches, of himself asleep on the sofa,
Rilke wrote for her the verses:

> Grief is a heavy soil, wherein
> some blissful meaning will darkly win
> its way to a flowering-tide;
> now, though, in you, my silent breast,
> all remains nameless and unexpressed:

things only get named outside.
Named but as doubt and as time decree,
till we've suddenly placed felicity
in between name and name.
And then, with the bright star overhead,
the white hind will purely tread
into the satisfied frame.[11]

It was Nanny Wunderly who finally found a suitable person, and on 15 October Frieda Baumgartner, a twenty-six-year-old farmer's daughter from Balsthal, near Solothurn, arrived to be introduced to her duties by Merline. It was apparent that this would take rather longer than the two or three days they had envisaged, but Rilke began at once as he meant to go on. 'Today my solitude should have started,' he wrote to Nikê on 17 October, 'and so it has in a way; I've been at my desk since early this morning and starting work on a long list of letters, which for me is always the approach to recollection': the fact that 'Mouky' was staying on a while longer would make no difference to his resolution.[12] Her presence was in fact a very good thing, sparing him from having to take hold of the leading-strings of the new establishment in its first tentative steps—and Frieda, willing but slow, and less experienced than they had been led to believe, obviously needed time to be ready for its independent running. 'Let's hope that I and Muzot have the right qualities to get her to blossom out,' he told Reinhart: 'at the moment she is more of a stalk still, and it would be something to see even a little leaf emerging.'[13]

Merline delayed her departure several times, and he did not see her off at Sierre until 8 November. Writing to her afterwards from the Bellevue, 'before going up to our good and loyal Muzot, which from now on will be mine with all the heart you have awakened in it', he urged her to continue with a good will: 'may God give us the assurance of doing the right thing and of not losing anything of the wealth He has showered upon us . . .'[14] 'It is not that Mouky does not understand,' he wrote to Simone Brüstlein, the friend who had stood by them during the crisis in Geneva, 'only that it is an inexpressible burden for her heart to follow it through.'[15]

By this time, the new stove for his study had been installed, and a new kitchen range into the bargain. With the other works in hand, and the arrival of a splendid wing-chair from Reinhart, Muzot bid fair soon to be 'complete', and Rilke, mindful of his dependence on Nikê not only for its budget but also for all the incidentals which would make it a worthy successor to Berg, urged her to come and view. From Reinhart she brought the good news that, pending consideration of the purchase, for which he was keen to have first refusal, he was preparing to renew the lease for a further six months; and a little later Rilke learned from Colonel Souvairan, the young Rauniers' guardian, that they were quite happy to leave the question of sale till after that: 'soyez bien heureux et tranquille dans votre château . . . travaillant de belles œuvres, avec la douce espérance qu'elles contribueront à améliorer quelque peu nos pauvres natures humaines.'[16] Nikê's visit—exactly a year since he had entered Berg—seemed to make Muzot ready for him to start his 'good winter'. The suit of armour had become a cloak, 'somewhat stiff, but nevertheless rather softer',[17] and a flow of parcels from her brought the hundred and one small additions needed to make him more comfortable. An occasional twinge of nostalgia for Berg—especially for its comforting open fireplace—was overcome in the thought that this time there could be no repetition of the fatal distractions there; through November and December his letters to Merline, though still tender, were less and less frequent as he turned with a lighter heart to his other correspondence.

Of some priority was a call from his family in Germany. In September Ruth had announced her engagement to Carl Sieber, a young lawyer, great-nephew of Johanna Westhoff and thus her second cousin. She had written that they were anxious to marry as soon as possible, when they would live on the Sieber estate at Liebau, in the Saxony Vogtland, south of Leipzig; a letter had already come from Sieber to his prospective father-in-law; and the question of what dowry he could manage for Ruth had taken on some urgency. There was a complication in an appeal also from Clara: Ruth's earlier engagement, now broken off, had been to the son of a friend, one of Clara's advisers and supporters in her house project at Bredenau, who had long looked forward to the union of their children, so that the change of heart had led to a distressing estrangement. Clara was thus not only facing a doubly lonely life, but was also in need of a further loan, for which she had addressed herself directly to Kippenberg as well as to her husband. Rilke, ready as always to meet his obligations as far as he could, and taking a distantly benevolent view of Ruth's future married life, put the problem in frank detail to the publisher, who alone could pronounce on what his account could afford with due regard for his own requirements.

He was himself sending half the sum Clara wanted, as a gift of course, not a loan (for once, the exchange worked in favour), and left it to his friend to send the balance and to decide on Ruth's dowry. But he also made it clear that he held firmly to the view he had expressed two years earlier, namely that the separation from Clara, whether or not formalized in a divorce, was for good, and that any help from him was as from a friend, not a husband. 'For the reality of my existence alone (not easy, but so essential), we must sooner or later reach the point of creating conditions that totally suit it for my life's work, and prevent it from being embroiled in another's fate.' Ruth must have as much as prudence in his own interests allowed—but there was no question of giving her any of his Munich furniture, which one day he hoped to recover for himself.[18]

Ruth was to celebrate her birthday on 12 December with an engagement party in Liebau, and Rilke asked Katharina to order a special cake as his contribution. Kippenberg, sensibly, invited Ruth over to Leipzig to talk over the matter of the dowry, and recommended a settlement of 50,000 marks, representing about half the balance in the account and the equivalent at the time of 1,500 Swiss francs. Rilke telegraphed his approval, and later, though with some reluctance, agreed it should be raised to 60,000—but no more. With these arrangements, and a belated birthday present of a photograph of his parents at their engagement, he seems to have felt his responsibilities towards his daughter discharged (though after the wedding in May he was to make her a small monthly allowance). What might appear neglect, he wrote to Carl Sieber, was in fact the sacrifice of family to work: if he were reproached for not having the strength for both, he could only point silently to 'those areas into which I have thrown all my capabilities', and await a final judgement.[19] 'A door closes,' he sighed to Nikê: 'maybe others open, it is after all *her* life, and I lack so many insights, not only into the present but also into the past, from which I was too distant and too diverted.'[20]

The engagement announcement had revealed his address to many old friends, and his correspondence list grew longer than ever. 'The letter-factory is in full-steam production,' he told Nikê on 1 December: over 180 pages had been sent off in a week, 'it goes by the metre, if not the kilometre! Must be done: for only on the other side comes the valley of real solitude, and then beyond, the ascent to the mountain range of work.'[21] He was modelling himself on that earlier time, he wrote in his letter to Alexander Taxis, congratulating him on his seventieth birthday, 'the winter when this assiduous retirement into my shell was so wonderfully successful: the winter in Duino!'[22] His hopes of Muzot, though more mutedly expressed in his letters than at Berg, were the stronger in the knowledge that his solitude was more assured here, and from the feeling that in the Valais he had finally discovered the true greatness of Switzerland 'this generous and so unused landscape' which Jean Strohl had aptly described as 'fresh from the Creation', still steaming as it were.[23]

Here too he had the advantage of a French-speaking environment—not as paradoxical as it might seem, for he had always felt his best work came when he was not surrounded by the sounds of everyday German. And above all, he had the inspiration of Valéry, whose scattered and not easily accessible works Gide had been helping him to collect, and whom he enthusiastically recommended to all his friends.

About twenty-five years ago there appeared a remarkable essay (*L'Introduction à la méthode de Léonard de Vinci*) which he has now—in 1919—published with an extraordinarily fine preface. But to begin with Mallarmé meant to find oneself, with the next half-step forward, standing in silence, 'dans un silence d'art très pur'. And this is what happened. Valéry fell silent and studied mathematics. And only recently ... did the necessity of aesthetic expression make itself felt again (all the purer for the interruption) in the man of fifty. Everything he has produced since then is extremely individual and important.[24]

If another could produce after so long a silence, then there must be hope for himself. In Valéry's 'Palme', he wrote to Princess Marie, came the words

> Patience, patience
> patience dans l'azur,
> chaque goutte de silence
> est la chance d'un fruit mûr!—

'If I could have a hope like that for my silence.'[25]

Thanking Kippenberg for his financial proposals, he told him of his good fortune at having Muzot assured for longer. A little pocket-money for himself would not come amiss, but that could be left till the mark was stronger, and it was perhaps just as well he should lack the means to leave, even for a day, the tower which so exactly met his needs for the work he hoped to do. Whether it would be granted him to fulfil the 'supreme task', he could not foretell; meanwhile he welcomed the publisher's proposal for a complete edition of the works, but suggested it might await the completion of the Michelangelo translations, also a task for this winter perhaps. He said he hoped for a visit— 'if I happen to have gone deep into my workings, then I'll still welcome you, in Pit No. So-and-so, by the light of the miner's lamp!'[26]—but in reality was glad it was not likely for some time yet.

His 'silence', virtually complete withdrawal from all human contact, was at last attained, and even animals were kept at arm's length. A stray cat which had attached itself to the household, and was useful to keep the mice in check, was an acceptable companion in its sovereign independence, but he drew the line at the offer of a dog. Frieda was turning out well and her competence improving daily, but, not surprisingly, she had a tendency to 'make "conversation" out of thin threads' even when his turned back emphasized his wish for silence, and he missed the perfect, instinctive discretion of Leni. To Nanny Wunderly, who exercised a remote control by letter of Frieda's activities, he appealed for a gentle hint to the willing girl, whom he was of course most anxious not to hurt: not to make a thing of it, but just to indicate that, now the 'correspondence time' was nearing its end, the master would no doubt be starting his real work, and it would be advisable only to speak when spoken to. He was not complaining, of course; but at times *any* words were too much, 'and often more disturbing is the mere apprehension that any moment it may happen (which with Leni, for instance, was never the case!)'[27] It was a relief when the good Colonel Souvairan cancelled his invitation for New Year's Day, so that he was not obliged to break his vow of silence: 'je [le] vois comme un consentement de Dieu que je reste dans ma solitude sans l'interrompre même pour un si aimable appel.'[28]

The 'correspondence time' in fact lasted well into January. Whether or not as a result of a hint from Nanny, Frieda learned her place in dealing with her unusual master, whose never-failing courtesy earned her respect and admiration. He for his part realized how lucky he was to have someone who could be content with so lonely a life, sitting of an evening with her handwork or reading after he had retired to his study; and on Christmas Eve, before they went over together to light candles in the St. Anne chapel and she joined neighbours for the midnight mass in Sierre, he saw to it that her presents should include a copy of his translation of Gide's *Enfant prodigue*, *Mitsou* of course, and Stifter's *Indian Summer*, dedicated to 'the quiet, loyal helper and good companion at Muzot, for her lonely evenings this winter'.[29] His copies of *Mitsou* had long been available, and made excellent presents to accompany his Christmas letters, especially to the many friends who had not heard from him for a long time. Lou was one: and this time his end-of-year report, though it lacked the optimism of that from Berg, and did not minimize his difficulty in finding concentration, was expressive of a quiet confidence in the therapy of 'this most literal solitude' at Muzot.[30]

One letter which reached him as a result of Ruth's engagement had roused in him deeper feelings than the event itself. It was from Gertrud Ouckama Knoop, whose daughter Wera, before the war a playmate of Ruth's in Munich, beautiful and showing graceful promise as a dancer, had died at the age of only nineteen a year after the war had ended. Rilke, who had known and liked the father, Gerhart Knoop, since their meeting in Paris in 1909, had made a point of seeing the family whenever he was in Munich; after Gerhart's sudden death in 1913 he had written a moving letter to his widow, and negotiated for her with the Insel over her husband's unpublished works; and Wera and her sister had once come to tea with him. It was natural that her mother should write to him about Ruth: but she will have been surprised to receive sixteen closely-written pages in reply, for though she admired him she had been closer to Clara and Ruth, and they had only occasionally corresponded. To her, at the end of November, he unburdened himself as to no other at this time, not even to Lou or Marie Taxis. She heard his resigned, almost indifferent acceptance of Ruth's marriage; his desperate need for total solitude and the disastrous effect of human intercourse upon his creative powers; the spiritual injury inflicted by the war years and his doubts whether his work would ever justify the lavish aid of his friends; the new chapter that had opened for him in the Valais and his search now, not so much for aesthetic expression, as for the inner core of his own being; the revelation that had come through Valéry—and at the very end, almost as a postscript, the real reason for this lengthy confidence. Wera, who had died so young, seemed a presence to him: he hoped her mother would one day tell him more about her.[31]

On New Year's Day he received from Gertrud an account of the illness and death of this young girl he had scarcely known: how while still a child 'the art of movement and metamorphosis innate in her body and mind' had astounded all who saw her dance, how then, with puberty, quite unexpectedly, she had told her mother that she could, or would, no longer dance. With the onset of the inexplicable glandular trouble that was soon to cause her death, she took up music, then finally abandoned that for drawing, 'as if the dancing which had been denied were still manifesting itself in her, but more and more gently and discreetly'.[32] It was a moving story, seeming to lay upon him an obligation, 'an overwhelming sense of duty towards my inmost being',[33] and though he could not yet see its fulfilment, the idea of dance as metamorphosis, which he encountered too now in Valéry's *L'âme et la danse*, quickened his imagination.

Towards the middle of January he promised himself a 'letter Lent'. He had written hundreds, and the prodigious effort simply had to be brought to an end if he was ever to begin the 'ascent to the mountain range of work'. Translation, as often before, could perhaps start him up the slope. Valéry's Leonardo preface, the *Eupalinos* dialogue or *L'âme et la danse* were tempting tasks, but must wait, he felt, until he had progressed further himself. A good preliminary, however, and in its way something of a continuity, would be to take up anew the version of a Latin letter of Petrarch's which he had begun in Paris and had to abandon there. Strohl in Zurich, who had been keeping him supplied with books, speedily obliged with the original text and a dictionary, and the 'little task' seemed to appeal.[34] The local carpenter had now finally delivered a standing-desk ordered some time before—essential equipment for real work—but the letter-pen still made its demands felt. He seemed constitutionally incapable of leaving a letter unanswered or of neglecting one he owed: and it was only by a supreme effort of will that on 31 January he laid this 'indescribably over-worked' instrument aside and proclaimed his resolve to let it lie for the whole of February. For time was slipping by: 'days, nights, days, nights, I never realized that such big pages as those I have now could be turned so swiftly.'[35] (Letters to Nanny Wunderly, of course did not count: thinking aloud to her had become as natural to him as breathing.)

Mountain heights or mine depths were expressive metaphors to convey the isolation his work demanded: but the notion of dogged perseverance to the goal was far from apposite. The Elegies had been begun, and their whole cycle perceived in outline, in an abrupt tempest of inspiration at Duino, now a whole decade back in time; the inspiration had briefly returned in Paris and Munich; it had to return again if they were to be completed. Rodin's 'toujours travailler' could no longer be the precept for the 'heart-work/on all the images imprisoned within you', and no amount of chipping away at the seam in the search for gold, or struggling forward in the quest for the mountain peak, could substitute, it seemed, for the sudden burst of 'inner dictation'. All he could do was seek the right conditions, prepare himself by routine word-smith work—letters, transcriptions from his reading, translations—and hope. 'Concentration is terribly hard,' he complained to Nikê on 1 February, 'even eating is a distraction, and the hours between meals seem too short for anything whole to be done ... if only one could eat for half a year, then spend the other half meditating, so that there did not have to be this constant shift of focus ...'[36]

The very next day, quite as unexpectedly as at Duino, came the turn. The spirit was suddenly upon him: but, to his own surprise, what he began to write was not the continuation of the Elegies, but a sequence of 'Sonnets to Orpheus', which as they progressed revealed themselves as a memorial to Wera Knoop. In three days he completed a cycle of twenty-five, in a free handling of the classic sonnet form, and on 7 February sent off to Gertrud Knoop a transcript of what had been 'granted' him. She would see at once, he said, why she had to be the first to have the cycle: for, although only one sonnet was a direct invocation of Wera, it was her spirit that 'controlled and impelled' the whole, had 'penetrated more and more—even though so mysteriously that I only gradually realized it—this irresistible and for me profoundly moving act of creation'.[37] His original he sent the same day to Strohl, 'tout chaud encore', 'une dictée intérieure, toute spontanée' which had made him abandon the translation for which his friend had been so helpful.[38]

The sonnets had come to him at the standing-desk. Now, as he completed their transcription, and as if in answer to the imperative call of inspiration, there arrived a second desk, which Nike, knowing the delay with the first, had ordered. On this he took up the Elegies again. That night and the following day the Seventh and Eighth were written—'I am way over my head in writing', he cried in a brief note to Nike, and, at last, not the stuff of letters.[39] Elegies and Sonnets were 'of the same birth'[40]—as he awoke on 9 February, there was another sonnet ready almost complete in his mind, a hymn to spring, which he dispatched at once to Gertrud to replace one of the earlier cycle which he had felt somehow empty. And then, straight away, he started a continuation of the 'Antistrophes' begun in the summer of 1912, to constitute, as he thought now, the Fifth Elegy. In the afternoon he walked down to the post-office and sent off a telegram to Nike—'Seven Elegies now mostly completed . . . Joy and miracle'[41]—and on the road back there flooded in the remainder of the Sixth and Ninth, whose fragments had been with him since Duino and Ronda. These too were completed as he worked on late into the night. 'My dear friend,' he wrote to Kippenberg,

though I can scarcely hold the pen after days of overwhelming obedience in the spirit—to *you*, before I try to sleep, I must give the news:
I am over the mountain!
At last! The Elegies are there. And can be published this year (or whenever you feel is the right moment). Nine great ones, about the length of those you already know; and then a second part, which I will call 'Fragments' . . . This was larger than life—I have groaned aloud through these days, as I did that time in Duino—but even then, after that struggle, I never knew that *such* a storm of spirit and heart could break over one! And that it could be survived! . . . I went out, in the cold moonlight, and stroked my little Muzot like a big animal—the old walls that have granted me this. And Duino that was shattered.
The whole is to be called:
The Duino Elegies.

... And: my dear friend: *this*: that *you* have made this possible for me, been so patient with me: *ten* years! Thanks! and that you always believed in me! *thanks!*[42]

In her last letter, of over a month before, Merline had recalled the anniversary of the crisis in Geneva when he had rushed to her side, and had not concealed from him that she was ill again. If she had nursed a faint hope that his reaction would be the same, she was disappointed, for he did not even reply; but at least now he could send her the good news of his salvation, for which she had created the conditions and which could not have come without her sacrifice. From the tempest which had swept over him, he was still a-tremble, he told her: 'mais voilà, j'ai vaincu. . . . That which weighed heaviest on me, and gave me the most anguish, is done, and gloriously, as I think'.[43]

It seems he felt that the 'supreme task' had been accomplished—the closing Elegy, the Tenth, of which he had had the first glimpse in Duino, already existed in the version completed just before the war. 'Oh Nikê, petite Victoire, fièrement ailée à jamais, how surely you winged on ahead, unperturbed, always . . . Victory! Victory!' He wrote of looking forward now to the calm after the storm, to something more everyday, 'quiet, human tasks':[44] but his storm was not yet over. On 11 February he wrote the Tenth almost completely anew, save for the opening lines from Duino, and even more jubilant letters went off to Nikê, to Marie Taxis, and to Lou.

Finally, Princess, the blessèd, how blessèd, day when I can tell you of the conclusion—as far as I can see—of the Elegies! Ten! From the last great one . . . always intended to be the last . . . my hand still trembles! . . . All in a few days, it was an incredible storm, a hurricane in the spirit . . . every fibre in me, every tissue, cracked. But now it exists. Is. Is. Amen. . . .

One [the Eighth] I have dedicated to Kassner. The whole is yours, Princess, how should it not be! It will be called:

The Duino Elegies.

In the book (for I cannot give you what from the start has belonged to you) will stand the words:

The property of . . .

He would not send her yet a transcript of the new poems, for he wanted her to hear them first from his lips—'soon, I hope'.[45]

For Nikê however he made a transcript of the whole, adding to the four Elegies already in a little parchment volume from Soglio, so that there should be another full copy deposited in her care. And to accompany his letter to Lou he made copies of the Sixth, Eighth, and Tenth to put with those she already had. 'Just think!' he wrote:

I have been allowed to survive to this point. Through everything. Miracle. Grace. . . . And imagine, *one more* thing, in another connection, just beforehand (in the 'Sonnets to Orpheus' . . . suddenly, written in the beginning of the storm . . .) I wrote, *made*, the horse, you know, the free, joyous white stallion with the hobble on his fetlock who sprang out in a gallop towards us one evening in a Volga meadow—

how

I made him, as an 'ex-voto' for Orpheus!—What is time? *When* is the present? Across so many years he sprang out, in his total happiness, to me, into my wide-open feeling
...*

Now I know myself again. My heart was as though truncated while the Elegies were not done. Now they are. They exist. . . .[46]

Through these few days he had been as one possessed, oblivious to rest or food—though, as Frieda later recalled, he had his normal simple meals, if with some irregularity. He was to be grateful for the stability of her placid temperament 'while Muzot sailed the high seas of the spirit'; for the flood tide had not yet abated. On 13 February came another sonnet, which he added to the cycle; and then, on the following day, in 'a radiant after-storm', yet another Elegy, the 'Saltimbanques', from the associations of Hertha Koenig's Picasso and Père Rollin's family of tumblers seen long ago in Paris. It was a day of 'sacred, elemental disorder'. Holding to his original scheme of the work, however, in which the powerful Tenth must remain the last, he decided to insert this new one, dedicated to Hertha, as the Fifth, replacing the earlier 'Antistrophes' which he felt less suited to the elegy form. Receiving back from Strohl his original manuscript of the 'Orpheus' poems, he began then to 'spin this thread further': and in the space of nine days, in a final burst of inspiration, wrote a stream of further sonnets, to form a second cycle. His productive wealth was such now that he could allow himself to be selective, he exulted to Nikê. 'What a world of grace we are living in! . . . The only thing we really own, is patience, but what a capital that represents—and what interest it bears, in due time!'[48] On 23 February he completed the manuscript of his second part of the 'Sonnets to Orpheus', in its final form of twenty-nine poems.

The fracture in his life had finally been mended, the 'broken-off surfaces' re-joined. He had the sensation of being once more 'in step' with himself, his

---

* But what shall I offer you, Master, say
  you who taught all creatures to hear?—
  The remembered evening of one spring day,
  in Russia: a horse drawing near . . .

  White, coming up from the village alone,
  on one fetlock a tethering-block,
  to spend the night alone, on his own:
  how gaily he tossed the shock

  of his mane in time to his mounting mood
  on that rudely encumbered race!
  How they leapt, the springs of the equine blood!

  He had followed the call of space.
  He sang and he listened—your cycle swept
  unbrokenly through him.
  His image: accept.
  (I. 20)[47]

own contemporary again, after the long years of frustration.[49] In his obsession with the great project of the Elegies, it had come to signify for him the culmination of his life's work: now the failure at Berg had been gloriously redeemed, and it was no wonder that he should feel an inordinate pride in the achievement. From its inception in Duino, the shape of the cycle had been clear in his mind, starting from the limitations of the human condition and ending in a final affirmation of man's place, and more especially the place of the poet, in the Whole—in terms of the symbol he had chosen, a progress from the celebration of the 'terrifying' Angel to that of the 'consentient' Angel. What had eluded him since the war years had been the ability to find expression for the turning-point, from the essentially negative burden of the Second Elegy, and particularly the bitter tone of the Fourth, written in 1915, to the jubilation he had foreshadowed in the opening lines of the Tenth that had stood ready since Duino—the singing of 'ecstatic praises to angels saying yes'. His recurring lament over the threads broken by the war reflected this inability to project his mind back to where he had stood in January 1912. The 'childhood' elegy begun in Berg had brought him close, but it lacked the positive, affirmatory note he sought.

It was only in the complete solitude of Muzot, free from all distractions, and above all from those of love, that inspiration gave him the words to turn the tide of his poetry from lament to praise—at first not in the missing Elegies, but in the unexpected form of the sonnets, where instead of the Angel, self-sufficient being standing beyond the transient world of humanity, the pervading figure is that of Orpheus, the supreme god of poetry, of whom all poets are but fleeting metamorphoses, as Rilke had said long ago in his lecture on Rodin.[50]

> Erect no memorial stone. Let the rose
> bloom every year to remind us of him.
> Because it's Orpheus. His metamorphosis
> is in this, and this. No other name
>
> should trouble us. Once and for all,
> when there's song, it's Orpheus. He comes and goes.
> Isn't it enough that now and then he's able
> to outlive the bowl of roses a few days? . . .
>   (I. 5)
> To praise, that's it! Called to praise,
> he came like ore out of the silence
> of stone. Oh, his heart's a perishable press
> of a wine that's eternal for men. . . .
>   (I. 7)[51]

At Berg Rilke had read Ovid's *Metamorphoses*; over his desk now at Muzot was pinned a reproduction Merline had found of Cima da Conegliano's Orpheus drawing; the Orphic myth—his power over animals and trees, his descent into the underworld—was peculiarly fitting as a symbolic expression of Rilke's ideas of the unity of life and death and especially of the poet's vocation. It was natural then that the framework should suggest itself, and even more natural that as he wrote the figure of Wera Knoop, snatched so early from a life of dance and music, should come to mind:

> you who evaporated,
> the unquellable cry's beautiful playmate.

> Dancer first, whose body, full of hesitation, paused
> suddenly, as if her youth were being cast in bronze;
> mourning and listening. Then, from the great
> creators music fell into her transformed heart.—[52]

The sonnets mused, in sensuous and highly concentrated images, on many themes and problems that had preoccupied him: love, death, childhood, the relationship of plants, animals, and inanimate things to human consciousness, the joys and inadequacy of transient earthly existence. Dominant however was the theme of the Orphic, the poetic mission: praise of creation, praise of the world in all its manifestations, praise even in lament. A month earlier, in a dedicatory verse to a copy of *Malte*, he had written:

> Oh, tell us, poet, what do you do?
> —I praise.
> But those dark, deadly, devastating ways,
> how do you bear them, suffer them?
> —I praise.
> And the Nameless, beyond guess or gaze,
> how can you still call and conjure it?
> —I praise . . .[53]

Now, in the sonnets:

> Over what's passing and changing,
> freer and wider,
> your overture is lasting,
> god with the lyre.

> Pain's beyond our grasp,
> love hasn't been learned,
> and whatever eliminates

> us in death is still secret.
> Only the Song above the land
> blesses and celebrates.[54]

That praise was the key to the locked door of his Elegiac cycle. When he had first conceived it, he had spoken of 'getting beyond Man and passing over . . . to the Angels'[55]—'on my return from immersion in things and animals . . . lo and behold! the next but one, the Angelic, was set before me: so I've skipped over humanity . . .'[56] But humanity, the here and now, was not to be thus passed over. From the joyous mood of the 'spring' sonnet, a memory of children singing to tambourine and triangle in a little church at Ronda—

> Earth, lucky earth on vacation,
> play with the children now. We long
> to catch you, happy earth. The happiest will win—[57]

sprang the Seventh Elegy: the celebration of human existence—'Being here's glorious'—and the assertion of Man's potential, through his greatest works of art, to attain the intensity of Being that is the Angel's.

> Pillars, pylons, the Sphinx, the cathedral's striving
> grey thrust out of its crumbling or alien city.
> Wasn't it a miracle? Oh, Angel, marvel. That's us,
> us, O great one. Tell them *that's* what we could do.
> My breath's too short for its praise.[58]

The door stood open now to the rest of the Elegies: developing in a fugue-like composition the themes of the first four, but progressing from lament for the limitations and transitoriness of Man, which only the early departed, the hero or the great lovers seem to transcend, to joy in his (that is, the poet's) ability to attain to the Whole, to raise 'externality' to the 'Absolute'. The Eighth, counterpoint to the affirmation of the Seventh, again stressed those limitations:

> All other creatures look into the Open
> with their whole eyes. But our eyes,
> turned inward, are set all around it like snares
>
> . . . .
>
> And we, spectators, always, everywhere,
> looking *at* everything and never *from!*[59]

and the Fifth, the last to be written, the even more transient life of the travelling acrobats, playthings of some unknown 'insatiable will', assembled on their 'threadbare carpet' to suggest the ultimate loneliness of man.[60] But in the Ninth he answered the question 'Why have to be human, and, shunning Destiny, long for Destiny?' We are here '*once* each, only *once. Once* and no more'. But it is our ability, and the poet's vocation, to express the things of this earth,

> to say them in a way that the things themselves
> never dreamed of existing so intensely,

that makes possible the transformation of the material world into the invisible Whole:

> Earth, isn't this what you want: to resurrect
> in us invisibly? Isn't it your dream
> to be invisible one day? Earth! Invisible!
> What's your urgent charge, if not transformation?
> Earth, my love, I will.

In submission to this task 'to speak and testify', poet/man is freed from the fear of death, earth's 'sacred idea', 'that intimate friend'.

> Look, I am living. On what? Neither childhood nor future
> are growing less. . . . Supernumerous existence
> wells up in my heart—

an infinite realm, beyond the reach of number and time, in which being and non-being are one.[61]

Since his early years, Rilke had held the idea that death is merely the unillumined side of life. Now, equally instinctively, he had found his way to the Buddhist conception of the external and the inner world as only 'two sides of the same fabric, in which the threads of all forces and of all events, of all forms of consciousnes and of their objects, are woven into an inseparable net of endless, mutually conditional relations'[62] (the conception, indeed, that seems to be indicated today by the quantum theory of atomic physics). It led him to reject his earlier fragmentary Tenth Elegy, which held only lament for the 'nights of anguish' and man's deep roots in suffering, and as he emerged from the 'terrifying vision' to write the Elegy anew, showing the complementarity of sorrow and joy in the journey beyond the half-life of earth's Vanity Fair to the realm of 'supernumerous existence'.

> But if the endlessly dead awakened a symbol in us,
> perhaps they would point to the catkins hanging from the bare
> branches of the hazel-trees, or
> would evoke the raindrops that fall onto the dark earth in springtime.
>
> And we, who have always thought
> of happiness as *rising*, would feel
> the emotion that almost overwhelms us
> whenever a happy thing *falls*.[63]

In his scheme of things there was no place for Christianity, 'from which I ever more passionately distance myself'. His 'Angel', he explained later, had nothing in common with the figures of the Christian heaven—if anything it owed more to those of Islam: it was there merely to symbolize the complete transformation of the visible into the invisible 'higher form of reality'.[64] Immediately after completing the Tenth Elegy, in fact, he had committed to paper the rejection of Christ, as a superfluous interpolation between God and man, which had been his conviction since his early years and which had grown even stronger in his acquaintance in Spain with Islam. Not intended for publication (for he never presumed to offer his personal views as example or precept[65]), his exposition took the form of a fictitious letter from a young worker to Verhaeren:[66] an appeal to the poet of the 'here and now' to confirm him in his direct approach to God from this life, from the senses, and his rejection of Christianity's disparagement of our earthly existence, and sex in particular, as sinful. Rilke's objection to all modern religions, Christianity included, as he put it in a later, real letter, was that they offered merely consolation for death instead of a way to come to terms with it and understand it. What was needed was a key 'to read the word "death" *without* negation; as the moon, so life undoubtedly has a side permanently turned away from us, which is not its opposite, but its complement, to bring it to perfection, to the full count, to the truly whole sphere and roundness of *existence*. . . . Life's word is always Yes and No at the same time. But death . . . is the final Yes, says only Yes . . .'[67]

It was significant that, of the second sequence of sonnets that immediately followed the completion of the Elegies, Rilke's own favourite was the central thirteenth:

> Be ahead of all Departure, as if it were
> behind you like the winter that's just passed.
>
> . . . .
>
> Be here among the vanishing in the realm of entropy,
> be a ringing glass that shatters as it rings.
>
> Be—and at the same time know the implication
> of non-being, the endless ground of your inner vibration,
> so you can fulfil it fully just this once . . .[68]

and that he should place the last he wrote, on 23 February, at the head of the cycle:

> Breath, you invisible poem!
> Steady sheer exchange between the cosmos
> and our being. Counterpoise
> in which I rhythmically become.
>
> Single wave whose
> gradual sea I am; sparest
> of all possible seas—
> winning the universe.
>
> How many regions in space have been
> inside me already. Many winds
> are like my son.
>
> You, air, still full of places once mine,
> do you know me? You, once
> my words' sphere, leaf, and smooth rind.[69]

Sonnets and Elegies were 'of the same essence', as he wrote three years later to his Polish translator. 'There is neither a Here nor a Beyond, but only the great Unity, in which the beings superior to us, the "Angels", have their abode.' The involuntary start with the Sonnets, and their relation to Wera Knoop's early death, had drawn him 'to the centre of that realm whose depths and influence we, unbounded on any side, share with the dead and with those to come. ... In that supreme "open" World, all *exist*—one cannot say "simultaneously", for it is precisely the discontinuation of time which determines their existence. The past plunges everywhere into a deep Being.' It behoves man therefore to look upon all the forms of his earthly existence, not as time-conditioned and thus transient, but as the stepping-stones to the higher realm.

The Elegies show us at this work, the work of continual conversion of the visible and tangible we hold dear into the invisible vibration and agitation of our own nature, which introduces new vibration-numbers into the vibration-spheres of the universe. (For, since the various materials in the cosmos are only different exponents of vibration, we prepare in this way, not only intensities of a spiritual kind, but—who knows?—new substances, metals, nebulae, stars.)[70]

Rilke's words here seem in striking anticipation of the modern perception in physics of the universe as 'a dynamic web of inseparable energy patterns',[71] and in his poetic notion of past, present, and future he comes close to the space-time concept of relativity. It was perhaps no accident that, reading early in April 1922 of Einstein's lectures in Paris, and without any real knowledge of his theories, he should feel instinctively that ideas were at work here which could be of capital importance to save our age from condemnation by future generations as only negative and sinister. He regretted his ignorance of these discoveries: 'it may be that exclusion from what is happening in mathematics and the natural sciences will bar one for ever from the intrinsic flavour of the fruit that will be ripened in the uncertain climate of this century.'[72]

This was pure instinct. What he wrote in his letters, both fictitious and real, and later in his gloss to the translator on the 'meaning' of the Elegies, was an intellectualization of ideas which he had reached through feeling rather than by logical thought or philosophical introspection. Not for nothing had he described the experience of these remarkable February weeks as a storm, a submission to the spirit. In the stillness of Muzot it had come upon him literally as a seizure, releasing him for the 'heart-work' he had sought since 1915. The Sonnets and Elegies burst forth of themselves, in a flood of images from his memories and associations, while he was only half conscious of the philosophical construct they would reveal, feeling only that 'singing is Being' and that '*this* is the time for what can be said'.[73]

> How a bird's cry can move us ...
> Any once-created crying.
> But even children playing
> in the open cry beyond real cries.
>
> Cry accident. They drive their screams'
> wedges into those interstices
> of cosmic space (in which bird-cries
> go unharmed, as men go into dreams).

Oh where are we? Freer and freer,
like kites torn loose, tattered by wind,
we race in midair, edged with laughter.

Singing god, order the criers,
so they awake resounding like a current
carrying the head and the lyre.[74]

2

'The root of the trouble refuses to be discovered'
(To Anton Kippenberg, 1.1.1924)

She had cried for joy at his first news, wrote Lou Salomé: 'not only joy, but something more powerful, as though a curtain had been divided, rent apart, and suddenly everything was quiet and certain and present and good'. She could picture him to herself after this achievement, 'as you were in the old days, like a boy in glance and happy bearing: and the hope that moved you then, what you demanded of life so insistently as the one single necessity, is now as though fulfilled'. He was well aware, he said, of the reaction she warned could follow such an effort: 'after being thrown like this, I must fall somewhere—but . . . if I could be granted the patience, the abiding endurance to reach this point, I ought to be able to summon up a small subsidiary patience to see me through less good days.'[1] For the moment, however, in the early spring sunshine as February drew to a close, he felt only euphoria, and the dangers of over-relaxation seemed remote as he busied himself in making copies of the work, in whole or in part, for the friends he felt should have them.

One for Kippenberg, who had said he would not yet be able to visit him, was of course a priority, and he sent him the last six Elegies on 23 February, ready for publication when he should see fit. The manuscript of the Sonnets he enclosed with a separate letter to Katharina, feeling that—like the *Life of Mary*—they were a lesser work, and leaving it to her to judge whether they were worthy of publication, in full or in extract. It was not until the 'great day' of 7 June, when the Princess finally came to Sierre and he brought her up to Muzot to hear him read all the Elegies, and then, in her room in the Bellevue the next day, read through to her the complete Sonnet cycles, that he came to realize himself just how closely related the two works were, 'how each in its way appropriates and communicates the same motifs'.[2]

The occasion was unforgettable for Princess Marie. 'Secret, tiny low rooms with ancient furniture—flowers, flowers everywhere, among them the five-petalled, flame-coloured rose. . . . we went up to the study—a room filled with books, a feeling of devotion. Next to it the small bedroom and the little chapel . . . It all looks as though it had been expressly created for the poet. At last, standing at his desk as he always does, he began to read. . . . As he read—

wonderfully, as only he can—I could feel my heart throbbing louder and louder, and the tears running down my cheeks. There are no words for this experience. The next day ... the Sonnets. Fifty-seven of them, and not one too many. Every word a jewel. Some of them make one's heart stand still. ... .'[3]

Before her visit, he had been almost alarmed at the prospect of resuming human contact after his long 'fast': 'Muzotien endurci', he was not yet ready to bear the talk social intercourse would demand, and he felt he must wean himself carefully from 'the breasts of work'.[4] He was thankful to be able to continue in isolation, even deciding against a visit from Ruth before her marriage, which had been arranged for 18 May and which he did not plan to attend. At the end of March he spent a few days in Zurich, with the opportunity to see Nanny Wunderly, and Jean Strohl, but even then was impatient to return to his refuge.

With his love of flowers, he was anxious to improve the garden, which the terms of the lease left to the Rauniers but which they were agreeable to share; and soon he was immersed in detailed discussions with Frieda—more at home in this sphere than in the kitchen—and with the local gardeners and Nanny Wunderly on how to fill the front with standard and bush roses and find climbers for the walls. Left a free hand by Reinhart, he took a keen interest in the doings of the gardeners. Muzot resounded to the cry 'oui, mais il est trop jeune', he reported to Nanny: it turned out to be a question of the manure for the rose-beds—'it seems, I don't know why, we need venerable, respectable, uncommonly experienced manure'.[5] Years before, seeing a bed of 'La France' in the Luxembourg Gardens, he had longed for the day when he could have such a one of his own, 'to sit before it, when I am old, and turn it into words which contain everything I will know then'.[6] Now his delight was unbounded at the prospect of 'a host of roses, a whole people of roses, the rose-miracle!'

It was the first time since Westerwede, over twenty years before, that he had had the feeling of four walls of his own and the privilege of creating his own garden, and although Muzot's future was still uncertain, he indulged himself in a sense of settled proprietorship which he had never before experienced, even in the first weeks together with Clara. The dream of sharing some such place with a silent beloved as protector of his solitude had vanished with his successive disappointments. He was content now, in his forty-seventh year, to settle for life alone, with the less disturbing, if not always satisfactory, service of Frieda, and to shield himself from the distractions love would inevitably bring. Merline's response to his good news of the Elegies had been over-shadowed by her own difficulties, and it was many weeks before he replied. She had written to Nanny Wunderly of her idea of contriving a return to Switzerland, perhaps by taking a post as a companion, and he was quite dispassionate in his comments to Nanny on this impractical notion. He was ready to have 'Mouky' at Muzot, which owed so much to her, for a while during the summer, and to do all he could for the boys' future education, writing to interest Gide in helping to install Pierre at school in Paris; but for all his protestations of love, he was clearly not prepared to allow it to predominate in his life. Merline was on her way to become almost as much a voice from the past as Loulou Albert-Lazard, who in March, with a presentiment that something important had happened for him, ventured to write after four years' silence, sending him some reproductions of her work and to whom he replied in the brotherly tones of a fellow artist.

Other possible buyers for Muzot were now in the offing, and although Colonel Souvairan was keeping them at bay until Reinhart had reached his decision, it was evident that it should not be too long delayed. Rilke, reporting this in April, was scrupulous to urge his benefactor to take no account of his own wishes, delighted though he would be to remain as his steward: 'the great work which Muzot had to protect has been done, and stands whole and completed.'[7] Reinhart had been expected, with Nanny, at Easter, but her illness deferred their visit, and it was not until 27 April that the Muzot guest-book which she had had prepared was inaugurated with a suitable verse from Rilke to his 'liege lord at the end of the wonderfully fruitful winter of 1921/22'.[8] Reinhart was clearly set upon the purchase, and after his return to Winterthur his final offer to Souvairan of 37,500 francs for the property, including almost all the contents, was accepted on 12 May, Rilke signing the contract on his behalf a week later. 'Vous êtes maintenant chez vous!' wrote the Colonel, who had always had his interest at heart;[9] and Reinhart asked nothing better than to leave Muzot at Rilke's disposal for as long as he wished.

All his life the poet had been fortunate in the generosity of friends and patrons, but this gesture was the most important ever, and at the same time the most appropriate. Loans or more usually gifts of money had often seen him through difficult times, especially those from Fischer and the Cassirers, but he had been anything but a sensible manager; the family legacy, and the Wittgenstein bequest, had gone like chaff in the wind; and he would surely have foundered without Kippenberg's prudent monthly allocations against his current and expected royalty income. He had rarely lacked offers of temporary hospitality, but it had hardly ever proved congenial, and at most his circumstances, even alone in Paris, had given him relatively short spells in which his work could prosper. The Ainmillerstrasse apartment in Munich, as he began to gather things of his own around him, had seemed a step towards stability: but his lack of isolation there and his innate aversion to Germany had combined with his depression over the war to stifle his pleasure in it. Muzot was his first chance of a real home and stable existence, and a better gift than money, which he would have been incapable of using wisely: he had little ready cash of his own, as the inflation rapidly eroded his substantial balance in Germany, but he could rely on the backing of Nanny Wunderly and the Reinharts for his day-to-day needs. And it cannot be denied that the role of chatelain held great appeal, as he drove Princess Marie up in a hired *calèche* and showed her with some pride the domain in which her Elegies had been finished.

In one sense, however, this change of fortune came too late. Whatever the vicissitudes of his hand-to-mouth life of the previous ten years, the one great task had been always before him: in the calm now after the storm of its achievement, he was left without the sense of purpose it had given him, and he could not escape the feeling that his acceptance of this opportunity of a settled existence was under something like false pretences. The reaction had inevitably set in after the extreme tension of February, not least physically in the need for an inordinate amount of sleep and in a vague but persistent malaise. It was brought home to him once again how, in single-minded pursuit of his art, he had denied himself the beneficial counterbalance some poets had found in the exercise of a different profession—Mallarmé as teacher, Carossa as doctor—which could alleviate the withdrawal symptoms after creative effort. Less exacting tasks lay to hand—during March and April he made a translation of Valéry's *Ebauche d'un serpent*—but emulation of Rodin's example was no longer possible for him, and he viewed the summer ahead with a certain depression.

His rootlessness in life, he said later, had been partly due to his welcome for any change of scene that offered itself after such periods of intensity, for this was the best way both to rest and to prepare for the new start.[10] Now, however, he could not bring himself to move. After the Princess's departure he stayed for the rest of June at the Bellevue, while Frieda took a holiday, and the necessity of supervising from there the watering of the garden, which after a late start had begun to flourish in the hot weather, was a welcome excuse for avoiding any call further afield, even to Meilen. There were many invitations—from Pia Valmarana in Italy; Sidie Nádherný, Mary Dobržensky and of course the Princess in Bohemia; Gide, who wanted him to join the 'Entretiens de Pontigny'; and especially tempting, from the Purtscher-Wydenbrucks in his supposed homeland of Carinthia—but he knew he was not likely to find with any of these the restful change he should have, and in any case he must on no account miss the Kippenbergs, who had at last arranged their visit to him for late in July. For a time it looked as though his presence would be required in Vienna, following the death of his cousin Irene's son Oswald von Kutschera, who had made him his residual heir, but—affected though he was by this early disappearance of a friend and one of the few remaining members of his Prague family—he was relieved in the end not to have to revisit Austria. As for Germany, scene of strikes, unrest, and increasing lawlessness, nothing would have dragged him there. The assassination of Walther Rathenau, on 24 June, filled him with horror: he felt it was the destruction of the 'last man of wisdom' who could have kept Germany under control.[11] It made him all the more anxious to offer Merline a holiday from Berlin, in the Muzot where she was 'née-invitée', and with Reinhart's approval it was arranged that she would come in July, leaving Pierre behind in Berlin but placing Baltusz in the Beatenberg holiday home. She was not to forget her artist's materials, he wrote: 'you must become the painter of the Valais . . . What splendour, the gentle shadows, the purity of this country's "traits" . . . but who am I telling!'[12]

She had just been installed in the hastily-furnished guest-room on the upper floor when the Kippenbergs arrived at the Bellevue on 21 July. They came up to Muzot each day, and their brief stay was very harmonious, Rilke reported to Nanny—though Kippenberg's appreciation of the excellent cigars she had sent, on his urgent request, had come close to eclipsing his enjoyment of the reading of the Elegies. They agreed upon the contents of the six-volume *Collected Works*; Elegies and Sonnets were to be published as soon as the increasingly difficult conditions in Germany allowed; the Sonnets, which he read to Katharina alone, he pressed into her hand in the form of a dedicated manuscript as they boarded their train in Sierre; and they took with them the manuscript of the second cycle of 'Count C. W.' Rilke could feel more than satisfied with the visit.

It had been in his mind to leave Merline to herself at Muzot, at least for part of the summer: but once she was there the effort of moving seemed too great, and he was once more preoccupied with her troubles. He was shocked at the change in her since the happier days in Geneva. The growing chaos in Berlin, her unavailing efforts to make a living from her art as costs soared, and above all the seeming impossibility of ever realizing her dream of returning to Paris and a French environment, had brought her near to despair. The unexpected arrival of a substantial sum of money from Werner Reinhart, however, shook Rilke out of his lethargy: he began to think of a visit later to Paris himself, having heard from the Czech Legation that his effects might at last be released, and meanwhile decided to take a short break with Merline, joining Baltusz in Beatenberg. When they returned to Muzot, early in September, Merline seemed more relaxed, but he himself had not been able entirely to shake off his malaise—and now new difficulties awaited him. Frieda, after such long independence, began to resent the presence of another woman in the house, and, after what she felt was unjustified criticism from Merline, gave a month's notice, pleading that she was needed at home in Balsthal.[13] A replacement engaged during October was unsatisfactory, and did not survive her month's trial. His hopes of another fruitful winter, therefore, looked like being frustrated just when he had made up his mind to it.

While Merline stayed on, the household's running was assured—but the last thing he wanted now was to share Muzot with her. '*Solitude* is the *only* possible thing for me,' he wrote to Nanny, 'anything else must be the exception, for a few hours or days, but never again so constant and lasting . . . If it were only another house, like Berg say, where people can keep themselves to themselves without seeming too purposeful about it; Muzot is like a mould for one living being only, with two it's overfilled, and (especially when extension outdoors is no longer possible) the result is a shapeless cast!'[14] For all his sympathy and understanding for her position, he found living with Merline an intolerable *énervement*. During November Frieda was persuaded to return, and he bent all his efforts to finding financial help for Merline that would take her off his hands. He had succeeded in interesting Georg Reinhart in the boys' future, and when Merline reluctantly left for Berlin with Baltusz, on 29 November, it was with the firm promise of his aid. In the end, Reinhart made 3,000 Swiss francs available to Rilke for the coming twelve months, to be sent on to her in appropriate instalments, for the family as a whole but primarily in the interests of the boys' schooling. With the now galloping inflation in Germany, the arrangement was a godsend for her, and Rilke's conscience was correspondingly relieved as he settled at last to his winter alone, 'la belle route de ma solitude'.[15]

During October, when it had seemed in jeopardy, he had momentarily regretted not having had the presence of mind to use Werner Reinhart's generous gift to better purpose for himself and Merline. Now that his 'main work was done', might it not have been the moment for them both to stake all on returning at once to France? She might have found her feet, in spite of everything; he, with the help of Gide and perhaps Valéry, could have reconnoitred the possibility of settling once again in Paris. It was too late for that now, but he did not abandon the idea of Paris one day, for which the final settlement of Oswald von Kutschera's estate might provide the funds. Meanwhile, his worry over the cost of Muzot, both to Nanny, who was meeting the household expenses, and to Werner, for whom the essential repairs were producing mounting bills, had been needless, they assured him, and nothing stood in the way of his winter there.

By comparison with that preceding, it would be no more than marking time, the 'inevitable pause between two periods of work'.[16] His plan, apart from dealing with the correspondence list and the proofs of Elegies and Sonnets, the first of which had already arrived with a discouraging flood of errors, was to concentrate on his translations, which were to form the final volume of the *Collected Works*. Here, however, even if no mountain range of work lay ahead, one peak remained to be conquered, lesser perhaps but just as important for him: Valéry. Snowed in at Muzot from the first days of December, as the household resumed its 'even and noiseless' course, he set about the task at once, and by February had made a rendering of almost all the poems of *Charmes*—'all these marvels, and I think I can say my work has been successful and blessed'.[17] As with his earlier translations—the *Sonnets from the Portuguese*, Gide's *Enfant prodigue*, Guérin's *Centaur*, the Michelangelo sonnets—his versions of Valéry were Rilkean re-creations rather than faithful transpositions of the original into German. With these 'summits of splendour', he felt he had never achieved so close an approach, and congratulated himself on his skill in retaining the same outward form of the verses: yet his images are often subtly different, and the thought sometimes elusively changed, resulting in a German poem with a beauty of its own but going beyond translation in the strict sense—'as if a piece written for the harpsichord were played on an organ'.[18] This may be why he found as great a pleasure in this work as in production of his own, while at the same time feeling he had achieved a *tour de force* of equivalence and continuing to consider Valéry—whose more cerebral poetry was in fact very different from his—as 'the one nearest to me among the poets of my generation'.[19]

Certainly it was a task which helped him through an indifferent and uneasy winter. His days followed a quiet and steady routine of letters, translation work, and reading. Without being actually ill, he still felt unaccountably off colour, and for a few days over Christmas subsisted only on soup. At times he needed ten, even twelve hours of sleep, at others suffered from insomnia. Any extra effort seemed to touch on an extreme sensitivity in the solar plexus, an area of the body to which he attributed almost mystical significance—'the central point of our orientation towards both the visible and the invisible'. Both he and the friends who heard his complaints and speculations about his indefinable malaise regarded it as the delayed reaction to the exhausting effort of the previous year, and he strove to make light of it. After the 'great works', as after *Malte*, he told Katharina Kippenberg, he stood before a new epoch: 'new courage, new despair . . .—oh endless novitiate!'[20]

His hopes of sending out the first copies of the Elegies at Christmas were disappointed: midnight on New Year's Eve found him at his desk still over the second proofs, and it was not until the summer that the first, limited, edition appeared. The *Inselschiff* for December, however, had carried a facsimile of his manuscript of the Fourth Elegy, and the *Almanach* for 1923 several earlier poems, including 'Exposed on the cliffs of the heart' and Count C. W.'s 'Karnak'. His one extravagance was on books, even though it meant shame-faced recourse to the Muzot fund or reliance on Nanny Wunderly's generosity: and in his wide reading he turned increasingly to French. Paul Morisse, formerly of the *Mercure de France* and now running a French bookshop in Zurich, had become a firm friend, not least through his connection with Valéry, and received a steady stream of orders for the latest publications— Romains, Larbaud, Colette, Jaloux, the 'Cahiers verts' as they appeared, as well as literary journals and new translations of Turgenev, Dostoevsky, even Chesterton. The special January number of the *Nouvelle Revue Française* devoted to Proust, whose work Rilke had followed with admiration since its first appearance, kept him up till two in the morning, with the revelation of his contemporary's achievement in devoting himself unswervingly to an inner call.

This self-expenditure on the world of society, quite free of ambition, verging on snobbery but saved by this search everywhere for something pure and powerful— which then gradually takes over his whole life, controlling everything, even sickness, with the one single aim. And finally this death, refusing all drugs, even in his agony improving the description of an agony, when the word 'Fin' had already been put to the last page.

'That is on one side of the Rhine,' he wrote to Nanny, 'on the other, adulation of Hauptmann for months on end. . . . On n'a qu'à choisir.' The contrast pointed up the revulsion which he had long felt for Germany and which turned now almost to hatred with the news he read of political and economic developments there and the crisis in Europe. He did not excuse the French occupation of the Ruhr and Rhineland, but laid the original blame at the door of the Germans—not a people, but a mass, ready and willing to be driven by megalomaniac 'ideas'; 'a league of evil instincts', all the worse for involving genuine intellectual values with them; without dignity or calm, and showing a feeling of community only when advantage beckoned. 'The "German God": under Wilhelm II, an NCO, and now, a sort of Ebert at half-mast.' The right moment for a change had been missed in 1919: now there seemed no hope. 'Really, there is nothing to which I stand more passionately opposed than this "Reich" . . . May Switzerland protect me until the day when I can find some far, far distant refuge, or disappear as a private individual in Paris, as a Czech citizen who can stroll along the *quais* and in the Luxembourg without ever bumping against the alarm bells of politics.'[21]

His antipathy towards Germany made him feel almost ashamed at having to use the German tongue—'if I did not know how distant from all this is the life and vibration of my language, the fact that nominally it comes from there, appears to belong there, would almost strike me to silence'—and he spoke, not altogether in jest, of resuming the study of Arabic he had dipped into on his North African tour. 'Then if, in ten years' time, a book of mine appears, the Insel will have to see about getting Arabic type to print it . . .'[22] German was not only prone to imprecision, against which all his work had been a constant struggle, for 'he was a poet, and hated the approximate'.[23] He also found its vocabulary poor in comparison with that of French. Gide recalled how in 1914 Rilke had remarked there was no word in German expressive enough for the palm of the hand: the German could talk at best of the 'hand surface', or of its back, *der Handrücken*, as though preferring the rough, impersonal outside to the 'warm, caressing, soft inside, *la paume*, which tells of the whole mystery of man!' In Gide's copy of Grimm's dictionary, he had found *Handteller*, 'plate of the hand'—'but it is *la paume* which is stretched out for alms, which serves as a bowl! what a confession, in this inadequacy of our language!'[24] When, from Etoy, he was in touch with Vildrac over corrections to his *Mitsou* preface, he had compared French with 'a beautiful vine ripened over the centuries' and cultivated according to well-defined laws: a language with a clarity and sureness which his own was far from having achieved.[25]

France, and its language and literature, in fact shed now the one ray of light on his gloomy view of Europe. He was well placed here, he wrote to Lou

Salomé in January, to judge how, at a level below politics, there were signs of a
hidden growth, and particularly in France. 'I don't know if you have been
following Proust, his influence is enormous—but it is not only his influence
that is bringing change, others, younger people, are achieving the same
effect.'[26] Meanwhile, it was gratifying to learn that Maurice Betz, a young
Alsatian writer, was translating part of *Malte* for publication in Paris, and he
asked Merline to try a sketch of himself for this first work of his to appear in
book form in French. Betz, it so happened, knew Claire Goll, and his news of
Rilke encouraged her to write, breaking their three years' silence and sending
him her most recent work; and it was significant that this reminder of a fleeting
but passionate affair should prompt in him, not German verses, but French,
jotted down on the back of her envelope:

> Ah moi à mon tour
> si je te lis, Liliane,
> c'est sans doute par amour
> que mon être s'inganne
> de la nuit et du jour
> et que je m'agite pour
> une goutte diaphane.[27]

By early March he could tell Kippenberg that the translation volume was
ready. He was ready too for a change from his monastic seclusion, and found
the many visitors who began to announce themselves more welcome than at
other times. Muzot's guest-room being hardly adequate, he mostly put them
up in Sierre, but was their host at tea or an occasional dinner (for which Frieda
was now rather more confident than before), the silver, glass, and china which
Nanny Wunderly had provided over the months arranged under his careful
supervision and lending distinction to his candle-lit table. It gave him
particular pleasure to be able, with a few Swiss francs, to buy train tickets for
Regina Ullmann and Ellen Delp to see Geneva, when their supply of inflated
marks was not sufficient to cover the extra journey. Easter became a real
festival for him, not only with the arrival of the first copies of the Sonnets, but
also from the visit of Werner Reinhart and two friends, the artist von Freyhold
and a young Australian violin virtuoso, Alma Moodie. Werner seemed this
time 'truly to take possession, to take Muzot (which fully stood the test) to his
heart', Rilke wrote to Nanny. Alma Moodie's Bach gave the old house 'its
great baptism of music'—'that, and the *Sonnets to Orpheus*, were like two
strings for the same part'.[28]

Frieda, who was to return home after Easter, and was already training her
replacement, was not forgotten at the feast. On Easter Day she received a little
card from the Easter hare, announcing his intention of laying his eggs in 'a new
summer hat': 'as he is old-fashioned and not able to pay attention to today's
modes, the undersigned begs to be assisted without delay in the selection of

this egg-basket'.[29] Her farewell present was an expensive bottle of perfume, so magnificent that she said she would have to hide it from her sister Rosa, who would surely covet it—and when he saw her off, on 6 April, she found he had bought another just like it for Rosa.[30]

In May Mary Dobržensky stayed in Sierre for two weeks, a frequent visitor to Muzot, and Rilke went with her to inspect a small château nearby which she thought of renting for a longer stay. It was owned by a doctor in Sierre, and they were shown round by his wife, Jeanne de Sépibus, entertaining her to tea afterwards at the Bellevue. She had no knowledge of German, and was quite unaware of Rilke's fame, but was captivated by his courtesy and charm. They became firm friends, Rilke often bringing her roses, spending quiet hours under the walnut tree in her garden and writing to her when he was away. Two years later she was bold enough to ask him—since she had heard he was a great poet—if he would write a poem for her in French, perhaps on her walnut tree. He smiled, and said he did not usually write to order, but would do his best: and a little later, invited to dine at Muzot, she found by her plate the carefully written holograph of 'Le noyer', with a single rose on the napkin:

> . . . Arbre qui peut-être
> pense au-dedans:
> antique Arbre-maître
> parmi les arbres servants!
>
> Arbre qui se domine,
> se donnant lentement
> la forme qui élimine
> les hasards du vent:
>
> plein de forces austères
> ton ombre claire nous rend
> une feuilles qui désaltère
> et des fruits persévérants.

Though she lived to a great age, she recalled to the end the years she had known Rilke as the 'most wonderful of my life'.[31]

Later in May the Princess arrived in Sierre, spending this time a week and taking Rilke for motor-car drives. It was disappointing not to be able to present her with the Elegies, but at least he could read her his Valéry versions, of which he had been making the first fair copy in a volume to present to Valéry, and provide her with the introduction she sought to Werner Reinhart. Kippenberg had meanwhile found a way to providing some francs from a Swiss account. With this slight augmentation of his pocket-money Rilke was able to leave Muzot from time to time during the summer—for Zurich, the Greifensee, Thun, Vevey and Villeneuve, Berne—without being always dependent on the hospitality and the motor cars of his friends. Escape was particularly welcome from the indifferent cooking of Frieda's replacement,

tions he mostly left untouched, and whom in the autumn he discharged even though Frieda's return was then uncertain. Paris, and the recovery of his papers which had finally been 'desequestrated', had to remain a dream for the moment. Merline was invited again in July, and this time he held to his resolve to leave her alone at Muzot for longer periods: they could talk together calmly now of her troubles, 'like the old friends we are',[32] and his efforts on her behalf were as intensive as ever, but the distance he wanted had been gained.

Despite the distractions of visitors and visits, however, his bodily unease persisted and sharpened. There was evidently something wrong abdominally, he was losing weight fast, and, convinced though he always was that his body ought to be able to heal itself, it had become clear that he must seek a doctor's aid. Towards the end of August, he entered a sanatorium at Schöneck, on Lake Lucerne, where the doctor in charge ('apparently because his daughter-in-law is a devoted reader of mine') insisted on carrying out his examination and the massage treatment personally. Rather grotesque, he found, 'to have an old gentleman pensively running his hands every morning over my body—a circus turn':[33] but it was in a way a relief to hear there was indeed some palpable evidence of an intestinal cramp, even though the cause remained obscure and the hot baths, massage, and electrical treatment over his month's stay seemed to have no effect.

A few days in Lucerne, and then with Guido von Salis, now established at Malans in the Grisons, which he had hoped would make a follow-up cure, brought no change. Thoughts of wider travel—to Paris perhaps, or Italy— were soon abandoned: a return to Muzot for the winter seemed the only possibility in his present condition. He was in no hurry to get there, however, until the redecoration which Merline was supervising was finished and he knew whether Frieda, once again appealed to, was prepared to return—despite her shortcomings, it was better than trying someone new. Meilen with Nanny Wunderly was a refuge for three weeks in October, followed by a short stay in Berne, and when he arrived back in Muzot at the end of the month all was settled. Frieda, after a short cookery course with Nanny to prepare her for the more invalid diet he would need, was reinstalled early in November, and Merline had made her plans: thanks to Gide's efforts, and to substantial provision from the balance of Georg Reinhart's funds, Pierre was at last to go to Paris, where he hoped to make a future for himself, while she would leave on 20 November for Beatenberg to spend the winter there with Baltusz.

Her resignation to her new role, as she prepared to leave him to his solitude, was badly shaken when Frieda answered the door one morning to an elegantly dressed and heavily made-up woman who asked to be announced to Rilke. It was Loulou Albert-Lazard, who had made a stop at Sierre on her way between France and Italy. The reply, through Merline, was that he could not see her, and to Frieda's alarm the visitor looked on the point of fainting away on the porch where she had been left standing. Merline, relenting, fetched Rilke, and retired with Frieda to the kitchen while he passed off this unexpected, but luckily brief, visitation as best he could—with a reading to Loulou from the Elegies, naturally, and the presentation of an inscribed copy.[34]

The stability of his circumstances, compared with the chaos in Germany where the inflation was now reaching unheard of heights, had induced a more sympathetic attitude towards his family. On the news in June that Ruth was expecting her first child, he had been able, for 48 Swiss francs, to send her a million marks (though he could not conceive the actual value of this fictitious fortune), and after the birth of Christine, in November, arranged for a similar Christmas present each for her and Ruth. Towards Clara, his earlier severity had mellowed. He had fallen in with Kippenberg's proposals for increasing help for her from his account, and was touched by her appreciation of the Elegies. The distance between them was no less, but their relationship was more cordial than it had been for years.

He was grateful for the protection of Muzot for yet another winter, and clung to the hope that the familiar conditions would set him right. But he still regarded it as temporary, and looked forward to the day when he could return to settle in France, in Paris, or Provence. His unblocked account with the Crédit Lyonnais, even if only a hundred odd francs, seemed a symbol of this future, and citizens of Czechoslovakia no longer needed a visa—'if the fancy takes me one day, all I have to do is jump into the train!' For the moment, however, after the pleasant enough months of wandering through Switzerland, he could only look back on what had been all in all a 'lost summer', and forward to another temporizing winter.[35] While this insidious malaise continued to beset him, his heart was not in the resumption even of the accustomed preliminary routine of correspondence, satisfying though it was to be able to distribute Christmas copies of the Elegies and Sonnets to his friends: and the work he hoped would follow was inhibited by the nagging feeling that his body was betraying him. He tried to believe that the 'magnificent agitation and achievement' of the Elegies had been a rejuvenation for him,[36] but the sense of reward from that great effort was increasingly overshadowed by its cost in bodily terms.

During December he felt so much worse that, in desperation, he telegraphed Georg Reinhart after Christmas for a recommendation to a doctor at the clinic of Valmont, in Glion above Montreux. Admitted there on 28 December, he spent three weeks under observation, while some routine treatment, as in Schöneck, was applied for a condition that in fact defied diagnosis, X-rays in January finding nothing apparently wrong. Valmont was a luxurious establishment, giving the maximum of personal attention and charging accordingly. Rilke, glad of the Swiss franc funds Kippenberg had been able to arrange, felt he was paying for the best, and Reinhart's Doctor

Haemmerli devoted much time to his puzzling case. He gained some weight, and 'objectively' his condition improved. The fact remained, however, that when he returned to Muzot on 20 January he felt no real change for the better, and the only profit was the conviction that in Haemmerli he had found the sympathetic and reliable adviser he was sure he would need.

The doctor—understandably, in the absence of identifiable physical symptoms, and accustomed as he was to the complaints of wealthy hypochondriacs—could not yet appreciate how deep the crisis of December had gone. In a sudden onset, the hitherto vague feeling of unease had developed into a brutal shock that Rilke felt to his very marrow, so powerful that he was terrified. He could not explain this covert onslaught: but somehow it had sapped the inner confidence which, even at his worst moments, had always seemed unshakeable, and whose absolute and ever more integrated unity with the body had been the well-spring of his art. He felt then a nameless fear that the defection of his body might destroy that unity, that a rift in his nature had been opened which might never be repaired. 'My body has been too much part of my joys of soul and spirit, too linked with the enthusiasms, the ecstasies, the transports of my being, for me to continue as "me" if that marvellous instrument should suddenly be out of tune . . .' Haemmerli might prove to be the 'interpreter of his nature' he had never before thought to need—but to become a 'patient' was an intolerable prospect. Lying at Valmont, he had felt as though transposed to 'another level of life', he wrote to Nanny Wunderly, 'perhaps that of the incurable, those who no longer take part'.[37] To submit would transform him into another being altogether, much as when he had been forced to put on uniform in 1915. Although he knew that something was fundamentally wrong with him—as indeed proved to be the case—he was determined to overcome it, to remain himself and not give way. To no one except Nanny did he reveal the fear that had smitten him. Others heard only of the 'less good chapters in his constitution' that had been opened, but which had to be 'read and understood'[38]—how he felt himself like a seed fallen on stony ground, how he was trying to regain the essential unity of body and spirit[39]—and none were particularly concerned over what seemed just another of his periodic depressions.

Haemmerli had welcomed his idea of a visit to Paris, indeed recommended some such radical change of surroundings; but he felt that at the moment it was too risky for his diet, and the doctor probably did not realize how important for him was the 'extreme solitude' of Muzot, 'even now that its main object has been attained'.[40] For what remained of the winter, *tant bien que mal*, he would resume the familiar routine: and, unplanned, it proved productive. Almost every day through February and March poems sprang to his pen— often occasional verses, or dedications to the copies of Elegies and Sonnets he was still sending away, but among them work of considerable power, such as 'Eros', written in February:

Masks! Masks! Or blind him! How can they endure
this flaming Eros gods and men obey,
bursting in summer-solstice on the pure
idyllic prologue to their vernal play?

How imperceptibly the conversation
takes a new, graver turn ... A cry ... And, there!
he's flung the nameless fascination
like a dim temple round the fated pair.

Lost, lost! O instantaneous perdition!
In brief divinity they cling.
Life turns, and Destiny begins her mission.
And within there weeps a spring.[41]

Stronger, however, was the impulse to use his second language, and the greater part of the notebooks he filled now with verse was in French. He delighted more and more in the quite different means of expression it offered for themes he had taken up in German, and in its suggestive power for those that came to him in the surroundings of Muzot. Certain words fascinated him—'verger' (orchard), for which German had no word with the same associations, or Valéry's 'absence'—and in the simple clarity of the language he found himself led along other paths. An 'Eros' emerged, at the same time as the German, in a form at once more concrete and differently evocative:

Là, sous la treille, parmi le feuillage
il nous arrive de le deviner:
son front rustique d'enfant sauvage
et son antique bouche mutilée ...

La grappe devant lui devient pesante
et semble fatiguée de sa lourdeur,
un court moment on frôle l'épouvante
de cet heureux trompeur.

. . . .
... Toi, qui indifférent et superbe,
humilies la bouche et exaltes le verbe
vers un ciel ignorant ...
Toi qui mutiles les êtres en les ajoutant
à l'ultime absence dont ils sont les fragments.[42]

Work at 'half-steam', perhaps, as he wrote to Dory von der Mühll in March, but all the same it gave a quiet satisfaction.[43] He had already sent Valéry the fair copy of his translations, and, hearing that there might be a chance of a meeting on Valéry's way through to Italy, he made bold to follow this up with one of his efforts, in French, 'dictated to me just when your letter arrived',[44] the first of a series of poems he would devote to his favourite 'Verger' theme:

Peut-être que si j'ai osé t'écrire,
langue prêtée, c'était pour employer
ce nom rustique dont l'unique empire
me tourmentait depuis toujours: Verger.

. . . .

Nom clair qui cache le printemps antique
tout aussi plein que transparent,
et qui dans ses syllabes symétriques
redouble tout et devient abondant.[45]

Valéry's praise of the 'strange grace' of these verses, 'giving me a direct and inestimable impression of your pure and deep poetry',[46] was a strong encouragement for Rilke's belief that his poetic gift could find expression, in different forms and rhythms, in French.

'Basically, one ought to write in all languages,' he had said during the war—the counterpart to his 'non-patriotism', which should be 'a jubilant and positive confession of belonging to the universal'[47]—and he had many times tried his hand in French, Russian, even Italian, though under no illusion that the results could ever rival his work in his native tongue. In French, these had been isolated attempts, under the stimulus of the passing moment, and even in Paris had been rare. Now he felt for the first time an impulse to 'active obedience to this admired language',[48] and the flow continued, in a progression which he found positively rejuvenating, for the rest of the year, alongside and often parallel with poems in German. He may well have felt too, as Boris Pasternak later surmised, that in German he had reached the very limit of abstraction and was unable to return to those 'details of the beginning without which the artist's word cannot emerge—in French he could become a beginner again'.[49]

These 'superfluities' to the great work, as he called them, were a help through the bad days which still plagued him from time to time. When Valéry spent a few hours at Muzot on 6 April—the French flag hoisted on the old tower, and a willow planted afterwards, in honour of an occasion so significant for Rilke—he was appalled at the thought of everlasting winters spent in such isolation, amid a melancholy landscape and in 'such abuse of intimacy with silence'. He could feel instinctively, though he had no German, how favourable this 'terrifying peace' could be for Rilke's art: but he feared for him, he wrote the following year, 'in this transparency of too monotonous a life through whose identical days there comes a distinct glimpse of death.'[50]

Through this winter and spring, however, Rilke's seclusion was anything but total. The chatelain of Muzot was accessible now to his neighbours, often taking tea with Jeanne de Sépibus; many friends from further afield in Switzerland came by; and Valéry's visit was the prelude to others as the late spring drew into summer. Jean Rudolf von Salis, then a student, recalled his host's 'natural laughter' and the resonance of his strong baritone voice as he read some of the Valéry translations—an impression of 'sovereign artistry'. 'Here stood not merely a poet, but a man ... with masculine rigour.'[51] At Easter the Swiss flag was raised to mark the arrival of Werner Reinhart, who brought Alma Moodie again and the Austrian composer Ernst Křenek; at the end of April the Kippenbergs once more spent a few days in Sierre, and discussed possible publication of the translations. During May Clara and her brother Helmuth came to stay at Muzot for a week. It was Rilke's first meeting with his wife since the end of the war, and was to be their last—a brief crossing of their separate paths which, however, he found now curiously satisfying, as he showed her the setting for the life he had chosen, the flourishing garden with its roses, and listened to her account of Ruth and little Christine, 'a sort of elementary course in the art of being a grandfather. Mais j'ai peu de talent'.[52] He arranged for them to stay with Nanny Wunderly on the return journey, for which he paid, and was content to hear from both women how quickly they had become friends.

It had been for him a meeting free from emotion, an exchange of news and reminiscences between old friends. With Merline too he had gained a similar detachment. Nanny Wunderly had been apprehensive of the effect on him if she were to return to Muzot, but he was able to reassure her that neither of them thought of any such return. 'M. is one of those people who, having once received a payment at some counter, keep coming back to it even when the official assures them nothing has come in under their name.' He had now done all he could for her, she was finally leaving for Paris in May, Baltusz having already gone ahead, and he could only hope that, after having sailed so long in troubled waters, she would find an even keel there.[53] Though her letters still sometimes betrayed her hopeless passion, their correspondence was now increasingly on the safer ground of literature and art. It was ironic that, having achieved a stability of solitary existence and an emotional independence he had rarely before known, he should find them undermined by the illness that would not leave him.

Princess Marie's itinerary this year did not include Muzot: now in her seventieth year, she had been advised to seek a cure at Bad Ragaz. Rilke, who had been taken with the old-fashioned elegance of the spa as he passed through from Soglio, planned to join her there in the hope that the change would do him good. His finances at least were healthy, thanks to the revaluation of the mark and further remittances from Kippenberg, and a generous contribution from Reinhart to 'the travel and holiday account of the faithful steward'. It had given him 'a freedom of movement and freedom from care that a steward can seldom have enjoyed through the centuries', he wrote in gratitude, though he confessed he would be leaving the fresh summer surroundings of Muzot with some regret.[54] He made first a leisurely motor tour with Nanny Wunderly, through Vaud, Neuchâtel, and Berne, taking the opportunity of a consultation with Dr Haemmerli in Valmont, before arriving in Ragaz on 28 June.

Though the spa had taken on new life since the war, with the advent of the
automobile and a largely Anglo-Saxon clientele (Mary Pickford and Douglas
Fairbanks were there during Rilke's stay), the Hotel Hof Ragaz, where he
lodged with the Prince and Princess, still preserved something of the
nineteenth-century atmosphere, with its Empire furniture and a horse-drawn
onmibus to and from the station. He could indulge his nostalgia for a past age
to the full, even though few remained of the traditional *Kurgäste*: 'today's are
not the right actors to animate appropriately the noble scene of avenues and
lawns. (Quel public!)'[55] The hotels, however, still had good carriages, he was
glad to find, 'at last I had the opportunity again (one of my greatest pleasures
since I was a boy) of riding in the country in a landau',[56] to revisit the Salis
family at Schloss Bothmar in Malans.

His days passed quietly in walks, absorbing the thrice-daily offerings of the
orchestra, taking a holiday from letters and seeking refuge from the crowd to
read to the Princess in her private drawing-room. She found his poems in
French attractive, but 'not the voice of the great angels, not the "primeval
breath of the sea"' that had come to him in Capri, and felt that for him they
were no more than a stimulating game.[57] Though the game continued
occasionally in the relaxation of Ragaz, the return to a German ambience
brought more inspiration in his native tongue, in a series of poems 'In the
Churchyard at Ragaz', some of which can rank with his finest work, and in the
continuation of a correspondence in verse which had started in May with a
poem addressed to him by the young Erika Mitterer in Vienna.[58]

After the Princess's departure, on 10 July, he was finding it so beneficial that
he stayed on for two more weeks, venturing towards the end to try the thermal
baths, which he had at first thought might be too exhausting, but which now
he could not praise too highly. The radioactivity and chemical composition,
and especially the temperature, at body heat, gave him an uncommon feeling
of well-being, and seemed to restore the harmony of body he had lacked. With
Nanny Wunderly, who came on a short visit, he made the excursion to Bad
Pfäfers and through the grandiose Tamina Gorge up to the source. The
'ancient healing spring' flowed noiselessly from a cave which reminded him of
the Pecherskaya Monastery below Kiev: 'how similar, I thought, may be the
forces which, exerting their influence from the depths of the earth, create *there*
a miracle of death and *here* give promise of one which, in infinite benevolence,
stands on the side of life!' In the gorge itself the roar of the waters in their
narrow channel recalled his notion of a 'primeval sound' subsisting in physical
manifestations: the great cleft might have been hollowed out not only by the
action of the waters, but also perhaps by their sound through the millennia, the
walls 'acoustically smoothed' just as the interior of cathedrals might be
influenced by the waves of sound from the organ. Experiment, he was
convinced, would one day establish that the world is largely the play of such
interactions, and that the different stimuli offered to our senses are somewhere
tangential, meeting 'on some as yet undiscovered periphery'.[59]

When he finally left at the end of the month, to spend a week with Nanny at Meilen, it was with the firm resolve to return one day to these springs which, as he wrote later,

> a terrestrial force warms to the very degree
> of the blood in our veins. Was ever a blessing so clear
> as this which Nature herself gives so exuberantly?
>
> Hostile and strange she often seems, in her preoccupation
> leaving us somewhere between quiet and unquietness;
> how she completes us, though, when she gives us her authorization:
> purely, from out of the depths, meeting our hesitantness.[60]

Meanwhile, he had conscientiously devoted his evenings to the preparation for Kippenberg of the Valéry translation manuscript, recruiting an excellent secretary to take his dictation from the drafts, the only fair copy having been sent to the poet. It was dispatched from Meilen, and the volume was published in 1925 for the Insel in an elegant limited edition by the Cranach Press, with an initial by Eric Gill and a dedication to Werner Reinhart, 'most hospitable friend'.[61]

Returning to Muzot on 2 August, he found the price had to be paid for his holiday from correspondence. In spite of a mountain of letters, however, his 'second lyre' began again to sound—a whole series of poems in French, 'dedicated to the Valais, true "Quatrains valaisans"', which, as he wrote to Nanny Wunderly, he would use 'to support my future application for Swiss nationality, there is no better proof that I have this country in the blood':

> Pays, arrêté à mi-chemin
> entre la terre et les cieux
> aux voix d'eau et d'airain,
> doux et dur, jeune et vieux,
>
> comme une offrande levée
> vers d'accueillantes mains:
> beau pays achevé,
> chaud comme le pain!
>   (2)
>
> Chemins qui ne mènent nulle part
> entre deux prés
> que l'on dirait avec art
> de leur but détournés,
>
> chemins qui souvent n'ont
> devant eux rien d'autre en face
> que le pur espace
> et la saison.
>   (31)[62]

The appearance of such 'regional poetry' from his pen was the first since his 'Offerings to the Lares' of his real homeland, nearly thirty years before— such was the rejuvenation he found in writing French verse—and the harsh picture of Prague he had retained since leaving it had now softened. Describing the old city for Strohl, who was about to pay a visit there, he said his friend would readily appreciate what the splendid buildings of its past had meant for his childhood.[63] He felt he owed much to his distant memories, and was full of hope too for the future of the new Czechoslovakia, under the statesmanlike guidance of Masaryk, to whom he had paid tribute already in 1921. It was not ingratitude that kept him from returning, but the recollection of his unhappy family life there. The memories of that, certainly, had been vividly revived for him with the death in February of his only remaining cousin, Jaroslav's daughter, Paula, from whose estate he had been sent papers and family memorabilia. What he looked back on there, he told Nanny Wunderly, was grotesque in the extreme, 'de la province engourdie'; and as for his mother's side, the ancient grandmother and Phia herself growing old, it beggared description—'a perfect Guignol, played with sadly disjointed but unbreakable puppets. Heaven preserve me from having to look too closely'.[64] Even had Switzerland become impossible for him, it is clear that Czechoslovakia as a refuge would have been even more unthinkable than Germany: he preferred to remain 'sufficiently aloof from my native land to keep faith with it, independently, in the particular turns taken by its destiny'.[65] Whether or not he seriously entertained the idea of Swiss citizenship, the *Quatrains valaisans*—'so heartening for me as they sprang up in the language of the country to which I owe so much'[66]—were an affirmation of allegiance which now seemed to eclipse even that to France itself. Although Paris was still much in his mind, and he hoped to go before the year was out, it was for a visit of nostalgic reminiscence rather than of reconnaissance for eventual settling there.

One of the first to receive some of his early 'Vergers' poems had been Claire Goll. 'A long way from the Elegies', she had written in February, 'but they have connoisseur, or rather connoisseur-ess value ... Everything that comes from you finds its way direct to my heart ...'[67] She had hoped for a meeting while she was in Switzerland during the summer: but he had hesitated at her mention of 'fate'. 'I am alone, my Liliane,' he wrote on 2 June, 'and would love to show you my old tower and my hundred roses ... but I believe you should come *only* if you are mistaken in thinking it is a "fate" which I, however I am, impose on you. Otherwise it would be sad to meet again, instead of joyful, and I beg you, if you come, to give me just that—joy—the greater the better! ... Au revoir, Liliane of the beautiful arms and the heart full of songbirds.'[68] She had at once relieved him of the fear that she was seeking somehow to bind him: 'as if I wanted to bring you anything but joy! If the word "fate" disturbs you, I take it back. Now I know I may hear you again, all torment is gone.'[69] But in

August, after she had arrived in Zurich and he looked forward to her coming, he heard she was returning straight to Paris after all.

The news contributed to a certain restlessness he had felt since leaving Ragaz. It was getting too late to think of even a brief return there, and he was glad in September to accept the hospitality of Richard and Mieze Weininger, who were holidaying in Ouchy, Lausanne and whom he had not seen since 1916 in Vienna. They had reserved for him the best room in the Savoy Hotel, with a magnificent view of the lake: and in the luxurious change from his tower a further cycle of poems in French came readily, more than twenty tender and beautiful variations, mostly in quatrain form, on one of his cherished themes, 'Les Roses'.

> T'appuyant, fraîche claire
> rose, contre mon œil fermé—,
> on dirait mille paupières
> superposées
>
> contre la mienne chaude.
> Mille sommeils contre ma feinte
> sous laquelle je rôde
> dans l'odorant labyrinthe.[70]

Edmond Jaloux chanced to be in Lausanne at this time, and was struck, when he met Rilke, by the strange association in him of courtly politeness and embarrassment, as though he were instinctively afraid of any new acquaintance. In fact, Rilke was delighted to know the author whose work he had admired and whose appreciation of the *Malte* fragment in Betz's translation was the first he had read: 'for twenty-five years I have persisted in taking no notice of critiques of my work, but . . . your articles I always read too eagerly to stop at the threshold of this one.'[71] The few hours he spent with Jaloux he felt were 'splendid', and he hoped they would meet again soon: for Paris was now a serious project for October.

Until then, he planned to spend the time at Muzot bringing some order to his papers and, with the secretary Nanny Wunderly was recruiting for him, preparing fair copies of the considerable number of poems, both German and French, which had accumulated. It was a measure of the grip the illness had already gained that he should again have felt the need for an amanuensis. Apart from the dictation of *Malte*, he had never shied from the handwork of his profession, still less from the labour of copying his work for his friends or of his vast correspondence: 'after all, writing is my handicraft, and one must love not only the work itself . . . but also the manual labour that goes with it,' he had said during the intensive effort of the *New Poems*.[72] A measure too was his tendency now to welcome any distraction that offered, especially in interminable reminiscence, anecdote, and discussion with his many visitors.

Even when the secretary arrived he spent almost as much time taking her for walks and excursions as on the work she had been engaged for, and she did not fail to notice how he was now and then brought up sharply by pain.

In his effort to make light of his bodily trouble, a letter from Valéry, asking for a contribution in French to the new quarterly *Commerce* he was editing, came as a welcome stimulus, and a foretaste of Paris: 'perhaps you will think of bringing your copy in person, an idea which would give great pleasure here where you are rather better known than you may think.'[73] (The issue which appeared in December finally carried three of Rilke's French poems, the first of these to be published.) Prompted perhaps by this, he took advantage of the stenographer's presence to dictate, straight from the page, the first draft of a translation of Valéry's *Eupalinos* dialogue, capturing, as he thought, its 'sublime beauty' as if it had been his own work.[74]

It had delayed his departure, he wrote to Katharina Kippenberg on 3 October, 'but at least something gladdening and permanent will have been achieved.' In fact, as he confessed to Nanny Wunderly, his state of mind was such that salvation through travel seemed even more to be feared than his present 'persecution'. He felt 'as though at the bottom of a rubbish-heap, looking out on the open and harmless only through little gaps'. There was nothing to be done about it, help if there was any must come 'from the same source as the blessing of a great poem'.[75] Even though Kippenberg had already sent him funds for the Paris journey, he lingered on. His depression was fed by the disappointment of the *vendange*, so vital for this area of the Valais after the many months of labour which he had celebrated in verse sketches the previous year—the vine that 'wrestles with the solar giant' on the terraces like organ keyboards till it gives its 'more resonant ring' for the ear in receptive mouths'.[76] This time the yield was meagre and poor, and the Bacchanalian exuberance that usually crowned the year's work was missing. 'Summer and autumn this year are like two great mirrors which have sprung a crack: is that what deforms the image of the universe, or is it so singularly distorted in reality?'[77]

> Green seed-urn the poppies bear,—
> oh, and the fragile, the red
> petals the ignorant wind would snatch from it . . .
> How soon the son's sons are there,
> all so often outsped,
> each one so indefinite.
>
> And time goes plunging on with them into the deeps;
> what of the plungers survives?
> A faded picture and letters in yellowing heaps,
> and something none can describe in some lingering lives . . .[78]

It seemed a sign of the 'doom' he felt was overtaking him when he awoke late one morning to find the poplar at the crossroads below Muzot was being felled—the tree that had stood, on his first sight of his home, like an exclamation mark crying 'This is it!' 'I entered the sad date on a page of the guest-book, it makes a melancholy counterpart to the willow planted after Valéry's visit,' he told Nanny. 'You cannot imagine the change in the landscape since it has lost this great yardstick of the vertical—it seems quite flattened . . . That something so engraved on the mind can be lost to sight from one day to the next!'[79]

At the end of October he roused himself: he would either seek out Dr Haemmerli and try to gain some confidence for the Paris journey, or else try a consultation with a psychiatrist in Freiburg im Breisgau suggested earlier by Dory von der Mühll.[80] Either, he felt, would make more sense than 'this attempting to pull myself out by my own pigtail (which even for Münchhausen only made sense after he had safely reached firm ground to tell the tale)'. In the event, he saw Haemmerli, who was encouraging, but visiting Montreux afterwards he passed some 'abominable days',[81] and it was evident that he would have to return to Valmont before any longer journey could be thinkable. He entered the clinic once again, on 24 November, for a stay which lengthened into over six weeks. It was made more congenial by the presence of Nanny Wunderly, who was also a patient there during the time, and by the thought of seeing Paris again, 'the avenues of the Luxembourg and the beautiful loops of the Seine at Sèvres';[82] Kippenberg had undertaken to settle the high bill for Valmont, as well as assuring him of a monthly allowance of 500 francs from January; as before, however, there was no perceptible change in his condition. Almost in desperation he decided to leave straight for Paris on 6 January, 'to try and distract myself from an illness which seems only to thrive on the attention it got in Valmont'.[83]

3

'In my own blood I'm trapped,
The torture-chamber of my blood in which,
waking hostile from its rest, so much
ferments and stirs that is not part of me.'

(To Erika Mitterer)

He grasped at Paris as at a talisman, whose magic might once again prove its healing powers. Four years earlier, the familiar surroundings had been enough to restore the sense of continuity he had lost, and he had felt as little need for people as in the days before the war. This time, however, escaping from the illness he did not understand, in an abrupt break-out from the prison of the patient's bed, he had an almost feverish craving for human contact—and that was offered him in plenty. He was known now in France, if not as the great lyric poet of the Elegies and New Poems, at least as the author of *Malte* and of the French poems that had appeared in *Commerce*; the praise of Gide, Valéry, and Jaloux had brought him to notice; and the literary world of Paris was open to him as never before.

Settling in the Hotel Foyot, near the Luxembourg, he spent his first few days quietly, feeling an 'incorrigible country boy' in the unaccustomed whirl of the city:[1] but he was soon making his presence known. A large bunch of flowers, with a note 'à tout à l'heure!' came as a joyful surprise to Merline, whose flat was just around the corner, and they spent much time together during his stay. Betz, at work on the full translation of *Malte*, was delighted to have word, and they began a morning routine of going through his work, Rilke's penetrating comments and suggestions invaluable for him. Valéry was one of his first callers, but disappointingly was too busy to see him often; Gide too, who was mostly in the country, he saw only rarely; but their introductions—to Princess Bassiano, the American-born patron of *Commerce*, and to Charles Du Bos, with Gide one of the few to have firsthand knowledge of Rilke's work—were the prelude to an increasingly busy round of invitations. 'Every day I see a complete cast, enough for five acts,' he wrote to Marie Taxis, asking her to send her French versions of two of Kassner's works which Du Bos was interested in publishing.[2]

He called on Jaloux, and the Princess Bibesco; met Anna de Noailles again, and Mardrus, translator of the *Thousand and One Nights*; Giraudoux, Jean Cassou, Supervielle, and Martin du Gard, whose work he had admired from afar, and many others, such as St. John Perse or Ivan Bunin, who were new to him. Old friends were there to be fitted in to his crowded diary: Marianne Mitford, now von Goldschmidt-Rothschild in her third marriage, and in contrast, in the sad role of refugee, Helene Voronin, whom he had not seen since St. Petersburg; Claire Goll, who heard more of him than she saw, the gatherings she frequented seeming like revolving doors taking him out as she passed in, but who was spared a few hours; the Sakharoffs, and Georges Pitoëff, now established in Paris. For others, passing through, he was as ready as ever with his good offices. Hofmannsthal was a fellow guest at Princess Bassiano's in February, with Valéry and Paul Claudel, and for his journey to Morocco Rilke put him in touch with a travelling companion who would introduce him to Marshal Lyautey. For Thankmar von Münchhausen, seeking a visa for France, he arranged an introduction to Roland de Margerie, Embassy secretary in Berlin, whose beautiful wife Jenny he had had the opportunity of meeting at lunch with her brother, Alfred Fabre-Luce. Marthe, however, now happily married to Jean Lurçat, was left waiting for weeks for a sign from him, and it was not until nearly the end of his stay that he visited them in Montmartre.

It was the end of a much longer stay, in fact, than he had ever envisaged. If a change was as good as a rest, he had written to Nanny Wunderly early on, he ought to be completely rejuvenated by conditions so diametrically opposed to those of Muzot. The constant talk left him exhausted, and he often longed for the peace of his tower, feeling as though swallowed up by the world of society like Jonah by the whale: but he was so persuaded of the therapeutic value of the change that he could not bring himself to leave, even after a severe influenza which kept him to his bed in April. Both Kippenberg and Nanny Wunderly came to his aid with the extra money he needed, not only for some essential purchases and to return hospitality with the occasional lunch at the Foyot, but also—biggest change of all from his one-time Paris life—to take taxis to his many engagements.

The city, he often felt, was no longer *his* Paris, the Paris that had formed him—his own fault, perhaps, for letting himself be drawn into the social whirl. But, as often as the whale 'spewed him up', he was 'astounded by the glorious waters . . . and the greatness and power of this world into which the monster so despotically throws me', by that 'indescribable completeness which makes this city, with all the aspects of its inexhaustible image, capable of building landscapes of the spirit, under the sweetest sky on earth'.[3] For one so used to solitary peace, his days were a frenetic round, but they still offered more leisurely delights: a walk every morning in the Luxembourg Gardens, the sport of language with Betz, for whom he often brought some trifle just acquired in an antique shop, a pause in the little sanctuary of St. Julien le Pauvre, visits to the marionette theatre of Julie Sazonova, with whom he could exchange reminiscences of St. Petersburg, or a quiet hour with Elisabeth Bergner. Occasionally there was even time and inspiration to write. In February, among his contributions to Paul Thun's new *European Review*, was a poem in German, written the previous October, 'Palm of the Hand',

> sole that has ceased to walk
> on anything but feeling . . .
> That appears in other hands,
> turning its own kind
> into a landscape:
> wanders, arrives in them,
> with arrival fills them—[4]

and, reminded of this contrast in the German and French vocabulary, he wrote a counterpart, 'La paume':

> Paume, doux lit froissé
> où des étoiles dormantes
> avaient laissé des plis
> en se levant vers le ciel.
>
> . . . .
>
> Ô les deux lits de mes mains,
> abandonnés et froids,
> légers d'un absent poids
> de ces astres d'airain.[5]

This, and one or two others written now, completed in May the manuscript of a selection of his French verse, to be published as *Vergers* by Gallimard the following year, together with the *Quatrains valaisans* which bore a dedication to Jeanne de Sépibus. By the end of June the *Malte* translation was finished, checked word for word by Rilke who was well pleased with the outcome. Betz and his wife were invited to join him and Merline in a celebratory lunch at the Bœuf à la mode, where their host, talkative and himself enjoying the wines he chose, showed an exuberant gaiety Betz had never seen in him before as they sat on until late in the afternoon. Jaloux undertook the publication as the first of a series of foreign prose works he was proposing to Emile-Paul, where he was literary editor, and *Malte* too appeared the following year.

The impression Rilke made in Paris was mixed. For many of the salon hostesses, even the American 'Amazon' Natalie Clifford Barney, he was a collector's item, but there were others, according to Jaloux, who refused to receive this 'German poet'. Valéry's admiration was such that he suggested putting him forward for the Legion of Honour (a proposal Rilke sensibly refused), and to some of his colleagues, like Du Bos and Martin Du Gard, he seemed the very incarnation of poetry: others however were put off by his strange manner and air of having just emerged from the depths. Raymond Schwab recalled being left as Rilke's sole audience at one gathering, as the poet, head on one side, a distant look in his eye and as though talking to himself, discoursed on the 'dictation' that came to him when writing verse, and his other listeners drifted away in boredom with the monologue. Later, no doubt, they became Rilke enthusiasts, said Schwab, but at the time they found him merely tedious.[6] In Jaloux's view, Rilke sacrificed himself needlessly in consorting with so many colourless and ephemeral figures of the social and literary scene, to the neglect of those who really appreciated him.

He had begun to realize this himself, and to realize too that his experiment of a cure by contrast had not succeeded. The constant putting off of his departure, he wrote on 26 June to Nanny Wunderly (who had been patiently watching over Muzot and filtering his correspondence), was in the hope of 'correcting certain errors of my life in Paris, of beginning again, from one day to the next, in a freer way. I am held as though in a vice, and ... my inner misfortune has not budged ... I'm evidently expiating the too great, too glorious freedom felt and acquired during my years of solitude and work.' His only consolation was that Muzot still stood, and he could soon be back there, 'to bring order to the booty of countless jumbled souvenirs, or perhaps, who knows, to bury them in a fruitful oblivion'.[7]

Among the souvenirs were the two cases of his papers he had collected at last from Gallimard, which a first glance had revealed to include not only the family seal and the faded daguerreotype of his father, but also bundles of letters, from Rodin, the Duse, and many others. The work on *Malte* too had revived memories—of the landscape of Provence in which he had set his

Prodigal Son, Les Baux, Aliscamps, Orange—and to Betz he spoke of perhaps developing these brief evocations in a further prose work, which might stand to the Elegies as *Malte* to the *New Poems* and the *Book of Images*. During July he began in fact to think of revisiting the south—Valéry's home country, as well as the exile of the Prodigal Son—on the return journey. He seemed still reluctant to leave, though Paris was growing more and more deserted. Claire Goll, meeting him again in August and herself far from well, found him looking weak and ill: 'how sad I am,' she wrote later, 'that we should have met again just at a time when the body transmitted its fatigue also to the soul. Grown thin spiritually.'[8] She, and Marthe, were the only friends to whom he made his farewell before deciding, suddenly, to take the train on 18 August for the south, accompanied by Merline.

They travelled, not to Provence, but through Burgundy; spent a night in Sierre, and then went on to Milan. Though Rilke spoke later of a 'pressing appointment' there, the journey was more likely by way of offering Merline a summer holiday before she returned to Paris without him. Her companionship during his long stay in Paris had been welcome, and he had continued his efforts to help her, Richard Weininger providing at his suggestion a subsidy for Pierre and Baltusz: but she knew full well there was no question of their resuming life together. At the end of August they spent a few days on Lake Maggiore, but an attack of food-poisoning he apparently suffered there made it advisable to return to Sierre, and by 1 September they were in the Bellevue again, where she looked after him until she left for Paris ten days later, her heart breaking at the sight of his dwindling figure on the platform.

For she knew, better than anyone, with what uncertain feelings he was approaching his next winter, and how deeply he was disturbed by the persistence of his mysterious indisposition. All in all, he confessed to Kippenberg after she had gone, he would reckon 1925 among the worst years he could ever recall since the torments of childhood—as then, he felt shaken to his physical roots, with the same sense of inescapability 'but even more deeply felt when life is no longer ahead of one'.[9] Ragaz with its soothing waters could perhaps relieve and restore him, and he decided on an end-of-season stay there before settling in to Muzot again: but arriving on 16 September he found the spa falling already into a precocious winter sleep, for the inclement weather was driving most of the visitors away early. The Hof Ragaz seemed likely to put up its shutters at the end of the month, and already there seemed more staff than guests. He was too late to see Princess Marie; Jeanne de Sépibus was there, but left after a few days, and Nanny Wunderly paid a short visit later; but it was a solitary life, reading, walking in the rain, alone with the spring's ceaseless chatter. 'I didn't expect so exclusive a tête-à-tête with her,' he wrote to Jeanne de Sépibus, 'but luckily she rattles on like Mme de Noailles, without waiting for the slightest response from poor me.'[10]

During his second week he was alarmed by a symptom quite unlike anything he had known before—swellings inside the mouth which made it almost impossible to speak—and he began to think it might be cancer. Spending the first week of October at Meilen, he went on to consult two doctors in Zurich, and also had the opportunity of a brief word with Haemmerli, who chanced to be there. None saw any indication of cancer: but as before he felt that Haemmerli's objective findings bore no relation to his actual, subjective condition. Haemmerli dismissed the swellings as merely cysts, and perhaps feeling that his patient's worries were all too subjective, actually suggested calling in Dr Mäder, a Zurich nerve specialist, though not with the idea of psychoanalysis.[11] Rilke however had no doubt that there were physical causes for his trouble, even if they could not yet be identified; and he returned to Muzot feeling he was still caught in the same inexplicable toils, a devilish 'circle of evil magic, enclosing me as in a Bruegel picture of hell', and with the same fear that his illness was transforming him into a totally different being.

> The doctors, seeking here and there, are still
> uncertain if my suffering's in their book
> of knowledge . . . and I myself still shun
> the transit to their hand from that of life.[12]

Accustomed as he was to reading aloud, and declaiming his own work as he wrote, the impediment from the swellings was especially distressing. 'Animal suffering gives me the urge to creep into hiding like an animal,' he had written from Valmont during his first stay there,[13] and he was grateful now for the hiding-place of his tower. Frieda was about to leave, this time for good, but her replacement, Ida Walthert, promised well, and the quiet Muzot routine was resumed. In a determined effort to fight against the malady, he sought distraction in clearing the backlog of his correspondence, and in ever wider reading in French, constantly adding orders from Morisse to the pile of books he had brought back from Paris. The reading was long, but the letters short, and to his friends, even at first to Nikê, he tended to gloss over his state of health, on which formerly they would have lacked no detail—a sign of how profoundly he felt himself on a downward path.

At the end of October, indeed, he drew up a will, sending it under sealed cover to Nanny Wunderly to be opened if the need arose. 'Puerile, perhaps, but the other evening I let myself write out, under a spontaneous dictation, some instructions in the event of a serious illness making it impossible for me to make certain dispositions. Knowing this paper in your hands, my dear, your hands faithful above all others, is one of the few consolations I can give myself in these infinitely painful and difficult days.'[14] Virtually propertyless, he had no need of any very specific testamentary dispositions. His concern was to ensure that, when the time came, he could be left to die his own death,

the dying which out of that same life evolves
in which he once had meaning, love and need[15]

—passing over to whatever might await him on the other side of life, 'towards the Open', without interference from the Christian church, which from his early years he had regarded as a superfluous intermediary and in the 'Letter from the Young Worker' denounced as downright pernicious:

1.   In case I should be overtaken by a grave illness and finally lose full control of my mental faculties, I beg, indeed *implore* my friends to ensure that any priestly support which might press itself forward is kept away from me. Bad enough that I had to admit the doctor as negotiator and middleman in the bodily distress of my nature; any clerical go-between would be an insult and an impediment to the movement of my soul towards the Open.
2.   Should I die in Muzot, or anywhere in Switzerland, I do not wish to be buried in Sierre, nor in Miège. . . .
3.   But I would prefer to be buried in the hilltop churchyard next to the old church at Raron. Its surrounding wall was one of the first spots from which I received the wind and light of this countryside, together with all the promises which it, with and in Muzot, was later to help me fulfil.

He went on to specify the headstone he wanted: if possible an old one, perhaps of the Empire period 'as was done in Vienna for my cousin's grave', inscribed simply with the coat of arms, the name, and below that the following epitaph:

> Rose, oh reiner Widerspruch, Lust,
> Niemandes Schlaf zu sein unter soviel
> Lidern
>
> (Rose, oh pure contradiction, delight
> in being nobody's sleep under so many
> eyelids).[16]

As to property, he mentioned only what was at Muzot. Nothing there he regarded as his own, save for any family pictures, which were to go to Ruth; the remainder, in so far as it did not belong to the house, was to be disposed of by Frau Wunderly in accord with her cousin Werner Reinhart, 'the owner of Muzot and my generous friend and benefactor'. The document ended:

6.   As after a certain age it was my habit from time to time to channel part of the productivity of my nature into letters, there is no objection to the publication of correspondence that may have been preserved in the hands of the addressees (should the Insel Verlag so propose).
7.   Of the pictures of myself, I consider none essentially valid, save those that may still exist, transiently, in the feeling and memory of some of my friends.[17]

He was not afraid of death. What haunted him, ever since the shock two years earlier that had brought him for the first time to Valmont, was the fear of being condemned to go on living as a patient, without ever regaining the unity of body and spirit which alone had made his work possible.

> For we are just the leaf and just the skin.
> But that great death which each one has within,
> that is the fruit around which all revolves:[18]

if that essential unity could not be restored, death when it came would not be his 'own death', the fruit which his life ought to bear. He felt already he was no longer himself—'I'm like an empty place, I don't exist, I'm not even identical with my affliction'[19]—and the fear of this alienation was fed by his 'phobia', as he called it, the apprehension that the increasingly painful symptoms of his body meant cancer.

Two days after sending off the Will, he turned to Lou Salomé, beginning a long letter in which he tried to describe, as factually as possible, the physical and especially the psychological evidences of his visitation: the gradual undermining of his 'dependable nature' by the great fear he had lived in for two years, which seemed perversely to have been nourished by his own obsession with it, 'a self-inflicted irritation', and threatened to drive him out of his mind. 'I don't know how I am to go on living like this.' It was a 'defeat', which he felt she would be able to understand and help him to overcome, perhaps even spending a few days at Muzot as his guest, a suggestion which had been in his mind for the past year. 'If only I had called to you long ago. Or if I had come to you and slipped my feet into my old hard sandals' [which still stood ready for him on the stairs at Loufried] 'I might have become "steadfast" again, like the tin soldier soldered back on to his flat base–plate. As I am, I stand askew, the first glance at these pages will tell you at what an angle.' The letter lay on his desk, however, unsealed and undispatched, as if he despaired of aid even from the one who possessed 'so many old dictionaries of the language of my complaints'.[20]

In the few poems of these days there were signs of a new departure in his work, exploring still further 'at the edge of the unsayable' and striving towards the expression of his notion of 'primeval sound', of the senses meeting 'on some as yet undiscovered periphery':[21]

> ### Gong
> Not meant for ears . . .: boom
> that like a deeper ear
> hears us, the seemingly hearing.
> Reversal of spaces. Draft
> of inner worlds outside . . .
>
> . . . .
>
> duration squeezed out of motion,
> star re-cast . . .: gong!
>
> . . . .

> wine on invisible lips,
> gale in the pillar that bears,
> rambler's fall to the path,
> our treason, to all . . .: gong![22]

With this theme, and that of 'Idol', both of which he had also essayed in French during the summer, he ventured towards the ultimate in synaesthesia, at the very 'borders of sensuous perception':

> God or goddess of the sleep of cats,
> devouring deity that in the dark
> mouth crushes ripe eye-berries,
> grape-juice of seeing grown sweet,
> everlasting light in the palate's crypt . . .[23]

He found a kindred 'concentrated imagery' in the works of the Berne artist Sophie Giauque, some of which he held for a while on loan: the rare ability to place their detail in 'a space wholly interior and imaginary, without recourse to that of reality imitated by all paintings (and by all poems for that matter) which are incapable of creating this transposed, profound, and intrinsic space'. The equivalent form in poetry in which to parallel her success, he thought, was the haiku, the art as it were of making 'a pill, its disparate elements combined by the event and by the emotion it excites, but subject always to the total absorption of this emotion by the simple felicity of the images. The visible is taken with a sure hand, picked like a ripe fruit, but weightless, for once set down it is compelled to convey the invisible'.[24] With a poem like 'Idol' he was finding his own way towards such concentration, but the stubborn betrayal of his body seemed to be holding him back.

'Work' now in fact became much more a preoccupation with the past, as he answered in careful detail his Polish translator's questionnaires on *Malte* and the Elegies and Sonnets, and delved into the papers recovered from Paris, 'memoirs of my dead life', as he called them to Nikê, quoting George Moore. A triste occupation, rereading and ordering these old pocket-books and letters—all cold to the touch, 'and yet warmer than I am now—strangely too, still "me", even if dead, with more meaning than anything in the letters and papers of my last stay in Paris'.[25] It was as though he were already looking through his *Nachlass*, the literary remains for which he had made no provision in his testament: and to his passion for meticulous order in his papers was added an impulse to give them some shape by a selection of the work he considered worthy of survival. In a leather-bound volume he began to transcribe scattered poems and prose pieces, chosen 'From Pocket-books and Notes, in random order, 1925', some from as early as 1906, but most written after the Elegies.

He was reticent in his letters about his illness, even to Nikê, whose concern was growing, and he had a horror of well-meant advice from Ida if she should suspect how ill he was. The swellings in his mouth persisted, and he began to feel similar symptoms in throat and tongue—so much so, that at the end of November he decided to return to Valmont: 'any certainty would be better than this long torment.'[26] A retreat there would bring the added blessing of escape from his fiftieth birthday, 'this terrible fourth of December' which he implored Nikê to protect him from. To his dismay, however, he learned that Haemmerli was to be away until the middle of December. He considered consulting other clinics in his absence, but it seemed better to wait until he could go to Valmont, though he was vexed by the thought that Haemmerli could at least have seen him before leaving and advised him whether it was right to wait.

> He's in the wrong who stands
> tired towards life and more fatigued towards death.
>
> I, once ready with affirmation of both,
> now dread the fight whose name is sickness;
> suddenly, against its imminence, there fail in me
> space of the heart and measure in the spirit.[27]

In such a state, he was anything but braced for the ordeal of his birthday, which as he had feared was the occasion for a deluge of letters, telegrams, and presents from friends far and near. A big apple-gathering basket was scarcely enough to hold them, and some at least had to be answered. 'Quelle corvée, quelle inutilité,' he wrote to Nikê: 'of course in fairness, love is there, but where is *that* love which does not cause trouble? Yours, my dear, is almost the only exception.'[28] How gladly he would have crept unnoticed through this day, he told Princess Marie, with his appreciation of her message and apologies for so long a silence: an 'interrupted being', he would soon be exchanging his solitary freedom for Valmont again, 'which has become a sort of annexe to Muzot these past two years.'[29]

He could not do more than write essential letters—to the Kippenbergs, who had not only arranged for flowers to be sent up from the Bellevue, but also sent the *Inselschiff* number marking the day; to Ruth, who had sent delightful photographs of his granddaughter and whose own birthday was near; to Werner Reinhart; to Hans Wunderly, and of course to Nanny, whose thoughtful present of a warm dressing-gown had been accompanied by a thousand-franc note. With his thanks to Jean Strohl, who had sent a ginkgo tree, he described how he had been able to plant it during a brief mild spell, for it to rediscover in the Valais soil its 'ancient plant consciousness' and recall the sleeping atoms 'of which some, once part of the mother-trees, had been stirred by the temple gong'.[30] One curiosity he could not help but reply to: an epistle signed by all the staff and students of Edinburgh University German Department, expressing their admiration and respect for his 'personality as poet' and their gratitude for the works he had given the world.[31]

A few days after his birthday he decided on impulse to mark it in his own way. He had been concerned at the deterioration of the little St. Anne chapel, which the descendants of the eighteenth-century builder were too poor to maintain: and when he heard from Vienna that the Kutschera inheritance could be expected to yield him an income, he made a donation of a thousand francs for the restoration of roof and windows. 'Not everyone can have St. Anne for a neighbour, and she must not get rheumatism.'[32] It was a work of piety towards the past and to the memory of the builder, of course, rather than of any sympathy for the Catholic church, but the gesture gave him great satisfaction.

Significantly, however, he sent off on 8 December the letter to Lou written over a month earlier: everything in it still stood, he added, his 'phobia' was even stronger than before, and although he would not suggest her coming in the now bitter winter conditions, he begged for at least a few lines of advice. Her long reply, which came a few days later, can have given him little of the help he had hoped for. He himself felt, even if the doctors did not, that his bodily distress was more than merely a reflection of his state of mind, but he had put his case to her in the terms they were accustomed to use to each other—in her 'dictionaries of the language of his complaints' the vocabulary had always been that of psychology rather than of medicine. Her recent experience as a practitioner of psychoanalysis inevitably inclined her still further to this approach, in a case where her knowledge of the physical symptoms was necessarily inadequate. She compared his 'self-inflicted irritation' with the guilt complexes of childhood, and his painful throat condition with an earlier incidence of haemorrhoids which, in spite of his then fears of malignancy, had been 'neurotically over-conditioned' and subsided as he regained mental stability. He had always been granted the power of sublimation through his work: what he was now experiencing, she thought, was the reverse side of that divine grace, but just as much a part of it. To feel and know that, he had only to read his own Elegies. 'Nothing is to blame here': all he needed was to recover his confidence in himself, as he had always succeeded in doing in the past.[33]

Whether or not he drew any comfort for the spirit from the thoroughly Freudian analysis, it made no difference to his physical condition, and he was still desperate to seek the doctor's help. On 20 December, as soon as Haemmerli was back, he was readmitted to Valmont. The first examination revealed that the swellings in the mouth were more widespread than he had thought, and Haemmerli, though he still saw no grounds for his 'phobia', was at last seriously concerned. The plain truth, however, was that there was no explanation, or even any effective relief for his pain, and he prepared for yet another Christmas and New Year in Valmont even more dispirited than before.

4

'Though in their mortal anguish men are dumb,
To me a god has given to tell my suffering.'

(Goethe, *Tasso*)

It was exactly a year, he wrote to Kippenberg on 8 January 1926, since he had
ventured the leap to Paris, from this same room in Valmont. It seemed
unlikely this time to provide such a springboard—unless for 'the dive inward',
in search of a new firm base for a nature 'that has become so unsteady'. He
could talk of his hopes of this 'decisive battle';[1] but the first weeks gave no
ground whatever for encouragement. Haemmerli could not have been more
attentive, and as before was ready for long discussions with his patient,
keeping him busy with a routine treatment of massage and special baths, and
doing his best to reassure him with the 'objective' improvements he claimed to
detect. Like all doctors at a loss, he put his faith in time, and rest, and
eventually another change of air—Rome, for instance, where Princess Marie
was urging Rilke to join her. For the patient, however, this optimism seemed
as hollow as ever. While he followed the doctor's arguments with a curious
detachment, it was quite clear to him that they did not bear upon the cause of
the malady which continued to hold him in its 'fatal circle'; and his experience in
Paris left him little inclined to try such a change again. Nevertheless, having
placed himself in the best hands available, he was prepared to wait in patience
and see what came of it, with a melancholy feeling of being 'held prisoner, exiled
and shut out from life', but never abandoning hope of relief and recovery. 'I
shall not get out of this trouble until I've found some way to take a cure into my
own hands—in the end no one can achieve it but myself.'[2]

He surrounded himself with 'innumerable books', scarcely a week passing
without an order to Morisse as he continued eagerly to follow what was being
produced in France. Not content with merely recommending to his friends
books that aroused his particular enthusiasm, he would send for copies for
them too—Giraudoux's *Bella*, Jouve's *Paulina 1880*, or *Le navire aveugle*,
Jean Barreyre's novel which he felt was his own special discovery. Every day
was an anniversary of the time in Paris, he wrote to Reinhart in February;[3] and
the images recalled to the 'empty screen' of his Valmont existence were those
of the colleagues he had most admired in Paris—Jean Cassou, Supervielle, and
Jaloux, with all of whom he exchanged cordial letters. He was particularly
anxious not to miss anything from Valéry's pen, and encouraged Kippenberg
in the idea of becoming Valéry's sole publisher in German.

French literature seemed to offer an unheard of wealth for his admiration.
His own spontaneous verses in the language he saw as a modest learner's
tribute not only to his adopted country but also 'to France and to Paris the
incomparable, which for my development and in my memory signify a whole
world'.[4] Receiving the proofs of his *Vergers* volume in March, he thoroughly

approved of the final selection Merline had made from the over-long manuscript he had left with her, some of the half-forgotten poems coming as a pleasant surprise, and he gladly agreed to publication of some of the 'Quatrains valaisans' in the *Revue de Genève*. The *Malte* translation was also now in proof in Paris; and when he learned that Betz was preparing a special number of the *Cahiers du mois*, 'Reconnaissance à Rilke', he was only too eager to help him with biographical and other details, even sending a further selection of verses in French from his *carnet de poche*, as well as putting him in touch with the Insel for their archive of critical assessments of his work—a notable departure for one who had always held himself aloof from such publicity, and who would certainly have demurred at collaborating in any similar enterprise in Germany.

The view from the limbo of Valmont was not exclusively towards France, however. In Italy too he thought to discern the attainment of new heights not only in literature, with the lyrical poetry of Ungaretti, but also in political life, as exemplified in an 'admirable speech' of Mussolini's. When the Italian lady to whom he expressed this rather surprising sentiment protested that for her the Duce was far from admirable, that she abhorred the violence of the regime, and that liberty was the *sine qua non* of a civilized country, she was treated to long letters in which he argued that an excess of liberty was the world's disease: humanity, like nature itself, needed order enforced by a modicum of violence. He understood little of politics, he admitted: but it seemed to him that there, as in poetry, humanitarian intentions were of little use. Perhaps it was because he was a patient now, that he preached a regime and a remedy which entailed a measure of authority and force, and a curtailment of liberty. At all events, the Italy of 1926 was demonstrating her vigour and good will, in contrast to the disarray of her neighbours. Certainly, Germany since 1870 had shown the appalling dangers of nationalism; but the abstract ideas of 'internationalism' and 'humanity' were scarcely less dangerous for the health of Europe.'

More interesting than this divagation into politics (where he adduced some support from articles by Gonzague de Reynold and Valéry Larbaud) was the statement of his own poetic theory from which he drew the debatable parallel. Much as he admired a writer like Romain Rolland, he wrote, he could not possibly be an adherent of any tendentious purpose in art. 'Poetry which *sets out* to console, or to help, or to support some noble conviction would be a kind of weakness ... what decides, is not some charitable and merciful intention, but the obedience to an authoritarian dictation which seeks neither good nor evil (of which we know so little) but quite simply commands us to work out our feelings, our ideas, all the transports of our being, according to the superior order which so far transcends us as to be for ever beyond our understanding.' Submission to the dictates of some mysterious higher order had always been his conception of the poet's role: what was lacking now was the physical well-being to support it. 'My plans ... are still at the larval stage, and if one day a butterfly should emerge from one of these chrysalides, shall I really follow it?'[6]

His treatment, such as it was as Haemmerli cast around for something effective, lasted a full three months, without bringing any appreciable change except for some improvement in the mouth condition. Between subventions from Kippenberg and Reinhart, the cost of his long-drawn-out stay in the 'absurdly expensive' clinic was basically covered, but it was a constant worry, even if often dismissed with humour in his letters: 'when you sit up in the quiet of the bath, you can hear this diabolical establishment crunching money ... I often ask myself whether any physical organism can really benefit from something which has such a wasting effect on so sensitive a part as the purse ...'[7] He was acutely depressed by the apparent lack of progress, and by the prospect of being still there at Easter after three consecutive New Years—this 'long novel of my life (or of an interlude in it)' which went by the title of Valmont and whose end was still a secret.[8] But, apart from Nanny Wunderly, none of his correspondents heard more than a tone of melancholy acceptance of his tedious lot, which as often as not he would make light of.

He tended to avoid the 'exotic millionaires' who made up most of the population, but there were one or two fellow patients whose company was a restful distraction and who shared his interests. The arrival in March of Lalli Horstmann, a young friend of Marianne Mitford's, whom he had last seen in wartime Berlin, was particularly welcome, 'my first real joy for months', as he wrote in a note, accompanied by a single rose, offering her his help and advice 'as a Swiss of seven years' standing'. He sent her books, and as soon as she was well enough came to spend his Sunday evenings in her room, one of the few with a fireplace, a consolation he had missed since Schloss Berg. Like Elya Nevar and many others before her, she was a charmed and willing audience for his long monologues of reminiscence and a pupil for his guidance in literature, especially French. She remarked his depression, but was struck by his avoidance of any mention of physical suffering: 'he laughed easily, seeing the funny side of people and events, and avoided anything which might have upset him.'[9]

At Easter his treatment was relaxed, and he could lead a 'more or less normal life'.[10] Haemmerli was unwilling to release him yet, but sorties to Montreux or Vevey became possible. This change, and the advent of spring, inspired him to write a few 'Easter eggs', quatrains in French, which he distributed to Lalli, 'as a proof of the harmlessness of my French productivity', and to Merline and other friends in Paris, and for Nanny Wunderly 'Le Christ ressuscité':

> Comment rester avec ce corps, comme un grain
> blessé afin qu'il repousse,
> dans ce tertre d'impatience tout plein
> sous la printanière secousse?

Comment isoler ce cœur végétal
de l'environnante Nature
qui professe que nul n'arrête le mal
à moins qu'il le transfigure.[11]

Signs, it might be thought, of a subjective improvement at last: but writing to
Nanny Wunderly a few days later he avowed he was no better, to himself
indeed seeming worse than when he arrived, 'my whole condition unfit for life
in freedom'. Her coming visit was his one gleam of hope, the only counsel and
support which could help him. Since Haemmerli was to be away for a while, he
determined to move temporarily to the nearby Hotel Victoria in Glion, an
annexe to the clinic but at least charging only normal hotel prices. 'Like a baby
that has tottered to the nearest support, I shall see whether I can get further on
my own or must return to the safety of grandpa's wing-chair.'[12]

Haemmerli was probably not loth to grant him this parole, for more outside
interests might well relieve the morbid introspection to which his patient was
prone and which negated any improvement in his physical condition. Through
April and May, therefore, Rilke remained on the clinic books, but it was now
an open prison: and the limited freedom seemed to brighten his outlook.
During Nikê's stay of a week at Glion they made excursions to Sierre and to
Vevey, where he bought a table and a Louis-Quatorze chair for the Muzot
study, and also found two painted wooden candlesticks for the St. Anne
chapel, where the repairs had now been completed under the supervision of
Jeanne de Sépibus.

Muzot, both house and garden, claimed his attention. While in Sierre with
Nikê he put in hand repairs to the chimney, the defective state of which had
made it a serious fire hazard, and in May, on another visit, was able to plan
some reorganization of the long-neglected garden, with welcome expert advice
from a young nurse with an interest in horticulture, Antoinette de Bonstetten.
Her family had been mentioned to him, before he left Munich, by the Swiss
savant Gustav Schneeli, and early in 1924, hearing of her interest in his work,
he had sent her the Elegies and Sonnets.[13] They had corresponded then for a
time, but it was not until his appeal for a visit to the 'Valmont detainee'[14] that
they had met. She had become a regular Friday caller there from her work in
Geneva, and he was glad of her counsel for his gardening projects. Thanks to
her, he saw Muzot about to start a new life: 'ces quelques parterres vagues se
repenseront, comme dirait Valéry', and their new order would brighten the
tower which had become rather morose through the gloom of its master and
his prolonged absence.[15] His letters to her between their meetings, with a
charm in the French not often paralleled in his German, were an indication of
the good influence of these new interests and of his ability to forget for a while
his deeper concerns.

He went several times to Lausanne, once taking lunch with Jaloux and his
wife—an evocation of Paris; in Montreux he found a cordial welcome over tea

with Madame Revilliod, 'une compatriote', for she was a daughter of his admired President Masaryk; and before Lalli Horstmann left they spent a day together in Vevey. Chance meetings reawakened memories of the more distant past: Poul Bjerre, the Swedish neurologist whom he had last seen with Lou in Munich before the war, told him of the recent death of Ellen Key—her last days 'no less Balzacian than those of Rodin, it seems,' he wrote to Nanny Wunderly: 'how full of dangers life is, how pitiless right to the last moment'[16]—and in Vevey he met the August von der Heydts, whose hospitality he had enjoyed in Elberfeld on his lecture tour twenty years earlier. Though well spaced, his excursions were nevertheless tiring—Lalli noticed how he sank back with eyes closed on the drive back with her—and in the company of people he knew less well he still felt inhibited, 'intimidated' by the mouth trouble. Yet he seemed determined to break out from the 'fictional plane' of Valmont, rather than sit there waiting, at ruinous expense, in the vain hope that one day 'this good Haemmerli will come in and say: now I *know* what has to be done to get you out of your long and persistent torment'.[17]

The fact was that Haemmerli could do nothing for him, and he might as well stand on his own feet. On the last day of May he crossed the threshold to freedom, taking his mysterious troubles with him. A whole long winter seemed to have been sacrificed in vain, his sole activity getting used to 'one of those rooms which, under the pretext of being your own, persist in remaining no one's':[18] but, as he wrote to Reinhart, at least he might have gained in strength to hold out against the inevitable in his condition, and where possible, to ignore it.[19] The Bellevue at Sierre once more made temporary quarters until Muzot was fit to receive him again. The chimney repairs had necessitated renewing one whole wall of his study, and on his daily visits much thought and endless discussion were required before he could decide exactly how it should be redecorated (the 'young intelligent painter' engaged was thankful to be self-employed, when so often interrupted in the work with the offer of a cigar and a chat).[20] Antoinette de Bonstetten's plan for the remodelling of the garden was a satisfying prospect for the autumn, and meanwhile he could enjoy the glory of his roses, the profusion of a flame-coloured eglantine coming as a compensation for the failure of the willow planted to mark Valéry's visit:

> Gente églantine,
> couple simple et fine
> que personne n'a remplie de pétales
> pour qu'elle reste égale
> à son origine . . .[21]

Immersion in the affairs of house and garden was a welcome aid in the effort to ignore his illness. Henri Gaspoz, who as a lad had been a useful errand runner and help about the house from Rilke's first days at Muzot, still recalls with gratitude the poet's interest in his future: thanks to Rilke's intervention with Werner Reinhart and Henry Détraz, owner of the nearby aluminium works at Chippis where Gaspoz was employed in an unskilled job, the way was opened to a course of study for him, and he was able later to return to a successful career as engineer with the firm.* There was distraction for Rilke too with the sense of release for his pen now that he was no longer the patient of Valmont—not only in more French verses, under the stimulus of the Valais summer, but also in another Elegy, directly inspired by a new relationship which the recent months had brought.

Among the greetings for his fiftieth birthday had been one from Leonid Pasternak, in Germany, and in his reply he had praised some impressive verses by Leonid's son Boris he had seen in French translation in Valéry's *Commerce*. For Boris, in Moscow, the news that his work was known and appreciated by one whom he considered the greatest living European poet, came 'like an electrical short-circuit of the soul'. In a letter to Rilke which his father sent on (at that time there was no mail communication between Switzerland and the USSR), he said that he felt 'as though born again': it seemed designed by fate that, on the very day he heard of Rilke's praise for his work, he should have received a poem, 'true and genuine as none of us in the USSR today will write', from Marina Tsvetayeva, living in emigration in Paris, whose admiration for Rilke was no less than his own. He made bold to ask Rilke to send her one of his latest works, perhaps the Elegies: an answer in this form, through her, would be his assurance that his letter had not been a presumption on the kindness of one who was and would ever remain a 'revelation' for him.[22] Receiving it in Valmont, in the early days of May, Rilke had been moved as by 'the stir of a beat of wings'. In an instinctive reaching out towards these two younger poets, he had written immediately to Marina, with his regret not to have met her in Paris, enclosing a fervent reply for her to forward to Boris, and sending her the Sonnets and the Elegies, with the dedication:

> We touch each other. With what? with beat of wings,
> with distances themselves we touch and meet.
> Alone *one* poet dwells—sometimes the one
> who bears him comes towards his *former* bearer.[23]

For her he was the very 'embodiment of poetry': and her reply, from the Vendée coast, had been a dithyramb of love—'because you are a *power*, the rarest'—looking up to him 'as to a protective mountain'.[24] Even before receiving the two volumes of her verse she was sending, he had felt her already 'entered in my inner map', he wrote on 10 May: 'somewhere between Moscow and Toledo I've made a space for the rush of your ocean.'[25] He had been drawn to this unknown poet almost as to another Benvenuta, but this time in

*After his retirement, Henri Gaspoz and his wife established a foundation to provide an annual prize for work in art and letters. The first award, to the Valais sculptor Vitali, was for a bust of Rilke, which Gaspoz presented to the town of Sierre, as a mark of his gratitude to the poet. The unveiling ceremony in the Jardin public there took place on 28 September 1984.

instinctive confidence that she was an equal, who wanted nothing but to write and pour out her life and her thoughts, in a response to his he had never found with Magda von Hattingberg. The Elegy that he addressed to her now, in the first days in Sierre, celebrated the affinity in their poetry and the union of praise and lament in the poet's (and the lover's) mission:

> Oh, the losses into the All, Marina, the stars that are falling!
> We can't make it larger, wherever we fling, to whatever
> star we go! Numbered for all time are the parts of the Whole.
> Neither can one who falls diminish the sacred number.
> Every abandoning plunge dives to the source and is healed.
> Can it, then, all be a game, reappearance of sameness, displacement,
> nowhere a name and scarce anywhere storable gain?
> Waves, Marina, we're sea! Depths, Marina, we're heaven.
> Earth, Marina, we're earth, we're thousand times spring, we're soaring
> larks an outbreaking song flings to where eyes cannot see.
>
> .   .   .   .
>
> Praise my dearest, let us be lavish with praise.
> Nothing belongs to us.
>
> .   .   .   .
>
>   Gods long ago discovered
> how to juggle with halves. We, drawn into the cycle,
> filled ourselves out to a whole like the disc of the moon.
> Even in time of wane, in the weeks of gradual turning,
> none could ever again help us to fullness except,
> lonely, that walk of our own over the slumberless landscape.[26]

Their brief correspondence has been aptly likened to that of 'conspirators, accomplices privy to a secret unknown to those around them',[27] each seeing in the other a poet related in spirit and equal in power. 'On the island where we were born—all are like us,' wrote Marina to Boris Pasternak;[28] and Rilke's immediate recognition of her genius has been amply confirmed by the judgement of posterity. But he was in no condition now to embark on the flowing stream of letters such a relationship would once have called forth. He soon began to find too much for him the effort of responding to Marina's overpowering style, the almost surrealistic play with words made possible by her astonishing command of German. After the sudden burst of inspiration in the Elegy, he needed more placid pursuits as he moved back to Muzot, in a life he felt inexorably slowing down—the slippered ease of confidences to Nanny Wunderly (who, however, heard nothing of Tsvetayeva); the satisfying work of completing the translation of Valéry's 'Narcisse' and writing an occasional short poem; the relaxation of a walk with Jeanne de Sépibus, or a visit with Détraz to the Chippis works.

He had already collected his earlier French production in a manuscript book which he entitled 'Tendres impôts à la France', some of the poems being included in the final selection for *Vergers*. The later verses he now added to a manuscript 'Exercices et évidences', but of these again some were included in the *Les Roses* cycle, which he was preparing for separate publication, and in another of variations on the window theme, *Les Fenêtres*, which Merline was to illustrate with engravings and was trying to place in Paris. Meanwhile *Vergers, suivis des Quatrains valaisans*, was at last out, and he found great pleasure in distributing his copies with the usual careful dedications, among others to Valéry, Gide, Jean Cassou, and Jules Supervielle—'admirable poète que j'aime'—and especially to Jeanne de Sépibus, 'for her to take irrevocable possession of her *pied-à-terre* in this orchard now in the public domain', and inscribing for her, in front of the Quatrains, a few additional verses. Valéry wrote his admiration for the 'astonishingly delicate strangeness of your French sound', and his pleasure at the news of the translation of 'Narcisse'—'an unbelievable fortune for me that you and I should exist at the same time in this infernal age'; while Gide found in Rilke's French verse 'a new joy, its quality a little different and more rare perhaps, more delicate, subtler'.[29]

The resumption of this literary life, however gratifying, was essentially superficial, a façade concealing his illness from his friends but inadequate to help him himself to forget it. It was symptomatic that he should once more be seeking a secretary. He became increasingly restless, and sought both company and movement. Princess Marie was due in Ragaz in July, and he made plans to join her there: his departure was put off from day to day, however, chiefly because of the fluctuations in his condition, but then, as July wore on, through the diversion of younger and more attractive society, bringing echoes of his stay in Paris—visits which he did not want to miss, as he wrote to Nanny Wunderly.

Elisabeth Bergner had sent him a telegram for his fiftieth birthday, and he had taken some trouble in finding her address to thank her. When she heard of his illness, she decided to include Muzot in her summer holiday itinerary, and on 13 July drove up with her companion Viola Bosshardt. The hour or two's visit they had planned lengthened into an overnight stay, when their host continued reading them one poem after another the night through, ignoring Elisabeth's protests that he ought to rest, and holding her enthralled while Viola dropped into a sound sleep on the sofa. Just before they left in the morning, he suddenly asked what was her favourite fruit: 'I knew it,' he said when she replied cherries; and leading them into the garden showed them a young cherry tree with the hole dug ready for planting. There and then it was installed, in memory of her visit.[30] About the same time, hearing from Dory von der Mühll that Jenny de Margerie was holidaying from Berlin with her two little sons in Lausanne, he wrote that, although he was on the point of leaving for Ragaz, he would postpone his departure if she could spend a day with him. She was one of the very few of his admirers in Paris, the previous year, who knew anything of his earlier work—a copy of the *Book of Hours* was already then a treasured possession—and her call at Muzot on 17 July, if more formal in character than Elisabeth Bergner's, was no less unforgettable for her. His nostalgia for Paris was so apparent that she went away with the idea of offering him later the use of their apartment there, unoccupied during her husband's tour in Berlin.[31]

His 'tristes maux' were still with him, he had written from Sierre, as he waited for Jenny de Margerie's train, in a letter to Nanny Wunderly with the news that in two days' time he would at last be coming through Zurich on his way to Ragaz.[32] That he should have gone out of his way to attract such company, when the Princess was impatiently awaiting him in the soothing atmosphere of Ragaz, speaks for his feeling now that he must seize every moment life still offered of enjoying youth and beauty.

Princess Marie's stay was almost at an end by the time he arrived in the Hotel Hof-Ragaz, and she was by no means well, with severe bronchitis. He devoted his first week entirely to her, 'hours full and charming, at every moment of which we both felt how much they had been needed'.[33] When she left, on 27 July, it was with the promise of a meeting later in the year in Paris. He began now in earnest with the cure he had missed on his earlier visits, conscientiously taking the thermal baths daily: the waters, clear and unusually abundant, seemed to give promise of exceptional efficacy, and he settled to a longer stay than originally intended in the hope that their special powers might bring him relief.

Far from seeking solitude, he was as gregarious as he had been in Paris; and although, like the previous year, the onset of wet weather in August began to thin out the guests, many remained to interest him: well-to-do Swiss whom he already knew or knew of, Austrians, Germans, Dutch, and Belgians. Mostly with their families, they were only too pleased to make the acquaintance of a distinguished poet who was so ready to talk, read from his work, compose verses for them in French or German with equal facility and press on them copies of *Vergers* or the French *Malte* with charming dedications. He had brought with him his translation of 'Narcisse', which had delighted the Princess in their short time together, and which he was able to read also to Nanny Wunderly, when she exchanged the early snow of Pontresina for the milder climate of Ragaz in the first week of August. They took drives in the hotel carriage out to the nearby Grisons, revisiting the gardens of Schloss Bothmar at Malans and calling for the first time at a former von Salis mansion at Maienfeld, Schloss Salenegg. Another old friend who stayed a short while was Eva Cassirer, whom he had not seen since before the war, and she too listened to 'Narcisse'.

Nanny Wunderly found him much restored, very 'entrain'; and 'cette vie au ralenti', as he looked back on it later, was peculiarly attractive to him, not least through the presence of the young. Meeting Beppy Veder, twenty-five, a promising singer studying in Basle, who had joined her parents from Holland in the nearby Quellenhof Hotel, he felt 'rich in a new joy', and could not resist sending over for her the proofs he had just received of his poems to appear in the next Insel Almanach.[34] Even if she could not fully appreciate them, 'even if . . . every object of my inner zeal should turn out strange to you, let that remain which you laid in my hands when we first met, *before* any word was spoken: an infinitely joyous trust in your life itself . . .' Her existence, he wrote after her departure, had given 'an ever surer delight' to those privileged to meet her in Ragaz.[35]

> With the first reaching of your hand alone
> your very self into my hand you gifted:
> as in the first pulsating organ-tone
> one hears the whole insurgent song uplifted,
>
> with offering, modulation, triumphing.
> How I perceived the waiting it had ended!
> And how its mighty opening transcended
> at once my hearing and my hearkening![36]

Delightful too, throughout his stay, was a 'quite ravishing little Belgian girl, a delicious child', as he wrote to Nanny Wunderly before she came. He had never seen such perfection, almost frightening when one knew how soon it must fade: 'so beautiful, so accomplished in her gestures, so measured, so intelligent'. Normally ill at ease in the presence of little children, he was quite captivated by Reine—'could one call her Se-reine?'—a child of six who, regarding him quizzically one day, said 'You look like a unicorn'. (Singular clairvoyance, thought Jaloux later, when he heard of this: 'so exactly Rilke physically and morally, a unicorn'. And Rilke himself may well have been reminded of his evocation of that 'never-credited white creature' in the *New Poems*, twenty years earlier, 'its gaze checked by nothing here beneath, / projecting pictures into space . . .'[37])

He stayed on until the end of August, reluctant to leave surroundings which helped him for a while to be oblivious of his illness and which stimulated the production of a quite remarkable quantity of verse. It was for the most part occasional, and in French, but included two long poems which showed undiminished mastery in German—'The Willow of Salenegg', and the lines inspired by the final verse of a poem of Count Lanckoroński's.

> 'No intellect, no ardour is redundant':
> to make one through the other more abundant
> is what we're for, and some are singled out
> for purest victory in that contention . . .
>
> . . . .

> In slumber also they continue seers:
> from dream and being, from laughter and from tears
> a meaning gathers ... which if they can seize,
> and kneel to Life and Death in adoration,
> another measure for the whole creation
> is given us in those right-angled knees.[38]

In this work, and in that on Salenegg, celebrating the miracle of the centuries-old willow there, which had thrust a new root down from its crown through the decaying trunk to take on new life, there was a spirit of affirmation, the expression perhaps of a fundamental faith in his own recovery, offsetting the melancholy and sense of farewell which pervaded many of the French quatrains and fragments:

> Comment te faire encore hésiter, bel été ...
>
> C'est la vie au ralenti,
> c'est le cœur à rebours,
> c'est une espérance et demie:
> trop et trop peu à son tour ...[39]

The Weiningers were staying at Ouchy, and their invitation to join them again there provided a welcome excuse for putting off his return to Muzot: its solitude he had come almost to fear, he had written to Beppy Veder, asking her to come and see him there—'I need just such prospects to make the return to my Valais home bearable'.[40] Certainly he had no thought of another 'winter of work' in his tower. A short stay to complete his Valéry translations with a secretary's aid, and then perhaps the south of France, by the sea, was the plan he put to Kippenberg now, with a request for an additional allowance to cover these expenses. Meanwhile, comfortably installed in the Hotel Savoy again, as the Weiningers' guest, he could make a transition from Ragaz, enjoying their company and that of Jaloux; interview a Russian girl who sounded suitable as secretary; and, best of all, be well placed for a crossing of the lake to see Valéry himself, who he discovered was on holiday at Anthy, near Thonon.

Betz's 'Reconnaissance à Rilke' had just appeared—an exceptional tribute to a living poet, and unique at the time as an international celebration of one of German tongue. For Merline, who had seen some of the proofs, Valéry's introductory letter to Rilke was of a 'politesse écrasante', typically man-of-the-world:[41] but its addressee, writing to propose himself for a visit to Anthy, found it exquisite—'an open letter which remains deliciously closed between us, I make myself small so that the world may read it over my shoulder'. Having never read anything of this kind, he claimed, 'except for that earlier article of Ellen Key's', his head was quite turned by the appreciations assembled here from all quarters of Europe, and 'something of a long-standing innocence thereby lost'.[42]

His day with Valéry, on 13 September, was the high point of this interlude in Lausanne. He was full of his translation of 'Narcisse', though it was in vain that he continued to urge his idol to write the prose study on this theme he had had vaguely in mind—to create 'a few steps of sacred marble to lead up to the temple of Narcissus'.[43] The Rilke photographed that day, and remembered by Valéry, looked smiling and youthful; he spoke of their meeting again perhaps later, when Valéry was in Vienna, and showed no outward sign of any illness. He returned, however, to a night made sleepless by abdominal cramps. He was still plagued by the same 'terrible and ridiculous obsession', he wrote to Nanny Wunderly a few days later, 'which follows me everywhere, and makes me latch on to new impressions and new people with the despair of one who wants to be saved by some miracle from without. And yet this miracle ought to be achieved *within* me . . . You cannot imagine what a life I'm leading, what a circle without exit I've been going round for years.'[44]

In the cosmopolitan society of Lausanne, however, there was no shortage of 'new people' for him. He was particularly attracted by Harriet Cohen, later to become famous as a pianist, whom he met several times and once accompanied to Geneva. To transcribe for her his verses of 1913 to the 'beloved, lost in advance' (then still unpublished) showed that the dream of the ideal woman was still with him even in this troubled time. She kept a tender memory of the encounter for long afterwards, even though disappointed to learn that the poem had not, as she then thought, been written to her.

Before his visit to Valéry, reading alone in the Savoy garden, he had been noticed by Jaloux, who was at another table with friends; among them was a young Egyptian woman, also a guest in the hotel, tall and of breathtaking beauty, who spoke to Jaloux with enthusiasm and emotion of her latest discovery, *Malte Laurids Brigge* in its French version. Astounded when he was able to point out the author, she pressed him for an introduction. The presence in the hotel of such a beautiful figure had naturally not gone unremarked by Rilke: and when he heard from Jaloux that his name meant something to her, he sent her a note at once—for fear, as he said, that he might have to leave before his friend could arrange for them to meet. Nimet, daughter of Ahmed Khairy Pasha, a court official in Cairo, French-educated and married at eighteen, had been some years in Switzerland, where her husband, Aziz Elwi Bey, was gravely ill in a sanatorium at Leysin. She had lost both her parents, and an elder sister, while still very young; and it was this early experience of death, Jaloux thought, which lent her an air of detachment from the superficial life of a wealthy *mondaine* she was leading in Lausanne. It may also explain the feelings *Malte* had aroused in her, and her admiration for the author.

Rilke saw much of her during the rest of his stay, which extended for nearly a week after the Weiningers had left. He was struck by the deep understanding she showed for his novel—'une compréhension essentielle qu'aucun consentement concernant "M. L. Brigge" n'a jamais su égaler: et les Cahiers existent pourtant depuis dix-sept ans!' He spent almost a whole night reading it again in the copy she lent him, marvelling that all these 'présences' had been hers for an instant, 'votre ineffable présence en vous-même'.[45] It was a new, if somewhat alarming, experience too to be whirled off in her car at a speed never approached by the sedate chauffeurs of Marie Taxis or Nanny Wunderly. Most of all he was beguiled by her Oriental beauty, the profile like that of royal statues he had seen in Egypt, the dark golden-brown of the eyes, the perfect skin and long delicate hands. Thanking Jaloux for the lunch he gave at his home for them both, he urged him to erect a small monument on his table 'at the spot where Mme E's gloves reposed, before they obeyed the act of assumption which filled them with angels'.[46] As he left on 20 September, he invited her to spend a day at Muzot as soon as she could.

Meanwhile he had been well pleased with the young secretary who had presented herself at the Savoy. Genia Tchernosvitova seemed intelligent and capable as well as charming, and it was arranged for her to accompany him back to Sierre, where he would put her up at the Bellevue. Their work began immediately—the final redaction of the Valéry dialogues *Eupalinos* and *L'âme et la danse* which he had long had in draft—and by 9 October they were completed. The daily stint was often interrupted when sunshine beckoned to a walk, or by visitors. During this time Nanny Wunderly arrived with a friend to stay at the Bellevue, and Nimet Elwi drove up to Muzot only a few days after his return. His appearance came as something of a shock to Nanny Wunderly, who had not seen him since Ragaz. Catching sight of him from a distance in the hotel, she thought he looked 'miserable, frightened, pale as though after a serious illness'; but his lively manner when they met soon dispelled the impression.[47] When he came to see her off, on 5 October, he arrived with both hands bandaged: as he picked roses for Nimet Elwi, a thorn had entered deep into the left hand, causing a severe inflammation, and immediately afterwards there came a painful infection under a nail on the right. He was reluctant for her to go—'I can still hear him say "I think this is only just beginning",' she wrote later;[48] but, persuading him to stay for a while at the Bellevue, she felt some relief in the thought that he would be under Genia's devoted care there.

After finishing the Valéry dictation, he took Genia off to Lausanne, where the Vieux-Colombier company was performing and Mauriac was to speak on 'La défense du roman'. For her it was a delightful trip, with all the zest of playing truant, she recalled: after the evening at the play they joined a party of artists at Chailly which went on till three in the morning, spent the next day quietly in the sumptuous surroundings of the Hotel Savoy, and after Mauriac's lecture returned on 14 October to Sierre, stopping for a choice candle-lit dinner at Vevey *en route*. Work began again the next day, on a further translation from Valéry, his article on 'Tante' Berthe Morisot; but the autumn was so beautiful that Rilke insisted on breaking off to spend the rest of the day together at Sion.

The enjoyment of this excursion cost him dear. Returning, he had to take to his bed with what seemed to be a gastric influenza, and although the feverish condition soon abated, he was laid low for nearly two weeks. He was in no state to face a winter in Muzot, he told Kippenberg, reporting on his progress with the translations, and was firmly decided on closing it up, to go to the south of France. Life at the Bellevue too, where alterations were in hand, was becoming uncomfortable. As though in preparation for his departure, he had the idea of classifying his correspondence while he still had the services of Genia. She brought the countless bundles of letters down from Muzot in suitcases, and he began to sort them, with infinite patience, while she prepared a large envelope for each correspondent and transported them back as they were completed. His condition obstinately refused to improve, however. During November, he was eating little, and with a constriction in the throat and an unaccountable cough began to feel himself back in the toils he had so long tried to ignore. News from Nanny Wunderly that Clara was expected in Switzerland, and that she had invited her to stay, made him unreasonably irritable: if it was on his account, he absolutely refused to see her 'and have her offering me her pitying Christian Science curiosity. If she insisted on seeing me, I'd leave at once over some frontier or other.'[49]

'Quel temps perdu!' he complained to Nanny. 'I would have liked to do so much more with Genia's charming aid, in the few days left to her with me — and instead she has had to become a nurse.' It was a torture for him to be obliged to exhibit his weakness to a friend, instead of to an impersonal professional; he felt like a sick dog who tries to hide and is put out by any sympathy if found. He would not hear of seeing a doctor, or take anything that 'smelled of the pharmacy', and struggled to restore himself, continuing as normal a life as he could.[50] He pursued his correspondence with A. A. M. Stols, a Dutch bibliophile publisher, on a possible reissue of his *Vergers*, in an enlarged edition; and took the trouble, ill as he felt, to write a long letter to Georg Reinhart asking for financial support for Regina Ullmann — a sharp contrast with his almost brutal attitude towards Clara. It was an effort that daily became more strained, and the von der Mühlls, who called to see him on 14 November, were appalled at his wasted appearance and evident fatigue.

Marianne von Goldschmidt-Rothschild had written inviting him to Berlin from December, while, unknown to him, other friends were planning alternative refuges. Jenny de Margerie had almost completed the redecoration of her Paris apartment, which she intended to offer him; and Marie Taxis, who had had encouraging news of his health from Valéry in Vienna, was thinking of bringing him to Rome in the spring. His own idea, however, was still the south of France — perhaps the Côte des Maures, a peaceful spot, as he heard from a friend, that was as yet undiscovered by tourists. The Tessin, which Nanny Wunderly suggested, would be a poor substitute — 'that *presque-Italie* which is becoming more and more a refuge for the Germans. Imagine, Hermann Hesse in Castagnola, and tomorrow perhaps Wilhelm II at Monte Verità.'[51] Kippenberg, though pointing out that his account was considerably overdrawn for the moment, had been reassuring on his finances. 'To reach any kind of future at all, I must first get over this sufficiently precarious present,' he wrote with his thanks, on 15 November. 'I know your advice is first of all to make sure of *that*, with all available resources.'[52]

He tried still to convince himself that he could do it unaided, getting up when he could and often taking walks with Genia, even up as far as Muzot. After much pain and sleepless nights, however, when a persistent dysentery following the gastric influenza began to show signs of suppuration, he could see no alternative to seeking help in Valmont again, and by the end of the month held out no longer. Genia, who was to leave for Paris in a day or two, accompanied him on 30 November to the sanatorium. As they talked in the train from Sierre, his 'amazing inner youthfulness' had the upper hand over his suffering, it seemed to her; but in the car taking them up from Montreux he was once more the 'infinitely fragile patient needing every possible care'.[53]

Haemmerli was away when he arrived, and not expected back for over a week: but this time there was no doubt of the diagnosis. The blood test indicated an acute myelogenous leukaemia—then, as now, incurable—and it was evident to the doctors that it was already at an advanced stage. It took a particularly painful form in his case, the first manifestations in the hand infections and the intestines being soon followed by outbreaks of black pustules, as with septicaemia, on the skin and later in mouth and nose. His strength began rapidly to ebb under the 'unspeakable tortures'[54] to which he was exposed. At his request, Nanny Wunderly prepared and sent off to his correspondents over a hundred printed cards saying he was too ill to write, but in the first week he was still able to pen what to him were essential letters: a recommendation to friends in Paris for Genia, whose future there was uncertain, and to Stols, with his regret at being unable to contribute to the planned 'Hommage des écrivains étrangers à Paul Valéry', the offer of his translation of 'Tante Berthe' and the manuscript of the *Les Roses* cycle, in the hope of seeing it published 'dans vos belles éditions'.[55] A reply to Richard Weininger, however, who had written with proposals about the Kutschera inheritance, he left to Nanny, asking her to give Weininger his power of attorney to deal as he should see fit. 'Day and night, day and night . . . Hell!' he wrote her on 8 December—and the hopeless feeling of abnegation, of having to become the patient and 'learn this absurd vocation under the eye of the doctors . . . In this business I'm the loser! . . . Dr Haemmerli is to return tomorrow. What a surprise I have for him here, poor chap.' He asked her too if initially the Valmont bills might be sent to Werner Reinhart: 'I'll arrange matters with Kippenberg later, but for the moment I can't do anything, not even sign my name properly.'[56]

Learning from Haemmerli by telephone how gravely ill Rilke was, she hurried to Valmont the next evening. Her presence seemed to comfort him—

'you bring me life,' he told her[57]—and she stayed at hand, after Genia's departure the only visitor he could bear to see. He would not consider allowing them to alarm his family or friends: his one desire, according to Haemmerli, was to see no one who 'might arouse the thought of the seriousness of his condition, which he determinedly concealed even from himself', confident in spite of his suffering that he would yet recover.[58] The only exception was Lou, and on 13 December he managed to pencil a short letter to her.

My dear, so you see, *this* was what my watchful nature has been preparing me for, forewarning me, these three years: and now it's finding it hard, hard to win through, after so long expending itself in trying self-help, corrections, slight adjustments . . . Lou, I can't tell you how many hells—you know how I was always able to integrate pain, physical, really great pain, into my way of life, if only as an exception and for it to become a way back to freedom. And now. It's smothering me. Cutting me off. Day and night! Where to find the courage? Dear, dear Lou, the doctor is writing to you, Mrs Wunderly too, who has come so helpfully for a few days. I have a good and understanding nurse, and I believe the doctor, seeing me again for the fourth time in three years, is in the right. But—the hells . . .[59]

'You know everything about him, from the beginning until now,' ran Nanny Wunderly's letter accompanying this. 'You know his boundless belief in you— he said: Lou must be told everything—perhaps she will know of some consolation.' Haemmerli sent her a full and detailed account of his condition, as Rilke had asked him to do, 'in the confidence that you as his true friend will be able to buoy up in our unfortunate patient his still unshaken will to live and his hope—to reveal the prognosis to him seems to me dangerous at the moment'.[60]

Lou, though she wrote often, could find no consolation. He himself did not write again: and she felt he knew, must know, it was the end. With Haemmerli, from whom he had never concealed his negative attitude towards doctors in general, but in whom personally he had great faith, he could talk freely and at length of his symptoms and convince himself each day that the treatment proposed and the calling in of specialists were in accord with his own ideas. He did not want to hear what the disease was called, preferring to regard it as peculiar to himself, and accepting his condition rather 'as an inevitable mystery, which ought not to be analysed too closely'.[61] Haemmerli remarked how in their long talks he would studiously avoid any mention of the possibility of death.

Through the first weeks of December he became progressively weaker, and was grateful for Nanny Wunderly's presence in the afternoons, as she read to him and dealt with essential letters. The fever and unremitting pain he faced with immense courage, determined not to accept any drugs that might make him lose consciousness: but it was heartbreaking for her to have to sit powerless to help him. His pencil was still often in his hand. To Kassner, asking him to tell the Princess as much as he thought fit, and to Weininger, he wrote of his 'miserable and infinitely painful' illness, 'which will be anything but temporary': 'a little-known change in the blood cells is causing the most horrible processes all over my body. And I'm learning to get used to the incommensurable, anonymous pain ... a hard lesson. ... I have every conceivable care here, but there is practically nothing that can be done for my relief'.[62] In his notebook, a last fragment gave poetic expression to his torment:

> Now come, the last that I can recognize,
> pain, utter pain, fierce in the body's texture.
> As once in the mind I burned, so now I burn
> in you; the wood resisted, long denied
> acceptance to the flame you blazed at me,
> but now I feed you and in you I flare.
> My mildness here in your hot rage must turn
> to hellish rage, hell-fury, kindled there.
> Quite pure of forethought, futureless and free
> I mounted suffering's tangled, criss-crossed pyre,
> so sure there was no purchase to acquire
> for this heart's future, all its store now silent.
> What burns there, so transmuted, is that I?
> Into this fire I drag no memory.
> To be alive, alive: to be outside.
> And I ablaze. With no one who knows me. ...[63]

Kippenberg, apprised by Haemmerli, begged his 'beloved friend' to have no worries over the costs—'what is mine, is yours!'—and arranged for a Leipzig specialist to attend.[64] Nanny Wunderly, in the sad knowledge that there could be no hope, took it upon herself on 15 December to write to Clara, who arrived two days later. 'Terribly disturbed', Rilke would not let her be admitted, and she had to leave again without being able to see him.[65] But he sent Ruth a 'Christmas embrace for you all, Christine, Carl' on 20 December: 'Be happy, joyous, confident, life is still the same, good thing';[66] and to Supervielle, the following day, who had sent him his poems:

I think of you, poet, friend, and as I do, I think too on the world, poor remnant of a vase which remembers being of the earth. (Mais cet abus de nos sens et de leur 'dictionnaire' par la douleur qui le feuillette!'[67]

He was in unimaginable pain, he wrote in a brief note to Nimet Elwi Bey; the doctors might have a name for this suffering, 'but us it teaches only three or four cries in which our voice is unrecognizable—our voice which was so trained in nuances! Point de fleurs, Madame, je vous en supplie, leur présence excite les démons dont la chambre est pleine. Mais ce qui m'est venu *avec* les fleurs, s'ajoutera à la grâce de l'invisible. Oh merci!'[68]

He seemed not yet to have given up hope. In a letter the following day, 23 December, to Merline, who had not heard from him for a month and was not even sure that he was in Valmont, he spoke of being shut up there 'for a long time'. 'Humbly, miserably ill, I can only beg you to believe that I have all possible care . . . If your loving heart were to counsel you to come, you would be ill-advised. . . . Ma chère Merline!'[69] But it was the last letter he could write. Thereafter even being read to seemed too much for him, and it was clear to Nanny Wunderly that he realized life was ebbing. 'Help me to *my* death,' he said to her suddenly. 'I do not want the doctors' death, I want my freedom.' And again: 'Life can give me no more—I have been on all its heights. . . . Never forget, my dear, that life is a thing of splendour!'[70] By 28 December he was extremely weak, dozing but asking Haemmerli not to let him lose consciousness: 'he would press my hand instead of answering, to speak left him out of breath.'[71] At midnight he went into a coma, while Nanny Wunderly and the doctor kept vigil, and lay thus for a time, until at 3.30 in the morning of 29 December he raised his head, eyes wide open, and fell back dead in Haemmerli's arms.

For Nanny Wunderly it was an inexpressible relief to know him released at last from torment. As he lay there—the thin, almost brown face still marked by the skin outbreaks, the growth of beard dark against the pillow, the heavy lids closed under the massive brow—he looked to her like some priestly figure, 'from Persia perhaps, or India, a sage come from afar to a short span on earth and lying now lifeless, his martyrdom at an end'.[72] To her fell now the sad task of the survivor, the telegrams and letters, a visit to Raron with Reinhart to arrange for the grave there in accordance with Rilke's wishes. The few friends who could make the journey began to arrive, among them Anton and Katharina Kippenberg, Loulou Albert-Lazard, and Regina Ullmann. On Sunday 2 January 1927, a sunny but bitter cold day, he was laid to rest in Raron, after a short (Catholic) service, with Bach from the organ and Alma Moodie's violin: against the wall of the little church high above the Rhône valley, one of the first places to bring him 'the wind and the light' of the countryside where he had at last achieved his greatest work, and—symbolically—at the linguistic border where French and German meet.

Each of the few mourners present, said Eduard Korrodi in a brief oration, was a representative of a host of Rilke's brothers in spirit, scattered through many lands, who must find comfort for his loss in the lasting fabric of his work; and he quoted from the First Elegy the lines:

> They've finally no more need of us, the early departed,
> one's gently weaned from terrestrial things as one mildly
> outgrows the breasts of a mother. But we, that have need of
> such mighty secrets, we, for whom sorrow's so often
> source of blessedest progress, could we exist without them?[73]

As the frozen earth closed the grave, the Valais dramatist René Morax spoke for those who had known Rilke only through his 'second lyre': 'Adieu, grand poète!' A little later, Princess Marie's laurel wreath was laid at the tomb, 'au poète incomparable, au cher et fidèle ami'.

Epilogue

—◦❧❦◦—

'Believe me, nothing moves me so deeply as the incredible,
unprecedented miraculousness of my existence, which from
the beginning followed such an impossible plot and yet has
progressed from deliverance to deliverance'

(To Emil von Gebsattel, 14.1.1912)

Rilke's death was mourned in memorial essays, orations, and ceremonies in
many lands—Germany and Austria, Czechoslovakia, France and Poland,
Scandinavia and Italy, even England. To many who wrote or spoke of him, he
was known only through his published work, and even to those who had been
more privileged, his life seemed 'enveloped in silence and mystery', as Stefan
Zweig wrote.[1] His work appeared to show him as the poet of death, who,
picturing life in all its manifestations, praised it as the preparation for that
other realm which alone would reveal its true purpose. In Vienna, where two
In memoriam gatherings took place, with readings from the works and music
played by Magda von Hattingberg, Alexander Lernet-Holenia's prologue for
the second was spoken by a herald in tabard emblazoned with the greyhound
of the Carinthian Rilkes: 'death for him was not an exit, it was a condition
sempiternal to which the exhausted and those with great plans withdraw in
order to live on ... Death for him was full of existence.'[2]

He was seen too, in these early tributes, as the model of the pure poet, with
single-minded purpose steering 'the ship of his life against the current of
bourgeois society' (Katherina Kippenberg).[3] His 'heroically fulfilled striving
for lyrical expression' was visible only in his work, said Zweig in his memorial
oration in Munich: 'No one has fully known his inner life ... devout
stonemason on the never-to-be-completed cathedral of the language', he toiled
softly, 'silently as with all great work, remote from the world like all that is
perfect'.[4] The other poets he had known, wrote Jaloux, were poets only
through their mind—outside their work, they were as other men: but Rilke
had led him 'into a universe of his own, to which I was admitted only as
though by a miracle ... one felt him without interests on earth, his face ever
turned towards those verities which are never expressed'.[5] Kassner struck a
more balanced note, pointing out that Rilke's asceticism and religiosity were
far removed in fact from the impression given by his work, and stressing in
anecdote and reminiscence his human qualities; but he extolled the 'priceless,
wonderful homogeneity' of life and work. 'Rilke was poet and personality even
when simply washing his hands.'[6]

The *laudatio funebris* is seldom the place to seek a settled judgement of the departed. In the case of Rilke, whose life had already taken on an aura of legend, it is all the more surprising to find assessments on the morrow of his death which still stand half a century later. They saw in him a unique phenomenon, a poet exclusively dedicated to his mission, even though the intensity of the struggle this had meant for him was as yet scarcely perceived; and although much of his work, indeed some of his finest, was then still unknown, there was unanimous acknowledgement that he had attained heights of lyrical expression rarely before seen. These propositions, though sometimes assailed and often qualified in the vast literature that has accumulated since round his figure, will remain the corner-stones of any study of Rilke.

Outwardly one of endless vicissitudes, in its essence his life followed a constant course. A rootless wanderer, seeking now solitude, now society, apparently seizing every possibility of change chance might offer, he nevertheless steadfastly held to his aim: through the alchemy of the gift he felt within him, to transform to the gold of poetic expression a personal perception of the world of man and of nature,

> as might be with the eyelids, utter
> reply to what the butterflies out-flutter,
> and learn to fathom what a flower infers.[7]

Time mellowed the arrogance of the young René, who had cried 'there is no one like me, there never has been'; but it did not weaken the sense of mission which ran like a thread through his life, unbroken though often perilously fragile—the yardstick against which he tried to measure all his decisions and the guide he instinctively followed in every action.

Many who met him gained the impression of a life of 'metaphysical remoteness'.[8] His appeals for advice and aid, in which he would constantly stress his inability to cope with practical details, seemed to mark him as living in a world of his own, the very image of the poet in the clouds. He was certainly without forethought in spending the money that came his way, in blithe confidence that the supply would somehow be renewed. Yet he had a very clear idea of the conditions he needed, and showed an almost spinsterish care in their planning, an attention to detail that most people have neither the time nor the patience for. 'Nothing ever left Rilke's hands that was not perfect,' said Stefan Zweig[9]—be it a letter, adapted always completely to the correspondent and entirely rewritten if there was a blemish, a book returned impeccably wrapped, or a holograph poem or dedication: and there was the same perfectionism in his daily habits or in the continual packing for his moves. In his temporary homes, and sometimes in other people's, he surrounded himself with small possessions carefully chosen and arranged—the standing-desk, its precise measurements always to hand for a new order; icons or prints; fine porcelain; vases and bowls for the flowers he was never without.

The passion for order in his papers and for meticulous organization of the smaller affairs of life found a sharp contrast in his apparent passivity over major decisions, often interminably procrastinating until some providential dispensation cast the die for him or, as he liked to think, his instinct guided him to the right move. It was as though, instead of living, he was letting himself *be* lived: holding himself in readiness for the moments of those 'terrific tensions of inner experience over which one has no control', and enduring the intervals between, all the harder 'because I have neglected everything outside my work'.[10] When he quoted Kassner's aphorism, 'The way from inwardness to greatness lies through sacrifice', as being 'both for me and against me', it was in recognition both of his aim and of the struggle to which he feared he might prove unequal.

In contrast to the background and circumstances of many of his contemporaries—Hofmannsthal, Rudolf Borchardt, Stefan Zweig, Rudolf Alexander Schröder—Rilke's were anything but propitious for the life he had chosen, and to sustain it would have been impossible without the favour of protection. He was fortunate to live in an age when patrons, and a publisher, could still be found ready to give it, fortunate too to have so many friends willing to aid in smoothing the difficulties in his path. The search for such an 'unpossessingly protective hand'[11] in a companion for his life, however, proved fruitless. 'Without shelter, here on the cliffs of the heart', he was impelled time and again to seek it in the love of a woman—'you who are almost protection, where no one / protects'[12]—and time and again the hope was frustrated. He described himself once to Lou Salomé as forever 'standing at the telescope, ascribing to every approaching woman a bliss which was certainly never to be found with any one of them: my own bliss, the bliss I once found in my most solitary hours'[13]—a diagnosis which did not hold him back, however, from plunging three months later into the adventure with Benvenuta.

So it remained throughout his life. The experience was endlessly repeated, both in his deeper love-affairs and in the more fleeting episodes of erotic attraction which he could never resist. The ideal woman for him could probably never be found, thought Princess Marie; 'yet he cannot live without the atmosphere of a woman around him . . . then comes the flight, the moment when he withdraws from any tie, and the old pain and sorrow.'[14] (According to Hofmannsthal, the Princess even went as far as to say that Rilke 'was incapable of feeling either friendship or love, and *knew it*, and suffered endlessly thereby.')[15] His was ever a 'fugitive heart': he knew that he was 'a betrayer of feeling', that 'people are bad for me', found indeed, at forty-four, that 'in the realm of intensified feeling' he was terrified, 'as if since childhood I've known only the dungeons in the castle of love'.[16] Yet in solitude he still longed 'to see a woman's two hands busying themselves of an evening, almost spiritually, with some manual task',[17] and it would not be long before he reached out again for the hand of another, only then once more to have to withdraw his own. The

Martha that was Nanny Wunderly gave him at last the absolute devotion that
caused no trouble, but it freed him only for still another failure in the attempt
to find the ideal woman. An incomparable spinner of words, he could find
expression for love in a thousand images and transcendent flights of emotion
that made him irresistible to a Merline or a Benvenuta, but to give what its
reality demanded remained impossible for him. 'Love lives on words and dies
with deeds':[18] the incidental remark in Marina Tsvetayeva's last letter to him
could well epitomize Rilke's inability to reconcile love with work.

'Whenever I was under an obligation to life, or sought a tie with it, I found
it impossible, and I withdrew myself,' as he said once.[19] From this refusal of the
responsibilities life lays upon the ordinary mortal, he fashioned a philosophy
which, as has been rightly observed, is a pre-eminent characteristic of his work
as of his life.[20] 'Why do people who love each other separate before there is any
need?' he wrote in 1909. 'Because it is after all so very temporary a thing, to be
together and to love one another. ... Our existence is a continuous flow of
vicissitudes, each perhaps no less intense than its successor, and the next, and
the next after that which comes with death. And just as we must part for ever
[then] ... so we must ... at any moment be ready to give each other up, let be
and not hold each other back.'[21] To see this as 'our most fruitful and sublime
truth' may well have been a rationalization of a fundamental weakness, the fear
of facing up to the obligations of love, marriage, and family. Be that as it may,
the important fact is that it was from this process of approach and withdrawal
that his creative power seemed to spring. Thus, no matter what the suffering
each breaking off caused, he could not desist from renewing the search,
suspecting that each longed for beloved would be 'lost from the start' but in
the conviction that the experience would bring him closer to the 'future's
fullness'.[22] 'Every happy space is child or grandchild of parting.'[23]

Many other of his ideas were no more than variations on the theme—the
idealization of love without possession, and the Prodigal Son 'beseeching them
not to love him'; the celebration of the felicity of the early-departed, or of
marriage as a union of guardians of each other's solitude. Developed early, and
held forth as doctrines to the end of his life, they all reflect the fundamental
narcissism of his work. Striving towards 'inwardness', his poetry remains
essentially personal and self-centred, however paradigmatically presented. His
letters, beneath the charm, the touches of humour, the empathy with his
correspondent, and the philosophical flights, reveal the same eternal preoccupation with himself, his art, and his recurring existential crises; and it was
natural that he should regard such compulsive self-expression as 'part of the
productivity of my nature',[24] envisaging their publication one day both as
works of art in themselves and as a facet of the inwardness to which he aspired.
Superfluous as it was to maintain such a vast network of connections, he did so
for the '"cause", for that which is my work, in the end all my letters impart a
vibration, a trace of its intensity'.[25]

Living for words, and enabled by a series of remarkable 'deliverances' to survive on his own terms and do nothing else but write, he reached out towards experience of the senses in the real life he praised, but constantly drew back again into an essentially unreal existence, 'ahead of all departure', to transform into the language peculiarly his own the 'glorious tapestry' of the world and of human emotion.[26] In the process, he transformed himself. The Rilke that emerges from the poetry and the letters is a construct, an ideal self, 'the figure I am making for myself outside, more validly, more permanently. ... Who knows who I am? I move on, ever changing.'[27] As Philip Larkin said, in another context, to live exclusively as a poet would mean going around *pretending* to be oneself. The women who loved or mothered Rilke, even Lou Salomé, the friends who were so eager to help him, were probably as far from knowing the real person as many who are beguiled by his words today or who add another stone of interpretation to the mounting edifice of Rilke scholarship.

'Transforming is not lying':[28] the fascination of his story lies in the interplay between the empirical self, the man who actually lived this extraordinary life, and the poet who strove to be 'among the vanishing in the realms of entropy', 'a ringing glass that shatters as it rings':

> as the arrow endures the string, and in the gathering momentum
> becomes more than itself. Because to stay is to be nowhere.[29]

Abbreviations

The following abbreviations are used in the Notes (for full titles, refer to the Bibliography).

Benvenuta	[Hattingberg] *Rilke und Benvenuta*, 1943.
Betz	*Rilke in Frankreich*, 1938.
Betz²	*Rilke in Paris*, 1948.
BL	British Library, London.
Blätter	*Blätter der Rilke-Gesellschaft*.
Br. 1, 2, etc.	Volume publications of Rilke's letters, serial numbers as in the Bibliography, Section II.
Brutzer	*Rilkes russische Reisen*, 1934.
BStB	Bayerische Staatsbibliothek, Munich.
Butler	*Rilke*, Cambridge, 1941 (reprint 1973).
Byong	*Rilkes Militärschulerlebnis . . .*, 1973.
Capra	*The Tao of Physics*, 1978.
Cardiff	B. J. Morse papers, University College, Cardiff.
Casellato	*La veneziana 'misteriosa' . . .*, 1977.
Clary	Rilke letters to Dorothea von Ledebur, in possession of Gräfin von Clary, Salzburg.
CSR	National Museum Archives, Prague.
Dernière Amitié	*La dernière amitié de Rilke* (Jaloux), 1949.
DLA	Deutsches Literaturarchiv, Marbach a.N.
Drozhzhin	'Der Dichter R. M. Rilke', 1929.
Ekner	'Rilke, Ellen Key och Sverige', 1965.
Ficker	'Rilke und der unbekannte Freund', 1954.
GB	Gothenburg Universitetsbibliotek.
Goll	*La poursuite du vent*, 1976.
Goll²	*Rilke et les femmes*, 1955.
Houghton	Houghton Library, Harvard University.
HK	Hertha Koenig, *Rilkes Mutter*, 1963.
Jaloux	*Rilke*, 1927.
JNUL	Jewish National and University Library, Jerusalem.
Jonas, 'Huf'	'Rilke und Fritz Huf', 1974.
Kat.	*Katalog*, Sonderausstellung Rilke, Marbach, 1975.
KB	Kunglige Biblioteket, Stockholm.
KBCop.	Kongelige Biblioteket, Copenhagen.
LAG	Landsarkivet, Gothenburg.
LAL	Loulou Albert-Lasard, *Wege mit Rilke*, 1952.
LAS	Lou Andreas-Salomé, *Lebensrückblick*, 1974.
Leppin	'Der neunzehnjährige Rilke', 1927.
Les Lettres	*Rilke: Inédits, études . . .*, 1952.
LUL	Universitetsbibliotek, Lund.

Mason	*Rilke, Leben und Werk*, 1964.
Mason[2]	*Rilke, Europe and the English-speaking World*, 1961.
Mauser	'Lettere di Rilke a Carlo Placci', 1956.
Mises	Obermüller *et al.* (ed.): *Katalog der Rilke-Sammlung Mises*, 1966.
MStB	Stadtbibliothek, Munich.
Mühll	Von der Mühll: 'Erinnerungen an Rilke', 1945.
Pfeiffer	'Rilke und die Psychoanalyse', 1976.
Pfeiffer[2]	'Denn Rilke starb "trostlos",' 1982.
Pittsburgh	German Literature Center, Pittsburgh.
PMB	*Paula Modersohn-Becker, Briefe* ..., 1979, ed. Busch/Von Reinken.
RA	Rilke-Archiv, Gernsbach.
Reconnaissance	*Reconnaissance à Rilke*, 1926.
Reventlow	*Marbacher Magazin* 8 (1978).
Salis	*Rilkes Schweizer Jahre*, 1975.
Schnack	*Rilke-Chronik*, 1975.
Schnack[2]	*Rilke in Ragaz*, 1981.
Scholz	*Eine Jahrhundertwende*, 1936.
Sieber	*René Rilke*, 1932.
Sieber, RA	MS biography, Rilke-Archiv, Gernsbach.
Sieber[2]	'Rilke und Worpswede', 1941.
Simenauer	*Rilke—Legende und Mythos*, 1953.
SLB	Schweizerische Landesbibliothek, Berne.
Šolle	'Neznámé Dopisy R. M. Rilka', 1975.
Stargardt	Auction catalogues of J. A. Stargardt, Marburg.
StBPKB	Staatsbibliothek (Preussischer Kulturbesitz), Berlin.
StdFr.	Buchheit (ed.), *Stimmen der Freunde*, 1931.
Storck	'Rilkes "Linzer Episode"', 1981.
Storck[2]	'Rilkes Briefe an Marianne Mitford', 1982.
Storck[3]	'Unbekannter Brief an Kippenberg', 1974.
Storck Diss.	'Rilke als Briefschreiber', dissertation, 1957.
Studer-Kiefer	MS album on Rilke, 1963–71, SLB.
Studien	*Rilke-Studien zu Werk* ..., 1976.
SW	*Sämtliche Werke*, 1955–66.
Tagebücher	*Tagebücher aus der Frühzeit*, 1973
Taxis	*Erinnerungen an Rilke*, 1966.
Trebitsch	*Chronicle of a Life*, 1953.
Testament	Rilke, *Das Testament*, 1975.
UBr.	Universität Bremen, Bibliothek.
Unseld	'*Das Tagebuch*' Goethes ..., 1978.
Voronin	Stahl *et al*, 'Letters of Rilke to Helene ***', 1960.
Weimar	Goethe- und Schiller-Archiv, Weimar.
Werfel	'Begegnungen mit Rilke', 1976.
WNB	Nationalbibliothek, Vienna.
Wohltmann	*Rilke in Worpswede*, 1952.
WStB	Stadt- und Landesbibliothek, Vienna
Wydenbruck	*Rilke*, 1949 (reprint 1972).
ZE	Stefan Zweig Estate, London.

Notes

I
A Boyhood in Bohemia
1875–1896

1 Motto: KB.

  1 Phia Rilke, 17 Dec. 1922 (quot. Sieber, 63–4).
  2 To Jenny Oltersdorf, 28 July 1911, and Nora Goudstikker, 4 Apr. 1897 (DLA).
  3 *Br.* 8: 37; *Br.* 8: 332.
  4 15 Apr. 1904 (*Br.* 31: 146).
  5 *SW* i. 149.
  6 Benvenuta, 22.
  7 To Ellen Key, 14 Feb. 1904 (KB).
  8 *Br.* 40: 145–6.

2 Motto: KB.

  1 6 Aug. 1883 (quot. Sieber, 84).
  2 To Werner Reinhart, 28 May 1924 (SLB).
  3 17 Mar 1926 (Quot. Schnack, 13).
  4 Sieber, 82, 85.
  5 *Br.* 27: 78.
  6 Byong, 35–62.
  7 Ibid. 63–4.
  8 Quot. Sieber, 159–60.
  9 To Ellen Key, 14 Feb. 1904 (KB).
  10 *Br.* 8: 37–8.
  11 To Valerie von David-Rhonfeld, 4 Dec. 1894 (quot. Leppin, 632).
  12 *SW* iii. 813.
  13 Quot. Sieber, 97.
  14 Quot. Leppin, 632.

3 Motto: quot. Sieber, 159–60.

  1 Quot. Sieber, 103–4.
  2 Quot. Schnack, 20.
  3 *SW* iii. 415.
  4 *SW* iii. 415–16.
  5 Byong, 51–4.
  6 Sieber, 108.
  7 To Helene and Tissa *** (quot. Storck, 123–4).
  8 Quot. in letter from Maj.-Gen. Sedlakowitz to Rilke, 16 Jan. 1921 (SLB).
  9 Arnold Wimhölzel's account (quot. Storck, 125–7).
  10 Quot. Sieber, 109–10.
  11 *Br.* 8: 38.
  12 Letters to Kastner, Mar.–June 1892 (auction catalogue 6, Dorotheum, Vienna, 1980).

13 Quot. Schnack, 22.
14 Sieber, 112.
15 Quot. in letter from Sedlakowitz to Rilke, 5 Oct. 1920 (SLB; Sieber, 159–60).
16 To Valerie, 4 Dec. 1894 (quot. Leppin, 631).
17 3 Mar. 1904 (KB).
18 *Br.* 13: 10.
19 Quot. Leppin, 631–3.
20 *SW* iv. 483.
21 Quot. Sieber, 127.

4 Motto: *SW* iv. 533.

 1 Quot. Schnack, 36.
 2 29 Jan. 1896 (CSR).
 3 Quot. Schnack, 40.
 4 Richard von Mises, *Br.* 22: 4–5.
 5 Sieber, 129–30.
 6 *Br.* 8: 13.
 7 *Br.* 22: 14.
 8 To Ottilie Malybrock-Stieler, ?Jan. 1896 (CSR).
 9 *Br.* 22: 28.
10 Ibid. 21–3.
11 Ibid. 31–2.
12 To Arthur Schnitzler, Apr. 1896 (quot. Schnack, 44).
13 *Br.* 22: 32–3.
14 *Br.* 15, ii: 459.
15 *Br.* 22: 23.
16 *SW* v, 304–5.
17 *Br.* 24: 22.
18 *Br.* 22: 40.
19 To Hans Olden, ?autumn 1896 (Sieber, RA).
20 To Richard Zoozmann, 10 Aug. 1896 (Copy Houghton; Mises 545).
21 Sieber, 134.
22 *Br.* 8: 23.
23 Trebitsch, 56–63.
24 Schnack, 48.
25 To Richard Zoozmann, 20 Aug. 1896 (Copy Houghton; Mises 545).
26 *Br.* 24: 32.
27 *SW* iv, 512 ff.

II
Munich, Russia, and
Wörpswede
1896–1902

Motto: *Br.* 31: 96.
1 Motto: *SW* iii. 550.

 1 *SW* iv. 536.
 2 *Br.* 22: 59.

3 Sieber, RA.
4 To Phia Rilke, 8 Dec. 1896 (Sieber, RA).
5 *Kat.*, 35.
6 *Br.* 8: 26–7.
7 Ibid.
8 *Br.* 24: 37–8.
9 *SW* iii. 823.
10 *SW* iii. 549–51.
11 *SW* iii. 551.
12 Letters to F. V. Krejči, Jan. 1897 (Šolle).
13 *Br.* 8: 30–1.
14 *SW* iii. 777.
15 *Br.* 15, ii: 460.
16 *Br.* 8: 35.
17 Ibid. 32.
18 *SW* iii. 489–92.
19 *SW* iii. 147–51.
20 *Br.* 30: 245–6.
21 *SW* iv. 556.
22 *Kat.*, 52; *Br.* 15, ii: 461.
23 Nachwort, *Niels Lyhne* (Leipzig, n.d.), 255.
24 *SW* vi. 1021–2.
25 Quot. Schnack, 56.
26 To Wilhelm von Scholz, 30 Mar. 1897 (Copy Houghton; Mises 548).
27 *Br.* 8: 35.
28 To Nora Goudstikker, 28/9 Mar. and 4 Apr. 1897 (DLA).
29 To Nora Goudstikker, 2 Apr. and 3 Apr. 1897 (DLA).
30 *Br.* 8: 37–42.
31 Reventlow, 6.
32 18 May 1897 (quot. Sieber, RA).
33 To Franziska zu Reventlow, 6 July 1902 (Copy Houghton; Mises 551).
34 29 Apr. 1897 (DLA).
35 *SW* i. 103.
36 to Nora Goudstikker, 29 Apr. 1897 (DLA).
37 *SW* iii. 565.

2

1 18 May 1897 (quot. Sieber, RA).
2 LAS 43.
3 Curt Paul Janz, *Friedrich Nietzsche* (Munich, 1978), ii. 171.
4 *Br.* 31: 7–8.
5 Cf. Ernst Pfeiffer's summary, *Br.* 31: 488–90.
6 *Br.* 31: 10.
7 *SW* iii. 572.
8 *Br.* 31: 11–13.
9 LAS 138.
10 *Br.* 31: 22, 16, 18, 20.

11 Ibid. 21.
12 To Phia Rilke, 7 Oct. 1897 (quot. Sieber, RA).
13 LAS 138.
14 *Br.* 31: 26. See Ernst Pfeiffer's note, ibid. 496–7, concerning the slight difference in the final version in *SW* i. 313.
15 LAS 288.
16 *Br.* 31: 26.
17 To Ludwig Ganghofer, 7 Oct. 1897 (MStB).
18 Ibid., and to Phia Rilke, 7 Oct. 1897 (quot. Sieber, RA).
19 To Bonz, 19 Oct. 1897 (Mises 493) and 25 Oct. 1897 (quot. Schnack 64).
20 *SW* i. 103.
21 *SW* iv. 98.
22 To Bonz, 15 Feb. 1898 (Mises 493).
23 8 Mar. 1898 (ibid.).
24 *SW* iii. 605.
25 To Julius Hart, 26 Mar. 1898 (copy Pittsburgh); to Hugo Salus, 1 Apr. 1898 (quot. Sieber, RA).
26 *Tagebücher*, 21–3.
27 To Hugo Salus, 16 Apr. 1898 (quot. Sieber, RA).
28 *Tagebücher*, 19, 13, 17, 25, 27, 28.
29 *SW* iii. 615–6.
30 *Tagebücher*, 29.
31 Ibid. 28, 33–4, 46.
32 Ibid. 74.
33 Ibid. 65.
34 To Franziska zu Reventlow, 18 June 1898 (copy Houghton; Mises 551).
35 *Tagebücher*, 115.
36 Ibid. 118–19.
37 11 July 1898 (Houghton; Mises 493).
38 To Alfred Roller, 21 July 1898 (WStB, quot. Schnack 74); to Phia Rilke, 27 July 1898 (quot. Sieber, RA).
39 *Tagebücher*, 126.
40 To Phia Rilke, 7 Sept. 1898 (quot. Sieber, RA).
41 To Phia Rilke, 28 Nov. 1898 (quot. ibid.).
42 *Br.* 8: 60.
43 To Phia Rilke, 29 Dec. 1898 (quot. Sieber[2]).
44 Heinrich Vogeler, *Erinnerungen* (Berlin, 1952), 101.
45 *SW* iii. 636.
46 29 Dec. 1898 (Voronin, 149).
47 *Br.* 8: 62.
48 Ibid. 64.
49 *Br.* 41: 41.
50 (?18) Mar. 1899 (quot. Sieber, RA).
51 Letters of 9 Mar., 21 Mar., and 20 Apr. 1899 (Houghton; Mises 493).
52 22 Apr. 1899 (quot. Sieber, RA).
53 *Br.* 1: 8.

3 Motto: Quot. Schnack 93.

1 Schnack, 84.

2 *Br.* 31: 142–3.

3 To Bonz, 10 May 1899(NS) (Houghton; Mises 493); to Phia Rilke, 4 May 1899 (NS) (quot. Schnack, 85) and 29 Apr. 1899(NS) (quot. Brutzer, 29). Rilke usually dated his letters from Russia according to the Old Style: they are given here their New Style (NS) datings.

4 *Br.* 1: 15.

5 Voronin, 154.

6 Ibid. 156.

7 7 June 1899 (quot. Schnack, 86, and Sieber, RA).

8 To Ilse Sadee, 13 Mar. 1912 (quot. Sieber, RA).

9 To Dr L., 29 Mar. 1902 (quot. ibid.).

10 *Br.* 8: 68–9.

11 To Emil Faktor, 3 June 1899 (DLA, quot. *Kat.*, 74).

12 Voronin, 157, 158, 160.

13 *Br.* 8: 493.

14 *Br.* 31: 37.

15 *Br.* 8: 72, 73.

16 Quot. Schnack, 91.

17 To Emil Faktor, 22 July 1899 (DLA, quot. Schnack, 88).

18 *SW* iii. 361.

19 *SW* iii. 334.

20 *Br.* 19, 54.

21 Cf. Walter Simon, 'Philologische Untersuchungen zu R. M. Rilkes "Cornet"', *Blätter* 2 (1973), 28–31.

22 *SW* i. 245.

23 *SW* ii. 265.

24 *Tagebücher*, 134, 166, 172.

25 Ibid. 137–44.

26 *SW* iv. 288.

27 27 Oct. 1899 (copy Houghton; Mises 551).

28 5 Dec. 1899 (quot. Brutzer, 1).

29 14 July 1899 (Houghton; Mises 493).

30 *Almanach der Insel für 1900*, quot. in *Die Insel: eine Ausstellung* (DLA, 1965), 15.

31 10 Dec. 1899 (quot. Schnack, 94).

32 Vogeler, op. cit., 74.

33 *Br.* 8: 76–7.

34 Ibid. 78.

35 27 Mar. 1900 (quot. Sieber, RA).

36 24 Mar. 1900 (Houghton; Mises 551).

37 Lou Andreas-Salomé, unpublished diary (courtesy Ernst Pfeiffer).

38 *Br.* 50: 19.

39 P. D. Ettinger, 'Erinnerungen an Rainer Maria Rilke', *Prager Presse*, no. 215 (7 Aug. 1932).

40 21 May 1900 (quot. Brutzer, 4–5).

41 Ibid.

42 Lou Andreas-Salomé, diary.
43 Quot. Schnack, 101.
44 *Br.* 1: 39–42.
45 Cf. *SW* vi. 967 ff.
46 6 June 1900 (quot. Brutzer, 6).
47 Lou Andreas-Salomé, diary.
48 Ibid. 19–21 June 1900.
49 Ibid. 24 June 1900.
50 Drozhzhin, 228.
51 *Br.* 8: 100–1.
52 Lou Andreas-Salomé, diary July 1900.
53 Drozhzhin, 230.
54 To Phia Rilke, 30 July 1900 (quot. Sieber, RA).
55 *Br.* 31: 42–3.
56 To Phia Rilke, 18 Aug. 1900 (quot. Brutzer, 29–30).
57 Quot. Brutzer, 7.
58 LAS 146.
59 Quot. *Br.* 31: 49.

4 Motto: *Br.* 1: 141.

1 Clara Rilke, in an interview for an unidentified paper, *c.* 1954 (SLB).
2 Wohltmann, 10.
3 28/29 Aug. 1900 (quot. Sieber[2]).
4 *Tagebücher*, 196–8.
5 Ibid. 198.
6 Wohltmann, 10.
7 *Tagebücher*, 204.
8 *PMB* 245.
9 Ibid. 233.
10 Ibid. 149.
11 *SW* i. 375.
12 *Tagebücher*, 216, 214, 237, 238.
13 Ibid. 247.
14 Ibid. 250.
15 Ibid. 253, 256, 271–2, 264, 276.
16 Ibid. 282, 283, 296, 289.
17 *Br.* 8: 107.
18 Ibid. 105, 110–11.
19 Ibid. 117.
20 5 Nov. 1900 (quot. Sieber[2]).
21 *SW* iii. 706, 704.
22 *PMB* 245.
23 *Br.* 8: 129, 137.
24 *Tagebücher*, 324.
25 *Br.* 8: 145.
26 *Tagebucher*, 346–9.
27 *Br.* 31: 51.

28 Ibid. 507.
29 Quot. Sieber, RA.
30 *Br.* 1: 91.
31 Ibid. 92, 97.
32 *SW* iii. 729.
33 From Schmargendorf, 15 Feb. 1901 (quot. Sieber, RA).
34 *Br.* 31: 55
35 Ibid. 56.
36 From Netzlers Hotel, Berlin, 16 Feb. 1901 (quot. Sieber, RA).
37 18 Feb. 1901 (quot. ibid.).
38 *Br.* 1: 99.
39 Quot. Schnack, 121.
40 *Br.* 31: 53–5.
41 *SW* iii. 738.
42 *Br.* 1: 141.
43 Ibid. 108.
44 To Ellen Key, 22 Mar. 1904 (KB).

5 Motto: *Br.* 1: 109.

1 *Br.* 31: 258.
2 Quot. Scholz, 218.
3 *Br.* 1: 109.
4 Ibid. 103–4.
5 The portraits, whose present location is unknown, are reproduced in Richard Pettit's *Rilke in und nach Worpswede* (Worpswede, 1983).
6 2 Sept. and 10 Oct. 1901 (quot. Sieber[2]).
7 *Br.* 1: 110.
8 *SW* i. 307–8.
9 *SW* i. 323, 339.
10 13 Dec. and 16 Dec. 1901 (quot. Schnack, 130–1).
11 *Br.* 1: 135.
12 *Br.* 3: 146.
13 *SW* iii. 755.
14 16 Dec. 1901 (*Br.* 1: 131 ff.) and end Dec. 1901 (StBPKB).
15 *Br.* 1: 137; to P. D. Ettinger, ?Jan. 1902 (quot. Asadowsky, 'Briefe nach Russland', in *Rilke-Studien* (Berlin, 1976), 207.
16 *Br.* 1: 143.
17 ?January 1902 (quot. Asadowsky, op. cit.).
18 *SW* v. 8.
19 *Br.* 1: 154.
20 Ibid. 182.
21 Ibid. 137, 141.
22 24 Aug. 1902 (quot. *SW* iii. 863).
23 *PMB* 309.
24 26 June 1902 (UBr.).
25 *Br.* 1: 183.
26 *Br.* 16: 1–7.

27 *Br.* 48: 35.
28 *SW* i. 477.
29 To Arthur Holitscher, 31 July 1902 (quot. Schnack, 147).
30 Br. 1: 191.

III
Paris, Rome and Sweden
1902–1905

Motto: *Br.* 2: 43.

1 Motto: *Br.* 2: 57.
1 Ibid. 21–2.
2 *Br.* 8: 246, 247.
3 End Aug. 1902 (quot. Sieber, RA).
4 *Br.* 8: 250–3.
5 *Br.* 42: 18.
6 24 Sept. 1902 (quot. Sieber[2]).
7 6 Sept. 1902 (KB).
8 To Oskar Zwintscher, 18 Oct. 1902 (quot. Schnack, 153).
9 *Br.* 16: 266–8.
10 *Br.* 2: 52; *Br.* 8: 294.
11 *SW* iii. 757; *SW* i. 400, 398.
12 *SW* i. 505.
13 *SW* v. 145.
14 *SW* v. 200.
15 To Verlag Greiner & Pfeifer, Stuttgart, 27 Jan. 1903 (Stargardt 620, 88).
16 *Br.* 48: 89.
17 *Br.* 8: 304.
18 *PMB* 334, 309.
19 *SW* iii. 769, 768.
20 *Br.* 13: 12.
21 *Br.* 8: 344.
22 *SW* i. 343–66 (last two stanzas trans. Leishman).
23 *Br.* 8: 436.
24 Lou Andreas-Salomé to Eva Cassirer, 5 Mar. 1933 (SLB).
25 *Br.* 8: 321.
26 To Gerhart Hauptmann, 17 June 1903 (StBPKB).
27 *Br.* 31: 56–7.
28 Ibid. 58–9.
29 Ibid. 62–4.
30 *SW* v. 145.
31 *Br.* 31: 65–74.
32 Ibid. 76–8.
33 Ibid. 79.
34 Ibid. 96–8.
35 Ibid. 105, 103.
36 To Ellen Key, 25 July 1903 (KB).

37 *Br.* 31: 118.

2 Motto: KB.

  1 *Br.* 13: 28.
  2 To Ellen Key, 3 Nov. 1903 (KB).
  3 *Br.* 2: 131.
  4 *Br.* 31: 121.
  5 *Br.* 48: 257.
  6 16 Jan 1904 (quot. Schnack, 175–6).
  7 14 Feb. 1904 (KB).
  8 *SW* i. 542, 549, 540.
  9 *Br.* 31: 139.
10 Ibid. 145, 160.
11 Ibid. 139, 145.
12 Ibid. 154, 157, 158.
13 Ibid. 160, 162.
14 Ibid. 174.
15 10 May 1904 (KB).
16 30 May 1904 (KB).
17 *Br.* 31: 177.
18 To Ernst Norlind, 14 and 20 June 1904 (LUL).
19 *Br.* 31: 177.
20 Ibid. 178; *Br.* 2: 170.

3 Motto: KB.

  1 *Br.* 9: 11.
  2 Ibid. 14.
  3 27 June 1904 (KB).
  4 July 1904 (quot. Sieber, RA).
  5 *Br.* 9: 21.
  6 Ernst Norlind's diary (unpublished typescript in German, LUL).
  7 26 June 1904 (KB, quot. Reidar Ekner, 'Rainer Maria Rilke, Ernst Norlind och Hans Larsson', *Nordisk Tidskrift för vetenskap, konst och industri*, 3 (1965), 128).
  8 *Br.* 9: 11.
  9 *Br.* 31: 178.
10 *Br.* 9: 38, 39.
11 Ibid. 39, 40, 47.
12 *Br.* 13: 50, 47.
13 *Br.* 16: 41.
14 *Br.* 31: 180.
15 Ernst Norlind's diary (LUL).
16 Quot. Wydenbruck, 111–12.
17 23 Sept. 1904 (LAG).
18 *Br.* 31: 186.
19 *Br.* 9: 54; to the Gibsons, 6 Oct. 1904 (LAG).
20 *Br.* 31: 183–5.
21 Ibid. 185–7.
22 Ibid. 187–9.

23 *Br.* 2: 224.
24 Ibid. 225.
25 Quot. Ekner, 28.
26 To Ellen Key, 2 Nov. 1904 (KB).
27 *Br.* 2: 227, 229–30.
28 Ibid. 226.
29 *Br.* 31: 192.
30 Ibid. 194.
31 29 Nov. 1904 (KB).
32 *Br.* 48: 281.

4 Motto: *Br.* 9: 78.
 1 To Jimmy Gibson, 18 Dec. 1904 (LAG).
 2 *Br.* 31: 196.
 3 To Jimmy Gibson, 18 Dec. 1904 (LAG).
 4 6 Jan. 1905 to Ellen Key (KB) and Jimmy Gibson (LAG); to Jimmy Gibson, 26 Feb. 1905 (LAG).
 5 To Ellen Key, 15 Feb. 1905 (KB).
 6 *Br.* 31: 196–8.
 7 19 Jan. 1905 (LAG).
 8 2 Mar. 1905 (KB).
 9 To Ellen Key, 9 Mar. 1905 (KB).
 10 To Eva Solmitz, 18 Mar. 1905 (SLB).
 11 Quot. Schnack, 208.
 12 To Ellen Key, 30 Mar. 1905 (KB); to Luise von Schwerin, undated (quot. Sieber, RA).
 13 *Br.* 31: 201.
 14 To Anna Schewitz-Hellmann, 24 Apr. 1905 (DLA).
 15 *Br.* 31: 204, 203, 200.
 16 Ibid. 203–6.
 17 To Ellen Key, 7 June 1905 (KB).
 18 *Br.* 31: 206.
 19 *Br.* 9: 75, 71.
 20 Ibid. 75–6.
 21 Ibid. 81–2.
 22 *Br.* 16: 45.
 23 *Br.* 9: 86.
 24 *Br.* 2: 250.
 25 Ibid. 251

IV
France, Italy, and North Africa
1905–1911

Motto: *SW* vi. 728.
1 Motto: *Br.* 31: 209.
 1 *Br.* 2: 255.
 2 Ibid. 257–8.

3 Ibid. 258, 259.
4 To Gudrun von Uexküll, 25 Sept. 1905 (Stargardt 620, 90).
5 Ibid.; *Br.* 2: 262–3.
6 To Marie Herzfeld, 10 Nov. 1905 (BL).
7 *Br.* 16: 50–1.
8 To Lizzie Gibson, 4 Nov. 1905 (LAG).
9 6 Nov. 1905 (KB)
10 To Lizzie Gibson, 4 Nov. 1905 (LAG).
11 To Marie Herzfeld, 10 Nov. 1905 (BL).
12 *Br.* 2: 274.
13 *Br.* 31: 209, 214.
14 *SW* i. 496.
15 Stefan Zweig to Ellen Key, 9 Feb. 1906 (KB).
16 8 Nov. 1905 (quot. Schnack, 224).
17 *Br.* 48: 167.
18 Quot. Ingeborg Schnack/Renate Scharffenberg, 'Ein Brief Rilkes an Karl von der
   Heydt (1905)', *Blätter* 7/8 (1980/1), 53.
19 *Br.* 3: 156.
20 To Marie Herzfeld, 22 Feb. 1906 (BL).
21 Quot. *Kat.*, 123.
22 *Br.* 9: 117.
23 20 Dec. 1905 (quot. Sieber, RA).
24 *Br.* 2: 291.
25 To Paula Modersohn-Becker, 23 Feb. 1906 (RA).
26 *Br.* 2: 296–8.
27 7 Feb. 1906 (quot. Sieber, RA).
28 *Br.* 2: 290, 294, 295, 300.
29 *Br.* 9: 119–20.
30 Ibid. 122.
31 Ibid. 121–2.
32 To Ellen Key, undated (early Apr. 1906) (KB).
33 *Br.* 2: 123–5.
34 *Br.* 9: 130.
35 *Br.* 2: 316.
36 To Gerhart Hauptmann, 19 Apr. 1906 (StBPKB).
37 *Br.* 2: 315.
38 To Gerhart Hauptmann, 19 Apr. 1906 (StBPKB).
39 *Br.* 2: 319.
40 *Br.* 16: 67–8.
41 *Br.* 9: 132–3.

2 Motto: *Br.* 3: 305.

1 *Br.* 9: 137, 138.
2 *Br.* 16: 68–9.
3 *Br.* 2: 325.
4 21 May 1906 (BL).
5 *Br.* 9: 141.

6 *Br.* 35: 21.
7 *Br.* 3: 19, 32, 33.
8 Ibid. 37, 38.
9 *Br.* 48: 186.
10 *Br.* 3: 17.
11 13 June 1906 (Houghton; Mises 554).
12 *Br.* 3: 42, 43.
13 Ibid. 46.
14 *StdFr.* 92.
15 31 July 1906 (Houghton; Mises 554).
16 28 July 1906 (KBCop.).
17 To Dora Herxheimer (Houghton; Mises 554); undated, probably 10 Aug. 1906.
18 To Mathilde Vollmoeller, 20 Aug. 1906 (quot. Schnack, 249).
19 Sieber, RA.
20 *Br.* 3: 78.
21 *Br.* 42: 44.
22 S. Fischer to Rilke, 2 Nov. 1906 (SLB).
23 *Br.* 3: 94–5.
24 *Br.* 7: 15–16.
25 *Br.* 3: 104; to Dora Herxheimer, 29 Nov. 1906 (Houghton; Mises 554).
26 *Br.* 3: 107.
27 6 Dec. 1906 (quot. Sieber, RA).
28 *Br.* 3: 121; *Br.* 31: 221; *Br.* 3: 119.
29 *Br.* 3: 121; *Br.* 25: 20.
30 *Br.* 3: 118, 117.
31 To Gustaf af Geijerstam, 16 Dec. 1906 (GB).
32 *Br.* 31: 221.
33 *Br.* 3: 132, 133, 136.
34 Ibid. 146–7.
35 To Geijerstam, 7 Feb. 1907 (GB).
36 *Br.* 3: 136.
37 Ibid. 144, 150.
38 *SW* ii. 332 (trans. Leishman).
39 *Br.* 3: 186.
40 *SW* ii. 11 (trans. Leishman).
41 *Br.* 3: 155.
42 3 Jan. 1907 (SLB).
43 *SW* i. 552, 546, 600, 518.
44 *Br.* 3: 164–6.
45 Ibid. 213, 214, 216, 215, 213.
46 Ibid. 221.
47 9 Feb. 1907 (KB).
48 *Br.* 3: 211, 212.
49 Ibid. 183, 186.
50 Ibid. 226.
51 Cf. B. J. Morse, 'Rainer Maria Rilke and English Literature' (privately reprinted from *German Life and Letters*, 1948), 5.

52 *Br.* 7: 22.
53 *Br.* 3: 252.
54 To Ellen Key, 18 Apr. 1907 (KB).
55 To Geijerstam, 12 Apr. and 25 May 1907 (GB).
56 *Br.* 3: 263.
57 Ibid. 237.
58 Ibid. 273, 265, 271, 272, 276.
59 *SW* i. 530 (trans. Mason).
60 *Br.* 31: 94.
61 *Br.* 3: 279–80.
62 5 July 1907 (quot. Sieber, RA).
63 To Clara, 4 Aug. 1907 (quot. Sieber, RA); *Br.* 3: 301.
64 14 July 1907 (Houghton; Mises 554).
65 *Br.* 3: 295.
66 Ibid. 371, 369.
67 Ibid. 390.

3 Motto: *Br.* 16: 125.

 1 *Br.* 3: 339.
 2 *Br.* 47: 19.
 3 *Br.* 4: 11, 10.
 4 Ibid. 16, 15.
 5 5 Nov. 1907 (Houghton; Mises 505).
 6 *Br.* 4: 17.
 7 Felix Braun: *Das Licht der Welt* (Vienna, 1949), 557.
 8 To Mathilde Vollmoeller, 22 Nov. 1907 (SLB).
 9 *Br.* 4: 23.
10 *Br.* 16: 76.
11 *Br.* 40: 48; *Br.* 4: 26; to Lili Schalk, 23 Nov. 1907 (quot. Sieber, RA).
12 *Br.* 4: 26–7.
13 25 Nov. 1907 (quot. Sieber, RA).
14 Casellato, 40–1.
15 *Br.* 19: 7–8.
16 *Br.* 40: 53.
17 *Br.* 15, i: 229.
18 *Br.* 19: 82.
19 To Emma von Ehrenfels, 30 Dec. 1907 (quot. Sieber, RA).
20 *Br.* 40: 59.
21 *Br.* 16: 83.
22 30 Dec. 1907, *Br.* 35: 29 (also *Br.* 4: 27, wrongly dated 30 Nov. 1907).
23 *Br.* 25: 25.
24 14 Mar. 1908 (quot. Schnack, 301).
25 3 Apr. 1908 (SLB).
26 11 Mar. 1908 (quot. Sieber, RA).
27 *Br.* 7: 44–5.
28 To Clara, 11 Mar. 1908 (quot. Sieber, RA).
29 To Clara, 14 Apr. 1908 (quot. ibid.).

30 *Br.* 16: 90–1.
31 To Eva Solmitz, 19 May 1908 (SLB).
32 To Gudrun von Uexküll, 1 June 1908 (quot. Sieber, RA).
33 2 July 1908 (quot. ibid.).
34 *Br.* 40: 69.
35 To Clara, 3 July 1908 (quot. Sieber, RA).
36 To Eva Solmitz, 11 Aug. 1908 (SLB).
37 *Br.* 7: 47.
38 20 Aug. 1908 (quot. Schnack, 309).
39 *Br.* 16: 99.
40 *Br.* 4: 42.
41 *Br.* 16: 100.
42 *Br.* 25: 45.
43 3 Sept. 1908 (Houghton; Mises 554).
44 *SW* v. 657–8.
45 *Br.* 4: 95.
46 Ibid. 54, 55.
47 *Br.* 19: 34–5.
48 *Br.* 4: 47.
49 *Br.* 40: 79, 80, 82.
50 *SW* vi. 924, 937, 941, 946.
51 *Br.* 40: 89.
52 *SW* i. 654 (trans. Leishman).
53 *SW* i. 662–4 (trans. Leishman).
54 9 June 1909 (BStB).
55 *Br.* 10: 57.
56 To Ellen Key, 9 Oct. 1908 (KB).
57 5 Oct. 1908 (KB, quot. Ekner, 42).
58 9 Oct. 1908 (KB).
59 *Br.* 40: 90.
60 *Br.* 19: 40; *Br.* 16: 125.
61 *Br.* 16: 127–8.
62 21 Dec. 1908 (quot. Sieber, RA).
63 31 Dec. 1908 and 2 Jan. 1909 (DLA, incomplete in *Br.* 7: 58–63).
64 *Br.* 7: 63.
65 *Br.* 25: 45.
66 Lou Andreas-Salomé, *Rainer Maria Rilke* (Leipzig, 1928), 43. Cf. Pfeiffer, 262.
67 *Br.* 7: 72.
68 *Br.* 19: 46.
69 *Br.* 4: 69.
70 *Br.* 31: 226.
71 2 Sept. 1909 (SLB).
72 5 Sept. 1909 (SLB).
73 *Br.* 31: 230.
74 To Madeleine de Broglie, 11 Oct. 1909 (quot. Schnack, 335).
75 *Br.* 31: 230–1, 233.
76 *SW* vi. 943.

77 *Br.* 7: 85.
78 To Heime Magdalene Kawerau, 17 Nov. 1909 (SLB).
79 16 Oct. 1909 (quot. Sieber, RA).
80 *SW* vi. 1026–7.
81 *Br.* 40: 109.
82 25 Oct. 1909 (LAG).
83 *Br.* 40: 109.
84 Taxis, 7.
85 Ibid.
86 *Br.* 30: 8.

4 Motto: *Br.* 7: 98.
 1 To Mathilde Vollmoeller, 10 Jan. 1910 (SLB copy extract).
 2 *Br.* 16: 145.
 3 *SW* vi. 946.
 4 Butler, 211, 205.
 5 Mason, 73.
 6 *Br.* 30: 10.
 7 Ibid. 12.
 8 *Br.* 10: 93.
 9 *Br.* 43: 20.
10 *Blätter* 5 (1978), 21.
11 *Br.* 30: 12.
12 *Br.* 7: 98; to Mathilde Vollmoeller, 3 Apr. 1910 (quot. Schnack, 347–8).
13 *Br.* 4: 112–13
14 *Br.* 40: 79.
15 *Br.* 31: 240.
16 To Mathilde Vollmoeller, 3 Apr. 1910 (SLB).
17 *Br.* 4: 101.
18 *Br.* 30: 15.
19 *Br.* 4: 101.
20 *Br.* 19: 58–60.
21 *Br.* 4: 100.
22 *Br.* 7: 103.
23 To Anton Kippenberg, 25 May 1910 (DLA).
24 8 Aug. 1910 (DLA).
25 *Br.* 34: 14; *Br.* 40: 125.
26 *Br.* 30: 26; *SW* ii. 377.
27 To Phia Rilke, 6 Sept. 1910 (quot. Sieber, RA).
28 *Br.* 4: 113.
29 *Br.* 40: 126–7.
30 To Clara, 30 Sept. 1910 (quot. Sieber, RA); *Br.* 16: 157.
31 To Anton Kippenberg, 20 Oct. 1910 (DLA, quot. Schnack, 356); Kippenberg's reply, 22 Oct. 1910 (Weimar).
32 *Br.* 7: 108–9; *Br.* 30: 29.
33 *Br.* 4: 114.
34 Ibid. 115.

35 Ibid. 116.
36 To Clara, early Dec. 1910 (quot. Sieber, RA).
37 *Br.* 4: 117–18.
38 19 Dec. 1910 (quot. Sieber, RA).
39 *Br.* 118–19; to Clara, 1 Jan. 1911 (quot. Sieber, RA).
40 *Br.* 25: 62 (the reading 'am unendlich Überlegenen' from Sieber, RA).
41 To Mary Dobržensky, 19 Feb. 1922 (SLB).
42 *Br.* 34: 15–16.
43 *Br.* 4: 119–20.
44 To Phia Rilke, 13 Jan. 1911 (quot. Sieber, RA); *Br.* 40: 325.
45 *Br.* 4: 121.
46 To Clara, 29 Jan. 1911 (quot. Sieber, RA).
47 *Br.* 7: 112.
48 4 Apr. 1911 (DLA).
49 *Br.* 44: 1074.
50 28 July 1911 (DLA, quot. Schnack, 378).
51 Cf. *Br.* 30: 901.
52 *Br.* 10: 125.
53 *Br.* 7: 113–15, 118.
54 Quot. Schnack, 366.

V
Duino and Spain
1911–1913

1 Motto: *Br.* 10: 141.

1 29 Mar. 1911 (quot. Sieber, RA).
2 *Br.* 43: 26–7.
3 *SW* ii. 119.
4 *Br.* 4: 128–9.
5 To Mathilde Vollmoeller, 25 Apr. 1911 (quot. Schnack, 368).
6 To Clara, 3 May 1911 (quot. Sieber, RA).
7 *Br.* 43: 27; to Ivo Hauptmann, 14 May 1911 (DLA).
8 *Br.* 30: 37.
9 Katharina Kippenberg, *Rainer Maria Rilke—Ein Beitrag* (Zurich/Wiesbaden, 1948, 4th edn.), 155.
10 22 May 1911 (DLA).
11 To Clara, *c.* 20 June 1911 (quot. Sieber, RA).
12 To Erica von Scheel, 4 June 1911 (DLA, quot. Kat., 156).
13 *Br.* 30: 44.
14 *Br.* 10: 141–2; Kassner, *Rilke: Gesammelte Erinnerungen*, ed. Klaus Bohnenkamp (Pfullingen, 1976), 7.
15 *Br.* 32: 56, 62.
16 To Mathilde Vollmoeller, 3 June 1911 (quot. Schnack, 372); to Erica von Scheel, 4 June 1911 (DLA).
17 *Br.* 30: 50.

18 *SW* ii. 379.
19 *Br.* 40: 84.
20 *SW* ii. 382–3.
21 *Br.* 40: 132, 182.
22 28 June 1911 (DLA, abridged in *Br.* 7: 129–31).
23 8 July 1911 (quot. Schnack, 376).
24 *Br.* 43: 133–4.
25 14 July 1911 (DLA).
26 *Br.* 30: 69.
27 Ibid. 52; Taxis, 23.
28 To Clara, 23 July 1911 (quot. Sieber, RA).
29 To Jenny Oltersdorf, 28 July 1911 (DLA).
30 *Br.* 7: 132, 133; *Br.* 30: 55.
31 Quot. Sieber, RA.
32 *Br.* 40: 133.
33 *Br.* 30: 59.
34 *Br.* 15, i: 314.
35 *Br.* 40: 136; *Br.* 30: 68.
36 *Br.* 30: 63–6.
37 *Br.* 40: 201.
38 To Josef Stark, 9 Dec. 1911 (DLA).
39 Ibid.
40 *Br.* 7: 146.
41 Ibid. 149–50.

2 Motto: *Br.* 34: 35.
  1 *Br.* 25: 66.
  2 Taxis, 35–6.
  3 *Br.* 40: 137.
  4 To Wilhelm von Scholz, 31 Jan. 1898 (*SW* vi, 1158–9).
  5 *Br.* 19: 62.
  6 To Erica von Scheel, end Nov. and *c.* 13 Dec. 1911 (DLA).
  7 *Br.* 4: 142.
  8 *Br.* 30: 75–6.
  9 *Br.* 40: 138.
 10 20 Dec. 1911 (Weimar).
 11 *Br.* 7: 152.
 12 *Br.* 31: 250.
 13 Cf. Pfeiffer, 267.
 14 *SW* ii. 39 (trans. Leishman).
 15 *Br.* 31: 242.
 16 *SW* ii. 39–40 (trans. Leishman).
 17 *Br.* 31: 240, 250.
 18 *SW* ii. 40 (trans. Leishman).
 19 *Br.* 31: 238–41.
 20 *Br.* 4: 169.
 21 *Br.* 31: 250–1.

22 *Br.* 30: 82.
23 9 Jan 1912 (SLB).
24 *Br.* 30: 85, 90.
25 *Br.* 18: 17, 16.
26 Taxis, 48–9; *SW* i. 685 (trans. Poulin).
27 *Br.* 31: 241.
28 *SW* i. 685, 721 (trans. Poulin).
29 *SW* i. 686, 687 (trans. Poulin).
30 *SW* i. 689–92 (trans. Poulin).
31 *Br.* 30: 97.
32 *Almanach der Psychoanalyse* (Vienna, 1926), 35.
33 Simenauer, 136.
34 Pfeiffer, 266.
35 *Br.* 31: 252–3.
36 Ibid. 255–6.
37 *Br.* 40: 144.
38 *Br.* 30: 100–1.
39 *Br.* 4: 200; *Br.* 31: 263–4.
40 *Br.* 7: 163, 174.
41 Algernon Blackwood to B. J. Morse, 28 Sept. 1949 and 7 Mar. 1950 (Cardiff).
42 *Br.* 30: 131.
43 *Br.* 31: 259–61.
44 13 and 17 Apr. 1912 (SLB).
45 *Br.* 4: 226.

3 Motto: *SW* ii. 51.
1 *Br.* 7: 174; to Anton Kippenberg, 14 Mar. 1912 (Weimar).
2 *Br.* 7: 173.
3 *Br.* 30: 149, 158.
4 Ibid. 162, 163.
5 To Pia Valmarana, June 1912 (SLB).
6 *Br.* 40: 154.
7 1 July 1912 (Mauscr, 221; quot. Schnack, 406)
8 *Br.* 30: 171.
9 Ibid. 181.
10 Taxis, 63.
11 *SW* ii. 387 (trans. Leishman).
12 *SW* ii. 42–3 (trans. Morse).
13 *Br.* 40: 156.
14 *Br.* 7: 178.
15 4 Sept. 1912 (SLB).
16 *Br.* 40: 158, 161.
17 *Br.* 6: 282; Taxis, 74; *Br.* 7: 179–80.
18 To Eva Cassirer, 18 Oct. 1912 (SLB).
19 *Br.* 7: 186.
20 *Br.* 30: 218.
21 To Pia Valmarana, 3 Nov. 1912 (SLB); *Br.* 30: 219.

22 15 Nov. 1912 (SLB).
23 *Br.* 40: 165–6; *Br.* 10: 267.
24 7 Nov. 1912 (quot. Sieber, RA).
25 To Gerhard Ouckama Knoop, 9 Nov. 1912 (DLA).
26 To Mathilde Vollmoeller, 14 Nov. 1912 (quot. Schnack, 414); *Br.* 10: 266.
27 *Br.* 30: 229.
28 To Frl. von Schenk, 12 Jan 1913 (DLA).
29 *SW* ii. 388 (trans. Leishman, adapted).
30 *Br.* 30: 239–40.
31 10 and 23 Dec. 1912 (Houghton; Mises 511).
32 Ibid. 10 Dec. 1912.
33 *Br.* 30: 246; to Pascha Taxis, 10 Dec. 1912 (Houghton; Mises 511); to Pia Valmarana, 16 Dec. 1912 (SLB).
34 *Br.* 43: 38.
35 *Br.* 31: 273–5.
36 *Br.* 7: 198.
37 *Br.* 31: 275.
38 Ibid. 279.
39 *SW* ii. 43–6 (trans. Leishman, adapted).
40 Quot. Storck Diss., App. 129.
41 To Eva Cassirer, 11 Jan. 1913 (SLB).
42 *SW* vi. 1038, 1040–1.
43 *SW* ii. 48 (trans. Leishman).
44 *SW* i. 706–7 (trans. Poulin).
45 *Br.* 7: 193–4.
46 16 Jan. 1913 (Mauser, 218).
47 Anton Kippenberg to Rilke, 16 Jan. 1913 (Weimar).
48 To Clara, 23 Feb. 1913 (quot. Sieber, RA).
49 *Br.* 40: 175–6.

VI
A World at War
1913–1919

1 Motto: *Br.* 4: 363.
1 *Br.* 30: 271, 275.
2 27 Feb. 1913 (quot. Sieber, RA).
3 *Br.* 7: 202; to Pia Valmarana, 22 Mar. 1913 (SLB).
4 *Br.* 30: 277, 278.
5 Ibid. 279, 280.
6 *Br.* 40: 177.
7 *Br.* 7: 202.
8 To Stefan Zweig, 15 Mar. 1913 (JNUL).
9 *Br.* 7: 204.
10 20 Mar. 1913 (Houghton; Mises 554).
11 *Br.* 16: 177.

12 15 Mar. 1913 (JNUL).
13 *Br.* 30: 281; to Ellen Key, 5 Apr. 1913 (KB).
14 Stefan Zweig's diary, 17 Mar. 1913 (ZE; Frankfurt a.M. 1984, 51–2).
15 *Br.* 30: 281, 290, 285.
16 Stefan Zweig's diary, 5 Apr. 1913 (ZE; op. cit. 63).
17 *Br.* 40: 181–2.
18 *Br.* 16: 178.
19 Quot. LAL, 51–2.
20 To Pia Valmarana, 14 Apr. 1913 (SLB).
21 *Br.* 30: 294.
22 *Br.* 40: 192; to Pia Valmarana, 19 June 1913 (SLB).
23 Hedwig Bernhard's diary, 28 June 1913 (quot. *Kat.*, 180).
24 6 July 1913 (DLA).
25 21 July 1913 (DLA).
26 *Br.* 31: 288.
27 Quot. Pfeiffer, 281.
28 *SW* ii. 57 (trans. Leishman).
29 Quot. Pfeiffer, 281.
30 *Br.* 30: 303; to Ellen Key, 21 July 1913 (KB, quot. Schnack, 433).
31 *Br.* 34: 60.
32 *Br.* 31: 289, 290.
33 *Br.* 30: 303.
34 *Br.* 43: 43.
35 8 Aug. 1913 (DLA).
36 7 Aug. 1913 (SLB).
37 *SW* ii. 61–2 (trans. Leishman, adapted).
38 14 Aug. 1913 (quot. Schnack, 437).
39 *SW* vi. 1055.
40 *SW* ii. 396–7 (trans. Leishman).
41 *Br.* 30: 309.
42 14 Aug. 1913 (Weimar).
43 16 Aug. 1913 (quot. Schnack, 438).
44 1 and 2 Sept. 1913 (SLB).
45 To Pia Valmarana, 17 Sept. 1913 (SLB).
46 *Br.* 27: 127.
47 *Br.* 30: 322.
48 Ibid. 323.
49 *SW* vi. 1064.
50 *Br.* 30: 323, 324.
51 Werfel, 242.
52 *Br.* 31: 304, 305.
53 *Br.* 43: 50; to Leopold von Kalckreuth, 27 Oct. 1913 (Houghton; Mises 555).
54 *Br.* 31: 304.
55 24 and 29 Oct. 1913 (SLB).
56 *Br.* 40: 202.
57 *Br.* 30: 329.
58 To Pia Valmarana, 16 Nov. 1913 (SLB).

59 Letter (possibly to May Knoop), 29 Dec. 1913 (Houghton; Mises 514); to Eva Cassirer, 29 Oct. 1913 (SLB).
60 *SW* i. 693–6 (trans. Poulin).
61 *SW* i. 708 (trans. Poulin, first two lines; trans. Leishman/Spender, third line).
62 *Br.* 40: 205–7.
63 *Br.* 30: 341.
64 *SW* ii. 79 (trans. Mitchell, adapted). It seems likely that this poem was written *before* the encounter with Benvenuta.
65 *Br.* 30: 345.
66 *Br.* 43: 63; Rilke's notebook, Jan. 1914 (quot. Storck Diss., 133).
67 *Br.* 27: 16.
68 Ibid. 17–19.
69 25 Jan. 1914 (Mauser, 220–1).
70 *Br.* 27: 22, 27, 28.
71 Ibid. 30, 31, 32.
72 *Br.* 31: 322.
73 Ibid. 323; *Br.* 27: 39–44.
74 Ibid. 47, 48.
75 15 Feb. 1914 (unpublished portion, DLA).
76 *Br.* 27: 90–1.
77 *Br.* 31: 323, 313.
78 *Br.* 27: 118.
79 13 Feb. 1914 (SLB).
80 *Br.* 27: 133, 140, 147.
81 *Br.* 31: 321.
82 *SW* vi. 1235–6.
83 *Br.* 31: 310.
84 *Br.* 30: 369; to Anton Kippenberg, 18 Mar. 1914 (DLA).
85 Benvenuta, 77.
86 Ibid. 144–5.
87 Benvenuta, 154. The poems did not survive (cf. *SW* vi. 1538).
88 Kassner to Rilke, 25 Aug. 1919 (*Modern Austrian Literature*, vol. 15, nos. 3/4 (1982), 228).
89 Benvenuta, 238.
90 27 Apr. 1914 (DLA).
91 To Pia Valmarana, 8 May 1914 (SLB).
92 *Br.* 40: 215–16.
93 *Br.* 7: 277; *Br.* 30: 382.
94 7 June 1914 (DLA).
95 *Br.* 31: 321–8.
96 *SW* ii. 80–1 (trans. Leishman, adapted).
97 *SW* ii. 417.
98 *Br.* 31: 329; *SW* ii. 82–4 (trans. Mitchell).
99 *Br.* 31: 336, 340, 347.

2 Motto: *Br.* 5: 25.

1 *Br.* 7: 279.

2 Ibid. 270.
3 Quot. Storck³, 28.
4 *Br.* 5: 10.
5 *Br.* 4: 372.
6 *SW* ii. 86–92 (last six lines trans. Leishman).
7 *Br.* 5: 9–10.
8 *Br.* 31: 353.
9 *SW* ii. 92–4 (trans. Leishman, adapted).
10 LAL 14.
11 *SW* ii. 219 (trans. Leishman).
12 *SW* ii. 94–5 (trans. Mitchell).
13 LAL 27.
14 Ibid. 52–3.
15 Ibid. 45.
16 *SW* ii. 224 (trans. Leishman).
17 Ficker, 239.
18 *Br.* 30: 391.
19 LAL 42.
20 Harry Graf Kessler, 25 Nov. 1914 (quot. Schnack, 487).
21 *Br.* 43: 83; to Pia Valmarana, 21 Oct. 1914 (SLB); *Br.* 5: 25.
22 DLA (extr. quot. Storck², 51).
23 Marianne Friedländer-Fuld was thus, for a short time, aunt by marriage to the six Mitford sisters, daughters of the second Lord Redesdale—a connection which would doubtless have interested Nancy but have been of less appeal to Unity or Diana.
24 *Br.* 30: 397.
25 *SW* ii. 95 (trans. Leishman).
26 *Br.* 30: 397.
27 28 Dec. 1914 (DLA, quot. Storck³, 30).
28 4 Jan. 1915 (ibid. 31).
29 To Hertha Koenig, 4 Jan. 1915 (*Blätter* 5 (1978), 11).
30 18 Jan. 1915 (DLA, quot. Storck², 63).
31 4 Nov. 1914 (DLA).
32 Hertha Koenig (*Blätter* (1978), 11).
33 15 Jan. 1915 (DLA, quot. Storck², 62).
34 *Br.* 40: 231.
35 *Br.* 30: 400.
36 Ibid. 408, 404, 409.
37 *Br.* 31: 369, 371.
38 Burte, Autobiographisches Fragment (copy SLB).
39 *Br.* 5: 33.
40 To Pia Valmarana, 19 Feb. 1915 (SLB).
41 *Br.* 30: 425.
42 LAL 55–6.
43 *Br.* 30: 418; to Alexander Taxis, 30 Apr. 1915 (Houghton; Mises 511).
44 *Br.* 31: 366.
45 Sieber, RA.

46 *Br.* 31: 374–5.
47 *SW* ii. 99–100 (trans. Leishman).
48 *Br.* 5: 47.
49 26 June 1915 (*Blätter* 5 (1978), 13).
50 To Ellen Delp, 6 Sept. 1915 (MStB).
51 Burte, Autobiographisches Fragment (copy SLB).
52 Sieber, RA.
53 To Marianne Mitford, 28 May 1915 (quot. Storck², 72).
54 To Lizzie Gibson, 28 Oct. 1915 (LAG).
55 To Ilse Erdmann, 11 Sept. 1915 (quot. Schnack, 511).
56 To Erica Hauptmann, 18 Aug. 1915 (DLA, quot. *Kat.*, 205–6).
57 Quot. Schnack, 504 (wrongly dated 'early June').
58 To Erica Hauptmann, 10 Aug. 1915 (DLA, quot. *Kat.*, 201).
59 To Ellen Delp, 6 Sept. 1915 (MStB).
60 To Marianne Mitford, 6 Sept. 1915 (DLA, quot. Storck², 80); *Br.* 30: 438.
61 5 Oct. 1915 (DLA, quot. Storck², 33–6).
62 HK 7.
63 *SW* ii. 101–2 (trans. Leishman).
64 To Marianne Mitford, 15 Oct. 1915 (quot. Schnack, 514).
65 *Br.* 5: 78.
66 To Marianne Mitford, 15 Oct. 1915 (*Br.* 38: 50).
67 *c.* 20 Oct. 1915 (BStB).
68 To Ellen Delp, 3 Nov. 1915 (MStB) and Jomar Förste, 1 Nov. 1915 (Unseld, Plate viii).
69 *Br.* 5: 90–1, 93.
70 *SW* ii. 103–4 (trans. Mitchell). Unseld, Plate iv, shows a facsimile of part of the Taschenbuch original, with the reading 'an ihrer *Rundung* in *vergangner* Schrift' for line 7.
71 To Else Jaffé, 14 Nov. 1915 (DLA).
72 *Br.* 15, ii: 47.
73 *SW* ii. 435–8 (trans. Leishman).
74 Quot. Pfeiffer, 285.
75 Jacob Steiner, *Rilkes Duineser Elegien* (Berne/Munich, 2nd edn., 1969), 54; *SW* i, 693 (trans. Poulin).
76 *SW* ii. 438 (trans. Leishman, adapted).
77 Unseld, 159–60; to Else Jaffé, 14 Nov. 1915 (DLA, quot. Schnack, 517).
78 *SW* i. 697–700 (trans. Mitchell).
79 To Philipp Schey-Rothschild, 25 Nov. 1915 (quot. Schnack, 518).

3 Motto: *Br.* 31: 376.
1 Quot. Sieber, R.A.
2 Stefan Zweig's diary, 16 Jan. 1916 (ZE; op. cit., 245–6).
3 Ginzkey, 'Rainer Maria Rilke der Infanterist', *Zeit und Menschen meiner Jugend*, 1943.
4 *Br.* 32 (German edn.), 97.
5 *Br.* 7: 298.
6 26 Feb. 1916 (DLA, quot. *Kat.*, 211–12).

7 *Br.* 7: 301.
8 *Br.* 40: 257.
9 *Br.* 30: 472.
10 To Loulou Albert-Lazard, 4 Mar. 1916 (quot. Schnack, 530).
11 To Richard Weininger, 28 Mar. 1916 (WNB).
12 *Br.* 43: 96.
13 *Br.* 31: 379; *Br.* 44: 166.
14 LAL 148.
15 *Br.* 40: 261.
16 Ibid. 262.
17 *Br.* 34: 170.
18 To Prince Wilhelm von Stolberg-Wernigerode, 9 Aug. 1916 (quot. Sieber, RA).
19 To Magda von Hattingberg, 2 Oct. 1914 (DLA).
20 *Br.* 34: 162, 177.
21 18 Sept. 1916 (DLA).
22 27 Sept. 1916 (quot. Schnack, 541).
23 To Philipp Schey-Rothschild, 25 Dec. 1916 (copy DLA); to Mieze Weininger, 31 Dec. 1916 (WNB); *Br.* 40: 268–9.
24 *Br.* 40: 266.
25 28 Sept. 1916 (copy Pittsburgh; quot. Schnack, 541).
26 LAL 123.
27 *Br.* 40: 267–8.
28 To Adrienne Sachs, 1 Dec. 1916 (quot. Storck Diss., App. 100).
29 To Mieze Weininger, 31 Dec. 1916 (WNB) and Marianne Mitford, 24 Jan. 1917 (copy Pittsburgh; quot. Schnack, 552).
30 *Br.* 31: 376; to Mieze Weininger, 9 Dec. 1916 (WNB); *Br.* 30: 501.
31 Quot. Sieber, RA.
32 *Br.* 7: 311–12; *Br.* 34: 229.
33 To Kurt Wolff, 28 Mar. 1917 (Wolff, *Briefwechsel eines Verlegers 1911–1936*, Frankfurt a.M., 1966, 145–6).
34 *Br.* 5: 137; *Br.* 37. 31.
35 Hausenstein, *StdFr.*, 89.
36 To Sophie Liebknecht, 22 June 1917 (RA) and from her, 18 Aug. 1917 (DLA, quot. *Kat.*, 231).
37 *Br.* 7. 313.
38 2 July 1917 (DLA).
39 To Anton Kippenberg, 5 July 1917 (DLA).

4 Motto: 'Requiem für die Gefallenen Europas—Rezitativ I'

1 To Mieze Weininger, 24 July 1917 (WNB, quot. Schnack, 564).
2 To Hedwig Jaenichen-Woermann, 18 Aug. 1917 (DLA).
3 To Sophie Liebknecht, 3 and 23 Aug. 1917 (RA).
4 *Br.* 34: 244.
5 To Mieze Weininger, 5 Oct. 1917 (WNB, quot. Schnack, 572).
6 *Br.* 34: 250.
7 To Dorothea von Ledebur, 5 Oct. 1917 (Clary).
8 To Dorothea von Ledebur, 29 Oct. 1917 (Clary).

9 To Clara, 15 Nov. 1917 (quot. Sieber, RA).
10 To Dorothea von Ledebur, 29 Oct. 1917 (Clary).
11 *Br.* 5: 165.
12 Ibid. 166.
13 To Dorothea von Ledebur, 14 Nov. 1917 (Clary).
14 Kessler's diary (Bernhard Zeller, *Jahrbuch der dt. Schiller-Gesellschaft*, xii (1968), 82–4).
15 To Dorothea von Ledebur, 14 Nov. 1917 (Clary).
16 Mehring, 'Einige Erinnerungen an Rilke' (*Literarische Welt* (1927), no. 2), 2.
17 Quot. Bassermann, *Der späte Rilke* (Munich, 1947), 263. Cf. William L. Moran, 'Rilke and the Gilgamesh Epic', *Journal of Cuneiform Studies*, vol. 32, no. 4 (Oct. 1980), 208–10.
18 *Br.* 5: 192, 191.
19 *Br.* 40: 277; *Br.* 34: 268.
20 *Br.* 5: 169–70.
21 *Br.* 40: 278–9.
22 To Stefan Zweig, 20 Sept. 1917 (JNUL).
23 To Elisabeth von Schmidt-Pauli, 3 Dec. 1917 (*Neue Rundschau*, vol. 38, no. 9, Sept. 1927).
24 27 Dec. 1917 (DLA).
25 To Dorothea von Ledebur, 24 Jan. 1918 (Clary).
26 To Clara, 8 Dec. 1917 (quot. Sieber, RA).
27 *Br.* 34: 257.
28 To Dorothea von Ledebur, 24 Jan. 1918 (Clary).
29 To Marianne Mitford, 12 Mar. 1918 (Copy Pittsburgh; quot. Schnack, 593).
30 To Walther Rathenau, 10 and 18 Mar. 1918 (RA).
31 *Br.* 31: 388.
32 *Br.* 7: 323; *Br.* 34: 291–2.
33 To Adrienne Sachs, 29 May 1918 (DLA); to Gräfin von Courten, 11 Oct. 1918 (quot. Sieber, RA).
34 10 May 1918 (quot. Sieber, RA).
35 Hertha Koenig, *Blätter* 5 (1978), 27–8.
36 2 July 1918 (quot. Sieber, RA).
37 *Br.* 5: 212–13.
38 10 Aug. 1918 (copy Pittsburgh; quot. Schnack, 601).
39 *Br.* 30: 557.
40 *Br.* 23: 21, 27.
41 To Hertha Koenig, 16 Sept. 1918 (DLA).
42 *Br.* 7: 328.
43 *Br.* 48: 201.
44 To Anni Mewes, 6 Nov. 1918 (BStB, quot. Schnack, 608–9).
45 *Br.* 5: 207–8.
46 Ibid. 206.
47 Ibid. 209; to Anni Mewes, 6 Nov. 1918 (BStB; quot. Storck Diss., App. 131).
48 *Br.* 5: 214.
49 *Br.* 23: 40.
50 To Dr Erich Katzenstein-Erler, 15 Nov. 1918 (quot. Schnack, 612).

51 Alfred Wolfenstein, 'Erinnerungen an Rilke', *Basler National-Zeitung*, 15 Feb. 1942 (quot. *Kat.*, 235).
52 Goll, 88.
53 Goll², 22–3.
54 *Br.* 20: 6.
55 *SW.* ii. 69.
56 *Br.* 20: 8–9.
57 To Phia Rilke, 8 Dec. 1918 (quot. Sieber, RA).
58 To Clara, 15 Dec. 1918 (quot. ibid.).
59 *Br.* 5: 215.
60 *Br.* 34: 322, 323; *Br.* 31: 383.
61 *Br.* 31: 381.
62 *Br.* 30: 570, 572.
63 From Anton Kippenberg, 20 Jan. 1919 (DLA, quot. Schnack, 622); to Kippenberg, 9 Feb. 1919 (DLA).
64 *Br.* 34: 328.
65 To Ludwig Landshoff, 5 Mar. 1919 (MStB).
66 *Br.* 40: 285.
67 *Br.* 5: 226, 227.
68 Undated letter to an unknown woman (Houghton; Mises 523). In view of that of 5 Feb. 1919 to Gräfin Stauffenberg (*Br.* 5: 228), the date here is probably January 1919, rather than June as given in Mises 523.
69 *Br.* 15, ii: 118.
70 *SW.* vi. 1041–2.
71 *Br.* 31: 382–3, 394.
72 *Br.* 34: 332–3.
73 Pfeiffer, 301.
74 Thomas Mann, *Tagebücher 1918–1921* (Frankfurt a.M., 1979), 668.
75 *Br.* 7: 338.
76 To Annette Kolb, 21 Mar. 1919 (MStB; quot. Schnack, 634).

VII
Prelude in Switzerland
1919–1921

 1 Motto: *Br.* 21: 13.
 1 To Clara, 20 June 1919 (quot. Sieber, RA).
 2 *Br.* 5: 270; *Br.* 7: 344, 345; to Phia Rilke, 6 July 1919 (quot. Sieber, RA).
 3 Inga Junghanns, *StdFr.*, 105–9.
 4 *Br.* 34: 357.
 5 *Br.* 5: 284, 259.
 6 To Elisabeth von Schmidt-Pauli, 14 Aug. 1919 (*Neue Rundschau*, vol. 38, no. 9, Sept. 1927). Not included in *Br.* 5: 261 ff.
 7 *Br.* 5: 261, 255.
 8 *SW.* vi. 1085 ff.; *Br.* 44: 143.
 9 9 Sept. 1919 (Rilke Collection, Sierre).
 10 To Yvonne von Wattenwyl, 26 Sept. 1919 (quot. Schnack, 660).

11 *Br.* 30: 587.
12 *Br.* 7: 347.
13 *Br.* 33: 15–16.

2 Motto: *Br.* 30: 588.

  1 *Br.* 26: 103.
  2 *SW.* vi. 1096–8.
  3 Salis, 49.
  4 To Anton Kippenberg, 31 Oct. 1919 (DLA).
  5 *Br.* 44: 20.
  6 *Br.* 5: 278.
  7 Mühll.
  8 *Br.* 33: 22.
  9 *Br.* 44: 1203.
10 Ibid. 59.
11 To Fritz Huf, 12 Nov. 1919 (Jonas, 'Huf'; quot. Schnack, 665).
12 16 Dec. 1919 (SLB).
13 *Br.* 44: 44, 46.
14 *Br.* 15, ii: 167.
15 30 Dec. 1919 (Rilke Collection, Sierre; quot. Schnack, 674).
16 *Br.* 14: 16.
17 To Eva Cassirer, 20 Aug. 1908 (SLB).
18 *Br.* 44: 81.
19 Ibid. 105–6.
20 Ibid. 139, 1176–8.
21 31 Oct. 1919 (DLA).
22 *Br.* 44: 71.

3 Motto: *Br.* 28: 41.

  1 *Br.* 33: 44.
  2 4 Mar. 1920 (SLB).
  3 *Br.* 44: 218.
  4 Letters to Hans Buchli, 23 Mar.–13 May 1920 (SLB); *Br.* 44: 223.
  5 22 Feb. 1920 (SLB).
  6 *Br.* 20: 19.
  7 *Br.* 30: 597.
  8 To Resi Hardy, 24 June 1920 (DLA).
  9 *Br.* 30: 611.
10 *Br.* 31: 421–2.
11 1 Aug. 1920 (SLB).
12 To Pia Valmarana, 28 July 1920, and Mary Dobržensky, 16 Aug. 1920 (SLB).
13 *Br.* 44: 296.
14 *Br.* 30: 620.
15 *Br.* 44: 306.
16 *SW.* ii. 637.
17 *Br.* 28: 18, 30; *SW.* ii. 243 (trans. Leishman).
18 *Br.* 28: 35, 32.
19 *Br.* 44: 320, 321–2.

20 Ibid. 311.
21 *Br.* 28: 41, 42, 45, 59.
22 Ibid. 53, 54.
23 Ibid. 69–70.
24 *Br.* 44: 330.
25 *Br.* 28: 77, 80.
26 *Br.* 5: 323; *Br.* 44, 332–3; to Mieze Weininger, 21 Nov. 1920 (WNB).
27 *Br.* 28: 85–6.
28 8 Nov. 1920 (SLB).
29 *Br.* 7: 364–5.

4
 1 *Br.* 44: 338.
 2 To Lily Ziegler, 2 Dec. 1920, and Mary Dobržensky, 19 Nov. 1920 (SLB).
 3 To Fanette Clavel, 1 Dec. 1920 (SLB).
 4 To Hans Reinhart, 29 Nov. 1920 (SLB).
 5 25 Nov. 1920 (SLB).
 6 *Br.* 28: 91, 124.
 7 *Br.* 44: 347.
 8 *SW.* vi. 1099–1103.
 9 *SW.* ii. 123 (trans. Hamburger).
10 *Br.* 44: 349.
11 *SW.* ii. 119 (trans. Leishman).
12 Sieber, 160.
13 *SW.* ii. 130 (trans. Leishman, adapted).
14 WNB.
15 *SW.* ii. 130–2 (trans. Leishman, adapted).
16 *Br.* 44: 353.
17 *Br.* 5: 351–5.
18 To Paul Adler, 3 June 1921 (Stargardt 630, 107).
19 *Br.* 44: 370.
20 *Br.* 28: 125–6.
21 Ibid. 136.
22 Ibid. 213–19.
23 *Br.* 30: 639.
24 44: 406.
25 *Testament*, 27.
26 Valéry, 'Préface à l'essai d'explication du Cimetière marin par G. Cohen' (*Variété III*, Paris, 1946), 56.
27 *Br.* 30: 639.
28 Quot. Bassermann, *Der späte Rilke*, 360.
29 *Testament*, 7–12.
30 Ibid. 18, 22, 35.
31 Ibid. 51, 52.
32 *Br.* 28: 343.
33 *Testament*, 39.
34 *Testament*, 31.

35 *Br.* 28: 335.
36 The Prieuré at Etoy, now in private hands, has a plaque in the porch recording Rilke's stay there.
37 31 May 1921 (DLA, part only in *Br.* 7: 387).
38 Taxis, 106–7.
39 *Br.* 44: 493.
40 Ibid. 496.

VIII
Muzot and Valmont
1921–1926

1 Motto: *SW.* i. 718 (trans. Poulin).

1 *Br.* 44: 499, 500.
2 Ibid. 509.
3 20 July 1921 (SLB).
4 From Werner Reinhart, 29 July 1921 (SLB).
5 *Br.* 44: 513.
6 Ibid. 522, 521.
7 To Werner Reinhart, 7 Oct. 1921 (SLB).
8 *Br.* 44: 516.
9 To Frida Strohl, 13 Sept. 1921 (Pittsburgh).
10 7 Oct. 1921 (SLB).
11 *SW.* ii. 247 (trans. Leishman).
12 *Br.* 44: 567.
13 19 Oct. 1921 (SLB).
14 *Br.* 28: 368.
15 28 Nov. 1921 (SLB).
16 To Werner Reinhart, 11 Dec. 1921 (SLB).
17 Quot. Salis, 123.
18 To Anton Kippenberg, 25 Nov. 1921 (DLA, unpublished portion).
19 *Br.* 15, ii: 256.
20 *Br.* 44: 596.
21 Ibid. 585.
22 26 Nov. 1921 (Houghton; Mises 511).
23 To Louis Gauchat, 1 Dec. 1921 (SLB).
24 *Br.* 31: 438–9.
25 *Br.* 30: 686.
26 *Br.* 7: 404, 407.
27 *Br.* 44: 594–5.
28 To Souvairan, 1 Jan. 1922 (SLB).
29 *Br.* 44: 1265–6.
30 *Br.* 31: 438.
31 *Br.* 6: 41 ff.
32 *Br.* 18: 60–1.
33 *Br.* 6: 84.
34 To Jean Strohl, 6 Jan. 1922 (Pittsburgh).

35 *Br.* 37: 202; *Br.* 6: 93.
36 *Br.* 44: 658–9.
37 *Br.* 6: 98.
38 7 Feb. 1922 (Pittsburgh).
39 *Br.* 44: 667.
40 *Br.* 6: 333.
41 *Br.* 44: 668.
42 *Br.* 7: 409–10.
43 *Br.* 28: 393.
44 *Br.* 44: 668, 669.
45 *Br.* 30: 697–9.
46 *Br.* 31: 444–5.
47 *SW.* i. 743–4 (trans. Leishman).
48 *Br.* 44: 673, 672, 675.
49 To Werner Reinhart, 14 Feb. 1922 (SLB).
50 *SW.* v. 215.
51 *SW.* i. 733, 735 (trans. Poulin).
52 *SW.* i. 747 (trans. Poulin).
53 *SW.* ii. 249 (trans. Leishman, adapted).
54 *SW.* i. 743 (trans. Poulin).
55 Quot. Storck Diss., App. 129.
56 *Br.* 4: 275.
57 *SW.* i. 744 (trans. Poulin).
58 *SW.* i. 710, 712 (trans. Poulin).
59 *SW.* i. 714, 716 (trans. Poulin).
60 *SW.* i. 701.
61 *SW.* i. 717–20 (trans. Poulin; third quotation trans. Leishman/Spender).
62 Lama Govinda, quot. Capra, 147.
63 *SW.* i. 721 (trans. Poulin), 726 (trans. Mitchell).
64 *Br.* 6: 334, 337.
65 *Br.* 21: 60.
66 *SW.* vi 1111–27.
67 *Br.* 18: 53, 55.
68 *SW.* i. 759 (trans. Poulin).
69 *SW.* i. 751 (trans. Poulin).
70 *Br.* 6: 333, 334, 335.
71 Capra, 85.
72 To Jean Strohl, 13 Apr. 1922 (Pittsburgh).
73 *SW.* i. 732, 718.
74 *SW.* i. 768 (trans. Poulin).

2   Motto: *Br.* 7: 444.

 1 *Br.* 31: 446–8.
 2 *Br.* 44: 755, 756.
 3 Taxis, 112.
 4 *Br.* 44: 697, 739, 733.
 5 Ibid. 715.

6 *Br.* 3: 293.

7 19 Apr. 1922 (SLB).

8 *SW.* ii. 251.

9 12 May 1922 (SLB).

10 *Br.* 18: 47–8.

11 *Br.* 44: 770.

12 *Br.* 28: 407.

13 Frieda Baumgartner to the author, Mar. 1979.

14 *Br.* 44: 798–9.

15 To Antoine Contat, 8 Nov. 1922 (quot. Schnack, 819).

16 To Jean Strohl, 10 Jan. 1923 (Pittsburgh).

17 *Br.* 44: 822; to Paul Morisse, 10 Feb. 1923 (SLB).

18 *Br.* 6: 178; Salis, 183.

19 *Br.* 33: 111.

20 *Br.* 30: 740; *Br.* 34: 484.

21 *Br.* 44: 851, 855, 850.

22 Ibid. 849.

23 *SW.* vi. 863.

24 Quot. Salis, 177.

25 *Br.* 44: 448.

26 *Br.* 31: 455.

27 *Br.* 19: 3.

28 *Br.* 44: 886.

29 Studer-Kiefer, iii (SLB).

30 Frieda Baumgartner to the author, Apr. 1979.

31 Jeanne de Sépibus to the author, 23 Apr. 1977; Studer-Kiefer, iv. 266–72 (SLB); *SW.* ii. 658–9.

32 *Br.* 44: 905.

33 Ibid. 907.

34 Frieda Baumgartner to the author, Mar. 1979.

35 *Br.* 44: 932; Salis, 187.

36 To Renée Alberti, 4 Sept. 1923 (quot. Sieber, RA).

37 *Br.* 44: 962.

38 Quot. Salis, 188.

39 To Alma Moodie, 31 Mar. 1924 (letter auctioned Berlin, Nov. 1980).

40 *Br.* 44: 963.

41 *SW.* ii. 158 (trans. Leishman).

42 *SW.* ii. 526, 527.

43 11 Mar. 1924 (SLB).

44 22 Feb. 1924 (*Mesa*, No. 4, Spring 1952, 34).

45 *SW.* ii. 531, 532.

46 20 Mar. 1924 (quot. Schnack, 908).

47 To Marie von Mutius, 15 Jan. 1918 (quot. Betz, 53–4).

48 *Br.* 32 (German edn.): 182.

49 *Br.* 50: 209.

50 *Reconnaissance*, 9–10.

51 Quot. Schnack, 913.

52 *Br.* 30: 806; to Werner Reinhart, 22 May 1924 (SLB).

53 *Br.* 44: 977, 980.

54 From Werner Reinhart, 17 June 1924 and Rilke's reply, 18 June 1924 (SLB),

55 *Br.* 18: 95.

56 To Dorothea von Ledebur, 9 Aug. 1924 (Clary).

57 Taxis, 115.

58 *SW.* ii. 168–74; 279 ff.

59 Schnack[2], 85–7.

60 *SW.* ii. 274 (trans. Leishman).

61 Schnack, 1003.

62 *Br.* 44, 1011; *SW.* ii. 557, 569.

63 4 Sept. 1924 (Pittsburgh).

64 *Br.* 44: 874.

65 *Br.* 6: 346.

66 *Br.* 44: 1021.

67 15 Feb. 1924 (DLA).

68 *Br.* 20: 28.

69 15 June 1924 (DLA).

70 *SW.* ii. 577.

71 To Edmond Jaloux, 12 Sept. 1924 (SLB).

72 To Dora Herxheimer, 14 July 1907 (Houghton; Mises 554).

73 27 Sept. 1924 (quot. Schnack, 944).

74 *Br.* 44: 1025.

75 *Br.* 34: 545; *Br.* 44: 1022–3.

76 *SW.* ii. 146–7.

77 *Br.* 44: 1023.

78 *SW.* ii. 502 (trans. Leishman).

79 *Br.* 44: 1022, 1032.

80 The psychiatrist in question was Dr Arthur Muthmann (1875–1957), a follower of
    Freud's method, with a practice at the time in Freiburg i. Br. According to a
    statement by Dr Heinrich Meng (1887–1972) in March 1952 (Simenauer, 688),
    Rilke did in fact undergo analysis with Muthmann 'during his last years'. In a later
    communication on 3 March 1970 (Pfeiffer, 311), Meng said that the treatment
    lasted a week, but was broken off, Rilke's excuse for this being that Lou considered
    it too dangerous for him as a poet, even though he had at first claimed it was
    undertaken on her advice. Pfeiffer considers that Meng's visit to Lou on 2–3
    January 1933, noted without comment in her diary, was to inform her of this late
    attempt with analysis, which Rilke had concealed from her, and which she would
    have found quite contrary to his earlier attitude (Pfeiffer[2], 300–1). If this were so, it
    would certainly put Rilke's letter to her of 31 Oct.–8 Dec. 1925, and her reply of 12
    Dec. 1925 (cf. pp. 384 and 387 above) in a different light. However, according to
    Rilke's correspondence with Dory von der Mühll (SLB) between 14 Apr. 1924,
    when he first mentioned her suggestion of consulting Muthmann, and 17 Jan.
    1925, he had not followed it up by then. After his return from Paris, in August 1925
    and up to his readmission to Valmont on 20 December that year, the only possible
    times not strictly accounted for in which he might have gone to see Muthmann
    were: 9–13 Oct. (from Zurich), 15–18 Oct. and 21–23 Oct. (from Muzot). Taking

account of the travelling time, these would each give at most two or three sessions, and Rilke would hardly have allowed so short a time for an undertaking of such importance. It seems inconceivable, in any case, that from Nanny Wunderly—his close confidante at this time, though not of course in the same sense as Lou—he would have concealed a *journey* to Freiburg i.Br., or to Basle, from where Dory had earlier offered to drive him to Muthmann, even if he did not wish to reveal that his object was an attempt with analysis. The categorical statements by Meng seem, admittedly, to leave no room for doubt. However, in view of the above considerations, I remain of the opinion that this 'secret analysis' remains unproven until and unless further evidence is forthcoming.

81 *Br.* 44: 1031, 1036.
82 Quot. Salis, 199–200.
83 *Br.* 36: 66–7.

3 Motto: *SW.* ii. 314.

1 To Yvonne von Wattenwyl, 16 Jan. 1925 (Rilke Collection, Sierre).
2 *Br.* 30: 819.
3 20 Feb. 1925, to Mieze Weininger (WNB, quot. Schnack, 971) and Ellen Delp (MStB).
4 *SW.* ii. 178 (trans. Hamburger).
5 *SW.* ii. 519–20.
6 Betz², 95–6.
7 *Br.* 44: 1058–9.
8 2 Sept. 1925 (DLA).
9 *Br.* 7: 495.
10 *Br.* 15, ii: 473.
11 Cf. Note 80 above.
12 *Br.* 31: 476; *SW.* ii. 314.
13 To Mary Dobržensky, 17 Jan. 1924 (SLB).
14 *Br.* 44: 1062.
15 *SW.* i. 347 (trans. Leishman, adapted).
16 *Br.* 44: 1192; *SW.* ii. 185 (trans. Hamburger).
17 *Br.* 44: 1193.
18 *SW.* i. 347 (trans. Leishman).
19 *Br.* 44: 1074.
20 *Br.* 31: 475–8.
21 Quot. Schnack², 86.
22 *SW.* ii. 186 (trans. Hamburger).
23 *SW.* ii. 185–6 (trans. Hamburger).
24 *Br.* 15, ii: 488–90.
25 *Br.* 44: 1073, 1074.
26 Ibid. 1080.
27 *SW.* ii. 317.
28 *Br.* 44: 1087.
29 *Br.* 30: 841.
30 17 Dec. 1925 (Pittsburgh).
31 Quot. Schnack, 1017.

32 *Br.* 44: 1089.
33 *Br.* 31: 478–82.

4

1 *Br.* 7: 509; to Dory von der Mühll, 7 Feb. 1926 (SLB).
2 To Werner Reinhart, 19 Feb. 1926 (SLB); *Br.* 28: 562.
3 19 Feb. 1926 (SLB).
4 *Br.* 6: 378.
5 *Br.* 36: 77, 82–98.
6 Ibid. 84, 108.
7 To Werner Reinhart, 24 Feb. 1926 (SLB); *Br.* 37: 244.
8 *Br.* 44: 1135.
9 *Les Lettres*, 205–6, 209.
10 *Br.* 44: 1120.
11 *Les Lettres*, 209–10; *SW.* ii. 676–7.
12 *Br.* 44: 1122, 1123.
13 With letter of 29 Feb. 1924 (courtesy Mme A. Vincens-de Bonstetten).
14 *Br.* 45: 29.
15 Ibid. 43.
16 *Br.* 44: 1130.
17 Ibid. 1122; to Edmond Jaloux, 5 May 1926 (SLB); *Br.* 44: 1130.
18 *Br.* 32 (German edn.): 181 (retranslated from French original).
19 3 June 1926 (SLB).
20 To Léonie Contat, 8 July 1926 (*Rilke en Valais*, 187); Studer-Kiefer, ii. 146 ff. (SLB).
21 *SW.* ii. 626.
22 *Br.* 50: 76–8.
23 Ibid. 128, 105.
24 Ibid. 105, 108.
25 Ibid. 112.
26 *SW.* ii. 271–3 (trans. Leishman).
27 Konstantin Asadovsky, *Br.* 50: 53.
28 *Br.* 50: 147.
29 Quot. Schnack, 1055, 1058, 1059.
30 Elisabeth Bergner to the author, 30 Sept. 1978.
31 Jenny de Margerie to the author, 15 Sept. 1983. When Valéry arrived in Berlin later in 1926, she organized a reading by Elisabeth Bergner of Rilke's translations; but her hope that Rilke might attend was disappointed.
32 *Br.* 44: 1150.
33 Ibid. 1151.
34 Schnack^2, 137, 124; *Br.* 44: 1155.
35 *Br.* 6: 393.
36 *SW.* ii. 509–10 (trans. Leishman).
37 *Br.* 44: 115; Schnack^2, 122–3; *SW.* i. 507 (trans. Leishman).
38 *SW.* ii. 276–7 (trans. Leishman).
39 *SW.* ii. 742, 684.
40 Quot. Schnack^2, 127.

41 *Br.* 28: 591.
42 To Valéry, 5 Sept. 1926 (quot. Schnack, 1072–3).
43 Quot. Schnack, 1060.
44 *Br.* 44: 1158–9.
45 *Dernière Amitié*, 197, 204.
46 To Jaloux, 20 Sept. 1926 (SLB; *Dernière Amitié*, 132–3).
47 *Br.* 33: 132.
48 Nanny Wunderly to Mieze Weininger, 16 Jan. 1927 (WNB).
49 *Br.* 44: 1167.
50 Ibid. 1166.
51 Ibid. 1170.
52 DLA.
53 Quot. Schnack, 1087.
54 Quot. ibid. 1088.
55 Ibid.
56 *Br.* 44: 1171–2.
57 Nanny Wunderly to Mieze Weininger, 16 Jan. 1927 (WNB).
58 *Br.* 30: 955.
59 *Br.* 31: 482–3.
60 Ibid. 618, 619.
61 *Br.* 30: 956.
62 Ibid. 884; to Richard Weininger, 19 Dec. 1926 (WNB).
63 *SW.* ii. 511 (trans. Hamburger).
64 Quot. Schnack, 1090.
65 Nanny Wunderly to Mieze Weininger, 16 Jan. 1927 (WNB).
66 Quot. Sieber, RA.
67 Quot. Schnack, 1091.
68 *Dernière Amitié*, 211–12.
69 *Br.* 28: 601–2.
70 *Br.* 33: 135; quot. Salis, 277.
71 *Br.* 30: 957.
72 Salis, 283.
73 *SW.* i. 688 (trans. Leishman/Spender).

Epilogue

Motto: *Br.* 4: 170.

1 Stefan Zweig to André Suarès, 4 Jan. 1927 (courtesy Mme Roland de Margerie).
2 *Philobiblon*, vol. viii, no. 10 (1935) (8).
3 *Inselschiff*, vol. viii, no. 2, 82.
4 Stefan Zweig, *Abschied von Rilke* (Tübingen, 1927), 25, 30.
5 Jaloux, 41–2, 58.
6 *Inselschiff*, vol. viii, no. 2, 125.
7 *SW.* ii. 277 (trans. Leishman).
8 Wilhelm Hausenstein, *StdFr.*, 90.
9 *Die Welt von gestern* (London and Stockholm, n.d.), 153.
10 To Manon zu Solms-Laubach, 12 Jan. 1912 (*Br.* 4: 166, 165).
11 *SW.* ii. 463.
12 *SW.* ii. 95, 137.
13 21 Oct. 1913 (*Br.* 31: 305).
14 Taxis, 107.
15 Hugo von Hofmannsthal to Dory von der Mühll, 1929 (*Neue Zürcher Zeitung*, 6 Oct. 1982).
16 To Nanny Wunderly, 26 Dec. 1919 (*Br.* 44: 63); to Sidie Nádherný, 30 Mar. 1913 (*Br.* 40: 181).
17 To Julie von Nordeck zu Rabenau, 2 Jan. 1912 (*Br.* 4: 154).
18 22 May 1926 (*Br.* 50: 238).
19 Benvenuta, 236.
20 Mason[2], 176.
21 To Elisabeth Schenk zu Schweinsberg, 4 Nov. 1909 (*Br.* 4: 80–1).
22 *SW.* ii 42.
23 *SW.* i. 759.
24 *Br.* 44: 1193.
25 Ibid. 105–6
26 *SW.* i. 759, 765.
27 To Ilse Jahr, 2 Dec. 1922 (*Br.* 6: 154).
28 *SW.* ii. 266.
29 *SW.* i. 759, 687 (trans. Poulin).

Bibliography

—◦❧❧◦—

I
Rilke's Works

Sämtliche Werke, vols i–vi, ed. Ernst Zinn, Frankfurt a.M., 1955–66.
Tagebücher aus der Frühzeit, ed. Ernst Zinn, Frankfurt a.M., 1973.
Übertragungen, ed. Ernst Zinn and Karin Wais, Frankfurt a.M., 1975.
Das Testament, ed. Ernst Zinn, Frankfurt a.M., 1975.

II
Rilke's Letters

The successive publications of the letters having followed a sometimes confusing course, it seems most practical to list the principal ones numerically, in the approximate order of their appearance. The references in the Notes are to these numbers (*Br.* 1, 2, etc.) Publisher, except where otherwise stated, is the Insel Verlag (Leipzig, Wiesbaden, or Frankfurt a.M.), and the date of the edition used is in brackets.

1 *Briefe und Tagebücher aus der Frühzeit 1899–1902* (1931).
2 *Briefe 1902–1906* (1929).
3 *Briefe 1906–1907* (1930).
4 *Briefe 1907–1914* (1933).
5 *Briefe 1914–1921* (1937).
6 *Briefe aus Muzot 1921–1926* (1935).
7 *Briefe an seinen Verleger* (enlarged 2 vol. ed. 1949).
8 *Briefe 1892–1904* (1939).
9 *Briefe 1904–1907* (1939).
10 *Briefe 1907–1914* (1939).
11 *Briefe 1914–1921* (1938—identical with 5 above).
12 *Briefe aus Muzot 1921–1926* (1937).
13 *Briefe an einen jungen Dichter* (Insel-Bücherei no. 406, n.d.).
14 *Briefe an eine junge Frau* (Insel-Bücherei no. 409, n.d.).
15 *Briefe*: vol. i 1897–1914, vol. ii 1914–1926 (1950).
16 *Lettres à Rodin* (Paris, 1931).
17 *Dreizehn Briefe an Oskar Zwintscher* (Gesellschaft der Bücherfreunde zu Chemnitz, 1931).
18 *Briefe an Gräfin Sizzo* (1977).
19 *Lettres à une amie vénitienne* (to Mimi Romanelli) (Milan, 1941).
20 *Briefe an eine Freundin* (to Claire Goll) (Aurora, NY, 1944).
21 *Briefe an R. R. Junghanns und Rudolf Zimmermann* (Olten, 1945).

22 *Briefe an Baronesse von Oe.* (New York, 1945).
23 *Freundschaft mit R. M. Rilke* (Briefe an Elya Nevar) (Berne-Bümpliz, 1946).
24 *Briefe, Verse und Prosa aus dem Jahre 1896* (New York, 1946).
25 *Briefe an das Ehepaar S. Fischer* (Zurich, 1952).
26 *Briefe an eine Reisegefährtin* (to Albertina Casani) (Vienna, 1947).
27 *Briefwechsel mit Benvenuta* (Esslingen, 1954).
28 *Rainer Maria Rilke et Merline: Correspondance* (Zurich, 1954).
29 *Briefwechsel in Gedichten mit Erika Mitterer 1924–1926* (Werkausgabe vol. 3, 1975).
30 *Briefwechsel Rainer Maria Rilke und Marie von Thurn und Taxis* (joint edition with Niehans & Rokitansky, Zurich, 1961).
31 *Briefwechsel Rainer Maria Rilke und Lou Andreas-Salomé* (1975).
32 *Rainer Maria Rilke/André Gide: Correspondance 1909–1926* (Paris, 1952; German edn. Stuttgart/Wiesbaden, 1957).
33 *Briefe an Gudi Nölke* (1953).
34 *Briefwechsel Rainer Maria Rilke und Katharina Kippenberg* (1954).
35 *Correspondance Rilke/André Gide/Emile Verhaeren* (Paris, 1955).
36 *Lettres milanaises 1921–1926* (to Duchesa Aurelia Gallarati-Scotti) (Paris, 1956).
37 *Briefwechsel Rainer Maria Rilke und Inga Junghanns* (1959).
38 *Marianne Gilbert: Le tiroir entr'ouvert* (including 31 lettres to Marianne Mitford, in often inaccurate French translation) (Paris, 1956).
39 'Briefwechsel Rilke/Arthur Schnitzler' (*Wort und Wahrheit*, vol. 13, no. 1 (1958), 232–98).
40 *Briefe an Sidonie Nádherný von Borutin* (1973).
41 Briefwechsel Rilke/Hofmannsthal 1899–1925 (1978).
42 *Briefe an Ernst Hardt* (Marbach a.N., 1975)
43 *Briefwechsel Rilke/Helene von Nostitz* (1976).
44 *Briefe an Nanny Wunderly-Volkart*, vols. i. and ii (1977).
45 *Lettres autour d'un jardin* (to Antoinette de Bonstetten) (Paris, 1977).
46 'Briefe an Rolf Ungern-Sternberg' (*Sinn und Form*, vol. 29, no. 2 (1977), 300–42).
47 'Lettres à Madonna' (Madeleine de Broglie) (*Journal de Genève*, 21–2 Jan. 1961).
48 *Briefe an Axel Juncker* (1979).
49 *Briefwechsel Rilke/Anita Forrer* (1982).
50 *Briefwechsel Rilke/Marina Zwetajewa/Boris Pasternak* (1983).

Note: works containing other letters of Rilke's are marked * in IV.

III
Translations into English

Hamburger, Michael, *An Unofficial Rilke*, London, 1981.

Hull, R. F. C., *Selected Letters 1902–1926*, London, 1946.

Leishman, J. B., *From the Remains of Count C. W.*, London, 1952.

—— *Selected Works*, vol. ii: *Poetry*, London, 1976.

—— *Poems 1906–1926*, London, 1976.

Leishman, J. B., and Spender, Stephen, *Duino Elegies*, London, 1975.

Linton, John, *The Notebooks of Malte Laurids Brigge*, London, 1972.

Mason, Eudo C., in *Rilke*, Edinburgh/London, 1963.

Mitchell, Stephen, *The Selected Poetry*, New York, 1982.

Morse, B. J., *Six Poems done into English*, Cardiff, 1945.

—— *Duino Elegies done into English*, South Wales, 1941.

Poulin, A., Jr., *Duino Elegies and the Sonnets to Orpheus*, Boston, 1977.

IV
Secondary Literature

*Albert-Lasard, Lou, *Wege mit Rilke*, Frankfurt a.M., 1952.

Andreas-Salomé, Lou, *Rainer Maria Rilke*, Leipzig, 1928.

—— *Lebensrückblick*, ed. Ernst Pfeiffer, Frankfurt a.M. 1974 (Insel-Taschenbuch 54).

Angelloz, J.-F., *Rilke*, Paris, 1952.

Bassermann, Dieter, *Der andere Rilke*, Bad Homburg, 1961.

—— *Der späte Rilke*, Munich, 1947.

Bauer, Marga, *Rainer Maria Rilke und Frankreich*, Berne, 1931.

*Baumgartner, Frieda, 'Wie ich den grossen Dichter Rainer Maria Rilke erleben durfte', offprint, 'Lueg nit verby', Derendingen, 1967.

Bergman, Marianne, *Rilkes kontakt med Ellen Key och hennes betydelse för honom och hans verk*, Stockholm, dissertation, n.d.

*Betz, Maurice, *Rilke in Frankreich*, Vienna, 1938.

*—— *Rilke in Paris*, Zurich, 1948.

*Blüher, Hans, *Werke und Tage*, Munich, 1953.

Braun, Felix, *Das Licht der Welt*, Vienna, 1949.

*—— *Zeitgefährten*, Munich, 1963.

*Brutzer, Sophie, *Rilkes russische Reisen*, Stallüpönen, 1934.

Buchheit, Gerd (ed.), *Rainer Maria Rilke: Stimmen der Freunde*, Freiburg i.Br., 1931.

Buddeberg, Else, *Rainer Maria Rilke: eine innere Biographie*, Stuttgart, 1955.

Busch, Günter, and Von Reinken, Liselotte (eds.), *Paula Modersohn-Becker in Briefen und Tagebüchern*, Frankfurt a.M., 1979.

Butler, E. M., *Rainer Maria Rilke*, Cambridge, 1941; reprint New York, 1973.

Byong-Ock Kim, *Rilkes Militärschulerlebnis und das Problem des verlorenen Sohnes*, Bonn, 1973.

Capra, Fritjof, *The Tao of Physics*, London, 1978.

Carossa, Hans, *Führung und Geleit*, Leipzig, 1933.

Casellato, Pietro, *La veneziana 'misteriosa' di Rainer Maria Rilke*, Venice, 1977.

Casey, Timothy J., *Rainer Maria Rilke: A Centenary Essay*, London, 1976.

Centro Studi 'Rainer Maria Rilke e il suo tempo', Duino/Trieste, *Atti degli Convegni* 1–9 (1972–80).

Černý, Václav, *Rilke, Prag, Böhmen und die Tschechen*, Prague, 1966.

*Delp, Ellen, *Regina Ullmann: eine Biographie der Dichterin*, Einsiedeln/Zurich, 1960.

—— 'Erinnerung', *Philobiblon*, vol. 8, no. 10 (1935), 483–7.

Demetz, Peter, *René Rilkes Prager Jahre*, Düsseldorf, 1953.

Die Insel, Eine Ausstellung zur Geschichte des Verlags unter Anton und Katharina Kippenberg, Marbach a.N., Deutsches Literaturarchiv, 1965.

Drozhzhin, S. D., 'Der deutsche Dichter Rainer Maria Rilke—Erinnerungen'. *Inselschiff* vol. x, no. 3 (1929), 225–33.

Ekner, Reidar, 'Rilke, Ellen Key och Sverige', *Samlaren*, Tidskrift för svensk literaturhistorisk forskning (1965), 5–43.

—— 'Rainer Maria Rilke, Ernst Norlind och Hans Larsson', *Nordisk tidskrift för vetenskap, konst och industri* 3 (1965), 127–41.

—— 'Rilke och Gustaf af Geijerstam: en vänskap', *Svensk Litteraturtidskrift* 2 (1965) 76–85.

Faesi, Robert, *Rainer Maria Rilke*, Zurich/Leipzig/Vienna, 2nd edn., 1921.

*Ficker, Ludwig von, 'Rilke und der unbekannte Freund', *Der Brenner*, no. 18 (1954), 234–48.

Fischer, Brigitte B., *Sie schrieben mir*, Zurich, 1978.

Fleischmann, Joseph, 'Zur Geschichte der Familie Rilke in Türmitz'. *Inselschiff*, vol. xvii, no. 1 (1935), 8–14.

*Gebser, J., *Rilke und Spanien*, Zurich, 1945.

*Glauert, Barbara, 'Wie auf eine Goldwaage gelegt—zu einem unveröffentlichten Briefwechsel zwischen Rilke und Mathilde Vollmoeller', *Frankfurter Zeitung*, 22 Aug. 1970, and *Stimme der Pfalz*, vol. 23, nos. 5/6 (1972), 6–9.

*—— '"Liliane": Rainer Maria Rilke und Claire Studer in ihren Briefen 1918–1925', *Börsenblatt für den dt. Buchhandel*, 23 Jan. 1976 (Aus dem Antiquariat, A1–11).

*Goldstücker, Eduard, 'Rainer Maria Rilke und Franz Werfel: zur Geschichte ihrer Beziehungen', *Acta Univ. Carolinae*, Philolog. 3 (1960), Germanistica Pragensia I, 37–71.

Goll, Claire, *La Poursuite du vent*, Paris, 1976.

*—— *Rilke et les femmes*, Paris, 1955.

*Hauptmann, Erica, 'Unbekannte Briefe von Rainer Maria Rilke', *Die Welt*, 11 Sept. 1948.

Hamburger, Käthe, 'Rilkes svenska resa', *Bonniers Lit. Magasin*, vol. 13, no. 7 (Sept. 1944).

*[Hattingberg, Magda von], *Rilke und Benvenuta. Ein Buch des Dankes*, Vienna, 1943.

Herzog, Wilhelm, *Menschen, denen ich begegnet bin*. Berne/Munich, 1959.

*Hirschfeld, C., 'Rilke-Erinnerungen Valéry von David-Rhonfelds', *Die Horen*, vol. 5, no. viii (1928/9).

*Hoefert, Siegfried, 'Rilkes Briefe an Max Halbe', *Euphorion* 61 (1967), 187–95.

Holthusen, Hans-Egon, *Rainer Maria Rilke in Selbstzeugnissen und Dokumenten*, Hamburg, 1967.

Insel-Almanach auf das Jahr 1977, 'Rainer Maria Rilke 1875–1975: eine Dokumentation', Frankfurt a.M., 1976.

Italiaander, Rolf, 'Rainer Maria Rilke: aus den Briefen an Ivo Hauptmann und seine Frau Erica', '. . . und liess eine Taube fliegen': Almanach für Kunst und Dichtung, Reinbek/Hamburg, 1948.

Jaloux, Edmond, *Rainer Maria Rilke*, Paris, 1927.

*—— *La Dernière amitié de Rainer Maria Rilke*, Paris, 1949.

Jonas, Klaus W., 'Rainer Maria Rilkes Handschriften', *Philobiblon*, vol. xv, nos. 1/2 (1971), 1–100.

*—— 'Rilke und Clotilde Sakharoff', *Börsenblatt für den dt. Buchhandel* 69 (31 Aug. 1973), A313–21.

*—— 'Rilke und Fritz Huf', *Die Tat*, Zurich, no. 115 (18 May 1974).

*—— 'Rilke und Paul Thun-Hohenstein', *Jb. des Wiener Goethe-Vereins*, vol. 79 (1975), 78–99.

*—— 'Richard Beer-Hofmann und Rilke', *Modern Austrian Literature*, vol. 8, nos. 3/4 (1975).

*—— 'Rilke und Mechtilde Lichnowsky', *Neue Zürcher Zeitung*, 9–10 Aug. 1980.

Kassner, Rudolf, *Rilke: Gesammelte Erinnerungen*, ed. Klaus Bohnenkamp, Pfullingen, 1976.

Kippenberg, Katharina, *Rainer Maria Rilke: ein Beitrag*, Zurich/Wiesbaden, 1948 (4th edn.).

Koenig, Hertha, *Rilkes Mutter*, Pfullingen, 1963.

Kohlschmidt, Werner, *Rainer Maria Rilke*, Lübeck, 1948.

*Leppin, Paul, 'Der neunzehnjährige Rilke', *Die Literatur*, vol. 29, no. 11 (1927), 630–4.

Leppmann, Wolfgang, *Rilke: sein Leben, seine Welt, sein Werk*, Berne, 1981.

*Luck, Rätus, '"Winterthur, dieses berühmte Winterthur . . .": Rainer Maria Rilke und die Eulachstadt', *Winterthurer Jahrbuch* (1979), 7–38.

Marbacher Magazin 8 (1978), 'Franziska zu Reventlow—Schwabing um die Jahrhundertwende', Deutsches Literaturarchiv, Marbach a.N.

Mark, Paul J. (ed.), *Die Familie Pasternak: Erinnerungen, Berichte*, Geneva, 1975.

Mason, Eudo C., *Rainer Maria Rilke: sein Leben und sein Werk*, Göttingen, 1964.

—— *Rilke, Europe and the English-speaking World*, Cambridge, 1961.

*Mauser, Wolfram, 'Lettere di Rilke a Carlo Placci', *Rivista de Letterature Moderne e Comparate*, vol. ix, no. 3 (July–Sept. 1956), 217–23.

*Milne, H. J. M., 'The Letters of Rilke, Hofmannsthal, Malwida von Meysenbug and others to Marie Herzfeld', *British Museum Quarterly* xiii (1938/9).

Modern Austrian Literature, vol. 15, nos. 3/4 (1982) (Special Rilke isue).

Modersohn-Becker, Paula, see Busch, Günter.

Morse, B. J., 'Rainer Maria Rilke and English Literature' and 'Contemporary English Poets and Rilke', Privately reprinted from *German Life and Letters*, NS i (1947/48).

—— 'Rainer Maria Rilke and the Occult', *Journal of Experimental Metaphysics*, July 1945, Oct. 1945, and Jan. 1946.

Naville-Wertheimer, Marga, *Arbeitsstunden mit Rainer Maria Rilke*, Zurich, 1962.

Obermüller, Paul, Steiner, Herbert and Zinn, Ernst (eds.), *Katalog der Rilke-Sammlung von Richard von Mises*, Frankfurt a.M., 1966.

Osann, Christiane, *Rainer Maria Rilke: der Weg eines Dichters*, Zurich, 1941.

Parry, Idris, *Hand to Mouth and other essays*, Manchester, 1981.

Pettit, Richard, *Rainer Maria Rilke in und nach Worpswede*, Worpswede, 1983.

Petzet, H. W., *Das Bildnis des Dichters*, Frankfurt a.M., 1976.

—— *Von Worpswede nach Moskau: Heinrich Vogeler*, Cologne, 1977 (4th edn.).

Pfeiffer, Ernst, 'Rilke und die Psychoanalyse', *Literaturwiss. Jb. der Görresgesellschaft*, NS, vol. 17 (1976), 247–320.

—— 'Zugang zu Rilke', ibid., vol. 18 (1977, 204–18.

—— 'Denn Rainer starb "trostlos"—eine Betrachtung', ibid., vol. 23 (1982), 297–304.

—— (ed.) *Lou Andreas-Salomé: Eintragungen, letzte Jahre*, Frankfurt a.M. 1982.

Rainer Maria Rilke: Inédits, études et notes, ed. André Silvaire, Paris, 1952.

Rainer Maria Rilke 1875–1975, Katalog der Ausstellung des Deutschen Literaturarchivs, Marbach a.N., ed. Joachim W. Storck, Stuttgart, 1975.

Razumovsky, Maria, *Marina Zwetajewa—Mythos und Wahrheit*, Vienna, 1981.

Reconnaissance à Rilke. Les Cahiers du mois 23/24, Paris, August 1926.

*Rie, Robert, 'Drei unveröffentlichte Briefe Rilkes', *Wort in der Zeit* (1958), 4.

Rilke en Valais. Suisse Romande, vol. 3, no. 4 (15 Sept. 1939), 148–206.

Rilke et la France, Hommages et souvenirs, Paris, 1943.

*Rilke-Gesellschaft, *Blätter* 1–10 (1972–83).

Rilke heute: Beziehungen und Wirkungen, vol. i. (ed. Ingeborg Solbrig and Joachim W. Storck), vol. ii, Frankfurt a. M., 1975, 1976.

*'Rilkes Briefe an seine Haushälterin' (Ida Walthert; ed. anon.), *Annabelle*, vol. 8, no. 94, Christmas 1945.

Rilke-Studien zu Werk und Wirkungsgeschichte, Berlin/Weimar, 1976.

Ritzer, Walter, *Rainer Maria Rilke: Bibliographie*, Vienna, 1951.

Salis, Jean Rudolf von, *Rilkes Schweizer Jahre*, Frankfurt a.M, 1975 (Suhrkamp Taschenbuch 289).

—— 'Zu Rilkes Lebensgeschichte—ein biographischer Essay', *Im Lauf der Jahre*, 319–77, Zurich, 1962.

—— *Grenzüberschreitungen: ein Lebensbericht*, pt. 1, Zurich, 1975.

—— 'Rainer Maria Rilke im Wallis', *Raron—Burg und Kirche*, 177–94, Basle, 1972.

*Schmidt-Pauli, Elisabeth, *Rainer Maria Rilke: ein Gedenkbuch*, Basle, 1940.

Schnack, Ingeborg (ed.), *Rilkes Leben und Werk im Bild*, Wiesbaden, 1956.

—— *Rainer Maria Rilkes Erinnerungen an Marburg und das hessische Land*, Marburg: N. G. Elwert, 2nd. edn., 1963.

*—— *Rainer Maria Rilke: Chronik seines Lebens und seines Werkes*, 2 vols., Frankfurt a.M. 1975.

*—— *Rilke in Ragaz*, Bad Ragaz, 2nd edn., 1981.

Scholz, Wilhelm von, *Eine Jahrhundertwende*, Leipzig, 1936.

Schwarz, Egon, *Das verschluckte Schluchzen*: Poesie und Politik bei Rainer Maria Rilke, Frankfurt a.M., 1972.

*Sieber, Carl, *René Rilke*, Leipzig, 1932.

—— Biographical sequel to *René Rilke*, unpublished manuscript, Rilke-Archiv.

—— 'Die Ahnen Rilkes', *Inselschiff*, vol. xii, no. 4 (1931).

—— 'Rainer Maria Rilkes Briefwerk', *Inselschiff*, vol. xiv, no. 4 (1933).

—— 'Rilke und Worpswede', *Stader Archiv*, NS (1941), bk. no. 31.

Simenauer, Erich, *Rainer Maria Rilke: Legende und Mythos*, Berne, 1953.

*Šolle, Zdeněk, 'Neznámé Dopisy R. M. Rilka v Československých Archivech', *Studie o Rukopisech* xiv (1975), Prague.

*Stahl, E. L., Boutchik, Vladimir, and Mitchell, Stanley, 'Letters of Rainer' Maria Rilke to Helene ***', *Oxford Slavonic Papers*, vol. ix (1960), 129–64.

Steiner, Jacob, *Rilkes Duineser Elegien*, Berne/Munich, 2nd edn., 1969.

*Storck, Joachim W., *Rainer Maria Rilke als Briefschreiber*, Dissertation, Freiburg i.Br., 1957.

*—— 'Ein unbekannter Brief Rilkes an Anton Kippenberg', *Jb. der dt. Schillergesellschaft* xviii (1974), 23–36.

—— 'Politisches Bewusstsein beim späten Rilke', *Recherches Germaniques*, 8 (1978).

*—— '"Die Rose von Locarno": ein Kapitel aus dem Briefwechsel Rainer Maria Rilkes mit Wilhelm Hausenstein', *Jb. der dt. Schillergesellschaft* xxiii (1979), 94–116.

*—— 'René Rilkes "Linzer Episode"', *Blätter der Rilke-Gesellschaft* 7–8 (1980/1), 111–34.

*—— '"Zeitgenosse dieser Weltschande", Briefe Rilkes an Marianne Mitford . . . aus dem Kriegsjahr 1915', *Jb. der dt. Schillergesellschaft*, xxvi (1982), 40–80.

*—— 'Rainer Maria Rilkes Begegnung mit Wilhelm Muehlon', *Recherches Germaniques*, 12 (1982), 221–35.

Studer-Kiefer, Ella, Illustrated scrapbook/manuscript on Rilke's years in Switzerland, 1963–1971 (SLB).

Thurn und Taxis, Marie von, *Erinnerungen an Rainer Maria Rilke*, trans. Georg Blokesch, Frankfurt a.M., 1966 (Insel-Bücherei no. 888).

Trebitsch, Siegfried, *Chronicle of a Life*, London, 1953.

*Ullmann, Regina, *Erinnerungen an Rilke*, St. Gallen, n.d.

Unseld, Siegfried, *Der Autor und sein Verleger*, Frankfurt a.M., 1978.

—— *'Das Tagebuch' Goethes und Rilkes 'Sieben Gedichte'*, Frankfurt a.M., 1978 (Insel-Bücherei no. 1000).

Van Heerikhuizen, F. W., *Rainer Maria Rilke: his Life and Work*, trans. F. G. Renier and Anne Cliff, London, 1951.

Vogeler, Heinrich, *Erinnerungen*, ed. Erich Weinert, Berlin, 1952.

Von der Mühll, Theodora (Dory), 'Erinnerungen an Rilke', Radio talk, 10 June 1945 (unpublished, SLB).

Werfel, Franz, 'Begegnungen mit Rilke', *Sudetenland* xviii (1976).

Wocke, Helmut, *Rilke und Italien*, Giessen, 1940.

*Wohltmann, Heinrich, *Otto Modersohn*, Stade, 1941.

*—— *Rainer Maria Rilke in Worpswede*, Hamburg, 2nd edn., 1952.

*Wolff, Kurt, *Briefwechsel eines Verlegers 1911–1963*, Frankfurt a.M., 1966.

Wydenbruck, Nora, *Rilke, Man and Poet*, London, 1949 (reprint Westport, Conn., 1972).

Zech, Paul, *Rainer Maria Rilke*, Dresden, 1930.

*Zermatten, Maurice, *Les Années valaisannes de Rilke*, Sierre, 1951.

*—— *Der Ruf der Stille: Rilkes Walliser Jahre*, Zurich, 1954.

*—— *Les Dernières années de Rainer Maria Rilke*, Fribourg, 1975.

Zweig, Stefan, *Abschied von Rilke*, Tübingen, 1927.

—— *Die Welt von gestern*, London/Stockholm, n.d. (1945).

Index of Rilke's Works

—◦❦◦—

Page numbers in italics refer to the Notes.

General Index

—◦❧◦—

Page numbers in italics refer to the Notes.